Walter Wood

VICTORIAN POETRY

VICTORIAN

TEN MAJOR POETS

Edited with introductions and notes by

ROBERT BERNARD MARTIN
Princeton University

RANDOM HOUSE · NEW YORK

POETRY

Tennyson

Browning

Arnold

Meredith

D. G. Rossetti

Christina Rossetti

Swinburne

Hardy

Hopkins

Housman

Contents

Contents

Contents

Contents

ACKNOWLEDGMENTS

From *Collected Poems* by Thomas Hardy:

"The Curate's Kindness"
"1967"
"The Man He Killed"
"Channel Firing"
"The Convergence of the Twain"
"Ah, Are You Digging on My Grave?"
"The Newcomer's Wife"
"A Poet"
"In Church"
"The Blinded Bird"
"The Oxen"
"At a Country Fair"
"He Fears His Good Fortune"

"In Time of 'The Breaking of Nations'"
"Neutral Tones"
"At an Inn"
"Drummer Hodge"
"Shelley's Skylark"
"I Said to Love"
"God-Forgotten"
"Song of Hope"
"Puzzled Game-Birds"
"The Darkling Thrush"
"The Self-Unseeing"
"The Division"

Reprinted by permission of The Macmillan Company; Macmillan & Company Ltd.; the Trustees of the Hardy Estate; and The Macmillan Company of Canada Limited.

"Snow in the Suburbs"   "Epitaph on a Pessimist"

Copyright 1925, 1953 by The Macmillan Company. Reprinted by permission of The Macmillan Company; Macmillan & Company Ltd.; the Trustees of the Hardy Estate; and The Macmillan Company of Canada Limited.

From *Poems of Gerard Manley Hopkins*, Third Edition, edited by Robert Bridges and W. H. Gardner. Copyright 1948 by Oxford University Press, Inc. Reprinted by permission.

From "A Shropshire Lad" by A. E. Housman:

"Loveliest of trees, the cherry now"
"When smoke stood up from Ludlow"
"When I was one-and-twenty"
"To an Athlete Dying Young"
"Bredon Hill"
"The lads in their hundreds to Ludlow come in for the fair"

"Is my team ploughing"
"On Wenlock Edge"
"White in the moon the long road lies"
"With rue my heart is laden"
"Hughley Steeple"
"'Terence, this is stupid stuff'"

I should like to acknowledge with thanks the clerical help of Mr. Robert
Patten in the preparation of this volume.

The date in brackets on the right side of the column at the end
of a poem indicates its first major publication; a date in italics
on the left side is that of its composition.

General Introduction

The Victorian poets remain a remarkably healthy lot when we consider how often their immediate demise has been predicted. Even one of the greatest of them, Matthew Arnold, could write of the poets of his own day that "Achilles ponders in his tent,/The kings of modern thought are dumb," and, in complimenting the writers of an earlier age on their "tireless powers," concludes sadly that "We mark them, but they are not ours." Arnold's remarks were directed to Byron, Shelley, and the French writer Sénancour; it is perhaps not inappropriate to wonder how many non-specialist readers would ever have heard of the latter were it not that Arnold's poetry has proved considerably more long-lived than he suspected. For one reason or another, critics since Arnold (and before, for that matter) have feared that the poetry of the last seventy years of the nineteenth century would dissolve, leaving not a rack behind. In 1934 James Stephens said that only the novels of Emily and Charlotte Brontë and perhaps Trollope, out of the vastness of Victorian prose, continued to have any meaning in the twentieth century, and he feared a like fate for the poetry of the period.

On my desk lie two collections of the best-known English poems, from the medieval period to our own century. The older of the two was compiled in 1939 by Sir Arthur Quiller-Couch, who picked the end of the First World War as the final date for his choices; roughly a quarter of the book is taken up with the poetry of the Victorian period. The second collection appeared in 1956, edited by Howard F. Lowry and Willard Thorp, and it includes poems written as recently as 1955; the proportion of Victorian poetry is even larger than in the earlier volume. "Q" might be accused of favoring the poems written in his own lifetime, but one could hardly make the same accusation of Professors Lowry and Thorp. Interest in Victorian poetry is scarcely flagging, as anyone can testify who tries to keep up with the flood of criticism of the Victorians that appears each year.

But if concern with the Victorian poets is waxing rather than waning, it is true all the same that the quality of that concern has undergone many changes in the past century, and most of those changes have resulted from the consideration of the role of the poet and the function of poetry.

During the youth of the earlier Victorians, Shelley had written his great *Defence of Poetry,* setting forth the ideal of the poet as the bardic voice of humanity. He ended on an inspiriting—and perhaps wishful—note: "Poets are the hierophants of an unapprehended inspiration; the mirrors of the gigantic shadows which futurity casts upon the present; the words which express what they understand not; the trumpets which sing to battle, and feel not what they inspire; the influence which is moved not, but moves. Poets are the unacknowledged legislators of the world." For Shelley the operative word of the last sentence was probably "legislators"; to many of his successors "unacknowledged" must have seemed to carry a larger burden of meaning.

The early Victorian critics and reading public increasingly demanded that their poets take on a vatic role, and few men, even poets, can always resist the temptation to prophesy. What that prophetic role meant to the public was frequently quite different, however, from what it meant to the poet. To the large body of middle-class readers, the poet's function was to concoct a bland pottage containing equal parts of versified moralizing and easy, impeccable sentiment, neither of which would disturb his readers' complacency or lead them into hard, uncomfortable thought. The invitation to consider contemporary social or moral problems was actually a request for reassurance that the subjects of the Queen lived in the best of all possible worlds. For some minor poets the lures of acclamation were too potent; the works of such versifiers as Martin Tupper show how a pinched talent could achieve astonishing popularity by couching commonplace reflections in equally commonplace rhythms, and how those works have sunk into the depths of literary history with scarcely a ripple to show their passing. In our own understated day, *bard* and *prophet* seem peculiarly Victorian words for poets, pompous in their assumptions; the contemporary usage of the terms held out the vatic titles with one hand while withdrawing their functions with the other.

The greater Victorian poets, like men of perception in all ages, displayed an abundant concern with morality in its wider sense, for the consideration of man and his life necessarily involves a moral view of the universe of a more complex kind than that demanded by the public. The giants of Victorian poetry gave more than their readers had asked for. Not surprisingly, the poets' views were frequently incongruent with those of their contemporaries, since the very condition of genius—or even talent— makes it difficult for the creator to accept unhesitatingly the assumptions of the mass of men. That the poets should have been unsympathetic with the aims of the Industrial Revolution, and with the rampant striving for material success that succeeded it, was probably a foregone conclusion. What was more remarkable was that many of them did not withdraw completely from the consideration of contemporary problems. It would be hard, however, to find in our own day a poetic parallel for the eagerness with which the major Victorian poets considered the outstanding political, scientific, and theological issues of the day. The examination of the social and intellectual problems of their contemporaries fused with the traditional matter of poetry: love, death, immortality, spiritual aspiration, the natural world, the legendary past, the passing of beauty, and the hundred other themes that re-echo through the ages since primitive man first began to sing. As a result, the province of Victorian poetry was far larger (and probably richer in consequence) than it is today. There were few aspects of life with which the poets failed to deal, and many of them would have felt that they were abrogating their own powers had they neglected the problems of their contemporaries. Charles Kingsley, a minor poet but one who saw the necessity for the relationship between poetry and contemporary life, once wrote of his own poetic limitations that "the power of metaphor & analogue—the instinctive vision of a connexion between all things in heaven & earth, which Poets *must* have, is very weak in me; & therefore I shall never be a great poet." Kingsley was not pointing out only the necessity for metaphorical and analogical consistency within a single poem; he was speaking for the wide vision that sees all of life as potential material for the poet.

The problem for the Victorian poet, then, was not of the

suitability of subjects but of how to connect his perceptions with those of his audience. Professor E. D. H. Johnson, in his influential study, *The Alien Vision of Victorian Poetry,* has demonstrated the painful dilemma in which the poets found themselves when they were aware that their own insights did not coincide with those of their age. The public's ideal man of letters was an essayist like Carlyle or Ruskin, or a novelist like Dickens or George Eliot, apparently choosing his themes primarily for their direct social significance. It is not surprising, therefore, that the poets alternated between direct social statement and a more private, metaphorical statement (which was usually fortunate for their poetry) of the issues of the day and the conditions out of which they arose. Tennyson's themes are much the same in "The Palace of Art," "The Lady of Shalott," and *Maud,* but to a Victorian reader interested in the conflict between private and public perception, the desertion of the Palace and the death of the Lady were conclusions less immediately comprehensible than the setting-forth of Maud's lover for the war in the Crimea. To modern readers, however, the conclusions of the two earlier poems are more generally satisfactory, since they are evolved from the inner life of the poem rather than, as one feels is true of the conclusion to *Maud,* taking their meaning from events external to the poem. It is probably fair to say that all three poems are concerned with problems that beset the Victorians but that, for posterity, less direct reference to specific contemporary events results in more satisfactory poetic experience. Arnold is the classic case of the poet who felt the necessity of addressing himself directly to contemporary problems and, at the same time, recognized his inability to write great poetry without resorting to myth for his metaphor. He felt that the straightforward treatment of his own age meant a lessening of quality in his poetry, but a metaphorical statement meant the loss of communication with his readers. Arnold's solution—the abandonment of poetry for the essay—perhaps answered his own needs, but it was neither satisfactory nor reassuring for poets at large.

The experience of a twentieth-century reader of Victorian poetry, however, is probably less that of coming upon a body of work whose subject is specifically the nineteenth century than that of reading highly introspective, self-absorbed poetry that constantly turns to the consciousness and the experience of the poet as a reference point—poetry informed with a distress or malaise of the mind and the heart. Comedy there is, to be sure, but the dry irony of Hardy and Housman, the grotesque humor of Browning, and the detached comic sense of Meredith are far from characterizing the age. Like a recurrent echo, the theme of isolation, both poetic and personal, reverberates in the great poetry. Browning was probably the only major poet of the period in whose work the sorrow of alienation is seldom heard, and even Browning's characters are frequently misunderstood, unable to communicate, or frustrated by an uncomprehending world. "The eternal note of sadness," of which Arnold wrote in "Dover Beach," sounds through the poetry of the whole period, more like a full orchestration of sorrow than a single reverberant note.

While some of the poets mourned the loss of the link between their own conceptions and those of their contemporaries, others ended by denying the need of such a link. It is one of the critical clichés—and, like most truisms, it has a great measure of truth—that, in reaction to the moral strenuousness of their own society, such poets as Swinburne and Rossetti (and, at a somewhat later date, Housman) discarded in both their poetry and their personal lives all the preconceptions of morals and conduct that are usually labelled *Victorian*. For them, beauty and intensity of experience took the place of the intellectual and moral preoccupations of their elders, and order came to mean primarily an aesthetic order. But, like most rebels, they were bound by the very conventions against which they reacted, for those conventions defined the limits of their rebellion. In their preoccupation with defying tradition, Swinburne and Rossetti seem as Victorian as do the traditions themselves.

No one could say reasonably that Hardy, Meredith, Christina Rossetti, and Hopkins were unconcerned with Victorian views of man, but they were less concerned with strictly contemporary problems than with the eternal kinship of man with the universe. The chief subject of Meredith's poetry was the relationship of human beings with Nature and their half-comic, half-tragic divorce from her ageless rhythms. Hardy was obsessed with the plight of man in an uncomprehending, ruthless chain of circumstance that totally ignored his strivings and his individuality. Christina Rossetti and Hopkins turned to beliefs that long antedated the reign of Queen Victoria and that reduced the immediacy of the problems of that age to irrelevancy.

Obviously, such a diverse and heterogeneous group is not

adequately described by lumping them together as Victorians; the historical accident of their having lived during the Queen's long reign did not insure a complete community of their interests. And yet the term persists, indicating some likeness between them. If there is such a likeness, it is probably in their passionate concern with duty and with morality in the broadest sense of that term. But *Victorian* must not be construed as meaning rigid or hypocritical, nor must *morality* be equated with narrowness or Puritanism. Morality meant, as it has since the morning of history, the duty of man in the world; what had changed was that man was no longer sure of the meaning of the world. The search for that meaning, and hence for man's duty, occupied a good part of Victorian poetry.

After the First World War, the reign of Queen Victoria seemed distant indeed. Social mores were—to put it mildly—changed; the religious views of most men were considerably different from those of their grandfathers, and the word *Victorian* began to take on overtones of stuffiness and outmoded earnestness. Naturally enough, the poetry of the 1920's and the 1930's reflected the society in which it arose, and the critics of the times began searching Victorian poetry for the qualities most apparent in the new poetry being written by their own contemporaries. Between the First and the Second World Wars, criticism of Victorian poetry consisted mainly of careful consideration of mood, tone, diction, imagery, and metrics, as the young Turks of criticism impatiently tossed to the winds the "subjects" of the poems and concentrated instead on their formal aspects. (Perhaps even more than poets and novelists, critics are apt to be intolerant of the preoccupations of those who have preceded them.) It is no accident that the most popular of the Victorian poets was the newly-discovered Gerard Manley Hopkins, for his metrics and imagery afforded plenty of critical puzzles to be solved, so that the solid Roman Catholic doctrine that informed his poetry could be dismissed as almost irrelevant. It is to this period of criticism that we certainly owe a revitalized way of looking at the Victorians, a consideration of them as careful literary artists rather than mere versifying moralizers. This criticism is still immensely valuable because it pointed out a new path by which to come to the same body of poetry, and also because it provided a healthy corrective to the excesses of moral and historical studies that preceded it.

Today the most popular form of criticism of Victorian poetry seems to be the investigation of the intellectual currents of the age implicit in the poems, the tracking down of the philosophical forebears of the poets. It is a type of criticism that, pushed to its logical extremes, becomes almost a judgment of the philosophical validity of the preconceptions of the poet. If the method sometimes seems to lose sight of the fact that the work being investigated is a poem, not a piece of consistent philosophy, it at least brings one to another approach to the same body of poetry. Perhaps it is not important which method of criticism we pursue so long as we ultimately come to deeper understanding of the work itself.

All good poetry must be subjected to many kinds of criticism, and only the best will stand up to investigation by many kinds of intelligence. The moral, the historical, the formal, and the philosophical methods have served to put much of Victorian poetry in perspective, to indicate those poets and works most worthy of being read by posterity. The present anthology is a personal attempt to cut down to size the formidable *corpus* of Victorian poetry, offering as an introduction to the college student only those writers and works that seem to me to have emerged in the second half of the twentieth century with undiminished vitality and interest. This is not to suggest that other poems have not done so as well, but that this is a representative selection of the best.

To the student beset with doubts as to how to "come at" a poem or what critical method to employ, it might be well to recommend the words of Miss Helen Gardner, writing of the function of the critic—and the reader:

> The primary critical act is a judgement, the decision that a certain piece of writing has significance and value. It asserts a hold in some way upon my intellect, which entertains the propositions which it makes. It appeals through my senses and imagination to my capacity to recognize order and harmony and to be delighted by them. It appeals also to my experience as a human being, to my conscience and moral life. I put the triad in this order because in literature, whose medium is words, unintelligibility prevents recognition of the presence of either beauty or wisdom. We must feel that the work "makes sense," even if at first only in patches, if we are to feel its value. But, of course, in experience we are not conscious of these different kinds of value as distinct. It is only for purposes of analysis, and when we come to try to ration-

alize our responses, that we separate what is in a work of art
not separable; what it says, how it says it, and why what it
says is important to us.*

With the good sense that characterizes her writing, Miss Gardner insists that her own distinctions are irrelevant in the most
deeply felt experiences one has in art, when one is content to
forget her triad and to perceive the work of art as a unity.
When the perceptions are quickened, one grasps a poem as a
whole and forgets the routes by which he arrived at this unity.

A Victorian statement of the same point of view was enunciated by John Henry Newman, who was a not-inconsiderable
poet himself. In this case Newman was writing of what he called
Real Assent, the kind of assent directed toward assertions based
on the whole trend of our experience. Because of this foundation,
he wrote, the assent is too rich to be sharply limited, is always
liable to be unfolded further, and is likely to vary from one person
to another: "The reasons of . . . conviction are too delicate, too
intricate; nay, they are in part invisible, except to those who from
circumstances have an intellectual perception of what does not
appear to the many." Real Assent, Newman continues, addresses
the mind "both through the intellect and through the imagination,
creating a certitude of its truth by arguments too various for
enumeration, too personal and deep for words, too powerful and
concurrent for refutation." In this context Newman was referring
to religious conversion, but for him there was a close kinship between the reception of poetry and the reception of grace. "One
and the same teaching," he wrote, "is in different aspects both
object and proof, and elicits one complex act both of inference
and assent." And so it is with the best poetry, whether Victorian
or not.

ROBERT BERNARD MARTIN

Princeton, 1963.

* Helen Gardner, *The Business of Criticism,* Oxford: The Clarendon Press,
1959, pp. 6-7.

General Bibliography

VICTORIAN BACKGROUND AND CRITICISM

Appleman, Philip, Madden, William A., and Wolff, Michael, *1859: Entering an Age of Crisis*. Indiana University Press, Bloomington, 1959.

Batho, Edith Clara, and Dobrée, Bonamy, *The Victorians and After, 1830-1914*. Dover, New York, 1952.

Beach, Joseph W. *The Concept of Nature in Nineteenth-Century Poetry*. Macmillan, New York, 1936.

Buckley, Jerome Hamilton, *The Victorian Temper: A Study in Literary Culture*. Harvard University Press, Cambridge, 1951. *good, but difficult. need bkgrd.*

Cooke, John D., and Stevenson, Lionel, *English Literature of the Victorian Period*. Appleton-Century-Crofts, New York, 1949.

Halévy, Elie, *Victorian Years, 1841-1895* (vol. IV of *History of the English People in the Nineteenth Century*), trans. by E. I. Watkin and D. A. Barker. Benn, London, 1951. *very good*

Holloway, John, *The Victorian Sage: Studies in Argument*. Macmillan, London, 1953.

Hough, Graham, *The Last Romantics*. Duckworth, London, 1949. *good on Keats*

Johnson, Edward Dudley Hume, *The Alien Vision of Victorian Poetry: Sources of the Poetic Imagination in Tennyson, Browning, and Arnold*. Princeton University Press, Princeton, 1952. *best*

Parrott, Thomas Marc, and Martin, Robert Bernard, *A Companion to Victorian Literature*. Scribner, New York, 1955. *pretensious*

Randall, John Herman, *The Making of the Modern Mind*. Houghton Mifflin, Boston, 1940. *one of best*

Stevenson, Lionel, *Darwin Among the Poets*. University of Chicago Press, Chicago, 1932.

Trevelyan, George Macaulay, *British History in the Nineteenth Century, and After, 1782-1919*. Longmans, Green, London, 1937.

Warren, Alba Houghton, *English Poetic Theory, 1825-1865*. Princeton University Press, Princeton, 1950.

Wright, Austin, ed., *Victorian Literature: Modern Essays in Criticism*. Oxford University Press, New York, 1961. *one of best*

Young, George Malcolm, *Victorian England: Portrait of an Age*. Oxford University Press, London, 1936. *best of age*

VICTORIAN POETRY

Alfred Tennyson

[1809-1892]

Alfred Tennyson was the fourth of the twelve children of a country parson, George Tennyson of Somersby, Lincolnshire. The elder Tennyson was a brilliant but disappointed and neurotic man who had been disinherited by his autocratic father. Throughout Alfred's boyhood his father's black depression and alcoholism threw a shadow over the happiness of the family. Tennyson's upbringing was free and somewhat unconventional, and all of his life he retained his awkward rustic manners and a distinct country accent in his speech. Part of his early education was in a grammar school in Louth, but most of it was received under his father's tutelage in the library of Somersby Rectory. By the time he was fifteen, he was already at home in the classics as well as in much of English literature. Like his brothers, Alfred wrote a great deal of poetry as a boy, most of it derivative and undistinguished when judged by mature standards, but unusually good for his age.

In 1827 Tennyson's first published poetry appeared in the anonymous *Poems by Two Brothers*, of which Alfred had written more than half. The following year he matriculated at Trinity College, Cambridge, where a new world opened to him. He was soon invited to join "The Apostles," a club for intellectual discussion composed of some of the most brilliant young men in Cambridge. With his new friends he began to read Wordsworth, Shelley, and Keats, and to talk of philosophy, religion, social duty, and poetry. Among the Apostles was Arthur Henry Hallam, regarded as the most promising man in Cambridge. Hallam, an Etonian, came of a cultivated family. He was learned, polished in his manners, articulate, gay, charming—in short, everything that the graceless, hulking Tennyson was not. The friendship that developed rapidly between the two was, in some ways, the most important human contact Tennyson ever made; Hallam was certainly closer to him than any of Tennyson's family had been.

In 1830 Tennyson published *Poems, Chiefly Lyrical,* to which Hallam had originally intended to add some of his own poetry. The summer of that year Tennyson and Hallam travelled to France and Spain. By this time Hallam had become engaged to Tennyson's sister Emily.

After withdrawing from Cambridge without a degree, Tennyson published another volume of *Poems* in 1832. In both this volume and the one that preceded it, there is already present the sense of melancholy and isolation that was to haunt his poetry during the rest of his life. "Mariana" is concerned with loneliness; "The Lady of Shalott" tells of that lady's disastrous attempt to break out of her isolation; "The Lotos-Eaters" is an extended dialectic between the opposing claims of the social contract and the individual retreating from it. Significantly, these poems have often been read as considerations of the role of the poet, of the question of whether art is a private or a public function. In "The Palace of Art" and later in *In Memoriam,* Tennyson seems to decide in favor of the public role, but it remained a question that perplexed him until his death.

The unfriendly reviews of the 1832 volume were shattering to Tennyson. His depression was deepened intolerably in 1833 by the prostrating news that Hallam had died suddenly in Vienna. In 1836 Tennyson became engaged to Emily Sellwood, but the engagement was broken, at least partially because he was too poor to support a wife.

It was not until 1842 that he published more poetry, although in the period since the 1832 volume, he had been writing constantly and had been carefully repolishing many of the poems from the earlier work. The critics were kinder to the 1842 *Poems,* and Tennyson's reputation began rising. In 1847 he published *The Princess,* a long narrative poem about the education and emancipation of women.

The year 1850 marked the great watershed in Tennyson's life. By this time he was able to offer a more secure future to Miss Sellwood, and in June of this year they were married. In April Wordsworth died, and the position of Poet Laureate was offered to Tennyson, who accepted it. Perhaps symbolically, he is said to have been presented to the Queen that autumn as Laureate wearing the same suit of court clothes that Wordsworth had worn on the occasion of his own presentation. In any case, after this he was to occupy a position in Victorian poetry even more commanding than that which Wordsworth had filled in the Romantic period; perhaps more than any other poet of the time he is the archetypal figure of the Victorian poet and prophet. Probably no other poet has ever had such wide popularity or become so wealthy from the sales of his work; certainly, he is the only poet in English history given a peerage in recognition of his talents.

Even more important for poetry, however, was the publication in 1850 of what most modern critics regard as Tennyson's greatest poem—perhaps the greatest of the whole period: *In Memoriam*. Since Hallam's death seventeen years before, Tennyson had been sporadically writing lyrics that wrestled with his own sense of bereavement, which paralleled his attempts to come to terms with his religious doubt, the brute facts of evolution, his perception of the low state of morality and aspiration in England, and his questioning of his own function as poet. The poems were not written originally with any thought of publication, and the order in which they were composed was not that in which they were published. It was only some fifteen years after Hallam's death that Tennyson perceived that the lyrics could be put into a coherent whole. After deciding to print them, he rearranged them and wrote a number of "bridge" passages to make their progress smoother, probably composing the introductory poem last. Even after the initial publication he continued smoothing out the poem into its present form.

In Memoriam is a mixture of autobiographical fact and more general considerations. For example, one might cite the imaginative accompanying of Hallam's body from Vienna, where he died, to Clevedon in the west of England, where he was buried. It is hard to believe that these lyrics do not reflect the actual grief of Tennyson during the period shortly after the death of his friend, yet in section II the poet appears to be writing of an actual visit to the churchyard where Hallam was buried, when, to be coldly factual, Hallam was really laid to rest in the chancel of Clevedon church and Tennyson did not visit the spot until many years later. " 'I' is not always the author speaking of himself," wrote Tennyson, "but the voice of the human race speaking thro' him." It is therefore dangerous to read too much literal autobiography into the poem as a whole, although it is obviously true to life in its larger considerations. To give the poem form, the temporal framework is compressed into about three years after Hallam's death, with the epilogue taking place in 1842.

The individual strands of the poem are not easy to separate, for Tennyson's questioning of religious faith was strengthened by his own grief over Hallam, the general fear that evolutionary discoveries threatened revealed religion, and his perception of the horrible disparity between what man is and what religion sometimes seemed to postulate that he is. The reader should remember that Tennyson was writing from one to three decades before Darwin's *Origin of Species*, and that much of his evolutionary fact he had learned from Charles Lyell's *Principles of Geology*. The realization that many species had disappeared, leaving behind nothing but their fossil remains, seemed to postulate that Nature was undirected, careless of both species and individual, and that the true perception was of a Nature "red in tooth and claw," fighting for physical survival and offering nothing beyond death. Tennyson's final position is that God exists and is a God of love, that evolution is directed by Him and is working toward a higher type of man, of whom Hallam has been an example, and that there is a continuity of communication between individuals, both in the afterlife and when they are separated by death. The epilogue, which seems at first reading to be somewhat incongruously tacked on to the end of the poem, since it celebrates the wedding of Tennyson's sister Cecilia (and not of his sister Emily, who had been engaged to Hallam), is actually a prophecy of a better race in the persons of the children of the marriage. The connection is one of general ideas rather than of strict biography.

The one hundred and thirty-one lyrics of *In Memoriam* are divided into four major sections: the first of these (I-XXVII) takes us to the first Christmas after Hallam's death; the second section (XXVIII-LXXVII) is intended to cover the year following, up to the second Christmas; the third section (LXXVIII-CIII) takes us as far as the third Christmas, the first the Tennyson family has spent away from Somersby; the final section (CIV-CXXXI), with its new note of reconciliation to Hallam's death, is concluded with the marriage epilogue. Paralleling this movement in time is the increasing adjustment of the poet's mind to the facts of change, moving from despair in the first section, to doubt in the second, hope in the third, and faith in the concluding section. Yet this scheme makes the development seem more linear than it actually is, for the poet alternates in his moods, and in each section there is both progressive and retrogressive movement; it is only in the totality of each section that one can say that the poet moves forward into a progressively healthier state of mind. Concurrent with the poet's change from private grief to a faith in the fate of mankind, there is a consideration of the function of the poet, moving from Tennyson's conception of poetry as mere release from emotion, in the first section, to his recognition in the final section of the poet's necessity to speak for mankind.

There are other kinds of pairs and groups in the poem as well. For example, lyrics II and XXXIX both deal with the yew tree Tennyson imagines growing by Hallam's grave, but the interval between the two lyrics significantly alters the poet's tone in addressing the tree. A similar kind of pairing can be seen in the two lyrics (VII and CXIX) that describe Hallam's house in London. Less formally, the whole poem is shot through with verbal echoes, repeated under different circumstances. On occasion Tennyson groups several lyrics dealing with the same subject; lyrics LIII-LVI, for example, are concerned with evolution, LX-LXV consider whether the dead retain memories of their earthly life; LXXIII-LXXVII treat the general subject of fame.

Tennyson called *Maud,* published five years after *In Memoriam,* his "little Hamlet," intending to indicate the parallel between the introspective, disillusioned central figure of the Shakespearean tragedy and his own work. *Maud* is a "monodrama," spoken entirely by one person; it is a series of lyrics alternating with soliloquies. Like *In Memoriam,* it records the progress of the individual from unhealthy self-questioning to his regeneration in the service of mankind as a whole. Where, in the earlier poem, the motive power had been supplied by the friendship with Hallam, in *Maud* the narrator first learns through romantic love and is then able to generalize to a wider conception of his relationship with the whole human race. Time has dimmed the glory of the resolution of the final section, in which the hero finds his regeneration by taking part in the Crimean War, but the section should probably be read with less specific reference to a particular war than to the sense of human fellowship which the narrator finally attains.

The nameless narrator of the poem is the son of a former associate of Maud's father; the hero's father has apparently committed suicide over a business venture, in the little hollow where the narrator finally kills Maud's brother. In his despair the narrator goes mad, is committed to an asylum in France, and is finally redeemed by his devotion to the common good. The story, however, is less important than the splendid lyrics and the progression of character indicated in the discontinuous sections. Both in its psychological penetration and its attempt to force the lyric into a substitute for an older style of narrative poetry, *Maud* is a brilliant experiment. It is worth noticing, too, how Tennyson has anticipated here the symbolist poetry of the later part of the century.

For almost thirty years after the appearance of *Maud*, Tennyson wrote primarily in longer and larger forms. His epic retelling of the Arthurian legend in the *Idylls of the King* appeared between 1859 and 1885, and during the same years he made several attempts at neo-Shakespearean drama, but his genius was never for the theater, and the plays were comparative failures.

In 1883 he was elevated by the Queen to the peerage as Baron Tennyson of Aldworth and Faringford. By then he was a legend in his own lifetime, a hero to the general public, who bought his poetry by the tens of thousands of volumes. It is at least arguable that his extreme popularity (and perhaps his sense of being a public figure as Poet Laureate) led him occasionally into themes he was not equipped to handle, but besides the poems now forgotten, he wrote much fine poetry in his old age. When he was buried in Westminster Abbey in 1892, England mourned one of its greatest poets.

BIBLIOGRAPHY

The standard editions of Tennyson's poetry are the *Complete Works* (6 vols., ed. Hallam Tennyson, Macmillan, New York, 1908) and the *Complete Poetical Works* (ed. W. J. Rolfe, Houghton Mifflin, Boston,

1898). The text of the poems in this anthology follows the latter volume.

Biography and Criticism:

Baum, Paull F., *Tennyson Sixty Years After*. University of North Carolina Press, Chapel Hill, 1948.

Bradley, A. C., *A Commentary on Tennyson's "In Memoriam"*. Macmillan, London, 1929.

Buckley, Jerome H., *Tennyson: the Growth of a Poet*. Harvard University Press, Cambridge, 1960.

Johnson, E. D. H., *The Alien Vision of Victorian Poetry: Sources of the Poetic Imagination in Tennyson, Browning, and Arnold*. Princeton University Press, Princeton, 1952. best

Nicholson, Harold G., *Tennyson: Aspects of His Life, Character, and Poetry*. Constable, London, 1949. Sims likes

Tennyson, Charles, *Alfred Tennyson*. Macmillan, New York, 1949.

Tennyson, Hallam, *Alfred Lord Tennyson: a Memoir*. 2 vols. Macmillan, New York, 1898.

MARIANA

"Mariana in the moated grange."
MEASURE FOR MEASURE.

With blackest moss the flower-plots
   Were thickly crusted, one and all:
The rusted nails fell from the knots
   That held the pear to the gable-wall.
The broken sheds look'd sad and strange:
   Unlifted was the clinking latch;
   Weeded and worn the ancient thatch
Upon the lonely moated grange.
    She only said, "My life is dreary,
      He cometh not," she said;   10
    She said, "I am aweary, aweary,
      I would that I were dead!"

Her tears fell with the dews at even;
   Her tears fell ere the dews were dried;
She could not look on the sweet heaven,
   Either at morn or eventide.
After the flitting of the bats,
   When thickest dark did trance the sky,
   She drew her casement-curtain by,
And glanced athwart the glooming flats.   20
    She only said, "The night is dreary,
      He cometh not," she said;
    She said, "I am aweary, aweary,
      I would that I were dead!"

Upon the middle of the night,
   Waking she heard the night-fowl crow:
The cock sung out an hour ere light:
   From the dark fen the oxen's low
Came to her: without hope of change,
   In sleep she seem'd to walk forlorn,   30
   Till cold winds woke the gray-eyed morn
About the lonely moated grange.

She only said, "The day is dreary,
    He cometh not," she said;
She said, "I am aweary, aweary,
    I would that I were dead!"

About a stone-cast from the wall
    A sluice with blacken'd waters slept,
And o'er it many, round and small,
    The cluster'd marish-mosses crept.   40
Hard by a poplar shook alway,
    All silver-green with gnarled bark:
For leagues no other tree did mark
The level waste, the rounding gray.
    She only said, "My life is dreary,
        He cometh not," she said;
    She said, "I am aweary, aweary,
        I would that I were dead!"

And ever when the moon was low,
    And the shrill winds were up and away,   50
In the white curtain, to and fro,
    She saw the gusty shadow sway.   *substance of reality*
But when the moon was very low,
    And wild winds bound within their cell,
    The shadow of the poplar fell
Upon her bed, across her brow.
    She only said, "The night is dreary,
        He cometh not," she said;
    She said, "I am aweary, aweary,
        I would that I were dead!"   60

All day within the dreamy house,
    The doors upon their hinges creak'd;
The blue fly sung in the pane; the mouse
    Behind the mouldering wainscot shriek'd,   *as life unbearable*
Or from the crevice peer'd about.
    Old faces glimmer'd thro' the doors,
    Old footsteps trod the upper floors,
Old voices call'd her from without.
    She only said, "My life is dreary,
        He cometh not," she said;   70

She said, "I am aweary, aweary,
  I would that I were dead!"

The sparrow's chirrup on the roof,
  The slow clock ticking, and the sound
Which to the wooing wind aloof
  The poplar made, did all confound
Her sense; but most she loathed the hour
  When the thick-moted sunbeam lay
  Athwart the chambers, and the day
Was sloping toward his western bower.   80
  Then, said she, "I am very dreary,
    He will not come," she said;
  She wept, "I am aweary, aweary,
    O God, that I were dead!"

                                [1830]

Sense of isolation + decay

THE LADY OF SHALOTT

PART I

On either side the river lie
Long fields of barley and of rye,
That clothe the wold and meet the sky;
And thro' the field the road runs by
    To many-tower'd Camelot;
And up and down the people go,
Gazing where the lilies blow
Round an island there below,
    The island of Shalott.

Willows whiten, aspens quiver,   10
Little breezes dusk and shiver
Thro' the wave that runs for ever
By the island in the river
    Flowing down to Camelot.
Four gray walls and four gray towers
Overlook a space of flowers,

And the silent isle imbowers
 The Lady of Shalott.

By the margin, willow-veil'd,
Slide the heavy barges trail'd   20
By slow horses; and unhail'd
The shallop flitteth silken-sail'd
  Skimming down to Camelot:
But who hath seen her wave her hand?
Or at the casement seen her stand?
Or is she known in all the land,
 The Lady of Shalott?

Only reapers, reaping early
In among the bearded barley,
Hear a song that echoes cheerly   30
From the river winding clearly,
  Down to tower'd Camelot:
And by the moon the reaper weary,
Piling sheaves in uplands airy,
Listening, whispers, " 'T is the fairy
 Lady of Shalott."

PART II

There she weaves by night and day
A magic web with colours gay.
She has heard a whisper say,
A curse is on her if she stay   40
  To look down to Camelot.
She knows not what the curse may be,
And so she weaveth steadily,
And little other care hath she,
 The Lady of Shalott.

And moving thro' a mirror clear
That hangs before her all the year,
Shadows of the world appear.
There she sees the highway near
  Winding down to Camelot: 50
There the river eddy whirls,
And there the surly village-churls,

And the red cloaks of market girls,
     Pass onward from Shalott.

Sometimes a troop of damsels glad,
An abbot on an ambling pad,
Sometimes a curly shepherd-lad,
Or long-hair'd page in crimson clad,
     Goes by to tower'd Camelot;
And sometimes thro' the mirror blue   60
The knights come riding two and two:
She hath no loyal knight and true,
     The Lady of Shalott.

But in her web she still delights
To weave the mirror's magic sights,
For often thro' the silent nights
A funeral, with plumes and lights
     And music, went to Camelot:
Or when the moon was overhead,
Came two young lovers lately wed;   70
"I am half sick of shadows," said
     The Lady of Shalott.

PART III

A bow-shot from her bower-eaves,
He rode between the barley-sheaves,
The sun came dazzling thro' the leaves,
And flamed upon the brazen greaves
     Of bold Sir Lancelot.
A red-cross knight for ever kneel'd
To a lady in his shield,
That sparkled on the yellow field,   80
     Beside remote Shalott.

The gemmy bridle glitter'd free,
Like to some branch of stars we see
Hung in the golden Galaxy.
The bridle bells rang merrily
     As he rode down to Camelot;

---

[76] *greaves:* leg armor.

And from his blazon'd baldric slung
A mighty silver bugle hung,
And as he rode his armour rung,
  Beside remote Shalott.   90

All in the blue unclouded weather
Thick-jewell'd shone the saddle-leather,
The helmet and the helmet-feather
Burn'd like one burning flame together,
  As he rode down to Camelot;
As often thro' the purple night,
Below the starry clusters bright,
Some bearded meteor, trailing light,
  Moves over still Shalott.

His broad clear brow in sunlight glow'd; 100
On burnish'd hooves his war-horse trode;
From underneath his helmet flow'd
His coal-black curls as on he rode,
  As he rode down to Camelot.
From the bank and from the river
He flash'd into the crystal mirror,
"Tirra lirra," by the river
  Sang Sir Lancelot.

She left the web, she left the loom,
She made three paces thro' the room, 110
She saw the water-lily bloom,
She saw the helmet and the plume,
  She look'd down to Camelot.
Out flew the web and floated wide;
The mirror crack'd from side to side;
"The curse is come upon me," cried
  The Lady of Shalott.

PART IV

In the stormy east-wind straining,
The pale yellow woods were waning,
The broad stream in his banks complaining, 120
Heavily the low sky raining
  Over tower'd Camelot;

Down she came and found a boat
Beneath a willow left afloat,
And round about the prow she wrote
  The Lady of Shalott.

And down the river's dim expanse,
Like some bold seër in a trance,
Seeing all his own mischance,
With a glassy countenance   130
    Did she look to Camelot.
And at the closing of the day
She loosed the chain, and down she lay,
The broad stream bore her far away,
    The Lady of Shalott.

Lying, robed in snowy white
That loosely flew to left and right—
The leaves upon her falling light—
Thro' the noises of the night
    She floated down to Camelot;   140
And as the boat-head wound along
The willowy hills and fields among,
They heard her singing her last song,
    The Lady of Shalott,—

Heard a carol, mournful, holy,
Chanted loudly, chanted lowly,
Till her blood was frozen slowly,
And her eyes were darken'd wholly,
    Turn'd to tower'd Camelot.
For ere she reach'd upon the tide   150
The first house by the water-side,
Singing in her song she died,
    The Lady of Shalott.

Under tower and balcony,
By garden-wall and gallery,
A gleaming shape she floated by,
Dead-pale between the houses high,
    Silent into Camelot.
Out upon the wharfs they came,

Knight and burgher, lord and dame,   160
And round the prow they read her name,
    The Lady of Shalott.

Who is this? and what is here?
And in the lighted palace near
Died the sound of royal cheer;
And they cross'd themselves for fear,
    All the knights at Camelot:
But Lancelot mused a little space;
He said, "She has a lovely face;
God in His mercy lend her grace,   170
    The Lady of Shalott."

                              [1832, 1842]

ŒNONE

There lies a vale in Ida, lovelier
Than all the valleys of Ionian hills.
The swimming vapour slopes athwart the glen,
Puts forth an arm, and creeps from pine to pine,
And loiters, slowly drawn. On either hand
The lawns and meadow-ledges midway down
Hang rich in flowers, and far below them roars
The long brook falling thro' the cloven ravine
In cataract after cataract to the sea.
Behind the valley topmost Gargarus   10
Stands up and takes the morning; but in front
The gorges, opening wide apart, reveal
Troas and Ilion's column'd citadel,

Œnone: a nymph of Mt. Ida, near Troy, who loved Paris, son of King Priam
of Troy. Paris judged the contest of beauty between Herè (queen of
heaven), Pallas (goddess of wisdom), and Aphroditè (goddess of love and
beauty). He awarded the golden apple to Aphroditè, and in return she gave
him the love of Helen, for whom he deserted Œnone. His abduction of
Helen caused the Trojan war.
10 *Gargarus:* highest peak of Mt. Ida.
13 *Troas and Ilion:* Ilion (Troy) was the capital of the district of Troas.

The crown of Troas.
               Hither came at noon
Mournful Œnone, wandering forlorn
Of Paris, once her playmate on the hills.
Her cheek had lost the rose, and round her neck
Floated her hair or seem'd to float in rest.
She, leaning on a fragment twined with vine,
Sang to the stillness, till the mountain-shade   20
Sloped downward to her seat from the upper cliff.

   "O mother Ida, many-fountain'd Ida,
Dear mother Ida, harken ere I die.
For now the noonday quiet holds the hill;
The grasshopper is silent in the grass;
The lizard, with his shadow on the stone,
Rests like a shadow, and the winds are dead.
The purple flower droops; the golden bee
Is lily-cradled: I alone awake.
My eyes are full of tears, my heart of love,   30
My heart is breaking, and my eyes are dim,
And I am all aweary of my life.

   "O mother Ida, many-fountain'd Ida,
Dear mother Ida, harken ere I die.
Hear me, O Earth, hear me, O Hills, O Caves
That house the cold crown'd snake! O Mountain Brooks,
I am the daughter of a River-God,
Hear me, for I will speak, and build up all
My sorrow with my song, as yonder walls
Rose slowly to a music slowly breathed,   40
A cloud that gather'd shape: for it may be
That, while I speak of it, a little while
My heart may wander from its deeper woe.

   "O mother Ida, many-fountain'd Ida,
Dear mother Ida, harken ere I die.
I waited underneath the dawning hills;
Aloft the mountain lawn was dewy-dark,
And dewy-dark aloft the mountain pine:

---

³⁹ *yonder walls:* The walls of Troy were supposed to have risen to the sound
of Apollo's lyre.

Beautiful Paris, evil-hearted Paris,
Leading a jet-black goat white-horn'd, white-hooved,   50
Came up from reedy Simois all alone.

"O mother Ida, harken ere I die.
Far off the torrent call'd me from the cleft;
Far up the solitary morning smote
The streaks of virgin snow. With down-dropt eyes
I sat alone: white-breasted like a star
Fronting the dawn he moved; a leopard skin
Droop'd from his shoulder, but his sunny hair
Cluster'd about his temples like a God's;
And his cheek brighten'd as the foam-bow brightens   60
When the wind blows the foam, and all my heart
Went forth to embrace him coming ere he came.

"Dear mother Ida, harken ere I die.
He smiled, and opening out his milk-white palm
Disclosed a fruit of pure Hesperian gold,
That smelt ambrosially, and while I look'd
And listen'd, the full-flowing river of speech
Came down upon my heart:
                      'My own Œnone,
Beautiful-brow'd Œnone, my own soul,
Behold this fruit, whose gleaming rind ingraven   70
"For the most fair," would seem to award it thine,
As lovelier than whatever Oread haunt
The knolls of Ida, loveliest in all grace
Of movement, and the charm of married brows.'

"Dear mother Ida, harken ere I die.
He prest the blossom of his lips to mine,
And added, 'This was cast upon the board,
When all the full-faced presence of the Gods
Ranged in the halls of Peleus; whereupon
Rose feud, with question unto whom 't were due: 80
But light-foot Iris brought it yester-eve,

---

[79] *Peleus:* king of Thessaly, who married Thetis, a sea nymph, and invited to his wedding all the gods except Eris, goddess of discord. The angry Eris threw among the guests a golden apple marked "For the fairest"; Paris was asked to judge the claimants for the apple.
[81] *Iris:* messenger of the gods.

Delivering, that to me, by common voice
Elected umpire, Herè comes to-day,
Pallas and Aphroditè, claiming each
This meed of fairest. Thou, within the cave
Behind yon whispering tuft of oldest pine,
Mayst well behold them unbeheld, unheard
Hear all, and see thy Paris judge of Gods.'

   "Dear mother Ida, harken ere I die.
It was the deep midnoon: one silvery cloud   90
Had lost his way between the piney sides
Of this long glen. Then to the bower they came,
Naked they came to that smooth-swarded bower,
And at their feet the crocus brake like fire,
Violet, amaracus, and asphodel,
Lotos and lilies; and a wind arose,
And overhead the wandering ivy and vine,
This way and that, in many a wild festoon
Ran riot, garlanding the gnarled boughs
With bunch and berry and flower thro' and thro'.   100

   "O mother Ida, harken ere I die.
On the tree-tops a crested peacock lit,
And o'er him flow'd a golden cloud, and lean'd
Upon him, slowly dropping fragrant dew.
Then first I heard the voice of her to whom
Coming thro' Heaven, like a light that grows
Larger and clearer, with one mind the Gods
Rise up for reverence. She to Paris made
Proffer of royal power, ample rule
Unquestion'd, overflowing revenue   110
Wherewith to embellish state, 'from many a vale
And river-sunder'd champaign clothed with corn,
Or labour'd mine undrainable of ore.
Honour,' she said, 'and homage, tax and toll,
From many an inland town and haven large,
Mast-throng'd beneath her shadowing citadel
In glassy bays among her tallest towers.'

---

102 *peacock:* sacred to Herè, whose arrival he announces.

"O mother Ida, harken ere I die.
Still she spake on and still she spake of power,
'Which in all action is the end of all;
Power fitted to the season; wisdom-bred
And throned of wisdom—from all neighbour crowns
Alliance and allegiance, till thy hand
Fail from the sceptre-staff. Such boon from me,
From me, Heaven's Queen, Paris, to thee king-born,—
A shepherd all thy life, but yet king-born,—
Should come most welcome, seeing men, in power
Only, are likest Gods, who have attain'd
Rest in a happy place and quiet seats
Above the thunder, with undying bliss
In knowledge of their own supremacy.'

"Dear mother Ida, harken ere I die.
She ceased, and Paris held the costly fruit
Out at arm's-length, so much the thought of power
Flatter'd his spirit; but Pallas where she stood
Somewhat apart, her clear and bared limbs
O'erthwarted with the brazen-headed spear
Upon her pearly shoulder leaning cold,
The while, above, her full and earnest eye
Over her snow-cold breast and angry cheek
Kept watch, waiting decision, made reply:

" 'Self-reverence, self-knowledge, self-control,
These three alone lead life to sovereign power.
Yet not for power (power of herself
Would come uncall'd for) but to live by law,
Acting the law we live by without fear;
And, because right is right, to follow right
Were wisdom in the scorn of consequence.'

"Dear mother Ida, harken ere I die.
Again she said: 'I woo thee not with gifts.
Sequel of guerdon could not alter me
To fairer. Judge thou me by what I am,
So shalt thou find me fairest.
                              Yet, indeed,
If gazing on divinity disrobed

Thy mortal eyes are frail to judge of fair,
Unbias'd by self-profit, oh! rest thee sure
That I shall love thee well and cleave to thee,
So that my vigour, wedded to thy blood,
Shall strike within thy pulses, like a God's,
To push thee forward thro' a life of shocks,   160
Dangers, and deeds, until endurance grow
Sinew'd with action, and the full-grown will,
Circled thro' all experiences, pure law,
Commeasure perfect freedom.'
                                        Here she ceas'd,
And Paris ponder'd, and I cried, 'O Paris,
Give it to Pallas!' but he heard me not,
Or hearing would not hear me, woe is me!

    "O mother Ida, many-fountain'd Ida,
Dear mother Ida, harken ere I die.
Idalian Aphroditè beautiful,   170
Fresh as the foam, new-bathed in Paphian wells,
With rosy slender fingers backward drew
From her warm brows and bosom her deep hair
Ambrosial, golden round her lucid throat
And shoulder: from the violets her light foot
Shone rosy-white, and o'er her rounded form
Between the shadows of the vine-bunches
Floated the glowing sunlights, as she moved.

    "Dear mother Ida, harken ere I die.
She with a subtle smile in her mild eyes,   180
The herald of her triumph, drawing nigh
Half-whisper'd in his ear, 'I promise thee
The fairest and most loving wife in Greece.'
She spoke and laugh'd: I shut my sight for fear;
But when I look'd, Paris had raised his arm,
And I beheld great Herè's angry eyes,
As she withdrew into the golden cloud,
And I was left alone within the bower;
And from that time to this I am alone,
And I shall be alone until I die.   190

---

170 *Idalian:* Idalium and Paphos were towns in Cyprus sacred to Aphroditè.

"Yet, mother Ida, harken ere I die.
Fairest—why fairest wife? am I not fair?
My love hath told me so a thousand times.
Methinks I must be fair, for yesterday,
When I past by, a wild and wanton pard,
Eyed like the evening star, with playful tail
Crouch'd fawning in the weed. Most loving is she?
Ah me, my mountain shepherd, that my arms
Were wound about thee, and my hot lips prest
Close, close to thine in that quick-falling dew   200
Of fruitful kisses, thick as Autumn rains
Flash in the pools of whirling Simois!

"O mother, hear me yet before I die.
They came, they cut away my tallest pines,
My tall dark pines, that plumed the craggy ledge
High over the blue gorge, and all between
The snowy peak and snow-white cataract
Foster'd the callow eaglet—from beneath
Whose thick mysterious boughs in the dark morn
The panther's roar came muffled, while I sat
Low in the valley. Never, never more
Shall lone Œnone see the morning mist
Sweep thro' them; never see them overlaid
With narrow moon-lit slips of silver cloud,
Between the loud stream and the trembling stars.

"O mother, hear me yet before I die.
I wish that somewhere in the ruin'd folds,
Among the fragments tumbled from the glens,
Or the dry thickets, I could meet with her
The Abominable, that uninvited came   220
Into the fair Peleïan banquet-hall,
And cast the golden fruit upon the board,
And bred this change; that I might speak my mind,
And tell her to her face how much I hate
Her presence, hated both of Gods and men.

---

195 *pard:* leopard or panther.
220 *The Abominable:* Eris.

"O mother, hear me yet before I die.
Hath he not sworn his love a thousand times,
In this green valley, under this green hill,
Even on this hand, and sitting on this stone?
Seal'd it with kisses? water'd it with tears?   230
O happy tears, and how unlike to these!
O happy Heaven, how canst thou see my face?
O happy earth, how canst thou bear my weight?
O death, death, death, thou ever-floating cloud,
There are enough unhappy on this earth,
Pass by the happy souls, that love to live;
I pray thee, pass before my light of life,
And shadow all my soul, that I may die.
Thou weighest heavy on the heart within,
Weigh heavy on my eyelids; let me die.   240

"O mother, hear me yet before I die.
I will not die alone, for fiery thoughts
Do shape themselves within me, more and more,
Whereof I catch the issue, as I hear
Dead sounds at night come from the inmost hills,
Like footsteps upon wool. I dimly see
My far-off doubtful purpose, as a mother
Conjectures of the features of her child
Ere it is born: her child!—a shudder comes
Across me: never child be born of me,   250
Unblest, to vex me with his father's eyes!

"O mother, hear me yet before I die.
Hear me, O earth. I will not die alone,
Lest their shrill happy laughter come to me
Walking the cold and starless road of death
Uncomforted, leaving my ancient love
With the Greek woman. I will rise and go
Down into Troy, and ere the stars come forth
Talk with the wild Cassandra, for she says

---

242 *I will not die alone:* When Paris, wounded in the Trojan war, came to
Œnone to be cured, she refused to help him; after his death she killed herself.
259 *Cassandra:* daughter of Priam; she had the power of prophecy, but no
one would believe what she foresaw.

A fire dances before her, and a sound   260
Rings ever in her ears of armed men.
What this may be I know not, but I know
That, wheresoe'er I am by night and day,
All earth and air seem only burning fire."

[1832, 1842]

THE PALACE OF ART

to ——
With the Following Poem

I send you here a sort of allegory
(For you will understand it) of a soul,
A sinful soul possess'd of many gifts,
A spacious garden full of flowering weeds,
A glorious Devil, large in heart and brain,
That did love Beauty only (Beauty seen
In all varieties of mould and mind)
And Knowledge for its beauty; or if Good,
Good only for its beauty, seeing not
That Beauty, Good, and Knowledge are three sisters   10
That doat upon each other, friends to man,
Living together under the same roof,
And never can be sunder'd without tears.
And he that shuts Love out, in turn shall be
Shut out from Love, and on her threshold lie
Howling in outer darkness. Not for this
Was common clay ta'en from the common earth
Moulded by God, and temper'd with the tears
Of angels to the perfect shape of man.

THE PALACE OF ART

I built my soul a lordly pleasure-house,
    Wherein at ease for aye to dwell.
I said, "O Soul, make merry and carouse,
    Dear soul, for all is well."

to——: The poem is probably dedicated to Richard Chevenix Trench, one of
the "Apostles" at Cambridge.

A huge crag-platform, smooth as burnish'd brass,
    I chose. The ranged ramparts bright
From level meadow-bases of deep grass
      Suddenly scaled the light.

Thereon I built it firm. Of ledge or shelf
    The rock rose clear, or winding stair.   10
My soul would live alone unto herself
      In her high palace there.

And "while the world runs round and round," I said,
    "Reign thou apart, a quiet king,
Still as, while Saturn whirls, his stedfast shade
      Sleeps on his luminous ring."

To which my soul made answer readily:
    "Trust me, in bliss I shall abide
In this great mansion that is built for me,
      So royal-rich and wide."   20

   .   .   .   .   .

Four courts I made, East, West and South and North,
    In each a squared lawn, wherefrom
The golden gorge of dragons spouted forth
      A flood of fountain-foam.

And round the cool green courts there ran a row
    Of cloisters, branch'd like mighty woods,
Echoing all night to that sonorous flow
      Of spouted fountain-floods.

And round the roofs a gilded gallery
    That lent broad verge to distant lands,   30
Far as the wild swan wings, to where the sky
      Dipt down to sea and sands.

From those four jets four currents in one swell
    Across the mountain stream'd below
In misty folds, that floating as they fell
      Lit up a torrent-bow.

---

15 *Saturn:* the shadow of Saturn seems without motion when thrown upon the bright ring surrounding the planet.

And high on every peak a statue seem'd
   To hang on tiptoe, tossing up
A cloud of incense of all odour steam'd
    From out a golden cup.   40

So that she thought, "And who shall gaze upon
   My palace with unblinded eyes,
While this great bow will waver in the sun,
    And that sweet incense rise?"

For that sweet incense rose and never fail'd,
   And, while day sank or mounted higher,
The light aërial gallery, golden-rail'd,
    Burnt like a fringe of fire.

Likewise the deep-set windows, stain'd and traced,
   Would seem slow-flaming crimson fires   50
From shadow'd grots of arches interlaced,
    And tipt with frost-like spires.

      .   .   .   .

Full of long-sounding corridors it was,
   That over-vaulted grateful gloom,
Thro' which the livelong day my soul did pass,
    Well-pleased, from room to room.

Full of great rooms and small the palace stood,
   All various, each a perfect whole
From living Nature, fit for every mood
    And change of my still soul.   60

For some were hung with arras green and blue,
   Showing a gaudy summer-morn,
Where with puff'd cheek the belted hunter blew
    His wreathed bugle-horn.

One seem'd all dark and red,—a tract of sand,
   And some one pacing there alone,
Who paced for ever in a glimmering land,
    Lit with a low large moon.

One show'd an iron coast and angry waves.
   You seem'd to hear them climb and fall   70

And roar rock-thwarted under bellowing caves,
    Beneath the windy wall.

And one, a full-fed river winding slow
    By herds upon an endless plain,
The ragged rims of thunder brooding low,
    With shadow-streaks of rain.

And one, the reapers at their sultry toil.
    In front they bound the sheaves. Behind
Were realms of upland, prodigal in oil,
    And hoary to the wind.   80

And one a foreground black with stones and slags,
    Beyond, a line of heights: and higher
All barr'd with long white cloud the scornful crags,
    And highest, snow and fire.

And one, an English home,—gray twilight pour'd
    On dewy pastures, dewy trees,
Softer than sleep,—all things in order stored,
    A haunt of ancient Peace.

Nor these alone, but every landscape fair,
    As fit for every mood of mind,   90
Or gay, or grave, or sweet, or stern, was there
    Not less than truth design'd.

    .   .   .   .   .

Or the maid-mother by a crucifix,
    In tracts of pasture sunny-warm,
Beneath branch-work of costly sardonyx
    Sat smiling, babe in arm.

Or in a clear-wall'd city on the sea,
    Near gilded organ-pipes, her hair
Wound with white roses, slept Saint Cecily;
    An angel look'd at her.   100

Or thronging all one porch of Paradise
    A group of Houris bow'd to see

---

[99] *Saint Cecily:* patron saint of music.
[102] *Houris:* nymphs of perfect beauty in Islamic paradise.

The dying Islamite, with hands and eyes
    That said, We wait for thee.

Or mythic Uther's deeply-wounded son
    In some fair space of sloping greens
Lay, dozing in the vale of Avalon,
    And watch'd by weeping queens.

Or hollowing one hand against his ear,
    To list a foot-fall, ere he saw   110
The wood-nymph, stay'd the Ausonian king to hear
    Of wisdom and of law.

Or over hills with peaky tops engrail'd,
    And many a tract of palm and rice,
The throne of Indian Cama slowly sail'd
    A summer fann'd with spice.

Or sweet Europa's mantle blew unclasp'd, *Greek*
    From off her shoulder backward borne:
From one hand droop'd a crocus; one hand grasp'd
    The mild bull's golden horn.   120

Or else flush'd Ganymede, his rosy thigh
    Half-buried in the Eagle's down,
Sole as a flying star shot thro' the sky
    Above the pillar'd town.

Nor these alone; but every legend fair
    Which the supreme Caucasian mind
Carved out of Nature for itself, was there,
    Not less than life, design'd.

     .   .   .   .   .

Then in the towers I placed great bells that swung,
    Moved of themselves, with silver sound;   130

---

[105] *Uther's deeply-wounded son:* King Arthur, who was taken by three queens, after his death, to the island paradise of Avalon.
[111] *Ausonian:* Italian. Numa, an early Roman king, was taught by the nymph Egeria.
[115] *Cama:* Hindu god of love.
[117] *Europa:* princess abducted by Zeus in the form of a bull.
[121] *Ganymede:* beautiful youth abducted by the eagle of Zeus to become cup-bearer to the gods.

And with choice paintings of wise men I hung
   The royal dais round.

For there was Milton like a seraph strong,
   Beside him Shakespeare bland and mild;
And there the world-worn Dante grasp'd his song,
   And somewhat grimly smiled.

And there the Ionian father of the rest;
   A million wrinkles carved his skin;
A hundred winters snow'd upon his breast,
   From cheek and throat and chin.   140

Above, the fair hall-ceiling stately-set
   Many an arch high up did lift,
And angels rising and descending met
   With interchange of gift.

Below was all mosaic choicely plann'd
   With cycles of the human tale
Of this wide world, the times of every land
   So wrought, they will not fail.

The people here, a beast of burden slow,
   Toil'd onward, prick'd with goads and stings;   150
Here play'd a tiger, rolling to and fro
   The heads and crowns of kings;

Here rose an athlete, strong to break or bind
   All force in bonds that might endure,
And here once more like some sick man declined,
   And trusted any cure.

But over these she trod; and those great bells
   Began to chime. She took her throne;
She sat betwixt the shining oriels,
   To sing her songs alone.   160

---

137 *Ionian father:* Homer.
159 *oriels:* bay windows.

And thro' the topmost oriels' coloured flame
    Two godlike faces gazed below,—
Plato the wise, and large-brow'd Verulam,
    The first of those who know.

And all those names that in their motion were
    Full-welling fountain-heads of change,
Betwixt the slender shafts were blazon'd fair
    In diverse raiment strange;

Thro' which the lights, rose, amber, emerald, blue,
    Flush'd in her temples and her eyes,   170
And from her lips, as morn from Memnon, drew
    Rivers of melodies.

No nightingale delighteth to prolong
    Her low preamble all alone,
More than my soul to hear her echo'd song
    Throb thro' the ribbed stone;

Singing and murmuring in her feastful mirth,
    Joying to feel herself alive,
Lord over Nature, lord of the visible earth,
    Lord of the senses five;   180

Communing with herself: "All these are mine,
    And let the world have peace or wars,
'T is one to me." She—when young night divine
    Crown'd dying day with stars,

Making sweet close of his delicious toils—
    Lit light in wreaths and anadems,
And pure quintessences of precious oils
    In hollow'd moons of gems,

To mimic heaven; and clapt her hands and cried,
    "I marvel if my still delight   190

---

163 *Verulam:* Francis Bacon, Lord Verulam.
171 *Memnon:* whose statue in Egypt was believed to give forth music when the dawn's light fell upon it.
186 *anadems:* garlands.

In this great house so royal-rich and wide
    Be flatter'd to the height.

"O all things fair to sate my various eyes!
    O shapes and hues that please me well!
O silent faces of the Great and Wise,
    My Gods, with whom I dwell!

"O Godlike isolation which art mine,
    I can but count thee perfect gain,
What time I watch the darkening droves of swine
    That range on yonder plain.   200

"In filthy sloughs they roll a prurient skin,
    They graze and wallow, breed and sleep;
And oft some brainless devil enters in,
    And drives them to the deep."

Then of the moral instinct would she prate
    And of the rising from the dead,
As hers by right of full-accomplish'd Fate;
    And at the last she said:

"I take possession of man's mind and deed.
    I care not what the sects may brawl.   210
I sit as God holding no form of creed,
    But contemplating all."

            .   .   .   .   .

Full oft the riddle of the painful earth
    Flash'd thro' her as she sat alone,
Yet not the less held she her solemn mirth,
    And intellectual throne.

And so she throve and prosper'd; so three years
    She prosper'd: on the fourth she fell,
Like Herod, when the shout was in his ears,
    Struck thro' with pangs of hell.   220

Lest she should fail and perish utterly,
    God, before whom ever lie bare

---

219 *Herod:* In *Acts* 12: 21-23 Herod is struck down as the people are praising
him, because he does not give God the glory.

The abysmal deeps of Personality,
    Plagued her with sore despair.

When she would think, where'er she turn'd her sight
    The airy hand confusion wrought,
Wrote, "Mene, mene," and divided quite
    The kingdom of her thought. *mind*

Deep dread and loathing of her solitude
    Fell on her, from which mood was born   230
Scorn of herself; again, from out that mood
    Laughter at her self-scorn.

"What! is not this my place of strength," she said,
    "My spacious mansion built for me,
Whereof the strong foundation-stones were laid
    Since my first memory?"

But in dark corners of her palace stood
    Uncertain shapes; and unawares
On white-eyed phantasms weeping tears of blood,
    And horrible nightmares,   240

And hollow shades enclosing hearts of flame,
    And, with dim fretted foreheads all,
On corpses three-months-old at noon she came,
    That stood against the wall.

A spot of dull stagnation, without light
    Or power of movement, seem'd my soul,
Mid onward-sloping motions infinite
    Making for one sure goal:

A still salt pool, lock'd in with bars of sand,
    Left on the shore; that hears all night   250
The plunging seas draw backward from the land
    Their moon-led waters white:

---

227 *"Mene, mene"*: the beginning of the mysterious phrase written on the wall of Belshazzar's palace. In *Daniel* 5: 26 it is interpreted as "God hath numbered thy kingdom, and finished it."

A star that with the choral starry dance
 Join'd not, but stood, and standing saw
The hollow orb of moving Circumstance
  Roll'd round by one fix'd law.

Back on herself her serpent pride had curl'd.
 "No voice," she shriek'd in that lone hall,
"No voice breaks thro' the stillness of this world:
  One deep, deep silence all!"   260

She, mouldering with the dull earth's mouldering sod,
 Inwrapt tenfold in slothful shame,
Lay there exiled from eternal God,
  Lost to her place and name;

And death and life she hated equally,
 And nothing saw, for her despair,
But dreadful time, dreadful eternity,
  No comfort anywhere;

Remaining utterly confused with fears,
 And ever worse with growing time,   270
And ever unrelieved by dismal tears,
  And all alone in crime.

Shut up as in a crumbling tomb, girt round
 With blackness as a solid wall,
Far off she seem'd to hear the dully sound
  Of human footsteps fall:

As in strange lands a traveller walking slow,
 In doubt and great perplexity,
A little before moon-rise hears the low
  Moan of an unknown sea;   280

And knows not if it be thunder, or a sound
 Of rocks thrown down, or one deep cry
Of great wild beasts; then thinketh, "I have found
  A new land, but I die."

---

255 *hollow . . . Circumstance:* the sphere of the heavens.

She howl'd aloud, "I am on fire within.
     There comes no murmur of reply.
What is it that will take away my sin,
     And save me lest I die?"

So when four years were wholly finished,
     She threw her royal robes away.
"Make me a cottage in the vale," she said,
     "Where I may mourn and pray.

"Yet pull not down my palace towers that are
     So lightly, beautifully built:
Perchance I may return with others there
     When I have purged my guilt."

*this but hedged yet 290
divided mind
something wrong
so involve self,
if involve self,
may destroy self*

[1832, 1842]

THE LOTOS-EATERS

"Courage!" he said, and pointed toward the land,
"This mounting wave will roll us shoreward soon."
In the afternoon they came unto a land
In which it seemed always afternoon.
All round the coast the languid air did swoon,
Breathing like one that hath a weary dream.
Full-faced above the valley stood the moon;
And, like a downward smoke, the slender stream
Along the cliff to fall and pause and fall did seem.

A land of streams! some, like a downward smoke,   10
Slow-dropping veils of thinnest lawn, did go;
And some thro' wavering lights and shadows broke,
Rolling a slumbrous sheet of foam below.
They saw the gleaming river seaward flow
From the inner land; far off, three mountain-tops,
Three silent pinnacles of aged snow,

---

[1] *he:* Odysseus urging his mariners on their return home. The story of their
encounter with the lotos-eaters is told in Book IX of the *Odyssey*.

Stood sunset-flush'd; and, dew'd with showery drops,
Up-clomb the shadowy pine above the woven copse. *thicket*

The charmed sunset linger'd low adown
In the red West: thro' mountain clefts the dale   20
Was seen far inland, and the yellow down
Border'd with palm, and many a winding vale
And meadow, set with slender galingale;
A land where all things always seem'd the same!
And round about the keel with faces pale,
Dark faces pale against that rosy flame,
The mild-eyed, melancholy Lotos-eaters came.

Branches they bore of that enchanted stem,
Laden with flower and fruit, whereof they gave
To each; but whoso did receive of them,   30
And taste, to him the gushing of the wave
Far, far away did seem to mourn and rave
On alien shores; and if his fellow spake,
His voice was thin, as voices from the grave;
And deep-asleep he seem'd, yet all awake,
And music in his ears his beating heart did make.

They sat them down upon the yellow sand,
Between the sun and moon upon the shore;
And sweet it was to dream of Fatherland,
Of child, and wife, and slave; but evermore   40
Most weary seem'd the sea, weary the oar,
Weary the wandering fields of barren foam.
Then some one said, "We will return no more;"
And all at once they sang, "Our island home
Is far beyond the wave; we will no longer roam."

Choric Song

I

There is sweet music here that softer falls
Than petals from blown roses on the grass,
Or night-dews on still waters between walls
Of shadowy granite, in a gleaming pass,—

---

[23] *galingale:* fragrant herb.

Music that gentlier on the spirit lies,
Than tired eyelids upon tired eyes;
Music that brings sweet sleep down from the blissful skies.
Here are cool mosses deep,
And thro' the moss the ivies creep,
And in the stream the long-leaved flowers weep, 10
And from the craggy ledge the poppy hangs in sleep.

II

Why are we weigh'd upon with heaviness, *is sense / of doubt*
And utterly consumed with sharp distress,
While all things else have rest from weariness?
All things have rest: why should we toil alone,
We only toil, who are the first of things,
And make perpetual moan,
Still from one sorrow to another thrown;
Nor ever fold our wings,
And cease from wanderings, 20
Nor steep our brows in slumber's holy balm;
Nor harken what the inner spirit sings,
"There is no joy but calm!"
Why should we only toil, the roof and crown of things?

III

Lo! in the middle of the wood, *peace + security / of nature*
The folded leaf is woo'd from out the bud
With winds upon the branch, and there
Grows green and broad, and takes no care,
Sun-steep'd at noon, and in the moon
Nightly dew-fed; and turning yellow 30
Falls, and floats adown the air.
Lo! sweeten'd with the summer light,
The full-juiced apple, waxing over-mellow, *word hints dante*
Drops in a silent autumn night.
All its allotted length of days,
The flower ripens in its place,
Ripens, and fades, and falls, and hath no toil,
Fast-rooted in the fruitful soil.

IV

Hateful is the dark-blue sky,
Vaulted o'er the dark-blue sea.   40
Death is the end of life; ah, why
Should life all labour be?
Let us alone. Time driveth onward fast,
And in a little while our lips are dumb.
Let us alone. What is it that will last?
All things are taken from us, and become
Portions and parcels of the dreadful Past.
Let us alone. What pleasure can we have
To war with evil? Is there any peace
In ever climbing up the climbing wave?   50
All things have rest, and ripen toward the grave
In silence; ripen, fall, and cease:
Give us long rest or death, dark death, or dreamful ease.

V

How sweet it were, hearing the downward stream,
With half-shut eyes ever to seem
Falling asleep in a half-dream!
To dream and dream, like yonder amber light,
Which will not leave the myrrh-bush on the height;
To hear each other's whisper'd speech;
Eating the Lotos day by day,   60
To watch the crisping ripples on the beach,
And tender curving lines of creamy spray;
To lend our hearts and spirits wholly
To the influence of mild-minded melancholy;
To muse and brood and live again in memory,
With those old faces of our infancy
Heap'd over with a mound of grass,
Two handfuls of white dust, shut in an urn of brass!

VI

Dear is the memory of our wedded lives,
And dear the last embraces of our wives   70
And their warm tears; but all hath suffer'd change:
For surely now our household hearths are cold;
Our sons inherit us; our looks are strange;

And we should come like ghosts to trouble joy.
Or else the island princes over-bold
Have eat our substance, and the minstrel sings
Before them of the ten years' war in Troy,
And our great deeds, as half-forgotten things.
Is there confusion in the little isle?
Let what is broken so remain.   80
The Gods are hard to reconcile;
'T is hard to settle order once again.
There *is* confusion worse than death,
Trouble on trouble, pain on pain,
Long labour unto aged breath,
Sore task to hearts worn out by many wars
And eyes grown dim with gazing on the pilot-stars.

VII

But, propt on beds of amaranth and moly,
How sweet (while warm airs lull us, blowing lowly)
With half-dropt eyelid still,   90
Beneath a heaven dark and holy,
To watch the long bright river drawing slowly
His waters from the purple hill—
To hear the dewy echoes calling
From cave to cave thro' the thick-twined vine—
To watch the emerald-colour'd water falling
Thro' many a woven acanthus-wreath divine!
Only to hear and see the far-off sparkling brine,
Only to hear were sweet, stretch'd out beneath the pine.

VIII

The Lotos blooms below the barren peak;   100
The Lotos blows by every winding creek;
All day the wind breathes low with mellower tone;
Thro' every hollow cave and alley lone
Round and round the spicy downs the yellow Lotos-dust is
    blown.
We have had enough of action, and of motion we,
Roll'd to starboard, roll'd to larboard, when the surge was
    seething free,

---

88 *amaranth:* unfading flower. *moly:* magical herb.
97 *acanthus:* sacred plant whose leaves were used in garlands.

Where the wallowing monster spouted his foam-fountains in
the sea.
Let us swear an oath, and keep it with an equal mind,
In the hollow Lotos-land to live and lie reclined
On the hills like Gods together, careless of mankind.   110
For they lie beside their nectar, and the bolts are hurl'd
Far below them in the valleys, and the clouds are lightly
curl'd
Round their golden houses, girdled with the gleaming world;
Where they smile in secret, looking over wasted lands,
Blight and famine, plague and earthquake, roaring deeps and
fiery sands,
Clanging fights, and flaming towns, and sinking ships, and praying
hands.
But they smile, they find a music centered in a doleful song
Steaming up, a lamentation and an ancient tale of wrong,
Like a tale of little meaning tho' the words are strong;
Chanted from an ill-used race of men that cleave the soil,   120
Sow the seed, and reap the harvest with enduring toil,
Storing yearly little dues of wheat, and wine and oil;
Till they perish and they suffer—some, 't is whisper'd—down
in hell
Suffer endless anguish, others in Elysian valleys dwell,
Resting weary limbs at last on beds of asphodel.
Surely, surely, slumber is more sweet than toil, the shore
Than labour in the deep mid-ocean, wind and wave and
oar;
Oh, rest ye, brother mariners, we will not wander more.

[1832, 1842]

---

124 *Elysian:* referring to Elysium, Greek paradise where grew the *asphodel,*
a kind of narcissus.

MORTE D'ARTHUR

So all day long the noise of battle roll'd
Among the mountains by the winter sea;
Until King Arthur's table, man by man,
Had fallen in Lyonness about their lord,
King Arthur: then, because his wound was deep,
The bold Sir Bedivere uplifted him,
Sir Bedivere, the last of all his knights,
And bore him to a chapel nigh the field,
A broken chancel with a broken cross,
That stood on a dark strait of barren land.   10
On one side lay the Ocean, and on one
Lay a great water, and the moon was full.
    Then spake King Arthur to Sir Bedivere:
"The sequel of to-day unsolders all
The goodliest fellowship of famous knights
Whereof this world holds record. Such a sleep
They sleep—the men I loved. I think that we
Shall never more, at any future time,
Delight our souls with talk of knightly deeds,
Walking about the gardens and the halls   20
Of Camelot, as in the days that were.
I perish by this people which I made,—
Tho' Merlin sware that I should come again
To rule once more; but let what will be, be,
I am so deeply smitten thro' the helm
That without help I cannot last till morn.
Thou therefore take my brand Excalibur,
Which was my pride: for thou rememberest how
In those old days, one summer noon, an arm
Rose up from out the bosom of the lake,   30
Clothed in white samite, mystic, wonderful,

Morte D'Arthur: Tennyson's chief source was Malory's *Morte D'Arthur*,
Book XXI. The poem, with some changes, became "The Passing of Arthur"
in the *Idylls of the King,* Tennyson's epic account of the court at Camelot.
4 *Lyonness:* legendary country south of Cornwall, later covered by the sea.
23 *Merlin:* chief magician of Arthur's court.
27 *brand:* sword.
31 *samite:* heavy silken fabric.

Holding the sword—and how I row'd across
And took it, and have worn it, like a king;
And, wheresoever I am sung or told
In aftertime, this also shall be known.
But now delay not: take Excalibur,
And fling him far into the middle mere:
Watch what thou seëst, and lightly bring me word."
    To him replied the bold Sir Bedivere:
"It is not meet, Sir King, to leave thee thus,   40
Aidless, alone, and smitten thro' the helm—
A little thing may harm a wounded man;
Yet I thy hest will all perform at full,
Watch what I see, and lightly bring thee word."
    So saying, from the ruin'd shrine he stept,
And in the moon athwart the place of tombs,
Where lay the mighty bones of ancient men,
Old knights, and over them the sea-wind sang
Shrill, chill, with flakes of foam. He, stepping down
By zig-zag paths and juts of pointed rock,   50
Came on the shining levels of the lake.
    There drew he forth the brand Excalibur,
And o'er him, drawing it, the winter moon,
Brightening the skirts of a long cloud, ran forth
And sparkled keen with frost against the hilt;
For all the haft twinkled with diamond sparks,
Myriads of topaz-lights, and jacinth-work
Of subtlest jewellery. He gazed so long
That both his eyes were dazzled, as he stood,
This way and that dividing the swift mind,   60
In act to throw; but at the last it seem'd
Better to leave Excalibur conceal'd
There in the many-knotted waterflags,
That whistled stiff and dry about the marge.
So strode he back slow to the wounded King.
    Then spake King Arthur to Sir Bedivere:
"Hast thou perform'd my mission which I gave?
What is it thou hast seen? or what hast heard?"
    And answer made the bold Sir Bedivere:
"I heard the ripple washing in the reeds,   70

---

[57] *jacinth-work:* jewelry of orange gems.

And the wild water lapping on the crag."
To whom replied King Arthur, faint and pale:
"Thou hast betray'd thy nature and thy name,
Not rendering true answer, as beseem'd
Thy fealty, nor like a noble knight;
For surer sign had follow'd, either hand,
Or voice, or else a motion of the mere.
This is a shameful thing for men to lie.
Yet now, I charge thee, quickly go again,
As thou art lief and dear, and do the thing   80
I bade thee, watch, and lightly bring me word."
Then went Sir Bedivere the second time
Across the ridge, and paced beside the mere,
Counting the dewy pebbles, fix'd in thought;
But when he saw the wonder of the hilt,
How curiously and strangely chased, he smote
His palms together, and he cried aloud:
"And if indeed I cast the brand away,
Surely a precious thing, one worthy note,
Should thus be lost for ever from the earth,   90
Which might have pleased the eyes of many men.
What good should follow this, if this were done?
What harm, undone? deep harm to disobey,
Seeing obedience is the bond of rule.
Were it well to obey then, if a king demand
An act unprofitable, against himself?
The King is sick, and knows not what he does.
What record, or what relic of my lord
Should be to aftertime, but empty breath
And rumours of a doubt? but were this kept,   100
Stored in some treasure-house of mighty kings,
Some one might show it at a joust of arms,
Saying, 'King Arthur's sword, Excalibur,
Wrought by the lonely maiden of the Lake.
Nine years she wrought it, sitting in the deeps
Upon the hidden bases of the hills.'
So might some old man speak in the aftertime
To all the people, winning reverence.
But now much honour and much fame were lost."
So spake he, clouded with his own conceit,   110
And hid Excalibur the second time,

And so strode back slow to the wounded King.
      Then spoke King Arthur, breathing heavily:
"What is it thou hast seen? or what hast heard?"
      And answer made the bold Sir Bedivere:
"I heard the water lapping on the crag,
And the long ripple washing in the reeds."
      To whom replied King Arthur, much in wrath:
"Ah, miserable and unkind, untrue,
Unknightly, traitor-hearted! Woe is me!   120
Authority forgets a dying king,
Laid widow'd of the power in his eye
That bow'd the will. I see thee what thou art,
For thou, the latest-left of all my knights,
In whom should meet the offices of all,
Thou wouldst betray me for the precious hilt;
Either from lust of gold, or like a girl
Valuing the giddy pleasure of the eyes.
Yet, for a man may fail in duty twice,
And the third time may prosper, get thee hence;   130
But if thou spare to fling Excalibur,
I will arise and slay thee with my hands."
      Then quickly rose Sir Bedivere, and ran,
And, leaping down the ridges lightly, plunged
Among the bulrush beds, and clutch'd the sword,
And strongly wheel'd and threw it. The great brand
Made lightnings in the splendour of the moon,
And flashing round and round, and whirl'd in an arch,
Shot like a streamer of the northern morn,
Seen where the moving isles of winter shock   140
By night, with noises of the Northern Sea.
So flash'd and fell the brand Excalibur;
But ere he dipt the surface, rose an arm
Cloth'd in white samite, mystic, wonderful,
And caught him by the hilt, and brandish'd him
Three times, and drew him under in the mere.
And lightly went the other to the King.
      Then spoke King Arthur, drawing thicker breath:
"Now see I by thine eyes that this is done.
Speak out: what is it thou hast heard, or seen?"   150

---

139 *northern morn:* the northern lights.
140 *moving isles:* icebergs.

And answer made the bold Sir Bedivere:
"Sir King, I closed mine eyelids, lest the gems
Should blind my purpose, for I never saw,
Nor shall see, here or elsewhere, till I die,
Not tho' I live three lives of mortal men,
So great a miracle as yonder hilt.
Then with both hands I flung him, wheeling him;
But when I look'd again, behold an arm,
Clothed in white samite, mystic, wonderful,
That caught him by the hilt, and brandish'd him　　160
Three times, and drew him under in the mere."
　　And answer made King Arthur, breathing hard:
"My end draws nigh; 't is time that I were gone.
Make broad thy shoulders to receive my weight,
And bear me to the margin; yet I fear
My wound hath taken cold, and I shall die."
　　So saying, from the pavement he half rose,
Slowly, with pain, reclining on his arm,
And looking wistfully with wide blue eyes
As in a picture. Him Sir Bedivere　　170
Remorsefully regarded thro' his tears,
And would have spoken, but he found not words;
Then took with care, and kneeling on one knee,
O'er both his shoulders drew the languid hands,
And rising bore him thro' the place of tombs.
　　But, as he walk'd, King Arthur panted hard,
Like one that feels a nightmare on his bed
When all the house is mute. So sigh'd the King,
Muttering and murmuring at his ear, "Quick, quick!
I fear it is too late, and I shall die."　　180
But the other swiftly strode from ridge to ridge,
Clothed with his breath, and looking, as he walk'd,
Larger than human on the frozen hills.
He heard the deep behind him, and a cry
Before. His own thought drove him like a goad.
Dry clash'd his harness in the icy caves
And barren chasms, and all to left and right
The bare black cliff clang'd round him, as he based
His feet on juts of slippery crag that rang
Sharp-smitten with the dint of armed heels—　　190
And on a sudden, lo! the level lake,

And the long glories of the winter moon.
    Then saw they how there hove a dusky barge,
Dark as a funeral scarf from stem to stern,
Beneath them; and descending they were ware
That all the decks were dense with stately forms
Black-stoled, black-hooded, like a dream—by these
Three Queens with crowns of gold: and from them rose
A cry that shiver'd to the tingling stars,
And, as it were one voice, an agony   200
Of lamentation, like a wind, that shrills
All night in a waste land, where no one comes,
Or hath come, since the making of the world.
    Then murmur'd Arthur, "Place me in the barge,"
And to the barge they came. There those three Queens
Put forth their hands, and took the King, and wept.
But she that rose the tallest of them all
And fairest laid his head upon her lap,
And loosed the shatter'd casque, and chafed his hands,
And call'd him by his name, complaining loud,   210
And dropping bitter tears against his brow
Striped with dark blood: for all his face was white
And colourless, and like the wither'd moon
Smote by the fresh beam of the springing east;
And all his greaves and cuisses dash'd with drops
Of onset; and the light and lustrous curls—
That made his forehead like a rising sun
High from the dais-throne—were parch'd with dust,
Or, clotted into points and hanging loose,
Mix'd with the knightly growth that fringed his lips.   220
So like a shatter'd column lay the King;
Not like that Arthur who, with lance in rest,
From spur to plume a star of tournament,
Shot thro' the lists at Camelot, and charged
Before the eyes of ladies and of kings.
    Then loudly cried the bold Sir Bedivere,
"Ah! my Lord Arthur, whither shall I go?
Where shall I hide my forehead and my eyes?
For now I see the true old times are dead,
When every morning brought a noble chance,   230

215-16 *And all his greaves . . . Of onset:* i.e., with his thigh- and leg-armor sprinkled with blood from the battle.

And every chance brought out a noble knight.
Such times have been not since the light that led
The holy Elders with the gift of myrrh.
But now the whole Round Table is dissolved
Which was an image of the mighty world;
And I, the last, go forth companionless,
And the days darken round me, and the years,
Among new men, strange faces, other minds."
    And slowly answer'd Arthur from the barge:
"The old order changeth, yielding place to new,   240
And God fulfils Himself in many ways,
Lest one good custom should corrupt the world.
Comfort thyself: what comfort is in me?
I have lived my life, and that which I have done
May He within Himself make pure! but thou,
If thou shouldst never see my face again,
Pray for my soul. More things are wrought by prayer
Than this world dreams of. Wherefore, let thy voice
Rise like a fountain for me night and day.
For what are men better than sheep or goats   250
That nourish a blind life within the brain,
If, knowing God, they lift not hands of prayer
Both for themselves and those who call them friend?
For so the whole round earth is every way
Bound by gold chains about the feet of God.
But now farewell. I am going a long way
With these thou seest—if indeed I go
(For all my mind is clouded with a doubt)
To the island-valley of Avilion;
Where falls not hail, or rain, or any snow,   260
Nor ever wind blows loudly; but it lies
Deep-meadow'd, happy, fair with orchard-lawns
And bowery hollows crown'd with summer sea,
Where I will heal me of my grievous wound."
    So said he, and the barge with oar and sail
Moved from the brink, like some full-breasted swan
That, fluting a wild carol ere her death,
Ruffles her pure cold plume, and takes the flood
With swarthy webs. Long stood Sir Bedivere

---

259 *Avilion:* Avalon, Arthurian paradise.

Revolving many memories, till the hull   270
Look'd one black dot against the verge of dawn,
And on the mere the wailing died away.

[1842]

ULYSSES

It little profits that an idle king,
By this still hearth, among these barren crags,
Match'd with an aged wife, I mete and dole
Unequal laws unto a savage race,
That hoard, and sleep, and feed, and know not me.
I cannot rest from travel: I will drink
Life to the lees: all times I have enjoy'd
Greatly, have suffer'd greatly, both with those
That loved me, and alone; on shore, and when
Thro' scudding drifts the rainy Hyades   10
Vext the dim sea: I am become a name;
For always roaming with a hungry heart
Much have I seen and known,—cities of men
And manners, climates, councils, governments,
Myself not least, but honour'd of them all,—
And drunk delight of battle with my peers,
Far on the ringing plains of windy Troy.
I am a part of all that I have met;
Yet all experience is an arch wherethro'
Gleams that untravell'd world, whose margin fades   20
For ever and for ever when I move.
How dull it is to pause, to make an end,
To rust unburnish'd, not to shine in use!
As tho' to breathe were life. Life piled on life
Were all too little, and of one to me
Little remains: but every hour is saved
From that eternal silence, something more,

Ulysses: Odysseus, king of the island of Ithaca, to which he has returned after the Trojan war. Tennyson's major source for this poem was Dante's *Inferno*, XXVI.
10 *Hyades*: cluster of stars supposed to predict the rainy season.

A bringer of new things; and vile it were
For some three suns to store and hoard myself,
And this gray spirit yearning in desire
To follow knowledge like a sinking star,
Beyond the utmost bound of human thought.
  This is my son, mine own Telemachus,
To whom I leave the sceptre and the isle,—
Well-loved of me, discerning to fulfil
This labour, by slow prudence to make mild
A rugged people, and thro' soft degrees
Subdue them to the useful and the good.
Most blameless is he, centred in the sphere
Of common duties, decent not to fail
In offices of tenderness, and pay
Meet adoration to my household gods,
When I am gone. He works his work, I mine.
  There lies the port; the vessel puffs her sail:
There gloom the dark, broad seas. My mariners,
Souls that have toil'd, and wrought, and thought with me,—
That ever with a frolic welcome took
The thunder and the sunshine, and opposed
Free hearts, free foreheads,—you and I are old;
Old age hath yet his honour and his toil;
Death closes all: but something ere the end,
Some work of noble note, may yet be done,
Not unbecoming men that strove with Gods.
The lights begin to twinkle from the rocks;
The long day wanes; the slow moon climbs; the deep
Moans round with many voices. Come, my friends,
'T is not too late to seek a newer world.
Push off, and sitting well in order smite
The sounding furrows; for my purpose holds
To sail beyond the sunset, and the baths
Of all the western stars, until I die.
It may be that the gulfs will wash us down:
It may be we shall touch the Happy Isles,
And see the great Achilles, whom we knew.
Tho' much is taken, much abides; and tho'
We are not now that strength which in old days

---

63 *Happy Isles:* Elysium, paradise.

Moved earth and heaven, that which we are, we are,—
One equal temper of heroic hearts,
Made weak by time and fate, but strong in will
To strive, to seek, to find, and not to yield.   70

[1842]

seek in death as in life? or else to the end as stoic self-sufficient

TITHONUS

The woods decay, the woods decay and fall, *leo a sound of Cassandra*
The vapours weep their burthen to the ground, *m*
Man comes and tills the field and lies beneath, *Agamemnon*
And after many a summer dies the swan.
Me only cruel immortality
Consumes: I wither slowly in thine arms,
Here at the quiet limit of the world,
A white-hair'd shadow roaming like a dream
The ever-silent spaces of the East,
Far-folded mists, and gleaming halls of morn.   10
   Alas! for this gray shadow, once a man—
So glorious in his beauty and thy choice,
Who madest him thy chosen, that he seem'd
To his great heart none other than a God!
I ask'd thee, "Give me immortality."
Then didst thou grant mine asking with a smile,
Like wealthy men who care not how they give.
But thy strong Hours indignant work'd their wills,
And beat me down and marr'd and wasted me,
And tho' they could not end me, left me maim'd   20
To dwell in presence of immortal youth,
Immortal age beside immortal youth,
And all I was, in ashes. Can thy love,
Thy beauty, make amends, tho' even now,
Close over us, the silver star, thy guide,
Shines in those tremulous eyes that fill with tears
To hear me? Let me go; take back thy gift:

In this perfect place of withdrawal is decay

Tithonus: a mortal beloved by the goddess of the dawn, who secured immortality for him but forgot to secure perpetual youth as well, so that he grew older and more withered until he begged for death.

sensuous appeal

of physical

Why should a man desire in any way
To vary from the kindly race of men,
Or pass beyond the goal of ordinance
Where all should pause, as is most meet for all?
　A soft air fans the cloud apart; there comes
A glimpse of that dark world where I was born.
Once more the old mysterious glimmer steals
From thy pure brows, and from thy shoulders pure,
And bosom beating with a heart renew'd.
Thy cheek begins to redden thro' the gloom,
Thy sweet eyes brighten slowly close to mine,
Ere yet they blind the stars, and the wild team
Which love thee, yearning for thy yoke, arise,　　40
And shake the darkness from their loosen'd manes,
And beat the twilight into flakes of fire.
　Lo! ever thus thou growest beautiful
In silence, then before thine answer given
Departest, and thy tears are on my cheek.
　Why wilt thou ever scare me with thy tears,
And make me tremble lest a saying learnt,
In days far-off, on that dark earth, be true?
"The Gods themselves cannot recall their gifts."
　Ay me! ay me! with what another heart　　50
In days far-off, and with what other eyes
I used to watch—if I be he that watch'd—
The lucid outline forming round thee; saw
The dim curls kindle into sunny rings;
Changed with thy mystic change, and felt my blood
Glow with the glow that slowly crimson'd all
Thy presence and thy portals, while I lay,
Mouth, forehead, eyelids, growing dewy-warm
With kisses balmier than half-opening buds
Of April, and could hear the lips that kiss'd　　60
Whispering I knew not what of wild and sweet,
Like that strange song I heard Apollo sing,
While Ilion like a mist rose into towers.
　Yet hold me not for ever in thine East:
How can my nature longer mix with thine?
Coldly thy rosy shadows bathe me, cold

Keats

---

39 *wild team:* steeds that draw the chariot of dawn.

Are all thy lights, and cold my wrinkled feet
Upon thy glimmering thresholds, when the steam
Floats up from those dim fields about the homes
Of happy men that have the power to die,   70
And grassy barrows of the happier dead.
Release me, and restore me to the ground;
Thou seest all things, thou wilt see my grave:
Thou wilt renew thy beauty morn by morn;
I earth in earth forget these empty courts,
And thee returning on thy silver wheels.

[1860]

THE SPLENDOUR FALLS

The splendour falls on castle walls
    And snowy summits old in story;
The long light shakes across the lakes,
    And the wild cataract leaps in glory.
Blow, bugle, blow, set the wild echoes flying:
Blow, bugle; answer, echoes, dying, dying, dying.

O hark, O hear! how thin and clear,
    And thinner, clearer, farther going!
O sweet and far from cliff and scar
    The horns of Elfland faintly blowing!   10
Blow, let us hear the purple glens replying:
Blow, bugle; answer, echoes, dying, dying, dying.

O love, they die in yon rich sky,
    They faint on hill or field or river;
Our echoes roll from soul to soul,
    And grow for ever and for ever.
Blow, bugle, blow, set the wild echoes flying;
And answer, echoes, answer, dying, dying, dying.

[1850]

The Splendour Falls: This lyric was added to *The Princess* in 1850.

IN MEMORIAM A.H.H.

OBIIT MDCCCXXXIII

Strong Son of God, immortal Love,
  Whom we, that have not seen thy face,
  By faith, and faith alone, embrace,
Believing where we cannot prove;

Thine are these orbs of light and shade;
  Thou madest Life in man and brute;
  Thou madest Death; and lo, thy foot
Is on the skull which thou hast made.

Thou wilt not leave us in the dust:
  Thou madest man, he knows not why,   10
  He thinks he was not made to die;
And thou hast made him: thou art just.

Thou seemest human and divine,
  The highest, holiest manhood, thou:
  Our wills are ours, we know not how;
Our wills are ours, to make them thine.

Our little systems have their day;
  They have their day and cease to be:
  They are but broken lights of thee,
And thou, O Lord, art more than they.   20

We have but faith: we cannot know;
  For knowledge is of things we see;
  And yet we trust it comes from thee,
A beam in darkness: let it grow.

Let knowledge grow from more to more,
  But more of reverence in us dwell;
  That mind and soul, according well,
May make one music as before,

But vaster. We are fools and slight;
  We mock thee when we do not fear: 30

But help thy foolish ones to bear;
Help thy vain worlds to bear thy light.

Forgive what seem'd my sin in me;
   What seem'd my worth since I began;
   For merit lives from man to man,
And not from man, O Lord, to thee.

Forgive my grief for one removed,
   Thy creature, whom I found so fair.
   I trust he lives in thee, and there
I find him worthier to be loved.   40

Forgive these wild and wandering cries,
   Confusions of a wasted youth;
   Forgive them where they fail in truth,
And in thy wisdom make me wise.

1849

I

I held it truth, with him who sings
   To one clear harp in divers tones,
   That men may rise on stepping-stones
Of their dead selves to higher things.

But who shall so forecast the years
   And find in loss a gain to match?
   Or reach a hand thro' time to catch
The far-off interest of tears?

Let Love clasp Grief lest both be drown'd,
   Let darkness keep her raven gloss:
   Ah, sweeter to be drunk with loss,   10
To dance with death, to beat the ground,

Than that the victor Hours should scorn
   The long result of love, and boast,
   "Behold the man that loved and lost,
But all he was is overworn."

I 1 *him:* Goethe.

II

Old Yew, which graspest at the stones
  That name the under-lying dead,
  Thy fibres net the dreamless head,
Thy roots are wrapt about the bones.

The seasons bring the flower again,
  And bring the firstling to the flock;
  And in the dusk of thee the clock
Beats out the little lives of men.

O, not for thee the glow, the bloom,
  Who changest not in any gale,   10
  Nor branding summer suns avail
To touch thy thousand years of gloom:

And gazing on thee, sullen tree,
  Sick for thy stubborn hardihood,
  I seem to fail from out my blood
And grow incorporate into thee.

III

O Sorrow, cruel fellowship,
  O Priestess in the vaults of Death,
  O sweet and bitter in a breath,
What whispers from thy lying lip?

"The stars," she whispers, "blindly run;   *no God, no order*
  A web is woven across the sky;   *no reason for death*
  From out waste places comes a cry,
And murmurs from the dying sun:

"And all the phantom, Nature, stands—
  With all the music in her tone,   10
  A hollow echo of my own,—
  A hollow form with empty hands."   *complete negation*

And shall I take a thing so blind,
  Embrace her as my natural good;

II 7 *clock:* church-tower clock in the churchyard where the yew grows.
III 13 *a thing so blind:* Sorrow.

Or crush her, like a vice of blood,
Upon the threshold of the mind?

IV

To Sleep I give my powers away;
  My will is bondsman to the dark;
  I sit within a helmless bark,
And with my heart I muse and say:

O heart, how fares it with thee now,
  That thou should'st fail from thy desire,
  Who scarcely darest to inquire,
"What is it makes me beat so low?"

Something it is which thou hast lost,
  Some pleasure from thine early years.
  Break, thou deep vase of chilling tears,
That grief hath shaken into frost!

Such clouds of nameless trouble cross
  All night below the darken'd eyes;
  With morning wakes the will, and cries,
"Thou shalt not be the fool of loss."

V

I sometimes hold it half a sin
  To put in words the grief I feel;
  For words, like Nature, half reveal
And half conceal the Soul within.

But, for the unquiet heart and brain,
  A use in measured language lies;
  The sad mechanic exercise,
Like dull narcotics, numbing pain.

In words, like weeds, I'll wrap me o'er,
  Like coarsest clothes against the cold:
  But that large grief which these enfold
Is given in outline and no more.

10

10

V 9 *weeds:* clothing.

VI

One writes, that "Other friends remain,"
   That "Loss is common to the race"—
   And common is the commonplace,
And vacant chaff well meant for grain.

That loss is common would not make
   My own less bitter, rather more:
   Too common! Never morning wore
To evening, but some heart did break.

not lessened by fact that all loose

O father, wheresoe'er thou be,
   Who pledgest now thy gallant son;   10
   A shot, ere half thy draught be done,
Hath still'd the life that beat from thee.

O mother, praying God will save
   Thy sailor,—while thy head is bow'd,
   His heavy-shotted hammock-shroud
Drops in his vast and wandering grave.

Ye know no more than I who wrought
   At that last hour to please him well;
   Who mused on all I had to tell,
And something written, something thought;   20

Expecting still his advent home;
   And ever met him on his way
   With wishes, thinking, "here to-day,"
Or "here to-morrow will he come."

O somewhere, meek, unconscious dove,
   That sittest ranging golden hair;
   And glad to find thyself so fair,
Poor child, that waitest for thy love!

For now her father's chimney glows
   In expectation of a guest;   30
   And thinking "this will please him best,"
She takes a riband or a rose;

For he will see them on to-night;
  And with the thought her colour burns;
  And, having left the glass, she turns
Once more to set a ringlet right;

And, even when she turn'd, the curse
  Had fallen, and her future lord
  Was drown'd in passing thro' the ford,
Or kill'd in falling from his horse.   40

O, what to her shall be the end?
  And what to me remains of good?
  To her, perpetual maidenhood,
And unto me no second friend.

VII

Dark house, by which once more I stand
  Here in the long unlovely street,
  Doors, where my heart was used to beat
So quickly, waiting for a hand,

A hand that can be clasp'd no more—
  Behold me, for I cannot sleep,
  And like a guilty thing I creep
At earliest morning to the door.

He is not here; but far away
  The noise of life begins again,   10
  And ghastly thro' the drizzling rain
On the bald street breaks the blank day.

VIII

A happy lover who has come
  To look on her that loves him well,
  Who 'lights and rings the gateway bell,
And learns her gone and far from home;

He saddens, all the magic light
  Dies off at once from bower and hall,

VII 1 *Dark house:* Hallam's house in Wimpole Street, London.

And all the place is dark, and all
The chambers emptied of delight:

So find I every pleasant spot
   In which we two were wont to meet,   10
   The field, the chamber, and the street,
For all is dark where thou art not.

Yet as that other, wandering there
   In those deserted walks, may find
   A flower beat with rain and wind,
Which once she foster'd up with care;

So seems it in my deep regret,
   O my forsaken heart, with thee
   And this poor flower of poesy
Which, little cared for, fades not yet.   20

But since it pleased a vanish'd eye,
   I go to plant it on his tomb,
   That if it can it there may bloom,
Or dying, there at least may die.

IX

Fair ship, that from the Italian shore
   Sailest the placid ocean-plains
   With my lost Arthur's loved remains,
Spread thy full wings, and waft him o'er.

So draw him home to those that mourn
   In vain; a favourable speed
   Ruffle thy mirror'd mast, and lead
Thro' prosperous floods his holy urn.

All night no ruder air perplex
   Thy sliding keel, till Phosphor, bright   10
   As our pure love, thro' early light
Shall glimmer on the dewy decks.

IX 1 *ship:* The ship bringing Hallam's body to England sailed from Trieste.
10 *Phosphor:* the morning star.

Sphere all your lights around, above;
    Sleep, gentle heavens, before the prow;
    Sleep, gentle winds, as he sleeps now,
My friend, the brother of my love;

My Arthur, whom I shall not see
    Till all my widow'd race be run;
    Dear as the mother to the son,
More than my brothers are to me.   20

X

bon voyage

I hear the noise about thy keel;
    I hear the bell struck in the night:
    I see the cabin-window bright;
I see the sailor at the wheel.

Thou bring'st the sailor to his wife,
    And travell'd men from foreign lands;
    And letters unto trembling hands;
And, thy dark freight, a vanish'd life.

So bring him; we have idle dreams:
    This look of quiet flatters thus   10
    Our home-bred fancies: O, to us,
The fools of habit, sweeter seems

man feels it better to lie under sod than sea

To rest beneath the clover sod,
    That takes the sunshine and the rains,
    Or where the kneeling hamlet drains
The chalice of the grapes of God;

Than if with thee the roaring wells
    Should gulf him fathom-deep in brine;
    And hands so often clasp'd in mine,
Should toss with tangle and with shells.   20

XI

Calm is the morn without a sound,
    Calm as to suit a calmer grief,

X 15-6 *Or where . . . of God:* in the vault of a country church beneath the
communion rail.

And only thro' the faded leaf
The chestnut pattering to the ground:

Calm and deep peace on this high wold,
    And on these dews that drench the furze,
    And all the silvery gossamers
That twinkle into green and gold:

Calm and still light on yon great plain
    That sweeps with all its autumn bowers,   10
    And crowded farms and lessening towers,
To mingle with the bounding main:

Calm and deep peace in this wide air,
    These leaves that redden to the fall;
    And in my heart, if calm at all,
If any calm, a calm despair:

Calm on the seas, and silver sleep,
    And waves that sway themselves in rest,
    And dead calm in that noble breast
Which heaves but with the heaving deep.   20

XII

Lo, as a dove when up she springs
    To bear thro' Heaven a tale of woe,
    Some dolorous message knit below
The wild pulsation of her wings;

Like her I go; I cannot stay;
    I leave this mortal ark behind,
    A weight of nerves without a mind,
And leave the cliffs, and haste away

O'er ocean-mirrors rounded large,
    And reach the glow of southern skies,   10
    And see the sails at distance rise,
And linger weeping on the marge,

feels wild despair, nature doesn't reflect his feelings

in conflict with nature

XI 11 *lessening:* diminishing in the distance.

And saying, "Comes he thus, my friend?
　Is this the end of all my care?"
　And circle moaning in the air,
"Is this the end? Is this the end?"

And forward dart again, and play
　About the prow, and back return
　To where the body sits, and learn
That I have been an hour away.　　　　　20

XIII

Tears of the widower, when he sees
　A late-lost form that sleep reveals,
　And moves his doubtful arms, and feels
Her place is empty, fall like these;

dreamy stupor

Which weep a loss for ever new,
　A void where heart on heart reposed;
　And, where warm hands have prest and closed,
Silence, till I be silent too;

Which weep the comrade of my choice,
　An awful thought, a life removed,
　The human-hearted man I loved,
A Spirit, not a breathing voice.　　　　　10

death seems unnatural

love was of Spiritual

Come, Time, and teach me, many years,
　I do not suffer in a dream;
　For now so strange do these things seem,
Mine eyes have leisure for their tears;

something to be learned from this period or time will sooth

My fancies time to rise on wing,
　And glance about the approaching sails,
　As tho' they brought but merchants' bales,
And not the burthen that they bring.　　　　　20

XIV

If one should bring me this report,
　That thou hadst touch'd the land to-day,
　And I went down unto the quay,
And found thee lying in the port;

And standing, muffled round with woe,
   Should see thy passengers in rank
   Come stepping lightly down the plank,
And beckoning unto those they know;

And if along with these should come
   The man I held as half-divine;   10
   Should strike a sudden hand in mine,
And ask a thousand things of home;

And I should tell him all my pain,
   And how my life had droop'd of late,
   And he should sorrow o'er my state
And marvel what possess'd my brain;

And I perceived no touch of change,
   No hint of death in all his frame,
   But found him all in all the same,
I should not feel it to be strange.   20

not able to accept H's death as real

XV

To-night the winds begin to rise
   And roar from yonder dropping day:
   The last red leaf is whirl'd away,
The rooks are blown about the skies;

The forest crack'd, the waters curl'd,
   The cattle huddled on the lea;
   And wildly dash'd on tower and tree
The sunbeam strikes along the world:

And but for fancies, which aver
   That all thy motions gently pass
   Athwart a plane of molten glass,
I scarce could brook the strain and stir

his woe like pain of glass that separates him

That makes the barren branches loud;
   And but for fear it is not so,
   The wild unrest that lives in woe
Would dote and pore on yonder cloud

That rises upward always higher,
    And onward drags a labouring breast,
    And topples round the dreary west,
A looming bastion fringed with fire.   20

XVI

What words are these have fallen from me?
    Can calm despair and wild unrest
    Be tenants of a single breast,
Or sorrow such a changeling be?

Or doth she only seem to take
    The touch of change in calm or storm;
    But knows no more of transient form
In her deep self, than some dead lake

That holds the shadow of a lark
    Hung in the shadow of a heaven?   10
    Or has the shock, so harshly given,
Confused me like the unhappy bark

That strikes by night a craggy shelf,
    And staggers blindly ere she sink?
    And stunn'd me from my power to think
And all my knowledge of myself;

And made me that delirious man
    Whose fancy fuses old and new,
    And flashes into false and true,
And mingles all without a plan?   20

XVII

Thou comest, much wept for: such a breeze
    Compell'd thy canvas, and my prayer
    Was as the whisper of an air
To breathe thee over lonely seas.

XV 20 In stanzas three to five, the poet says that he fancies Hallam at rest;
if it were not for this fancy, he could not bear the tumult of the autumn
storm. If he did not, at the same time, fear that the fancy was false, he
could seek solace in identifying himself with the great cloud, fringed with
sunset fire, toiling on in sorrow. In both this and the following poem, he is
confused by the alternation of comfort and doubt.

For I in spirit saw thee move
    Thro' circles of the bounding sky,
    Week after week: the days go by:
Come quick, thou bringest all I love.

Henceforth, wherever thou may'st roam,
    My blessing, like a line of light,   10
    Is on the waters day and night,
And like a beacon guards thee home.

So may whatever tempest mars
    Mid-ocean spare thee, sacred bark;
    And balmy drops in summer dark
Slide from the bosom of the stars;

So kind an office hath been done,
    Such precious relics brought by thee;
    The dust of him I shall not see
Till all my widow'd race be run.   20

XVIII

'T is well; 't is something; we may stand
    Where he in English earth is laid,
    And from his ashes may be made
The violet of his native land.

'T is little; but it looks in truth
    As if the quiet bones were blest
    Among familiar names to rest
And in the places of his youth.

Come then, pure hands, and bear the head
    That sleeps or wears the mask of sleep,   10
    And come, whatever loves to weep,
And hear the ritual of the dead.

Ah yet, even yet, if this might be,
    I, falling on his faithful heart,
    Would breathing thro' his lips impart
The life that almost dies in me;

[handwritten marginalia:] Pastoral (see later in 2nd sec / tradition which buried / Nature present. / Sorry softened by nature*

That dies not, but endures with pain,
    And slowly forms the firmer mind,
    Treasuring the look it cannot find,
The words that are not heard again.   20

XIX

The Danube to the Severn gave
    The darken'd heart that beat no more;
    They laid him by the pleasant shore,
And in the hearing of the wave.

There twice a day the Severn fills;
    The salt sea-water passes by,
    And hushes half the babbling Wye,
And makes a silence in the hills.

The Wye is hush'd nor moved along,
    And hush'd my deepest grief of all,   10
    When fill'd with tears that cannot fall,
I brim with sorrow drowning song.

The tide flows down, the wave again
    Is vocal in its wooded walls;
    My deeper anguish also falls,
And I can speak a little then.

XX

The lesser griefs that may be said,
    That breathe a thousand tender vows,
    Are but as servants in a house
Where lies the master newly dead;

Who speak their feeling as it is,
    And weep the fulness from the mind:
    "It will be hard," they say, "to find
Another service such as this."

XIX 1 *Danube . . . Severn:* Hallam died in Vienna on the Danube and was
buried in Clevedon on the Severn near the point where it widens into the
Bristol Channel. The tide comes up the Bristol Channel into the Severn and
thence into its tributary, the Wye.

My lighter moods are like to these,
    That out of words a comfort win;   10
    But there are other griefs within,
And tears that at their fountain freeze;

For by the hearth the children sit
    Cold in that atmosphere of Death,
    And scarce endure to draw the breath,
Or like to noiseless phantoms flit:

But open converse is there none,
    So much the vital spirits sink
    To see the vacant chair, and think,
"How good! how kind! and he is gone."   20

XXI

I sing to him that rests below,
    And, since the grasses round me wave,
    I take the grasses of the grave,
And make them pipes whereon to blow.

The traveller hears me now and then,
    And sometimes harshly will he speak:
    "This fellow would make weakness weak,
And melt the waxen hearts of men."

Another answers, "Let him be,
    He loves to make parade of pain,   *accuse of
    That with his piping he may gain   playing openly
The praise that comes to constancy."   10 his grief*

A third is wroth: "Is this an hour
    For private sorrow's barren song,
    When more and more the people throng
The chairs and thrones of civil power?

"A time to sicken and to swoon,
    When Science reaches forth her arms
    To feel from world to world, and charms
Her secret from the latest moon?"   20

XXI 18 *arms:* telescopes.
20 *latest moon:* probably oblique reference to the discovery of Neptune in 1846.

Behold, ye speak an idle thing:
    Ye never knew the sacred dust:
    I do but sing because I must,
And pipe but as the linnets sing:

And one is glad; her note is gay,
    For now her little ones have ranged;
    And one is sad; her note is changed,
Because her brood is stolen away.

XXII

The path by which we twain did go,
    Which led by tracts that pleased us well,
    Thro' four sweet years arose and fell,
From flower to flower, from snow to snow;

And we with singing cheer'd the way,
    And, crown'd with all the season lent,
    From April on to April went,
And glad at heart from May to May:

But where the path we walk'd began
    To slant the fifth autumnal slope,   10
    As we descended following Hope,
There sat the Shadow fear'd of man;

Who broke our fair companionship,
    And spread his mantle dark and cold,
    And wrapt thee formless in the fold,
And dull'd the murmur on thy lip,

And bore thee where I could not see
    Nor follow, tho' I walk in haste,
    And think that somewhere in the waste
The Shadow sits and waits for me.   20

XXIII

Now, sometimes in my sorrow shut,
    Or breaking into song by fits,
    Alone, alone, to where he sits,
The Shadow cloak'd from head to foot,

Who keeps the keys of all the creeds,
    I wander, often falling lame,
    And looking back to whence I came,
Or on to where the pathway leads;

And crying, How changed from where it ran
    Thro' lands where not a leaf was dumb;
    But all the lavish hills would hum
The murmur of a happy Pan:

When each by turns was guide to each,
    And Fancy light from Fancy caught,
    And Thought leapt out to wed with Thought
Ere Thought could wed itself with Speech;

And all we met was fair and good,
    And all was good that Time could bring,
    And all the secret of the Spring
Moved in the chambers of the blood;

And many an old philosophy
    On Argive heights divinely sang,
    And round us all the thicket rang
To many a flute of Arcady.

XXIV

And was the day of my delight
    As pure and perfect as I say?
    The very source and fount of Day
Is dash'd with wandering isles of night.

If all was good and fair we met,
    This earth had been the Paradise
    It never look'd to human eyes
Since our first Sun arose and set.

And is it that the haze of grief
    Makes former gladness loom so great?

XXIII 12 *Pan:* Greek god of shepherds and flocks.
22 *Argive:* Greek.
24 *Arcady:* Greek region of untroubled calm, home of pastoral poetry.

The lowness of the present state,
That sets the past in this relief?

Or that the past will always win
  A glory from its being far,
  And orb into the perfect star
We saw not when we moved therein?

XXV

I know that this was Life,—the track
  Whereon with equal feet we fared;
  And then, as now, the day prepared
The daily burden for the back.

But this it was that made me move
  As light as carrier-birds in air;
  I loved the weight I had to bear,
Because it needed help of Love:

Nor could I weary, heart or limb,
  When mighty Love would cleave in twain   10
  The lading of a single pain,
And part it, giving half to him.

XXVI

Still onward winds the dreary way;
  I with it; for I long to prove
  No lapse of moons can canker Love,
Whatever fickle tongues may say.

And if that eye which watches guilt
  And goodness, and hath power to see
  Within the green the moulder'd tree,
And towers fallen as soon as built—

O, if indeed that eye foresee
  Or see (in Him is no before)   10
  In more of life true life no more
And Love the indifference to be,

XXIV 15 *And orb into the perfect star:* i.e., and appear to become a perfectly round star.

if A.T. is wrong in trying to maintain this love, if life only covers what is really death, then A.T. may go to.

Then might I find, ere yet the morn
    Breaks hither over Indian seas,
    That Shadow waiting with the keys,
To shroud me from my proper scorn.

for thinking there was something to their spiritual friendship.

XXVII

I envy not in any moods
    The captive void of noble rage,
    The linnet born within the cage,
That never knew the summer woods:

I envy not the beast that takes
    His license in the field of time,
    Unfetter'd by the sense of crime,
To whom a conscience never wakes;

Nor, what may count itself as blest,
    The heart that never plighted troth   10
    But stagnates in the weeds of sloth;
Nor any want-begotten rest.

Resol: hours mock, but to have loved is better

I hold it true, whate'er befall;
    I feel it, when I sorrow most;
    'T is better to have loved and lost
Than never to have loved at all.

— end 1st group section

↓ continued life of dead

XXVIII

The time draws near the birth of Christ:
    The moon is hid; the night is still;
    The Christmas bells from hill to hill
Answer each other in the mist.

first Christmas after death

Four voices of four hamlets round,
    From far and near, on mead and moor,
    Swell out and fail, as if a door
Were shut between me and the sound:

Each voice four changes on the wind,
    That now dilate, and now decrease,   10

XXVI 16 *proper scorn:* contempt of self.
XXVIII 1 *birth of Christ:* Christmas of 1833, the first after Hallam's death.
9 *changes:* sequences in which bells are rung.

Peace and goodwill, goodwill and peace,
Peace and goodwill, to all mankind.

This year I slept and woke with pain,
　I almost wish'd no more to wake,
　And that my hold on life would break
Before I heard those bells again:

But they my troubled spirit rule,
　For they controll'd me when a boy;
　They bring me sorrow touch'd with joy,
The merry, merry bells of Yule.　　　　　　20

XXIX

With such compelling cause to grieve
　As daily vexes household peace,
　And chains regret to his decease,
How dare we keep our Christmas-eve;

Which brings no more a welcome guest
　To enrich the threshold of the night
　With shower'd largess of delight
In dance and song and game and jest?

Yet go, and while the holly boughs
　Entwine the cold baptismal font,　　　　　10
　Make one wreath more for Use and Wont,
That guard the portals of the house;

Old sisters of a day gone by,
　Gray nurses, loving nothing new;
　Why should they miss their yearly due
Before their time? They too will die.

XXX

With trembling fingers did we weave
　The holly round the Christmas hearth;
　A rainy cloud possess'd the earth,
And sadly fell our Christmas-eve.

At our old pastimes in the hall
　We gamboll'd, making vain pretence

how can household be happy

Of gladness, with an awful sense
Of one mute Shadow watching all.

We paused: the winds were in the beech:
   We heard them sweep the winter land;   10
   And in a circle hand-in-hand
Sat silent, looking each at each.

Then echo-like our voices rang;
   We sung, tho' every eye was dim,
   A merry song we sang with him
Last year: impetuously we sang:

We ceased: a gentler feeling crept
   Upon us: surely rest is meet:
   "They rest," we said, "their sleep is sweet,"
And silence follow'd, and we wept.   20

Our voices took a higher range;
   Once more we sang: "They do not die
   Nor lose their mortal sympathy,
Nor change to us, although they change;

"Rapt from the fickle and the frail
   With gather'd power, yet the same,
   Pierces the keen seraphic flame
From orb to orb, from veil to veil."

Rise, happy morn, rise, holy morn,
   Draw forth the cheerful day from night: 30
   O Father, touch the east, and light
The light that shone when Hope was born.

XXXI

When Lazarus left his charnel-cave,
   And home to Mary's house return'd,
   Was this demanded—if he yearn'd
To hear her weeping by his grave?

XXXI 1 *Lazarus: John* 11 and 12 tell how Christ raised Lazarus from the
dead, and how his sister Mary anointed Christ's feet.

"Where wert thou, brother, those four days?"
　　There lives no record of reply,
　　Which telling what it is to die
Had surely added praise to praise.

From every house the neighbours met,
　　The streets were fill'd with joyful sound,　　10
　　A solemn gladness even crown'd
The purple brows of Olivet.

Behold a man raised up by Christ!
　　The rest remaineth unreveal'd;
　　He told it not; or something seal'd
The lips of that Evangelist.

Love leads, to Love in Christian sense.

XXXII

Her eyes are homes of silent prayer,
　　Nor other thought her mind admits
　　But, he was dead, and there he sits,
And he that brought him back is there.

Then one deep love doth supersede
　　All other, when her ardent gaze
　　Roves from the living brother's face,
And rests upon the Life indeed.

All subtle thought, all curious fears,
　　Borne down by gladness so complete,　　10
　　She bows, she bathes the Saviour's feet
With costly spikenard and with tears.

Thrice blest whose lives are faithful prayers,
　　Whose loves in higher love endure;
　　What souls possess themselves so pure,
Or is there blessedness like theirs?

---

12 *Olivet:* hill near Jerusalem.
16 *Evangelist:* St. John.
XXXII 1 *Her:* Mary's

XXXIII

O thou that after toil and storm
    Mayst seem to have reach'd a purer air,
    Whose faith has centre everywhere,
Nor cares to fix itself to form,

emotional religion
not for him

Leave thou thy sister when she prays,
    Her early Heaven, her happy views;
    Nor thou with shadow'd hint confuse
A life that leads melodious days.

intellect rather than emotion

Her faith thro' form is pure as thine,
    Her hands are quicker unto good:
    Oh, sacred be the flesh and blood
To which she links a truth divine!

10

See thou, that countest reason ripe
    In holding by the law within,
    Thou fail not in a world of sin,
And even for want of such a type.

XXXIV

My own dim life should teach me this,
    That life shall live for evermore,
    Else earth is darkness at the core,
And dust and ashes all that is;

life continues

This round of green, this orb of flame,
    Fantastic beauty; such as lurks
    In some wild Poet, when he works
Without a conscience or an aim.

What then were God to such as I?
    'T were hardly worth my while to choose
    Of things all mortal, or to use
A little patience ere I die;

needs intellectual faith

10

XXXIII In this lyric, the man of intellectual religion, independent of forms, is warned not to disturb the simple faith of others, learned in childhood; in following only his own conscience, the rationalist may sin through lacking literal belief in Christ.

'T were best at once to sink to peace,
   Like birds the charming serpent draws,
   To drop head-foremost in the jaws
Of vacant darkness and to cease.

best to stop this sorrowing

XXXV

Yet if some voice that man could trust
   Should murmur from the narrow house,
   "The cheeks drop in; the body bows;
Man dies: nor is there hope in dust:"

nothing beyond grave

Might I not say? "Yet even here,
   But for one hour, O Love, I strive
   To keep so sweet a thing alive:"
But I should turn mine ears and hear

love survive death

The moanings of the homeless sea,
   The sound of streams that swift or slow   10
   Draw down Æonian hills, and sow
The dust of continents to be;

Love reflection of spiritual love

And Love would answer with a sigh,
   "The sound of that forgetful shore
   Will change my sweetness more and more,
Half-dead to know that I shall die."

O me, what profits it to put
   An idle case? If Death were seen
   At first as Death, Love had not been,
Or been in narrowest working shut,   20

Mere fellowship of sluggish moods,
   Or in his coarsest Satyr-shape
   Had bruised the herb and crush'd the grape,
And bask'd and batten'd in the woods.

must be love in larger than sexual

XXXV 2 *narrow house:* grave.
11 *Æonian:* ages old.
19 *as Death:* as total extinction.
22 *Satyr-shape:* brutish form of love.
24 *batten'd:* fed grossly.

XXXVI

Tho' truths in manhood darkly join,
  Deep-seated in our mystic frame,
  We yield all blessing to the name
Of Him that made them current coin;

For Wisdom dealt with mortal powers,
  Where truth in closest words shall fail,
  When truth embodied in a tale
Shall enter in at lowly doors.

And so the Word had breath, and wrought
  With human hands the creed of creeds   10
  In loveliness of perfect deeds,
More strong than all poetic thought;

Which he may read that binds the sheaf,
  Or builds the house, or digs the grave,
  And those wild eyes that watch the wave
In roarings round the coral reef.

XXXVII

Urania speaks with darken'd brow: *may be asked*
  "Thou pratest here where thou art least;   *too much*
  This faith has many a purer priest,
And many an abler voice than thou.

"Go down beside thy native rill,
  On thy Parnassus set thy feet,
  And hear thy laurel whisper sweet
About the ledges of the hill."

And my Melpomene replies,
  A touch of shame upon her cheek: 10

XXXVI 1-2 *Tho' truths . . . frame:* i.e., man intuits the truths which Christ made manifest.
9 *the Word:* according to Tennyson, "the Revelation of the Eternal Thought of the Universe."
XXXVII 1 *Urania:* the goddess of astronomy used by Milton as the "Heavenly Muse" of exalted poetry.
6 *Parnassus:* Greek mountain sacred to the muses.
9 *Melpomene:* the muse of elegy, hence less exalted than Urania.

"I am not worthy even to speak
Of thy prevailing mysteries;

"For I am but an earthly Muse,
    And owning but a little art
    To lull with song an aching heart,
And render human love his dues;

[handwritten: should speak of human not divine]

"But brooding on the dear one dead,
    And all he said of things divine,
    (And dear to me as sacred wine
To dying lips is all he said),   20

"I murmur'd, as I came along,
    Of comfort clasp'd in truth reveal'd;
    And loiter'd in the master's field,
And darken'd sanctities with song."

XXXVIII

With weary steps I loiter on,
    Tho' always under alter'd skies
    The purple from the distance dies,
My prospect and horizon gone.

[handwritten: can't feel spring no purpose in his action]

No joy the blowing season gives,
    The herald melodies of spring,
    But in the songs I love to sing
A doubtful gleam of solace lives.

If any care for what is here
    Survive in spirits render'd free,
    Then are these songs I sing of thee   10
Not all ungrateful to thine ear.

XXXIX

Old warder of these buried bones,
    And answering now my random stroke
    With fruitful cloud and living smoke,
Dark yew, that graspest at the stones

XXXVIII 5 *blowing:* blossoming.
XXXIX This lyric was first published with the rest of *In Memoriam* in 1872.
3 *fruitful cloud:* cloud of pollen from the blossoming yew.

And dippest toward the dreamless **head**,
  To thee too comes the golden hour
  When flower is feeling after flower;
But Sorrow,—fixt upon the dead,

And darkening the dark graves of men,—
  What whisper'd from her lying lips?   10
  Thy gloom is kindled at the tips,
And passes into gloom again.

XL

Could we forget the widow'd hour
  And look on Spirits breathed away,
  As on a maiden in the day
When first she wears her orange-flower!

When crown'd with blessing she doth rise
  To take her latest leave of home,
  And hopes and light regrets that come
Make April of her tender eyes;

And doubtful joys the father move,
  And tears are on the mother's face,   10
  As parting with a long embrace
She enters other realms of love;

Her office there to rear, to teach,
  Becoming as is meet and fit
  A link among the days, to knit
The generations each with each;

And, doubtless, unto thee is given
  A life that bears immortal fruit
  In those great offices that suit
The full-grown energies of heaven.   20

Ay me, the difference I discern!
  How often shall her old fireside
  Be cheer'd with tidings of the bride,
How often she herself return,

what will dead be like after death?

And tell them all they would have told,
    And bring her babe, and make her boast,
    Till even those that miss'd her most
Shall count new things as dear as old:

But thou and I have shaken hands,
    Till growing winters lay me low;   30
    My paths are in the fields I know,
And thine in undiscover'd lands.

XLI

Thy spirit ere our fatal loss
    Did ever rise from high to higher;
    As mounts the heavenward altar-fire,
As flies the lighter thro' the gross.

But thou art turn'd to something strange,
    And I have lost the links that bound
    Thy changes; here upon the ground,
No more partaker of thy change.

Deep folly! yet that this could be—
    That I could wing my will with might   10
    To leap the grades of life and light,
And flash at once, my friend, to thee.

For tho' my nature rarely yields
    To that vague fear implied in death,
    Nor shudders at the gulfs beneath,
The howlings from forgotten fields;

Yet oft when sundown skirts the moor
    An inner trouble I behold,
    A spectral doubt which makes me cold,
That I shall be thy mate no more,   20

Tho' following with an upward mind
    The wonders that have come to thee,

XLI 15-16 *gulfs beneath . . . forgotten fields:* the terror of the underworld
and the torments of the damned.

Thro' all the secular to-be,
But evermore a life behind.

XLII

I vex my heart with fancies dim:
    He still outstript me in the race;
    It was but unity of place
That made me dream I rank'd with him.

And so may Place retain us still,
    And he the much-beloved again,
    A lord of large experience, train
To riper growth the mind and will:

And what delights can equal those
    That stir the spirit's inner deeps,   10
    When one that loves but knows not, reaps
A truth from one that loves and knows?

XLIII

If Sleep and Death be truly one,
    And every spirit's folded bloom
    Thro' all its intervital gloom
In some long trance should slumber on;

Unconscious of the sliding hour,
    Bare of the body, might it last,
    And silent traces of the past
Be all the colour of the flower:

So then were nothing lost to man;
    So that still garden of the souls   10
    In many a figured leaf enrolls
The total world since life began;

---

23 *secular to-be:* future of the world.

XLIII In this lyric, the poet considers the possibility of death being like a
sleep before a future awakening; the sleeping soul is like a flower with its
petals folded for the night. In the garden of sleeping flowers, all history is
contained, for the souls of all men are there.

3 *intervital:* between lives.

11 *enrolls:* encloses.

assuming life after-death on faith.

And love will last as pure and whole
   As when he loved me here in Time,
   And at the spiritual prime
Rewaken with the dawning soul.

XLIV

How fares it with the happy dead?
   For here the man is more and more;
   But he forgets the days before
God shut the doorways of his head.

soul with new consciousness in death

The days have vanish'd, tone and tint,
   And yet perhaps the hoarding sense
   Gives out at times (he knows not whence)
A little flash, a mystic hint;

And in the long harmonious years
   (If Death so taste Lethean springs),
   May some dim touch of earthly things
Surprise thee ranging with thy peers.

   10

If such a dreamy touch should fall,
   Oh, turn thee round, resolve the doubt;
   My guardian angel will speak out
In that high place, and tell thee all.

that it would know of previous life in heaven

XLV

The baby new to earth and sky,
   What time his tender palm is prest
   Against the circle of the breast,
Has never thought that "this is I:"

soul won't entirely forget

But as he grows he gathers much,
   And learns the use of "I" and "me,"
   And finds "I am not what I see,
And other than the things I touch."

---

15 *prime:* dawn.
XLIV 2 *For here the man is more and more:* i.e., on earth the dead man is increasingly remembered.
3 *he:* the dead man.
4 *God shut the doorways of his head:* the closing of the organs of sense in death.

So rounds he to a separate mind
From whence clear memory may begin,
As thro' the frame that binds him in
His isolation grows defined.

This use may lie in blood and breath,
Which else were fruitless of their due,
Had man to learn himself anew
Beyond the second birth of Death.

XLVI

We ranging down this lower track,
The path we came by, thorn and flower,
Is shadow'd by the growing hour,
Lest life should fail in looking back.

So be it: there no shade can last
In that deep dawn behind the tomb,
But clear from marge to marge shall bloom
The eternal landscape of the past;

remembered past life

in future rejoicing

A lifelong tract of time reveal'd;
The fruitful hours of still increase;
Days order'd in a wealthy peace,
And those five years its richest field.

10

O Love, thy province were not large,
A bounded field, nor stretching far;
Look also, Love, a brooding star,
A rosy warmth from marge to marge.

XLVII

That each, who seems a separate whole,
Should move his rounds, and fusing all

XLVI This section suggests that earthly memory of pain and joy is short, but
in eternity all the past is remembered. The five years of the friendship of
Hallam and Tennyson, although short ("nor stretching far"), will be revealed as the "richest field" of time.

XLVII Tennyson is concerned with denying the idea that souls lose their
identity and merge into a general soul; at least the souls of friends will have
a personal reunion before losing identity.

The skirts of self again, should fall
Remerging in the general Soul,

Is faith as vague as all unsweet:
    Eternal form shall still divide
    The eternal soul from all beside;
And I shall know him when we meet:

And we shall sit at endless feast,
    Enjoying each the other's good: 10
    What vaster dream can hit the mood
Of Love on earth? He seeks at least

Upon the last and sharpest height,
    Before the spirits fade away,
    Some landing-place, to clasp and say,
"Farewell! We lose ourselves in light."

XLVIII

If these brief lays, of Sorrow born,
    Were taken to be such as closed
    Grave doubts and answers here proposed,
Then these were such as men might scorn:

Her care is not to part and prove;
    She takes, when harsher moods remit,
    What slender shade of doubt may flit,
And makes it vassal unto love:

And hence, indeed, she sports with words,
    But better serves a wholesome law,   10
    And holds it sin and shame to draw
The deepest measure from the chords;

Nor dare she trust a larger lay,
    But rather loosens from the lip
    Short swallow-flights of song, that dip
Their wings in tears, and skim away.

XLVIII 5 *part:* dissect.

XLIX

From art, from nature, from the schools,
  Let random influences glance,
  Like light in many a shiver'd lance
That breaks about the dappled pools:

The lightest wave of thought shall lisp,
  The fancy's tenderest eddy wreathe,
  The slightest air of song shall breathe
To make the sullen surface crisp.

And look thy look, and go thy way,
  But blame not thou the winds that make   10
  The seeming-wanton ripple break,
The tender-pencill'd shadow play.

Beneath all fancied hopes and fears
  Ay me, the sorrow deepens down,
  Whose muffled motions blindly drown
The bases of my life in tears.

L

Be near me when my light is low,
  When the blood creeps, and the nerves prick
  And tingle; and the heart is sick,
And all the wheels of Being slow.

Be near me when the sensuous frame
  Is rack'd with pangs that conquer trust;
  And Time, a maniac scattering dust,
And Life, a Fury slinging flame.

Be near me when my faith is dry,
  And men the flies of latter spring,
  That lay their eggs, and sting and sing   10
And weave their petty cells and die.

XLIX 1 *schools:* of thought.
8 *crisp:* ripple.

Be near me when I fade away,
　To point the term of human strife,
　And on the low dark verge of life
The twilight of eternal day.

out of sorrow

LI

Do we indeed desire the dead
　Should still be near us at our side?
　Is there no baseness we would hide?
No inner vileness that we dread?

Shall he for whose applause I strove,
　I had such reverence for his blame,
　See with clear eye some hidden shame
And I be lessen'd in his love?

I wrong the grave with fears untrue:
　Shall love be blamed for want of faith?
　There must be wisdom with great Death:
The dead shall look me thro' and thro'.

Be near us when we climb or fall:
　Ye watch, like God, the rolling hours
　With larger other eyes than ours,
To make allowance for us all.

LII

I cannot love thee as I ought,
　For love reflects the thing beloved;
　My words are only words, and moved
Upon the topmost froth of thought.

"Yet blame not thou thy plaintive song,"
　The Spirit of true love replied;
　"Thou canst not move me from thy side,
Nor human frailty do me wrong.

"What keeps a spirit wholly true
　To that ideal which he bears?

10

L 14 *term:* conclusion.

What record? not the sinless years
That breathed beneath the Syrian blue:

"So fret not, like an idle girl,
    That life is dash'd with flecks of sin.
    Abide: thy wealth is gather'd in,
When Time hath sunder'd shell from pearl."

[handwritten: T. will have his happiness in end]

LIII

How many a father have I seen,
    A sober man, among his boys,
    Whose youth was full of foolish noise,
Who wears his manhood hale and green:

[handwritten: without experience life is not full trust in good.]

And dare we to this fancy give,
    That had the wild oat not been sown,
    The soil, left barren, scarce had grown
The grain by which a man may live?

Or, if we held the doctrine sound
    For life outliving heats of youth,
    Yet who would preach it as a truth
To those that eddy round and round?

10

Hold thou the good: define it well:
    For fear divine Philosophy
    Should push beyond her mark, and be
Procuress to the Lords of Hell.

LIV

Oh, yet we trust that somehow good
    Will be the final goal of ill,
    To pangs of nature, sins of will,
Defects of doubt, and taints of blood;

That nothing walks with aimless feet;
    That not one life shall be destroy'd,

LII 11 *the sinless years:* Christ's life (the record of which is insufficient to
keep man sinless).
LIII 5 *give:* give assent.

Or cast as rubbish to the void,
When God hath made the pile complete;

That not a worm is cloven in vain;
  That not a moth with vain desire
  Is shrivell'd in a fruitless fire,
Or but subserves another's gain.

Behold, we know not anything;
  I can but trust that good shall fall
  At last—far off—at last, to all,
And every winter change to spring.

So runs my dream: but what am I?
  An infant crying in the night;
  An infant crying for the light;
And with no language but a cry.

                    LV

The wish, that of the living whole
  No life may fail beyond the grave,
  Derives it not from what we have
The likest God within the soul?

Are God and Nature then at strife,
  That Nature lends such evil dreams?
  So careful of the type she seems,
So careless of the single life,

That I, considering everywhere
  Her secret meaning in her deeds,
  And finding that of fifty seeds
She often brings but one to bear,

I falter where I firmly trod,
  And falling with my weight of cares
  Upon the great world's altar-stairs
That slope thro' darkness up to God,

LV 7 *type:* species.

I stretch lame hands of faith, and grope,
  And gather dust and chaff, and call
  To what I feel is Lord of all,
And faintly trust the larger hope.   20

LVI

"So careful of the type?" but no.
  From scarped cliff and quarried stone
  She cries, "A thousand types are gone:
I care for nothing, all shall go.

"Thou makest thine appeal to me:
  I bring to life, I bring to death:
  The spirit does but mean the breath:
I know no more." And he, shall he,

Man, her last work, who seem'd so fair,
  Such splendid purpose in his eyes,
  Who roll'd the psalm to wintry skies,
Who built him fanes of fruitless prayer,   10

Who trusted God was love indeed
  And love Creation's final law—
  Tho' Nature, red in tooth and claw
With ravine, shriek'd against his creed—

Who loved, who suffer'd countless ills,
  Who battled for the True, the Just,
  Be blown about the desert dust,
Or seal'd within the iron hills?   20

No more? A monster then, a dream,
  A discord. Dragons of the prime,
  That tare each other in their slime,
Were mellow music match'd with him.

O life as futile, then, as frail!
  O for thy voice to soothe and bless!

LVI 2 *scarped:* cut away.
3 *She:* Nature.
12 *fanes:* temples.
16 *ravine:* rapacity.

What hope of answer, or redress?
Behind the veil, behind the veil.

LVII

Peace; come away: the song of woe
  Is after all an earthly song:
  Peace; come away: we do him wrong
To sing so wildly: let us go.

Come; let us go: your cheeks are pale;
  But half my life I leave behind:
  Methinks my friend is richly shrined;
But I shall pass; my work will fail.

Yet in these ears, till hearing dies,
  One set slow bell will seem to toll   10
  The passing of the sweetest soul
That ever look'd with human eyes.

I hear it now, and o'er and o'er,
  Eternal greetings to the dead;
  And "Ave, Ave, Ave," said,
"Adieu, adieu" for evermore.

LVIII

In those sad words I took farewell:
  Like echoes in sepulchral halls,
  As drop by drop the water falls
In vaults and catacombs, they fell;

And, falling, idly broke the peace
  Of hearts that beat from day to day,
  Half-conscious of their dying clay,
And those cold crypts where they shall cease.

The high Muse answer'd: "Wherefore grieve
  Thy brethren with a fruitless tear?   10
  Abide a little longer here,
And thou shalt take a nobler leave."

LVII 15 *Ave:* hail.
LVIII 9 *Muse:* Urania.

LIX

O Sorrow, wilt thou live with me
   No casual mistress, but a wife,
   My bosom-friend and half of life;
As I confess it needs must be;

O Sorrow, wilt thou rule my blood,
   Be sometimes lovely like a bride,
   And put thy harsher moods aside,
If thou wilt have me wise and good.

My centred passion cannot move.
   Nor will it lessen from to-day;   10
   But I'll have leave at times to play
As with the creature of my love;

And set thee forth, for thou art mine,
   With so much hope for years to come,
   That, howsoe'er I know thee, some
Could hardly tell what name were thine.

LX

He past; a soul of nobler tone:
   My spirit loved and loves him yet,
   Like some poor girl whose heart is set
On one whose rank exceeds her own.

He mixing with his proper sphere,
   She finds the baseness of her lot,
   Half jealous of she knows not what,
And envying all that meet him there.

The little village looks forlorn;
   She sighs amid her narrow days,   10
   Moving about the household ways,
In that dark house where she was born.

The foolish neighbours come and go,
   And tease her till the day draws by:

LIX This section was added in 1851.

At night she weeps, "How vain am I!
How should he love a thing so low?"

LXI

If, in thy second state sublime,
   Thy ransom'd reason change replies
   With all the circle of the wise,
The perfect flower of human time;

And if thou cast thine eyes below,
   How dimly character'd and slight,
   How dwarf'd a growth of cold and night,
How blanch'd with darkness must I grow!

Yet turn thee to the doubtful shore,
   Where thy first form was made a man;   10
   I loved thee, Spirit, and love, nor can
The soul of Shakspeare love thee more.

LXII

Tho' if an eye that's downward cast
   Could make thee somewhat blench or fail,
   Then be my love an idle tale,
And fading legend of the past;

And thou, as one that once declined,
   When he was little more than boy,
   On some unworthy heart with joy,
But lives to wed an equal mind;

And breathes a novel world, the while
   His other passion wholly dies,   10
   Or in the light of deeper eyes
Is matter for a flying smile.

LXIII

Yet pity for a horse o'er-driven,
   And love in which my hound has part,

LXI 12 *Shakspeare:* the poet is saying that his love equals the love displayed by Shakespeare in his sonnets.

Can hang no weight upon my heart
In its assumptions up to heaven;

And I am so much more than these,
 As thou, perchance, art more than I,
 And yet I spare them sympathy,
And I would set their pains at ease.

So mayst thou watch me where I weep,
 As, unto vaster motions bound,   10
 The circuits of thine orbit round
A higher height, a deeper deep. *H. fuller understanding*

LXIV

Dost thou look back on what hath been,
 As some divinely gifted man,
 Whose life in low estate began
And on a simple village green;

Who breaks his birth's invidious bar,
 And grasps the skirts of happy chance,
 And breasts the blows of circumstance,
And grapples with his evil star;

Who makes by force his merit known
 And lives to clutch the golden keys, 10
 To mould a mighty state's decrees,
And shape the whisper of the throne;

And moving up from high to higher,
 Becomes on Fortune's crowning slope
 The pillar of a people's hope,
The centre of a world's desire;

Yet feels, as in a pensive dream,
 When all his active powers are still,
 A distant dearness in the hill,
A secret sweetness in the stream, 20

LXIV 10 *golden keys:* symbolic of official position.

The limit of his narrower fate,
  While yet beside its vocal springs
  He play'd at counsellors and kings,
With one that was his earliest mate;

Who ploughs with pain his native lea
  And reaps the labour of his hands,
  Or in the furrow musing stands;
"Does my old friend remember me?"

LXV

Sweet soul, do with me as thou wilt;
  I lull a fancy trouble-tost
  With "Love's too precious to be lost,
A little grain shall not be spilt."

And in that solace can I sing,
  Till out of painful phases wrought
  There flutters up a happy thought,
Self-balanced on a lightsome wing:

Since we deserved the name of friends,
  And thine effect so lives in me,   10
  A part of mine may live in thee
And move thee on to noble ends.

LXVI

You thought my heart too far diseased;
  You wonder when my fancies play
  To find me gay among the gay,
Like one with any trifle pleased.

The shade by which my life was crost,
  Which makes a desert in the mind,
  Has made me kindly with my kind,
And like to him whose sight is lost;

Whose feet are guided thro' the land,
  Whose jest among his friends is free,   10

LXVI 1 *You:* probably not Hallam but a living friend.

Who takes the children on his knee,
And winds their curls about his hand:

He plays with threads, he beats his chair
   For pastime, dreaming of the sky;
   His inner day can never die,
His night of loss is always there.

LXVII

[handwritten: nights sleep ↓]

When on my bed the moonlight falls,
   I know that in thy place of rest
   By that broad water of the west,
There comes a glory on the walls:

Thy marble bright in dark appears,
   As slowly steals a silver flame
   Along the letters of thy name,
And o'er the number of thy years.

The mystic glory swims away;
   From off my bed the moonlight dies;   10
   And closing eaves of wearied eyes
I sleep till dusk is dipt in gray:

[handwritten: relation & sleep of T. & H.'s rest]

And then I know the mist is drawn
   A lucid veil from coast to coast,
   And in the dark church like a ghost
Thy tablet glimmers to the dawn.

LXVIII

When in the down I sink my head,
   Sleep, Death's twin-brother, times my breath;
   Sleep, Death's twin-brother, knows not Death,
Nor can I dream of thee as dead:

I walk as ere I walk'd forlorn,
   When all our path was fresh with dew,
   And all the bugle breezes blew
Reveillée to the breaking morn.

But what is this? I turn about,
   I find a trouble in thine eye,   10

Which makes me sad I know not why,
Nor can my dream resolve the doubt:

But ere the lark hath left the lea
   I wake, and I discern the truth;
   It is the trouble of my youth
That foolish sleep transfers to thee.

LXIX

[handwritten margin note: death related to Spring]

I dream'd there would be Spring no more,
   That Nature's ancient power was lost:
   The streets were black with smoke and frost,
They chatter'd trifles at the door:

I wander'd from the noisy town,
   I found a wood with thorny boughs:
   I took the thorns to bind my brows,
I wore them like a civic crown:

I met with scoffs, I met with scorns
   From youth and babe and hoary hairs:
   They call'd me in the public squares
The fool that wears a crown of thorns:

[handwritten margin note: fool for sacrifices to mourning]

They call'd me fool, they call'd me child:
   I found an angel of the night;
   The voice was low, the look was bright;
He look'd upon my crown and smiled:

He reach'd the glory of a hand,
   That seem'd to touch it into leaf:
   The voice was not the voice of grief,
The words were hard to understand.   20

[handwritten margin note: this affection is good in Angel's sight]

LXX

I cannot see the features right,
   When on the gloom I strive to paint
   The face I know; the hues are faint
And mix with hollow masks of night;

Cloud-towers by ghostly masons wrought,
   A gulf that ever shuts and gapes,

A hand that points, and palled shapes
In shadowy thoroughfares of thought;

And crowds that stream from yawning doors,
   And shoals of pucker'd faces drive;   10
     Dark bulks that tumble half alive,
And lazy lengths on boundless shores;

Till all at once beyond the will
   I hear a wizard music roll,
     And thro' a lattice on the soul
Looks thy fair face and makes it still.

LXXI

Sleep, kinsman thou to death and trance
   And madness, thou hast forged at last
     A night-long Present of the Past
In which we went thro' summer France.

Hadst thou such credit with the soul?
   Then bring an opiate trebly strong,
     Drug down the blindfold sense of wrong,
That so my pleasure may be whole;

While now we talk as once we talk'd
   Of men and minds, the dust of change,   10
     The days that grow to something strange,
In walking as of old we walk'd

Beside the river's wooded reach,
   The fortress, and the mountain ridge,
     The cataract flashing from the bridge,
The breaker breaking on the beach.

LXXII

Risest thou thus, dim dawn, again,
   And howlest, issuing out of night,
     With blasts that blow the poplar white,
And lash with storm the streaming pane?

LXXI 4 *summer France:* reference to Tennyson's trip to France with Hallam
in 1830.
LXXII 1 *dawn:* of the anniversary of Hallam's death.

Day, when my crown'd estate begun
   To pine in that reverse of doom,
   Which sicken'd every living bloom,
And blurr'd the splendour of the sun;

Who usherest in the dolorous hour
   With thy quick tears that make the rose   10
   Pull sideways, and the daisy close
Her crimson fringes to the shower;

Who might'st have heaved a windless flame
   Up the deep East, or, whispering, play'd
   A chequer-work of beam and shade
Along the hills, yet look'd the same.

As wan, as chill, as wild as now;
   Day, mark'd as with some hideous crime,
   When the dark hand struck down thro' time,
And cancell'd nature's best: but thou,   20

Lift as thou may'st thy burthen'd brows
   Thro' clouds that drench the morning star,
   And whirl the ungarner'd sheaf afar,
And sow the sky with flying boughs,

And up thy vault with roaring sound
   Climb thy thick noon, disastrous day;
   Touch thy dull goal of joyless gray,
And hide thy shame beneath the ground.

LXXIII

So many worlds, so much to do,
   So little done, such things to be,
   How know I what had need of thee,
For thou wert strong as thou wert true?

The fame is quench'd that I foresaw,
   The head hath miss'd an earthly wreath:
   I curse not nature, no, nor death;
For nothing is that errs from law.

We pass; the path that each man trod
   Is dim, or will be dim, with weeds: 10
   What fame is left for human deeds
In endless age? It rests with God.

O hollow wraith of dying fame,
   Fade wholly, while the soul exults,
   And self-infolds the large results
Of force that would have forged a name.

LXXIV

As sometimes in a dead man's face,
   To those that watch it more and more,
   A likeness, hardly seen before,
Comes out—to some one of his race;

So, dearest, now thy brows are cold,
   I see thee what thou art, and know
   Thy likeness to the wise below,
Thy kindred with the great of old.

But there is more than I can see,
   And what I see I leave unsaid,   10
   Nor speak it, knowing Death has made
His darkness beautiful with thee.

LXXV

I leave thy praises unexpress'd
   In verse that brings myself relief,
   And by the measure of my grief
I leave thy greatness to be guess'd;

What practice howsoe'er expert
   In fitting aptest words to things,
   Or voice the richest-toned that sings,
Hath power to give thee as thou wert?

I care not in these fading days
   To raise a cry that lasts not long,   10

LXXIII 14-16 *the soul exults . . . name:* i.e., the soul rejoices in the forces
that would have made Hallam famous.

And round thee with the breeze of song
To stir a little dust of praise.

Thy leaf has perish'd in the green,
   And, while we breathe beneath the sun,
   The world which credits what is done
Is cold to all that might have been.

So here shall silence guard thy fame;
   But somewhere, out of human view,
   Whate'er thy hands are set to do
Is wrought with tumult of acclaim.   20

LXXVI

Take wings of fancy, and ascend,
   And in a moment set thy face
   Where all the starry heavens of space
Are sharpen'd to a needle's end;

Take wings of foresight; lighten thro'
   The secular abyss to come,
   And lo, thy deepest lays are dumb
Before the mouldering of a yew;

And if the matin songs, that woke
   The darkness of our planet, last,   10
   Thine own shall wither in the vast,
Ere half the lifetime of an oak.

Ere these have clothed their branchy bowers
   With fifty Mays, thy songs are vain;
   And what are they when these remain
The ruin'd shells of hollow towers?

LXXVII

What hope is here for modern rhyme
   To him, who turns a musing eye

LXXVI ⁴ *needle's end:* farthest point of perspective in vision.
⁶ *secular:* lasting for ages.
⁷ *thy:* Tennyson's; presumably the poet is speaking to himself in this section.
⁹ *matin songs:* of early poets.

On songs, and deeds, and lives, that lie
Foreshorten'd in the tract of time?

These mortal lullabies of pain
   May bind a book, may line a box,
   May serve to curl a maiden's locks;
Or when a thousand moons shall wane

A man upon a stall may find,
   And, passing, turn the page that tells   10
   A grief, then changed to something else,
Sung by a long-forgotten mind.

But what of that? My darken'd ways
   Shall ring with music all the same;
   To breathe my loss is more than fame,
To utter love more sweet than praise.

LXXVIII

Again at Christmas did we weave
   The holly round the Christmas hearth;
   The silent snow possess'd the earth,
And calmly fell our Christmas-eve:

The yule-clog sparkled keen with frost,
   No wing of wind the region swept,
   But over all things brooding slept
The quiet sense of something lost.

As in the winters left behind,
   Again our ancient games had place,   10
   The mimic picture's breathing grace,
And dance and song and hoodman-blind.

Who show'd a token of distress?
   No single tear, no mark of pain:
   O sorrow, then can sorrow wane?
   O grief, can grief be changed to less?

LXXVIII 5 *yule-clog:* yule log.
11 *mimic . . . grace:* charades or *tableaux vivants.*

O last regret, regret can die!
   No—mixt with all this mystic frame,
   Her deep relations are the same,
But with long use her tears are dry.   20

LXXIX

"More than my brothers are to me,"—
   Let this not vex thee, noble heart!
   I know thee of what force thou art
To hold the costliest love in fee.

But thou and I are one in kind,
   As moulded like in Nature's mint;
   And hill and wood and field did print
The same sweet forms in either mind.

For us the same cold streamlet curl'd
   Thro' all his eddying coves; the same   10
   All winds that roam the twilight came
In whispers of the beauteous world.

At one dear knee we proffer'd vows,
   One lesson from one book we learn'd,
   Ere childhood's flaxen ringlet turn'd
To black and brown on kindred brows.

And so my wealth resembles thine,
   But he was rich where I was poor,
   And he supplied my want the more
As his unlikeness fitted mine.   20

LXXX

If any vague desire should rise,
   That holy Death ere Arthur died
   Had moved me kindly from his side,
And dropt the dust on tearless eyes;

Then fancy shapes, as fancy can,
   The grief my loss in him had wrought,

LXXIX The section is addressed to Tennyson's brother.

A grief as deep as life or thought,
But stay'd in peace with God and man.

I make a picture in the brain;
   I hear the sentence that he speaks;
   He bears the burthen of the weeks,
But turns his burthen into gain.

If T. had
gone first,
10
H. would have
found gain in
the loss

His credit thus shall set me free;
   And, influence-rich to soothe and save,
   Unused example from the grave
Reach out dead hands to comfort me.

LXXXI

Could I have said while he was here,
   "My love shall now no further range;
   There cannot come a mellower change,
For now is love mature in ear."

Love, then, had hope of richer store:
   What end is here to my complaint?
   This haunting whisper makes me faint,
"More years had made me love thee more."

Death made love
more deep
Death than not
10 been grief
but beneficial

But Death returns an answer sweet:
   "My sudden frost was sudden gain,
   And gave all ripeness to the grain
It might have drawn from after-heat."

LXXXII

I wage not any feud with Death
   For changes wrought on form and face;
   No lower life that earth's embrace
May breed with him, can fright my faith.

Death has been
meaningful

Eternal process moving on,
   From state to state the spirit walks;
   And these are but the shatter'd stalks,
Or ruin'd chrysalis of one.

LXXX 8 *stay'd:* endured.
15 *Unused:* imaginary.

Nor blame I Death, because he bare
  The use of virtue out of earth: 10
  I know transplanted human worth
Will bloom to profit, otherwhere.

For this alone on Death I wreak
  The wrath that garners in my heart:
  He put our lives so far apart
We cannot hear each other speak.

LXXXIII

Dip down upon the northern shore,
  O sweet new-year delaying long;
  Thou doest expectant nature wrong;
Delaying long, delay no more.

What stays thee from the clouded noons,
  Thy sweetness from its proper place?
  Can trouble live with April days,
Or sadness in the summer moons?

Bring orchis, bring the foxglove spire,
  The little speedwell's darling blue, 10
  Deep tulips dash'd with fiery dew,
Laburnums, dropping-wells of fire.

O thou, new-year, delaying long,
  Delayest the sorrow in my blood,
  That longs to burst a frozen bud
And flood a fresher throat with song.

LXXXIV

When I contemplate all alone
  The life that had been thine below,
  And fix my thoughts on all the glow
To which thy crescent would have grown;

I see thee sitting crown'd with good,
  A central warmth diffusing bliss

LXXXII 14 *garners:* accumulates.

In glance and smile, and clasp and kiss,
On all the branches of thy blood;

Thy blood, my friend, and partly mine;
   For now the day was drawing on,   10
   When thou should'st link thy life with one
Of mine own house, and boys of thine

Had babbled "Uncle" on my knee;
   But that remorseless iron hour
   Made cypress of her orange flower,
Despair of Hope, and earth of thee.

I seem to meet their least desire,
   To clap their cheeks, to call them mine.
   I see their unborn faces shine
Beside the never-lighted fire.   20

I see myself an honour'd guest,
   Thy partner in the flowery walk
   Of letters, genial table-talk,
Or deep dispute, and graceful jest;

While now thy prosperous labour fills
   The lips of men with honest praise,
   And sun by sun the happy days
Descend below the golden hills

With promise of a morn as fair;
   And all the train of bounteous hours   30
   Conduct, by paths of growing powers,
To reverence and the silver hair;

Till slowly worn her earthly robe,
   Her lavish mission richly wrought,
   Leaving great legacies of thought,
Thy spirit should fail from off the globe;

What time mine own might also flee,
   As link'd with thine in love and fate,

LXXXIV 9 *partly mine:* Tennyson's sister was engaged to Hallam.

And, hovering o'er the dolorous strait
To the other shore, involved in thee,   40

Arrive at last the blessed goal,
    And He that died in Holy Land
    Would reach us out the shining hand,
And take us as a single soul.

What reed was that on which I leant?
    Ah, backward fancy, wherefore wake
    The old bitterness again, and break
The low beginnings of content?

LXXXV

This truth came borne with bier and pall,
    I felt it, when I sorrow'd most,
    'T is better to have loved and lost,
Than never to have loved at all—

O true in word, and tried in deed,
    Demanding, so to bring relief
    To this which is our common grief,
What kind of life is that I·lead;

And whether trust in things above
    Be dimm'd of sorrow, or sustain'd;   10
    And whether love for him have drain'd
My capabilities of love;

Your words have virtue such as draws
    A faithful answer from the breast,
    Thro' light reproaches, half exprest,
And loyal unto kindly laws.

My blood an even tenor kept,
    Till on mine ear this message falls,
    That in Vienna's fatal walls
God's finger touch'd him, and he slept.   20

LXXXV addressed to Edmund Lushington. His marriage to Tennyson's sister
Cecilia is celebrated in the Epilogue.

The great Intelligences fair
  That range above our mortal state,
  In circle round the blessed gate,
Received and gave him welcome there;

And led him thro' the blissful climes,
  And show'd him in the fountain fresh
  All knowledge that the sons of flesh
Shall gather in the cycled times.

But I remain'd, whose hopes were dim,
  Whose life, whose thoughts were little worth,   30
  To wander on a darken'd earth,
Where all things round me breathed of him.

O friendship, equal-poised control,
  O heart, with kindliest motion warm,
  O sacred essence, other form,
O solemn ghost, O crowned soul!

Yet none could better know than I,
  How much of act at human hands
  The sense of human will demands
By which we dare to live or die.   40

Whatever way my days decline,
  I felt and feel, tho' left alone,
  His being working in mine own,
The footsteps of his life in mine;

A life that all the Muses deck'd
  With gifts of grace, that might express
  All-comprehensive tenderness,
All-subtilising intellect:

And so my passion hath not swerved
  To works of weakness, but I find
  An image comforting the mind,
And in my grief a strength reserved.   *seeks new friend, but not to replace old friend*

---

28 *cycled times:* future ages.

Likewise the imaginative woe,
　　That loved to handle spiritual strife,
　　Diffused the shock thro' all my life,
But in the present broke the blow.

My pulses therefore beat again
　　For other friends that once I met;
　　Nor can it suit me to forget
The mighty hopes that make us men.　　　　60

I woo your love: I count it crime
　　To mourn for any overmuch;
　　I, the divided half of such
A friendship as had master'd Time;

Which masters Time indeed, and is
　　Eternal, separate from fears:
　　The all-assuming months and years
Can take no part away from this:

But Summer on the steaming floods,
　　And Spring that swells the narrow brooks,　　70
　　And Autumn, with a noise of rooks,
That gather in the waning woods,

And every pulse of wind and wave
　　Recalls, in change of light or gloom,
　　My old affection of the tomb,
And my prime passion in the grave:

My old affection of the tomb,
　　A part of stillness, yearns to speak:
　　"Arise, and get thee forth and seek
A friendship for the years to come.　　　　80

"I watch thee from the quiet shore;
　　Thy spirit up to mine can reach;
　　But in dear words of human speech
We two communicate no more."

---

60 *hopes:* of immortality.
67 *all-assuming:* all-consuming.

And I, "Can clouds of nature stain
  The starry clearness of the free?
  How is it? Canst thou feel for me
Some painless sympathy with pain?"

And lightly does the whisper fall:
  " 'T is hard for thee to fathom this;   90
  I triumph in conclusive bliss,
And that serene result of all."

So hold I commerce with the dead;
  Or so methinks the dead would say;
  Or so shall grief with symbols play
And pining life be fancy-fed.

Now looking to some settled end,
  That these things pass, and I shall prove
  A meeting somewhere, love with love,
I crave your pardon, O my friend;   100

If not so fresh, with love as true,
  I, clasping brother-hands, aver
  I could not, if I would, transfer
The whole I felt for him to you.

For which be they that hold apart
  The promise of the golden hours?
  First love, first friendship, equal powers,
That marry with the virgin heart.

Still mine, that cannot but deplore,
  That beats within a lonely place,   110
  That yet remembers his embrace,
But at his footstep leaps no more,

My heart, tho' widow'd, may not rest
  Quite in the love of what is gone,
  But seeks to beat in time with one
That warms another living breast.

105-6 *For which be . . . golden hours?:* i.e., What keeps me from new joy?

Ah, take the imperfect gift I bring,
   Knowing the primrose yet is dear,
   The primrose of the later year,
As not unlike to that of Spring.   120

LXXXVI

new sense of joy in Spring

Sweet after showers, ambrosial air,
   That rollest from the gorgeous gloom
   Of evening over brake and bloom
And meadow, slowly breathing bare

The round of space, and rapt below
   Thro' all the dewy-tassell'd wood,
   And shadowing down the horned flood
In ripples, fan my brows and blow

finds purpose in Spring.

if H. content, so should be

The fever from my cheek, and sigh
   The full new life that feeds thy breath   10
   Throughout my frame, till Doubt and Death,
Ill brethren, let the fancy fly

From belt to belt of crimson seas
   On leagues of odour streaming far,
   To where in yonder orient star
A hundred spirits whisper "Peace."

LXXXVII

I past beside the reverend walls
   In which of old I wore the gown;
   I roved at random thro' the town,
And saw the tumult of the halls;

doesn't feel horror of dying des père

And heard once more in college fanes
   The storm their high-built organs make,
   And thunder-music, rolling, shake
The prophet blazon'd on the panes;

LXXXVI 4-5 *breathing bare . . . space:* i.e., blowing the clouds from the sky.
7 *horned:* winding.
13 *belt to belt of crimson seas:* belts of color reflected from the sunset.
LXXXVII 1 *walls:* of Trinity College, Cambridge.

And caught once more the distant shout,
  The measured pulse of racing oars   10
  Among the willows; paced the shores
And many a bridge, and all about

The same gray flats again, and felt
  The same, but not the same; and last
  Up that long walk of limes I past
To see the rooms in which he dwelt.

Another name was on the door:
  I linger'd; all within was noise
  Of songs, and clapping hands, and boys
That crash'd the glass and beat the floor;   20

Where once we held debate, a band
  Of youthful friends, on mind and art,
  And labour, and the changing mart,
And all the framework of the land;

When one would aim an arrow fair,
  But send it slackly from the string;
  And one would pierce an outer ring,
And one an inner, here and there;

And last the master-bowman, he,
  Would cleave the mark. A willing ear   30
  We lent him. Who but hung to hear
The rapt oration flowing free

From point to point, with power and grace
  And music in the bounds of law,
  To those conclusions when we saw
The God within him light his face,

And seem to lift the form, and glow
  In azure orbits heavenly-wise;

---

21 *band:* the "Apostles."
29 *he:* Hallam.

And over those ethereal eyes
The bar of Michael Angelo?   40

LXXXVIII

only occasional grief.

Wild bird, whose warble, liquid sweet,
   Rings Eden thro' the budded quicks,
   O, tell me where the senses mix,
O, tell me where the passions meet,

Whence radiate: fierce extremes employ
   Thy spirits in the darkening leaf,
   And in the midmost heart of grief
Thy passion clasps a secret joy:

And I—my harp would prelude woe—
   I cannot all command the strings;   10
   The glory of the sum of things
Will flash along the chords and go.

LXXXIX

89-104
communion with dead

Witch-elms that counterchange the floor
   Of this flat lawn with dusk and bright;
   And thou, with all thy breadth and height
Of foliage, towering sycamore;

How often, hither wandering down,
   My Arthur found your shadows fair,
   And shook to all the liberal air
The dust and din and steam of town!

He brought an eye for all he saw;
   He mixt in all our simple sports;   10
   They pleased him, fresh from brawling courts
And dusty purlieus of the law.

O joy to him in this retreat,
   Immantled in ambrosial dark,

---

40 *bar of Michael Angelo:* Hallam is said to have had a ridge of bone above
his eyes resembling that in the face of Michelangelo.
LXXXVIII 1 *bird:* nightingale.
2 *quicks:* hedges.
LXXXIX 1 *counterchange:* dapple.
12 *law:* Hallam studied law in London after leaving Cambridge.

To drink the cooler air, and mark
The landscape winking thro' the heat!

O sound to rout the brood of cares,
　　The sweep of scythe in morning dew,
　　The gust that round the garden flew,
And tumbled half the mellowing pears!　　20

O bliss, when all in circle drawn
　　About him, heart and ear were fed
　　To hear him, as he lay and read
The Tuscan poets on the lawn;

Or in the all-golden afternoon
　　A guest, or happy sister, sung,
　　Or here she brought the harp and flung
A ballad to the brightening moon:

Nor less it pleased in livelier moods,
　　Beyond the bounding hill to stray,　　30
　　And break the livelong summer day
With banquet in the distant woods;

Whereat we glanced from theme to theme,
　　Discuss'd the books to love or hate,
　　Or touch'd the changes of the state,
Or threaded some Socratic dream;

But if I praised the busy town,
　　He loved to rail against it still,
　　For "ground in yonder social mill
We rub each other's angles down,　　40

"And merge," he said, "in form and gloss
　　The picturesque of man and man."
　　We talk'd: the stream beneath us ran,
The wine-flask lying couch'd in moss,

Or cool'd within the glooming wave;
　　And last, returning from afar,

---

²⁴ *Tuscan poets:* Petrarch and Dante.

Before the crimson-circled star
Had fallen into her father's grave,

And brushing ankle-deep in flowers,
    We heard behind the woodbine veil   50
    The milk that bubbled in the pail,
And buzzings of the honied hours.

XC

He tasted love with half his mind,
    Nor ever drank the inviolate spring
    Where nighest heaven, who first could fling
This bitter seed among mankind;

That could the dead, whose dying eyes
    Were closed with wail, resume their life,
    They would but find in child and wife
An iron welcome when they rise:

'T was well, indeed, when warm with wine,
    To pledge them with a kindly tear,   10
    To talk them o'er, to wish them here,
To count their memories half divine;

But if they came who past away,
    Behold their brides in other hands;
    The hard heir strides about their lands,
And will not yield them for a day.

Yea, tho' their sons were none of these,
    Not less the yet-loved sire would make
    Confusion worse than death, and shake
The pillars of domestic peace.   20

Ah, dear, but come thou back to me:
    Whatever change the years have wrought,

---

47 *crimson-circled star:* Venus, the evening star, figuratively the child of the sun.

XC 1 *He:* the man who first suggested that the dead would be unwelcome should they return to earth.

I find not yet one lonely thought
That cries against my wish for thee.

XCI

When rosy plumelets tuft the larch,
    And rarely pipes the mounted thrush;
    Or underneath the barren bush
Flits by the sea-blue bird of March;

Come, wear the form by which I know
    Thy spirit in time among thy peers;
    The hope of unaccomplish'd years
Be large and lucid round thy brow.

When summer's hourly-mellowing change
    May breathe, with many roses sweet,
    Upon the thousand waves of wheat,
That ripple round the lonely grange;

Come: not in watches of the night,
    But where the sunbeam broodeth warm,
    Come, beauteous in thine after form,
And like a finer light in light.

XCII

If any vision should reveal
    Thy likeness, I might count it vain
    As but the canker of the brain;
Yea, tho' it spake and made appeal

To chances where our lots were cast
    Together in the days behind,
    I might but say, I hear a wind
Of memory murmuring the past.

Yea, tho' it spake and bared to view
    A fact within the coming year;
    And tho' the months, revolving near,
Should prove the phantom-warning true,

XCI 4 *sea-blue bird:* kingfisher.

They might not seem thy prophecies,
But spiritual presentiments,
And such refraction of events
As often rises ere they rise.

XCIII

I shall not see thee. Dare I say
No spirit ever brake the band
That stays him from the native land
Where first he walk'd when claspt in clay?

No visual shade of some one lost,
But he, the Spirit himself, may come
Where all the nerve of sense is numb;
Spirit to Spirit, Ghost to Ghost.

Oh, therefore from thy sightless range
With gods in unconjectured bliss,   10
Oh, from the distance of the abyss
Of tenfold-complicated change,

Descend, and touch, and enter; hear
The wish too strong for words to name;
That in this blindness of the frame
My Ghost may feel that thine is near.

XCIV

How pure at heart and sound in head,
With what divine affections bold
Should be the man whose thought would hold
An hour's communion with the dead.

In vain shalt thou, or any, call
The spirits from their golden day,
Except, like them, thou too canst say,
My spirit is at peace with all.

They haunt the silence of the breast,
Imaginations calm and fair,   10

XCIII 9 *sightless:* invisible.

The memory like a cloudless air,
The conscience as a sea at rest;

But when the heart is full of din,
   And doubt beside the portal waits,
   They can but listen at the gates,
And hear the household jar within.

XCV

By night we linger'd on the lawn,
   For underfoot the herb was dry;
   And genial warmth; and o'er the sky
The silvery haze of summer drawn;

And calm that let the tapers burn
   Unwavering: not a cricket chirr'd:
   The brook alone far-off was heard,
And on the board the fluttering urn:

And bats went round in fragrant skies,
   And wheel'd or lit the filmy shapes   10
   That haunt the dusk, with ermine capes
And woolly breasts and beaded eyes;

While now we sang old songs that peal'd
   From knoll to knoll, where, couch'd at ease,
   The white kine glimmer'd, and the trees
Laid their dark arms about the field.

But when those others, one by one,
   Withdrew themselves from me and night,
   And in the house light after light
Went out, and I was all alone,   20

A hunger seized my heart; I read
   Of that glad year which once had been,
   In those fallen leaves which kept their green,   *sign of rebirth*
The noble letters of the dead:

XCV 8 *fluttering urn:* bubbling tea-urn.
10 *filmy shapes:* night moths.

And strangely on the silence broke
  The silent-speaking words, and strange
  Was love's dumb cry defying change
To test his worth; and strangely spoke

The faith, the vigour, bold to dwell
  On doubts that drive the coward back,   30
  And keen thro' wordy snares to track
Suggestions to her inmost cell.

So word by word, and line by line,
  The dead man touch'd me from the past,
  And all at once it seem'd at last
The living soul was flash'd on mine,

And mine in this was wound, and whirl'd
  About empyreal heights of thought,
  And came on that which is, and caught
The deep pulsations of the world,   40

Æonian music measuring out
  The steps of Time—the shocks of Chance—
  The blows of Death. At length my trance
Was cancell'd, stricken thro' with doubt.

Vague words! but ah, how hard to frame
  In matter-moulded forms of speech,
  Or even for intellect to reach
Thro' memory that which I became:

Till now the doubtful dusk reveal'd
  The knolls once more where, couch'd at ease,   50
  The white kine glimmer'd, and the trees
Laid their dark arms about the field:

And suck'd from out the distant gloom
  A breeze began to tremble o'er
  The large leaves of the sycamore,
And fluctuate all the still perfume,

---

38 *empyreal:* celestial.
41 *Æonian:* ages-long.

And gathering freshlier overhead,
 Rock'd the full-foliaged elms, and swung
 The heavy-folded rose, and flung
The lilies to and fro, and said,   60

"The dawn, the dawn," and died away;
 And East and West, without a breath,
 Mixt their dim lights, like life and death,
To broaden into boundless day.

XCVI

You say, but with no touch of scorn,
 Sweet-hearted, you, whose light-blue eyes
 Are tender over drowning flies,
You tell me, doubt is Devil-born.

I know not: one indeed I knew
 In many a subtle question versed,
 Who touch'd a jarring lyre at first,
But ever strove to make it true:

Perplext in faith, but pure in deeds,
 At last he beat his music out.   10
 There lives more faith in honest doubt,
Believe me, than in half the creeds.

He fought his doubts and gather'd strength,
 He would not make his judgment blind,
 He faced the spectres of the mind
And laid them: thus he came at length

To find a stronger faith his own;
 And Power was with him in the night,
 Which makes the darkness and the light,
And dwells not in the light alone,   20

But in the darkness and the cloud,
 As over Sinaï's peaks of old,

XCVI 1 *You:* a woman of uncomplicated faith.
5 *one:* probably Hallam, although part of this section sounds as if Tennyson were describing himself.

While Israel made their gods of gold,
Altho' the trumpet blew so loud.

XCVII

My love has talk'd with rocks and trees;
   He finds on misty mountain-ground
   His own vast shadow glory-crown'd;
He sees himself in all he sees.

Two partners of a married life—
   I look'd on these and thought of thee
   In vastness and in mystery,
And of my spirit as of a wife.

These two—they dwelt with eye on eye,
   Their hearts of old have beat in tune,   10
   Their meetings made December June,
Their every parting was to die.

Their love has never past away;
   The days she never can forget
   Are earnest that he loves her yet,
Whate'er the faithless people say.

Her life is lone, he sits apart;
   He loves her yet, she will not weep,
   Tho' rapt in matters dark and deep
He seems to slight her simple heart.   20

He thrids the labyrinth of the mind,
   He reads the secret of the star,
   He seems so near and yet so far,
He looks so cold: she thinks him kind.

She keeps the gift of years before,
   A wither'd violet is her bliss:

---

23 *gods of gold:* The Israelites were worshipping the golden calf while God
spoke to Moses amid darkness and cloud on Mt. Sinai (see *Exodus* 19: 16-25
and 32: 1-6).
XCVII 15 *earnest:* pledge.

She knows not what his greatness is,
For that, for all, she loves him more.

For him she plays, to him she sings
    Of early faith and plighted vows;   30
    She knows but matters of the house,
And he, he knows a thousand things.

Her faith is fixt and cannot move,
    She darkly feels him great and wise,
    She dwells on him with faithful eyes,
"I cannot understand: I love."

XCVIII

You leave us: you will see the Rhine,
    And those fair hills I sail'd below,
    When I was there with him; and go
By summer belts of wheat and vine

To where he breathed his latest breath,
    That City. All her splendour seems
    No livelier than the wisp that gleams
On Lethe in the eyes of Death.

Let her great Danube rolling fair
    Enwind her isles, unmark'd of me: 10
    I have not seen, I will not see
Vienna; rather dream that there,

A treble darkness, Evil haunts
    The birth, the bridal; friend from friend
    Is oftener parted, fathers bend
Above more graves, a thousand wants

Gnarr at the heels of men, and prey
    By each cold hearth, and sadness flings
    Her shadow on the blaze of kings:
And yet myself have heard him say,   20

XCVIII The section is addressed to the poet's brother Charles, who was going to Vienna on his wedding trip.
17 *Gnarr:* snarl.

That not in any mother town
  With statelier progress to and fro
  The double tides of chariots flow
By park and suburb under brown

Of lustier leaves; nor more content,
  He told me, lives in any crowd,
  When all is gay with lamps, and loud
With sport and song, in booth and tent,

Imperial halls, or open plain;
  And wheels the circled dance, and breaks   30
  The rocket molten into flakes
Of crimson or in emerald rain.

XCIX

Risest thou thus, dim dawn, again, *pered of 92*
  So loud with voices of the birds,
  So thick with lowings of the herds,
Day, when I lost the flower of men;

Who tremblest thro' thy darkling red
  On yon swollen brook that bubbles fast
  By meadows breathing of the past,
And woodlands holy to the dead;

Who murmurest in the foliaged eaves
  A song that slights the coming care,   10
  And Autumn laying here and there
A fiery finger on the leaves;

Who wakenest with thy balmy breath
  To myriads on the genial earth,
  Memories of bridal, or of birth,
And unto myriads more, of death.

Oh, wheresoever those may be,
  Betwixt the slumber of the poles,

---

21 *mother town:* metropolis.
XCIX 1 *dim dawn:* second anniversary of Hallam's death.

To-day they count as kindred souls;
They know me not, but mourn with me.   20

C

I climb the hill: from end to end
    Of all the landscape underneath,
    I find no place that does not breathe
Some gracious memory of my friend;

No gray old grange, or lonely fold,
    Or low morass and whispering reed,
    Or simple stile from mead to mead,
Or sheepwalk up the windy wold;

Nor hoary knoll of ash and haw
    That hears the latest linnet trill,   10
    Nor quarry trench'd along the hill
And haunted by the wrangling daw;

Nor runlet tinkling from the rock;
    Nor pastoral rivulet that swerves
    To left and right thro' meadowy curves,
That feed the mothers of the flock;

But each has pleased a kindred eye,
    And each reflects a kindlier day;
    And, leaving these, to pass away,
I think once more he seems to die.   20

CI

101 – 102
leaving of home.

Unwatch'd, the garden bough shall sway,
    The tender blossom flutter down,
    Unloved, that beech will gather brown,
This maple burn itself away;

Unloved, the sun-flower, shining fair,
    Ray round with flames her disk of seed,
    And many a rose-carnation feed
With summer spice the humming air;

C In this and two following sections, Tennyson considers leaving his childhood home at Somersby in order to move near London.

Unloved, by many a sandy bar,
   The brook shall babble down the plain,   10
   At noon or when the Lesser Wain
Is twisting round the polar star;

Uncared for, gird the windy grove,
   And flood the haunts of hern and crake;
   Or into silver arrows break
The sailing moon in creek and cove;

Till from the garden and the wild
   A fresh association blow,
   And year by year the landscape grow
Familiar to the stranger's child;   20

As year by year the labourer tills
   His wonted glebe, or lops the glades;
   And year by year our memory fades
From all the circle of the hills.

CII

We leave the well-beloved place
   Where first we gazed upon the sky;
   The roofs that heard our earliest cry
Will shelter one of stranger race.

We go, but ere we go from home,
   As down the garden-walks I move,
   Two spirits of a diverse love
Contend for loving masterdom.

One whispers, "Here thy boyhood sung
   Long since its matin song, and heard   10
   The low love-language of the bird
In native hazels tassel-hung."

The other answers, "Yea, but here
   Thy feet have stray'd in after hours

CI 11 *Lesser Wain:* Ursa Minor, the Little Dipper.
14 *hern and crake:* heron and corn crake.
18 *blow:* blossom.
22 *glebe:* farmland attached to a rectory.

With thy lost friend among the bowers,
And this hath made them trebly dear."

These two have striven half the day,
    And each prefers his separate claim,
    Poor rivals in a losing game,
That will not yield each other way.   20

I turn to go: my feet are set
    To leave the pleasant fields and farms;
    They mix in one another's arms
To one pure image of regret.

CIII

On that last night before we went
    From out the doors where I was bred,
    I dream'd a vision of the dead,
Which left my after-morn content.

contact with H.

Methought I dwelt within a hall,
    And maidens with me: distant hills
    From hidden summits fed with rills
A river sliding by the wall.

The hall with harp and carol rang.
    They sang of what is wise and good   10
    And graceful. In the centre stood
A statue veil'd, to which they sang;

H. as symbol of greater race to come.

And which, tho' veil'd, was known to me,
    The shape of him I loved, and love
    For ever: then flew in a dove
And brought a summons from the sea:

And when they learnt that I must go,
    They wept and wail'd, but led the way
    To where a little shallop lay
At anchor in the flood below;   20

CIII 6 *maidens:* the muses.

And on by many a level mead,
   And shadowing bluff that made the banks,
   We glided winding under ranks
Of iris and the golden reed;

And still as vaster grew the shore
   And roll'd the floods in grander space,
   The maidens gather'd strength and grace
And presence, lordlier than before;

And I myself, who sat apart
   And watch'd them, wax'd in every limb;   30
   I felt the thews of Anakim,
The pulses of a Titan's heart;

As one would sing the death of war,
   And one would chant the history
   Of that great race which is to be,
And one that shaping of a star;

Until the forward-creeping tides
   Began to foam, and we to draw
   From deep to deep, to where we saw
A great ship lift her shining sides.   40

The man we loved was there on deck,
   But thrice as large as man he bent
   To greet us. Up the side I went,
And fell in silence on his neck:

Whereat those maidens with one mind
   Bewail'd their lot; I did them wrong:
   "We served thee here," they said, "so long,
And wilt thou leave us now behind?"

So rapt I was, they could not win
   An answer from my lips, but he   50
   Replying, "Enter likewise ye
And go with us:" they enter'd in.

---

31 *Anakim:* plural of Anak, descended from giants.

And while the wind began to sweep
    A music out of sheet and shroud,
    We steer'd her toward a crimson cloud
That landlike slept along the deep.

CIV

The time draws near the birth of **Christ**;
    The moon is hid, the night is still;
    A single church below the hill
Is pealing, folded in the mist.

A single peal of bells below,
    That wakens at this hour of rest
    A single murmur in the breast,
That these are not the bells I know.

Like strangers' voices here they sound,
    In lands where not a memory strays,   10
    Nor landmark breathes of other days,
But all is new unhallow'd ground.

CV

To-night ungather'd let us leave
    This laurel, let this holly stand:
    We live within the stranger's land,
And strangely falls our Christmas-eve.

Our father's dust is left alone
    And silent under other snows:
    There in due time the woodbine blows,
The violet comes, but we are gone.

No more shall wayward grief abuse
    The genial hour with mask and mime;   10
    For change of place, like growth of time,
Has broke the bond of dying use.

Let cares that petty shadows cast,
    By which our lives are chiefly proved,

CIV 9 *here:* Tennyson's new home in Epping Forest, near London.
CV 5 *Our father's dust:* Tennyson's father was buried at Somersby.

A little spare the night I loved,
And hold it solemn to the past.

But let no footstep beat the floor,
    Nor bowl of wassail mantle warm;
    For who would keep an ancient form
Thro' which the spirit breathes no more?   20

Be neither song, nor game, nor feast;
    Nor harp be touch'd, nor flute be blown;
    No dance, no motion, save alone
What lightens in the lucid east

Of rising worlds by yonder wood.
    Long sleeps the summer in the seed;
    Run out your measured arcs, and lead
The closing cycle rich in good.

CVI

Ring out, wild bells, to the wild sky,
    The flying cloud, the frosty light:
    The year is dying in the night;
Ring out, wild bells, and let him die.

Ring out the old, ring in the new,
    Ring, happy bells, across the snow:
    The year is going, let him go;
Ring out the false, ring in the true.

Ring out the grief that saps the mind,
    For those that here we see no more;   10
    Ring out the feud of rich and poor,
Ring in redress to all mankind.

Ring out a slowly dying cause,
    And ancient forms of party strife;
    Ring in the nobler modes of life,
With sweeter manners, purer laws.

---

18 *mantle:* foam.

Ring out the want, the care, the sin,
  The faithless coldness of the times;
  Ring out, ring out my mournful rhymes,
But ring the fuller minstrel in.   20

Ring out false pride in place and blood,
  The civic slander and the spite;
  Ring in the love of truth and right,
Ring in the common love of good.

Ring out old shapes of foul disease;
  Ring out the narrowing lust of gold;
  Ring out the thousand wars of old,
Ring in the thousand years of peace.

Ring in the valiant man and free,
  The larger heart, the kindlier hand;   30
  Ring out the darkness of the land,
Ring in the Christ that is to be.

CVII

It is the day when he was born,
  A bitter day that early sank
  Behind a purple-frosty bank
Of vapour, leaving night forlorn.

The time admits not flowers or leaves
  To deck the banquet. Fiercely flies
  The blast of North and East, and ice
Makes daggers at the sharpen'd eaves,

And bristles all the brakes and thorns
  To yon hard crescent, as she hangs   10
  Above the wood which grides and clangs
Its leafless ribs and iron horns

Together, in the drifts that pass
  To darken on the rolling brine

CVII 10 *crescent:* moon.
11 *grides:* clashes.

Horatian ode from Alcaeus, greek

That breaks the coast. But fetch the wine,
　Arrange the board and brim the glass;

sense of larger purpose

Bring in great logs and let them lie,
　To make a solid core of heat;
　Be cheerful-minded, talk and treat
Of all things even as he were by;　　　　20

We keep the day. With festal cheer,
　With books and music, surely we
　Will drink to him, whate'er he be,
And sing the songs he loved to hear.

CVIII

I will not shut me from my kind,
　And, lest I stiffen into stone,
　I will not eat my heart alone,
Nor feed with sighs a passing wind:

What profit lies in barren faith,
　And vacant yearning, tho' with might
　To scale the heaven's highest height,
Or dive below the wells of Death?

What find I in the highest place,
　But mine own phantom chanting hymns?　　10
　And on the depths of death there swims
The reflex of a human face.

gain from experiencing sorrow

I'll rather take what fruit may be
　Of sorrow under human skies:
　'T is held that sorrow makes us wise,
Whatever wisdom sleep with thee.

CIX

Contemplated character of H.

Heart-affluence in discursive talk
　From household fountains never dry;

CVIII 12 *reflex:* reflection.
16 *Whatever wisdom . . . thee:* Hallam's wisdom, distinct from that of the
poet.

The critic clearness of an eye,
That saw thro' all the Muses' walk;

Seraphic intellect and force
    To seize and throw the doubts of man;
    Impassion'd logic, which outran
The hearer in its fiery course;

High nature amorous of the good,
    But touch'd with no ascetic gloom;   10
    And passion pure in snowy bloom
Thro' all the years of April blood;

A love of freedom rarely felt,
    Of freedom in her regal seat
    Of England; not the schoolboy heat,
The blind hysterics of the Celt;

And manhood fused with female grace
    In such a sort, the child would twine
    A trustful hand, unask'd, in thine,
And finds his comfort in thy face;   20

All these have been, and thee mine eyes
    Have look'd on: if they look'd in vain,
    My shame is greater who remain,
Nor let thy wisdom make me wise.

CX

Thy converse drew us with delight,
    The men of rathe and riper years:
    The feeble soul, a haunt of fears,
Forgot his weakness in thy sight.

On thee the loyal-hearted hung,
    The proud was half disarm'd of pride,
    Nor cared the serpent at thy side
To flicker with his double tongue.

CIX 4 *Muses' walk:* the realm of the muses.
CX 2 *rathe:* young, precocious.

The stern were mild when thou wert by,
   The flippant put himself to school   10
   And heard thee, and the brazen fool
And soften'd, and he knew not why;

While I, thy nearest, sat apart,
   And felt thy triumph was as mine;
   And loved them more, that they were thine,
The graceful tact, the Christian art;

Nor mine the sweetness or the skill,
   But mine the love that will not tire,
   And, born of love, the vague desire
That spurs an imitative will.   20

CXI

The churl in spirit, up or down
   Along the scale of ranks, thro' all,
   To him who grasps a golden ball,
By blood a king, at heart a clown;

The churl in spirit, howe'er he veil
   His want in forms for fashion's sake,
   Will let his coltish nature break
At seasons thro' the gilded pale:

For who can always act? but he,
   To whom a thousand memories call.   10
   Not being less but more than all
The gentleness he seem'd to be,

Best seem'd the thing he was, and join'd
   Each office of the social hour
   To noble manners, as the flower
And native growth of noble mind;

Nor ever narrowness or spite,
   Or villain fancy fleeting by,

CXI 3 *golden ball:* symbolic of sovereignty.
8 *gilded pale:* façade of artificial manners.

Drew in the expression of an eye,
Where God and Nature met in light; 20

And thus he bore without abuse
The grand old name of gentleman,
Defamed by every charlatan,
And soil'd with all ignoble use.

CXII

High wisdom holds my wisdom less,
That I, who gaze with temperate eyes
On glorious insufficiencies,
Set light by narrower perfectness.

But thou, that fillest all the room
Of all my love, art reason why
I seem to cast a careless eye
On souls, the lesser lords of doom.

For what wert thou? some novel power
Sprang up for ever at a touch, 10
And hope could never hope too much,
In watching thee from hour to hour,

Large elements in order brought,
And tracts of calm from tempest made,
And world-wide fluctuation sway'd
In vassal tides that follow'd thought.

CXIII

'T is held that sorrow makes us wise;
Yet how much wisdom sleeps with thee
Which not alone had guided me,
But served the seasons that may rise;

For can I doubt, who knew thee keen
In intellect, with force and skill
To strive, to fashion, to fulfil—
I doubt not what thou wouldst have been:

CXII 2-4 *gaze . . . narrower perfectness:* i.e., look without enthusiasm on
either noble imperfections or narrow perfection.

A life in civic action warm,
   A soul on highest mission sent,   10
   A potent voice of Parliament,
A pillar steadfast in the storm,

Should licensed boldness gather force,
   Becoming, when the time has birth,
   A lever to uplift the earth
And roll it in another course,

With thousand shocks that come and go,
   With agonies, with energies,
   With overthrowings, and with cries,
And undulations to and fro.   20

CXIV

Who loves not Knowledge? Who shall rail
   Against her beauty? May she mix
   With men and prosper! Who shall fix
Her pillars? Let her work prevail.

But on her forehead sits a fire:
   She sets her forward countenance
   And leaps into the future chance,
Submitting all things to desire.

Half-grown as yet, a child, and vain—
   She cannot fight the fear of death.   10
   What is she, cut from love and faith,
But some wild Pallas from the brain

Of Demons? fiery-hot to burst
   All barriers in her onward race
   For power. Let her know her place;
She is the second, not the first.

A higher hand must make her mild,
   If all be not in vain; and guide

CXIV 4 *pillars:* limits, as the Pillars of Hercules (Gibraltar) were the limit
of the known world of the ancients.
12 *Pallas:* Pallas Athena, goddess of wisdom, was born from the brain of
Zeus.

Her footsteps, moving side by side
With Wisdom, like the younger child: 20

For she is earthly of the mind,
　　But Wisdom heavenly of the soul.
　　O friend, who camest to thy goal
So early, leaving me behind,

I would the great world grew like thee,
　　Who grewest not alone in power
　　And knowledge, but by year and hour
In reverence and in charity.

CXV

Now fades the last long streak of snow,
　　Now burgeons every maze of quick
　　About the flowering squares, and thick
By ashen roots the violets blow.

Now rings the woodland loud and long,
　　The distance takes a lovelier hue,
　　And drown'd in yonder living blue
The lark becomes a sightless song.

Now dance the lights on lawn and lea,
　　The flocks are whiter down the vale,   10
　　And milkier every milky sail
On winding stream or distant sea;

Where now the seamew pipes, or dives
　　In yonder greening gleam, and fly
　　The happy birds, that change their sky
To build and brood; that live their lives

From land to land; and in my breast
　　Spring wakens too; and my regret
　　Becomes an April violet,
And buds and blossoms like the rest.   20

CXV 2 *maze of quick:* hedge enclosing a garden or field.

CXVI

Is it, then, regret for buried time
    That keenlier in sweet April wakes,
    And meets the year, and gives and takes
The colours of the crescent prime?

Not all: the songs, the stirring air,
    The life re-orient out of dust,
    Cry thro' the sense to hearten trust
In that which made the world so fair.

Not all regret: the face will shine
    Upon me, while I muse alone;
    And that dear voice, I once have known,
Still speak to me of me and mine:

Yet less of sorrow lives in me
    For days of happy commune dead;
    Less yearning for the friendship fled,
Than some strong bond which is to be.

CXVII

O days and hours, your work is this
    To hold me from my proper place,
    A little while from his embrace,
For fuller gain of after bliss:

That out of distance might ensue
    Desire of nearness doubly sweet;
    And unto meeting when we meet,
Delight a hundredfold accrue,

For every grain of sand that runs,
    And every span of shade that steals,
    And every kiss of toothed wheels,
And all the courses of the suns.

CXVIII

Contemplate all this work of Time,
    The giant labouring in his youth;

CXVII 11 *toothed wheels:* cogs in a clock.

Nor dream of human love and truth,
As dying Nature's earth and lime;

But trust that those we call the dead
    Are breathers of an ampler day
    For ever nobler ends. They say,
The solid earth whereon we tread

In tracts of fluent heat began,
    And grew to seeming-random forms,   10
    The seeming prey of cyclic storms,
Till at the last arose the man;

Who throve and branch'd from clime to clime,
    The herald of a higher race,
    And of himself in higher place,
If so he type this work of time

Within himself, from more to more;
    Or, crown'd with attributes of woe
    Like glories, move his course, and show
That life is not as idle ore,   20

But iron dug from central gloom,
    And heated hot with burning fears,
    And dipt in baths of hissing tears,
And batter'd with the shocks of doom

To shape and use. Arise and fly
    The reeling Faun, the sensual feast;
    Move upward, working out the beast,
And let the ape and tiger die.

CXIX

Doors, where my heart was used to beat
    So quickly, not as one that weeps
    I come once more; the city sleeps;
I smell the meadow in the street;

CXVIII 16-17 *If so he type . . . Within himself:* i.e., if man himself is typical
of the work of time (evolution).

I hear a chirp of birds; I see
     Betwixt the black fronts long-withdrawn
     A light-blue lane of early dawn,
And think of early days and thee,

And bless thee, for thy lips are bland,
     And bright the friendship of thine eye;   10
     And in my thoughts with scarce a sigh
I take the pressure of thine hand.

CXX

I trust I have not wasted breath:
     I think we are not wholly brain,
     Magnetic mockeries; not in vain,
Like Paul with beasts, I fought with Death;

Not only cunning casts in clay:
     Let Science prove we are, and then
     What matters Science unto men,
At least to me? I would not stay.

Let him, the wiser man who springs
     Hereafter, up from childhood shape   10
     His action like the greater ape,
But I was *born* to other things.

CXXI

Sad Hesper o'er the buried sun
     And ready, thou, to die with him,
     Thou watchest all things ever dim
And dimmer, and a glory done:

The team is loosen'd from the wain,
     The boat is drawn upon the shore;
     Thou listenest to the closing door,
And life is darken'd in the brain.

CXX 3 *Magnetic mockeries:* i.e., mere puppets responding to stimuli.
4 *Paul . . . Death:* See *I Corinthians* 15: 32, where St. Paul speaks of the
battle against disbelief in immortality as one fought with beasts.
CXXI 1 *Hesper:* The evening star (Hesper) and the morning star (Phosphor)
are both the same planet, Venus, symbol of love.

Bright Phosphor, fresher for the night,
   By thee the world's great work is heard   10
   Beginning, and the wakeful bird;
Behind thee comes the greater light:

The market boat is on the stream,
   And voices hail it from the brink;
   Thou hear'st the village hammer clink,
And see'st the moving of the team.

Sweet Hesper-Phosphor, double name
   For what is one, the first, the last,
   Thou, like my present and my past,
Thy place is changed; thou art the same.   20

CXXII

Oh, wast thou with me, dearest, then,
   While I rose up against my doom,
   And yearn'd to burst the folded gloom,
To bare the eternal Heavens again,

To feel once more, in placid awe,
   The strong imagination roll
   A sphere of stars about my soul,
In all her motion one with law;

If thou wert with me, and the grave
   Divide us not, be with me now,   10
   And enter in at breast and brow,
Till all my blood, a fuller wave,

Be quicken'd with a livelier breath,
   And like an inconsiderate boy,
   As in the former flash of joy,
I slip the thoughts of life and death;

And all the breeze of Fancy blows,
   And every dew-drop paints a bow,
   The wizard lightnings deeply glow,
And every thought breaks out a rose.   20

CXXII 16 *slip:* escape.

CXXIII

There rolls the deep where grew the tree.
   O earth, what changes hast thou seen!
   There where the long street roars, hath been
The stillness of the central sea.

The hills are shadows, and they flow
   From form to form, and nothing stands;
   They melt like mist, the solid lands,
Like clouds they shape themselves and go.

But in my spirit will I dwell,
   And dream my dream, and hold it true;   10
   For tho' my lips may breathe adieu,
I cannot think the thing farewell.

CXXIV

That which we dare invoke to bless;
   Our dearest faith; our ghastliest doubt;
   He, They, One, All; within, without;
The Power in darkness whom we guess;

I found Him not in world or sun,
   Or eagle's wing, or insect's eye;
   Nor thro' the questions men may try,
The petty cobwebs we have spun:

If e'er when faith had fallen asleep,
   I heard a voice, "believe no more,"   10
   And heard an ever-breaking shore
That tumbled in the Godless deep;

A warmth within the breast would melt
   The freezing reason's colder part,
   And like a man in wrath the heart
Stood up and answer'd, "I have felt."

No, like a child in doubt and fear:
   But that blind clamour made me wise;
   Then was I as a child that cries,
But, crying, knows his father near;   20

And what I am beheld again
  What is, and no man understands;
  And out of darkness came the hands
That reach thro' nature, moulding men.

CXXV

Whatever I have said or sung,
  Some bitter notes my harp would give,
  Yea, tho' there often seem'd to live
A contradiction on the tongue,

Yet Hope had never lost her youth;
  She did but look through dimmer eyes;
  Or Love but play'd with gracious lies,
Because he felt so fix'd in truth:

And if the song were full of care,
  He breathed the spirit of the song;
  And if the words were sweet and strong
He set his royal signet there;

Abiding with me till I sail
  To seek thee on the mystic deeps,
  And this electric force, that keeps
A thousand pulses dancing, fail.

CXXVI

Love is and was my Lord and King,
  And in his presence I attend
  To hear the tidings of my friend,
Which every hour his couriers bring.

Love is and was my King and Lord,
  And will be, tho' as yet I keep
  Within his court on earth, and sleep
Encompass'd by his faithful guard,

And hear at times a sentinel
  Who moves about from place to place,

CXXV 15 *electric force:* animal vitality, thought of as magnetic.

And whispers to the worlds of space,
In the deep night, that all is well.

CXXVII

And all is well, tho' faith and form
    Be sunder'd in the night of fear;
    Well roars the storm to those that hear
A deeper voice across the storm,

Proclaiming social truth shall spread,
    And justice, even tho' thrice again
    The red fool-fury of the Seine
Should pile her barricades with dead.

But ill for him that wears a crown,
    And him, the lazar, in his rags: 10
    They tremble, the sustaining crags;
The spires of ice are toppled down,

And molten up, and roar in flood;
    The fortress crashes from on high,
    The brute earth lightens to the sky,
And the great Æon sinks in blood,

And compass'd by the fires of Hell;
    While thou, dear spirit, happy star,
    O'erlook'st the tumult from afar,
And smilest, knowing all is well.   20

CXXVIII

The love that rose on stronger wings,
    Unpalsied when he met with Death,
    Is comrade of the lesser faith
That sees the course of human things.

No doubt vast eddies in the flood
    Of onward time shall yet be made,

CXXVII 7 *red fool-fury of the Seine:* referring to revolution in France, although it is not clear which one is meant.
9-10 *him that wears . . . the lazar:* i.e., both king and beggar will be swept away.
16 *great Æon:* presumably the present age.

And throned races may degrade;
Yet, O ye mysteries of good,

Wild Hours that fly with Hope and Fear,
   If all your office had to do   10
   With old results that look like new;
If this were all your mission here,

To draw, to sheathe a useless sword,
   To fool the crowd with glorious lies,
   To cleave a creed in sects and cries,
To change the bearing of a word,

To shift an arbitrary power,
   To cramp the student at his desk,
   To make old bareness picturesque
And tuft with grass a feudal tower;   20

Why, then my scorn might well descend
   On you and yours. I see in part
   That all, as in some piece of art,
Is toil coöperant to an end.

CXXIX

Dear friend, far off, my lost desire,
   So far, so near in woe and weal;
   O loved the most, when most I feel
There is a lower and a higher;

Known and unknown; human, divine;
   Sweet human hand and lips and eye;
   Dear heavenly friend that canst not die,
Mine, mine, for ever, ever mine;

Strange friend, past, present, and to be;
   Loved deeplier, darklier understood;   10
   Behold, I dream a dream of good,
And mingle all the world with thee.

CXXX

Thy voice is on the rolling air;
   I hear thee where the waters run;

Thou standest in the rising sun,
And in the setting thou art fair.

What art thou then? I cannot guess;
But tho' I seem in star and flower
To feel thee some diffusive power,
I do not therefore love thee less:

My love involves the love before;
My love is vaster passion now;   10
Tho' mix'd with God and Nature thou,
I seem to love thee more and more.

Far off thou art, but ever nigh;
I have thee still, and I rejoice;
I prosper, circled with thy voice;
I shall not lose thee tho' I die.

CXXXI

O living will that shalt endure
When all that seems shall suffer shock,
Rise in the spiritual rock,
Flow thro' our deeds and make them pure,

That we may lift from out of dust
A voice as unto him that hears,
A cry above the conquer'd years
To one that with us works, and trust,

With faith that comes of self-control,
The truths that never can be proved   10
Until we close with all we loved,
And all we flow from, soul in soul.

———— —

O true and tried, so well and long,
Demand not thou a marriage lay;

CXXXI 3 *spiritual rock:* Christ.
1 *true and tried:* Edmund Lushington. The epilogue celebrates the marriage
of Lushington to Tennyson's sister Cecilia on 10 October 1842. Tennyson
wrote that his poem "begins with a funeral and ends with a marriage."

In that it is thy marriage day
Is music more than any song.

Nor have I felt so much of bliss
   Since first he told me that he loved
   A daughter of our house; nor proved
Since that dark day a day like this;

Tho' I since then have number'd o'er
   Some thrice three years: they went and came,   10
   Remade the blood and changed the frame,
And yet is love not less, but more;

No longer caring to embalm
   In dying songs a dead regret,
   But like a statue solid-set,
And moulded in colossal calm.

Regret is dead, but love is more
   Than in the summers that are flown,
   For I myself with these have grown
To something greater than before;   20

Which makes appear the songs I made
   As echoes out of weaker times,
   As half but idle brawling rhymes,
The sport of random sun and shade.

But where is she, the bridal flower,
   That must be made a wife ere noon?
   She enters, glowing like the moon
Of Eden on its bridal bower:

On me she bends her blissful eyes
   And then on thee; they meet thy look   30
   And brighten like the star that shook
Betwixt the palms of Paradise.

Oh, when her life was yet in bud,
   He too foretold the perfect rose.
   For thee she grew, for thee she grows
For ever, and as fair as good.

And thou art worthy; full of power;
    As gentle; liberal-minded, great,
    Consistent; wearing all that weight
Of learning lightly like a flower.   40

But now set out: the noon is near,
    And I must give away the bride;
    She fears not, or with thee beside
And me behind her, will not fear.

For I that danced her on my knee,
    That watch'd her on her nurse's arm,
    That shielded all her life from harm,
At last must part with her to thee;

Now waiting to be made a wife,
    Her feet, my darling, on the dead;   50
    Their pensive tablets round her head,
And the most living words of life

Breathed in her ear. The ring is on,
    The "wilt thou" answer'd, and again
    The "wilt thou" ask'd, till out of twain
Her sweet "I will" has made you one.

Now sign your names, which shall be read,
    Mute symbols of a joyful morn,
    By village eyes as yet unborn;
The names are sign'd, and overhead   60

Begins the clash and clang that tells
    The joy to every wandering breeze;
    The blind wall rocks, and on the trees
The dead leaf trembles to the bells.

O happy hour, and happier hours
    Await them. Many a merry face
    Salutes them—maidens of the place,
That pelt us in the porch with flowers.

---

50 *the dead:* reference to the graves beneath the church and the memorials
on the walls.

O happy hour, behold the bride
   With him to whom her hand I gave.   70
   They leave the porch, they pass the grave
That has to-day its sunny side.

To-day the grave is bright for me,
   For them the light of life increased,
   Who stay to share the morning feast,
Who rest to-night beside the sea.

Let all my genial spirits advance
   To meet and greet a whiter sun;
   My drooping memory will not shun
The foaming grape of eastern France.   80

It circles round, and fancy plays,
   And hearts are warm'd and faces bloom,
   As drinking health to bride and groom
We wish them store of happy days.

Nor count me all to blame if I
   Conjecture of a stiller guest,
   Perchance, perchance, among the rest,
And, tho' in silence, wishing joy.

But they must go, the time draws on,
   And those white-favour'd horses wait;   90
   They rise, but linger; it is late;
Farewell, we kiss, and they are gone.

A shade falls on us like the dark
   From little cloudlets on the grass,
   But sweeps away as out we pass
To range the woods, to roam the park,

Discussing how their courtship grew,
   And talk of others that are wed,
   And how she look'd, and what he said,
And back we come at fall of dew.   100

---

80 *foaming grape of eastern France:* champagne.

Again the feast, the speech, the glee,
　　The shade of passing thought, the wealth
　　Of words and wit, the double health,
The crowning cup, the three-times-three,

And last the dance;—till I retire:
　　Dumb is that tower which spake so loud,
　　And high in heaven the streaming cloud,
And on the downs a rising fire:

And rise, O moon, from yonder down,
　　Till over down and over dale　　　　　　110
　　All night the shining vapour sail
And pass the silent-lighted town,

The white-faced halls, the glancing rills,
　　And catch at every mountain head,
　　And o'er the friths that branch and spread
Their sleeping silver thro' the hills;

And touch with shade the bridal doors,
　　With tender gloom the roof, the wall;
　　And breaking let the splendour fall
To spangle all the happy shores　　　　　　120

By which they rest, and ocean sounds,
　　And, star and system rolling past,
　　A soul shall draw from out the vast
And strike his being into bounds,

And, moved thro' life of lower phase,
　　Result in man, be born and think,
　　And act and love, a closer link
Betwixt us and the crowning race

Of those that, eye to eye, shall look
　　On knowledge; under whose command　　　130
　　Is Earth and Earth's, and in their hand
　　Is Nature like an open book;

---

[115] *friths:* inlets of the sea.
[123] *soul:* i.e., the married couple will conceive a child, whose soul will be encased in a body.

*part of process
we leading to more
perfect man.*

\ No longer half-akin to brute,
    For all we thought and loved and did,
    And hoped, and suffer'd, is but seed
Of what in them is flower and fruit;

Whereof the man, that with me trod
    This planet, was a noble type
    Appearing ere the times were ripe,
That friend of mine who lives in God,   140

That God, which ever lives and loves,
    One God, one law, one element,
    And one far-off divine event,
To which the whole creation moves.

         [1850]

MAUD

A Monodrama

PART I

I

I

I hate the dreadful hollow behind the little wood;
Its lips in the field above are dabbled with blood-red
    heath,
The red-ribb'd ledges drip with a silent horror of blood,
And Echo there, whatever is ask'd her, answers "Death."

II

For there in the ghastly pit long since a body was found,
His who had given me life—O father! O God! was it
    well?—
Mangled, and flatten'd, and crush'd, and dinted into the
    ground;
There yet lies the rock that fell with him when he fell.

III

Did he fling himself down? who knows? for a vast specu-
    lation had fail'd,
And ever he mutter'd and madden'd, and ever wann'd
    with despair,   10
And out he walk'd when the wind like a broken world-
    ling wail'd,
And the flying gold of the ruin'd woodlands drove thro'
    the air.

IV

I remember the time, for the roots of my hair were stirr'd
By a shuffled step, by a dead weight trail'd, by a
    whisper'd fright,
And my pulses closed their gates with a shock on my
    heart as I heard
The shrill-edged shriek of a mother divide the shudder-
    ing night.

V

Villainy somewhere! whose? One says, we are villains all.
Not he: his honest fame should at least by me be main-
    tained:
But that old man, now lord of the broad estate and the
    Hall,
Dropt off gorged from a scheme that had left us flaccid
    and drain'd.   20

VI

Why do they prate of the blessings of Peace? we have
    made them a curse,
Pickpockets, each hand lusting for all that is not its own;
And lust of gain, in the spirit of Cain, is it better or worse
Than the heart of the citizen hissing in war on his own
    hearthstone?

VII

But these are the days of advance, the works of the men
    of mind,

When who but a fool would have faith in a tradesman's
    ware or his word?
Is it peace or war? Civil war, as I think, and that of a kind
The viler, as underhand, not openly bearing the sword.

VIII

Sooner or later I too may passively take the print
Of the golden age—why not? I have neither hope nor
    trust;   30
May make my heart as a millstone, set my face as a flint,
Cheat and be cheated, and die—who knows? we are
    ashes and dust.

IX

Peace sitting under her olive, and slurring the days gone
    by,
When the poor are hovell'd and hustled together, each
    sex, like swine,
When only the ledger lives, and when only not all men
    lie;
Peace in her vineyard—yes!—but a company forges the
    wine.

X

And the vitriol madness flushes up in the ruffian's head,
Till the filthy by-lane rings to the yell of the trampled
    wife,
And chalk and alum and plaster are sold to the poor for
    bread,
And the spirit of murder works in the very means of life,   40

XI

And Sleep must lie down arm'd, for the villainous centre-
    bits
Grind on the wakeful ear in the hush of the moonless
    nights,
While another is cheating the sick of a few last gasps, as
    he sits
To pestle a poison'd poison behind his crimson lights.

---

41 *centre-bits:* burglars' tools.

XII

When a Mammonite mother kills her babe for a burial
    fee,
And Timour-Mammon grins on a pile of children's bones,
Is it peace or war? better, war! loud war by land and by
    sea,
War with a thousand battles, and shaking a hundred
    thrones.

XIII

For I trust if an enemy's fleet came yonder round by the
    hill,
And the rushing battle-bolt sang from the three-decker
    out of the foam,   50
That the smooth-faced, snub-nosed rogue would leap
    from his counter and till,
And strike, if he could, were it but with his cheating
    yardwand, home.—

XIV

What! am I raging alone as my father raged in his mood?
Must *I* too creep to the hollow and dash myself down and
    die
Rather than hold by the law that I made, nevermore to
    brood
On a horror of shatter'd limbs and a wretched swindler's
    lie?

XV

Would there be sorrow for *me?* there was *love* in the
    passionate shriek,
Love for the silent thing that had made false haste to
    the grave—
Wrapt in a cloak, as I saw him, and thought he would
    rise and speak
And rave at the lie and the liar, ah God, as he used to rave.   60

---

46 *Timour:* Tamerlane, Mongolian conqueror of the fourteenth century.
Mammon: god of wealth; his followers are Mammonites.

XVI

I am sick of the Hall and the hill, I am sick of the moor
  and the main.
Why should I stay? can a sweeter chance ever come to
  me here?
Oh, having the nerves of motion as well as the nerves of
  pain,
Were it not wise if I fled from the place and the pit and
  the fear?

not mentally well at beginning

XVII

Workmen up at the Hall!—they are coming back from
  abroad;
The dark old place will be gilt by the touch of a millionaire:
I have heard, I know not whence, of the singular beauty
  of Maud;
I play'd with the girl when a child; she promised then to
  be fair.

man resp. for father's death returns to Hall

XVIII

Maud, with her venturous climbings and tumbles and
  childish escapes,
Maud, the delight of the village, the ringing joy of the Hall,   70
Maud, with her sweet purse-mouth when my father dan-
  gled the grapes,
Maud, the beloved of my mother, the moon-faced darling
  of all,—

XIX

What is she now? My dreams are bad. She may bring me
  a curse.
No, there is fatter game on the moor; she will let me alone.
Thanks, for the fiend best knows whether woman or man
  be the worse.
I will bury myself in myself, and the Devil may pipe to his
  own.

further alternation

II

Long have I sigh'd for a calm: God grant I may find it at
   last!
It will never be broken by Maud; she has neither savour nor
   salt,
But a cold and clear-cut face, as I found when her carriage
   past,
Perfectly beautiful: let it be granted her: where is the fault?   80
All that I saw (for her eyes were downcast, not to be seen)
Faultily faultless, icily regular, splendidly null,
Dead perfection, no more; nothing more, if it had not been
For a chance of travel, a paleness, an hour's defect of the
   rose,
Or an underlip, you may call it a little too ripe, too full,
Or the least little delicate aquiline curve in a sensitive nose,
From which I escaped heart-free, with the least little touch
   of spleen. *escapes her cold beauty without attraction*
did not escape, protested too much

Cold and clear-cut face, why come you so cruelly meek,
Breaking a slumber in which all spleenful folly was
   drown'd?
Pale with the golden beam of an eyelash dead on the cheek,   90
Passionless, pale, cold face, star-sweet on a gloom profound;
Womanlike, taking revenge too deep for a transient wrong
Done but in thought to your beauty, and ever as pale as
   before
Growing and fading and growing upon me without a
   sound,
Luminous, gemlike, ghostlike, deathlike, half the night long
Growing and fading and growing, till I could bear it no
   more,
But arose, and all by myself in my own dark garden ground,
Listening now to the tide in its broad-flung shipwrecking
   roar,
Now to the scream of a madden'd beach dragg'd down by
   the wave,
Walk'd in a wintry wind by a ghastly glimmer, and found   100
The shining daffodil dead, and Orion low in his grave.

IV

I

A million emeralds break from the ruby-budded lime
In the little grove where I sit—ah, wherefore cannot I be
Like things of the season gay, like the bountiful season
    bland,
When the far-off sail is blown by the breeze of a softer
    clime,
Half-lost in the liquid azure bloom of a crescent of sea,
The silent sapphire-spangled marriage ring of the land?

II

Below me, there, is the village, and looks how quiet and
    small!
And yet bubbles o'er like a city, with gossip, scandal, and
    spite;
And Jack on his ale-house bench has as many lies as a Czar;   110
And here on the landward side, by a red rock, glimmers the
    Hall;
And up in the high Hall-garden I see her pass like a light;
But sorrow seize me if ever that light be my leading star!

III

When have I bow'd to her father, the wrinkled head of the
    race?
I met her to-day with her brother, but not to her brother I
    bow'd:
I bow'd to his lady-sister as she rode by on the moor;
But the fire of a foolish pride flash'd over her beautiful face.
O child, you wrong your beauty, believe it, in being so
    proud;
Your father has wealth well-gotten, and I am nameless and
    poor.

IV

I keep but a man and a maid, ever ready to slander and
    steal;   120
I know it, and smile a hard-set smile, like a stoic, or like
A wiser epicurean, and let the world have its way:
For nature is one with rapine, a harm no preacher can heal;

The Mayfly is torn by the swallow, the sparrow spear'd by
   the shrike,
And the whole little wood where I sit is a world of plunder
   and prey. *nature not kind, world is cruel*

V

We are puppets, Man in his pride, and Beauty fair in her
   flower;
Do we move ourselves, or are moved by an unseen hand at a
   game
That pushes us off from the board, and others ever succeed?
Ah yet, we cannot be kind to each other here for an hour;
We whisper, and hint, and chuckle, and grin at a brother's
   shame;   130
However we brave it out, we men are a little breed.

VI

A monstrous eft was of old the Lord and Master of Earth,
For him did his high sun flame, and his river billowing ran,
And he felt himself in his force to be Nature's crowning
   race.
As nine months go to the shaping an infant ripe for his birth,
So many a million of ages have gone to the making of man:
He now is first, but is he the last? is he not too base?

better type of man may come

VII

The man of science himself is fonder of glory, and vain,
An eye well-practised in nature, a spirit bounded and poor;
The passionate heart of the poet is whirl'd into folly and
   vice.   140
I would not marvel at either, but keep a temperate brain;
For not to desire or admire, if a man could learn it, were
   more
Than to walk all day like the sultan of old in a garden of
   spice.

between man of science, poet

---

124 *shrike:* butcherbird.
132 *eft:* lizard.

VIII

For the drift of the Maker is dark, an Isis hid by the veil.
Who knows the ways of the world, how God will bring them
    about?
Our planet is one, the suns are many, the world is wide.
Shall I weep if a Poland fall? shall I shriek if a Hungary
    fail?
Or an infant civilisation be ruled with rod or with knout?
I have not made the world, and He that made it will guide.

continued
withdrawal

IX

Be mine a philosopher's life in the quiet woodland ways,   150
Where if I cannot be gay let a passionless peace be my lot,
Far-off from the clamour of liars belied in the hubbub of
    lies;
From the long-neck'd geese of the world that are ever
    hissing dispraise
Because their natures are little, and, whether he heed it or
    not,
Where each man walks with his head in a cloud of
    poisonous flies.

will not last

like Thorton

X

And most of all would I flee from the cruel madness of love
The honey of poison-flowers and all the measureless ill.
Ah, Maud, you milk-white fawn, you are all unmeet for a
    wife.
Your mother is mute in her grave as her image in marble
    above;
Your father is ever in London, you wander about at your
    will;   160
You have but fed on the roses and lain in the lilies of life.

no motheress in maud

not experienced, less pleasant, so have no feelings

V

I

A voice by the cedar tree
In the meadow under the Hall!

---

144 *Isis:* Egyptian fertility goddess.
148 *knout:* whip with knots in it.

She is singing an air that is known to me,
A passionate ballad gallant and gay,
A martial song like a trumpet's call!
Singing alone in the morning of life,
In the happy morning of life and of May,
Singing of men that in battle array,
Ready in heart and ready in hand, 170
March with banner and bugle and fife
To the death, for their native land.

II

Maud with her exquisite face,
And wild voice pealing up to the sunny sky,
And feet like sunny gems on an English green,
Maud in the light of her youth and her grace,
Singing of Death, and of Honour that cannot die,
Till I well could weep for a time so sordid and mean,
And myself so languid and base.

III

Silence, beautiful voice! 180
Be still, for you only trouble the mind
With a joy in which I cannot rejoice,
A glory I shall not find.
Still! I will hear you no more,
For your sweetness hardly leaves me a choice
But to move to the meadow and fall before
Her feet on the meadow grass, and adore,
Not her, who is neither courtly nor kind,
Not her, not her, but a voice.

attraction only of voice & power of words

VI

I

Morning arises stormy and pale, 190
No sun, but a wannish glare
In fold upon fold of hueless cloud;
And the budded peaks of the wood are bow'd,
Caught, and cuff'd by the gale:
I had fancied it would be fair.

II

Whom but Maud should I meet
Last night, when the sunset burn'd
On the blossom'd gable-ends
At the head of the village street,
Whom but Maud should I meet?   200
And she touch'd my hand with a smile so sweet,
She made me divine amends
For a courtesy not return'd.

III

And thus a delicate spark
Of glowing and growing light
Thro' the livelong hours of the dark
Kept itself warm in the heart of my dreams,
Ready to burst in a colour'd flame;
Till at last, when the morning came
In a cloud, it faded, and seems   210
But an ashen-gray delight.

IV

What if with her sunny hair,
And smile as sunny as cold,
She meant to weave me a snare
Of some coquettish deceit,
Cleopatra-like as of old
To entangle me when we met,
To have her lion roll in a silken net
And fawn at a victor's feet?

V

Ah, what shall I be at fifty   220
Should Nature keep me alive,
If I find the world so bitter
When I am but twenty-five?
Yet, if she were not a cheat,
If Maud were all that she seem'd,
And her smile were all that I dream'd,
Then the world were not so bitter
But a smile could make it sweet.

VI

What if, tho' her eye seem'd full
Of a kind intent to me,   230
What if that dandy-despot, he,
That jewell'd mass of millinery,
That oil'd and curl'd Assyrian Bull
Smelling of musk and of insolence,
Her brother, from whom I keep aloof,
Who wants the finer politic sense
To mask, tho' but in his own behoof,
With a glassy smile his brutal scorn—
What if he had told her yestermorn
How prettily for his own sweet sake   240
A face of tenderness might be feign'd,
And a moist mirage in desert eyes,
That so, when the rotten hustings shake
In another month to his brazen lies,
A wretched vote may be gain'd?

VII

For a raven ever croaks, at my side,
Keep watch and ward, keep watch and ward,
Or thou wilt prove their tool.
Yea, too, myself from myself I guard,
For often a man's own angry pride   250
Is cap and bells for a fool.

VIII

Perhaps the smile and tender tone
Came out of her pitying womanhood,
For am I not, am I not, here alone
So many a summer since she died,
My mother, who was so gentle and good?
Living alone in an empty house,
Here half-hid in the gleaming wood,
Where I hear the dead at midday moan,
And the shrieking rush of the wainscot mouse,   260

---

233 *Assyrian Bull:* Maud's brother is compared to the human-faced bulls of
ancient Assyrian sculpture, represented with curled hair.
243 *hustings:* platform from which political nominations were made.

And my own sad name in corners cried,
When the shiver of dancing leaves is thrown
About its echoing chambers wide,
Till a morbid hate and horror have grown
Of a world in which I have hardly mixt,
And a morbid eating lichen fixt
On a heart half-turn'd to stone.

IX

O heart of stone, are you flesh, and caught
By that you swore to withstand?
For what was it else within me wrought   270
But, I fear, the new strong wine of love,
That made my tongue so stammer and trip
When I saw the treasured splendour, her hand,
Come sliding out of her sacred glove,
And the sunlight broke from her lip?

X

I have play'd with her when a child;
She remembers it now we meet.
Ah, well, well, well, I *may* be beguiled
By some coquettish deceit.
Yet, if she were not a cheat,   280
If Maud were all that she seem'd,
And her smile had all that I dream'd,
Then the world were not so bitter
But a smile could make it sweet.

VII

I

Did I hear it half in a doze
    Long since, I know not where?
Did I dream it an hour ago,
    When asleep in this arm-chair?

II

Men were drinking together,
    Drinking and talking of me: 290
"Well, if it prove a girl, the boy
    Will have plenty: so let it be."

III

Is it an echo of something
    Read with a boy's delight,
Viziers nodding together
    In some Arabian night?

IV

Strange, that I hear two men,
    Somewhere, talking of me;
"Well, if it prove a girl, my boy
    Will have plenty: so let it be."   300

VIII

She came to the village church,
And sat by a pillar alone;
An angel watching an urn
Wept over her, carved in stone;
And once, but once, she lifted her eyes,
And suddenly, sweetly, strangely blush'd
To find they were met by my own;
And suddenly, sweetly, my heart beat stronger
And thicker, until I heard no longer
The snowy banded, dilettante,   310
Delicate-handed priest intone;
And thought, is it pride? and mused and sigh'd,
"No surely, now it cannot be pride."

IX

I was walking a mile,
More than a mile from the shore,
The sun look'd out with a smile
Betwixt the cloud and the moor;
And riding at set of day
Over the dark moor land,
Rapidly riding far away,   320
She waved to me with her hand.
There were two at her side,
Something flash'd in the sun,
Down by the hill I saw them ride,
In a moment they were gone:

Like a sudden spark
Struck vainly in the night,
Then returns the dark
With no more hope of light.

X

I

Sick, am I sick of a jealous dread?   330
Was not one of the two at her side
This new-made lord, whose splendour plucks *one of arir₃ts*
The slavish hat from the villager's head?
Whose old grandfather has lately died,
Gone to a blacker pit, for whom
Grimy nakedness dragging his trucks
And laying his trams in a poison'd gloom
Wrought, till he crept from a gutted mine   *industrial*
Master of half a servile shire,
And left his coal all turn'd into gold   340
To a grandson, first of his noble line,
Rich in the grace all women desire,
Strong in the power that all men adore,
And simper and set their voices lower,
And soften as if to a girl, and hold
Awe-stricken breaths at a work divine,
Seeing his gewgaw castle shine,
New as his title, built last year,
There amid perky larches and pine,
And over the sullen-purple moor   350
(Look at it) pricking a cockney ear.

II

What, has he found my jewel out?   *jealous*
For one of the two that rode at her side
Bound for the Hall, I am sure was he;
Bound for the Hall, and I think for a bride.
Blithe would her brother's acceptance be.
Maud could be gracious too, no doubt,
To a lord, a captain, a padded shape,
A bought commission, a waxen face,
A rabbit mouth that is ever agape—   360

Bought? what is it he cannot buy?
And therefore splenetic, personal, base,
A wounded thing with a rancorous cry,
At war with myself and a wretched race,
Sick, sick to the heart of life, am I.

III

Last week came one to the county town,
To preach our poor little army down,
And play the game of the despot kings,
Tho' the state has done it and thrice as well:
This broad-brimm'd hawker of holy things,   370
Whose ear is cramm'd with his cotton, and rings
Even in dreams to the chink of his pence,
This huckster put down war! can he tell
Whether war be a cause or a consequence?
Put down the passions that make earth Hell!
Down with ambition, avarice, pride,
Jealousy, down! cut off from the mind
The bitter springs of anger and fear;
Down too, down at your own fireside,
With the evil tongue and the evil ear,   380
For each is at war with mankind!

IV

I wish I could hear again
The chivalrous battle-song
That she warbled alone in her joy!
I might persuade myself then
She would not do herself this great wrong,
To take a wanton dissolute boy
For a man and leader of men.

V

Ah God, for a man with heart, head, hand,
Like some of the simple great ones gone   390
For ever and ever by,
One still strong man in a blatant land,
Whatever they call him, what care I,
Aristocrat, democrat, autocrat—one
Who can rule and dare not lie!

VI

And ah for a man to arise in me,
That the man I am may cease to be!

XI

I

O, let the solid ground
  Not fail beneath my feet
Before my life has found   400
  What some have found so sweet!
Then let come what come may,
What matter if I go mad,
I shall have had my day.

irresponsibility
after was not lillies

II

Let the sweet heavens endure,
  Not close and darken above me
Before I am quite quite sure
  That there is one to love me!
Then let come what come may
To a life that has been so sad,   410
I shall have had my day.

XII

I

Birds in the high Hall-garden
  When twilight was falling,
Maud, Maud, Maud, Maud,
  They were crying and calling.

II

Where was Maud? in our wood;
  And I—who else?—was with her,
Gathering woodland lilies,
  Myriads blow together.

III

Birds in our wood sang   420
  Ringing thro' the valleys,

Maud is here, here, here
In among the lilies.

IV

I kiss'd her slender hand,
   She took the kiss sedately;
Maud is not seventeen,
   But she is tall and stately.

V

I to cry out on pride
   Who have won her favour!
Oh, Maud were sure of Heaven   430
   If lowliness could save her!

VI

I know the way she went
   Home with her maiden posy,
For her feet have touch'd the meadows
   And left the daisies rosy.

VII

Birds in the high Hall-garden
   Were crying and calling to her,
Where is Maud, Maud, Maud?
   One is come to woo her.

VIII

Look, a horse at the door,   440
   And little King Charley snarling!
Go back, my lord, across the moor,
   You are not her darling.

XIII

I

Scorn'd, to be scorn'd by one that I scorn,
Is that a matter to make me fret?
That a calamity hard to be borne?

---

435 *rosy:* showing the pink undersides of the daisy petals.
441 *King Charley:* spaniel.

Well, he may live to hate me yet.
Fool that I am to be vext with his pride!
I past him, I was crossing his lands;
He stood on the path a little aside;   450
His face, as I grant, in spite of spite,
Has a broad-blown comeliness, red and white,
And six feet two, as I think, he stands;
But his essences turn'd the live air sick,
And barbarous opulence jewel-thick
Sunn'd itself on his breast and his hands.

II

Who shall call me ungentle, unfair?
I long'd so heartily then and there
To give him the grasp of fellowship;
But while I past he was humming an air,   460
Stopt, and then with a riding-whip
Leisurely tapping a glossy boot,
And curving a contumelious lip,
Gorgonised me from head to foot
With a stony British stare.

III

Why sits he here in his father's chair?
That old man never comes to his place:
Shall I believe him ashamed to be seen?
For only once, in the village street,
Last year, I caught a glimpse of his face,   470
A gray old wolf and a lean.
Scarcely, now, would I call him a cheat;
For then, perhaps, as a child of deceit,
She might by a true descent be untrue;
And Maud is as true as Maud is sweet:
Tho' I fancy her sweetness only due
To the sweeter blood by the other side;
Her mother has been a thing complete,
However she came to be so allied.
And fair without, faithful within,   480
Maud to him is nothing akin:

---

464 *Gorgonised:* turned to stone, as did the sight of the face of Medusa, one of the Gorgons.

Some peculiar mystic grace
Made her only the child of her mother,
And heap'd the whole inherited sin
On that huge scapegoat of the race,
All, all upon the brother.

IV

Peace, angry spirit, and let him be!
Has not his sister smiled on me?

XIV

I

Maud has a garden of roses
And lilies fair on a lawn;   490
There she walks in her state
And tends upon bed and bower,
And thither I climb'd at dawn
And stood by her garden-gate.
A lion ramps at the top,
He is claspt by a passion-flower.

II

Maud's own little oak-room
(Which Maud, like a precious stone
Set in the heart of the carven gloom,
Lights with herself, when alone   500
She sits by her music and books
And her brother lingers late
With a roystering company) looks
Upon Maud's own garden-gate:
And I thought as I stood, if a hand, as white
As ocean-foam in the moon, were laid
On the hasp of the window, and my Delight
Had a sudden desire, like a glorious ghost, to glide,
Like a beam of the seventh Heaven, down to my side,
There were but a step to be made.   510

III

The fancy flatter'd my mind,
And again seem'd overbold;

Now I thought that she cared for me,
Now I thought she was kind
Only because she was cold.

IV

I heard no sound where I stood
But the rivulet on from the lawn
Running down to my own dark wood;
Or the voice of the long sea-wave as it swell'd
Now and then in the dim-gray dawn;   520
But I look'd, and round, all round the house I beheld
The death-white curtain drawn;
Felt a horror over me creep,
Prickle my skin and catch my breath,
Knew that the death-white curtain meant but sleep,
Yet I shudder'd and thought like a fool of the sleep of death.

XV

So dark a mind within me dwells,
    And I make myself such evil cheer,
That if *I* be dear to some one else,
    Then some one else may have much to fear;   530
But if *I* be dear to some one else,
    Then I should be to myself more dear.
Shall I not take care of all that I think,
Yea even of wretched meat and drink,
If I be dear,
If I be dear to some one else?

XVI

I

This lump of earth has left his estate
The lighter by the loss of his weight;
And so that he find what he went to seek,
And fulsome Pleasure clog him, and drown   540
His heart in the gross mud-honey of town,
He may stay for a year who has gone for a week:
But this is the day when I must speak,
And I see my Oread coming down,

---

544 *Oread:* mountain nymph.

Oh, this is the day!
O beautiful creature, what am I
That I dare to look her way?
Think I may hold dominion sweet,
Lord of the pulse that is lord of her breast,
And dream of her beauty with tender dread,   550
From the delicate Arab arch of her feet
To the grace that, bright and light as the crest
Of a peacock, sits on her shining head,
And she knows it not: oh, if she knew it,
To know her beauty might half undo it!
I know it the one bright thing to save
My yet young life in the wilds of Time,
Perhaps from madness, perhaps from crime,
Perhaps from a selfish grave.

II

What, if she be fasten'd to this fool lord,   560
Dare I bid her abide by her word?
Should I love her so well if she
Had given her word to a thing so low?
Shall I love her as well if she
Can break her word were it even for me?
I trust that it is not so.

III

Catch not my breath, O clamorous heart,
Let not my tongue be a thrall to my eye,
For I must tell her before we part,
I must tell her, or die.   570

XVII

Go not, happy day,
    From the shining fields,
Go not, happy day,
    Till the maiden yields.
Rosy is the West,
    Rosy is the South,
Roses are her cheeks,

---

551 *Arab arch:* high instep.

And a rose her mouth.
When the happy Yes
     Falters from her lips,   580
Pass and blush the news
     Over glowing ships;
Over blowing seas,
     Over seas at rest,
Pass the happy news,
     Blush it thro' the West;
Till the red man dance
     By his red cedar-tree,
And the red man's babe
     Leap, beyond the sea.   590
Blush from West to East,
     Blush from East to West,
Till the West is East,
     Blush it thro' the West.
Rosy is the West,
     Rosy is the South,
Roses are her cheeks,
     And a rose her mouth.

XVIII

I

I have led her home, my love, my only friend.
There is none like her, none.   600
And never yet so warmly ran my blood
And sweetly, on and on
Calming itself to the long-wish'd-for end,
Full to the banks, close on the promised good.

II

None like her, none.
Just now the dry-tongued laurels' pattering talk
Seem'd her light foot along the garden walk,
And shook my heart to think she comes once more:
But even then I heard her close the door;
The gates of heaven are closed, and she is gone.   610

III

There is none like her, none,
Nor will be when our summers have deceased.
Oh, art thou sighing for Lebanon
In the long breeze that streams to thy delicious East,
Sighing for Lebanon,
Dark cedar, tho' thy limbs have here increased,
Upon a pastoral slope as fair,
And looking to the South and fed
With honey'd rain and delicate air,
And haunted by the starry head   620
Of her whose gentle will has changed my fate,
And made my life a perfumed altar-flame;
And over whom thy darkness must have spread
With such delight as theirs of old, thy great
Forefathers of the thornless garden, there
Shadowing the snow-limb'd Eve from whom she came?

IV

Here will I lie, while these long branches sway,
And you fair stars that crown a happy day
Go in and out as if at merry play,
Who am no more so all forlorn   630
As when it seem'd far better to be born
To labour and the mattock-harden'd hand
Than nursed at ease and brought to understand
A sad astrology, the boundless plan
That makes you tyrants in your iron skies,
Innumerable, pitiless, passionless eyes,
Cold fires, yet with power to burn and brand
His nothingness into man.

V

But now shine on, and what care I,
Who in this stormy gulf have found a pearl   640
The countercharm of space and hollow sky,
And do accept my madness, and would die
To save from some slight shame one simple girl?

---

634 *sad astrology:* modern astronomy, in which the stars seem estranged from
man.

VI

Would die; for sullen-seeming Death may give
More life to Love than is or ever was
In our low world, where yet 'tis sweet to live.
Let no one ask me how it came to pass;
It seems that I am happy, that to me
A livelier emerald twinkles in the grass,
A purer sapphire melts into the sea.   650

VII

Not die; but live a life of truest breath,
And teach true life to fight with mortal wrongs.
Oh, why should Love, like men in drinking-songs,
Spice his fair banquet with the dust of death?
Make answer, Maud my bliss,
Maud made my Maud by that long loving kiss,
Life of my life, wilt thou not answer this?
"The dusky strand of Death inwoven here
With dear Love's tie, makes Love himself more dear."

VIII

Is that enchanted moan only the swell   660
Of the long waves that roll in yonder bay?
And hark the clock within, the silver knell
Of twelve sweet hours that past in bridal white,
And died to live, long as my pulses play;
But now by this my love has closed her sight
And given false death her hand, and stolen away
To dreamful wastes where footless fancies dwell
Among the fragments of the golden day.
May nothing there her maiden grace affright!
Dear heart, I feel with thee the drowsy spell.   670
My bride to be, my evermore delight,
My own heart's heart, my ownest own, farewell;
It is but for a little space I go:
And ye meanwhile far over moor and fell
Beat to the noiseless music of the night!
Has our whole earth gone nearer to the glow
Of your soft splendours that you look so bright?

674 *ye:* the stars.

I have climb'd nearer out of lonely Hell.
Beat, happy stars, timing with things below,
Beat with my heart more blest than heart can tell,   680
Blest, but for some dark undercurrent woe
That seems to draw—but it shall not be so:
Let all be well, be well.

XIX

I

Her brother is coming back to-night,
Breaking up my dream of delight.

II

My dream? do I dream of bliss?
I have walk'd awake with Truth.
Oh, when did a morning shine
So rich in atonement as this
For my dark-dawning youth,   690
Darken'd watching a mother decline
And that dead man at her heart and mine:
For who was left to watch her but I?
Yet so did I let my freshness die.

III

I trust that I did not talk
To gentle Maud in our walk
(For often in lonely wanderings
I have cursed him even to lifeless things)
But I trust that I did not talk,
Not touch on her father's sin: 700
I am sure I did but speak
Of my mother's faded cheek
When it slowly grew so thin
That I felt she was slowly dying
Vext with lawyers and harass'd with debt;
For how often I caught her with eyes all wet,
Shaking her head at her son and sighing
A world of trouble within!

IV

And Maud too, Maud was moved
To speak of the mother she loved   710
As one scarce less forlorn,
Dying abroad and it seems apart
From him who had ceased to share her heart,
And ever mourning over the feud,
The household Fury sprinkled with blood
By which our houses are torn:
How strange was what she said,
When only Maud and the brother
Hung over her dying bed—
That Maud's dark father and mine   720
Had bound us one to the other,
Betrothed us over their wine,
On the day when Maud was born;
Seal'd her mine from her first sweet breath.
Mine, mine by a right, from birth till death.
Mine, mine—our fathers have sworn.

mad possess ire hess

V

But the true blood spilt had in it a heat
To dissolve the precious seal on a bond,
That, if left uncancell'd, had been so sweet:
And none of us thought of a something beyond,   730
A desire that awoke in the heart of the child,
As it were a duty done to the tomb,
To be friends for her sake, to be reconciled;
And I was cursing them and my doom,
And letting a dangerous thought run wild
While often abroad in the fragrant gloom
Of foreign churches—I see her there,
Bright English lily, breathing a prayer
To be friends, to be reconciled!

VI

But then what a flint is he!   740
Abroad, at Florence, at Rome,
I find whenever she touch'd on me
This brother had laugh'd her down,

And at last, when each came home,
He had darken'd into a frown,
Chid her, and forbid her to speak
To me, her friend of the years before;
And this was what had redden'd her cheek
When I bow'd to her on the moor.

VII

Yet Maud, altho' not blind   750
To the faults of his heart and mind,
I see she cannot but love him,
And says he is rough but kind,
And wishes me to approve him,
And tells me, when she lay
Sick once, with a fear of worse,
That he left his wine and horses and play,
Sat with her, read to her, night and day,
And tended her like a nurse.

VIII

Kind? but the death-bed desire   760
Spurn'd by this heir of the liar—
Rough but kind? yet I know
He has plotted against me in this,
That he plots against me still.
Kind to Maud? that were not amiss.
Well, rough but kind; why, let it be so:
For shall not Maud have her will?

IX

For, Maud, so tender and true,
As long as my life endures
I feel I shall owe you a debt   770
That I never can hope to pay,
And if ever I should forget
That I owe this debt to you
And for your sweet sake to yours,
Oh, then, what then shall I say?—
If ever I *should* forget,
May God make me more wretched
Than ever I have been yet!

X

So now I have sworn to bury
All this dead body of hate, 780
I feel so free and so clear
By the loss of that dead weight,
That I should grow light-headed, I fear,
Fantastically merry;
But that her brother comes, like a blight
On my fresh hope, to the Hall to-night.

XX

I

Strange, that I felt so gay,
Strange, that *I* tried to-day
To beguile her melancholy;
The Sultan, as we name him— 790
She did not wish to blame him—
But he vext her and perplext her
With his worldly talk and Folly:
Was it gentle to reprove her
For stealing out of view
From a little lazy lover
Who but claims her as his due?
Or for chilling his caresses
By the coldness of her manners,
Nay, the plainness of her dresses? 800
Now I know her but in two,
Nor can pronounce upon it
If one should ask me whether
The habit, hat, and feather,
Or the frock and gipsy bonnet
Be the neater and completer;
For nothing can be sweeter
Than maiden Maud in either.

II

But to-morrow, if we live,
Our ponderous squire will give 810
A grand political dinner

To half the squirelings near;
And Maud will wear her jewels,
And the bird of prey will hover,
And the titmouse hope to win her
With his chirrup at her ear.

III

A grand political dinner
To the men of many acres,
A gathering of the Tory,
A dinner and then a dance   820
For the maids and marriage-makers,
And every eye but mine will glance
At Maud in all her glory.

IV

For I am not invited,
But, with the Sultan's pardon,
I am all as well delighted,
For I know her own rose-garden,
And mean to linger in it
Till the dancing will be over;
And then, oh, then, come out to me   830
For a minute, but for a minute,
Come out to your own true lover,
That your true lover may see
Your glory also, and render
All homage to his own darling,
Queen Maud in all her splendour.

XXI

Rivulet crossing my ground,
And bringing me down from the Hall
This garden-rose that I found,
Forgetful of Maud and me,   840
And lost in trouble and moving round
Here at the head of a tinkling fall,
And trying to pass to the sea;
O rivulet, born at the Hall,
My Maud has sent it by thee

(If I read her sweet will right)
On a blushing mission to me,
Saying in odour and colour, "Ah, be
Among the roses to-night."

XXII

I

Come into the garden, Maud,　　　850
　　For the black bat, night, has flown,
Come into the garden, Maud,
　　I am here at the gate alone;
And the woodbine spices are wafted **abroad**,
　　And the musk of the rose is blown.

II

For a breeze of morning moves,
　　And the planet of Love is on high,
Beginning to faint in the light that she **loves**
　　On a bed of daffodil sky,
To faint in the light of the sun she loves,　　　860
　　To faint in his light, and to die.

III

All night have the roses heard
　　The flute, violin, bassoon;
All night has the casement jessamine stirr'd
　　To the dancers dancing in tune;
Till a silence fell with the waking bird,
　　And a hush with the setting moon.

IV

I said to the lily, "There is but one
　　With whom she has heart to be gay.
When will the dancers leave her alone?　　　870
　　She is weary of dance and play."
Now half to the setting moon are gone,
　　And half to the rising day;

---

857 *planet of Love:* Venus.

Low on the sand and loud on the stone
    The last wheel echoes away.

V

I said to the rose, "The brief night goes
    In babble and revel and wine.
O young lord-lover, what sighs are those,
    For one that will never be thine?
But mine, but mine," so I sware to the rose,   880
    "For ever and ever, mine."

VI

And the soul of the rose went into my blood,
    As the music clash'd in the hall;
And long by the garden lake I stood,
    For I heard your rivulet fall
From the lake to the meadow and on to the wood,
    Our wood, that is dearer than all;

VII

From the meadow your walks have left so sweet
    That whenever a March-wind sighs
He sets the jewel-print of your feet   890
    In violets blue as your eyes,
To the woody hollows in which we meet
    And the valleys of Paradise.

VIII

The slender acacia would not shake
    One long milk-bloom on the tree;
The white lake-blossom fell into the lake
    As the pimpernel dozed on the lea;
But the rose was awake all night for your sake,
    Knowing your promise to me;
The lilies and roses were all awake,   900
    They sigh'd for the dawn and thee.

IX

Queen rose of the rosebud garden of girls,
    Come hither, the dances are done,
In gloss of satin and glimmer of pearls,

Queen lily and rose in one;
Shine out, little head, sunning over with curls,
 To the flowers, and be their sun.

X

There has fallen a splendid tear
 From the passion-flower at the gate.
She is coming, my dove, my dear;   910
 She is coming, my life, my fate;
The red rose cries, "She is near, she is near;"
 And the white rose weeps, "She is late;"
The larkspur listens, "I hear, I hear;"
 And the lily whispers, "I wait."

XI

She is coming, my own, my sweet;
 Were it ever so airy a tread,
My heart would hear her and beat,
 Were it earth in an earthy bed;
My dust would hear her and beat,   920
 Had I lain for a century dead;
Would start and tremble under her feet,
 And blossom in purple and red.

PART II

I

I

"The fault was mine, the fault was mine"—
Why am I sitting here so stunn'd and still,
Plucking the harmless wild-flower on the hill?—
It is this guilty hand!—
And there rises ever a passionate cry
From underneath in the darkening land—
What is it, that has been done?
O dawn of Eden bright over earth and sky,
The fires of Hell brake out of thy rising sun,
The fires of Hell and of Hate;   10
For she, sweet soul, had hardly spoken a word,
When her brother ran in his rage to the gate,

He came with the babe-faced lord;
Heap'd on her terms of disgrace,
And while she wept, and I strove to be cool,
He fiercely gave me the lie,
Till I with as fierce an anger spoke,
And he struck me, madman, over the face,
Struck me before the languid fool,
Who was gaping and grinning by: 20
Struck for himself an evil stroke;
Wrought for his house an irredeemable woe;
For front to front in an hour we stood,
And a million horrible bellowing echoes broke
From the red-ribb'd hollow behind the wood,
And thunder'd up into Heaven the Christless code
That must have life for a blow.
Ever and ever afresh they seem'd to grow.
Was it he lay there with a fading eye?
"The fault was mine," he whisper'd, "fly!"   30
Then glided out of the joyous wood
The ghastly Wraith of one that I know;
And there rang on a sudden a passionate cry,
A cry for a brother's blood:
It will ring in my heart and my ears, till I die, till I die.

II

Is it gone? my pulses beat—
What was it? a lying trick of the brain?
Yet I thought I saw her stand,
A shadow there at my feet,
High over the shadowy land.   40
It is gone; and the heavens fall in a gentle rain,
When they should burst and drown with deluging storms
The feeble vassals of wine and anger and lust,
The little hearts that know not how to forgive:
Arise, my God, and strike, for we hold Thee just,
Strike dead the whole weak race of venomous worms,
That sting each other here in the dust;
We are not worthy to live.

---

16 *gave me the lie:* accused me of lying.
26 *Christless code:* of duelling.
32 *one that I know:* probably Maud.

II

I

See what a lovely shell,
Small and pure as a pearl,   50
Lying close to my foot,
Frail, but a work divine,
Made so fairily well
With delicate spire and whorl,
How exquisitely minute,
A miracle of design!

II

What is it? a learned man
Could give it a clumsy name.
Let him name it who can,
The beauty would be the same.

III

The tiny cell is forlorn,
Void of the little living will
That made it stir on the shore.
Did he stand at the diamond door
Of his house in a rainbow frill?
Did he push, when he was uncurl'd,
A golden foot or a fairy horn
Thro' his dim water-world?

IV

Slight, to be crush'd with a tap
Of my finger-nail on the sand,   70
Small, but a work divine,
Frail, but of force to withstand,
Year upon year, the shock
Of cataract seas that snap
The three-decker's oaken spine
Athwart the ledges of rock,
Here on the Breton strand!

II In this section, the deranged hero is exiled in Brittany; he is musing on a shell which Tennyson said symbolized the narrator's "first and highest nature preserved amid the storms of passion."

V

Breton, not Briton; here
Like a shipwreck'd man on a coast
Of ancient fable and fear—   80
Plagued with a flitting to and fro,
A disease, a hard mechanic ghost
That never came from on high
Nor ever arose from below,
But only moves with the moving eye,
Flying along the land and the main—
Why should it look like Maud?
Am I to be overawed
By what I cannot but know
Is a juggle born of the brain?   90

VI

Back from the Breton coast,
Sick of a nameless fear,
Back to the dark sea-line
Looking, thinking of all I have lost;
An old song vexes my ear;
But that of Lamech is mine.

VII

For years, a measureless ill,
For years, for ever, to part—
But she, she would love me still;
And as long, O God, as she   100
Have a grain of love for me,
So long, no doubt, no doubt,
Shall I nurse in my dark heart,
However weary, a spark of will
Not to be trampled out.

VIII

Strange, that the mind, when fraught
With a passion so intense
One would think that it well

---

96 *Lamech:* In *Genesis* 4:23 Lamech says, "I have slain a man to my wound-
ing, and a young man to my hurt."

Might drown all life in the eye,—
That it should, by being so overwrought,   110
Suddenly strike on a sharper sense
For a shell, or a flower, little things
Which else would have been past by!
And now I remember, I,
When he lay dying there,
I noticed one of his many rings
(For he had many, poor worm) and thought,
It is his mother's hair.

IX

Who knows if he be dead?
Whether I need have fled?   120
Am I guilty of blood?
However this may be,
Comfort her, comfort her, all things good,
While I am over the sea!
Let me and my passionate love go by,
But speak to her all things holy and high,
Whatever happen to me!
Me and my harmful love go by;
But come to her waking, find her asleep,
Powers of the height, Powers of the deep,   *doesn't know* [130]
And comfort her tho' I die!   *if is guilty*

III

Courage, poor heart of stone!
I will not ask thee why
Thou canst not understand
That thou art left for ever alone:
Courage, poor stupid heart of stone!—
Or if I ask thee why,   *dead to him*
Care not thou to reply:
She is but dead, and the time is at hand /
When thou shalt more than die.   140

---

[118] *mother's hair:* enclosed in a mourning ring.
[139] *She is but dead:* The narrator imagines that Maud has died.

IV

I

Oh, that 't were possible
After long grief and pain
To find the arms of my true love
Round me once again!

II

When I was wont to meet her
In the silent woody places
By the home that gave me birth,
We stood tranced in long embraces
Mixt with kisses sweeter, sweeter
Than anything on earth.   150

III

A shadow flits before me,
Not thou, but like to thee:
Ah, Christ, that it were possible
For one short hour to see
The souls we loved, that they might tell us
What and where they be!

IV

It leads me forth at evening,
It lightly winds and steals
In a cold white robe before me,
When all my spirit reels   160
At the shouts, the leagues of lights,
And the roaring of the wheels.

V

Half the night I waste in sighs,
Half in dreams I sorrow after
The delight of early skies;
In a wakeful doze I sorrow
For the hand, the lips, the eyes,
For the meeting of the morrow,

IV This lyric was originally published separately; Tennyson later elaborated
it into the whole of *Maud*.

The delight of happy laughter,
The delight of low replies.   170

VI

'T is a morning pure and sweet,
And a dewy splendour falls
On the little flower that clings
To the turrets and the walls;
'T is a morning pure and sweet,
And the light and shadow fleet;
She is walking in the meadow,
And the woodland echo rings;
In a moment we shall meet;
She is singing in the meadow,   180
And the rivulet at her feet
Ripples on in light and shadow
To the ballad that she sings.

VII

Do I hear her sing as of old,
My bird with the shining head,
My own dove with the tender eye?
But there rings on a sudden a passionate cry,
There is some one dying or dead,
And a sullen thunder is roll'd;
For a tumult shakes the city,   190
And I wake, my dream is fled;
In the shuddering dawn, behold,
Without knowledge, without pity,
By the curtains of my bed
That abiding phantom cold!

VIII

Get thee hence, nor come again,
Mix not memory with doubt,
Pass, thou deathlike type of pain,
Pass and cease to move about!
'T is the blot upon the brain   200
That *will* show itself without.

IX

Then I rise, the eave-drops fall,
And the yellow vapours choke
The great city sounding wide;
The day comes, a dull red ball
Wrapt in drifts of lurid smoke
On the misty river-tide.

X

Thro' the hubbub of the market
I steal, a wasted frame;
It crosses here, it crosses there,　　　　210
Thro' all that crowd confused and loud,
The shadow still the same;
And on my heavy eyelids
My anguish hangs like shame.

XI

Alas for her that met me,
That heard me softly call,
Came glimmering thro' the laurels
At the quiet evenfall,
In the garden by the turrets
Of the old manorial hall!　　　　220

XII

Would the happy spirit descend
From the realms of light and song,
In the chamber or the street,
As she looks among the blest,
Should I fear to greet my friend
Or to say "Forgive the wrong,"
Or to ask her, "Take me, sweet,
To the regions of thy rest"?

XIII

But the broad light glares and beats,
And the shadow flits and fleets　　　　230
And will not let me be;
And I loathe the squares and streets,

And the faces that one meets,
Hearts with no love for me:
Always I long to creep
Into some still cavern deep,
There to weep, and weep, and weep
My whole soul out to thee.

V

confined to asylum

I

Dead, long dead,
Long dead!   240
And my heart is a handful of dust,
And the wheels go over my head,
And my bones are shaken with pain,
For into a shallow grave they are thrust,
Only a yard beneath the street,
And the hoofs of the horses beat, beat,
The hoofs of the horses beat,
Beat into my scalp and my brain,
With never an end to the stream of passing feet,
Driving, hurrying, marrying, burying,   250
Clamour and rumble, and ringing and clatter,
And here beneath it is all as bad,
For I thought the dead had peace, but it is not so;
To have no peace in the grave, is that not sad?
But up and down and to and fro,
Ever about me the dead men go;
And then to hear a dead man chatter
Is enough to drive one mad.

II

Wretchedest age, since Time began,
They cannot even bury a man;   260
And tho' we paid our tithes in the days that are gone,
Not a bell was rung, not a prayer was read;
It is that which makes us loud in the world of the dead;
There is none that does his work, not one;
A touch of their office might have sufficed,

V In this section, the hero is confined in an insane asylum.

But the churchmen fain would kill their church,
As the churches have kill'd their Christ.

III

See, there is one of us sobbing,
No limit to his distress;
And another, a lord of all things, praying   270
To his own great self, as I guess;
And another, a statesman there, betraying
His party-secret, fool, to the press;
And yonder a vile physician, blabbing
The case of his patient—all for what?
To tickle the maggot born in an empty head,
And wheedle a world that loves him not,
For it is but a world of the dead.

IV

Nothing but idiot gabble!
For the prophecy given of old   280
And then not understood,
Has come to pass as foretold;
Not let any man think for the public good,
But babble, merely for babble.
For I never whisper'd a private affair
Within the hearing of cat or mouse,
No, not to myself in the closet alone,
But I heard it shouted at once from the top of the house;
Everything came to be known.
Who told *him* we were there?   290

V

Not that gray old wolf, for he came not back
From the wilderness, full of wolves, where he used to lie;
He has gather'd the bones for his o'ergrown whelp to crack;
Crack them now for yourself, and howl, and die.

VI

Prophet, curse me the blabbing lip,
And curse me the British vermin, the rat;

---

268 *us:* patients in the insane asylum.
291 *gray old wolf:* Maud's father.

I know not whether he came in the Hanover ship,
But I know that he lies and listens mute
In an ancient mansion's crannies and holes:
Arsenic, arsenic, sure, would do it,   300
Except that now we poison our babes, poor souls!
It is all used up for that.

VII

Tell him now: she is standing here at my head;
Not beautiful now, not even kind;
He may take her now; for she never speaks her mind,
But is ever the one thing silent here.
She is not *of* us, as I divine;
She comes from another stiller world of the dead,
Stiller, not fairer than mine.

VIII

But I know where a garden grows,   310
Fairer than aught in the world beside,
All made up of the lily and rose
That blow by night, when the season is good,
To the sound of dancing music and flutes:
It is only flowers, they had no fruits,
And I almost fear they are not roses, but blood;
For the keeper was one, so full of pride,
He linkt a dead man there to a spectral bride;
For he, if he had not been a Sultan of brutes,
Would he have that hole in his side?   320

IX

But what will the old man say?
He laid a cruel snare in a pit
To catch a friend of mine one stormy day;
Yet now I could even weep to think of it;
For what will the old man say
When he comes to the second corpse in the pit?

---

297 *Hanover ship:* allusion to the theory that the Norwegian rat first came into England on the ships of George I.

X

Friend, to be struck by the public foe,
Then to strike him and lay him low,
That were a public merit, far,
Whatever the Quaker holds, from sin;   330
But the red life spilt for a private blow—
I swear to you, lawful and lawless war
Are scarcely even akin.

XI

O me, why have they not buried me deep enough?
Is it kind to have made me a grave so rough,
Me, that was never a quiet sleeper?
Maybe still I am but half-dead;
Then I cannot be wholly dumb;
I will cry to the steps above my head
And somebody, surely, some kind heart will come   340
To bury me, bury me
Deeper, ever so little deeper.

PART III

I

My life has crept so long on a broken wing
Thro' cells of madness, haunts of horror and fear,
That I come to be grateful at last for a little thing:
My mood is changed, for it fell at a time of year
When the face of night is fair on the dewy downs,
And the shining daffodil dies, and the Charioteer
And starry Gemini hang like glorious crowns
Over Orion's grave low down in the west,
That like a silent lightning under the stars
She seem'd to divide in a dream from a band of the blest, 10
And spoke of a hope for the world in the coming wars—
"And in that hope, dear soul, let trouble have rest,

---

⁶ *Charioteer:* the constellation Auriga.
⁷ *Gemini:* another constellation.

Knowing I tarry for thee," and pointed to Mars
As he glow'd like a ruddy shield on the Lion's breast.

II

And it was but a dream, yet it yielded a dear delight
To have look'd, tho' but in a dream, upon eyes so fair,
That had been in a weary world my one thing bright;
And it was but a dream, yet it lighten'd my despair
When I thought that a war would arise in defence
   of the right,
That an iron tyranny now should bend or cease,   20
The glory of manhood stand on his ancient height,
Nor Britain's one sole God be the millionaire:
No more shall commerce be all in all, and Peace
Pipe on her pastoral hillock a languid note,
And watch her harvest ripen, her herd increase,
Nor the cannon-bullet rust on a slothful shore,
And the cobweb woven across the cannon's throat
Shall shake its threaded tears in the wind no more.

III

And as months ran on and rumour of battle grew,
"It is time, it is time, O passionate heart," said I   30
(For I cleaved to a cause that I felt to be pure and true),
"It is time, O passionate heart and morbid eye,
That old hysterical mock-disease should die."
And I stood on a giant deck and mix'd my breath
With a loyal people shouting a battle-cry,
Till I saw the dreary phantom arise and fly
Far into the North, and battle, and seas of death.

IV

Let it go or stay, so I wake to the higher aims
Of a land that has lost for a little her lust of gold,
And love of a peace that was full of wrongs and shames,   40
Horrible, hateful, monstrous, not to be told;
And hail once more to the banner of battle unroll'd!
Tho' many a light shall darken, and many shall weep
For those that are crush'd in the clash of jarring claims,

---

13 *Mars:* the planet symbolizing war, part of the constellation of Leo (the Lion), symbol of England.

Yet God's just wrath shall be wreak'd on a giant liar;
And many a darkness into the light shall leap,
And shine in the sudden making of splendid names,
And noble thought be freer under the sun,
And the heart of a people beat with one desire;
For the peace, that I deem'd no peace, is over and done,   50
And now by the side of the Black and the Baltic deep,
And deathful-grinning mouths of the fortress, flames
The blood-red blossom of war with a heart of fire.

v

Let it flame or fade, and the war roll down like a wind,
We have proved we have hearts in a cause, we are noble
    still,
And myself have awaked, as it seems, to the better mind;
It is better to fight for the good than to rail at the ill;
I have felt with my native land, I am one with my kind,
I embrace the purpose of God, and the doom assign'd.

[1855, 1856]

THE HIGHER PANTHEISM

The sun, the moon, the stars, the seas, the hills and the plains,—
Are not these, O Soul, the Vision of Him who reigns?

Is not the Vision He, tho' He be not that which He seems?
Dreams are true while they last, and do we not live in dreams?

Earth, these solid stars, this weight of body and limb,
Are they not sign and symbol of thy division from Him?

---

45 *liar:* Czar of Russia.
The Higher Pantheism: Pantheism is the doctrine that God is simply the
forces and laws manifested in the universe. Tennyson here says that God is
more than a totality of the universe, that the physical world is the tangible
expression ("the Vision") of God, who must therefore be greater than that
physical universe. See also Swinburne's parody of this poem, "The Higher
Pantheism in a Nutshell."

Dark is the world to thee: thyself art the reason why;
For is He not all but thou, that hast power to feel "I am I"?

Glory about thee, without thee; and thou fulfillest thy doom,
Making Him broken gleams and a stifled splendour and
   gloom.   10

Speak to Him, thou, for He hears, and Spirit with Spirit can
   meet—
Closer is He than breathing, and nearer than hands and feet.

God is law, say the wise; O Soul, and let us rejoice,
For if He thunder by law the thunder is yet His voice.

Law is God, say some: no God at all, says the fool;
For all we have power to see is a straight staff bent in a pool;

And the ear of man cannot hear, and the eye of man cannot
   see;
But if we could see and hear, this Vision—were it not He?

                                         [1869]

MERLIN AND THE GLEAM

I

O young Mariner,
You from the haven
Under the sea-cliff,
You that are watching
The gray Magician
With eyes of wonder,
I am Merlin,
And *I* am dying,
I am Merlin
Who follow The Gleam.   10

---

[8] *For is He . . . "I am I"?:* i.e., Is God not everything except the individual, who has self-consciousness, and is therefore separate from Him?
Merlin: the magician of King Arthur's court at Camelot.

II

Mighty the Wizard
Who found me at sunrise
Sleeping, and woke me
And learn'd me Magic!
Great the Master,
And sweet the Magic,
When over the valley,
In early summers,
Over the mountain,
On human faces,   20
And all around me,
Moving to melody,
Floated The Gleam.

III

Once at the croak of a Raven who crost it,
A barbarous people,
Blind to the magic,
And deaf to the melody,
Snarl'd at and cursed me.
A demon vext me,
The light retreated,   30
The landskip darken'd,
The melody deaden'd,
The Master whisper'd,
"Follow The Gleam."

IV

Then to the melody,
Over a wilderness
Gliding, and glancing at
Elf of the woodland,
Gnome of the cavern,
Griffin and Giant,   40
And dancing of Fairies
In desolate hollows,
And wraiths of the mountain,
And rolling of dragons

By warble of water,
Or cataract music
Of falling torrents,
Flitted The Gleam.

v

Down from the mountain
And over the level,   50
And streaming and shining on
Silent river,
Silvery willow,
Pasture and plowland,
Innocent maidens,
Garrulous children,
Homestead and harvest,
Reaper and gleaner,
And rough-ruddy faces
Of lowly labour,   60
Slided The Gleam—

vi

Then, with a melody
Stronger and statelier,
Led me at length
To the city and palace
Of Arthur the King;
Touch'd at the golden
Cross of the churches,
Flash'd on the Tournament,
Flicker'd and bicker'd   70
From helmet to helmet,
And last on the forehead
Of Arthur the blameless
Rested The Gleam.

vii

Clouds and darkness
Closed upon Camelot;
Arthur had vanish'd
I knew not whither,

The king who loved me,
And cannot die;   80
For out of the darkness
Silent and slowly
The Gleam, that had waned to a wintry glimmer
On icy fallow
And faded forest,
Drew to the valley
Named of the shadow,
And slowly brightening
Out of the glimmer,
And slowly moving again to a melody   90
Yearningly tender,
Fell on the shadow,
No longer a shadow,
But clothed with The Gleam.

VIII

And broader and brighter
The Gleam flying onward,
Wed to the melody,
Sang thro' the world;
And slower and fainter,
Old and weary,   100
But eager to follow,
I saw, whenever
In passing it glanced upon
Hamlet or city,
That under the Crosses
The dead man's garden,
The mortal hillock,
Would break into blossom;
And so to the land's
Last limit I came—   110
And can no longer,
But die rejoicing,
For thro' the Magic
Of Him the Mighty,
Who taught me in childhood,
There on the border
Of boundless Ocean,

And all but in Heaven
Hovers The Gleam.

IX

Not of the sunlight,   120
Not of the moonlight,
Not of the starlight!
O young Mariner,
Down to the haven,
Call your companions,
Launch your vessel,
And crowd your canvas,
And, ere it vanishes
Over the margin,
After it, follow it,   130
Follow The Gleam.

[1889]

CROSSING THE BAR

Sunset and evening star,
    And one clear call for me!
And may there be no moaning of the bar,
    When I put out to sea,

But such a tide as moving seems asleep,
    Too full for sound and foam,
When that which drew from out the boundless deep
    Turns again home.

Twilight and evening bell,
    And after that the dark!   10
And may there be no sadness of farewell,
    When I embark;

Crossing the Bar: Tennyson asked that this poem be placed at the end of all
editions of his poetry.

For tho' from out our bourne of Time and Place
 The flood may bear me far,
I hope to see my Pilot face to face
 When I have crost the bar.

[1889]

Robert Browning

[1812-1889]

Robert Browning was born into a properous suburban London family that almost seemed designed to produce a poet. His father was a mild, scholarly man who earned his living as an upper clerk in the Bank of England but saved his enthusiasm for painting and for collecting books, many of them volumes of poetry and of exotic, curious history; it is probably to the example of his father's passion for esoteric information that the poet owed his own magpie habit of storing his mind with curious fact. Mrs. Browning was half-Scottish, half-German. She was an excellent amateur pianist, and from her Browning learned his lifelong love of music. In Dulwich, only "a green half-hour's walk" through the fields from the Browning household in Camberwell, was the best gallery of painting then in London, and the young Robert there learned to admire the Italian painting that was to be the subject of so much of his poetry. In later life Browning himself became a competent musician and an enthusiastic, if not very successful, sculptor, and his son carried on the family tradition by becoming a professional painter.

From his mother Browning also learned the non-conformist piety that made him "passionately religious" in his boyhood. In later years he flirted briefly with atheism in emulation of Shelley, but most of his life he was a devout believer in the Incarnation of Christ and in personal immortality, although the exact forms his belief took might have puzzled some of the orthodox. In general, he preferred the more Evangelical forms of Protestantism, and there is an implicit hostility to the formality and doctrine of the Roman Catholic Church in much of his poetry.

The poet had the greater part of his education in this pleasant, cultivated household, where he preferred the place of petted, precocious son to the less flattering position he occupied in the day school he attended for about five years. His real education came from undisciplined but continuous reading in his father's extensive library. In addition, he learned to read Latin, Greek, French, and Italian. His first great poetic love was for Shelley, and though he later abandoned that poet's attitude toward religion, he learned from him an abiding passion for liberty and an admiration for rebellion.

As a child Browning wrote a good deal of poetry, most of which has not survived, although what remains shows that he was talented but still unformed in style and taste. His first published work was a long, introspective piece of disguised autobiography, *Pauline,* published anonymously in 1833. In spite of a favorable review or two, not a single copy of the poem was sold, and it was not republished for thirty-five years. *Paracelsus,* published two years later under Browning's name, is the study of a Renaissance alchemist and philosopher and his search for knowledge. It sold little better than *Pauline,* but it did attract the favorable notice of a number of perceptive reviewers, and it is still interesting as the first mature study Browning made of the seeker for knowledge. He described his purpose in *Paracelsus,* in the introduction, as

> . . . an attempt . . . to reverse the method usually adopted by writers whose aim it is to set forth any phenomena of the mind or the passions, by the operation of persons and events; and that, instead of having recourse to an external machinery of incidents to create and evolve the crisis I desire to produce, I have ventured to display somewhat minutely the mood itself in its rise and progress, and have suffered the agency by which it is influenced and determined, to be generally discernible in its effects alone, and subordinate throughout, if not altogether excluded: and this for a reason. I have endeavoured to write a poem, not a drama.

Whatever the merits of *Paracelsus,* Browning's remarks about it could stand for the rest of his output.

Because of the reception of *Paracelsus,* Browning met the great actor Macready, who asked him to write a play for him. Browning obliged with *Strafford,* a historical tragedy, which had a limited success in 1837. Although Browning's greatest talents are now recognized to be dramatic in nature, they were never the gifts of the theater; nonetheless, this was the first of several abortive attempts to write for the stage. None of them fared well on the boards. Perhaps a clue to his theatrical failure is given in his dedication of *Strafford* as a drama of "Action in Character, rather than Character in Action." The dedication sounds like an echo of the introduction to *Paracelsus,* with its disavowal of his intent to write drama.

Browning's last major poem before he really found his own niche in poetry was *Sordello,* a long and confusing study of a poet's mind and career; it is difficult reading but less so than most of Browning's contemporaries found it. The early poems and plays were not successes themselves, but they were the necessary preparation for the great works of his middle career.

Between 1841 and 1846, Browning was engaged in writing and publishing a series of pamphlets under the general title of *Bells and Pomegranates,* which contained several plays besides the three chief works for which it is remembered: *Pippa Passes,* 1841; *Dramatic Lyrics,* 1842; and *Dramatic Romances and Lyrics,* 1845. In all three of them he struck out in his own original direction. In *Pippa Passes,* instead of attempting a full-length drama, Browning took four melodramatic situations, complete with characters and dialogue, but concentrated on the moment of decision in each situation, discarding the preliminary plot and action that would be necessary in a play. In each of the four situations the decision of the characters is precipitated by the sound of the song of an innocent young girl who passes, unaware of the effect that she has on others. Browning here, as in *Strafford,* is concentrating on "Action in Character," i.e., on psychological penetration rather than on physical action. The poem is not a total success, but it pointed the way to the form with which Browning's name has always been associated, the dramatic monologue, which first appeared in *Dramatic Lyrics* and *Dramatic Romances and Lyrics,* and came to its perfection in *Men and Women,* 1855; *Dramatis Personae,* 1864; and *The Ring and the Book,* 1868-69.

The dramatic monologue of Browning has many ancestors (and untold descendants), but it is clear that one of the major

sources from which he drew heavily was the soliloquy as Shakespeare used it in his plays. In the soliloquy Browning found the
moment of arrested action, when the character's personality and
motives are laid bare before the audience, whether or not he is
aware of thus revealing himself. The effect of the soliloquy is
often dependent upon the dramatic irony of the spectator's understanding more than the character himself is able to perceive.
For instance, in the great soliloquies of Iago in *Othello* and
Edmund in *King Lear,* each of these magnificent villains unwittingly exposes layer after layer of unrecognized evil in his character at the very moment that he is giving superficially adequate
reasons to explain his actions. The triumph of these soliloquies
is that the speaker is simultaneously concealing the truth from
himself and revealing it to the audience. In such a dramatic
monologue as "My Last Duchess," Browning has the speaker put
forth a splendid defense of his murder of his first wife, but the
texture of his language and the unexamined assumptions that he
makes reveal to his hearer (and, more importantly, to the reader)
the unplumbed, almost insane depth of his arrogance and pride.
In "Soliloquy of the Spanish Cloister," the monk's thoughts show
us that it is he, not Brother Lawrence, who is the religious hypo-
crite. This kind of double vision in Browning is perhaps most
effective in studies of villainy, but he also used it admirably for
the greater psychological delineation of such characters as Cleon,
Abt Vogler, the Grammarian's disciple, Fra Lippo Lippi, Andrea,
and Caponsacchi, to name only a few. In each case, a listener is
postulated, whether it be the characters who hear Lippo and
Caponsacchi, and the recipient of Cleon's letter, or the reader,
who is the only one aware of Abt Vogler's thoughts.

After the reception of *Pauline* and *Sordello,* Browning was
abnormally sensitive to the association of his own feelings with
those of his characters; to *Dramatic Lyrics* he wrote a foreword
saying that the following poems "come properly enough, I
suppose, under the head of 'Dramatic Pieces'; being, though for
the most part Lyric in expression, always Dramatic in principle,
and so many utterances of so many imaginary persons, not mine."
To the modern reader the poems reveal a great deal about
Browning himself, although it is not necessary to associate him
directly with any particular speaker.

In 1845 began the most famous of literary romances, as
Browning paid court to Elizabeth Barrett, an invalid some six

years older than he and already considerably better known as a poet. Miss Barrett was a virtual prisoner in her father's house, where Browning went to visit her. For nearly two years they wrote each other a splendid series of letters about poetry, politics —and love. In the autumn of 1846 they were married secretly and fled to Italy to live almost all the rest of Mrs. Browning's life.

Browning had visited Italy before, but his long stay there after his marriage was the golden period of his life. With Mrs. Browning he shared an enthusiasm for the Risorgimento and the cause of Italian liberty, the world of painting and music opened up before him, the daily life of Italy was a warm-blooded embodiment of the passion of which he wrote. All around him were the mementoes of the Renaissance, with which he felt such kinship. It was not only the accident of physical propinquity that caused him to set so many of his poems in Italy; rather, it was the awareness that the volatile Italian temperament openly displayed the love, the hatred, the passion that existed in England but was kept concealed under a cool exterior. Italy, and particularly Florence, was a constant reminder of the time when poetry, music, painting, sculpture, and learning, his own preoccupations, were part of daily life. In the pages of Giorgio Vasari's biographies of the Renaissance artists he found ready-made many of the characters whom he was to treat in his own poetry. It is completely fitting that in the house in Venice where he died two lines from "De Gustibus" are carved into the wall:

> "Open my heart and you will see
> Graved inside of it, 'Italy.' "

After his wife's death in 1861, Browning and his son returned to England. His greatest poem still lay ahead of him, although he had been thinking about it since 1860. In 1864 he began writing *The Ring and the Book*, and by its publication in 1868-69 it had become a monumental work, some 21,000 lines long, twice the length of *Paradise Lost*. The poem is probably the best, and greatest, example of the attempt of the Victorian poet to grapple with the long narrative poem—even though it might be argued that it is dramatic, not narrative. In twelve books Browning considers the story of a murder and the subsequent trial in seventeenth-century Italy (an account of the events of the poem and its structure will be found in the headnote to "Guiseppe Caponsacchi"). What concerns Browning most is not the actual events (few of them are in doubt after the introductory book) but how they happened and why; ultimately, one might say that he is interested in the nature of truth lying behind action and motive. The poem is told chiefly in long dramatic monologues, and Browning never wrote the form more subtly or more convincingly. Each account of the events of the story is different from every other because of the personality of the speaker, and the way in which each speaker sees the events reveals his own personality. As an elementary example, one might cite the fact that Guido can see nothing but evil in Pompilia, since he is totally malignant himself. Caponsacchi thinks of Pompilia in terms of the archetypal figures of Andromeda, rescued from the monster by Perseus, and Debra, rescued from the dragon by St. George. He makes the equation of Pompilia and the maidens, and that of Guido and the monsters, but he never thinks of himself as Perseus or St. George. Pompilia thinks of him as St. George, but in her simplicity fails to think of herself as an unspotted sacrifice, as Andromeda and Debra were meant to be. Undoubtedly, as Professor W. C. De Vane has pointed out in an article in the *Yale Review* in 1947, Browning projected into the relationship between Pompilia-Andromeda-Debra and Caponsacchi-Perseus-St. George much of his own love for Mrs. Browning and his sense of having rescued her from her dragon-father. Many of Browning's favorite themes appear in the poem: the doctrine of the fateful hour when a man's ability to act is the test of his soul; the glorification of romantic love as a duty to God; the casting aside of conventional behavior in favor of a higher duty; the advocacy of intuitive knowledge over intellectual apprehension; the dislike of formalized religion that stifles the spirit within; and many more. The poem is a bold experiment, and it works. The complexity of viewpoint is masterfully handled, there is a constant inventiveness that keeps the repeated facts from becoming boring, and the speeches are constantly individual and characteristic.

After the publication of *The Ring and the Book,* Browning was accepted as one of the great poets of his day, and his declining years, during which he continued his writing with vitality, were full of honors. He died in his son's palace in Venice, and his remains are buried in Westminster Abbey.

Of all the Victorian poets, Browning, Meredith, and Hopkins, for various reasons, probably seem most contemporary to our own day. There has been no poet between Shakespeare and the twentieth century who was so fascinated as Browning by the unspoken drives that compel man; he had no hesitation about going into the minds of evil men or even madmen, fascinated but incapable of shock at what he saw. He understood perfectly, too, that motives and personalities are mixed: the reader feels in "The Bishop Orders His Tomb," for example, that the poet is quite aware of how shocking the bishop's behavior has been, without losing a real admiration for the lust for life and beauty that the corrupt prelate feels.

Like Meredith and Hopkins, Browning is willing to sacrifice surface smoothness and comprehensibility for the re-creation of mental processes; the connections between his ideas are often more associative than intellectual, and the diction consequently becomes difficult, even contorted. The speech of his characters is colloquial, often racy, and behind his metaphors lies a constant attempt to come to terms with metaphysical problems; it is not surprising that he so admired that god of modern poetry, John Donne.

Early in our own century it was fashionable to criticize Browning for his so-called optimism, quoting out of its ironical context the song of Pippa: "God's in his heaven—/All's right with the world!" If to be optimistic is to find more pleasure than pain in life, then the word applies to Browning, but it is also responsible for the leaping vitality of his poetry, in constant awareness of the necessity to live to the fullest extent of every moment. It is no wonder that Browning's place in English poetry has always been secure.

BIBLIOGRAPHY

The standard editions are *Complete Works of Robert Browning* (ed. Charlotte Porter and Helen A. Clarke, 12 vols., Crowell, New York, 1910) and *The Works of Robert Browning* (ed. F. G. Kenyon, 10 vols., Smith, Elder, London, 1912).

Biography and Criticism:

De Vane, William Clyde, *A Browning Handbook*. Second edition. Appleton-Century-Crofts, New York, 1955.

Griffin, W. Hall, and Minchin, Harry Christopher, *The Life of Robert Browning, With Notices of His Writings, His Family, and His Friends*. Methuen, London, 1910.

King, Roma A., Jr., *The Bow and the Lyre: The Art of Robert Browning*. University of Michigan Press, Ann Arbor, 1957.

Miller, Betty, *Robert Browning: A Portrait.* John Murray, London, 1952.

Orr, Alexandra Leighton [Mrs. Sutherland Orr], *The Life and Letters of Robert Browning,* rev. F. G. Kenyon. 2 vols. Houghton Mifflin, New York, 1908.

PORPHYRIA'S LOVER

The rain set early in to-night,
  The sullen wind was soon awake,
It tore the elm-tops down for spite,
  And did its worst to vex the lake:
  I listened with heart fit to break.
When glided in Porphyria; straight
  She shut the cold out and the storm,
And kneeled and made the cheerless grate
  Blaze up, and all the cottage warm;
  Which done, she rose, and from her form   10
Withdrew the dripping cloak and shawl,
  And laid her soiled gloves by, untied
Her hat and let the damp hair fall,
  And, last, she sat down by my side
  And called me. When no voice replied,
She put my arm about her waist,
  And made her smooth white shoulder bare,
And all her yellow hair displaced,
  And, stooping, made my cheek lie there,
  And spread, o'er all, her yellow hair,   20
Murmuring how she loved me—she
  Too weak, for all her heart's endeavour,
To set its struggling passion free
  From pride, and vainer ties dissever,
  And give herself to me for ever.
But passion sometimes would prevail,
  Nor could to-night's gay feast restrain
A sudden thought of one so pale
  For love of her, and all in vain:
  So, she was come through wind and rain.   30
Be sure I looked up at her eyes
  Happy and proud; at last I knew
Porphyria worshipped me; surprise
  Made my heart swell, and still it grew

Porphyria's Lover: originally printed under the title "Madhouse Cells," which is a clue to its meaning.

While I debated what to do.
That moment she was mine, mine, fair,
   Perfectly pure and good: I found
A thing to do, and all her hair
   In one long yellow string I wound
   Three times her little throat around,   40
And strangled her. No pain felt she;
   I am quite sure she felt no pain.
As a shut bud that holds a bee,
   I warily oped her lids: again
   Laughed the blue eyes without a stain.
And I untightened next the tress
   About her neck; her cheek once more
Blushed bright beneath my burning kiss:
   I propped her head up as before,
   Only, this time my shoulder bore   50
Her head, which droops upon it still:
   The smiling rosy little head,
So glad it has its utmost will,
   That all it scorned at once is fled,
   And I, its love, am gained instead!
Porphyria's love: she guessed not how
   Her darling one wish would be heard.
And thus we sit together now,
   And all night long we have not stirred,
   And yet God has not said a word!   60

[1836]

MY LAST DUCHESS

FERRARA

That's my last Duchess painted on the wall,
Looking as if she were alive. I call
That piece a wonder, now: Frà Pandolf's hands
Worked busily a day, and there she stands.

Ferrara: Browning's model for the narrator was probably the sixteenth-century Alfonso II, fifth Duke of Ferrara and last of the great Este family.
3 *Frà:* Brother. Brother Pandolf is imaginary.

Will 't please you sit and look at her? I said
"Frà Pandolf" by design, for never read
Strangers like you that pictured countenance,
The depth and passion of its earnest glance,
But to myself they turned (since none puts by
The curtain I have drawn for you, but I)   10
And seemed as they would ask me, if they durst,
How such a glance came there; so, not the first
Are you to turn and ask thus. Sir 't was not
Her husband's presence only, called that spot
Of joy into the Duchess' cheek: perhaps
Frà Pandolf chanced to say "Her mantle laps
Over my lady's wrist too much," or "Paint
Must never hope to reproduce the faint
Half-flush that dies along her throat:" such stuff
Was courtesy, she thought, and cause enough   20
For calling up that spot of joy. She had
A heart—how shall I say?—too soon made glad,
Too easily impressed; she liked whate'er
She looked on, and her looks went everywhere.
Sir, 't was all one! My favour at her breast,
The dropping of the daylight in the West,
The bough of cherries some officious fool
Broke in the orchard for her, the white mule
She rode with round the terrace—all and each
Would draw from her alike the approving speech,   30
Or blush, at least. She thanked men,—good! but thanked
Somehow—I know not how—as if she ranked
My gift of a nine-hundred-years-old name
With anybody's gift. Who'd stoop to blame
This sort of trifling? Even had you skill
In speech—(which I have not)—to make your will
Quite clear to such an one, and say, "Just this
Or that in you disgusts me; here you miss,
Or there exceed the mark"—and if she let
Herself be lessoned so, nor plainly set   40
Her wits to yours, forsooth, and made excuse,
—E'en then would be some stooping; and I choose
Never to stoop. Oh sir, she smiled, no doubt,
Whene'er I passed her; but who passed without

Much the same smile? This grew; I gave commands;
Then all smiles stopped together. <u>There she stands</u>
<u>As if alive.</u> Will 't please you rise? We'll meet   *Killed by*
The company below, then. I repeat,   *order of Duke*
The Count your master's known munificence
Is ample warrant that no just pretence   50
Of mine for dowry will be disallowed;
Though his fair daughter's self, as I avowed
At starting, is my object. Nay, we'll go
Together down, sir. Notice Neptune, though,
Taming a sea-horse, thought a rarity,
Which Claus of Innsbruck cast in bronze for me!

[1842]

Monk revealing hatred   **SOLILOQUY OF**
for Bro. Monk.   **THE SPANISH CLOISTER**

I

Gr-r-r—there go, my heart's abhorrence!
  Water your damned flower-pots, do!
If hate killed men, Brother Lawrence,
  God's blood, would not mine kill you!
What? your myrtle-bush wants trimming?
  Oh, that rose has prior claims—
Needs its leaden vase filled brimming?
  Hell dry you up with its flames!

II

At the meal we sit together:
  Salve tibi! I must hear   10
Wise talk of the kind of weather,
  Sort of season, time of year:
Not a plenteous cork-crop: scarcely

---

45 *commands:* Browning explained they "were that she should be put to death, or he might have had her shut up in a convent."
56 *Claus:* imaginary sculptor.
10 *Salve tibi!:* greetings to you. Here and in the following italicized lines, the narrator is repeating Brother Lawrence's remarks.

Dare we hope oak-galls, I doubt:
What's the Latin name for "parsley"?
What's the Greek name for Swine's Snout?

III

Whew! We'll have our platter burnished,
   Laid with care on our own shelf!
With a fire-new spoon we're furnished,
   And a goblet for ourself,   20
Rinsed like something sacrificial
   Ere 't is fit to touch our chaps—
Marked with L. for our initial!
   (He-he! There his lily snaps!)

IV

Saint, forsooth! While brown Dolores
   Squats outside the Convent bank
With Sanchicha, telling stories,
   Steeping tresses in the tank,
Blue-black, lustrous, thick like horsehairs,
   —Can't I see his dead eye glow,   30
Bright as 't were a Barbary corsair's?
   (That is, if he'd let it show!)

V

When he finishes refection,
   Knife and fork he never lays
Cross-wise, to my recollection,
   As do I, in Jesu's praise.
I the Trinity illustrate,
   Drinking watered orange-pulp—
In three sips the Arian frustrate;
   While he drains his at one gulp.   40

VI

Oh, those melons? If he's able
   We're to have a feast! so nice!
One goes to the Abbot's table,
   All of us get each a slice.

---

[31] *Barbary corsair:* North African pirate.
[39] *Arian:* The Arian heresy denied the doctrine of the Trinity.

How go on your flowers? None double?
    Not one fruit-sort can you spy?
Strange!—And I, too, at such trouble,
    Keep them close-nipped on the sly!

VII

There's a great text in Galatians,
    Once you trip on it, entails   50
Twenty-nine distinct damnations,
    One sure, if another fails:
If I trip him just a-dying,
    Sure of heaven as sure can be,
Spin him round and send him flying
    Off to hell, a Manichee?

VIII

Or, my scrofulous French novel
    On grey paper with blunt type!
Simply glance at it, you grovel
    Hand and foot in Belial's gripe: 60
If I double down its pages
    At the woeful sixteenth print,
When he gathers his greengages,
    Ope a sieve and slip it in 't?

IX

Or, there's Satan!—one might venture
    Pledge one's soul to him, yet leave
Such a flaw in the indenture
    As he'd miss till, past retrieve,
Blasted lay that rose-acacia
    We're so proud of! *Hy, Zy, Hine.* . .   70
'St, there's Vespers! *Plena gratiâ
    Ave, Virgo!* Gr-r-r—you swine!

[1842]

---

49 *Galatians:* probably 5: 19-21 or 3: 10, which refers to the twenty-nine
curses listed in *Deuteronomy* 28: 15-46.
56 *Manichee:* believer in the Manichean heresy, which postulates the equal
division of power between the forces of good and of evil.
70 *Hy, Zy, Hine:* There is no satisfactory explanation of this passage, but it
may be the beginning of a curse upon Brother Lawrence.
71-2 *Plena . . . Virgo!:* Hail, Virgin, full of grace.

HOME-THOUGHTS, FROM ABROAD

I

Oh, to be in England
Now that April's there,
And whoever wakes in England
Sees, some morning, unaware,
That the lowest boughs and the brushwood sheaf
Round the elm-tree bole are in tiny leaf,
While the chaffinch sings on the orchard bough
In England—now!

II

And after April, when May follows,
And the whitethroat builds, and all the swallows!   10
Hark, where my blossomed pear-tree in the hedge
Leans to the field and scatters on the clover
Blossoms and dewdrops—at the bent spray's edge—
That's the wise thrush; he sings each song twice over,
Lest you should think he never could recapture
The first fine careless rapture!
And though the fields look rough with hoary dew
All will be gay when noontide wakes anew
The buttercups, the little children's dower
—Far brighter than this gaudy melon-flower!   20

[1845]

THE BISHOP ORDERS HIS TOMB AT
SAINT PRAXED'S CHURCH

Rome, 15—

Vanity, saith the preacher, vanity!
Draw round my bed: is Anselm keeping back?
Nephews—sons mine . . . ah God, I know not! Well—
She, men would have to be your mother once,

---

[1] *Vanity:* see *Ecclesiastes* 1: 2.

Old Gandolf envied me, so fair she was!
What's done is done, and she is dead beside,
Dead long ago, and I am Bishop since,
And as she died so must we die ourselves,   *death non sense*
And thence ye may perceive the world's a dream.
Life, how and what is it? As here I lie   10
In this state-chamber, dying by degrees,
Hours and long hours in the dead night, I ask
"Do I live, am I dead?" Peace, peace seems all.   *not peaceful life*
Saint Praxed's ever was the church for peace;
And so, about this tomb of mine I fought
With tooth and nail to save my niche, ye know:
—Old Gandolf cozened me, despite my care;
Shrewd was that snatch from out the corner South
He graced his carrion with, God curse the same!
Yet still my niche is not so cramped but thence   20
One sees the pulpit o' the epistle-side,
And somewhat of the choir, those silent seats,
And up into the aery dome where live
The angels, and a sunbeam's sure to lurk:

can see material splendor

And I shall fill my slab of basalt there,
And 'neath my tabernacle take my rest,
With those nine columns round me, two and two,
The odd one at my feet where Anselm stands:

is really dead to all these things

Peach-blossom marble all, the rare, the ripe
As fresh-poured red wine of a mighty pulse.   30
—Old Gandolf with his paltry onion-stone,
Put me where I may look at him! True peach,
Rosy and flawless: how I earned the prize!
Draw close: that conflagration of my church
—What then? So much was saved if aught were missed!
My sons, ye would not be my death? Go dig
The white-grape vineyard where the oil-press stood,
Drop water gently till the surface sink,
And if ye find . . . Ah God, I know not, I! . . .
Bedded in store of rotten fig-leaves soft,   40
And corded up in a tight olive-frail,

---

21 *epistle-side:* side of the altar from which the epistle is read.
26 *tabernacle:* canopy over tomb.
31 *onion-stone:* inferior marble liable to peeling.
41 *olive-frail:* olive basket.

Some lump, ah God, of *lapis lazuli*,
Big as a Jew's head cut off at the nape,
Blue as a vein o'er the Madonna's breast . . .
Sons, all have I bequeathed you, villas, all,
That brave Frascati villa with its bath,
So, let the blue lump poise between my knees,
Like God the Father's globe on both his hands
Ye worship in the Jesu Church so gay,
For Gandolf shall not choose but see and burst!   50
Swift as a weaver's shuttle fleet our years:
Man goeth to the grave, and where is he?
Did I say basalt for my slab, sons? Black—
'T was ever antique-black I meant! How else
Shall ye contrast my frieze to come beneath?
The bas-relief in bronze ye promised me,
Those Pans and Nymphs ye wot of, and perchance
Some tripod, thyrsus, with a vase or so,
The Saviour at his sermon on the mount,
Saint Praxed in a glory, and one Pan   60
Ready to twitch the Nymph's last garment off,
And Moses with the tables . . . but I know
Ye mark me not! What do they whisper thee,
Child of my bowels, Anselm? Ah, ye hope
To revel down my villas while I gasp
Bricked o'er with beggar's mouldy travertine
Which Gandolf from his tomb-top chuckles at!
Nay, boys, ye love me—all of jasper, then!
'T is jasper ye stand pledged to, lest I grieve
My bath must needs be left behind, alas!   70
One block, pure green as a pistachio-nut,
There's plenty jasper somewhere in the world—
And have I not Saint Praxed's ear to pray
Horses for ye, and brown Greek manuscripts,
And mistresses with great smooth marbly limbs?
—That's if ye carve my epitaph aright,
Choice Latin, picked phrase, Tully's every word,

[Margin annotations: *pleasure he has saved* / *in return* / *wants to outdo Gandolf* / *Pagan Subject* / *pagan worship* / *from here out doubt in sons whether give him this good stuff*]

---

[58] *tripod, thyrsus:* The tripod was associated with the oracle of Delphi, the
thyrsus with Dionysus, god of fertility. Browning suggests an incongruous
mixture of classical and Christian motifs.
[60] *glory:* aureole, halo.
[66] *travertine:* white limestone full of holes.

No gaudy ware like Gandolf's second line—
Tully, my masters? Ulpian serves his need!   *medieval*
And then how I shall lie through centuries,   *Church* 80
And hear the blessed mutter of the mass,   *mass*
And see God made and eaten all day long,
And feel the steady candle-flame, and taste
Good strong thick stupefying incense-smoke!
For as I lie here, hours of the dead night,
Dying in state and by such slow degrees,
I fold my arms as if they clasped a crook,
And stretch my feet forth straight as stone can point,
And let the bedclothes, for a mortcloth, drop
Into great laps and folds of sculptor's-work: 90
And as yon tapers dwindle, and strange thoughts
Grow, with a certain humming in my ears,
About the life before I lived this life,
And this life too, popes, cardinals and priests,
Saint Praxed at his sermon on the mount,
Your tall pale mother with her talking eyes,
And new-found agate urns as fresh as day,
And marble's language, Latin pure, discreet,
—Aha, ELUCESCEBAT quoth our friend?
No Tully, said I, Ulpian at the best!   *been evil / but* 100
Evil and brief hath been my pilgrimage.   *look what I have*
All *lapis*, all, sons! Else I give the Pope   *got*
My villas! Will ye ever eat my heart?
Ever your eyes were as a lizard's quick,
They glitter like your mother's for my soul,
Or ye would heighten my impoverished frieze,
Piece out its starved design, and fill my vase
With grapes, and add a vizor and a Term,
And to the tripod ye would tie a lynx
That in his struggle throws the thyrsus down,   110

---

79 *Tully:* Marcus Tullius Cicero, Roman orator of impeccable style. *Ulpian:*
Domitius Ulpianus, late Latin writer of deteriorated style.
87 *crook:* bishop's staff.
89 *mortcloth:* funereal pall.
95 *Saint . . . mount:* The bishop's wandering mind confuses St. Praxed and
Christ.
99 ELUCESCEBAT: he was illustrious; an example of the poor Latin on Gandolf's tomb.
108 *vizor:* mask. *Term:* pedestal with bust.
109 *lynx:* associated with Dionysus.

To comfort me on my entablature
Whereon I am to lie till I must ask
"Do I live, am I dead?" There, leave me, there!
For ye have stabbed me with ingratitude
To death—ye wish it—God, ye wish it! Stone—
Gritstone, a-crumble! Clammy squares which sweat
As if the corpse they keep were oozing through—
And no more *lapis* to delight the world!
Well, go! I bless ye. Fewer tapers there,
But in a row: and, going, turn your backs   120
—Ay, like departing altar-ministrants,
And leave me in my church, the church for peace,
That I may watch at leisure if he leers—
Old Gandolf, at me, from his onion-stone,
As still he envied me, so fair she was!

[1845]

TIME'S REVENGES

I've a Friend, over the sea;
I like him, but he loves me.
It all grew out of the books I write;
They find such favour in his sight
That he slaughters you with savage looks
Because you don't admire my books.
He does himself though,—and if some vein
Were to snap to-night in this heavy brain,
To-morrow month, if I lived to try,
Round should I just turn quietly,   10
Or out of the bedclothes stretch my hand
Till I found him, come from his foreign land
To be my nurse in this poor place,
And make my broth and wash my face
And light my fire and, all the while,
Bear with his old good-humoured smile

---

116 *Gritstone:* sandstone.
Time's Revenges: See *Twelfth Night,* V, i, 384.

That I told him "Better have kept away
Than come and kill me, night and day,
With, worse than fever throbs and shoots,
The creaking of his clumsy boots."   20
I am as sure that this he would do,
As that Saint Paul's is striking two.
And I think I rather . . . woe is me!
—Yes, rather would see him than not see,
If lifting a hand could seat him there
Before me in the empty chair
To-night, when my head aches indeed,
And I can neither think nor read
Nor make these purple fingers hold
The pen; this garret's freezing cold!   30

And I've a Lady—there he wakes,
The laughing fiend and prince of snakes
Within me, at her name, to pray
Fate send some creature in the way
Of my love for her, to be down-torn,
Upthrust and outward-borne,
So I might prove myself that sea
Of passion which I needs must be!
Call my thoughts false and my fancies quaint
And my style infirm and its figures faint,   40
All the critics say, and more blame yet,
And not one angry word you get.
But, please you, wonder I would put
My cheek beneath that lady's foot
Rather than trample under mine
The laurels of the Florentine,
And you shall see how the devil spends
A fire God gave for other ends!
I tell you, I stride up and down
This garret, crowned with love's best crown,   50
And feasted with love's perfect feast,
To think I kill for her, at least,
Body and soul and peace and fame,

---

⁴⁶ *Florentine:* Dante; the narrator thinks less of being a better poet than
Dante than he does of being with the lady, even if it were only to be stepped
upon by her.

Alike youth's end and manhood's aim,
—So is my spirit, as flesh with sin,
Filled full, eaten out and in
With the face of her, the eyes of her,
The lips, the little chin, the stir
Of shadow round her mouth; and she
—I'll tell you,—calmly would decree   60
That I should roast at a slow fire,
If that would compass her desire
And make her one whom they invite
To the famous ball to-morrow night.

There may be heaven; there must be hell;
Meantime, there is our earth here—well!

[1845]

LOVE AMONG THE RUINS

I

Where the quiet-coloured end of evening smiles
    Miles and miles
On the solitary pastures where our sheep
    Half-asleep
Tinkle homeward thro' the twilight, stray or stop
    As they crop—
Was the site once of a city great and gay,
    (So they say)
Of our country's very capital, its prince
    Ages since   10
Held his court in, gathered councils, wielding far
    Peace or war.

II

Now,—the country does not even boast a tree
    As you see,
To distinguish slopes of verdure, certain rills
    From the hills

Intersect and give a name to, (else they run
    Into one)
Where the domed and daring palace shot its spires
    Up like fires   20
O'er the hundred-gated circuit of a wall
    Bounding all,
Made of marble, men might march on nor be pressed,
    Twelve abreast.

III

And such plenty and perfection, see, of grass
    Never was!
Such a carpet as, this summer-time, o'erspreads
    And embeds
Every vestige of the city, guessed alone,
    Stock or stone—   30
Where a multitude of men breathed joy and woe
    Long ago;
Lust of glory pricked their hearts up, dread of shame
    Struck them tame;
And that glory and that shame alike, the gold
    Bought and sold.

IV

Now,—the single little turret that remains
    On the plains,
By the caper overrooted, by the gourd
    Overscored,   40
While the patching houseleek's head of blossom winks
    Through the chinks—
Marks the basement whence a tower in ancient time
    Sprang sublime,
And a burning ring, all round, the chariots traced
    As they raced,
And the monarch and his minions and his dames
    Viewed the games.

---

[39] *caper:* shrub grown for its flowers used in seasoning.
[41] *houseleek:* European herb.

v

And I know, while thus the quiet-coloured eve
    Smiles to leave   50
To their folding, all our many-tinkling fleece
    In such peace,
And the slopes and rills in undistinguished grey
    Melt away—
That a girl with eager eyes and yellow hair
    Waits me there
In the turret whence the charioteers caught soul
    For the goal,
When the king looked, where she looks now, breathless, dumb
    Till I come.   60

vi

But he looked upon the city, every side,
    Far and wide,
All the mountains topped with temples, all the glades'
    Colonnades,
All the causeys, bridges, aqueducts,—and then,
    All the men!
When I do come, she will speak not, she will stand,
    Either hand
On my shoulder, give her eyes the first embrace
    Of my face,   70
Ere we rush, ere we extinguish sight and speech
    Each on each.

vii

In one year they sent a million fighters forth
    South and North,
And they built their gods a brazen pillar high
    As the sky,
Yet reserved a thousand chariots in full force—
    Gold, of course.
Oh heart! oh blood that freezes, blood that burns!
    Earth's returns   80

---

65 *causeys:* causeways.

For whole centuries of folly, noise and sin!
   Shut them in,
With their triumphs and their glories and the rest!
   Love is best.

[1855]

FRA LIPPO LIPPI

I am poor brother Lippo, by your leave!
You need not clap your torches to my face.
Zooks, what's to blame? you think you see a monk!
What, 't is past midnight, and you go the rounds,
And here you catch me at an alley's end
Where sportive ladies leave their doors ajar?
The Carmine's my cloister: hunt it up,
Do,—harry out, if you must show your zeal,
Whatever rat, there, haps on his wrong hole,
And nip each softling of a wee white mouse,   10
Weke, weke, that's crept to keep him company!
Aha, you know your betters! Then, you'll take
Your hand away that's fiddling on my throat,
And please to know me likewise. Who am I?
Why, one, sir, who is lodging with a friend
Three streets off—he's a certain . . . how d'ye call?
Master—a . . . Cosimo of the Medici,
I' the house that caps the corner. Boh! you were best!
Remember and tell me, the day you're hanged,
How you affected such a gullet's-gripe!   20
But you, sir, it concerns you that your knaves
Pick up a manner nor discredit you:
Zooks, are we pilchards, that they sweep the streets
And count fair prize what comes into their net?
He's Judas to a tittle, that man is! *artist's perception*

Fra Lippo Lippi: fifteenth-century Carmelite monk and painter. The scene
of the poem is a sidestreet of Florence where Lippo is questioned by the civil
guards who have stopped him late at night when he is absent from the palace
of Cosimo de' Medici, his patron and virtual ruler of the city.
23 *pilchards:* common fish.
25 *that man:* one of the guards.

Just such a face! Why, sir, you make amends.
Lord, I'm not angry! Bid your hangdogs go
Drink out this quarter-florin to the health
Of the munificent House that harbours me
(And many more beside, lads! more beside!)   30
And all's come square again. I'd like his face—
His, elbowing on his comrade in the door
With the pike and lantern,—for the slave that holds
John Baptist's head a-dangle by the hair
With one hand ("Look you, now," as who should say)
And his weapon in the other, yet unwiped!
It's not your chance to have a bit of chalk,
A wood-coal or the like? or you should see!
Yes, I'm the painter, since you style me so.
What, brother Lippo's doings, up and down,
You know them and they take you? like enough!
I saw the proper twinkle in your eye—
'Tell you, I liked your looks at very first.
Let's sit and set things straight now, hip to haunch.
Here's spring come, and the nights one makes up bands
To roam the town and sing out carnival,
And I've been three weeks shut within my mew,
A-painting for the great man, saints and saints
And saints again. I could not paint all night—
Ouf! I leaned out of window for fresh air.   50
There came a hurry of feet and little feet,
A sweep of lute-strings, laughs, and whifts of song,—
Flower o' the broom,
Take away love, and our earth is a tomb!
Flower o' the quince,
I let Lisa go, and what good in life since?
Flower o' the thyme—and so on. Round they went.
Scarce had they turned the corner when a titter
Like the skipping of rabbits by moonlight,—three slim shapes,
And a face that looked up . . . zooks, sir, flesh and blood,   60
That's all I'm made of! Into shreds it went,
Curtain and counterpane and coverlet,
All the bed-furniture—a dozen knots,
There was a ladder! Down I let myself,

---

[53] *Flower o' the broom:* This and the following italicized sections are portions of *stornelli*, improvised flower-songs.

Hands and feet, scrambling somehow, and so dropped,
And after them. I came up with the fun
Hard by Saint Laurence, hail fellow, well met,—
Flower o' the rose,
If I've been merry, what matter who knows?
And so as I was stealing back again   70
To get to bed and have a bit of sleep
Ere I rise up to-morrow and go work
On Jerome knocking at his poor old breast
With his great round stone to subdue the flesh,
You snap me of the sudden. Ah, I see!
Though your eye twinkles still, you shake your head—
Mine's shaved—a monk, you say—the sting's in that!
If Master Cosimo announced himself,
Mum's the word naturally; but a monk!
Come, what am I a beast for? tell us, now!   80
I was a baby when my mother died
And father died and left me in the street.
I starved there, God knows how, a year or two
On fig-skins, melon-parings, rinds and shucks,
Refuse and rubbish. One fine frosty day,
My stomach being empty as your hat,
The wind doubled me up and down I went.
Old Aunt Lapaccia trussed me with one hand,
(Its fellow was a stinger as I knew)
And so along the wall, over the bridge,   90
By the straight cut to the convent. Six words there,
While I stood munching my first bread that month:
"So, boy, you're minded," quoth the good fat father
Wiping his own mouth, 't was refection-time,—
"To quit this very miserable world?
Will you renounce" . . . "the mouthful of bread?" thought I;
By no means! Brief, they made a monk of me;
I did renounce the world, its pride and greed,
Palace, farm, villa, shop and banking-house,
Trash, such as these poor devils of Medici   100
Have given their hearts to—all at eight years old.

---

⁶⁷ *Saint Laurence:* church of San Lorenzo.
⁷³ *Jerome:* The ascetic saint of the fifth century was one of the Church Fathers.
⁸⁸ *trussed:* held up.

Well, sir, I found in time, you may be sure,
'T was not for nothing—the good bellyful,
The warm serge and the rope that goes all round,
And day-long blessed idleness beside!
"Let's see what the urchin's fit for"—that came next.
Not overmuch their way, I must confess.
Such a to-do! They tried me with their books:
Lord, they'd have taught me Latin in pure waste!
Flower o' the clove,   110
All the Latin I construe is, "amo" I love!
But, mind you, when a boy starves in the streets
Eight years together, as my fortune was,
Watching folk's faces to know who will fling
The bit of half-stripped grape-bunch he desires,
And who will curse or kick him for his pains,—
Which gentleman processional and fine,
Holding a candle to the Sacrament,
Will wink and let him lift a plate and catch
The droppings of the wax to sell again,   120
Or holla for the Eight and have him whipped,—
How say I?—nay, which dog bites, which lets drop
His bone from the heap of offal in the street,—
Why, soul and sense of him grow sharp alike,   *sharp observer*
He learns the look of things, and none the less   *& judge of character*
For admonition from the hunger-pinch.
I had a store of such remarks, be sure,
Which, after I found leisure, turned to use.
I drew men's faces on my copy-books,
Scrawled them within the antiphonary's marge,   130
Joined legs and arms to the long music-notes,
Found eyes and nose and chin for A's and B's,
And made a string of pictures of the world
Betwixt the ins and outs of verb and noun,
On the wall, the bench, the door. The monks looked black.
"Nay," quoth the Prior, "turn him out, d' ye say?
In no wise. Lose a crow and catch a lark.
What if at last we get our man of parts,   *corruption of*
We Carmelites, like those Camaldolese   *monastery*

---

121 *the Eight:* Florentine magistrates.
130 *antiphonary's marge:* margin of choir-book.
139 *Camaldolese:* monks of the convent of the Camaldoli.

And Preaching Friars, to do our church up fine   140
And put the front on it that ought to be!"
And hereupon he bade me daub away.
Thank you! my head being crammed, the walls a blank,
Never was such prompt disemburdening.
First, every sort of monk, the black and white,
I drew them, fat and lean: then, folk at church,
From good old gossips waiting to confess
Their cribs of barrel-droppings, candle-ends,—
To the breathless fellow at the altar-foot,
Fresh from his murder, safe and sitting there   150
With the little children round him in a row
Of admiration, half for his beard and half
For that white anger of his victim's son
Shaking a fist at him with one fierce arm,
Signing himself with the other because of Christ
(Whose sad face on the cross sees only this
After the passion of a thousand years)
Till some poor girl, her apron o'er her head,
(Which the intense eyes looked through) came at eve
On tiptoe, said a word, dropped in a loaf,   160
Her pair of earrings and a bunch of flowers
(The brute took growling), prayed, and so was gone.
I painted all, then cried " 'T is ask and have;
Choose, for more's ready!"—laid the ladder flat,
And showed my covered bit of cloister-wall.
The monks closed in a circle and praised loud
Till checked, taught what to see and not to see,
Being simple bodies,—"That's the very man!
Look at the boy who stoops to pat the dog!
That woman's like the Prior's niece who comes   170
To care about his asthma: it's the life!"
But there my triumph's straw-fire flared and funked;
Their betters took their turn to see and say:
The Prior and the learned pulled a face
And stopped all that in no time. "How? what's here?
Quite from the mark of painting, bless us all!

---

140 *Preaching Friars:* Dominicans.
148 *cribs:* small thefts.
150 *safe:* because of having taken sanctuary in the church.
172 *funked:* began to smoke.

Faces, arms, legs and bodies like the true
As much as pea and pea! it's devil's-game!
Your business is not to catch men with show,
With homage to the perishable clay,   180
But lift them over it, ignore it all,
Make them forget there's such a thing as flesh.
Your business is to paint the souls of men—
Man's soul, and it's a fire, smoke . . . no, it's not . . .
It's vapour done up like a new-born babe—
(In that shape when you die it leaves your mouth)
It's . . . well, what matters talking, it's the soul!
Give us no more of body than shows soul!
Here's Giotto, with his Saint a-praising God,
That sets us praising,—why not stop with him?   190
Why put all thoughts of praise out of our head
With wonder at lines, colours, and what not?
Paint the soul, never mind the legs and arms!
Rub all out, try at it a second time.
Oh, that white smallish female with the breasts,
She's just my niece . . . Herodias, I would say,—
Who went and danced and got men's heads cut off!
Have it all out!" Now, is this sense, I ask?
A fine way to paint soul, by painting body
So ill, the eye can't stop there, must go further
And can't fare worse! Thus, yellow does for white
When what you put for yellow's simply black,
And any sort of meaning looks intense
When all beside itself means and looks nought.
Why can't a painter lift each foot in turn,
Left foot and right foot, go a double step,
Make his flesh liker and his soul more like,
Both in their order? Take the prettiest face,
The Prior's niece . . . patron-saint—is it so pretty
You can't discover if it means hope, fear,   210
Sorrow or joy? won't beauty go with these?
Suppose I've made her eyes all right and blue,
Can't I take breath and try to add life's flash,
And then add soul and heighten them threefold?

---

189 *Giotto:* Giotto di Bondone, medieval painter of hieratic spirituality.
196 *Herodias:* It was Salome, daughter of Herodias, who received the head
of John the Baptist for her dancing.

Or say there's beauty with no soul at all— *worshiping divine*
(I never saw it—put the case the same—) *if get pleasure*
If you get simple beauty and nought else, *from the beautiful*
You get about the best thing God invents:
That's somewhat: and you'll find the soul you have missed,
Within yourself, when you return him thanks.   220
"Rub all out!" Well, well, there's my life, in short,
And so the thing has gone on ever since.
I'm grown a man no doubt, I've broken bounds:
You should not take a fellow eight years old
And make him swear to never kiss the girls.
I'm my own master, paint now as I please—
Having a friend, you see, in the Corner-house!
Lord, it's fast holding by the rings in front—
Those great rings serve more purposes than just
To paint a flag in, or tie up a horse!   230
And yet the old schooling sticks, the old grave eyes
Are peeping o'er my shoulder as I work,
The heads shake still—"It's art's decline, my son!
You're not of the true painters, great and old;   *other better artists*
Brother Angelico's the man, you'll find;
Brother Lorenzo stands his single peer:
Fag on at flesh, you'll never make the third!"
Flower o' the pine,
You keep your mistr . . . manners, and I'll stick to mine!
I'm not the third, then: bless us, they must know!   240
Don't you think they're the likeliest to know,
They with their Latin? So, I swallow my rage,
Clench my teeth, suck my lips in tight, and paint
To please them—sometimes do and sometimes don't;
For, doing most, there's pretty sure to come
A turn, some warm eve finds me at my saints—
A laugh, a cry, the business of the world—
(*Flower o' the peach,*
Death for us all, and his own life for each!)
And my whole soul revolves, the cup runs over,   250
The world and life's too big to pass for a dream,

---

228 *rings:* Lippo uses the decorative rings fastened in the palace wall for climbing in and out of his window.
235-6 *Angelico . . . Lorenzo:* Fra Angelico and Lorenzo Monaco were monastic painters of the generation before Lippo's.

And I do these wild things in sheer despite,
And play the fooleries you catch me at,
In pure rage! The old mill-horse, out at grass
After hard years, throws up his stiff heels so,
Although the miller does not preach to him
The only good of grass is to make chaff.
What would men have? Do they like grass or no—
May they or mayn't they? all I want's the thing
Settled for ever one way. As it is,   260
You tell too many lies and hurt yourself:
You don't like what you only like too much,
You do like what, if given you at your word,
You find abundantly detestable.
For me, I think I speak as I was taught;
I always see the garden and God there
A-making man's wife: and, my lesson learned,
The value and significance of flesh,
I can't unlearn ten minutes afterwards.

    You understand me: I'm a beast, I know.   270
But see, now—why, I see as certainly
As that the morning-star's about to shine,
What will hap some day. We've a youngster here
Comes to our convent, studies what I do,
Slouches and stares and lets no atom drop:
His name is Guidi—he'll not mind the monks—
They call him Hulking Tom, he lets them talk—
He picks my practice up—he'll paint apace,
I hope so—though I never live so long,
I know what's sure to follow. You be judged!   280
You speak no Latin more than I, belike;
However, you're my man, you've seen the world
—The beauty and the wonder and the power,
The shapes of things, their colours, lights and shades,
Changes, surprises,—and God made it all!
—For what? Do you feel thankful, ay or no,
For this fair town's face, yonder river's line,
The mountain round it and the sky above,
Much more the figures of man, woman, child,

---

[276] *Guidi:* Tommaso Guido, known as Masaccio, was probably Lippo's master, not his pupil.

These are the frame to? What's it all about?   290
To be passed over, despised? or dwelt upon,
Wondered at? oh, this last of course!—you say.
But why not do as well as say,—paint these
Just as they are, careless what comes of it?
God's works—paint anyone, and count it crime
To let a truth slip. Don't object, "His works
Are here already; nature is complete:
Suppose you reproduce her—(which you can't)
There's no advantage! you must beat her, then."
For, don't you mark? we're made so that we love   300
First when we see them painted, things we have passed
Perhaps a hundred times nor cared to see;
And so they are better, painted—better to us,
Which is the same thing. Art was given for that;
God uses us to help each other so,
Lending our minds out. Have you noticed, now,
Your cullion's hanging face? A bit of chalk,
And trust me but you should, though! How much more,
If I drew higher things with the same truth!
That were to take the Prior's pulpit-place,   310
Interpret God to all of you! Oh, oh,
It makes me mad to see what men shall do
And we in our graves! This world's no blot for us,
Nor blank; it means intensely, and means good:
To find its meaning is my meat and drink.
"Ay, but you don't so instigate to prayer!"
Strikes in the Prior: "when your meaning's plain
It does not say to folk—remember matins,
Or, mind you fast next Friday!" Why, for this
What need of art at all? A skull and bones,   320
Two bits of stick nailed crosswise, or, what's best,
A bell to chime the hour with, does as well.
I painted a Saint Laurence six months since
At Prato, splashed the fresco in fine style:
"How looks my painting, now the scaffold's down?"
I ask a brother: "Hugely," he returns—
"Already not one phiz of your three slaves
Who turn the Deacon off his toasted side,

---

323 *Saint Laurence:* who was martyred by roasting on a gridiron.
327 *phiz:* face.

But's scratched and prodded to our heart's content,
The pious people have so eased their own   330
With coming to say prayers there in a rage:
We get on fast to see the bricks beneath.
Expect another job this time next year,
For pity and religion grow i' the crowd—
Your painting serves its purpose!" Hang the fools!

—That is—you'll not mistake an idle word
Spoke in a huff by a poor monk, God wot,
Tasting the air this spicy night which turns
The unaccustomed head like Chianti wine!
Oh, the church knows! don't misreport me, now!   340
It's natural a poor monk out of bounds
Should have his apt word to excuse himself:
And hearken how I plot to make amends.
I have bethought me: I shall paint a piece
. . . There's for you! Give me six months, then go, see
Something in Sant' Ambrogio's! Bless the nuns!
They want a cast o' my office. I shall paint
God in the midst, Madonna and her babe,
Ringed by a bowery flowery angel-brood,
Lilies and vestments and white faces, sweet   350
As puff on puff of grated orris-root
When ladies crowd to Church at midsummer.
And then i' the front, of course a saint or two—
Saint John, because he saves the Florentines,
Saint Ambrose, who puts down in black and white
The convent's friends and gives them a long day,
And Job, I must have him there past mistake,
The man of Uz (and Us without the z,
Painters who need his patience). Well, all these
Secured at their devotions, up shall come   360
Out of a corner when you least expect,
As one by a dark stair into a great light,
Music and talking, who but Lippo! I!—

---

361 *corner:* In the corner of Lippo's "Coronation of the Virgin" is a figure
formerly supposed to be a self-portrait of Lippo but now believed to be of his
benefactor, another priest. The scroll in the picture has part of the Latin
phrase, *"Iste perfecit opus"* (l. 377), which may be translated as "This is he
who caused the work to be done."

paint self into picture of angelic hosts [handwritten marginal note]

Mazed, motionless and moonstruck—I'm the man!
Back I shrink—what is this I see and hear?
I, caught up with my monk's-things by mistake,
My old serge gown and rope that goes all round,
I, in this presence, this pure company!
Where's a hole, where's a corner for escape?
Then steps a sweet angelic slip of a th_ng   370
Forward, puts out a soft palm—"Not so fast!"
—Addresses the celestial presence, "nay—

God made all [handwritten marginal note]

He made you and devised you, after all,
Though he's none of you! Could Saint John there draw—
His camel-hair make up a painting-brush?
We come to brother Lippo for all that,

He who caused work to be done [handwritten marginal note]

Iste perfecit opus! So, all smile—
I shuffle sideways with my blushing face
Under the cover of a hundred wings

sensuous [handwritten marginal note]

Thrown like a spread of kirtles when you're gay   380
And play hot cockles, all the doors being shut,
Till, wholly unexpected, in there pops
The hothead husband! Thus I scuttle off
To some safe bench behind, not letting go
The palm of her, the little lily thing
That spoke the good word for me in the nick,
Like the Prior's niece . . . Saint Lucy, I would say.
And so all's saved for me, and for the church
A pretty picture gained. Go, six months hence!
Your hand, sir, and good-bye: no lights, no lights!   390
The street's hushed, and I know my own way back,
Don't fear me! There's the grey beginning. Zooks!

[1855]

---

380 *kirtles:* skirts.
381 *hot cockles:* children's game like blindman's buff; the game Lippo is sug-
gesting is not for children.

A TOCCATA OF GALUPPI'S

I

Oh, Galuppi, Baldassaro, this is very sad to find!
I can hardly misconceive you; it would prove me deaf and
blind;
But although I take your meaning, 't is with such a heavy
mind!

II

Here you come with your old music, and here's all the good
it brings.
What, they lived once thus at Venice where the merchants
were the kings,
Where Saint Mark's is, where the Doges used to wed the
sea with rings?

III

Ay, because the sea's the street there; and 't is arched by . . .
what you call
. . . Shylock's bridge with houses on it, where they kept
the carnival:
I was never out of England—it's as if I saw it all.

IV

Did young people take their pleasure when the sea was
warm in May?   10
Balls and masks begun at midnight, burning ever to mid-
day,
When they made up fresh adventures for the morrow, do
you say?

A Toccata of Galuppi's: Baldassare Galuppi was a Venetian composer of the
eighteenth century. A toccata is an improvisation designed to display the skill
of the performer. The speaker of this poem is a nineteenth-century English
scientist who is playing the toccata.
6 *rings:* Each year the rulers of Venice used to throw a ring into the sea to
indicate the marriage of city and sea.
8 *Shylock's bridge:* the Rialto.

V

Was a lady such a lady, cheeks so round and lips so red,—
On her neck the small face buoyant, like a bell-flower on
  its bed,
O'er the breast's superb abundance where a man might
  base his head?

VI

Well, and it was graceful of them—they'd break talk off
  and afford
—She, to bite her mask's black velvet—he, to finger on his
  sword,
While you sat and played Toccatas, stately at the clavichord?

VII

What? Those lesser thirds so plaintive, sixths diminished,
  sigh on sigh,
Told them something? Those suspensions, those solutions—
  "Must we die?"   20
Those commiserating sevenths—"Life might last! we can
  but try!"

VIII

"Were you happy?"—"Yes."—"And are you still as happy?"
  —"Yes. And you?"
—"Then, more kisses!"—"Did *I* stop them, when a million
  seemed so few?"
Hark, the dominant's persistence till it must be answered
  to!

IX

So, an octave struck the answer. Oh, they praised you, I
  dare say!
"Brave Galuppi! that was music! good alike at grave and
  gay!
I can always leave off talking when I hear a master play!"

X

Then they left you for their pleasure: till in due time, one
  by one,

Some with lives that came to nothing, some with deeds as
   well undone,
Death stepped tacitly and took them where they never
   see the sun.   30

XI

But when I sit down to reason, think to take my stand nor
   swerve,
While I triumph o'er a secret wrung from nature's close
   reserve,
In you come with your cold music till I creep thro' every
   nerve.

XII

Yes, you, like a ghostly cricket, creaking where a house was
   burned:
"Dust and ashes, dead and done with, Venice spent what
   Venice earned.
The soul, doubtless, is immortal—where a soul can be
   discerned.

XIII

"Yours for instance: you know physics, something of
   geology,
Mathematics are your pastime; souls shall rise in their
   degree;
Butterflies may dread extinction,—you'll not die, it cannot
   be!

XIV

"As for Venice and her people, merely born to bloom and
   drop,   40
Here on earth they bore their fruitage, mirth and folly were
   the crop:
What of soul was left, I wonder, when the kissing had to
   stop?

XV

"Dust and ashes!" So you creak it, and I want the heart to
   scold.

---

[43] *want*: lack.

Dear dead women, with such hair, too—what's become of
all the gold
Used to hang and brush their bosoms? I feel chilly and
grown old.

[1855]

AN EPISTLE

Containing the Strange Medical Experience of Karshish,
The Arab Physician

Karshish, the picker-up of learning's crumbs,
The not-incurious in God's handiwork
(This man's-flesh he hath admirably made,
Blown like a bubble, kneaded like a paste,
To coop up and keep down on earth a space
That puff of vapour from his mouth, man's soul)
—To Abib, all-sagacious in our art,
Breeder in me of what poor skill I boast,
Like me inquisitive how pricks and cracks
Befall the flesh through too much stress and strain,   10
Whereby the wily vapour fain would slip
Back and rejoin its source before the term,—
And aptest in contrivance (under God)
To baffle it by deftly stopping such:—
The vagrant Scholar to his Sage at home
Sends greeting (health and knowledge, fame with peace)
Three samples of true snakestone—rarer still,
One of the other sort, the melon-shaped,
(But fitter, pounded fine, for charms than drugs)
And writeth now the twenty-second time.   20

My journeyings were brought to Jericho:
Thus I resume. Who studious in our art
Shall count a little labour unrepaid?
I have shed sweat enough, left flesh and bone
On many a flinty furlong of this land.

---

17 *snakestone:* for curing snakebite.

Also, the country-side is all on fire
With rumours of a marching hitherward:
Some say Vespasian cometh, some, his son.
A black lynx snarled and pricked a tufted ear;
Lust of my blood inflamed his yellow balls: 30
I cried and threw my staff and he was gone.
Twice have the robbers stripped and beaten me,
And once a town declared me for a spy;
But at the end, I reach Jerusalem,
Since this poor covert where I pass the night,
This Bethany, lies scarce the distance thence
A man with plague-sores at the third degree
Runs till he drops down dead. Thou laughest here!
'Sooth, it elates me, thus reposed and safe,
To void the stuffing of my travel-scrip   40
And share with thee whatever Jewry yields.
A viscid choler is observable
In tertians, I was nearly bold to say;
And falling-sickness hath a happier cure
Than our school wots of: there's a spider here
Weaves no web, watches on the ledge of tombs,
Sprinkled with mottles on an ash-grey back;
Take five and drop them . . . but who knows his mind,
The Syrian runagate I trust this to?   *not sure Syrian will*
His service payeth me a sublimate   *deliv not*   50
Blown up his nose to help the ailing eye.
Best wait: I reach Jerusalem at morn,
There set in order my experiences,
Gather what most deserves, and give thee all—
Or I might add, Judæa's gum-tragacanth
Scales off in purer flakes, shines clearer-grained,
Cracks 'twixt the pestle and the porphyry,
In fine exceeds our produce. Scalp-disease

---

28 *Vespasian . . . son:* The Roman emperor invaded Palestine in A.D. 66,
his son Titus in A.D. 70.
36 *Bethany:* where lived Lazarus, whom Christ raised from the dead (*John,*
11).
43 *tertians:* fevers recurring every third day.
44 *falling-sickness:* epilepsy.
49 *runagate:* renegade.
50 *sublimate:* mercury powder used as medicine.
55 *gum-tragacanth:* medicinal gum.
57 *porphyry:* mortar made of porphyry.

Confounds me, crossing so with leprosy—
Thou hadst admired one sort I gained at Zoar—   60
But zeal outruns discretion. Here I end.

compelled to continue.

    Yet stay: my Syrian blinketh gratefully,
Protesteth his devotion is my price—
Suppose I write what harms not, though he steal?
I half resolve to tell thee, yet I blush,
What set me off a-writing first of all.
An itch I had, a sting to write, a tang!
For, be it this town's barrenness—or else
The Man had something in the look of him—
His case has struck me far more than 't is worth.   70
So, pardon if—(lest presently I lose
In the great press of novelty at hand
The care and pains this somehow stole from me)
I bid thee take the thing while fresh in mind,
Almost in sight—for, wilt thou have the truth?
The very man is gone from me but now,
Whose ailment is the subject of discourse.
Thus then, and let thy better wit help all!

result of exam of Lazarus

'T is but a case of mania—subinduced
By epilepsy, at the turning-point   80
Of trance prolonged unduly some three days:
When, by the exhibition of some drug
Or spell, exorcization, stroke of art
Unknown to me and which 't were well to know,
The evil thing out-breaking all at once
Left the man whole and sound of body indeed,—
But, flinging (so to speak) life's gates too wide,
Making a clear house of it too suddenly,

Lazarus had gl impse of heaven, value / are changed

The first conceit that entered might inscribe
Whatever it was minded on the wall   90
So plainly at that vantage, as it were,
(First come, first served) that nothing subsequent
Attaineth to erase those fancy-scrawls
The just-returned and new-established soul
Hath gotten now so thoroughly by heart
That henceforth she will read or these or none.
And first—the man's own firm conviction rests

That he was dead (in fact they buried him)
—That he was dead and then restored to life
By a Nazarene physician of his tribe: 100
—'Sayeth, the same bade "Rise," and he did rise.
"Such cases are diurnal," thou wilt cry.
Not so this figment!—not, that such a fume,
Instead of giving way to time and health,
Should eat itself into the life of life,
As saffron tingeth flesh, blood, bones and all!
For see, how he takes up the after-life.
The man—it is one Lazarus a Jew,
Sanguine, proportioned, fifty years of age,
The body's habit wholly laudable,   110
As much, indeed, beyond the common health
As he were made and put aside to show.
Think, could we penetrate by any drug
And bathe the wearied soul and worried flesh,
And bring it clear and fair, by three days' sleep!
Whence has the man the balm that brightens all?
This grown man eyes the world now like a child.
Some elders of his tribe, I should premise,
Led in their friend, obedient as a sheep,
To bear my inquisition. While they spoke,   120
Now sharply, now with sorrow,—told the case,—
He listened not except I spoke to him,
But folded his two hands and let them talk,
Watching the flies that buzzed: and yet no fool.
And that's a sample how his years must go.
Look, if a beggar, in fixed middle-life,
Should find a treasure,—can he use the same
With straitened habits and with tastes starved small,
And take at once to his impoverished brain
The sudden element that changes things,   130
That sets the undreamed-of rapture at his hand
And puts the cheap old joy in the scorned dust?
Is he not such an one as moves to mirth—
Warily parsimonious, when no need,
Wasteful as drunkenness at undue times?
All prudent counsel as to what befits

---

102 *diurnal:* everyday, common.
103 *fume:* hallucination.

The golden mean, is lost on such an one:
The man's fantastic will is the man's law.
So here—we call the treasure knowledge, say,
Increased beyond the fleshly faculty—   140
Heaven opened to a soul while yet on earth,
Earth forced on a soul's use while seeing heaven:
The man is witless of the size, the sum,
The value in proportion of all things,
Or whether it be little or be much.
Discourse to him of prodigious armaments
Assembled to besiege his city now,
And of the passing of a mule with gourds—
'T is one! Then take it on the other side,
Speak of some trifling fact,—he will gaze rapt   150
With stupor at its very littleness,
(Far as I see) as if in that indeed
He caught prodigious import, whole results;
And so will turn to us the bystanders
In ever the same stupor (note this point)
That we too see not with his opened eyes.
Wonder and doubt come wrongly into play,
Preposterously, at cross purposes.
Should his child sicken unto death,—why, look
For scarce abatement of his cheerfulness,   160
Or pretermission of the daily craft!
While a word, gesture, glance from that same child
At play or in the school or laid asleep,
Will startle him to an agony of fear,
Exasperation, just as like. Demand
The reason why—"'t is but a word," object—
"A gesture"—he regards thee as our lord,
Who lived there in the pyramid alone,
Looked at us (dost thou mind?) when, being young,
We both would unadvisedly recite   170
Some charm's beginning, from that book of his,
Able to bid the sun throb wide and burst
All into stars, as suns grown old are wont.
Thou and the child have each a veil alike
Thrown o'er your heads, from under which ye both

---

161 *pretermission:* interruption.

Stretch your blind hands and trifle with a match
Over a mine of Greek fire, did ye know!
He holds on firmly to some thread of life—
(It is the life to lead perforcedly)
Which runs across some vast distracting orb   180
Of glory on either side that meagre thread,
Which, conscious of, he must not enter yet—
The spiritual life around the earthly life:
The law of that is known to him as this,
His heart and brain move there, his feet stay here.
So is the man perplext with impulses
Sudden to start off crosswise, not straight on,
Proclaiming what is right and wrong across,
And not along, this black thread through the blaze—
"It should be" baulked by "here it cannot be."   190
And oft the man's soul springs into his face
As if he saw again and heard again
His sage that bade him "Rise" and he did rise.
Something, a word, a tick o' the blood within
Admonishes: then back he sinks at once
To ashes, who was very fire before,
In sedulous recurrence to his trade
Whereby he earneth him the daily bread;
And studiously the humbler for that pride,
Professedly the faultier that he knows   200
God's secret, while he holds the thread of life.
Indeed the especial marking of the man
Is prone submission to the heavenly will—
Seeing it, what it is, and why it is.
'Sayeth, he will wait patient to the last
For that same death which must restore his being
To equilibrium, body loosening soul
Divorced even now by premature full growth:
He will live, nay, it pleaseth him to live
So long as God please, and just how God please.   210
He even seeketh not to please God more
(Which meaneth, otherwise) than as God please.
Hence, I perceive not he affects to preach

Marginalia (handwritten): achieve vision of ultimate reward, not fit to live here

---

174-7 *Thou and the child . . . Greek fire:* i.e., man is like a child who has his eyes veiled and unwittingly holds a match over a mine of Greek fire, an explosive substance.

The doctrine of his sect whate'er it be,
Make proselytes as madmen thirst to do:
How can he give his neighbour the real ground,
His own conviction? Ardent as he is—
Call his great truth a lie, why, still the old
"Be it as God please" reassureth him.
I probed the sore as thy disciple should: 220
"How, beast," said I, "this stolid carelessness
Sufficeth thee, when Rome is on her march
To stamp out like a little spark thy town,
Thy tribe, thy crazy tale and thee at once?"
He merely looked with his large eyes on me.
The man is apathetic, you deduce?
Contrariwise, he loves both old and young,
Able and weak, affects the very brutes
And birds—how say I? flowers of the field—
As a wise workman recognizes tools   230
In a master's workshop, loving what they make.
Thus is the man as harmless as a lamb:
Only impatient, let him do his best,
At ignorance and carelessness and sin—
An indignation which is promptly curbed:
As when in certain travel I have feigned
To be an ignoramus in our art
According to some preconceived design,
And happed to hear the land's practitioners,
Steeped in conceit sublimed by ignorance,   240
Prattle fantastically on disease,
Its cause and cure—and I must hold my peace!

Thou wilt object—Why have I not ere this
Sought out the sage himself, the Nazarene
Who wrought this cure, inquiring at the source,
Conferring with the frankness that befits?
Alas! it grieveth me, the learned leech
Perished in a tumult many years ago,
Accused,—our learning's fate,—of wizardry,
Rebellion, to the setting up a rule   250
And creed prodigious as described to me.
His death, which happened when the earthquake fell

---

252 *earthquake:* at the time of Christ's crucifixion.

(Prefiguring, as soon appeared, the loss
To occult learning in our lord the sage
Who lived there in the pyramid alone)
Was wrought by the mad people—that's their wont!
On vain recourse, as I conjecture it,
To his tried virtue, for miraculous help—
How could he stop the earthquake? That's their way!
The other imputations must be lies: 260
But take one, though I loathe to give it thee,
In mere respect for any good man's fame.
(And after all, our patient Lazarus
Is stark mad; should we count on what he says?
Perhaps not: though in writing to a leech
'T is well to keep back nothing of a case.)
This man so cured regards the curer, then,
As—God forgive me! who but God himself,
Creator and sustainer of the world,
That came and dwelt in flesh on it awhile!   270
—'Sayeth that such an one was born and lived,
Taught, healed the sick, broke bread at his own house,
Then died, with Lazarus by, for aught I know,
And yet was . . . what I said nor choose repeat,
And must have so avouched himself, in fact,
In hearing of this very Lazarus
Who saith—but why all this of what he saith?
Why write of trivial matters, things of price
Calling at every moment for remark?
I noticed on the margin of a pool   280
Blue-flowering borage, the Aleppo sort,
Aboundeth, very nitrous. It is strange!

Thy pardon for this long and tedious case,
Which, now that I review it, needs must seem
Unduly dwelt on, prolixly set forth!
Nor I myself discern in what is writ
Good cause for the peculiar interest
And awe indeed this man has touched me with.
Perhaps the journey's end, the weariness
Had wrought upon me first. I met him thus: 290
I crossed a ridge of short sharp broken hills
Like an old lion's cheek teeth. Out there came

A moon made like a face with certain spots
  Multiform, manifold and menacing:
Then a wind rose behind me. So we met
In this old sleepy town at unaware,
The man and I. I send thee what is writ.
Regard it as a chance, a matter risked
To this ambiguous Syrian—he may lose,
Or steal, or give it thee with equal good.   300
Jerusalem's repose shall make amends
For time this letter wastes, thy time and mine;
Till when, once more thy pardon and farewell!

The very God! think, Abib; dost thou think?
So, the All-Great, were the All-Loving too—
So, through the thunder comes a human voice
Saying, "O heart I made, a heart beats here!
Face, my hands fashioned, see it in myself!
Thou hast no power nor mayst conceive of mine,
But love I gave thee, with myself to love,   310
And thou must love me who have died for thee!"
The madman saith He said so: it is strange.

[1855]

"CHILDE ROLAND TO
THE DARK TOWER CAME"

See Edgar's Song in LEAR

I

My first thought was, he lied in every word,
  That hoary cripple, with malicious eye
  Askance to watch the working of his lie
On mine, and mouth scarce able to afford
Suppression of the glee, that pursed and scored
  Its edge, at one more victim gained thereby.

Childe: son of a knight, not yet knighted himself.
Lear: III, iv, 173. Shakespeare gives no hint of the phantasmagoric, allegorical quest that Browning makes of the line.

II

What else should he be set for, with his staff?
    What, save to waylay with his lies, ensnare
    All travellers who might find him posted there,
And ask the road? I guessed what skull-like laugh   10
Would break, what crutch 'gin write my epitaph
    For pastime in the dusty thoroughfare,

III

If at his counsel I should turn aside
    Into that ominous tract which, all agree,
    Hides the Dark Tower. Yet acquiescingly
I did turn as he pointed: neither pride
Nor hope rekindling at the end descried,
    So much as gladness that some end might be.

IV

For, what with my whole world-wide wandering,
    What with my search drawn out thro' years, my hope   20
    Dwindled into a ghost not fit to cope
With that obstreperous joy success would bring,—
I hardly tried now to rebuke the spring
    My heart made, finding failure in its scope.

V

As when a sick man very near to death
    Seems dead indeed, and feels begin and end
    The tears and takes the farewell of each friend,
And hears one bid the other go, draw breath
Freelier outside, ("since all is o'er," he saith,
    "And the blow fallen no grieving can amend;")   30

VI

While some discuss if near the other graves
    Be room enough for this, and when a day
    Suits best for carrying the corpse away,
With care about the banners, scarves and staves:
And still the man hears all, and only craves
    He may not shame such tender love and stay.

VII

Thus, I had so long suffered in this quest,
　　Heard failure prophesied so oft, been writ
　　So many times among "The Band"—to wit,
The knights who to the Dark Tower's search addressed   40
Their steps—that just to fail as they, seemed best,
　　And all the doubt was now—should I be fit?

VIII

So, quiet as despair, I turned from him,
　　That hateful cripple, out of his highway
　　Into the path he pointed. All the day
Had been a dreary one at best, and dim
Was settling to its close, yet shot one grim
　　Red leer to see the plain catch its estray.

IX

For mark! no sooner was I fairly found
　　Pledged to the plain, after a pace or two,   50
　　Than, pausing to throw backward a last view
O'er the safe road, 't was gone; grey plain all round:
Nothing but plain to the horizon's bound.
　　I might go on; nought else remained to do.

X

So, on I went. I think I never saw
　　Such starved ignoble nature; nothing throve:
　　For flowers—as well expect a cedar grove!
But cockle, spurge, according to their law
Might propagate their kind, with none to awe,
　　You'd think; a burr had been a treasure-trove.   60

XI

No! penury, inertness and grimace,
　　In some strange sort, were the land's portion. "See
　　Or shut your eyes," said Nature peevishly,
"It nothing skills: I cannot help my case:

---

48 *estray:* wanderer.
58 *cockle, spurge:* weeds.
59 *with none to awe:* i.e., with no one to restrain them.

'T is the Last Judgment's fire must cure this place,
    Calcine its clods and set my prisoners free."

XII

If there pushed any ragged thistle-stalk
    Above its mates, the head was chopped; the bents
    Were jealous else. What made those holes and rents
In the dock's harsh swarth leaves, bruised as to baulk   70
All hope of greenness? 't is a brute must walk
    Pashing their life out, with a brute's intents.

XIII

As for the grass, it grew as scant as hair
    In leprosy; thin dry blades pricked the mud
    Which underneath looked kneaded up with blood.
One stiff blind horse, his every bone a-stare,
Stood stupefied, however he came there:
    Thrust out past service from the devil's stud!

XIV

Alive? he might be dead for aught I know,
    With that red gaunt and colloped neck a-strain,   80
    And shut eyes underneath the rusty mane;
Seldom went such grotesqueness with such woe;
I never saw a brute I hated so;
    He must be wicked to deserve such pain.

XV

I shut my eyes and turned them on my heart.
    As a man calls for wine before he fights,
    I asked one draught of earlier, happier sights,
Ere fitly I could hope to play my part.
Think first, fight afterwards—the soldier's art:
    One taste of the old time sets all to rights.   90

---

66 *calcine:* reduce to powder by fire.
68 *bents:* coarse grasses.
72 *pashing:* smashing by blow.
80 *colloped:* wrinkled.

XVI

Not it! I fancied Cuthbert's reddening face
   Beneath its garniture of curly gold,
   Dear fellow, till I almost felt him fold
An arm in mine to fix me to the place,
That way he used. Alas, one night's disgrace!
   Out went my heart's new fire and left it cold.

XVII

Giles then, the soul of honour—there he stands
   Frank as ten years ago when knighted first.
   What honest man should dare (he said) he durst.
Good—but the scene shifts—faugh! what hangman hands 100
Pin to his breast a parchment? His own bands
   Read it. Poor traitor, spit upon and curst!

XVIII

Better this present than a past like that;
   Back therefore to my darkening path again!
   No sound, no sight as far as eye could strain.
Will the night send a howlet or a bat?
I asked: when something on the dismal flat
   Came to arrest my thoughts and change their train.

XIX

A sudden little river crossed my path
   As unexpected as a serpent comes.   110
   No sluggish tide congenial to the glooms;
This, as it frothed by, might have been a bath
For the fiend's glowing hoof—to see the wrath
   Of its black eddy bespate with flakes and spumes.

XX

So petty yet so spiteful! All along,
   Low scrubby alders kneeled down over it;
   Drenched willows flung them headlong in a fit

---

91 *Cuthbert:* This knight and Giles (in the following stanza) have failed the quest.
106 *howlet:* owlet.
114 *bespate:* spattered.

Of mute despair, a suicidal throng:
The river which had done them all the wrong,
   Whate'er that was, rolled by, deterred no whit.   120

XXI

Which, while I forded,—good saints, how I feared
   To set my foot upon a dead man's cheek,
   Each step, or feel the spear I thrust to seek
For hollows, tangled in his hair or beard!
—It may have been a water-rat I speared,
   But, ugh! it sounded like a baby's shriek.

XXII

Glad was I when I reached the other bank.
   Now for a better country. Vain presage!
   Who were the strugglers, what war did they wage,
Whose savage trample thus could pad the dank   130
Soil to a plash? Toads in a poisoned tank,
   Or wild cats in a red-hot iron cage—

XXIII

The fight must so have seemed in that fell cirque.
   What penned them there, with all the plain to choose?
   No foot-print leading to that horrid mews,
None out of it. Mad brewage set to work
Their brains, no doubt, like galley-slaves the Turk
   Pits for his pastime, Christians against Jews.

XXIV

And more than that—a furlong on—why, there!
   What bad use was that engine for, that wheel,   140
   Or brake, not wheel—that harrow fit to reel
Men's bodies out like silk? with all the air
Of Tophet's tool, on earth left unaware,
   Or brought to sharpen its rusty teeth of steel.

130-1 *pad the dank / Soil to a plash:* i.e., tramp the damp earth into a puddle.
133 *fell cirque:* terrible amphitheatre.
135 *mews:* enclosure.
140 *engine:* presumably an instrument of torture.
143 *Tophet:* hell.

XXV

Then came a bit of stubbed ground, once a wood,
  Next a marsh, it would seem, and now mere earth
  Desperate and done with; (so a fool finds mirth,
Makes a thing and then mars it, till his mood
Changes and off he goes!) within a rood—
  Bog, clay and rubble, sand and stark black dearth.   150

XXVI

Now blotches rankling, coloured gay and grim,
  Now patches where some leanness of the soil's
  Broke into moss or substances like boils;
Then came some palsied oak, a cleft in him
Like a distorted mouth that splits its rim
  Gaping at death, and dies while it recoils.

XXVII

And just as far as ever from the end!
  Naught in the distance but the evening, naught
  To point my footstep further! At the thought,
A great black bird, Apollyon's bosom-friend,   160
Sailed past, nor beat his wide wing dragon-penned
  That brushed my cap—perchance the guide I sought.

XXVIII

For, looking up, aware I somehow grew,
  'Spite of the dusk, the plain had given place
  All round to mountains—with such name to grace
Mere ugly heights and heaps now stolen in view.
How thus they had surprised me,—solve it, you!
  How to get from them was no clearer case.

XXIX

Yet half I seemed to recognize some trick
  Of mischief happened to me, God knows when—   170
  In a bad dream perhaps. Here ended, then,
Progress this way. When, in the very nick

---

154 *palsied:* shaking.
160 *Apollyon:* the Devil.
161 *dragon-penned:* winged like a dragon.

Of giving up, one time more, came a click
   As when a trap shuts—you're inside the den!

XXX

Burningly it came on me all at once,
   This was the place! those two hills on the right,
   Crouched like two bulls locked horn in horn in fight;
While to the left, a tall scalped mountain . . . Dunce,
Dotard, a-dozing at the very nonce,
   After a life spent training for the sight!   180

XXXI

What in the midst lay but the Tower itself?
   The round squat turret, blind as the fool's heart,
   Built of brown stone, without a counterpart
In the whole world. The tempest's mocking elf
Points to the shipman thus the unseen shelf
   He strikes on, only when the timbers start.

XXXII

Not see? because of night perhaps?—why, day
   Came back again for that! before it left,
   The dying sunset kindled through a cleft:
The hills, like giants at a hunting, lay,   190
Chin upon hand, to see the game at bay,—
   "Now stab and end the creature—to the heft!"

XXXIII

Not hear? when noise was everywhere! it tolled
   Increasing like a bell. Names in my ears
   Of all the lost adventurers my peers,—
How such a one was strong, and such was bold,
And such was fortunate, yet each of old
   Lost, lost! one moment knelled the woe of years.

XXXIV

There they stood, ranged along the hill-sides, met
   To view the last of me, a living frame   200

---

[179] *nonce:* present time.
[185] *shelf:* reef.
[192] *heft:* strain, i.e., stab to the utmost.
[199] *they:* his "peers."

For one more picture! in a sheet of flame
I saw them and I knew them all. And yet
Dauntless the slug-horn to my lips I set,
    And blew *"Childe Roland to the Dark Tower came."*

[1855]

THE STATUE AND THE BUST

There's a palace in Florence, the world knows well,
And a statue watches it from the square,
And this story of both do our townsmen tell.

Ages ago, a lady there,
At the farthest window facing the East
Asked, "Who rides by with the royal air?"

The bridesmaids' prattle around her ceased;
She leaned forth, one on either hand;
They saw how the blush of the bride increased—

They felt by its beats her heart expand—   10
As one at each ear and both in a breath
Whispered, "The Great-Duke Ferdinand."

That self-same instant, underneath,
The Duke rode past in his idle way,
Empty and fine like a swordless sheath.

Gay he rode, with a friend as gay,
Till he threw his head back—"Who is she?"
—"A bride the Riccardi brings home to-day."

Hair in heaps lay heavily

---

203 *Dauntless:* i.e., in spite of the failure of the others. *slug-horn:* trumpet.
1 *palace:* of the Riccardi; now known as the Palazzo Antinori. Beneath one
of its windows is a niche for the bust of the poem, and facing this from the
Piazza Annunziata is the equestrian statue of the sixteenth-century Grand
Duke, Ferdinand de' Medici.

Over a pale brow spirit-pure—   20
Carved like the heart of a coal-black tree,

Crisped like a war-steed's encolure—
And vainly sought to dissemble her eyes
Of the blackest black our eyes endure.

And lo, a blade for a knight's emprise
Filled the fine empty sheath of a man,—
The Duke grew straightway brave and wise.

He looked at her, as a lover can;
She looked at him, as one who awakes:
The past was a sleep, and her life began.   30

Now, love so ordered for both their sakes,
A feast was held that selfsame night
In the pile which the mighty shadow makes.

(For Via Larga is three-parts light,
But the palace overshadows one,
Because of a crime which may God requite!

To Florence and God the wrong was done,
Through the first republic's murder there
By Cosimo and his cursed son.)

The Duke (with the statue's face in the square)   40
Turned in the midst of his multitude
At the bright approach of the bridal pair.

Face to face the lovers stood   *i'n moment, sees what*
A single minute and no more,   *may go on*
While the bridegroom bent as a man subdued—

Bowed till his bonnet brushed the floor—
For the Duke on the lady a kiss conferred,
As the courtly custom was of yore.

---

22 *encolure:* mane or neck.
25 *emprise:* enterprise.
35 *palace:* that of the Grand Duke. His family had deprived Florence of its
freedom and become its rulers.

In a minute can lovers exchange a word?
If a word did pass, which I do not think,   50
Only one out of the thousand heard.

That was the bridegroom. At day's brink
He and his bride were alone at last
In a bedchamber by a taper's blink.

Calmly he said that her lot was cast,
That the door she had passed was shut on her
Till the final catafalk repassed.

The world meanwhile, its noise and stir,
Through a certain window facing the East,
She could watch like a convent's chronicler.   60

Since passing the door might lead to a feast,
And a feast might lead to so much beside,
He, of many evils, chose the least.

"Freely I choose too," said the bride—
"Your window and its world suffice,"
Replied the tongue, while the heart replied—

"If I spend the night with that devil twice,
May his window serve as my loop of hell
Whence a damned soul looks on paradise!

"I fly to the Duke who loves me well,   70
Sit by his side and laugh at sorrow
Ere I count another ave-bell.

" 'T is only the coat of a page to borrow,
And tie my hair in a horse-boy's trim,
And I save my soul—but not to-morrow"—

(She checked herself and her eye grew dim)
"My father tarries to bless my state:
I must keep it one day more for him.

---

[57] *catafalk:* hearse.

"Is one day more so long to wait?
Moreover the Duke rides past, I know;   80
We shall see each other, sure as fate."

She turned on her side and slept. Just so!
So we resolve on a thing and sleep:
So did the lady, ages ago.

That night the Duke said, "Dear or cheap
As the cost of this cup of bliss may prove
To body or soul, I will drain it deep."

And on the morrow, bold with love,
He beckoned the bridegroom (close on call,
As his duty bade, by the Duke's alcove)   90

And smiled " 'T was a very funeral,
Your lady will think, this feast of ours,—
A shame to efface, whate'er befall!

"What if we break from the Arno bowers,
And try if Petraja, cool and green,
Cure last night's fault with this morning's flowers?"

The bridegroom, not a thought to be seen
On his steady brow and quiet mouth,
Said, "Too much favour for me so mean!

"But, alas! my lady leaves the South;   100
Each wind that comes from the Apennine
Is a menace to her tender youth:

"Nor a way exists, the wise opine,
If she quits her palace twice this year,
To avert the flower of life's decline."

Quoth the Duke, "A sage and a kindly fear.
Moreover Petraja is cold this spring:
Be our feast to-night as usual here!"

---

[95] *Petraja:* the Duke's country house near Florence, which stands on the banks of the River Arno.

And then to himself—"Which night shall bring
Thy bride to her lover's embraces, fool—   110
Or I am the fool, and thou art the king!

"Yet my passion must wait a night, nor cool—
For to-night the Envoy arrives from France
Whose heart I unlock with thyself, my tool.

"I need thee still and might miss perchance.
To-day is not wholly lost, beside,
With its hope of my lady's countenance:

"For I ride—what should I do but ride?
And passing her palace, if I list,
May glance at its window—well betide!"   120

So said, so done: nor the lady missed
One ray that broke from the ardent brow,
Nor a curl of the lips where the spirit kissed.

Be sure that each renewed the vow,
No morrow's sun should arise and set
And leave them then as it left them now.

But next day passed, and next day yet,
With still fresh cause to wait one day more
Ere each leaped over the parapet.

And still, as love's brief morning wore,   130
With a gentle start, half smile, half sigh,
They found love not as it seemed before.

They thought it would work infallibly,
But not in despite of heaven and earth:
The rose would blow when the storm passed by.

Meantime they could profit in winter's dearth
By store of fruits that supplant the rose:
The world and its ways have a certain worth:

And to press a point while these oppose
Were simple policy; better wait:
We lose no friends and we gain no foes. 140

*take no chance
middle of road*

Meantime, worse fates than a lover's fate,
Who daily may ride and pass and look
Where his lady watches behind the grate!

And she—she watched the square like a book
Holding one picture and only one,
Which daily to find she undertook:

When the picture was reached the book was done,
And she turned from the picture at night to scheme
Of tearing it out for herself next sun. 150

*each night she
plans to leave*

So weeks grew months, years; gleam by gleam
The glory dropped from their youth and love,
And both perceived they had dreamed a dream;

*They missed
their moment*

Which hovered as dreams do, still above:
But who can take a dream for a truth?
Oh, hide our eyes from the next remove!

One day as the lady saw her youth
Depart, and the silver thread that streaked
Her hair, and, worn by the serpent's tooth,

The brow so puckered, the chin so peaked,— 160
And wondered who the woman was,
Hollow-eyed and haggard-cheeked,

Fronting her silent in the glass—
"Summon here," she suddenly said,
"Before the rest of my old self pass,

"Him, the Carver, a hand to aid,
Who fashions the clay no love will change,
And fixes a beauty never to fade.

to make a bust

---

166 *Carver:* From the context, clearly one of the Della Robbia family, who
were famous sculptors, but the last of them would have been dead before the
time of the poem's action.

"Let Robbia's craft so apt and strange
Arrest the remains of young and fair,   170
And rivet them while the seasons range.

"Make me a face on the window there,
Waiting as ever, mute the while,
My love to pass below in the square!

"And let me think that it may beguile
Dreary days which the dead must spend
Down in their darkness under the aisle,

"To say, 'What matters it at the end?
I did no more while my heart was warm
Than does that image, my pale-faced friend.'   180

"Where is the use of the lip's red charm,
The heaven of hair, the pride of the brow,
And the blood that blues the inside arm—

"Unless we turn, as the soul knows how,
The earthly gift to an end divine?
A lady of clay is as good, I trow."

But long ere Robbia's cornice, fine,
With flowers and fruits which leaves enlace,
Was set where now is the empty shrine—

(And, leaning out of a bright blue space,   190
As a ghost might lean from a chink of sky,
The passionate pale lady's face—

Eyeing ever, with earnest eye
And quick-turned neck at its breathless stretch,
Some one who ever is passing by—)

The Duke had sighed like the simplest wretch
In Florence, "Youth—my dream escapes!
Will its record stay?" And he bade them fetch

Some subtle moulder of brazen shapes—

"Can the soul, the will, die out of a man
Ere his body find the grave that gapes?

"John of Douay shall effect my plan,
Set me on horseback here aloft,
Alive, as the crafty sculptor can,

"In the very square I have crossed so oft:
That men may admire, when future suns
Shall touch the eyes to a purpose soft,

"While the mouth and the brow stay brave in bronze—
Admire and say, 'When he was alive
How he would take his pleasure once!'

"And it shall go hard but I contrive
To listen the while, and laugh in my tomb
At idleness which aspires to strive."

So! While these wait the trump of doom,
How do their spirits pass, I wonder,
Nights and days in the narrow room?

Still, I suppose, they sit and ponder
What a gift life was, ages ago,
Six steps out of the chapel yonder.

Only they see not God, I know,
Nor all that chivalry of his,
The soldier-saints who, row on row,

Burn upward each to his point of bliss—
Since, the end of life being manifest,
He had burned his way thro' the world to this.

I hear you reproach, "But delay was best,
For their end was a crime."—Oh, a crime will do
As well, I reply, to serve for a test,

would have seen
God had run away
together.

life is prize
man must
grasp & seize.

As a virtue golden through and through,
Sufficient to vindicate itself   230
And prove its worth at a moment's view!

Must a game be played for the sake of pelf?
Where a button goes, 't were an epigram
To offer the stamp of the very Guelph.

The true has no value beyond the sham:
As well the counter as coin, I submit,
When your table's a hat, and your prize a dram.

need courage to
grasp moment

Stake your counter as boldly every whit,
Venture as warily, use the same skill,
Do your best, whether winning or losing it,   240

lovers lost
as did not
gamble

If you choose to play!—is my principle.
Let a man contend to the uttermost
For his life's set prize, be it what it will!

The counter our lovers staked was lost
As surely as if it were lawful coin:
And the sin I impute to each frustrate ghost

Is—the unlit lamp and the ungirt loin,
Though the end in sight was a vice, I say.
You of the virtue (we issue join)
How strive you? *De te, fabula!*   250

[1855]

---

232 *pelf:* money.
233-4 *Where a button . . . very Guelph:* i.e., when the stakes are buttons,
there is no point in offering genuine money stamped with the image of the
ruler (the Guelph).
237 *dram:* trifle; that is, in an unimportant game.
250 *De te, fabula!:* the story concerns you.

the story is told of you

THE LAST RIDE TOGETHER

I

I said—Then, dearest, since 't is so,
Since now at length my fate I know,
Since nothing all my love avails,
Since all, my life seemed meant for, fails,
    Since this was written and needs must be—
My whole heart rises up to bless
Your name in pride and thankfulness!
Take back the hope you gave,—I claim
Only a memory of the same,
—And this beside, if you will not blame,   10
    Your leave for one more last ride with me.

II

My mistress bent that brow of hers;
Those deep dark eyes where pride demurs
When pity would be softening through,
Fixed me a breathing-while or two
    With life or death in the balance: right!
The blood replenished me again;
My last thought was at least not vain:
I and my mistress, side by side
Shall be together, breathe and ride,   20
So, one day more am I deified.
    Who knows but the world may end to-night?

III

Hush! if you saw some western cloud
All billowy-bosomed, over-bowed
By many benedictions—sun's
And moon's and evening-star's at once—
    And so, you, looking and loving best,
Conscious grew, your passion drew
Cloud, sunset, moonrise, star-shine too,
Down on you, near and yet more near,   30
Till flesh must fade for heaven was here!—

Thus leant she and lingered—joy and fear!
  Thus lay she a moment on my breast.

IV

Then we began to ride. My soul
Smoothed itself out, a long-cramped scroll
Freshening and fluttering in the wind.
Past hopes already lay behind.
  What need to strive with a life awry?
Had I said that, had I done this,
So might I gain, so might I miss.   40
Might she have loved me? just as well
She might have hated, who can tell!
Where had I been now if the worst befell?
  And here we are riding, she and I.

V

Fail I alone, in words and deeds?
Why, all men strive and who succeeds?
We rode; it seemed my spirit flew,
Saw other regions, cities new,
  As the world rushed by on either side.
I thought,—All labour, yet no less   50
Bear up beneath their unsuccess.
Look at the end of work, contrast
The petty done, the undone vast,
This present of theirs with the hopeful past!
  I hoped she would love me; here we ride.

VI

What hand and brain went ever paired?
What heart alike conceived and dared?
What act proved all its thought had been?
What will but felt the fleshly screen?
  We ride and I see her bosom heave.   60
There's many a crown for who can reach.
Ten lines, a statesman's life in each!
The flag stuck on a heap of bones,
A soldier's doing! what atones?

---

62 *Ten lines:* brief obituary notices.

They scratch his name on the Abbey-stones.
My riding is better, by their leave.

VII

What does it all mean, poet? Well,
Your brains beat into rhythm, you tell
What we felt only; you expressed
You hold things beautiful the best,   70
    And pace them in rhyme so, side by side.
'T is something, nay 't is much: but then,
Have you yourself what's best for men?
Are you—poor, sick, old ere your time—
Nearer one whit your own sublime
Than we who never have turned a rhyme?
    Sing, riding's a joy! For me, I ride.

VIII

And you, great sculptor—so, you gave
A score of years to Art, her slave,
And that's your Venus, whence we turn   80
To yonder girl that fords the burn!
    You acquiesce, and shall I repine?
What, man of music, you grown grey
With notes and nothing else to say,
Is this your sole praise from a friend,
"Greatly his opera's strains intend,
But in music we know how fashions end!"
    I gave my youth; but we ride, in fine.

IX

Who knows what's fit for us? Had fate
Proposed bliss here should sublimate   90
My being—had I signed the bond—
Still one must lead some life beyond,
    Have a bliss to die with, dim-descried.
This foot once planted on the goal,
This glory-garland round my soul,
Could I descry such? Try and test!
    I sink back shuddering from the quest.

---

81 *burn:* brook.
90 *sublimate:* refine.

Earth being so good, would heaven seem best?
Now, heaven and she are beyond this ride.

X

And yet—she has not spoke so long!   100
What if heaven be that, fair and strong
At life's best, with our eyes upturned
Whither life's flower is first discerned,
    We, fixed so, ever should so abide?
What if we still ride on, we two
With life for ever old yet new,
Changed not in kind but in degree,
The instant made eternity,—
And heaven just prove that I and she
    Ride, ride together, for ever ride?   110

[1855]

ANDREA DEL SARTO

Called "The Faultless Painter"

But do not let us quarrel any more,
No, my Lucrezia; bear with me for once:
Sit down and all shall happen as you wish.
You turn your face, but does it bring your heart?
I'll work then for your friend's friend, never fear,
Treat his own subject after his own way,
Fix his own time, accept too his own price,
And shut the money into this small hand
When next it takes mine. Will it? tenderly?
Oh, I'll content him,—but to-morrow, Love!   10

Andrea del Sarto: Andrea d'Agnolo di Francesca di Luca, 1486-1531, known for the "design, colouring and invention" of his painting, which, however, lacked boldness and assurance. Browning follows the tradition that Andrea returned from the court of King Francis I of France, where he had done some of his best work, at the behest of his vicious wife, Lucrezia; when he returned to Florence he spent the king's money, intended for the purchase of paintings, in building a house for Lucrezia. The setting of the poem is the painter's house, looking over the Florentine suburb of Fiesole.

I often am much wearier than you think,
This evening more than usual, and it seems
As if—forgive now—should you let me sit
Here by the window with your hand in mine
And look a half-hour forth on Fiesole,
Both of one mind, as married people use,
Quietly, quietly the evening through,
I might get up to-morrow to my work
Cheerful and fresh as ever. Let us try.
To-morrow, how you shall be glad for this!   20
Your soft hand is a woman of itself,
And mine the man's bared breast she curls inside.
Don't count the time lost, neither; you must serve
For each of the five pictures we require:
It saves a model. So! keep looking so—
My serpentining beauty, rounds on rounds!
—How could you ever prick those perfect ears,
Even to put the pearl there! oh, so sweet—
My face, my moon, my everybody's moon,
Which everybody looks on and calls his,   30
And, I suppose, is looked on by in turn,
While she looks—no one's: very dear, no less.
You smile? why, there's my picture ready made,
There's what we painters call our harmony!
A common greyness silvers everything,—
All in a twilight, you and I alike
—You, at the point of your first pride in me
(That's gone you know),—but I, at every point;
My youth, my hope, my art, being all toned down
To yonder sober pleasant Fiesole.   40
There's the bell clinking from the chapel-top;
That length of convent-wall across the way
Holds the trees safer, huddled more inside;
The last monk leaves the garden; days decrease,
And autumn grows, autumn in everything.
Eh? the whole seems to fall into a shape
As if I saw alike my work and self
And all that I was born to be and do,
A twilight-piece. Love, we are in God's hand.
How strange now, looks the life he makes us lead;   50
So free we seem, so fettered fast we are!

I feel he laid the fetter: let it lie!
This chamber for example—turn your head—
All that's behind us! You don't understand
Nor care to understand about my art,
But you can hear at least when people speak:
And that cartoon, the second from the door
—It is the thing, Love! so such things should be—
/Behold Madonna!—I am bold to say.
I can do with my pencil what I know,   60
What I see, what at bottom of my heart
I wish for, if I ever wish so deep—
Do easily, too—when I say, perfectly,
\ I do not boast, perhaps: yourself are judge,
  Who listened to the Legate's talk last week,
And just as much they used to say in France.
At any rate 't is easy, all of it!
No sketches first, no studies, that's long past:
I do what many dream of, all their lives,
—Dream? strive to do, and agonize to do,   70
And fail in doing. I could count twenty such
On twice your fingers, and not leave this town,
Who strive—you don't know how the others strive
To paint a little thing like that you smeared
Carelessly passing with your robes afloat,—
Yet do much less, so much less, Someone says,
(I know his name, no matter)—so much less!
_Well, less is more, Lucrezia: I am judged.
| There burns a truer light of God in them,
/ In their vexed beating stuffed and stopped-up brain,   80
Heart, or whate'er else, than goes on to prompt
This low-pulsed forthright craftsman's hand of mine.
Their works drop groundward, but themselves, I know,
Reach many a time a heaven that's shut to me,
Enter and take their place there sure enough,
_Though they come back and cannot tell the world.
My works are nearer heaven, but I sit here.
The sudden blood of these men! at a word—
Praise them, it boils, or blame them, it boils too.

---

57 *cartoon:* preliminary sketch.
65 *Legate:* the Pope's representative.
76 *Someone:* Michelangelo.

I, painting from myself and to myself,   90
Know what I do, am unmoved by men's blame
Or their praise either. Somebody remarks
Morello's outline there is wrongly traced,
His hue mistaken; what of that? or else,
Rightly traced and well ordered; what of that?
Speak as they please, what does the mountain care?
Ah, but a man's reach should exceed his grasp,
Or what's a heaven for? All is silver-grey
Placid and perfect with my art: the worse!
I know both what I want and what might gain,   100
And yet how profitless to know, to sigh
"Had I been two, another and myself,
Our head would have o'erlooked the world!" No doubt.
Yonder's a work now, of that famous youth
The Urbinate who died five years ago.
('T is copied, George Vasari sent it me.)
Well, I can fancy how he did it all,
Pouring his soul, with kings and popes to see,
Reaching, that heaven might so replenish him,
Above and through his art—for it gives way;   110
That arm is wrongly put—and there again—
A fault to pardon in the drawing's lines,
Its body, so to speak: its soul is right,
He means right—that, a child may understand.
Still, what an arm! and I could alter it:
But all the play, the insight and the stretch—
Out of me, out of me! And wherefore out?
Had you enjoined them on me, given me soul,
We might have risen to Rafael, I and you!
Nay, Love, you did give all I asked, I think—   120
More than I merit, yes, by many times.
But had you—oh, with the same perfect brow,
And perfect eyes, and more than perfect mouth,
And the low voice my soul hears, as a bird
The fowler's pipe, and follows to the snare—

---

93 *Morello:* mountain near Florence.
105 *Urbinate:* Raphael was born in Urbino.
106 *Vasari:* Giorgio Vasari, pupil of Andrea, wrote *Lives of the Painters*,
from which Browning took the story of *Andrea,* as well as of several other
poems.

Had you, with these the same, but brought a mind!
Some women do so. Had the mouth there urged
"God and the glory! never care for gain.
The present by the future, what is that?
Live for fame, side by side with Agnolo!   130
Rafael is waiting: up to God, all three!"
I might have done it for you. So it seems:
Perhaps not. All is as God over-rules.
Beside, incentives come from the soul's self;
The rest avail not. Why do I need you?
What wife had Rafael, or has Agnolo?
In this world, who can do a thing, will not;
And who would do it, cannot, I perceive:
Yet the will's somewhat—somewhat, too, the power—
And thus we half-men struggle. At the end,   140
God, I conclude, compensates, punishes.
'T is safer for me, if the award be strict,
That I am something underrated here,
Poor this long while, despised, to speak the truth.
I dared not, do you know, leave home all day,
For fear of chancing on the Paris lords.
The best is when they pass and look aside;
But they speak sometimes; I must bear it all.
Well may they speak! That Francis, that first time,
And that long festal year at Fontainebleau!   150
I surely then could sometimes leave the ground,
Put on the glory, Rafael's daily wear,
In that humane great monarch's golden look,—
One finger in his beard or twisted curl
Over his mouth's good mark that made the smile,
One arm about my shoulder, round my neck,
The jingle of his gold chain in my ear,
I painting proudly with his breath on me,
All his court round him, seeing with his eyes,
Such frank French eyes, and such a fire of souls   160
Profuse, my hand kept plying by those hearts,—
And, best of all, this, this, this face beyond,
This in the background, waiting on my work,
To crown the issue with a last reward!

---

130 *Agnolo:* Michelangelo.

A good time, was it not, my kingly days?
And had you not grown restless . . . but I know—
'T is done and past; 't was right, my instinct said;
Too live the life grew, golden and not grey,
And I'm the weak-eyed bat no sun should tempt
Out of the grange whose four walls make his world.   170
How could it end in any other way?
You called me, and I came home to your heart.
The triumph was—to reach and stay there; since
I reached it ere the triumph, what is lost?
Let my hands frame your face in your hair's gold,
You beautiful Lucrezia that are mine!
"Rafael did this, Andrea painted that;
The Roman's is the better when you pray,
But still the other's Virgin was his wife—"
Men will excuse me. I am glad to judge   180
Both pictures in your presence; clearer grows
My better fortune, I resolve to think.
For, do you know, Lucrezia, as God lives,
Said one day Agnolo, his very self,
To Rafael . . . I have known it all these years . . .
(When the young man was flaming out his thoughts
Upon a palace-wall for Rome to see,
Too lifted up in heart because of it)
"Friend, there's a certain sorry little scrub
Goes up and down our Florence, none cares how,   190
Who, were he set to plan and execute
As you are, pricked on by your popes and kings,
Would bring the sweat into that brow of yours!"
To Rafael's!—And indeed the arm is wrong.
I hardly dare . . . yet, only you to see,
Give the chalk here—quick, thus the line should go!
Ay, but the soul! he's Rafael! rub it out!
Still, all I care for, if he spoke the truth,
(What he? why, who but Michel Agnolo?
Do you forget already words like those?)   200
If really there was such a chance, so lost,—
Is, whether you're—not grateful—but more pleased.
Well, let me think so. And you smile indeed!
This hour has been an hour! Another smile?
If you would sit thus by me every night

I should work better, do you comprehend?
I mean that I should earn more, give you more.
See, it is settled dusk now; there's a star;
Morello's gone, the watch-lights show the wall,
The cue-owls speak the name we call them by.   210
Come from the window, love,—come in, at last,
Inside the melancholy little house
We built to be so gay with. God is just.
King Francis may forgive me: oft at nights
When I look up from painting, eyes tired out,
The walls become illumined, brick from brick
Distinct, instead of mortar, fierce bright gold,
That gold of his I did cement them with!
Let us but love each other. Must you go?
That Cousin here again? he waits outside?   220
Must see you—you, and not with me? Those loans?
More gaming debts to pay? you smiled for that?
Well, let smiles buy me! have you more to spend?
While hand and eye and something of a heart
Are left me, work's my ware, and what's it worth?
I'll pay my fancy. Only let me sit
The grey remainder of the evening out,
Idle, you call it, and muse perfectly
How I could paint, were I but back in France,
One picture, just one more—the Virgin's face,   230
Not yours this time! I want you at my side
To hear them—that is, Michel Agnolo—
Judge all I do and tell you of its worth.
Will you? To-morrow, satisfy your friend.
I take the subjects for his corridor,
Finish the portrait out of hand—there, there,
And throw him in another thing or two
If he demurs; the whole should prove enough
To pay for this same Cousin's freak. Beside,
What's better and what's all I care about,   240
Get you the thirteen scudi for the ruff!
Love, does that please you? Ah, but what does he,
The Cousin! What does he to please you more?

---

[220] *Cousin:* the term by which they refer to Lucrezia's lover.

I am grown peaceful as old age to-night.
I regret little, I would change still less.
Since there my past life lies, why alter it?
The very wrong to Francis!—it is true
I took his coin, was tempted and complied,
And built this house and sinned, and all is said.
My father and my mother died of want.   250
Well, had I riches of my own? you see
How one gets rich! Let each one bear his lot.
They were born poor, lived poor, and poor they died:
And I have laboured somewhat in my time
And not been paid profusely. Some good son
Paint my two hundred pictures—let him try!
No doubt, there's something strikes a balance. Yes,
You loved me quite enough, it seems to-night.
This must suffice me here. What would one have?
In heaven, perhaps, new chances, one more chance—   260
Four great walls in the New Jerusalem,
Meted on each side by the angel's reed,
For Leonard, Rafael, Agnolo and me
To cover—the three first without a wife,
While I have mine! So—still they overcome
Because there's still Lucrezia,—as I choose.

Again the Cousin's whistle! Go, my Love.

[1855]

"DE GUSTIBUS—"

I

Your ghost will walk, you lover of trees,
　　(If our loves remain)
　　　In an English lane,
By a cornfield-side a-flutter with poppies.

---

263 *Leonard:* Leonardo da Vinci.
"De Gustibus": from the Latin proverb, *De gustibus non est disputandum*
(there is no disputing about tastes).

Hark, those two in the hazel coppice—
A boy and a girl, if the good fates please,
  Making love, say,—
  The happier they!
Draw yourself up from the light of the moon,
And let them pass, as they will too soon,   10
  With the bean-flowers' boon,
  And the blackbird's tune,
  And May, and June!

II

What I love best in all the world
Is a castle, precipice-encurled,
In a gash of the wind-grieved Apennine.
Or look for me, old fellow of mine,
(If I get my head from out the mouth
O' the grave, and loose my spirit's bands,
And come again to the land of lands)—   20
In a sea-side house to the farther South,
Where the baked cicala dies of drouth,
And one sharp tree—'t is a cypress—stands,
By the many hundred years red-rusted,
Rough iron-spiked, ripe fruit-o'ercrusted,
My sentinel to guard the sands
To the water's edge. For, what expands
Before the house, but the great opaque
Blue breadth of sea without a break?
While, in the house, for ever crumbles   30
Some fragment of the frescoed walls,
From blisters where a scorpion sprawls.
A girl bare-footed brings, and tumbles
Down on the pavement, green-flesh melons,
And says there's news to-day—the king
Was shot at, touched in the liver-wing,
Goes with his Bourbon arm in a sling:
—She hopes they have not caught the felons.
Italy, my Italy!

---

22 *cicala:* cicada.
35 *king:* the Bourbon Ferdinand II, tyrannous ruler of the Two Sicilies, lived in Naples.
36 *liver-wing:* right arm.

Queen Mary's saying serves for me—   40
　　　(When fortune's malice
　　　Lost her—Calais)—
Open my heart and you will see
Graved inside of it, "Italy."
Such lovers old are I and she:
So it always was, so shall ever be!

[1855]

CLEON

"As certain also of your own poets have said"—

Cleon the poet (from the sprinkled isles,
Lily on lily, that o'erlace the sea,
And laugh their pride when the light wave lisps "Greece")—
To Protus in his Tyranny: much health!

　　They give thy letter to me, even now:
I read and seem as if I heard thee speak.
The master of thy galley still unlades
Gift after gift; they block my court at last
And pile themselves along its portico
Royal with sunset, like a thought of thee: 10
And one white she-slave from the group dispersed
Of black and white slaves (like the chequer-work
Pavement, at once my nation's work and gift,
Now covered with this settle-down of doves),
One lyric woman, in her crocus vest
Woven of sea-wools, with her two white hands

---

40 *Queen Mary:* When Calais was taken from England in 1558, Queen Mary
of England is supposed to have said that the name of the city would be
found written on her heart after her death.
Cleon: The two major figures in this epistolary poem, Cleon, the complete
artist-intellectual, and Protus, the king and man of action, are imaginary;
Browning is using them to show the limits of the intellect and the Greek
mind.
As certain . . . have said: see *Acts* 17: 28-34.
4 *Tyranny:* here meaning only absolute power, not despotism.

Commends to me the strainer and the cup
Thy lip hath bettered ere it blesses mine.

Well-counselled, king, in thy munificence!
For so shall men remark, in such an act   20
Of love for him whose song gives life its joy,
Thy recognition of the use of life;
Nor call thy spirit barely adequate
To help on life in straight ways, broad enough
For vulgar souls, by ruling and the rest.
Thou, in the daily building of thy tower,—
Whether in fierce and sudden spasms of toil,
Or through dim lulls of unapparent growth,
Or when the general work 'mid good acclaim
Climbed with the eye to cheer the architect,—   30
Didst ne'er engage in work for mere work's sake—
Hadst ever in thy heart the luring hope
Of some eventual rest a-top of it,
Whence, all the tumult of the building hushed,
Thou first of men mightst look out to the East:
The vulgar saw thy tower, thou sawest the sun.
For this, I promise on thy festival
To pour libation, looking o'er the sea,
Making this slave narrate thy fortunes, speak
Thy great words, and describe thy royal face—   40
Wishing thee wholly where Zeus lives the most,
Within the eventual element of calm.

Thy letter's first requirement meets me here.
It is as thou hast heard, in one short life
I, Cleon, have effected all those things
Thou wonderingly dost enumerate.
That epos on thy hundred plates of gold
Is mine,—and also mine the little chant,
So sure to rise from every fishing-bark
When, lights at prow, the seamen haul their net.   50
The image of the sun-god on the phare,
Men turn from the sun's self to see, is mine;

what Cleon has done.

---

47 *epos:* epic.
51 *phare:* lighthouse.

[handwritten margin note: jack of all trades, master of none]

The Pœcile, o'er-storied its whole length,
As thou didst hear, with painting, is mine too.
I know the true proportions of a man
And woman also, not observed before;
And I have written three books on the soul,
Proving absurd all written hitherto,
And putting us to ignorance again.
For music,—why, I have combined the moods,   60
Inventing one. In brief, all arts are mine;
Thus much the people know and recognize,
Throughout our seventeen islands. Marvel not.
We of these latter days, with greater mind
Than our forerunners, since more composite,
Look not so great, beside their simple way,
To a judge who only sees one way at once,
One mind-point and no other at a time,—
Compares the small part of a man of us
With some whole man of the heroic age,   70
Great in his way—not ours, nor meant for ours.
And ours is greater, had we skill to know:
For, what we call this life of men on earth,
This sequence of the soul's achievements here
Being, as I find much reason to conceive,
Intended to be viewed eventually
As a great whole, not analyzed to parts,
But each part having reference to all,—
How shall a certain part, pronounced complete,
Endure effacement by another part?   80
Was the thing done?—then, what's to do again?
See, in the chequered pavement opposite,
Suppose the artist made a perfect rhomb,
And next a lozenge, then a trapezoid—
He did not overlay them, superimpose
The new upon the old and blot it out,
But laid them on a level in his work,
Making at last a picture; there it lies.
So, first the perfect separate forms were made,
The portions of mankind; and after, so,   90

[handwritten margin note: synthesizer the greatest]

---

53 *Pœcile:* the Portico in Athens.
60 *moods:* modes.

Occurred the combination of the same.
For where had been a progress, otherwise?
Mankind, made up of all the single men,—
In such a synthesis the labour ends.
Now mark me! those divine men of old time
Have reached, thou sayest well, each at one point
The outside verge that rounds our faculty;
And where they reached, who can do more than reach?
It takes but little water just to touch
At some one point the inside of a sphere,   100
And, as we turn the sphere, touch all the rest
In due succession: but the finer air
Which not so palpably nor obviously,
Though no less universally, can touch
The whole circumference of that emptied sphere,
Fills it more fully than the water did;
Holds thrice the weight of water in itself
Resolved into a subtler element.
And yet the vulgar call the sphere first full
Up to the visible height—and after, void;   110
Not knowing air's more hidden properties.
And thus our soul, misknown, cries out to Zeus
To vindicate his purpose in our life:
Why stay we on the earth unless to grow?
Long since, I imaged, wrote the fiction out,
That he or other god descended here
And, once for all, showed simultaneously
What, in its nature, never can be shown,
Piecemeal or in succession;—showed, I say,
The worth both absolute and relative   120
Of all his children from the birth of time,
His instruments for all appointed work.
I now go on to image,—might we hear
The judgment which should give the due to each,
Show where the labour lay and where the ease,
And prove Zeus' self, the latent everywhere!
This is a dream:—but no dream, let us hope,
That years and days, the summers and the springs,
Follow each other with unwaning powers.
The grapes which dye thy wine are richer far,   130
Through culture, than the wild wealth of the rock;

The suave plum than the savage-tasted drupe;
The pastured honey-bee drops choicer sweet;
The flowers turn double, and the leaves turn flowers;
That young and tender crescent-moon, thy slave,
Sleeping above her robe as buoyed by clouds,
Refines upon the women of my youth.
What, and the soul alone deteriorates?
I have not chanted verse like Homer, no—
Nor swept string like Terpander, no—nor carved   140
And painted men like Phidias and his friend:
I am not great as they are, point by point.
But I have entered into sympathy
With these four, running these into one soul,
Who, separate, ignored each other's art.
Say, is it nothing that I know them all?
The wild flower was the larger; I have dashed
Rose-blood upon its petals, pricked its cup's
Honey with wine, and driven its seed to fruit,
And show a better flower if not so large: 150
I stand myself. Refer this to the gods
Whose gift alone it is! which, shall I dare
(All pride apart) upon the absurd pretext
That such a gift by chance lay in my hand,
Discourse of lightly or depreciate?
It might have fallen to another's hand: what then?
I pass too surely: let at least truth stay!

    And next, of what thou followest on to ask.
This being with me as I declare, O king,
My works, in all these varicoloured kinds,   160
So done by me, accepted so by men—
Thou askest, if (my soul thus in men's hearts)
I must not be accounted to attain
The very crown and proper end of life?
Inquiring thence how, now life closeth up,
I face death with success in my right hand:

---

132 *drupe:* wild plum.
139-45 *Homer:* Cleon is saying that he is a less great poet than Homer, a less
accomplished musician than *Terpander*, a less skillful sculptor than *Phidias,*
and knows less of the arts of government than Pericles, *friend* of Phidias, but
that he combines part of the talents of each in himself, and so is broader than
they.

Purpose of life
Is in achievement
remembered in his works

Whether I fear death less than dost thyself
The fortunate of men? "For" (writest thou)
"Thou leavest much behind, while I leave nought.
Thy life stays in the poems men shall sing,   170
The pictures men shall study; while my life,
Complete and whole now in its power and joy,
Dies altogether with my brain and arm,
Is lost indeed; since, what survives myself?
The brazen statue to o'erlook my grave,
Set on the promontory which I named.
And that—some supple courtier of my heir
Shall use its robed and sceptred arm, perhaps,
To fix the rope to, which best drags it down.
I go then: triumph thou, who dost not go!"   180

　　Nay, thou art worthy of hearing my whole mind.
Is this apparent, when thou turn'st to muse
Upon the scheme of earth and man in chief,
That admiration grows as knowledge grows?
That imperfection means perfection hid,
Reserved in part, to grace the after-time?
If, in the morning of philosophy,
Ere aught had been recorded, nay perceived,
Thou, with the light now in thee, couldst have looked
On all earth's tenantry, from worm to bird,   190
Ere man, her last, appeared upon the stage—
Thou wouldst have seen them perfect, and deduced
The perfectness of others yet unseen.
Conceding which,—had Zeus then questioned thee

Final gift
of Zeus is
Consciousness

"Shall I go on a step, improve on this,
Do more for visible creatures than is done?"
Thou wouldst have answered, "Ay, by making each
Grow conscious in himself—by that alone.
All's perfect else: the shell sucks fast the rock,
The fish strikes through the sea, the snake both swims   200
And slides, forth range the beasts, the birds take flight,
Till life's mechanics can no further go—
And all this joy in natural life is put
Like fire from off thy finger into each,
So exquisitely perfect is the same.
But 't is pure fire, and they mere matter are;

It has them, not they it: and so I choose
For man, thy last premeditated work
(If I might add a glory to the scheme)
That a third thing should stand apart from both,   210
A quality arise within his soul,
Which, intro-active, made to supervise
And feel the force it has, may view itself,
And so be happy." Man might live at first
The animal life: but is there nothing more?
In due time, let him critically learn
How he lives; and, the more he gets to know
Of his own life's adaptabilities,
The more joy-giving will his life become.
Thus man, who hath this quality, is best.   220

But thou, king, hadst more reasonably said:
"Let progress end at once,—man make no step
Beyond the natural man, the better beast,
Using his senses, not the sense of sense."
In man there's failure, only since he left
The lower and inconscious forms of life.
We called it an advance, the rendering plain
Man's spirit might grow conscious of man's life,
And, by new lore so added to the old,
Take each step higher over the brute's head.   230
This grew the only life, the pleasure-house,
Watch-tower and treasure-fortress of the soul,
Which whole surrounding flats of natural life
Seemed only fit to yield subsistence to;
A tower that crowns a country. But alas,
The soul now climbs it just to perish there!
For thence we have discovered ('t is no dream—
We know this, which we had not else perceived)
That there's a world of capability
For joy, spread round about us, meant for us,   240
Inviting us; and still the soul craves all,
And still the flesh replies, "Take no jot more
Than ere thou clombst the tower to look abroad!
Nay, so much less as that fatigue has brought
Deduction to it." We struggle, fain to enlarge
Our bounded physical recipiency,

Increase our power, supply fresh oil to life,
Repair the waste of age and sickness: no,
It skills not life's inadequate to joy,
As the soul sees joy, tempting life to take.   250
They praise a fountain in my garden here
Wherein a Naiad sends the water-bow
Thin from her tube; she smiles to see it rise.
What if I told her, it is just a thread
From that great river which the hills shut up,
And mock her with my leave to take the same?
The artificer has given her one small tube
Past power to widen or exchange—what boots
To know she might spout oceans if she could?
She cannot lift beyond her first thin thread: 260
And so a man can use but a man's joy
While he sees God's. Is it for Zeus to boast,
"See, man, how happy I live, and despair—
That I may be still happier—for thy use!"
If this were so, we could not thank our lord,
As hearts beat on to doing; 't is not so—
Malice it is not. Is it carelessness?
Still, no. If care—where is the sign? I ask,
And get no answer, and agree in sum,
O king, with thy profound discouragement,   270
Who seest the wider but to sigh the more.
Most progress is most failure: thou sayest well.

    The last point now:—thou dost except a case—
Holding joy not impossible to one
With artist-gifts—to such a man as I
Who leave behind me living works indeed;
For, such a poem, such a painting lives.
What? dost thou verily trip upon a word,
Confound the accurate view of what joy is
(Caught somewhat clearer by my eyes than thine)   280
With feeling joy? confound the knowing how
And showing how to live (my faculty)
With actually living?—Otherwise
Where is the artist's vantage o'er the king?
Because in my great epos I display
How divers men young, strong, fair, wise, can act—

Is this as though I acted? if I paint,
Carve the young Phœbus, am I therefore young?
Methinks I'm older that I bowed myself
The many years of pain that taught me art!   290
Indeed, to know is something, and to prove   *many of emotion*
How all this beauty might be enjoyed, is more: *knows more*
But, knowing nought, to enjoy is something too.   *purely*
Yon rower, with the moulded muscles there,
Lowering the sail, is nearer it than I.
I can write love-odes: thy fair slave's an ode. *better to do /*
I get to sing of love, when grown too grey   *than know, /*
For being beloved: she turns to that young man,
The muscles all a-ripple on his back.   *knowing is*
I know the joy of kingship: well, thou art king!   300 *pacivity*

    "But," sayest thou—(and I marvel, I repeat,
To find thee trip on such a mere word) "what
Thou writest, paintest, stays; that does not die:
Sappho survives, because we sing her songs,
And Æschylus, because we read his plays!"
Why, if they live still, let them come and take
Thy slave in my despite, drink from thy cup,
Speak in my place. Thou diest while I survive?
Say rather that my fate is deadlier still,
In this, that every day my sense of joy   310
Grows more acute, my soul (intensified
By power and insight) more enlarged, more keen;
While every day my hairs fall more and more,
My hand shakes, and the heavy years increase—
The horror quickening still from year to year,
The consummation coming past escape
When I shall know most, and yet least enjoy—
When all my works wherein I prove my worth,
Being present still to mock me in men's mouths,
Alive still, in the praise of such as thou,   *horrible* 320
I, I the feeling, thinking, acting man,   *that all come to*
The man who loved his life so over-much,   *naught*
Sleep in my urn. It is so horrible,
I dare at times imagine to my need
Some future state revealed to us by **Zeus**,
Unlimited in capability

For joy, as this is in desire for joy,
—To seek which, the joy-hunger forces us:
That, stung by straitness of our life, made strait
On purpose to make prized the life at large—   330
Freed by the throbbing impulse we call death,
We burst there as the worm into the fly,
Who, while a worm still, wants his wings. But no!
Zeus has not yet revealed it; and alas,
He must have done so, were it possible!

   Live long and happy, and in that thought die:
Glad for what was! Farewell. And for the rest,
I cannot tell thy messenger aright
Where to deliver what he bears of thine
To one called Paulus; we have heard his fame   340
Indeed, if Christus be not one with him—
I know not, nor am troubled much to know.
Thou canst not think a mere barbarian Jew,
As Paulus proves to be, one circumcized,
Hath access to a secret shut from us?
Thou wrongest our philosophy, O king,
In stooping to inquire of such an one,
As if his answer could impose at all!
He writeth, doth he? well, and he may write.
Oh, the Jew findeth scholars! certain slaves   350
Who touched on this same isle, preached him and Christ;
And (as I gathered from a bystander)
Their doctrine could be held by no sane man.

[1855]

A GRAMMARIAN'S FUNERAL

Shortly After the Revival of Learning in Europe

Let us begin and carry up this corpse,
    Singing together.
Leave we the common crofts, the vulgar thorpes,
    Each in its tether
Sleeping safe on the bosom of the plain,
    Cared-for till cock-crow:
Look out if yonder be not day again
    Rimming the rock-row!
That's the appropriate country; there, man's thought,
    Rarer, intenser,   10
Self-gathered for an outbreak, as it ought,
    Chafes in the censer.
Leave we the unlettered plain its herd and crop;
    Seek we sepulture
On a tall mountain, cited to the top,
    Crowded with culture!
All the peaks soar, but one the rest excels;
    Clouds overcome it;
No! yonder sparkle is the citadel's
    Circling its summit.   20
Thither our path lies; wind we up the heights:
    Wait ye the warning?
Our low life was the level's and the night's;
    He's for the morning.
Step to a tune, square chests, erect each head,
    'Ware the beholders!
This is our master, famous calm and dead,
    Borne on our shoulders.

---

the Revival of Learning: that is, the time in the early Renaissance, when western Europe was rediscovering Greek thought and grammarians had to make the language clear, so that the Greek philosophy and literature would be available to other scholars. The speaker of the monologue is a disciple of the grammarian, taking his master's body to its burial place on the top of a mountain.

3 *common crofts, the vulgar thorpes:* the farms and villages of the common people.

Sleep, crop and herd! sleep, darkling thorpe and croft,
　　Safe from the weather!　　　　　　　　　　　30
He, whom we convoy to his grave aloft,
　　Singing together,
He was a man born with thy face and throat,
　　Lyric Apollo!
Long he lived nameless: how should spring take note
　　Winter would follow?
Till lo, the little touch, and youth was gone!
　　Cramped and diminished,
Moaned he, "New measures, other feet anon!
　　My dance is finished?"　　　　　　　　　　　40
No, that's the world's way: (keep the mountain-side,
　　Make for the city!)
He knew the signal, and stepped on with pride
　　Over men's pity;
Left play for work, and grappled with the world
　　Bent on escaping:
"What's in the scroll," quoth he, "thou keepest furled?
　　Show me their shaping,
Theirs who most studied man, the bard and sage,—
　　Give!"—So, he gowned him,　　　　　　　　　50
Straight got by heart that book to its last page:
　　Learned, we found him.
Yea, but we found him bald too, eyes like lead,
　　Accents uncertain:
"Time to taste life," another would have said,
　　"Up with the curtain!"
This man said rather, "Actual life comes next?
　　Patience a moment!
Grant I have mastered learning's crabbed text,
　　Still there's the comment.　　　　　　　　　60
Let me know all! Prate not of most or least,
　　Painful or easy!
Even to the crumbs I'd fain eat up the feast,
　　Ay, nor feel queasy."
Oh, such a life as he resolved to live,

---

34 *Apollo:* god of poetry and song.
45-6 *grappled . . . escaping:* i.e., wrestled to find the elusive meaning of life.
50 *gowned him:* wore a scholar's gown.

When he had learned it,
When he had gathered all books had to give!
   Sooner, he spurned it.
Image the whole, then execute the parts—
   Fancy the fabric   70
Quite, ere you build, ere steel strike fire from quartz,
   Ere mortar dab brick!

(Here's the town-gate reached: there's the market-place
   Gaping before us.)
Yea, this in him was the peculiar grace
   (Hearten our chorus!)
That before living he'd learn how to live—
   No end to learning:
Earn the means first—God surely will contrive
   Use for our earning.   80
Others mistrust and say, "But time escapes:
   Live now or never!"
He said, "What's time? Leave Now for dogs and apes!
   Man has Forever."
Back to his book then: deeper drooped his head:
   Calculus racked him:
Leaden before, his eyes grew dross of lead:
   Tussis attacked him.
"Now, master, take a little rest!"—not he!
   (Caution redoubled,   90
Step two abreast, the way winds narrowly!)
   Not a whit troubled
Back to his studies, fresher than at first,
   Fierce as a dragon
He (soul-hydroptic with a sacred thirst)
   Sucked at the flagon.
Oh, if we draw a circle premature,
   Heedless of far gain,
Greedy for quick returns of profit, sure
   Bad is our bargain!   100
Was it not great? did not he throw on God,

---

86 *Calculus:* gallstones.
88 *Tussis:* bronchitis.
95 *soul-hydroptic:* meaning both spiritually thirsty and afflicted with dropsy
of the soul.

(He loves the burthen)—
God's task to make the heavenly period
    Perfect the earthen?
Did not he magnify the mind, show clear
    Just what it all meant?
He would not discount life, as fools do here,
    Paid by instalment.
He ventured neck or nothing—heaven's success
    Found, or earth's failure: 110
"Wilt thou trust death or not?" He answered "Yes:
    Hence with life's pale lure!"
That low man seeks a little thing to do,
    Sees it and does it:
This high man, with a great thing to pursue,
    Dies ere he knows it.
That low man goes on adding one to one,
    His hundred's soon hit:
This high man, aiming at a million,
    Misses an unit.   120
That, has the world here—should he need the next,
    Let the world mind him!
This, throws himself on God, and unperplexed
    Seeking shall find him.
So, with the throttling hands of death at strife,
    Ground he at grammar;
Still, thro' the rattle, parts of speech were rife:
    While he could stammer
He settled *Hoti's* business—let it be!—
    Properly based *Oun*—   130
Gave us the doctrine of the enclitic *De*,
    Dead from the waist down.
Well, here's the platform, here's the proper place:
    Hail to your purlieus,
All ye highfliers of the feathered race,
    Swallows and curlews!
Here's the top-peak; the multitude below
    Live, for they can, there:
This man decided not to Live but Know—

129-31 *Hoti:* Hoti, *Oun,* and *De* are Greek particles, whose proper usage was
difficult to determine.
134 *purlieus:* haunts.

Bury this man there? 140
Here—here's the place, where meteors shoot, clouds form,
 Lightnings are loosened,
Stars come and go! Let joy break with the storm,
 Peace let the dew send!
Lofty designs must close in like effects: *never daring to grasp.*
 Loftily lying,
Leave him—still loftier than the world suspects,
 Living and dying.

[1855]

ABT VOGLER

*After He Has Been Extemporizing Upon the Musical
Instrument of His Invention*

I

Would that the structure brave, the manifold music I build,
 Bidding my organ obey, calling its keys to their work,
Claiming each slave of the sound, at a touch, as when Solomon
 willed
Armies of angels that soar, legions of demons that lurk,
Man, brute, reptile, fly,—alien of end and of aim,
 Adverse, each from the other heaven-high, hell-deep re-
 moved,—
Should rush into sight at once as he named the ineffable
 Name,
 And pile him a palace straight, to pleasure the princess he
 loved!

II

Would it might tarry like his, the beautiful building of mine,
 This which my keys in a crowd pressed and importuned
 to raise! 10

Abt Vogler: the early nineteenth-century German musician, the Abbe Georg
Joseph Vogler, inventor of a portable organ, who was famous for his im-
provisations.
[7] *ineffable Name:* the name of God. Solomon was said to own a seal bearing the name of God, which enabled him to summon supernatural help.

Ah, one and all, how they helped, would dispart now and
    now combine,
    Zealous to hasten the work, heighten their master his
        praise!
And one would bury his brow with a blind plunge down to
    hell,
    Burrow awhile and build, broad on the roots of things,
Then up again swim into sight, having based me my palace
    well,
    Founded it, fearless of flame, flat on the nether springs.

III

And another would mount and march, like the excellent
    minion he was,
    Ay, another and yet another, one crowd but with many a
        crest,
Raising my rampired walls of gold as transparent as glass,
    Eager to do and die, yield each his place to the rest: 20
For higher still and higher (as a runner tips with fire,
    When a great illumination surprises a festal night—
Outlining round and round Rome's dome from space to
    spire)
    Up, the pinnacled glory reached, and the pride of my soul
    was in sight.

IV

In sight? Not half! for it seemed, it was certain, to match
    man's birth,
    Nature in turn conceived, obeying an impulse as I;
And the emulous heaven yearned down, made effort to
    reach the earth,
    As the earth had done her best, in my passion, to scale the
    sky:
Novel splendours burst forth, grew familiar and dwelt with
    mine,

---

[16] *nether springs:* the fountains of the deep on which the universe rested.
[19] *rampired:* ramparted.
[23] *Rome's dome:* St. Peter's, illuminated for festivals.
[25-8] *to match man's birth . . . scale the sky:* i.e., nature copied man's creation and projected down from heaven to earth a structure equal to the musical structure of Vogler (which he compares to Solomon's palace) that
reaches from earth to heaven.

Not a point nor peak but found and fixed its wondering
    star;   30
Meteor-moons, balls of blaze: and they did not pale nor
    pine,
    For earth had attained to heaven, there was no more
    near nor far.

v

Nay more; for there wanted not who walked in the glare
    and glow,
    Presences plain in the place; or, fresh from the Protoplast,
Furnished for ages to come, when a kindlier wind should
    blow,
    Lured now to begin and live, in a house to their liking at
    last;
Or else the wonderful Dead who have passed through the
    body and gone,
    But were back once more to breathe in an old world
    worth their new:
What never had been, was now; what was, as it shall be
    anon;
    And what is,—shall I say, matched both? for I was made
    perfect too.   40

vi

All through my keys that gave their sounds to a wish of my
    soul,
    All through my soul that praised as its wish flowed visibly
    forth,
All through music and me! For think, had I painted the
    whole,
    Why, there it had stood, to see, nor the process so wonder-
    worth:
Had I written the same, made verse—still, effect proceeds
    from cause,
    Ye know why the forms are fair, ye hear how the tale is
    told;
It is all triumphant art, but art in obedience to laws,
    Painter and poet are proud in the artist-list enrolled:—

---

[34] *fresh from the Protoplast:* newly created of protoplasm.
[35] *Furnished:* intended.

VII

But here is the finger of God, a flash of the will that can,
   Existent behind all laws, that made them and, lo, they
      are!   50
And I know not if, save in this, such gift be allowed to man,
   That out of three sounds he frame, not a fourth sound, but
      a star.
Consider it well: each tone of our scale in itself is nought;
   It is everywhere in the world—loud, soft, and all is said:
Give it to me to use! I mix it with two in my thought:
   And, there! Ye have heard and seen: consider and bow the
      head!

VIII

Well, it is gone at last, the palace of music I reared;
   Gone! and the good tears start, the praises that come too
      slow;
For one is assured at first, one scarce can say that he feared,
   That he even gave it a thought, the gone thing was to go.   60
Never to be again! But many more of the kind
   As good, nay, better perchance: is this your comfort to me?
To me, who must be saved because I cling with my mind
   To the same, same self, same love, same God: ay, what
      was, shall be.

IX

Therefore to whom turn I but to thee, the effable Name?
   Builder and maker, thou, of houses not made with hands!
What, have fear of change from thee who art ever the same?
   Doubt that thy power can fill the heart that thy power ex-
      pands?
There shall never be one lost good! What was, shall live as
      before;
   The evil is null, is nought, is silence implying sound;   70
What was good shall be good, with, for evil, so much good
      more;

---

[49] *here:* in music. Vogler is saying that music is more Godlike than pictorial
art or poetry because it is not subject to laws and therefore is closer to the
creative power of God.
[52] *star:* harmony, greater than the sounds composing it.

On the earth the broken arcs; in the heaven, a perfect
  round.

X

All we have willed or hoped or dreamed of good shall exist;
  Not its semblance, but itself; no beauty, nor good, nor
    power
Whose voice has gone forth, but each survives for the melo-
  dist
  When eternity affirms the conception of an hour.
The high that proved too high, the heroic for earth too hard,
  The passion that left the ground to lose itself in the sky,
Are music sent up to God by the lover and the bard;
  Enough that he heard it once: we shall hear it by-and-by.   80

XI

And what is our failure here but a triumph's evidence
  For the fulness of the days? Have we withered or ago-
  nized?
Why else was the pause prolonged but that singing might is-
  sue thence?
  Why rushed the discords in but that harmony should be
    prized?
Sorrow is hard to bear, and doubt is slow to clear,
  Each sufferer says his say, his scheme of the weal and
  woe:
But God has a few of us whom he whispers in the ear;
  The rest may reason and welcome: 't is we musicians
  know.

XII

Well, it is earth with me; silence resumes her reign:
  I will be patient and proud, and soberly acquiesce.   90
Give me the keys. I feel for the common chord again,
  Sliding by semitones, till I sink to the minor,—yes,
And I blunt it into a ninth, and I stand on alien ground,
  Surveying awhile the heights I rolled from into the deep;
Which, hark, I have dared and done, for my resting-place is
    found,
  The C Major of this life: so, now I will try to sleep.

[1864]

RABBI BEN EZRA

I

Grow old along with me!
The best is yet to be,
The last of life, for which the first was made:
Our times are in His hand
Who saith "A whole I planned,
Youth shows but half; trust God: see all nor be afraid!"

[handwritten margin note: Some purpose in it is end]

II

Not that, amassing flowers,
Youth sighed "Which rose make ours,
Which lily leave and then as best recall?"
Not that, admiring stars,   10
It yearned "Nor Jove, nor Mars;
Mine be some figured flame which blends, transcends them all!"

III

Not for such hopes and fears
Annulling youth's brief years,
Do I remonstrate: folly wide the mark!
Rather I prize the doubt
Low kinds exist without,
Finished and finite clods, untroubled by a spark.

IV

Poor vaunt of life indeed,
Were man but formed to feed
On joy, to solely seek and find and feast:
Such feasting ended, then
As sure an end to men;
Irks care the crop-full bird? Frets doubt the maw-crammed
    beast?   20

[handwritten margin note: like more than joy alone]

Rabbi Ben Ezra: Abraham Ibn Ezra, twelfth-century Jewish scholar, astronomer, physician, mathematician, teacher, poet, and theologian, best known for his commentaries upon the Old Testament.
24 *Irks care . . . Frets doubt:* i.e., Does care irk . . . does doubt disturb . . . ?

V

Rejoice we are allied
To That which doth provide
And not partake, effect and not receive!
A spark disturbs our clod;
Nearer we hold of God
Who gives, than of His tribes that take, I must believe.   30

VI

Then, welcome each rebuff
That turns earth's smoothness rough,
Each sting that bids nor sit nor stand but go!
Be our joys three-parts pain!
Strive, and hold cheap the strain;
Learn, nor account the pang; dare, never grudge the throe!

VII

For thence,—a paradox
Which comforts while it mocks,—
Shall life succeed in that it seems to fail:
What I aspired to be,   40
And was not, comforts me:
A brute I might have been, but would not sink i' the scale.

VIII

What is he but a brute
Whose flesh has soul to suit,
Whose spirit works lest arms and legs want play?
To man, propose this test—
Thy body at its best,
How far can that project thy soul on its lone way?

IX

Yet gifts should prove their use:
I own the Past profuse   50
Of power each side, perfection every turn:
Eyes, ears took in their dole,

---

45 *Whose spirit . . . want play?*: i.e., whose spirit is subservient to bodily pleasures.

Brain treasured up the whole;
Should not the heart beat once "How good to live and learn"?

X

Not once beat "Praise be Thine!
I see the whole design,
I, who saw power, see now love perfect too:
 Perfect I call Thy plan:
 Thanks that I was a man!
Maker, remake, complete,—I trust what Thou shalt do!" 60

XI

. For pleasant is this flesh;
 Our soul, in its rose-mesh
Pulled ever to the earth, still yearns for rest;
 Would we some prize might hold
 To match those manifold
Possessions of the brute,—gain most, as we did best!

XII

Let us not always say
"Spite of this flesh to-day
I strove, made head, gained ground upon the whole!"
 As the bird wings and sings, 70
 Let us cry "All good things
Are ours, nor soul helps flesh more, now, than flesh helps soul!"

XIII

Therefore I summon age
To grant youth's heritage,
Life's struggle having so far reached its term:
 Thence shall I pass, approved
 A man, for aye removed
From the developed brute; a god though in the germ.

XIV

And I shall thereupon
Take rest, ere I be gone 80

---

[62] *rose-mesh:* the body, with its network of veins and arteries.
[74] *grant youth's heritage:* probably, to recognize the meaning of past experience.

Once more on my adventure brave and new:
    Fearless and unperplexed,
    When I wage battle next,
What weapons to select, what armour to indue.

XV

    Youth ended, I shall try
    My gain or loss thereby;
Leave the fire ashes, what survives is gold:
    And I shall weigh the same,
    Give life its praise or blame:
Young, all lay in dispute; I shall know, being old.   90

XVI

    For note, when evening shuts,
    A certain moment cuts
The deed off, calls the glory from the grey:
    A whisper from the west
    Shoots—"Add this to the rest,
Take it and try its worth: here dies another day."

XVII

    So, still within this life,
    Though lifted o'er its strife,
Let me discern, compare, pronounce at last,
    "This rage was right i' the main,   100
    That acquiescence vain:
The Future I may face now I have proved the Past."

XVIII

    For more is not reserved
    To man, with soul just nerved
To act to-morrow what he learns to-day:
    Here, work enough to watch
    The Master work, and catch
Hints of the proper craft, tricks of the tool's true play.

XIX

    As it was better, youth
    Should strive, through acts uncouth,   110
Toward making, than repose on aught found made:

So, better, age, exempt
　From strife, should know, than tempt
Further. Thou waitedest age: wait death nor be afraid!

XX

Enough now, if the Right
　And Good and Infinite
Be named here, as thou callest thy hand thine own,
　　With knowledge absolute,
　　Subject to no dispute
From fools that crowded youth, nor let thee feel alone.　120

XXI

Be there, for once and all,
　Severed great minds from small,
Announced to each his station in the Past!
　　Was I, the world arraigned,
　　Were they, my soul disdained,
Right? Let age speak the truth and give us peace at last!

XXII

Now, who shall arbitrate?
　Ten men love what I hate,
Shun what I follow, slight what I receive;
　　Ten, who in ears and eyes　　　　　　　　130
　　Match me: we all surmise,
They this thing, and I that: whom shall my soul believe?

XXIII

Not on the vulgar mass
　Called "work," must sentence pass,
Things done, that took the eye and had the price;
　　O'er which, from level stand,
　　The low world laid its hand,
Found straightway to its mind, could value in a trice:

XXIV

But all, the world's coarse thumb
　And finger failed to plumb,　　　　　　　　140
So passed in making up the main account;
　　All instincts immature,

All purposes unsure,
That weighed not as his work, yet swelled the man's amount:

XXV

Thoughts hardly to be packed
Into a narrow act,
Fancies that broke through language and escaped;
All I could never be,
All, men ignored in me,
This, I was worth to God, whose wheel the pitcher shaped. 150

XXVI

Ay, note that Potter's wheel,
That metaphor! and feel
Why time spins fast, why passive lies our clay,—
Thou, to whom fools propound,
When the wine makes its round,
"Since life fleets, all is change; the Past gone, seize to-day!"

XXVII

Fool! All that is, at all,
Lasts ever, past recall;
Earth changes, but thy soul and God stand sure:
What entered into thee, 160
That was, is, and shall be:
Time's wheel runs back or stops: Potter and clay endure.

XXVIII

He fixed thee mid this dance
Of plastic circumstance,
This Present, thou, forsooth, wouldst fain arrest:
Machinery just meant
To give thy soul its bent,
Try thee and turn thee forth, sufficiently impressed.

XXIX

What though the earlier grooves
Which ran the laughing loves 170
Around thy base, no longer pause and press?

---

150 *pitcher:* for the figure of God as potter and man the pot He makes, see
Isaiah 64: 8; *Jeremiah* 18: 2-6; *Romans* 9: 21.

What though, about thy rim,
Scull-things in order grim
Grow out, in graver mood, obey the sterner stress?

XXX

Look not thou down but up!
To uses of a cup,
The festal board, lamp's flash and trumpet's peal,
The new wine's foaming flow,
The Master's lips a-glow!
Thou, heaven's consummate cup, what need'st thou with
earth's wheel?   180

XXXI

But I need, now as then,
Thee, God, who mouldest men;
And since, not even while the whirl was worst,
Did I,—to the wheel of life
With shapes and colours rife,
Bound dizzily,—mistake my end, to slake Thy thirst:

XXXII

So, take and use Thy work:
Amend what flaws may lurk,
What strain o' the stuff, what warpings past the aim!
My times be in Thy hand!   190
Perfect the cup as planned!
Let age approve of youth, and death complete the same!

[1864]

CALIBAN UPON SETEBOS;
OR
NATURAL THEOLOGY IN
THE ISLAND

"Thou thoughtest that I was altogether such a one as thyself"

['Will sprawl, now that the heat of day is best,
Flat on his belly in the pit's much mire,
With elbows wide, fists clenched to prop his chin.
And, while he kicks both feet in the cool slush,
And feels about his spine small eft-things course,
Run in and out each arm, and make him laugh:
And while above his head a pompion-plant,
Coating the cave-top as a brow its eye,
Creeps down to touch and tickle hair and beard,
And now a flower drops with a bee inside,   10
And now a fruit to snap at, catch and crunch,—
He looks out o'er yon sea which sunbeams cross
And recross till they weave a spider-web
(Meshes of fire, some great fish breaks at times)
And talks to his own self, howe'er he please,
Touching that other, whom his dam called God.
Because to talk about Him, vexes—ha,
Could He but know! and time to vex is now,
When talk is safer than in winter-time.

Can talk about God as Setebos not around

Natural Theology: the attempt to estimate the character of God from the evidence of nature. It was, of course, given impetus by Darwinian theory. In the poem Browning imagines a creature, half-man, half-beast, speculating upon God and imagining Setebos, a capricious god made in Caliban's own image. Beyond Setebos, he imagines, there may be the "Quiet," a power without the capriciousness of Setebos. The character of Caliban is taken from *The Tempest,* which explains the references to Prospero, Miranda, and Ariel. In the poem Caliban refers to himself in the third person, or even drops the pronoun altogether, for fear of provoking the wrath of Setebos. Finally, he forgets his wariness and refers to himself in the first person. When the third person pronoun is capitalized ("He" or "Him"), Caliban is referring to Setebos. The sections in brackets are meant to be interior monologue, not spoken aloud.
Thou thoughtest . . . thyself: see *Psalms* 50: 21.
5 *eft-things:* lizards.
16 *dam:* mother.

Moreover Prosper and Miranda sleep   20
In confidence he drudges at their task,
And it is good to cheat the pair, and gibe,
Letting the rank tongue blossom into speech.]

Setebos, Setebos, and Setebos!
Thinketh, He dwelleth i' the cold o' the moon.

'Thinketh He made it, with the sun to match,
But not the stars; the stars came otherwise;
Only made clouds, winds, meteors, such as that:
Also this isle, what lives and grows thereon,
And snaky sea which rounds and ends the same.   30

'Thinketh, it came of being ill at ease:
He hated that He cannot change His cold,
Nor cure its ache. 'Hath spied an icy fish
That longed to 'scape the rock-stream where she lived,
And thaw herself within the lukewarm brine
O' the lazy sea her stream thrusts far amid,
A crystal spike 'twixt two warm walls of wave;
Only, she ever sickened, found repulse
At the other kind of water, not her life,
(Green-dense and dim-delicious, bred o' the sun)   40
Flounced back from bliss she was not born to breathe,
And in her old bounds buried her despair,
Hating and loving warmth alike: so He.

'Thinketh, He made thereat the sun, this isle,
Trees and the fowls here, beast and creeping thing.
Yon otter, sleek-wet, black, lithe as a leech;
Yon auk, one fire-eye in a ball of foam,
That floats and feeds; a certain badger brown
He hath watched hunt with that slant white-wedge eye
By moonlight; and the pie with the long tongue   50
That pricks deep into oakwarts for a worm,
And says a plain word when she finds her prize,
But will not eat the ants; the ants themselves
That build a wall of seeds and settled stalks

---

50 *pie:* magpie.

About their hole—He made all these and more,
Made all we see, and us, in spite: how else?
He could not, Himself, make a second self
To be His mate; as well have made Himself:
He would not make what he mislikes or slights,
An eyesore to Him, or not worth His pains: 60
But did, in envy, listlessness or sport,
Make what Himself would fain, in a manner, be—
Weaker in most points, stronger in a few,
Worthy, and yet mere playthings all the while,
Things He admires and mocks too,—that is it.
Because, so brave, so better though they be,
It nothing skills if He begin to plague.
Look now, I melt a gourd-fruit into mash,
Add honeycomb and pods, I have perceived,
Which bite like finches when they bill and kiss,—   70
Then, when froth rises bladdery, drink up all,
Quick, quick, till maggots scamper through my brain;
Last, throw me on my back i' the seeded thyme,
And wanton, wishing I were born a bird.
Put case, unable to be what I wish,
I yet could make a live bird out of clay:
Would not I take clay, pinch my Caliban
Able to fly?—for, there, see, he hath wings,
And great comb like the hoopoe's to admire,
And there, a sting to do his foes offence,   80
There, and I will that he begin to live,
Fly to yon rock-top, nip me off the horns
Of grigs high up that make the merry din,
Saucy through their veined wings, and mind me not.
In which feat, if his leg snapped, brittle clay,
And he lay stupid-like,—why, I should laugh;
And if he, spying me, should fall to weep,
Beseech me to be good, repair his wrong,
Bid his poor leg smart less or grow again,—
Well, as the chance were, this might take or else   90
Not take my fancy: I might hear his cry,
And give the mankin three sound legs for one,
Or pluck the other off, leave him like an egg,

---

79 *hoopoe:* crested bird.
83 *grigs:* grasshoppers.

[handwritten marginalia: Caliban thinks of self as God; intuits nature of divine; deity ltd. to what beast thinks.]

And lessoned he was mine and merely clay.
Were this no pleasure, lying in the thyme,
Drinking the mash, with brain become alive,
Making and marring clay at will? So He.

'Thinketh, such shows nor right nor wrong in Him,
Nor kind, nor cruel: He is strong and Lord.
'Am strong myself compared to yonder crabs   100
That march now from the mountain to the sea;
'Let twenty pass, and stone the twenty-first,
Loving not, hating not, just choosing so.
'Say, the first straggler that boasts purple spots
Shall join the file, one pincer twisted off;
'Say, this bruised fellow shall receive a worm,
And two worms he whose nippers end in red;
As it likes me each time, I do: so He.

Well then, 'supposeth He is good i' the main,
Placable if His mind and ways were guessed,   110
But rougher than His handiwork, be sure!
Oh, He hath made things worthier than Himself,
And envieth that, so helped, such things do more
Than He who made them! What consoles but this?
That they, unless through Him, do nought at all,
And must submit: what other use in things?
'Hath cut a pipe of pithless elder-joint
That, blown through, gives exact the scream o' the jay
When from her wing you twitch the feathers blue:
Sound this, and little birds that hate the jay   120
Flock within stone's throw, glad their foe is hurt:
Put case such pipe could prattle and boast forsooth
"I catch the birds, I am the crafty thing,
I make the cry my maker cannot make
With his great round mouth; he must blow through mine!"
Would not I smash it with my foot? So He.

But wherefore rough, why cold and ill at ease?
Aha, that is a question! Ask, for that,
What knows,—the something over Setebos
That made Him, or He, may be, found and fought,   130
Worsted, drove off and did to nothing, perchance.

There may be something quiet o'er His head,
Out of His reach, that feels nor joy nor grief,
Since both derive from weakness in some way.
I joy because the quails come; would not joy
Could I bring quails here when I have a mind:
This Quiet, all it hath a mind to, doth.
'Esteemeth stars the outposts of its couch,
But never spends much thought nor care that way.
It may look up, work up,—the worse for those   140
It works on! 'Careth but for Setebos
The many-handed as a cuttle-fish,
Who, making Himself feared through what He does,
Looks up, first, and perceives he cannot soar
To what is quiet and hath happy life;
Next looks down here, and out of very spite
Makes this a bauble-world to ape yon real,
These good things to match those as hips do grapes.
'T is solace making baubles, ay, and sport.
Himself peeped late, eyed Prosper at his books   150
Careless and lofty, lord now of the isle:
Vexed, 'stitched a book of broad leaves, arrow-shaped,
Wrote thereon, he knows what, prodigious words;
Has peeled a wand and called it by a name;
Weareth at whiles for an enchanter's robe
The eyed skin of a supple oncelot;
And hath an ounce sleeker than youngling mole,
A four-legged serpent he makes cower and couch,
Now snarl, now hold its breath and mind his eye,
And saith she is Miranda and my wife: 160
'Keeps for his Ariel a tall pouch-bill crane
He bids go wade for fish and straight disgorge;
Also a sea-beast, lumpish, which he snared,
Blinded the eyes of, and brought somewhat tame,
And split its toe-webs, and now pens the drudge
In a hole o' the rock and calls him Caliban;
A bitter heart that bides its time and bites.
'Play thus at being Prosper in a way,
Taketh his mirth with make-believes: so He.

---

148 *hips:* rough berries.
156 *oncelot:* ocelot.
157 *ounce:* leopard.

His dam held that the Quiet made all things   170
Which Setebos vexed only: 'holds not so.
Who made them weak, meant weakness He might vex.
Had He meant other, while His hand was in,
Why not make horny eyes no thorn could prick,
Or plate my scalp with bone against the snow,
Or overscale my flesh 'neath joint and joint,
Like an orc's armour? Ay,—so spoil His sport!
He is the One now: only He doth all.

'Saith, He may like, perchance, what profits Him.
Ay, himself loves what does him good; but why?   180
'Gets good no otherwise. This blinded beast
Loves whoso places flesh-meat on his nose,
But, had he eyes, would want no help, but hate
Or love, just as it liked him: He hath eyes.
Also it pleaseth Setebos to work,
Use all His hands, and exercise much craft,
By no means for the love of what is worked.
'Tasteth, himself, no finer good i' the world
When all goes right, in this safe summer-time,
And he wants little, hungers, aches not much,   190
Than trying what to do with wit and strength.
'Falls to make something: 'piled yon pile of turfs,
And squared and stuck there squares of soft white chalk,
And, with a fish-tooth, scratched a moon on each,
And set up endwise certain spikes of tree,
And crowned the whole with a sloth's skull a-top,
Found dead i' the woods, too hard for one to kill.
No use at all i' the work, for work's sole sake;
'Shall some day knock it down again: so He.

'Saith He is terrible: watch His feats in proof!   200
One hurricane will spoil six good months' hope.
He hath a spite against me, that I know,
Just as He favours Prosper, who knows why?
So it is all the same, as well I find.
'Wove wattles half the winter, fenced them firm
With stone and stake to stop she-tortoises

---

177 *orc:* sea monster.
205 *wattles:* twigs.

Crawling to lay their eggs here: well, one wave,
Feeling the foot of Him upon its neck,
Gaped as a snake does, lolled out its large tongue,
And licked the whole labour flat; so much for spite. 210
'Saw a ball flame down late (yonder it lies)
Where, half an hour before, I slept i' the shade:
Often they scatter sparkles: there is force!
'Dug up a newt He may have envied once
And turned to stone, shut up inside a stone.
Please Him and hinder this?—What Prosper does?
Aha, if He would tell me how! Not He!
There is the sport: discover how or die!
All need not die, for of the things o' the isle
Some flee afar, some dive, some run up trees; 220
Those at His mercy,—why, they please Him most
When . . . when . . . well, never try the same way twice!
Repeat what act has pleased, He may grow wroth.
You must not know His ways, and play Him off,
Sure of the issue. 'Doth the like himself:
'Spareth a squirrel that it nothing fears
But steals the nut from underneath my thumb,
And when I threat, bites stoutly in defence:
'Spareth an urchin that contrariwise,
Curls up into a ball, pretending death 230
For fright at my approach: the two ways please.
But what would move my choler more than this,
That either creature counted on its life
To-morrow and next day and all days to come,
Saying, forsooth, in the inmost of its heart,
"Because he did so yesterday with me,
And otherwise with such another brute,
So must he do henceforth and always."—Ay?
Would teach the reasoning couple what "must" means!
'Doth as he likes, or wherefore Lord? So He. 240

'Conceiveth all things will continue thus,
And we shall have to live in fear of Him
So long as He lives, keeps His strength: no change,
If He have done His best, make no new world
To please Him more, so leave off watching this,—
If He surprise not even the Quiet's self

Some strange day,—or, suppose, grow into it
As grubs grow butterflies: else, here are we,
And there is He, and nowhere help at all.

'Believeth with the life, the pain shall stop.   250
His dam held different, that after death
He both plagued enemies and feasted friends:
Idly! He doth His worst in this our life,
Giving just respite lest we die through pain,
Saving last pain for worst,—with which, an end.
(Meanwhile, the best way to escape His ire
Is, not to seem too happy.) 'Sees, himself,
Yonder two flies, with purple films and pink,
Bask on the pompion-bell above: kills both.
'Sees two black painful beetles roll their ball   260
On head and tail as if to save their lives:
Moves them the stick away they strive to clear.

Even so, 'would have Him misconceive, suppose
This Caliban strives hard and ails no less,
And always, above all else, envies Him;
Wherefore he mainly dances on dark nights,
Moans in the sun, gets under holes to laugh,
And never speaks his mind save housed as now:
Outside, 'groans, curses. If He caught me here,
O'erheard this speech, and asked "What chucklest at?"   270
'Would, to appease Him, cut a finger off,
Or of my three kid yearlings burn the best,
Or let the toothsome apples rot on tree,
Or push my tame beast for the orc to taste:
While myself lit a fire, and made a song
And sung it, "What I hate, be consecrate
To celebrate Thee and Thy state, no mate
For Thee; what see for envy in poor me?"
Hoping the while, since evils sometimes mend,
Warts rub away and sores are cured with slime,   280
That some strange day, will either the Quiet catch
And conquer Setebos, or likelier He
Decrepit may doze, doze, as good as die.

Thinks Setebos is present

[What, what? A curtain o'er the world at once!
Crickets stop hissing; not a bird—or, yes,
There scuds His raven that has told Him all!
It was fool's play, this prattling! Ha! The wind
Shoulders the pillared dust, death's house o' the move,
And fast invading fires begin! White blaze—
A tree's head snaps—and there, there, there, there, there,   290
His thunder follows! Fool to gibe at Him!
Lo! 'Lieth flat and loveth Setebos!
'Maketh his teeth meet through his upper lip,
Will let those quails fly, will not eat this month
One little mess of whelks, so he may 'scape!]

[1864]

From THE RING AND THE BOOK

Prefatory Note

[In 1860 on a bookstall in an open market in Florence, Browning found a vellum-bound collection of documents, in both print and manuscript, which the title-page said was "A Setting-forth of the entire Criminal Cause against Guido Franceschini, Nobleman of Arezzo, and his Bravoes, who were put to death in Rome, February 22, 1698. The first by beheading, the other four by the gallows. Roman Murder-Case. In which it is disputed whether and when a Husband may kill his Adulterous Wife without incurring the ordinary penalty." This volume, which Browning called *The Old Yellow Book,* and a few other contemporary documents gave him the plot for *The Ring and the Book.* Since the story is told from many points of view, the facts are occasionally disputable, but in general they are these:

In 1693 Count Guido Franceschini, an ugly, depraved, middle-aged member of an ancient, decadent family, was married secretly in Rome to a thirteen-year-old girl, Pompilia, thought to be the daughter of Pietro and Violante Comparini, by whom she had been reared. Guido was motivated by greed for the fortune he believed the Comparini to have; Violante concealed the marriage from her husband in her anxiety to assure Pompilia a marriage with a nobleman. Making the best of the situation when he discovered it, Pietro turned over his property (which was much less handsome than Guido believed) to Pompilia's new husband as her dowry, but he specified that he and his wife should live in Arezzo with Pompilia and Guido. After a few months of persecution by Guido, Pietro and Violante returned to Rome and began a suit for the return of the dowry, on the grounds that Pompilia was actually not their child but the daughter of a common prostitute, who had turned her baby over to Violante, who tricked Pietro into believing that Pompilia was their own child. The courts held that Pompilia was indeed legitimate, but awarded the dowry to Guido because he had been deceived.

After the departure of the Comparini from Arezzo, Guido (who, with some reason, felt that he had been tricked) began treating Pompilia with great cruelty and, even worse, to leave her exposed to the lascivious solicitations of his younger brother, a priest who lived in the same house. In despair Pompilia appealed for help to both civil and church authorities, but they sent her back to her husband. For three years Pompilia lived with her husband, until she conceived his child.

Meanwhile, Guido had apparently begun to plot to remove Pompilia from his life without losing her dowry. A handsome young priest, Giuseppe Caponsacchi, a nobleman of Arezzo, who had been somewhat worldly in his spiritual duties, was picked by Guido for the role of Pompilia's adulterous lover. Pompilia began to receive love letters, supposedly written by Caponsacchi but presumably written by Guido himself. At the same time Caponsacchi received ardent letters urging a meeting with Pompilia. Actually, Pompilia was illiterate and could not have written them as she was supposed to have done; they were the work of Guido and his mistress, Pompilia's serving-woman. Since Pompilia and Caponsacchi were innocent of adulterous intentions, the plot failed, but it did serve to make them aware of each other.

When Pompilia discovered that she was pregnant, she felt forced to escape from Guido for the sake of her unborn child. Knowing no one to whom she could turn for help, she begged Caponsacchi to take her to Rome, where she could live with her foster-parents. In April 1697 they left Arezzo together, driving without stop that night, the next day, the next night, and the following day. At last, too tired to go on, Pompilia had to rest in order to save the life of her child. The pair stayed the night at

an inn in Castelnuovo, a few miles from Rome in the papal ter-
ritories, and planned to go easily into Rome the next day. In the
morning Guido arrived before they could continue their journey;
his men overcame Caponsacchi, who was dressed as a courtier,
and went upstairs to find Pompilia asleep. Springing up, she
caught Guido's sword and tried to kill him but was unarmed by
his men, and she and Caponsacchi were arrested for adultery.

In the trial of Pompilia and Caponsacchi, the judges took a
lenient view and sentenced him to three years of banishment in
Civita Vecchia and remanded her to a convent run for the care of
fallen women. The sentence was unsatisfactory, for it assumed the
guilt of the pair and it failed to provide sufficient protection for
Pompilia from the wrath of Guido.

In December 1697 Pompilia gave birth to a son, Gaetano,
at the home of Pietro and Violante, where she had been allowed
to go under bond. Two weeks later Guido brought four villainous
helpers to the house of the Comparini with the intention of ab-
ducting the baby, taking revenge on Pompilia and her foster
parents, and securing all their property. They stabbed Pietro and
Violante to death and left Pompilia for dead after she had received twenty-two dagger wounds. She survived, however, long
enough to give her own account of the affair. The baby had been
taken away for safety and so escaped Guido.

At the trial of Guido and his ruffians there was no attempt
made to deny the actual killing of the Comparini, but Guido
pleaded the rights of a tricked and cuckolded husband. The court
sentenced Guido to beheading and his companions to hanging.
Because Guido had once taken minor orders in the Church, he
claimed papal jurisdiction and made an appeal for mercy to the
Pope, who denied his plea. Guido was executed in February
1698.

In a subsequent suit for Pompilia's property instituted by the
convent in which she had been placed (since the nuns inherited
the property of loose women in their care), Pompilia was declared innocent of adultery and her son was made heir to her
estate.

The setting of the poem is during and immediately after the
period when Guido and his ruffians were on trial for murder. The
whole poem is divided into twelve books. In Book I Browning
summarizes the plot, as drawn from *The Old Yellow Book*, and
explains his title. As a jeweller makes a ring from gold and alloy,

so he takes the crude material of the plot, adds the alloy of creative imagination to give it shape, then purges away the alloy
leaving only the pure gold of the essence of the story. Book I
concludes with the invocation of the spirit of Mrs. Browning
as "lyric Love." Books II, III, and IV present the differing views
of "Half-Rome," a cuckolded husband who naturally thinks Pompilia is guilty; "The Other Half-Rome," a libertine who thinks
that Pompilia and Caponsacchi are probably guilty but takes a
romantic view of the elopement; and "Tertium Quid," who treats
the whole affair as an intellectual exercise in determining guilt.
In Book V Guido presents his case as the representative of an
old family deceived by his wife and her friends and relatives.
Book VI is the monologue of Caponsacchi spoken at the trial of
Guido. Book VII is the testimony of Pompilia on her deathbed.
In the next three books we get the points of view of Guido's
lawyer, Pompilia's lawyer, and the Pope, who must review the
whole case. In Book XI Guido returns for a second monologue
just before his execution, changing from a suave and worldly
man to a frightened animal in his terror. Book XII contains
Browning's own account of the execution and includes a statement by Pompilia's confessor, who attests to her innocence and
saintliness.]

VI   .

GIUSEPPE CAPONSACCHI

Answer you, Sirs? Do I understand aright?
· Have patience! In this sudden smoke from hell,—
So things disguise themselves,—I cannot see
My own hand held thus broad before my face
And know it again. Answer you? Then that means
Tell over twice what I, the first time, told
Six months ago: 't was here, I do believe,
Fronting you same three in this very room,
I stood and told you: yet now no one laughs,
Who then . . . nay, dear my lords, but laugh you did,   10
As good as laugh, what in a judge we style
Laughter—no levity, nothing indecorous, lords!
Only,—I think I apprehend the mood:
There was the blameless shrug, permissible smirk,

The pen's pretence at play with the pursed mouth,
The titter stifled in the hollow palm
Which rubbed the eyebrow and caressed the nose,
When I first told my tale: they meant, you know,
"The sly one, all this we are bound believe!
Well, he can say no other than what he says.   20
We have been young, too,—come, there's greater guilt!
Let him but decently disembroil himself,
Scramble from out the scrape nor move the mud,—
We solid ones may risk a finger-stretch!"
And now you sit as grave, stare as aghast
As if I were a phantom: now 't is—"Friend,
Collect yourself!"—no laughing matter more—
"Counsel the Court in this extremity,
Tell us again!"—tell that, for telling which,
I got the jocular piece of punishment,   30
Was sent to lounge a little in the place
Whence now of a sudden here you summon me
To take the intelligence from just—your lips!
You, Judge Tommati, who then tittered most,—
That she I helped eight months since to escape
Her husband, was retaken by the same,
Three days ago, if I have seized your sense,—
(I being disallowed to interfere,
Meddle or make in a matter none of mine,
For you and law were guardians quite enough   40
O' the innocent, without a pert priest's help)—
And that he has butchered her accordingly,
As she foretold and as myself believed,—
And, so foretelling and believing so,
We were punished, both of us, the merry way:
Therefore, tell once again the tale! For what?
Pompilia is only dying while I speak!
Why does the mirth hang fire and miss the smile?
My masters, there's an old book, you should con
For strange adventures, applicable yet,   50
'T is stuffed with. Do you know that there was once
This thing: a multitude of worthy folk
Took recreation, watched a certain group
Of soldiery intent upon a game,—
How first they wrangled, but soon fell to play,

Threw dice,—the best diversion in the world.
A word in your ear,—they are now casting lots,
Ay, with that gesture quaint and cry uncouth,
For the coat of One murdered an hour ago!
I am a priest,—talk of what I have learned.   60
Pompilia is bleeding out her life belike,
Gasping away the latest breath of all,
This minute, while I talk—not while you laugh.

Yet, being sobered now, what is it you ask
By way of explanation? There's the fact!
It seems to fill the universe with sight
And sound,—from the four corners of this earth
Tells itself over, to my sense at least.
But you may want it lower set i' the scale,—
Too vast, too close it clangs in the ear, perhaps;   70
You'd stand back just to comprehend it more.
Well then, let me, the hollow rock, condense
The voice o' the sea and wind, interpret you
The mystery of this murder. God above!
It is too paltry, such a transference
O' the storm's roar to the cranny of the stone!

This deed, you saw begin—why does its end
Surprise you? Why should the event enforce
The lesson, we ourselves learned, she and I,
From the first o' the fact, and taught you, all in vain?   80
This Guido from whose throat you took my grasp,
Was this man to be favoured, now, or feared,
Let do his will, or have his will restrained,
In the relation with Pompilia? Say!
Did any other man need interpose
—Oh, though first comer, though as strange at the work
As fribble must be, coxcomb, fool that's near
To knave as, say, a priest who fears the world—
Was he bound brave the peril, save the doomed,
Or go on, sing his snatch and pluck his flower,   90
Keep the straight path and let the victim die?
I held so; you decided otherwise,

---

87 *fribble:* trifler.

Saw no such peril, therefore no such need
To stop song, loosen flower, and leave path. Law,
Law was aware and watching, would suffice,
Wanted no priest's intrusion, palpably
Pretence, too manifest a subterfuge!
Whereupon I, priest, coxcomb, fribble and fool,
Ensconced me in my corner, thus rebuked,
A kind of culprit, over-zealous hound   100
Kicked for his pains to kennel; I gave place
To you, and let the law reign paramount:
I left Pompilia to your watch and ward,
And now you point me—there and thus she lies!

Men, for the last time, what do you want with me?
Is it,—you acknowledge, as it were, a use,
A profit in employing me?—at length
I may conceivably help the august law?
I am free to break the blow, next hawk that swoops
On next dove, nor miss much of good repute?   110
Or what if this your summons, after all,
Be but the form of mere release, no more,
Which turns the key and lets the captive go?
I have paid enough in person at Civita,
Am free,—what more need I concern me with?
Thank you! I am rehabilitated then,
A very reputable priest. But she—
The glory of life, the beauty of the world,
The splendour of heaven, . . . well, Sirs, does no one move?
Do I speak ambiguously? The glory, I say,   120
And the beauty, I say, and splendour, still say I,
Who, priest and trained to live my whole life long
On beauty and splendour, solely at their source,
God,—have thus recognized my food in her,
You tell me, that's fast dying while we talk,
Pompilia! How does lenity to me
Remit one death-bed pang to her? Come, smile!
The proper wink at the hot-headed youth
Who lets his soul show, through transparent words,
The mundane love that's sin and scandal too!   130
You are all struck acquiescent now, it seems:
It seems the oldest, gravest signor here,

Even the redoubtable Tommati, sits
Chop-fallen,—understands how law might take
Service like mine, of brain and heart and hand,
In good part. Better late than never, law.
You understand of a sudden, gospel too
Has a claim here, may possibly pronounce
Consistent with my priesthood, worthy Christ,
That I endeavoured to save Pompilia?   140

                              Then
You were wrong, you see: that's well to see, though late:
That's all we may expect of man, this side
The grave, his good is—knowing he is bad:
Thus will it be with us when the books ope
And we stand at the bar on judgment-day.
Well then, I have a mind to speak, see cause
To relume the quenched flax by this dreadful light,
Burn my soul out in showing you the truth.
I heard, last time I stood here to be judged,   150
What is priest's-duty,—labour to pluck tares
And weed the corn of Molinism; let me
Make you hear, this time, how, in such a case,
Man, be he in the priesthood or at plough,
Mindful of Christ or marching step by step
With . . . what's his style, the other potentate
Who bids have courage and keep honour safe,
Nor let minuter admonition tease?—
How he is bound, better or worse, to act.
Earth will not end through this misjudgment, no!   160

---

152 *Molinism:* term used to describe both the doctrines of Luis Molina, a
sixteenth-century Spanish Jesuit priest, who asserted that grace is dependent
upon the will of the individual freely accepting it, and the doctrine of Quietism, propounded by Miguel Molinos, a seventeenth-century Spanish priest.
Quietism was a form of mysticism which stressed contemplation rather than
action, and a withdrawal from the world of the senses. Because it lessened
the importance of the Sacraments and ceremonies of the Church, Quietism
was declared heretical by the Roman Catholic Church in 1687, only a few
years before the action of the poem. Browning is using Molinism as a standard against which to judge the corrupt practices of the Church, and as a
guide for Caponsacchi in his rejection of obedience to the forms of the
Church rather than to their spirit.
156 *other potentate:* the devil.

For you and the others like you sure to come,
Fresh work is sure to follow,—wickedness
That wants withstanding. Many a man of blood,
Many a man of guile will clamour yet,
Bid you redress his grievance,—as he clutched
The prey, forsooth a stranger stepped between,
And there's the good gripe in pure waste! My part
Is done; i' the doing it, I pass away
Out of the world. I want no more with earth.
Let me, in heaven's name, use the very snuff   170
O' the taper in one last spark shall show truth
For a moment, show Pompilia who was true!
Not for her sake, but yours: if she is dead,
Oh, Sirs, she can be loved by none of you
Most or least priestly! Saints, to do us good,
Must be in heaven, I seem to understand:
We never find them saints before, at least.
Be her first prayer then presently for you—
She has done the good to me . . .

                          What is all this?   180
There, I was born, have lived, shall die, a fool!
This is a foolish outset:—might with cause
Give colour to the very lie o' the man,
The murderer,—make as if I loved his wife,
In the way he called love. He is the fool there!
Why, had there been in me the touch of taint,
I had picked up so much of knaves'-policy
As hide it, keep one hand pressed on the place
Suspected of a spot would damn us both.
Or no, not her!—not even if any of you   190
Dares think that I, i' the face of death, her death
That's in my eyes and ears and brain and heart,
Lie,—if he does, let him! I mean to say,
So he stop there, stay thought from smirching her
The snow-white soul that angels fear to take
Untenderly. But, all the same, I know
I too am taintless, and I bare my breast.
You can't think, men as you are, all of you,
But that, to hear thus suddenly such an end
Of such a wonderful white soul, that comes   200

Of a man and murderer calling the white black,
Must shake me, trouble and disadvantage. Sirs,
Only seventeen!

       Why, good and wise you are!
You might at the beginning stop my mouth:
So, none would be to speak for her, that knew.
I talk impertinently, and you bear,
All the same. This it is to have to do
With honest hearts: they easily may err,
But in the main they wish well to the truth.   210
You are Christians; somehow, no one ever plucked
A rag, even, from the body of the Lord,
To wear and mock with, but, despite himself,
He looked the greater and was the better. Yes,
I shall go on now. Does she need or not
I keep calm? Calm I'll keep as monk that croons
Transcribing battle, earthquake, famine, plague,
From parchment to his cloister's chronicle.
Not one word more from the point now!

          I begin. 220
Yes, I am one of your body and a priest.
Also I am a younger son o' the House
Oldest now, greatest once, in my birth-town
Arezzo, I recognize no equal there—
(I want all arguments, all sorts of arms
That seem to serve,—use this for a reason, wait!)
Not therefore thrust into the Church, because
O' the piece of bread one gets there. We were first
Of Fiesole, that rings still with the fame
Of Capo-in-Sacco our progenitor: 230
When Florence ruined Fiesole, our folk
Migrated to the victor-city, and there
Flourished,—our palace and our tower attest,
In the Old Mercato,—this was years ago,
Four hundred, full,—no, it wants fourteen just.
Our arms are those of Fiesole itself,
The shield quartered with white and red: a branch

---

203 *seventeen:* Pompilia's age at her death.

Are the Salviati of us, nothing more.
That were good help to the Church? But better still—
Not simply for the advantage of my birth　　　　240
I' the way of the world, was I proposed for priest;
But because there's an illustration, late
I' the day, that's loved and looked to as a saint
Still in Arezzo, he was bishop of,
Sixty years since: he spent to the last doit
His bishop's-revenue among the poor,
And used to tend the needy and the sick,
Barefoot, because of his humility.
He it was,—when the Granduke Ferdinand
Swore he would raze our city, plough the place　　　　250
And sow it with salt, because we Aretines
Had tied a rope about the neck, to hale
The statue of his father from its base
For hate's sake,—he availed by prayers and tears
To pacify the Duke and save the town.
This was my father's father's brother. You see,
For his sake, how it was I had a right
To the self-same office, bishop in the egg,
So, grew i' the garb and prattled in the school,
Was made expect, from infancy almost,　　　　260
The proper mood o' the priest; till time ran by
And brought the day when I must read the vows,
Declare the world renounced and undertake
To become priest and leave probation,—leap
Over the ledge into the other life,
Having gone trippingly hitherto up to the height
O'er the wan water. Just a vow to read!

I stopped short awe-struck. "How shall holiest flesh
Engage to keep such a vow inviolate,
How much less mine? I know myself too weak,　　　　270
Unworthy! Choose a worthier stronger man!"
And the very Bishop smiled and stopped my mouth
In its mid-protestation. "Incapable?
Qualmish of conscience? Thou ingenuous boy!
Clear up the clouds and cast thy scruples far!

---

245 *doit:* small coin; hence, a trifle.

I satisfy thee there's an easier sense
Wherein to take such vow than suits the first
Rough rigid reading. Mark what makes all smooth,
Nay, has been even a solace to myself!
The Jews who needs must, in their synagogue,   280
Utter sometimes the holy name of God,
A thing their superstition boggles at,
Pronounce aloud the ineffable sacrosanct,—
How does their shrewdness help them? In this wise;
Another set of sounds they substitute,
Jumble so consonants and vowels—how
Should I know?—that there grows from out the old
Quite a new word that means the very same—
And o'er the hard place slide they with a smile.
Giuseppe Maria Caponsacchi mine,   290
Nobody wants you in these latter days
To prop the Church by breaking your backbone,—
As the necessary way was once, we know,
When Diocletian flourished and his like.
That building of the buttress-work was done
By martyrs and confessors: let it bide,
Add not a brick, but, where you see a chink,
Stick in a sprig of ivy or root a rose
Shall make amends and beautify the pile!
We profit as you were the painfullest   300
O' the martyrs, and you prove yourself a match
For the cruelest confessor ever was,
If you march boldly up and take your stand
Where their blood soaks, their bones yet strew the soil,
And cry 'Take notice, I the young and free
And well-to-do i' the world, thus leave the world,
Cast in my lot thus with no gay young world
But the grand old Church: she tempts me of the two!'
Renounce the world? Nay, keep and give it us!
Let us have you, and boast of what you bring.   310
We want the pick o' the earth to practise with,
Not its offscouring, halt and deaf and blind
In soul and body. There's a rubble-stone
Unfit for the front o' the building, stuff to stow
In a gap behind and keep us weather-tight;
There's porphyry for the prominent place. Good lack!

Saint Paul has had enough and to spare, I trow,
Of ragged run-away Onesimus:
He wants the right-hand with the signet-ring
Of King Agrippa, now, to shake and use.   320
I have a heavy scholar cloistered up,
Close under lock and key, kept at his task
Of letting Fénelon know the fool he is,
In a book I promise Christendom next Spring.
Why, if he covets so much meat, the clown,
As a lark's wing next Friday, or, any day,
Diversion beyond catching his own fleas,
He shall be properly swinged, I promise him.
But you, who are so quite another paste
Of a man,—do you obey me? Cultivate   330
Assiduous that superior gift you have
Of making madrigals—(who told me? Ah!)
Get done a Marinesque Adoniad straight
With a pulse o' the blood a-pricking, here and there,
That I may tell the lady, 'And he's ours!' "

So I became a priest: those terms changed all;
I was good enough for that, nor cheated so;
I could live thus and still hold head erect.
Now you see why I may have been before
A fribble and coxcomb, yet, as priest, break word   340
Nowise, to make you disbelieve me now.
I need that you should know my truth. Well, then,
According to prescription did I live,
—Conformed myself, both read the breviary
And wrote the rhymes, was punctual to my place
I' the Pieve, and as diligent at my post
Where beauty and fashion rule. I throve apace,
Sub-deacon, Canon, the authority

---

[318] *Onesimus:* In Paul's Epistle to *Philemon* he asks forgiveness for his son Onesimus; in *Acts* 25 and 26, Agrippa, the king, is merciful to Paul. Browning's contrast is between the suppliant and the powerful.
[323] *Fénelon:* François de Salignac de La Mothe-Fénelon, 1651-1715, French prelate who supported Molinism.
[328] *swinged:* beaten.
[333] *Marinesque Adoniad:* Giambattista Marino told the love story of Adonis in *Adone*, 1623.
[346] *Pieve:* Santa Maria della Pieve, the church in Arezzo where Caponsacchi was priest.

For delicate play at tarocs, and arbiter
O' the magnitude of fan-mounts: all the while   350
Wanting no whit the advantage of a hint
Benignant to the promising pupil,—thus:
"Enough attention to the Countess now,
The young one; 't is her mother rules the roast,
We know where, and puts in a word: go pay
Devoir to-morrow morning after mass!
Break that rash promise to preach, Passion-week!
Has it escaped you the Archbishop grunts
And snuffles when one grieves to tell his Grace
No soul dares treat the subject of the day   360
Since his own masterly handling it (ha, ha!)
Five years ago,—when somebody could help
And touch up an odd phrase in time of need,
(He, he!)—and somebody helps you, my son!
Therefore, don't prove so indispensable
At the Pieve, sit more loose i' the seat, nor grow
A fixture by attendance morn and eve!
Arezzo's just a haven midway Rome—
Rome's the eventual harbour,—make for port,
Crowd sail, crack cordage! And your cargo be   370
A polished presence, a genteel manner, wit
At will, and tact at every pore of you!
I sent our lump of learning, Brother Clout,
And Father Slouch, our piece of piety,
To see Rome and try suit the Cardinal.
Thither they clump-clumped, beads and book in hand,
And ever since 't is meat for man and maid
How both flopped down, prayed blessing on bent pate
Bald many an inch beyond the tonsure's need,
Never once dreaming, the two moony dolts,   380
There's nothing moves his Eminence so much
As—far from all this awe at sanctitude—
Heads that wag, eyes that twinkle, modified mirth
At the closet-lectures on the Latin tongue
A lady learns so much by, we know where.
Why, body o' Bacchus, you should crave his rule
For pauses in the elegiac couplet, chasms

---

349 *tarocs:* card game.

Permissible only to Catullus! There!
Now go to duty: brisk, break Priscian's head
By reading the day's office—there's no help.   390
You've Ovid in your poke to plaster that;
Amen's at the end of all: then sup with me!"

    Well, after three or four years of this life,
In prosecution of my calling, I
Found myself at the theatre one night
With a brother Canon, in a mood and mind
Proper enough for the place, amused or no:
When I saw enter, stand, and seat herself
A lady, young, tall, beautiful, strange and sad.
It was as when, in our cathedral once,   400
As I got yawningly through matin-song,
I saw *facchini* bear a burden up,
Base it on the high-altar, break away
A board or two, and leave the thing inside
Lofty and lone: and lo, when next I looked,
There was the Rafael! I was still one stare,
When—"Nay, I'll make her give you back your gaze"—
Said Canon Conti; and at the word he tossed
A paper-twist of comfits to her lap,
And dodged and in a trice was at my back   410
Nodding from over my shoulder. Then she turned,
Looked our way, smiled the beautiful sad strange smile.
"Is not she fair? 'T is my new cousin," said he:
"The fellow lurking there i' the black o' the box
Is Guido, the old scapegrace: she's his wife,
Married three years since: how his Countship sulks!
He has brought little back from Rome beside,
After the bragging, bullying. A fair face,
And—they do say—a pocketful of gold
When he can worry both her parents dead.   420
I don't go much there, for the chamber's cold
And the coffee pale. I got a turn at first
Paying my duty: I observed they crouched
—The two old frightened family spectres—close

---

388 *Catullus:* The cardinal thinks of himself as a poet equal to Catullus.
389 *Priscian:* a Latin grammarian.
402 *facchini:* porters.

In a corner, each on each like mouse on mouse
I' the cat's cage: ever since, I stay at home.
Hallo, there's Guido, the black, mean and small,
Bends his brows on us—please to bend your own
On the shapely nether limbs of Light-skirts there
By way of a diversion! I was a fool   430
To fling the sweetmeats. Prudence, for God's love!
To-morrow I'll make my peace, e'en tell some fib,
Try if I can't find means to take you there."

That night and next day did the gaze endure,
Burnt to my brain, as sunbeam thro' shut eyes,
And not once changed the beautiful sad strange smile.
At vespers Conti leaned beside my seat
I' the choir,—part said, part sung—"*In ex-cel-sis*—
All's to no purpose; I have louted low,
But he saw you staring—*quia sub*—don't incline   440
To know you nearer: him we would not hold
For Hercules,—the man would lick your shoe
If you and certain efficacious friends
Managed him warily,—but there's the wife:
Spare her, because he beats her, as it is,
She's breaking her heart quite fast enough—*jam tu*—
So, be you rational and make amends
With little Light-skirts yonder—*in secula
Secu-lo-o-o-o-rum*. Ah, you rogue! Every one knows
What great dame she makes jealous: one against one,   450
Play, and win both!"
                        Sirs, ere the week was out,
I saw and said to myself, "Light-skirts hides teeth
Would make a dog sick,—the great dame shows spite
Should drive a cat mad: 't is but poor work this—
Counting one's fingers till the sonnet's crowned.
I doubt much if Marino really be
A better bard than Dante after all.
'T is more amusing to go pace at eve
I' the Duomo,—watch the day's last gleam outside   460
Turn, as into a skirt of God's own robe,
Those lancet-windows' jewelled miracle,—

---

439 *louted:* bent low in submission.
460 *Duomo:* cathedral.

Than go eat the Archbishop's ortolans,
Digest his jokes. Luckily Lent is near:
Who cares to look will find me in my stall
At the Pieve, constant to this faith at least—
Never to write a canzonet any more."

So, next week, 't was my patron spoke abrupt,
In altered guise. "Young man, can it be true
That after all your promise of sound fruit,   470
You have kept away from Countess young or old
And gone play truant in church all day long?
Are you turning Molinist?" I answered quick:
"Sir, what if I turned Christian? It might be.
The fact is, I am troubled in my mind,
Beset and pressed hard by some novel thoughts.
This your Arezzo is a limited world;
There's a strange Pope,—'t is said, a priest who thinks.
Rome is the port, you say: to Rome I go.
I will live alone, one does so in a crowd,   480
And look into my heart a little." "Lent
Ended,"—I told friends—"I shall go to Rome."

     One evening I was sitting in a muse
Over the opened "Summa," darkened round
By the mid-March twilight, thinking how my life   *Can only*
Had shaken under me,—broke short indeed   *think of*
And showed the gap 'twixt what is, what should be,—   *Pompilia*
And into what abysm the soul may slip,
Leave aspiration here, achievement there,
Lacking omnipotence to connect extremes—   490
Thinking moreover . . . oh, thinking, if you like,
How utterly dissociated was I
A priest and celibate, from the sad strange wife
Of Guido,—just as an instance to the point,
Nought more,—how I had a whole store of strengths
Eating into my heart, which craved employ,
And she, perhaps, need of a finger's help,—
And yet there was no way in the wide world
To stretch out mine and so relieve myself,—

---

[463] *ortolans:* European birds much prized as food.
[484] *"Summa":* the *Summa Theologiæ* of St. Thomas Aquinas.

How when the page o' the "Summa" preached its best, 500
Her smile kept glowing out of it, as to mock
The silence we could break by no one word,—
There came a tap without the chamber-door,
And a whisper; when I bade who tapped speak out,
And, in obedience to my summons, last
In glided a masked muffled mystery,
Laid lightly a letter on the opened book,
Then stood with folded arms and foot demure,
Pointing as if to mark the minutes' flight.

I took the letter, read to the effect   510
That she, I lately flung the comfits to,
Had a warm heart to give me in exchange,
And gave it,—loved me and confessed it thus,
And bade me render thanks by word of mouth,
Going that night to such a side o' the house
Where the small terrace overhangs a street
Blind and deserted, not the street in front:
Her husband being away, the surly patch,
At his villa of Vittiano.

                    "And you?"—I asked: 520
"What may you be?" "Count Guido's kind of maid—
Most of us have two functions in his house.
We all hate him, the lady suffers much,
'T is just we show compassion, furnish help,
Specially since her choice is fixed so well.
What answer may I bring to cheer the sweet
Pompilia?"

            Then I took a pen and wrote:
"No more of this! That you are fair, I know:
But other thoughts now occupy my mind.   530
I should not thus have played the insensible
Once on a time. What made you,—may one ask,—
Marry your hideous husband? 'T was a fault,
And now you taste the fruit of it. Farewell."

"There!" smiled I as she snatched it and was gone—
"There, let the jealous miscreant,—Guido's self,

Whose mean soul grins through this transparent trick,—
Be baulked so far, defrauded of his aim!
What fund of satisfaction to the knave,
Had I kicked this his messenger down stairs,   540
Trussed to the middle of her impudence,
And set his heart at ease so! No, indeed!
There's the reply which he shall turn and twist
At pleasure, snuff at till his brain grow drunk,
As the bear does when he finds a scented glove
That puzzles him,—a hand and yet no hand,
Of other perfume than his own foul paw!
Last month, I had doubtless chosen to play the dupe,
Accepted the mock-invitation, kept
The sham appointment, cudgel beneath cloak,   550
Prepared myself to pull the appointer's self
Out of the window from his hiding-place
Behind the gown of this part-messenger
Part-mistress who would personate the wife.
Such had seemed once a jest permissible:
Now I am not i' the mood."
                                Back next morn brought
The messenger, a second letter in hand.
"You are cruel, Thyrsis, and Myrtilla moans
Neglected but adores you, makes request   560
For mercy: why is it you dare not come?
Such virtue is scarce natural to your age.
You must love someone else; I hear you do,
The Baron's daughter or the Advocate's wife,
Or both,—all's one, would you make me the third—
I take the crumbs from table gratefully
Nor grudge who feasts there. 'Faith, I blush and blaze!
Yet if I break all bounds, there's reason sure.
Are you determinedly bent on Rome?
I am wretched here, a monster tortures me: 570
Carry me with you! Come and say you will!
Concert this very evening! Do not write!
I am ever at the window of my room
Over the terrace, at the *Ave*. Come!"

---

559 *Thyrsis, and Myrtilla:* conventional pastoral names of shepherd and shepherdess.

I questioned—lifting half the woman's mask
To let her smile loose. "So, you gave my line
To the merry lady?" "She kissed off the wax,
And put what paper was not kissed away,
In her bosom to go burn: but merry, no!
She wept all night when evening brought no friend,   580
Alone, the unkind missive at her breast;
Thus Philomel, the thorn at her breast too,
Sings" . . . "Writes this second letter?" "Even so!
Then she may peep at vespers forth?"—"What risk
Do we run o' the husband?"—"Ah,—no risk at all!
He is more stupid even than jealous. Ah—
That was the reason? Why, the man's away!
Beside, his bugbear is that friend of yours,
Fat little Canon Conti. He fears him,
How should he dream of you? I told you truth: 590
He goes to the villa at Vittiano—'t is
The time when Spring-sap rises in the vine—
Spends the night there. And then his wife's a child:
Does he think a child outwits him? A mere child:
Yet so full grown, a dish for any duke.
Don't quarrel longer with such cates, but come!"

I wrote "In vain do you solicit me.
I am a priest: and you are wedded wife,
Whatever kind of brute your husband prove.
I have scruples, in short. Yet should you really show   600
Sign at the window . . . but nay, best be good!
My thoughts are elsewhere." "Take her that!"
                                        "Again
Let the incarnate meanness, cheat and spy,
Mean to the marrow of him, make his heart
His food, anticipate hell's worm once more!
Let him watch shivering at the window—ay,
And let this hybrid, this his light-of-love
And lackey-of-lies,—a sage economy,—
Paid with embracings for the rank brass coin,—   610
Let her report and make him chuckle o'er

---

582 *Philomel:* the nightingale.

The break-down of my resolution now,
And lour at disappointment in good time!
—So tantalize and so enrage by turns,
Until the two fall each on the other like
Two famished spiders, as the coveted fly
That toys long, leaves their net and them at last!"
And so the missives followed thick and fast
For a month, say,—I still came at every turn
On the soft sly adder, endlong 'neath my tread.   620
I was met i' the street, made sign to in the church,
A slip was found i' the door-sill, scribbled word
'Twixt page and page o' the prayer-book in my place
A crumpled thing dropped even before my feet,
Pushed through the blind, above the terrace-rail,
As I passed, by day, the very window once.
And ever from corners would be peering up
The messenger, with the self-same demand
"Obdurate still, no flesh but adamant?
Nothing to cure the wound, assuage the throe   630
O' the sweetest lamb that ever loved a bear?"
And ever my one answer in one tone—
"Go your ways, temptress! Let a priest read, pray,
Unplagued of vain talk, visions not for him!
In the end, you'll have your will and ruin me!"

One day, a variation: thus I read:
"You have gained little by timidity.
My husband has found out my love at length,
Sees cousin Conti was the stalking-horse,
And you the game he covered, poor fat soul!   640
My husband is a formidable foe,
Will stick at nothing to destroy you. Stand
Prepared, or better, run till you reach Rome!
I bade you visit me, when the last place
My tyrant would have turned suspicious at,
Or cared to seek you in, was . . . why say, where?
But now all's changed: beside, the season's past
At the villa,—wants the master's eye no more.
Anyhow, I beseech you, stay away
From the window! He might well be posted there."   650

I wrote—"You raise my courage, or call up
My curiosity, who am but man.
Tell him he owns the palace, not the street
Under—that's his and yours and mine alike.
If it should please me pad the path this eve,
Guido will have two troubles, first to get
Into a rage and then get out again.
Be cautious, though: at the *Ave!*"

                    You of the Court!
When I stood question here and reached this point   660
O' the narrative,—search notes and see and say
If someone did not interpose with smile
And sneer, "And prithee why so confident
That the husband must, of all needs, not the wife,
Fabricate thus,—what if the lady loved?
What if she wrote the letters?"

                    Learned Sir,
I told you there's a picture in our church.
Well, if a low-browed verger sidled up
Bringing me, like a blotch, on his prod's point,   670
A transfixed scorpion, let the reptile writhe,
And then said "See a thing that Rafael made—
This venom issued from Madonna's mouth!"
I should reply, "Rather, the soul of you
Has issued from your body, like from like,
By way of the ordure-corner!"

                    But no less,
I tired of the same long black teasing lie
Obtruded thus at every turn; the pest
Was far too near the picture, anyhow: 680
One does Madonna service, making clowns
Remove their dung-heap from the sacristy.
"I will to the window, as he tempts," said I:
"Yes, whom the easy love has failed allure,
This new bait of adventure tempts,—thinks he.
Though the imprisoned lady keeps afar,
There will they lie in ambush, heads alert,
Kith, kin, and Count mustered to bite my heel.

---

676 *ordure-corner:* bowels.

No mother nor brother viper of the brood
Shall scuttle off without the instructive bruise!" 690

So, I went: crossed street and street: "The next street's turn,
I stand beneath the terrace, see, above,
The black of the ambush-window. Then, in place
Of hand's throw of soft prelude over lute,
And cough that clears way for the ditty last,"—
I began to laugh already—"he will have
'Out of the hole you hide in, on to the front,
Count Guido Franceschini, show yourself!
Hear what a man thinks of a thing like you,
And after, take this foulness in your face!'" 700

The words lay living on my lip, I made
The one turn more—and there at the window stood,
Framed in its black square length, with lamp in hand,
Pompilia; the same great, grave, griefful air
As stands i' the dusk, on altar that I know,
Left alone with one moonbeam in her cell,
Our Lady of all the Sorrows. Ere I knelt—
Assured myself that she was flesh and blood—
She had looked one look and vanished.
                              I thought—"Just so: 710
It was herself, they have set her there to watch—
Stationed to see some wedding-band go by,
On fair pretence that she must bless the bride,
Or wait some funeral with friends wind past,
And crave peace for the corpse that claims its due.
She never dreams they used her for a snare,
And now withdraw the bait has served its turn.
Well done, the husband, who shall fare the worse!"
And on my lip again was—"Out with thee,
Guido!" When all at once she re-appeared; 720
But, this time, on the terrace overhead,
So close above me, she could almost touch
My head if she bent down; and she did bend,
While I stood still as stone, all eye, all ear.

She began—"You have sent me letters, Sir:
I have read none, I can neither read nor write;

But she you gave them to, a woman here,
One of the people in whose power I am,
Partly explained their sense, I think, to me
Obliged to listen while she inculcates   730
That you, a priest, can dare love me, a wife,
Desire to live or die as I shall bid,
(She makes me listen if I will or no)
Because you saw my face a single time.
It cannot be she says the thing you mean;
Such wickedness were deadly to us both:
But good true love would help me now so much—
I tell myself, you may mean good and true.
You offer me, I seem to understand,
Because I am in poverty and starve,   740
Much money, where one piece would save my life.
The silver cup upon the altar-cloth
Is neither yours to give nor mine to take;
But I might take one bit of bread therefrom,
Since I am starving, and return the rest,
Yet do no harm: this is my very case.
I am in that strait, I may not dare abstain
From so much of assistance as would bring
The guilt of theft on neither you nor me;
But no superfluous particle of aid.   750
I think, if you will let me state my case,
Even had you been so fancy-fevered here,
Not your sound self, you must grow healthy now—
Care only to bestow what I can take.
That it is only you in the wide world,
Knowing me nor in thought nor word nor deed,
Who, all unprompted save by your own heart,
Come proffering assistance now,—were strange
But that my whole life is so strange: as strange
It is, my husband whom I have not wronged   760
Should hate and harm me. For his own soul's sake,
Hinder the harm! But there is something more,
And that the strangest: it has got to be
Somehow for my sake too, and yet not mine,
—This is a riddle—for some kind of sake
Not any clearer to myself than you,
And yet as certain as that I draw breath,—

I would fain live, not die—oh no, not die!
My case is, I was dwelling happily
At Rome with those dear Comparini, called 770
Father and mother to me; when at once
I found I had become Count Guido's wife:
Who then, not waiting for a moment, changed
Into a fury of fire, if once he was
Merely a man: his face threw fire at mine,
He laid a hand on me that burned all peace,
All joy, all hope, and last all fear away,
Dipping the bough of life, so pleasant once,
In fire which shrivelled leaf and bud alike,
Burning not only present life but past, 780
Which you might think was safe beyond his reach.
He reached it, though, since that beloved pair,
My father once, my mother all those years,
That loved me so, now say I dreamed a dream
And bid me wake, henceforth no child of theirs,
Never in all the time their child at all.
Do you understand? I cannot: yet so it is.
Just so I say of you that proffer help:
I cannot understand what prompts your soul,
I simply needs must see that it is so, 790
Only one strange and wonderful thing more.
They came here with me, those two dear ones, kept
All the old love up, till my husband, till
His people here so tortured them, they fled.
And now, is it because I grow in flesh
And spirit one with him their torturer,
That they, renouncing him, must cast off me?
If I were graced by God to have a child,
Could I one day deny God graced me so?
Then, since my husband hates me, I shall break 800
No law that reigns in this fell house of hate,
By using—letting have effect so much
Of hate as hides me from that whole of hate
Would take my life which I want and must have—
Just as I take from your excess of love
Enough to save my life with, all I need.
The Archbishop said to murder me were sin:
My leaving Guido were a kind of death

With no sin,—more death, he must answer for.
Hear now what death to him and life to you   810
I wish to pay and owe. Take me to Rome!
You go to Rome, the servant makes me hear.
Take me as you would take a dog, I think,
Masterless left for strangers to maltreat:
Take me home like that—leave me in the house
Where the father and the mother are; and soon
They'll come to know and call me by my name,
Their child once more, since child I am, for all
They now forget me, which is the worst o' the dream—
And the way to end dreams is to break them, stand,   820
Walk, go: then help me to stand, walk and go!
The Governor said the strong should help the weak:
You know how weak the strongest women are.
How could I find my way there by myself?
I cannot even call out, make them hear—
Just as in dreams: I have tried and proved the fact.
I have told this story and more to good great men,
The Archbishop and the Governor: they smiled.
'Stop your mouth, fair one!'—presently they frowned,
'Get you gone, disengage you from our feet!'   830
I went in my despair to an old priest,
Only a friar, no great man like these two,
But good, the Augustinian, people name
Romano,—he confessed me two months since:
He fears God, why then needs he fear the world?
And when he questioned how it came about
That I was found in danger of a sin—
Despair of any help from providence,—
'Since, though your husband outrage you,' said he,
'That is a case too common, the wives die   840
Or live, but do not sin so deep as this'—
Then I told—what I never will tell you—
How, worse than husband's hate, I had to bear
The love,—soliciting to shame called love,—
Of his brother,—the young idle priest i' the house
With only the devil to meet there. 'This is grave—
Yes, we must interfere: I counsel,—write
To those who used to be your parents once,

Of dangers here, bid them convey you hence!'
'But,' said I, 'when I neither read nor write?'   850
Then he took pity and promised 'I will write.'
If he did so,—why, they are dumb or dead:
Either they give no credit to the tale,
Or else, wrapped wholly up in their own joy
Of such escape, they care not who cries, still
I' the clutches. Anyhow, no word arrives.
All such extravagance and dreadfulness
Seems incident to dreaming, cured one way,—
Wake me! The letter I received this morn,
Said—if the woman spoke your very sense—   860
'You would die for me:' I can believe it now:
For now the dream gets to involve yourself.
First of all, you seemed wicked and not good,
In writing me those letters: you came in
Like a thief upon me. I this morning said
In my extremity, entreat the thief!
Try if he have in him no honest touch!
A thief might save me from a murderer.
'T was a thief said the last kind word to Christ:
Christ took the kindness and forgave the theft: 870
And so did I prepare what I now say.
But now, that you stand and I see your face,
Though you have never uttered word yet,—well, I know,
Here too has been dream-work, delusion too,
And that at no time, you with the eyes here,
Ever intended to do wrong by me,
Nor wrote such letters therefore. It is false,
And you are true, have been true, will be true.
To Rome then,—when is it you take me there?
Each minute lost is mortal. When?—I ask."   880

I answered "It shall be when it can be.
I will go hence and do your pleasure, find
The sure and speedy means of travel, then
Come back and take you to your friends in Rome.
There wants a carriage, money and the rest,—
A day's work by to-morrow at this time.
How shall I see you and assure escape?"

She replied, "Pass, to-morrow at this hour.
If I am at the open window, well:
If I am absent, drop a handkerchief 890
And walk by! I shall see from where I watch,
And know that all is done. Return next eve,
And next, and so till we can meet and speak!"
"To-morrow at this hour I pass," said I.
She was withdrawn.
                    Here is another point
I bid you pause at. When I told thus far,
Some one said, subtly, "Here at least was found
Your confidence in error,—you perceived
The spirit of the letters, in a sort, 900
Had been the lady's, if the body should be
Supplied by Guido: say, he forged them all!
Here was the unforged fact—she sent for you,
Spontaneously elected you to help,
—What men call, loved you: Guido read her mind,
Gave it expression to assure the world
The case was just as he foresaw: he wrote,
She spoke."
           Sirs, that first simile serves still,—
That falsehood of a scorpion hatched, I say, 910
Nowhere i' the world but in Madonna's mouth.
Go on! Suppose, that falsehood foiled, next eve
Pictured Madonna raised her painted hand,
Fixed the face Rafael bent above the Babe,
On my face as I flung me at her feet:
Such miracle vouchsafed and manifest,
Would that prove the first lying tale was true?
Pompilia spoke, and I at once received,
Accepted my own fact, my miracle
Self-authorized and self-explained,—she chose 920
To summon me and signify her choice.
Afterward,—oh! I gave a passing glance
To a certain ugly cloud-shape, goblin-shred
Of hell-smoke hurrying past the splendid moon
Out now to tolerate no darkness more,
And saw right through the thing that tried to pass
For truth and solid, not an empty lie:
"So, he not only forged the words for her

But words for me, made letters he called mine:
What I sent, he retained, gave these in place,   930
All by the mistress-messenger! As I
Recognized her, at potency of truth,
So she, by the crystalline soul, knew me,
Never mistook the signs. Enough of this—
Let the wraith go to nothingness again,
Here is the orb, have only thought for her!"

"Thought?" nay, Sirs, what shall follow was not thought:
I have thought sometimes, and thought long and hard.
I have stood before, gone round a serious thing,
Tasked my whole mind to touch and clasp it close,   940
As I stretch forth my arm to touch this bar.
God and man, and what duty I owe both,—
I dare to say I have confronted these
In thought: but no such faculty helped here.
I put forth no thought,—powerless, all that night
I paced the city: it was the first Spring.
By the invasion I lay passive to,
In rushed new things, the old were rapt away;
Alike abolished—the imprisonment
Of the outside air, the inside weight o' the world   950
That pulled me down. Death meant, to spurn the ground,
Soar to the sky,—die well and you do that.
The very immolation made the bliss;
Death was the heart of life, and all the harm
My folly had crouched to avoid, now proved a veil
Hiding all gain my wisdom strove to grasp:
As if the intense centre of the flame
Should turn a heaven to that devoted fly
Which hitherto, sophist alike and sage,
Saint Thomas with his sober grey goose-quill,   960
And sinner Plato by Cephisian reed,
Would fain, pretending just the insect's good,
Whisk off, drive back, consign to shade again.
Into another state, under new rule
I knew myself was passing swift and sure;
Whereof the initiatory pang approached,

---

961 *Cephisian:* The reedy river Cephisus ran through Athens, where Plato
lived.

Felicitous annoy, as bitter-sweet
As when the virgin-band, the victors chaste,
Feel at the end the earthly garments drop,
And rise with something of a rosy shame   970
Into immortal nakedness: so I
Lay, and let come the proper throe would thrill
Into the ecstasy and outthrob pain.

I' the grey of dawn it was I found myself
Facing the pillared front o' the Pieve—mine,
My church: it seemed to say for the first time
"But am not I the Bride, the mystic love
O' the Lamb, who took thy plighted troth, my priest,
To fold thy warm heart on my heart of stone
And freeze thee nor unfasten any more?   980
This is a fleshly woman,—let the free
Bestow their life-blood, thou art pulseless now!"
See! Day by day I had risen and left this church
At the signal waved me by some foolish fan,
With half a curse and half a pitying smile
For the monk I stumbled over in my haste,
Prostrate and corpse-like at the altar-foot
Intent on his *corona:* then the church
Was ready with her quip, if word conduced,
To quicken my pace nor stop for prating—"There!   990
Be thankful you are no such ninny, go
Rather to teach a black-eyed novice cards
Than gabble Latin and protrude that nose
Smoothed to a sheep's through no brains and much faith!"
That sort of incentive! Now the church changed tone—
Now, when I found out first that life and death
Are means to an end, that passion uses both,
Indisputably mistress of the man
Whose form of worship is self-sacrifice:
Now, from the stone lungs sighed the scrannel voice   1000
"Leave that live passion, come be dead with me!"
As if, i' the fabled garden, I had gone

---

988 *corona:* rosary.
1000 *scrannel:* hoarse.
1002 *fabled garden:* garden of the Hesperides, in which the golden apples
belonging to Hera were guarded by a dragon.

On great adventure, plucked in ignorance
Hedge-fruit, and feasted to satiety,
Laughing at such high fame for hips and haws,
And scorned the achievement: then come all at once
O' the prize o' the place, the thing of perfect gold,
The apple's self: and, scarce my eye on that,
Was 'ware as well o' the seven-fold dragon's watch.

Sirs, I obeyed. Obedience was too strange,—   1010
This new thing that had been struck into me
By the look o' the lady,—to dare disobey
The first authoritative word. 'T was God's.
I had been lifted to the level of her,
Could take such sounds into my sense. I said
"We two are cognisant o' the Master now;
She it is bids me bow the head: how true,
I am a priest! I see the function here;
I thought the other way self-sacrifice:
This is the true, seals up the perfect sum.   1020
I pay it, sit down, silently obey."

So, I went home. Dawn broke, noon broadened, I—
I sat stone-still, let time run over me.
The sun slanted into my room, had reached
The west. I opened book,—Aquinas blazed
With one black name only on the white page.
I looked up, saw the sunset: vespers rang:
"She counts the minutes till I keep my word
And come say all is ready. I am a priest.
Duty to God is duty to her: I think   1030
God, who created her, will save her too
Some new way, by one miracle the more,
Without me. Then, prayer may avail perhaps."
I went to my own place i' the Pieve, read
The office: I was back at home again
Sitting i' the dark. "Could she but know—but know
That, were there good in this distinct from God's,
Really good as it reached her, though procured
By a sin of mine,—I should sin: God forgives.
She knows it is no fear withholds me: fear?   1040
Of what? Suspense here is the terrible thing.

If she should, as she counts the minutes, come
On the fantastic notion that I fear
The world now, fear the Archbishop, fear perhaps
Count Guido, he who, having forged the lies,
May wait the work, attend the effect,—I fear
The sword of Guido! Let God see to that—
Hating lies, let not her believe a lie!"

Again the morning found me. "I will work,
Tie down my foolish thoughts. Thank God so far!   1050
I have saved her from a scandal, stopped the tongues
Had broken else into a cackle and hiss
Around the noble name. Duty is still
Wisdom: I have been wise." So the day wore.

At evening—"But, achieving victory,
I must not blink the priest's peculiar part,
Nor shrink to counsel, comfort: priest and friend—
How do we discontinue to be friends?
I will go minister, advise her seek
Help at the source,—above all, not despair: 1060
There may be other happier help at hand.
I hope it,—wherefore then neglect to say?"

There she stood—leaned there, for the second time,
Over the terrace, looked at me, then spoke:
"Why is it you have suffered me to stay
Breaking my heart two days more than was need?
Why delay help, your own heart yearns to give?
You are again here, in the self-same mind,
I see here, steadfast in the face of you,—
You grudge to do no one thing that I ask.   1070
Why then is nothing done? You know my need.
Still, through God's pity on me, there is time
And one day more: shall I be saved or no?"
I answered—"Lady, waste no thought, no word
Even to forgive me! Care for what I care—
Only! Now follow me as I were fate!
Leave this house in the dark to-morrow night,
Just before daybreak:—there's new moon this eve—
It sets, and then begins the solid black.

Descend, proceed to the Torrione, step   1080
Over the low dilapidated wall,
Take San Clemente, there's no other gate
Unguarded at the hour: some paces thence
An inn stands; cross to it; I shall be there."

She answered, "If I can but find the way.
But I shall find it. Go now!"

                                        I did go,
Took rapidly the route myself prescribed,
Stopped at Torrione, climbed the ruined place,
Proved that the gate was practicable, reached   1090
The inn, no eye, despite the dark, could miss,
Knocked there and entered, made the host secure:
"With Caponsacchi it is ask and have;
I know my betters. Are you bound for Rome?
I get swift horse and trusty man," said he.

Then I retraced my steps, was found once more
In my own house for the last time: there lay
The broad pale opened "*Summa*." "Shut his book,
There's other showing! 'T was a Thomas too
Obtained,—more favoured than his namesake here,—   1100
A gift, tied faith fast, foiled the tug of doubt,—
Our Lady's girdle; down he saw it drop
As she ascended into heaven, they say:
He kept that safe and bade all doubt adieu.
I too have seen a lady and hold a grace."

I know not how the night passed: morning broke;
Presently came my servant. "Sir, this eve—
Do you forget?" I started. "How forget?
What is it you know?" "With due submission, Sir,
This being last Monday in the month but one   1110
And a vigil, since to-morrow is Saint George,

1099 *Thomas:* Christ's apostle Thomas refused to believe in the resurrection
of Christ without physical proof (*John* 20: 24-29). An alternative to this
story is that Thomas was convinced by the girdle of the Virgin which she let
fall from heaven into his hands.

1111 *Saint George:* The actual date of the flight of Caponsacchi and Pompilia
was some five days later, but Browning put it on 23 April, St. George's day,
because of the symbolic fitness of St. George rescuing the maiden.

And feast day, and moreover day for copes,
And Canon Conti now away a month,
And Canon Crispi sour because, forsooth,
You let him sulk in stall and bear the brunt
Of the octave. . . . Well, Sir, 't is important!"
                                        "True!
Hearken, I have to start for Rome this night.
No word, lest Crispi overboil and burst!
Provide me with a laic dress! Throw dust   1120
I' the Canon's eye, stop his tongue's scandal so!
See there's a sword in case of accident."
I knew the knave, the knave knew me.

                                   And thus
Through each familiar hindrance of the day
Did I make steadily for its hour and end,—
Felt time's old barrier-growth of right and fit
Give way through all its twines, and let me go.
Use and wont recognized the excepted man,
Let speed the special service,—and I sped   1130
Till, at the dead between midnight and morn,
There was I at the goal, before the gate,
With a tune in the ears, low leading up to loud,
A light in the eyes, faint that would soon be flare,
Ever some spiritual witness new and new
In faster frequence, crowding solitude
To watch the way o' the warfare,—till, at last,
When the ecstatic minute must bring birth,
Began a whiteness in the distance, waxed
Whiter and whiter, near grew and more near,   1140
Till it was she: there did Pompilia come:
The white I saw shine through her was her soul's,
Certainly, for the body was one black,
Black from head down to foot. She did not speak,
Glided into the carriage,—so a cloud
Gathers the moon up. "By San Spirito,
To Rome, as if the road burned underneath!
Reach Rome, then hold my head in pledge, I pay
The run and the risk to heart's content!" Just that
I said,—then, in another tick of time,   1150
Sprang, was beside her, she and I alone.

So it began, our flight thro' dusk to clear,
Through day and night and day again to night
Once more, and to last dreadful dawn of all.
Sirs, how should I lie quiet in my grave
Unless you suffer me wring, drop by drop,
My brain dry, make a riddance of the drench
Of minutes with a memory in each,
Recorded motion, breath or look of hers,
Which poured forth would present you one pure glass, 1160
Mirror you plain,—as God's sea, glassed in gold,
His saints,—the perfect soul Pompilia? Men,
You must know that a man gets drunk with truth
Stagnant inside him! Oh, they've killed her, Sirs!
Can I be calm?
             Calmly! Each incident
Proves, I maintain, that action of the flight
For the true thing it was. The first faint scratch
O' the stone will test its nature, teach its worth
To idiots who name Parian—coprolite. 1170
After all, I shall give no glare—at best
Only display you certain scattered lights
Lamping the rush and roll of the abyss:
Nothing but here and there a fire-point pricks
Wavelet from wavelet: well!
             For the first hour
We both were silent in the night, I know:
Sometimes I did not see nor understand.
Blackness engulphed me,—partial stupor, say—
Then I would break way, breathe through the surprise, 1180
And be aware again, and see who sat
In the dark vest with the white face and hands.
I said to myself—"I have caught it, I conceive
The mind o' the mystery: 't is the way they wake
And wait, two martyrs somewhere in a tomb
Each by each as their blessing was to die;
Some signal they are promised and expect,—
When to arise before the trumpet scares:
So, through the whole course of the world they wait

1170 *Parian—coprolite:* Parian was marble from the island of Paros; coprolite
is fossilized excrement.

The last day, but so fearless and so safe!   1190
No otherwise, in safety and not fear,
I lie, because she lies too by my side."
You know this is not love, Sirs,—it is faith,
The feeling that there's God, he reigns and rules
Out of this low world: that is all; no harm!
At times she drew a soft sigh—music seemed
Always to hover just above her lips,
Not settle,—break a silence music too.

In the determined morning, I first found
Her head erect, her face turned full to me,   1200
Her soul intent on mine through two wide eyes.
I answered them. "You are saved hitherto.
We have passed Perugia,—gone round by the wood,
Not through, I seem to think—and opposite
I know Assisi; this is holy ground."
Then she resumed. "How long since we both left
Arezzo?"—"Years—and certain hours beside."

It was at . . . ah, but I forget the names!
'T is a mere post-house and a hovel or two;
I left the carriage and got bread and wine   1210
And brought it her. "Does it detain to eat?"
"They stay perforce, change horses,—therefore eat!
We lose no minute: we arrive, be sure!"
This was—I know not where—there's a great hill
Close over, and the stream has lost its bridge,
One fords it. She began—"I have heard say
Of some sick body that my mother knew,
'T was no good sign when in a limb diseased
All the pain suddenly departs,—as if
The guardian angel discontinued pain   1220
Because the hope of cure was gone at last:
The limb will not again exert itself,
It needs be pained no longer: so with me,
—My soul whence all the pain is past at once:
All pain must be to work some good in the end.
True, this I feel now, this may be that good,
Pain was because of,—otherwise, I fear!"

She said,—a long while later in the day,
When I had let the silence be,—abrupt—
"Have you a mother?" "She died, I was born."   1230
"A sister then?" "No sister." "Who was it—
What woman were you used to serve this way,
Be kind to, till I called you and you came?"
I did not like that word. Soon afterward—
"Tell me, are men unhappy, in some kind
Of mere unhappiness at being men,
As women suffer, being womanish?
Have you, now, some unhappiness, I mean,
Born of what may be man's strength overmuch,
To match the undue susceptibility,   1240
The sense at every pore when hate is close?
It hurts us if a baby hides its face
Or child strikes at us punily, calls names
Or makes a mouth,—much more if stranger men
Laugh or frown,—just as that were much to bear!
Yet rocks split,—and the blow-ball does no more,
Quivers to feathery nothing at a touch;
And strength may have its drawback, weakness 'scapes."

Once she asked, "What is it that made you smile,
At the great gate with the eagles and the snakes,   1250
Where the company entered, 't is a long time since?"
"—Forgive—I think you would not understand:
Ah, but you ask me,—therefore, it was this.
That was a certain bishop's villa-gate,
I knew it by the eagles,—and at once
Remembered this same bishop was just he
People of old were wont to bid me please
If I would catch preferment: so, I smiled
Because an impulse came to me, a whim—
What if I prayed the prelate leave to speak,   1260
Began upon him in his presence-hall
—'What, still at work so grey and obsolete?
Still rocheted and mitred more or less?
Don't you feel all that out of fashion now?
I find out when the day of things is done!' "

At eve we heard the *angelus:* she turned—
"I told you I can neither read nor write.
My life stopped with the play-time; I will learn,
If I begin to live again: but you—
Who are a priest—wherefore do you not read   1270
The service at this hour? Read Gabriel's song,
The lesson, and then read the little prayer
To Raphael, proper for us travellers!"
I did not like that, neither, but I read.

When we stopped at Foligno it was dark.
The people of the post came out with lights:
The driver said, "This time to-morrow, may
Saints only help, relays continue good,
Nor robbers hinder, we arrive at Rome."
I urged,—"Why tax your strength a second night?   1280
Trust me, alight here and take brief repose!
We are out of harm's reach, past pursuit: go sleep
If but an hour! I keep watch, guard the while
Here in the doorway." But her whole face changed,
The misery grew again about her mouth,
The eyes burned up from faintness, like the fawn's
Tired to death in the thicket, when she feels
The probing spear o' the huntsman. "Oh, no stay!"
She cried, in the fawn's cry, "On to Rome, on, on—
Unless 't is you who fear,—which cannot be!"   1290

We did go on all night; but at its close
She was troubled, restless, moaned low, talked at whiles
To herself, her brow on quiver with the dream:
Once, wide awake, she menaced, at arms' length
Waved away something—"Never again with you!
My soul is mine, my body is my soul's:
You and I are divided ever more
In soul and body: get you gone!" Then I—
"Why, in my whole life I have never prayed!
Oh, if the God, that only can, would help!   1300
Am I his priest with power to cast out fiends?
Let God arise and all his enemies
Be scattered!" By morn, there was peace, no sigh
Out of the deep sleep.

When she woke at last,
I answered the first look—"Scarce twelve hours more,
Then, Rome! There probably was no pursuit,
There cannot now be peril: bear up brave!
Just some twelve hours to press through to the prize:
Then, no more of the terrible journey!" "Then,   1310
No more o' the journey: if it might but last!
Always, my life-long, thus to journey still!
It is the interruption that I dread,—
With no dread, ever to be here and thus!
Never to see a face nor hear a voice!
Yours is no voice; you speak when you are dumb;
Nor face, I see it in the dark. I want
No face nor voice that change and grow unkind."
That I liked, that was the best thing she said.

In the broad day, I dared entreat, "Descend!"   1320
I told a woman, at the garden-gate
By the post-house, white and pleasant in the sun,
"It is my sister,—talk with her apart!
She is married and unhappy, you perceive;
I take her home because her heart is hurt;
Comfort her as you women understand!"
So, there I left them by the garden-wall,
Paced the road, then bade put the horses to,
Came back, and there she sat: close to her knee,
A black-eyed child still held the bowl of milk,   1330
Wondered to see how little she could drink,
And in her arms the woman's infant lay.
She smiled at me, "How much good this has done!
This is a whole night's rest and how much more!
I can proceed now, though I wish to stay.
How do you call that tree with the thick top
That holds in all its leafy green and gold
The sun now like an immense egg of fire?"
(It was a million-leaved mimosa.) "Take
The babe away from me and let me go!"   1340
And in the carriage "Still a day, my friend!
And perhaps half a night, the woman fears.
I pray it finish since it cannot last:
There may be more misfortune at the close,

And where will you be? God suffice me then!"
And presently—for there was a roadside-shrine—
"When I was taken first to my own church
Lorenzo in Lucina, being a girl,
And bid confess my faults, I interposed
'But teach me what fault to confess and know!'   1350
So, the priest said—'You should bethink yourself:
Each human being needs must have done wrong!'
Now, be you candid and no priest but friend—
Were I surprised and killed here on the spot,
A runaway from husband and his home,
Do you account it were in sin I died?
My husband used to seem to harm me, not . . .
Not on pretence he punished sin of mine,
Nor for sin's sake and lust of cruelty,
But as I heard him bid a farming-man   1360
At the villa take a lamb once to the wood
And there ill-treat it, meaning that the wolf
Should hear its cries, and so come, quick be caught,
Enticed to the trap: he practised thus with me
That so, whatever were his gain thereby,
Others than I might become prey and spoil.
Had it been only between our two selves,—
His pleasure and my pain,—why, pleasure him
By dying, nor such need to make a coil!
But this was worth an effort, that my pain   1370
Should not become a snare, prove pain threefold
To other people—strangers—or unborn—
How should I know? I sought release from that—
I think, or else from,—dare I say, some cause
Such as is put into a tree, which turns
Away from the north wind with what nest it holds,—
The woman said that trees so turn: now, friend,
Tell me, because I cannot trust myself!
You are a man: what have I done amiss?"
You must conceive my answer,—I forget—   1380
Taken up wholly with the thought, perhaps,
This time she might have said,—might, did not say—
"You are a priest." She said, "my friend."
                              Day wore,
We passed the places, somehow the calm went,

Again the restless eyes began to rove
In new fear of the foe mine could not see.
She wandered in her mind,—addressed me once
"Gaetano!"—that is not my name: whose name?
I grew alarmed, my head seemed turning too.   1390
I quickened pace with promise now, now threat:
Bade drive and drive, nor any stopping more.
"Too deep i' the thick of the struggle, struggle through!
Then drench her in repose though death's self pour
The plenitude of quiet,—help us, God,
Whom the winds carry!"

           Suddenly I saw
The old tower, and the little white-walled clump
Of buildings and the cypress-tree or two,—
"Already Castelnuovo—Rome!" I cried,   1400
"As good as Rome,—Rome is the next stage, think!
This is where travellers' hearts are wont to beat.
Say you are saved, sweet lady!" Up she woke.
The sky was fierce with colour from the sun
Setting. She screamed out "No, I must not die!
Take me no farther, I should die: stay here!
I have more life to save than mine!"
                    She swooned.
We seemed safe: what was it foreboded so?
Out of the coach into the inn I bore   1410
The motionless and breathless pure and pale
Pompilia,—bore her through a pitying group
And laid her on a couch, still calm and cured
By deep sleep of all woes at once. The host
Was urgent, "Let her stay an hour or two!
Leave her to us, all will be right by morn!"
Oh, my foreboding! But I could not choose.

I paced the passage, kept watch all night long.
I listened,—not one movement, not one sigh.
"Fear not: she sleeps so sound!" they said: but I   1420
Feared, all the same, kept fearing more and more,
Found myself throb with fear from head to foot,

---

¹³⁸⁹ *Gaetano:* the name Pompilia intended for her unborn son.

Filled with a sense of such impending woe,
That, at first pause of night, pretence of grey,
I made my mind up it was morn.—"Reach Rome,
Lest hell reach her! A dozen miles to make,
Another long breath, and we emerge!" I stood
I' the court-yard, roused the sleepy grooms. "Have out
Carriage and horse, give haste, take gold!" said I.
While they made ready in the doubtful morn,—   1430
'T was the last minute,—needs must I ascend
And break her sleep; I turned to go.

                                 And there
Faced me Count Guido, there posed the mean man
As master,—took the field, encamped his rights,
Challenged the world: there leered new triumph, there
Scowled the old malice in the visage bad
And black o' the scamp. Soon triumph suppled the tongue
A little, malice glued to his dry throat,
And he part howled, part hissed . . . oh, how he kept 1440
Well out o' the way, at arm's length and to spare!—
"My salutation to your priestship! What?
Matutinal, busy with book so soon
Of an April day that's damp as tears that now
Deluge Arezzo at its darling's flight?—
'T is unfair, wrongs feminity at large,
To let a single dame monopolize
A heart the whole sex claims, should share alike:
Therefore I overtake you, Canon! Come!
The lady,—could you leave her side so soon?   1450
You have not yet experienced at her hands
My treatment, you lay down undrugged, I see!
Hence this alertness—hence no death-in-life
Like what held arms fast when she stole from mine.
To be sure, you took the solace and repose
That first night at Foligno!—news abound
O' the road by this time,—men regaled me much,
As past them I came halting after you,
Vulcan pursuing Mars, as poets sing,—

1452 *undrugged:* Guido claimed that Pompilia had drugged him in order to
make her escape.
1459 *Mars:* The god of war, making love to Venus, was caught in a net by
her jealous husband Vulcan.

Still at the last here pant I, but arrive,   1460
Vulcan—and not without my Cyclops too,
The Commissary and the unpoisoned arm
O' the Civil Force, should Mars turn mutineer.
Enough of fooling: capture the culprits, friend!
Here is the lover in the smart disguise
With the sword,—he is a priest, so mine lies still.
There upstairs hides my wife the runaway,
His leman: the two plotted, poisoned first,
Plundered me after, and eloped thus far
Where now you find them. Do your duty quick!   1470
Arrest and hold him! That's done: now catch her!"
During this speech of that man,—well, I stood
Away, as he managed,—still, I stood as near
The throat of him,—with these two hands, my own,—
As now I stand near yours, Sir,—one quick spring,
One great good satisfying gripe, and lo!
There had he lain abolished with his lie,
Creation purged o' the miscreate, man redeemed,
A spittle wiped off from the face of God!
I, in some measure, seek a poor excuse   1480
For what I left undone, in just this fact
That my first feeling at the speech I quote
Was—not of what a blasphemy was dared,
Not what a bag of venomed purulence
Was split and noisome,—but how splendidly
Mirthful, how ludicrous a lie was launched!
Would Molière's self wish more than hear such man
Call, claim such woman for his own, his wife,
Even though, in due amazement at the boast,
He had stammered, she moreover was divine?   1490
She to be his,—were hardly less absurd
Than that he took her name into his mouth,
Licked, and then let it go again, the beast,
Signed with his slaver. Oh, she poisoned him,
Plundered him, and the rest! Well, what I wished
Was, that he would but go on, say once more
So to the world, and get his meed of men,
The fist's reply to the filth. And while I mused,

1461 *Cyclops:* Vulcan's workmen.
1497 *meed:* payment.

The minute, oh the misery, was gone!
On either idle hand of me there stood   1500
Really an officer, nor laughed i' the least:
They rendered justice to his reason, laid
Logic to heart, as 't were submitted them
"Twice two makes four."
                    "And now, catch her!"—he cried.
That sobered me. "Let myself lead the way—
Ere you arrest me, who am somebody,
Being, as you hear, a priest and privileged,—
To the lady's chamber! I presume you—men
Expert, instructed how to find out truth,   1510
Familiar with the guise of guilt. Detect
Guilt on her face when it meets mine, then judge
Between us and the mad dog howling there!"
Up we all went together, in they broke
O' the chamber late my chapel. There she lay,
Composed as when I laid her, that last eve,
O' the couch, still breathless, motionless, sleep's self,
Wax-white, seraphic, saturate with the sun
O' the morning that now flooded from the front
And filled the window with a light like blood.   1520
"Behold the poisoner, the adulteress,
—And feigning sleep too! Seize, bind!" Guido hissed.

She started up, stood erect, face to face
With the husband: back he fell, was buttressed there
By the window all aflame with morning-red,
He the black figure, the opprobrious blur
Against all peace and joy and light and life.
"Away from between me and hell!" she cried:
"Hell for me, no embracing any more!
I am God's, I love God, God—whose knees I clasp,   1520
Whose utterly most just award I take,
But bear no more love-making devils: hence!"
I may have made an effort to reach her side
From where I stood i' the door-way,—anyhow
I found the arms, I wanted, pinioned fast,
Was powerless in the clutch to left and right
O' the rabble pouring in, rascality
Enlisted, rampant on the side of hearth,

Home and the husband,—pay in prospect too!
They heaped themselves upon me. "Ha!—and him   1540
Also you outrage? Him, too, my sole friend,
Guardian and saviour? That I baulk you of,
Since—see how God can help at last and worst!"
She sprang at the sword that hung beside him, seized,
Drew, brandished it, the sunrise burned for joy
O' the blade, "Die," cried she, "devil, in God's name!"
Ah, but they all closed round her, twelve to one
—The unmanly men, no woman-mother made,
Spawned somehow! Dead-white and disarmed she lay.
No matter for the sword, her word sufficed   1550
To spike the coward through and through: he shook,
Could only spit between the teeth—"You see?
You hear? Bear witness, then! Write down . . . but no—
Carry these criminals to the prison-house,
For first thing! I begin my search meanwhile
After the stolen effects, gold, jewels, plate,
Money and clothes, they robbed me of and fled,
With no few amorous pieces, verse and prose,
I have much reason to expect to find."

When I saw that—no more than the first mad speech, 1560
Made out the speaker mad and a laughing-stock,
So neither did this next device explode
One listener's indignation,—that a scribe
Did sit down, set himself to write indeed,
While sundry knaves began to peer and pry
In corner and hole,—that Guido, wiping brow
And getting him a countenance, was fast
Losing his fear, beginning to strut free
O' the stage of his exploit, snuff here, sniff there,—
Then I took truth in, guessed sufficiently   1570
The service for the moment. "What I say,
Slight at your peril! We are aliens here,
My adversary and I, called noble both;
I am the nobler, and a name men know.
I could refer our cause to our own Court
In our own country, but prefer appeal
To the nearer jurisdiction. Being a priest,
Though in a secular garb,—for reasons good

I shall adduce in due time to my peers,—
I demand that the Church I serve, decide   1580
Between us, right the slandered lady there.
A Tuscan noble, I might claim the Duke:
A priest, I rather choose the Church,—bid Rome
Cover the wronged with her inviolate shield."

There was no refusing this: they bore me off,
They bore her off, to separate cells o' the same
Ignoble prison, and, separate, thence to Rome.
Pompilia's face, then and thus, looked on me
The last time in this life: not one sight since,
Never another sight to be! And yet   1590
I thought I had saved her. I appealed to Rome:
It seems I simply sent her to her death.
You tell me she is dying now, or dead;
I cannot bring myself to quite believe
This is a place you torture people in:
What if this your intelligence were just
A subtlety, an honest wile to work
On a man at unawares? 'T were worthy you.
No, Sirs, I cannot have the lady dead!
That erect form, flashing brow, fulgurant eye,   1600
That voice immortal (oh, that voice of hers!)
That vision in the blood-red day-break—that
Leap to life of the pale electric sword
Angels go armed with,—that was not the last
O' the lady! Come, I see through it, you find—
Know the manœuvre! Also herself said
I had saved her: do you dare say she spoke false?
Let me see for myself if it be so!
Though she were dying, a Priest might be of use,
The more when he's a friend too,—she called me   1610
Far beyond "friend." Come, let me see her—indeed
It is my duty, being a priest: I hope
I stand confessed, established, proved a priest?
My punishment had motive that, a priest
I, in a laic garb, a mundane mode,
Did what were harmlessly done otherwise.

1600 *fulgurant:* flashing like lightning.

I never touched her with my finger-tip
Except to carry her to the couch, that eve,
Against my heart, beneath my head, bowed low,
As we priests carry the paten: that is why   1620
—To get leave and go see her of your grace—
I have told you this whole story over again.
Do I deserve grace? For I might lock lips,
Laugh at your jurisdiction: what have you
To do with me in the matter? I suppose
You hardly think I donned a bravo's dress
To have a hand in the new crime; on the old,
Judgment's delivered, penalty imposed,
I was chained fast at Civita hand and foot—
She had only you to trust to, you and Rome,   1630
Rome and the Church, and no pert meddling priest
Two days ago, when Guido, with the right,
Hacked her to pieces. One might well be wroth;
I have been patient, done my best to help:
I come from Civita and punishment
As friend of the Court—and for pure friendship's sake
Have told my tale to the end,—nay, not the end—
For, wait—I'll end—not leave you that excuse!

When we were parted,—shall I go on there?
I was presently brought to Rome—yes, here I stood   1640
Opposite yonder very crucifix—
And there sat you and you, Sirs, quite the same.
I heard charge, and bore question, and told tale
Noted down in the book there,—turn and see
If, by one jot or tittle, I vary now!
I' the colour the tale takes, there's change perhaps;
'T is natural, since the sky is different,
Eclipse in the air now; still, the outline stays.
I showed you how it came to be my part
To save the lady. Then your clerk produced   1650
Papers, a pack of stupid and impure
Banalities called letters about love—
Love, indeed,—I could teach who styled them so,
Better, I think, though priest and loveless both!
"—How was it that a wife, young, innocent,
And stranger to your person, wrote this page?"—

"—She wrote it when the Holy Father wrote
The bestiality that posts thro' Rome,
Put in his mouth by Pasquin." "Nor perhaps
Did you return these answers, verse and prose,   1660
Signed, sealed and sent the lady? There's your hand!"
"—This precious piece of verse, I really judge,
Is meant to copy my own character,
A clumsy mimic; and this other prose,
Not so much even; both rank forgery:
Verse, quotha? Bembo's verse! When Saint John wrote
The tract 'De Tribus,' I wrote this to match."
"—How came it, then, the documents were found
At the inn on your departure?"—"I opine,
Because there were no documents to find   1670
In my presence,—you must hide before you find.
Who forged them hardly practised in my view;
Who found them waited till I turned my back."
"—And what of the clandestine visits paid,
Nocturnal passage in and out the house
With its lord absent? 'T is alleged you climbed" . . .
"—Flew on a broomstick to the man i' the moon!
Who witnessed or will testify this trash?"
"—The trusty servant, Margherita's self,
Even she who brought you letters, you confess,   1680
And, you confess, took letters in reply:
Forget not we have knowledge of the facts!"
"—Sirs, who have knowledge of the facts, defray
The expenditure of wit I waste in vain,
Trying to find out just one fact of all!
She who brought letters from who could not write,
And took back letters to who could not read,—
Who was that messenger, of your charity?"
"—Well, so far favours you the circumstance
That this same messenger . . . how shall we say? . . .   1690
Sub imputatione meretricis
Laborat,—which makes accusation null:

1659 *Pasquin:* the name of a statue in Rome on which it was the custom to post satirical or obscene verses.
1666 *Bembo:* Italian cardinal and writer.
1667 *'De Tribus':* De Tribus Impostoribus, blasphemous tract.
1691-2 *Sub . . . Laborat:* labors under the imputation of prostitution.

We waive this woman's:—nought makes void the next.
Borsi, called Venerino, he who drove,
O' the first night when you fled away, at length
Deposes to your kissings in the coach,
—Frequent, frenetic" . . . "When deposed he so?"
"After some weeks of sharp imprisonment" . . .
"—Granted by friend the Governor, I engage"—
"—For his participation in your flight!   1700
At length his obduracy melting made
The avowal mentioned" . . . "Was dismissed forthwith
To liberty, poor knave, for recompense.
Sirs, give what credit to the lie you can!
For me, no word in my defence I speak,
And God shall argue for the lady!"

                              So
Did I stand question, and make answer, still
With the same result of smiling disbelief,
Polite impossibility of faith   1710
In such affected virtue in a priest;
But a showing fair play, an indulgence, even,
To one no worse than others after all—
Who had not brought disgrace to the order, played
Discreetly, ruffled gown nor ripped the cloth
In a bungling game at romps: I have told you, Sirs—
If I pretended simply to be pure
Honest and Christian in the case,—absurd!
As well go boast myself above the needs
O' the human nature, careless how meat smells,   1720
Wine tastes,—a saint above the smack! But once
Abate my crest, own flaws i' the flesh, agree
To go with the herd, be hog no more nor less,
Why, hogs in common herd have common rights:
I must not be unduly borne upon,
Who just romanced a little, sowed wild oats,
But 'scaped without a scandal, flagrant fault.
My name helped to a mirthful circumstance:
"Joseph" would do well to amend his plea:
Undoubtedly—some toying with the wife,   1730
But as for ruffian violence and rape,

Potiphar pressed too much on the other side!
The intrigue, the elopement, the disguise,—well charged!
The letters and verse looked hardly like the truth.
Your apprehension was—of guilt enough
To be compatible with innocence,
So, punished best a little and not too much.
Had I struck Guido Franceschini's face,
You had counselled me withdraw for my own sake,
Baulk him of bravo-hiring. Friends came round,   1740
Congratulated, "Nobody mistakes!
The pettiness o' the forfeiture defines
The peccadillo: Guido gets his share:
His wife is free of husband and hook-nose,
The mouldy viands and the mother-in-law.
To Civita with you and amuse the time,
Travesty us 'De Raptu Helenæ!'
A funny figure must the husband cut
When the wife makes him skip,—too ticklish, eh?
Do it in Latin, not the Vulgar, then!   1750
Scazons—we'll copy and send his Eminence.
Mind—one iambus in the final foot!
He'll rectify it, be your friend for life!"
Oh, Sirs, depend on me for much new light
Thrown on the justice and religion here
By this proceeding, much fresh food for thought!

And I was just set down to study these
In relegation, two short days ago,
Admiring how you read the rules, when, clap,
A thunder comes into my solitude—   1760
I am caught up in a whirlwind and cast here,
Told of a sudden, in this room where so late
You dealt out law adroitly, that those scales,
I meekly bowed to, took my allotment from,
Guido has snatched at, broken in your hands,
Metes to himself the murder of his wife,

1732 *Potiphar:* for the story of Joseph and Potiphar's wife, see *Genesis* 39.
1747 *'De Raptu Helenæ':* concerning the rape of Helen. The reference is to the elopement that caused the Trojan war.
1751 *Scazons:* modifications of iambic trimeter in which the final foot has no iambus.

Full measure, pressed down, running over now!
Can I assist to an explanation?—Yes,
I rise in your esteem, sagacious Sirs,
Stand up a renderer of reasons, not   1770
The officious priest would personate Saint George
For a mock Princess in undragoned days.
What, the blood startles you? What, after all
The priest who needs must carry sword on thigh
May find imperative use for it? Then, there was
A Princess, was a dragon belching flame,
And should have been a Saint George also? Then,
There might be worse schemes than to break the bonds
At Arezzo, lead her by the little hand,
Till she reached Rome, and let her try to live?   1780
But you were law and gospel,—would one please
Stand back, allow your faculty elbow-room?
You blind guides who must needs lead eyes that see!
Fools, alike ignorant of man and God!
What was there here should have perplexed your wit
For a wink of the owl-eyes of you? How miss, then,
What's now forced on you by this flare of fact—
As if Saint Peter failed to recognize
Nero as no apostle, John or James,
Till someone burned a martyr, made a torch   1790
O' the blood and fat to show his features by!
Could you fail read this cartulary aright
On head and front of Franceschini there,
Large-lettered like hell's masterpiece of print,—
That he, from the beginning pricked at heart
By some lust, letch of hate against his wife,
Plotted to plague her into overt sin
And shame, would slay Pompilia body and soul,
And save his mean self—miserably caught
I' the quagmire of his own tricks, cheats and lies?   1800
—That himself wrote those papers,—from himself
To himself,—which, i' the name of me and her,
His mistress-messenger gave her and me,
Touching us with such pustules of the soul
That she and I might take the taint, be shown

1792 *cartulary:* collection of documents.
1804 *pustules:* pimples.

To the world and shuddered over, speckled so?
—That the agent put her sense into my words,
Made substitution of the thing she hoped,
For the thing she had and held, its opposite,
While the husband in the background bit his lips   1810
At each fresh failure of his precious plot?
—That when at the last we did rush each on each,
By no chance but because God willed it so—
The spark of truth was struck from out our souls—
Made all of me, descried in the first glance,
Seem fair and honest and permissible love
O' the good and true—as the first glance told me
There was no duty patent in the world
Like daring try be good and true myself,
Leaving the shows of things to the Lord of Show   1820
And Prince o' the Power of the Air. Our very flight,
Even to its most ambiguous circumstance,
Irrefragably proved how futile, false . . .
Why, men—men and not boys—boys and not babes—
Babes and not beasts—beasts and not stocks and stones!—
Had the liar's lie been true one pin-point speck,
Were I the accepted suitor, free o' the place,
Disposer of the time, to come at a call
And go at a wink as who should say me nay,—
What need of flight, what were the gain therefrom   1830
But just damnation, failure or success?
Damnation pure and simple to her the wife
And me the priest—who bartered private bliss
For public reprobation, the safe shade
For the sunshine which men see to pelt me by:
What other advantage,—we who led the days
And nights alone i' the house,—was flight to find?
In our whole journey did we stop an hour,
Diverge a foot from straight road till we reached
Or would have reached—but for that fate of ours—   1840
The father and mother, in the eye of Rome,
The eye of yourselves we made aware of us
At the first fall of misfortune? And indeed
You did so far give sanction to our flight,
Confirm its purpose, as lend helping hand,
Deliver up Pompilia not to him

She fled, but those the flight was ventured for.
Why then could you, who stopped short, not go on
One poor step more, and justify the means,
Having allowed the end?—not see and say   1850
"Here's the exceptional conduct that should claim
To be exceptionally judged on rules
Which, understood, make no exception here"—
Why play instead into the devil's hands
By dealing so ambiguously as gave
Guido the power to intervene like me,
Prove one exception more? I saved his wife
Against law: against law he slays her now:
Deal with him!

             I have done with being judged.   1860
I stand here guiltless in thought, word and deed,
To the point that I apprise you,—in contempt
For all misapprehending ignorance
O' the human heart, much more the mind of Christ,—
That I assuredly did bow, was blessed
By the revelation of Pompilia. There!
Such is the final fact I fling you, Sirs,
To mouth and mumble and misinterpret: there!
"The priest's in love," have it the vulgar way!
Unpriest me, rend the rags o' the vestment, do—   1870
Degrade deep, disenfranchise all you dare—
Remove me from the midst, no longer priest
And fit companion for the like of you—
Your gay Abati with the well-turned leg
And rose i' the hat-rim, Canons, cross at neck
And silk mask in the pocket of the gown,
Brisk Bishops with the world's musk still unbrushed
From the rochet; I'll no more of these good things:
There's a crack somewhere, something that's unsound
I' the rattle!   1880

         For Pompilia—be advised,
Build churches, go pray! You will find me there,
I know, if you come,—and you will come, I know.

1877 *musk:* perfume.

Why, there's a Judge weeping! Did not I say
You were good and true at bottom? You see the truth—
I am glad I helped you: she helped me just so.

But for Count Guido,—you must counsel there!
I bow my head, bend to the very dust,
Break myself up in shame of faultiness.
I had him one whole moment, as I said—   1890
As I remember, as will never out
O' the thoughts of me,—I had him in arm's reach
There,—as you stand, Sir, now you cease to sit,—
I could have killed him ere he killed his wife,
And did not: he went off alive and well
And then effected this last feat—through me!
Me—not through you—dismiss that fear! 'T was you
Hindered me staying here to save her,—not
From leaving you and going back to him
And doing service in Arezzo. Come,   1900
Instruct me in procedure! I conceive—
In all due self-abasement might I speak—
How you will deal with Guido: oh, not death!
Death, if it let her life be: otherwise
Not death,—your lights will teach you clearer! I
Certainly have an instinct of my own
I' the matter: bear with me and weigh its worth!
Let us go away—leave Guido all alone
Back on the world again that knows him now!
I think he will be found (indulge so far!)   1910
Not to die so much as slide out of life,
Pushed by the general horror and common hate
Low, lower,—left o' the very ledge of things,
I seem to see him catch convulsively
One by one at all honest forms of life,
At reason, order, decency and use—
To cramp him and get foothold by at least;
And still they disengage them from his clutch.
"What, you are he, then, had Pompilia once
And so forwent her? Take not up with us!"   1920
And thus I see him slowly and surely edged
Off all the table-land whence life upsprings
Aspiring to be immortality,

As the snake, hatched on hill-top by mischance,
Despite his wriggling, slips, slides, slidders down
Hill-side, lies low and prostrate on the smooth
Level of the outer place, lapsed in the vale:
So I lose Guido in the loneliness,
Silence and dusk, till at the doleful end,
At the horizontal line, creation's verge,　　　　1930
From what just is to absolute nothingness—
Whom is it, straining onward still, he meets?
What other man deep further in the fate,
Who, turning at the prize of a footfall
To flatter him and promise fellowship,
Discovers in the act a frightful face—
Judas, made monstrous by much solitude!
The two are at one now! Let them love their love
That bites and claws like hate, or hate their hate
That mops and mows and makes as it were love!　　　1940
There, let them each tear each in devil's-fun,
Or fondle this the other while malice aches—
Both teach, both learn detestability!
Kiss him the kiss, Iscariot! Pay that back,
That smatch o' the slaver blistering on your lip,
By the better trick, the insult he spared Christ—
Lure him the lure o' the letters, Aretine!
Lick him o'er slimy-smooth with jelly-filth
O' the verse-and-prose pollution in love's guise!
The cockatrice is with the basilisk!　　　　1950
There let them grapple, denizens o' the dark,
Foes or friends, but indissolubly bound,
In their one spot out of the ken of God
Or care of man, for ever and ever more!

Why, Sirs, what's this? Why, this is sorry and strange!
Futility, divagation: this from me
Bound to be rational, justify an act
Of sober man!—whereas, being moved so much,
I give you cause to doubt the lady's mind:
A pretty sarcasm for the world! I fear　　　　1960
You do her wit injustice,—all through me!

1950 *cockatrice . . . basilisk:* legendary serpents or lizards whose glances
caused death.

Like my fate all through,—ineffective help!
A poor rash advocate I prove myself.
You might be angry with good cause: but sure
At the advocate,—only at the undue zeal
That spoils the force of his own plea, I think?
My part was just to tell you how things stand,
State facts and not be flustered at their fume.
But then 't is a priest speaks: as for love,—no!
If you let buzz a vulgar fly like that   1970
About your brains, as if I loved, forsooth,
Indeed, Sirs, you do wrong! We had no thought
Of such infatuation, she and I:
There are many points that prove it: do be just!
I told you,—at one little roadside-place
I spent a good half-hour, paced to and fro
The garden; just to leave her free awhile,
I plucked a handful of Spring herb and bloom:
I might have sat beside her on the bench
Where the children were: I wish the thing had been, 1980
Indeed: the event could not be worse, you know:
One more half-hour of her saved! She's dead now, Sirs!
While I was running on at such a rate,
Friends should have plucked me by the sleeve: I went
Too much o' the trivial outside of her face
And the purity that shone there—plain to me,
Not to you, what more natural? Nor am I
Infatuated,—oh, I saw, be sure!
Her brow had not the right line, leaned too much,
Painters would say; they like the straight-up Greek: 1990
This seemed bent somewhat with an invisible crown
Of martyr and saint, not such as art approves.
And how the dark orbs dwelt deep underneath,
Looked out of such a sad sweet heaven on me!
The lips, compressed a little, came forward too,
Careful for a whole world of sin and pain.
That was the face, her husband makes his plea,
He sought just to disfigure,—no offence
Beyond that! Sirs, let us be rational!
He needs must vindicate his honour,—ay,   2000
Yet shirks, the coward, in a clown's disguise,
Away from the scene, endeavours to escape.

Now, had he done so, slain and left no trace
O' the slayer,—what were vindicated, pray?
You had found his wife disfigured or a corpse,
For what and by whom? It is too palpable!
Then, here's another point involving law:
I use this argument to show you meant
No calumny against us by that title
O' the sentence,—liars try to twist it so: 2010
What penalty it bore, I had to pay
Till further proof should follow of innocence—
Probationis ob defectum,—proof?
How could you get proof without trying us?
You went through the preliminary form,
Stopped there, contrived this sentence to amuse
The adversary. If the title ran
For more than fault imputed and not proved,
That was a simple penman's error, else
A slip i' the phrase,—as when we say of you   2020
"Charged with injustice"—which may either be
Or not be,—'t is a name that sticks meanwhile.
Another relevant matter: fool that I am!
Not what I wish true, yet a point friends urge:
It is not true,—yet, since friends think it helps,—
She only tried me when some others failed—
Began with Conti, whom I told you of,
And Guillichini, Guido's kinsfolk both,
And when abandoned by them, not before,
Turned to me. That's conclusive why she turned.   2030
Much good they got by the happy cowardice!
Conti is dead, poisoned a month ago:
Does that much strike you as a sin? Not much,
After the present murder,—one mark more
On the Moor's skin,—what is black by blacker still?
Conti had come here and told truth. And so
With Guillichini; he's condemned of course
To the galleys, as a friend in this affair,
Tried and condemned for no one thing i' the world,
A fortnight since by who but the Governor?—   2040
The just judge, who refused Pompilia help

2013 *Probationis ob defectum:* for lack of proof.

At first blush, being her husband's friend, you know.
There are two tales to suit the separate courts,
Arezzo and Rome: he tells you here, we fled
Alone, unhelped,—lays stress on the main fault,
The spiritual sin, Rome looks to: but elsewhere
He likes best we should break in, steal, bear off,
Be fit to brand and pillory and flog—
That's the charge goes to the heart of the Governor:
If these unpriest me, you and I may yet   2050
Converse, Vincenzo Marzi-Medici!
Oh, Sirs, there are worse men than you, I say!
More easily duped, I mean; this stupid lie,
Its liar never dared propound in Rome,
He gets Arezzo to receive,—nay more,
Gets Florence and the Duke to authorize!
This is their Rota's sentence, their Granduke
Signs and seals! Rome for me henceforward—Rome,
Where better men are,—most of all, that man
The Augustinian of the Hospital,   2060
Who writes the letter,—he confessed, he says,
Many a dying person, never one
So sweet and true and pure and beautiful.
A good man! Will you make him Pope one day?
Not that he is not good too, this we have—
But old,—else he would have his word to speak,
His truth to teach the world: I thirst for truth,
But shall not drink it till I reach the source.

Sirs, I am quiet again. You see, we are
So very pitiable, she and I,   2070
Who had conceivably been otherwise.
Forget distemperature and idle heat!
Apart from truth's sake, what's to move so much?
Pompilia will be presently with God;
I am, on earth, as good as out of it,
A relegated priest; when exile ends,
I mean to do my duty and live long.
She and I are mere strangers now: but priests

2051 *Marzi-Medici:* the governor of Arezzo. Caponsacchi means, if he is un-
frocked, to have a "conversation" (duel) with him.
2057 *Rota:* papal court dealing primarily with matrimonial cases.

priests should know the
emotions of people,
in order to help
them

Should study passion; how else cure mankind,
Who come for help in passionate extremes?   2080
I do but play with an imagined life
Of who, unfettered by a vow, unblessed
By the higher call,—since you will have it so,—
Leads it companioned by the woman there.
To live, and see her learn, and learn by her,
Out of the low obscure and petty world—
Or only see one purpose and one will
Evolve themselves i' the world, change wrong to right:
To have to do with nothing but the true,
The good, the eternal—and these, not alone   2090
In the main current of the general life,
But small experiences of every day,
Concerns of the particular hearth and home:
To learn not only by a comet's rush
But a rose's birth,—not by the grandeur, God—
But the comfort, Christ. All this, how far away!
Mere delectation, meet for a minute's dream!—
Just as a drudging student trims his lamp,
Opens his Plutarch, puts him in the place
Of Roman, Grecian; draws the patched gown close,   2100
Dreams, "Thus should I fight, save or rule the world!"—
Then smilingly, contentedly, awakes
To the old solitary nothingness.
So I, from such communion, pass content . . .

O great, just, good God! Miserable me!

[1868]

NEVER THE TIME AND THE PLACE

Never the time and the place
    And the loved one all together!
This path—how soft to pace!
    This May—what magic weather!
Where is the loved one's face?

In a dream that loved one's face meets mine,
   But the house is narrow, the place is bleak
Where, outside, rain and wind combine
   With a furtive ear, if I strive to speak,
   With a hostile eye at my flushing cheek,   10
With a malice that marks each word, each sign!
O enemy sly and serpentine,
   Uncoil thee from the waking man!
      Do I hold the Past
      Thus firm and fast
   Yet doubt if the Future hold I can?
This path so soft to pace shall lead
Thro' the magic of May to herself indeed!
Or narrow if needs the house must be,
Outside are the storms and strangers: we—   20
Oh, close, safe, warm sleep I and she,
   —I and she!

[1883]

Matthew Arnold

[1822-1888]

There is no true biography of Matthew Arnold and he wished there to be none, for his was a life without the wealth of external incident that makes good biography. Yet from his poetry and from his letters, curiously impersonal though they are, there emerges an intimacy of mind and emotion unlike that of any other Victorian poet, save, perhaps, Hopkins. It is this sense of nearness to brain and heart, although the nearness is couched in urbane, detached language, that has made Arnold seem to many modern readers the most immediate poet of his age.

Arnold was the second of the twelve children born in rapid, ecclesiastical fashion to the Rev. Thomas Arnold and his wife, the former Mary Penrose. If all men's histories are in part the history of their fathers, this was doubly true of Matthew Arnold. His father, although he has been embalmed in Lytton Strachey's phrase as an "Eminent Victorian," was one of the great men of his day. His posthumous fame has been chiefly as the foremost innovator of educational reform of the period, as the man who transformed the public schools of England from ill-run, dissolute, slack institutions into the finest examples of secondary education in the world, chiefly through the force of his own example as headmaster of Rugby. To his contemporaries he was also well known as an historian and as a social and religious critic. The elder Arnold found no division between learning, conduct, and religion; just as he thought of Rugby as producing a whole man, so he was concerned with government and Church as ministering equally to the minds, bodies, and hearts of men. His liberal views were more deeply impressed in the mind of Matthew Arnold than his son was to recognize for a long time. Thomas Arnold was a stern (if loving) father, whose somewhat schoolmasterly attitude toward government and religion was extended to his family. Naturally enough, his son absorbed many of his views, but, equally naturally, he reacted against the strenuous earnestness of his father. It has become a cliché in our own psychologically-minded era that "Sohrab and Rustum" is concerned with a fight to the death between father and son, and that Matthew Arnold delayed writing his great elegy to his father, "Rugby Chapel," until fifteen years after the latter's death.

Matthew Arnold was sent first to Winchester to school, then to Rugby. In 1841 he went to Oxford with a scholarship to Balliol, then the most intellectually distinguished of Oxford colleges. Clearly talented though he was, Arnold showed little to his friends at Balliol that could connect him with the great Dr. Arnold; he was a handsome, debonair young man with elegant, affected manners and wondrous waistcoats, seldom going to chapel, speaking often in French, ostensibly more devoted to dogs and horses than to his studies. What he later wrote in "The Austerity of Poetry" might be applied to him at this period: "young, gay, / Radiant, adorn'd outside a hidden ground / Of thought and of austerity within." The suave exterior concealed a troubled heart, the sparkling wit hid a divided mind, and he did not care to reveal his inner distress to most of his friends. One among them, Arthur Hugh Clough, was the exception. Clough was also interested in writing poetry, he too was upset by the feeling of being in a world whose ancient props were tumbling one by one, and to him Arnold revealed "the buried life" that others seldom saw. The correspondence that passed between Arnold and Clough is probably a better guide to the mind and the intellectual and emotional biography of Arnold than anything else ever written. For Arnold, Clough was always to be part of all that Oxford had meant so deeply to him; together the two friends (although forever disagreeing on poetry) discovered the pensive, detached spirit of poetry represented in the legend of the Scholar-Gipsy. And it was to the memory of Clough that Arnold dedicated *Thyrsis,* one of the three or four great elegies in the English language. The hills and flowers, streams, and scattered farms, among which he and Clough had wandered and where he liked to think the spirit of the Scholar-Gipsy still walked, drew from Arnold in these Oxfordshire poems an emotional richness of natural imagery hardly paralleled elsewhere in his poetry.

At Balliol, Arnold, fresh from the liberal but orthodox religious attitudes of his home, was plunged into the center of the High Church Oxford Movement, and, though he was never persuaded by it, he was much attracted to Newman and to the stern beauty of that Movement, which is probably reflected in his consideration of the austere liturgical life of the monks in "Stanzas from the Grande Chartreuse." Although such a life seemed to him anachronistic, Arnold could well envy its unquestioning sense of security. His own religious views became quite unorthodox, but to the end of his life he was moved by the beauty and example of Christianity, particularly in the Church of England. If he could not believe totally in the dogma of Christianity, he felt it was an unparalleled guide for conduct and morality, and the supreme example of his own definition of religion as morality touched with emotion. Of all the traditional guides that he mourned for in his poetry, religion was easily chief; he longed for its consolation, but could not accept intellectually any of its traditional formulations.

Arnold's classical studies, which had begun long before Oxford and which continued the rest of his life, were the most important single influence on his thinking. In both poetry and prose, he used the classics as a constant measure of the literature, the life, the intelligence of his own day. In them, he found the consolation of knowing that his own sense of isolation was part of a long tradition. The serenity of the Greeks in the face of despair, their intelligence, their beauty of mind and sense of proportion aroused his deepest envy. It was Sophocles, and not Shakespeare or a more modern writer, who, Arnold said, "saw life steadily, and saw it whole." Despite his love of the classics, Arnold took only a second class degree at Oxford in 1844, because he had not followed a disciplined course of reading. In 1845, after a brief interlude of teaching classics at Rugby, he was elected, in spite of his disappointing degree, to one of the most coveted positions in Oxford, a fellowship in Oriel College. In 1847 he became private secretary to Lord Lansdowne, a political peer, who a few years later secured him an inspectorship of schools, a position he occupied for more than thirty years.

Sometime in 1848 or 1849 Arnold seems to have met in Switzerland a French girl, the mysterious "Marguerite" of the love poems. Amid all the conjecture about her, there is little certainty as to who she was; most of what we can guess comes from the poems themselves. It is probable that she was from Paris, that she was strikingly beautiful, that she had had lovers before Arnold, that she was perhaps of lower social station than he, and that the whole affair was over within a year. The lyrics of "Switzerland" are concerned with Marguerite; probably a handful of other poems are as well. What is more striking than the subject of these poems is the reiteration of the isolation in the midst of life—the failure of romantic love to bring him a sense of unity. "The unplumb'd, salt, estranging sea" (which provides isolation in a literal sense) is an image repeated in "Tristram and Iseult" and "Dover Beach."

In 1849 Arnold brought out his first volume of poetry, *The Strayed Reveller and Other Poems*, enigmatically signed only with the letter "A." The title poem was the first consideration of a problem that was to occupy Arnold frequently in his poetry, the conflict of sensuality and reason. After a short time, the volume, which had attracted scant attention, was withdrawn from sale.

Empedocles on Etna and Other Poems, 1852, was also withdrawn after publication. *Poems*, 1853, contained Arnold's first major piece of criticism, the preface, in which he enunciated his intention of turning away from situations in poetry "in which the suffering finds no vent in action; in which a continuous state of mental distress is prolonged, unrelieved by incident, hope, or resistance; in which there is everything to be endured, nothing to be done." In other words, he intended to give his attention to poetry that was less introspective, less concerned with the personal and the contemporary, and more interested in appealing to the "great primary affections." In support of the preface, he published "Sohrab and Rustum," a deliberate attempt to achieve distance from his subject by a kind of classical objectivity. This volume reprinted from the earlier books those poems he wanted associated with his name; it also included one of the most beautiful poems he ever wrote, "The Scholar-Gipsy," which seems almost a direct refutation of the preface.

Poems, Second Series, 1855, was in large part the closing of the poetic part of Arnold's career, although it was followed in 1858 by *Merope,* an attempt at drama in the classical form, and *New Poems,* 1867, which (although it did contain "Dover Beach," "Thyrsis," and "Rugby Chapel") was somewhat misleadingly named, since it was primarily a reprinting of previously published poems.

In 1851 Arnold had married Miss Lucy Wightman, after his inspectorship of schools made marriage financially possible. As an inspector he worked long hard hours, enduring slow train journeys and uncomfortable hotels, both in England and while travelling on the Continent. In 1857 he was elected Professor of Poetry at Oxford, a chair which required but few lectures and which he could fill at the same time as his inspectorship.

There have been many conjectures as to why Arnold practically deserted poetry in his later life; certainly, his professorship and his inspectorship demanded most of his time, and, equally certainly, he could not have supported his growing family on the proceeds from his poetry. Perhaps, too, he felt his poetic powers failing ("I am past thirty," he had written to Clough, "and three parts iced over"), and he felt that the society in which he lived was a deeply unpoetic one, unproductive of great poetry. In any case, after his inauguration as Professor of Poetry, he turned almost all of his writing energies to criticism, initially of literature and then of society. His criticism of both was written in an Olympian, witty style greatly unlike that of his poetry, but he continued, in investigating literature and society, to regard them with the same awareness of tradition that he had brought to his poems. He attempted to teach his contemporaries to look at themselves and their institutions with a searching, Attic combination of pure intellect and a sense of proportion and beauty, qualities he felt conspicuously lacking in his own day. As he had said in "Stanzas from the Grande Chartreuse," he was "wandering between two worlds, one dead, / The other powerless to be born."

In 1883 Arnold made a lecture tour of the United States, and in 1886 he retired as inspector of schools. Two years later, he died suddenly from a heart attack, as his father had done a half century before.

It is a melancholy fact that Arnold himself never perceived the real reasons why his memory was to remain green. The writing of his later life was of such a high order as to make him one of the major critics in English, but it inspires admiration, not the love which readers of his poetry feel. Nor was it the objective treatment of a noble action in poetry, of which he spoke in the 1853 preface, that has made his poems have such continued meaning for readers a century later; it is the strong, direct emotion of his best poetry, the lyrical statement of a cosmic sadness, and the touching awareness of the beauty of what has passed. Even in so successful a narrative poem as "Sohrab and Rustum," it is the poignance of the relationship between father and son, not the sense of noble, animating action, that moves the reader. And the shifting of the poet's attention to the magnificent, objective conclusion of the Oxus takes its meaning from the emotions of father and son, fated to know each other only in death. Arnold had a particular affection for a quiet closing to a poem, objectifying what has gone before. In "Sohrab and Rustum," "The Scholar-Gipsy," and "Dover Beach," it is an effective device because it has immediate relevance to what has preceded it; in such closings as that of "Tristram and Iseult," it is perhaps less effective because the relevance is ambiguous.

Austerity, Requiescat, Resignation, Parting, Farewell, Isolation, Absence, Strayed, Faded, Despondency, Courage: a sense of quiet, Stoic, dignified melancholy haunts even the titles of Arnold's poems, and it is as the poet of the isolated soul that he will probably be remembered.

BIBLIOGRAPHY

The standard edition of the poetry is *The Poetical Works of Matthew Arnold* (ed. C. B. Tinker and H. F. Lowry. Oxford University Press, London, New York, and Toronto, 1950).

Biography and Criticism:

Allott, Kenneth, *Matthew Arnold.* Macmillan, London, 1955.

Baum, Paull F., *Ten Studies in the Poetry of Matthew Arnold.* Duke University Press, Durham, 1958. explication of evident

Duffin, Henry Charles, *Arnold the Poet.* Bowes and Bowes, London, 1962.

Tinker, C. B., and Lowry, H. F., *The Poetry of Matthew Arnold: a Commentary.* Oxford University Press, London, New York, and Toronto, 1940. accompany reading of poems

Trilling, Lionel, *Matthew Arnold.* Columbia University Press, New York, 1949. intellectual history

THE STRAYED REVELLER

The Portico of Circe's Palace. Evening.

A YOUTH.   CIRCE.

THE YOUTH. Faster, faster,
O Circe, Goddess,
Let the wild, thronging train,
The bright procession
Of eddying forms,
Sweep through my soul!

Thou standest, smiling
Down on me! thy right arm,
Leaned up against the column there,
Props thy soft cheek;   10
Thy left holds, hanging loosely,
The deep cup, ivy-cinctured,
I held but now.

Is it, then, evening
So soon? I see, the night-dews,
Cluster'd in thick beads, dim
The agate brooch-stones
On thy white shoulder;
The cool night-wind, too,
Blows through the portico,   20
Stirs thy hair, Goddess,
Waves thy white robe!

The Strayed Reveller: Ulysses and his men have come to the island of Ææa and the palace of the sorceress Circe, who has turned Ulysses' men into swine. The Youth, a would-be poet, has strayed into Circe's palace and drunk her wine, which has intoxicated him. He is a follower of Iacchus (Bacchus), god of wine and revel, and hence he wears the costume of the devotees of Bacchus, a fawn skin, and carries a thyrsus, a long rod wreathed with leaves. The rites of Bacchus were carried on with drink, dancing to the drum and flute, and debauchery.

CIRCE. /Whence art thou, sleeper?

THE YOUTH. When the white dawn first
               Through the rough fir-planks
               Of my hut, by the chestnuts,
               Up at the valley-head,
               Came breaking, Goddess!
               I sprang up, I threw round me
               My dappled fawn-skin;   30
               Passing out, from the wet turf,
               Where they lay, by the hut door,
               I snatch'd up my vine-crown, my fir-staff,
               All drench'd in dew—
               Came swift down to join
               The rout early gather'd
               In the town, round the temple,
               Iacchus' white fane
               On yonder hill.

               Quick I pass'd, following   40
               The wood-cutters' cart-track
               Down the dark valley;—I saw
               On my left, through the beeches,
               Thy palace, Goddess,
               Smokeless, empty!
               Trembling, I enter'd; beheld
               The court all silent,
               The lions sleeping,
               On the altar this bowl.
               I drank, Goddess!   50
               And sank down here, sleeping,
               On the steps of thy portico.

CIRCE. Foolish boy! Why tremblest thou?
          Thou lovest it, then, my wine?
          Wouldst more of it? See, how glows,
          Through the delicate, flush'd marble,
          The red, creaming liquor,

---

[57] *creaming:* foaming.

Strown with dark seeds!
Drink, then! I chide thee not,
Deny thee not my bowl.   60
Come, stretch forth thy hand, then—so!
Drink—drink again!

THE YOUTH. Thanks, gracious one!
Ah, the sweet fumes again!
More soft, ah me,
More subtle-winding
Than Pan's flute-music!
Faint—faint! Ah me,
Again the sweet sleep!

CIRCE. Hist! Thou—within there!
Come forth, Ulysses! *man of action oppos to poet.*
Art tired with hunting?
While we range the woodland,
See what the day brings. *conflict between ... contemplation + action*

ULYSSES. Ever new magic!
Hast thou then lured hither,
Wonderful Goddess, by thy art,
The young, languid-eyed Ampelus,
Iacchus' darling—
Or some youth beloved of Pan,   80
Of Pan and the Nymphs?
That he sits, bending downward
His white, delicate neck
To the ivy-wreathed marge
Of thy cup; the bright, glancing vine-leaves
That crown his hair,
Falling forward, mingling
With the dark ivy-plants—
His fawn-skin, half untied,
Smear'd with red wine-stains? Who is he,   90
That he sits, overweigh'd

---

78 *Ampelus:* handsome son of a nymph and a centaur.

By fumes of wine and sleep,
So late, in thy portico?
What youth, Goddess,—what guest
Of Gods or mortals?

CIRCE.   Hist! he wakes!
I lured him not hither, Ulysses.
Nay, ask him!

THE YOUTH.   Who speaks? Ah, who comes forth
To thy side, Goddess, from within?   100
How shall I name him?
This spare, dark-featured,
Quick-eyed stranger?
Ah, and I see too
His sailor's bonnet,
His short coat, travel-tarnish'd,
With one arm bare!—
Art thou not he, whom fame
This long time rumours
The favour'd guest of Circe, brought by the
        waves?   110
Art thou he, stranger?
The wise Ulysses,
Laertes' son?

ULYSSES.   I am Ulysses.
And thou, too, sleeper?
Thy voice is sweet.
It may be thou hast follow'd
Through the islands some divine bard,
By age taught many things,
Age and the Muses;   120
And heard him delighting
The chiefs and people
In the banquet, and learn'd his songs,
Of Gods and Heroes,
Of war and arts,

And peopled cities,
Inland, or built
By the grey sea.—If so, then hail!
I honour and welcome thee.

THE YOUTH. The Gods are happy.   130
They turn on all sides
Their shining eyes,
And see below them
The earth and men.

They see Tiresias
Sitting, staff in hand,
On the warm, grassy
Asopus bank,
His robe drawn over
His old, sightless head,   140
Revolving inly
The doom of Thebes.

They see the Centaurs *half man, half-horse, bestial*
In the upper glens
Of Pelion, in the streams,
Where red-berried ashes fringe
The clear-brown shallow pools,
With streaming flanks, and heads
Rear'd proudly, snuffing
The mountain wind.   150

They see the Indian
Drifting, knife in hand,

---

135 *Tiresias:* old, blind prophet who foresaw the defeat of Thebes; he is
imagined sitting by the river Asopus in Boeotia. He was stricken blind
through the wrath of Hera.
143 *Centaurs:* savage race living on Mt. Pelion in Thessaly, usually represented as half horse, half human.
151 *Indian:* the inhabitants of a Kashmir valley were thought to grow fruit
on a mat spread on the surface of a lake.

veil of blackness

*happy not
by action but by
drifting*

His frail boat moor'd to
A floating isle thick-matted
With large-leaved, low-creeping melon-plants,
And the dark cucumber.
He reaps, and stows them,
Drifting—drifting;—round him,
Round his green harvest-plot,
Flow the cool lake-waves,   160
The mountains ring them.

They see the Scythian   *man of destruction*
On the wide stepp, unharnessing
His wheel'd house at noon.
He tethers his beast down, and makes his meal—
Mares' milk, and bread
Baked on the embers;—all around
The boundless, waving grass-plains stretch,
    thick-starr'd
With saffron and the yellow hollyhock
And flag-leaved iris-flowers.   170
Sitting in his cart
He makes his meal; before him, for long miles,
Alive with bright green lizards,
And the springing bustard-fowl,
The track, a straight black line,
Furrows the rich soil; here and there
Clusters of lonely mounds
Topp'd with rough-hewn,
Grey, rain-blear'd statues, overpeer
The sunny waste.   180

They see the ferry
On the broad, clay-laden
Lone Chorasmian stream;—thereon,

---

162 *Scythian:* nomadic inhabitant of country northeast of Greece.
174 *bustard-fowl:* large game bird of Europe, Asia, and Africa, similar to a
plover.
183 *Chorasmian stream:* the river Oxus, the background of "Sohrab and
Rustum."

With snort and strain,
Two horses, strongly swimming, tow
The ferry-boat, with woven ropes
To either bow
Firm harness'd by the mane; a chief,
With shout and shaken spear,
Stands at the prow, and guides them; but astern   190
The cowering merchants, in long robes,
Sit pale beside their wealth
Of silk-bales and of balsam-drops,
Of gold and ivory,
Of turquoise-earth and amethyst,
Jasper and chalcedony,
And milk-barr'd onyx-stones.
The loaded boat swings groaning
In the yellow eddies;
The Gods behold them.   200
They see the Heroes
Sitting in the dark ship
On the foamless, long-heaving
Violet sea,
At sunset nearing
The Happy Islands.

These things, Ulysses,
The wise bards also
Behold and sing.
But oh, what labour!   210
O prince, what pain!

They too can see
Tiresias;—but the Gods,
Who give them vision,
Added this law:
That they should bear too   *poet & Centaur*
His groping blindness,
His dark foreboding,

---

206 *Happy Islands:* Greek paradise.

His scorn'd white hairs;
Bear Hera's anger   220
Through a life lengthen'd
To seven ages.

They see the Centaurs
On Pelion;—then they feel,
They too, the maddening wine
Swell their large veins to bursting; in wild pain
They feel the biting spears
Of the grim Laphithæ, and Theseus, drive,
Drive crashing through their bones; they feel
High on a jutting rock in the red stream   230
Alcmena's dreadful son
Ply his bow;—such a price
The Gods exact for song:
To become what we sing.

They see the Indian
On his mountain lake; but squalls
Make their skiff reel, and worms
In the unkind spring have gnawn
Their melon-harvest to the heart.—They see
The Scythian; but long frosts   240
Parch them in winter-time on the bare stepp,
Till they too fade like grass; they crawl
Like shadows forth in spring.

They see the merchants
On the Oxus stream;—but care
Must visit first them too, and make them pale.
Whether, through whirling sand,
A cloud of desert robber-horse have burst
Upon their caravan; or greedy kings,
In the wall'd cities the way passes through,   250

---

228 *Laphithæ:* warlike people who fought the Centaurs. Theseus, king of
Athens, and Hercules, son of Alcmena, aided the Lapithæ. The war repre-
sents the conflict of reason (the Greeks) with savagery.

Crush'd them with tolls; or fever-airs,
On some great river's marge,
Mown them down, far from home.

They see the Heroes
Near harbour;—but they share
Their lives, and former violent toil in Thebes,
Seven-gated Thebes, or Troy;
Or where the echoing oars
Of Argo first
Startled the unknown sea.   260

The old Silenus
Came, lolling in the sunshine,
From the dewy forest-coverts,
This way, at noon.
Sitting by me, while his Fauns
Down at the water-side
Sprinkled and smoothed
His drooping garland,
He told me these things.

But I, Ulysses,
Sitting on the warm steps,
Looking over the valley,
All day long, have seen,
Without pain, without labour,
Sometimes a wild-hair'd Mænad—
Sometimes a Faun with torches—
And sometimes, for a moment,
Passing through the dark stems
Flowing-robed, the beloved,
The desired, the divine,   280
Beloved Iacchus.

---

259 *Argo:* the ship of Jason, who sailed in quest of the golden fleece.
261 *Silenus:* foster father of Bacchus and eldest of the riotous satyrs.
275 *Mænad:* female participant in the orgiastic Bacchus worship.

Ah, cool night-wind, tremulous stars!
Ah, glimmering water,
Fitful earth-murmur,
Dreaming woods!
Ah, golden-hair'd, strangely smiling Goddess,
And thou, proved, much enduring,
Wave-toss'd Wanderer!
Who can stand still?
Ye fade, ye swim, ye waver before me—   290
The cup again!

Faster, faster,
O Circe, Goddess,
Let the wild, thronging train,
The bright procession
Of eddying forms,
Sweep through my soul!

[1849]

TO A FRIEND

Who prop, thou ask'st, in these bad days, my mind?
He much, the old man, who, clearest-soul'd of men,
Saw The Wide Prospect, and the Asian Fen,
And Tmolus' hill, and Smyrna's bay, though blind.
Much he, whose friendship I not long since won,
That halting slave, who in Nicopolis
Taught Arrian, when Vespasian's brutal son

Friend: Arthur Hugh Clough.
2 *old man:* Homer.
3 *Wide Prospect . . . Fen:* Arnold explained in a note that "Europe"
meant "The Wide Prospect," and "Asia" meant "the fen."
4 *Tmolus' hill . . . Smyrna's bay:* Tmolus is a mountain near Smyrna,
which claimed to be Homer's birthplace.
5 *he:* Epictetus, the Greek Stoic philosopher, had been a slave in Rome before going to the Grecian city of Nicopolis, where he became the mentor of
Flavius Arrian, a Greek historian. The Roman emperor Domitian drove from
Rome all the teachers of philosophy ("what most sham'd him").

Clear'd Rome of what most sham'd him. But be his *Sophocles*
My special thanks, whose even-balanc'd soul,
From first youth tested up to extreme old age,   10
Business could not make dull, nor Passion wild:
Who saw life steadily, and saw it whole: *tag line, for this must be detached.*
The mellow glory of the Attic stage;
Singer of sweet Colonus, and its child.

[1849]

SHAKESPEARE *also has distinct objectivity*

Others abide our question. Thou art free.
We ask and ask—Thou smilest and art still,
Out-topping knowledge. For the loftiest hill,
Who to the stars uncrowns his majesty,

Planting his steadfast footsteps in the sea,
Making the heaven of heavens his dwelling-place,
Spares but the cloudy border of his base
To the foil'd searching of mortality;

And thou, who didst the stars and sunbeams know,
Self-school'd, self-scann'd, self-honour'd, self-secure, *detached*
Didst tread on earth unguess'd at.—Better so!   16

All pains the immortal spirit must endure,
All weakness which impairs, all griefs which bow,
Find their sole speech in that victorious brow.

[1849]

---

8 *his:* referring to Sophocles, born at Colonus, one of whose great plays was
Oedipus at Colonus.

THE FORSAKEN MERMAN

Come, dear children, let us away;
Down and away below!
Now my brothers call from the bay,
Now the great winds shoreward blow,
Now the salt tides seaward flow;
Now the wild white horses play,
Champ and chafe and toss in the spray.
Children dear, let us away!
This way, this way!

Call her once before you go—   10
Call once yet!
In a voice that she will know:
"Margaret! Margaret!"
Children's voices should be dear
(Call once more) to a mother's ear;
Children's voices, wild with pain—
Surely she will come again!
Call her once and come away;
This way, this way!
"Mother dear, we cannot stay!   20
The wild white horses foam and fret."
Margaret! Margaret!

Come, dear children, come away down;
Call no more!
One last look at the white-wall'd town,
And the little grey church on the windy shore,
Then come down!
She will not come though you call all day;
Come away, come away!

Children dear, was it yesterday   30
We heard the sweet bells over the bay?
In the caverns where we lay,

---

⁶ *white horses:* waves.

Through the surf and through the swell,
The far-off sound of a silver bell?
Sand-strewn caverns, cool and deep,
Where the winds are all asleep;
Where the spent lights quiver and gleam,
Where the salt weed sways in the stream,
Where the sea-beasts, ranged all round,
Feed in the ooze of their pasture-ground;   40
Where the sea-snakes coil and twine,
Dry their mail and bask in the brine;
Where great whales come sailing by,
Sail and sail, with unshut eye,
Round the world for ever and aye?
When did music come this way?
Children dear, was it yesterday?

Children dear, was it yesterday
(Call yet once) that she went away?
Once she sate with you and me,   50
On a red gold throne in the heart of the sea,
And the youngest sate on her knee.
She comb'd its bright hair, and she tended it well,
When down swung the sound of a far-off bell.
She sigh'd, she look'd up through the clear green sea;
She said: "I must go, for my kinsfolk pray
In the little grey church on the shore to-day.
'Twill be Easter-time in the world—ah me!
And I lose my poor soul, Merman! here with thee."
I said: "Go up, dear heart, through the waves;   60
Say thy prayer, and come back to the kind sea-caves!"
She smiled, she went up through the surf in the bay.
Children dear, was it yesterday?

    Children dear, were we long alone?
"The sea grows stormy, the little ones moan;
Long prayers," I said, "in the world they say;
Come!" I said; and we rose through the surf in the bay.
We went up the beach, by the sandy down
Where the sea-stocks bloom, to the white-wall'd town;
Through the narrow paved streets, where all was still, 70
To the little grey church on the windy hill.

From the church came a murmur of folk at their prayers,
But we stood without in the cold blowing airs.
We climb'd on the graves, on the stones worn with rains,
And we gazed up the aisle through the small leaded panes.
She sate by the pillar; we saw her clear:
"Margaret, hist! come quick, we are here!
Dear heart," I said, "we are long alone;
The sea grows stormy, the little ones moan."
But, ah, she gave me never a look,   80
For her eyes were seal'd to the holy book!
Loud prays the priest; shut stands the door.
Come away, children, call no more!
Come away, come down, call no more!

    Down, down, down!
Down to the depths of the sea!
She sits at her wheel in the humming town,
Singing most joyfully.
Hark what she sings: "O joy, O joy,
For the humming street, and the child with its toy!   90
For the priest, and the bell, and the holy well;
For the wheel where I spun,
And the blessed light of the sun!"
And so she sings her fill,
Singing most joyfully,
Till the spindle drops from her hand,
And the whizzing wheel stands still.
She steals to the window, and looks at the sand,
And over the sand at the sea;
And her eyes are set in a stare;   100
And anon there breaks a sigh,
And anon there drops a tear,
From a sorrow-clouded eye,
And a heart sorrow-laden,
A long, long sigh;
For the cold strange eyes of a little Mermaiden
And the gleam of her golden hair.

    Come away, away children;
Come children, come down!
The hoarse wind blows coldly;   110

Lights shine in the town.
She will start from her slumber
When gusts shake the door;
She will hear the winds howling,
Will hear the waves roar.
We shall see, while above us
The waves roar and whirl,
A ceiling of amber,
A pavement of pearl.
Singing: "Here came a mortal,   120
But faithless was she!
And alone dwell for ever
The kings of the sea."

But, children, at midnight,
When soft the winds blow,
When clear falls the moonlight,
When spring-tides are low;
When sweet airs come seaward
From heaths starr'd with broom,
And high rocks throw mildly   130
On the blanch'd sands a gloom;
Up the still, glistening beaches,
Up the creeks we will hie,
Over banks of bright seaweed
The ebb-tide leaves dry.
We will gaze, from the sand-hills,
At the white, sleeping town;
At the church on the hill-side—
And then come back down.
Singing: "There dwells a loved one,   140
But cruel is she!
She left lonely for ever
The kings of the sea."

[1849]

RESIGNATION

To Fausta

To die be given us, or attain!
Fierce work it were, to do again.
So pilgrims, bound for Mecca, pray'd
At burning noon; so warriors said,
Scarf'd with the cross, who watch'd the miles
Of dust which wreathed their struggling files
Down Lydian mountains; so, when snows
Round Alpine summits, eddying rose,
The Goth, bound Rome-wards; so the Hun,
Crouch'd on his saddle, while the sun   10
Went lurid down o'er flooded plains
Through which the groaning Danube strains
To the drear Euxine;—so pray all,
Whom labours, self-ordain'd, enthrall;
Because they to themselves propose
On this side the all-common close
A goal which, gain'd, may give repose.
So pray they; and to stand again
Where they stood once, to them were pain;
Pain to thread back and to renew   20
Past straits, and currents long steer'd through.

his father / But milder natures, and more free—
Whom an unblamed serenity
Hath freed from passions, and the state
Of struggle these necessitate;
Whom schooling of the stubborn mind
Hath made, or birth hath found, resign'd—
These mourn not, that their goings pay
Obedience to the passing day.
These claim not every laughing Hour   30

Fausta: Arnold's sister Jane.
5 *Scarf'd with the cross:* wearing scarves on which were woven crosses: worn
by the Crusaders.
7 *Lydian:* of Lydia, in Asia Minor.
13 *Euxine:* the Black Sea.

For handmaid to their striding power;
Each in her turn, with torch uprear'd,
To await their march; and when appear'd,
Through the cold gloom, with measured race,
To usher for a destined space
(Her own sweet errands all forgone)
The too imperious traveller on.
These, Fausta, ask not this; nor thou,
Time's chafing prisoner, ask it now!

We left, just ten years since, you say,   40
That wayside inn we left to-day.
Our jovial host, as forth we fare,
Shouts greeting from his easy chair.
High on a bank our leader stands, *the father*
Reviews and ranks his motley bands,
Makes clear our goal to every eye—
The valley's western boundary.
A gate swings to! our tide hath flow'd
Already from the silent road.
The valley-pastures, one by one,   50
Are threaded, quiet in the sun;
And now beyond the rude stone bridge
Slopes gracious up the western ridge.
Its woody border, and the last
Of its dark upland farms is past—
Cool farms, with open-lying stores,
Under their burnish'd sycamores;
All past! and through the trees we glide,
Emerging on the green hill-side.
There climbing hangs, a far-seen sign,   60
Our wavering, many-colour'd line;
There winds, upstreaming slowly still
Over the summit of the hill.
And now, in front, behold outspread
Those upper regions we must tread!
Mild hollows, and clear heathy swells,
The cheerful silence of the fells.
Some two hours' march with serious air,
Through the deep noontide heats we fare;
The red-grouse, springing at our sound,   70

Skims, now and then, the shining ground;
No life, save his and ours, intrudes
Upon these breathless solitudes.
O joy! again the farms appear.
Cool shade is there, and rustic cheer;
There springs the brook will guide us down,
Bright comrade, to the noisy town.
Lingering, we follow down; we gain
The town, the highway, and the plain.
And many a mile of dusty way,   80
Parch'd and road-worn, we made that day;
But, Fausta, I remember well,
That as the balmy darkness fell
We bathed our hands with speechless glee
That night, in the wide-glimmering sea.

Once more we tread this self-same road,
Fausta, which ten years since we trod;
Alone we tread it, you and I,
Ghosts of that boisterous company.
Here, where the brook shines, near its head,   90
In its clear, shallow, turf-fringed bed;
Here, whence the eye first sees, far down,
Capp'd with faint smoke, the noisy town;
Here sit we, and again unroll,
Though slowly, the familiar whole.
The solemn wastes of heathy hill
Sleep in the July sunshine still;
The self-same shadows now, as then,
Play through this grassy upland glen;
The loose dark stones on the green way   100
Lie strewn, it seems, where then they lay;
On this mild bank above the stream,
(You crush them!) the blue gentians gleam.
Still this wild brook, the rushes cool,
The sailing foam, the shining pool!
These are not changed; and we, you say,
Are scarce more changed, in truth, than they.

The gipsies, whom we met below,
They, too, have long roam'd to and fro;

They ramble, leaving, where they pass,   110
Their fragments on the cumber'd grass.
And often to some kindly place
Chance guides the migratory race,
Where, though long wanderings intervene,
They recognise a former scene.
The dingy tents are pitch'd; the fires
Give to the wind their wavering spires;
In dark knots crouch round the wild flame
Their children, as when first they came;
They see their shackled beasts again   120
Move, browsing, up the gray-wall'd lane.
Signs are not wanting, which might raise
The ghost in them of former days—
Signs are not wanting, if they would;
Suggestions to disquietude.
For them, for all, time's busy touch,
While it mends little, troubles much.
Their joints grow stiffer—but the year
Runs his old round of dubious cheer;
Chilly they grow—yet winds in March,   130
Still, sharp as ever, freeze and parch;
They must live still—and yet, God knows,
Crowded and keen the country grows;
It seems as if, in their decay,
The law grew stronger every day.
So might they reason, so compare,
Fausta, times past with times that are.
But no!—they rubb'd through yesterday
In their hereditary way,
And they will rub through, if they can,   140
To-morrow on the self-same plan,
Till death arrive to supersede,
For them, vicissitude and need.

The poet, to whose mighty heart
Heaven doth a quicker pulse impart,
Subdues that energy to scan
Not his own course, but that of man.

---

135 *the law:* against trespassing.

Though he move mountains, though his day
Be pass'd on the proud heights of sway,
Though he hath loosed a thousand chains,   150
Though he hath borne immortal pains,
Action and suffering though he know—
He hath not lived, if he lives so.
He sees, in some great-historied land,
A ruler of the people stand,
Sees his strong thought in fiery flood
Roll through the heaving multitude;
Exults—yet for no moment's space
Envies the all-regarded place.
Beautiful eyes meet his—and he   160
Bears to admire uncravingly;
They pass—he, mingled with the crowd,
Is in their far-off triumphs proud.
From some high station he looks down,
At sunset, on a populous town;
Surveys each happy group, which fleets,
Toil ended, through the shining streets,
Each with some errand of its own—
And does not say: *I am alone.*
He sees the gentle stir of birth   170
When morning purifies the earth;
He leans upon a gate and sees
The pastures, and the quiet trees.
Low, woody hill, with gracious bound,
Folds the still valley almost round;
The cuckoo, loud on some high lawn,
Is answer'd from the depth of dawn;
In the hedge straggling to the stream,
Pale, dew-drench'd, half-shut roses gleam;
But, where the farther side slopes down,   180
He sees the drowsy new-waked clown
In his white quaint-embroider'd frock
Make, whistling, tow'rd his mist-wreathed flock—
Slowly, behind his heavy tread,
The wet, flower'd grass heaves up its head.
Lean'd on his gate, he gazes—tears
Are in his eyes, and in his ears
The murmur of a thousand years.

Before him he sees life unroll,
A placid and continuous whole—   190
That general life, which does not cease,
Whose secret is not joy, but peace;
That life, whose dumb wish is not miss'd
If birth proceeds, if things subsist;
The life of plants, and stones, and rain,
The life he craves—if not in vain
Fate gave, what chance shall not control,
His sad lucidity of soul.

You listen—but that wandering smile,
Fausta, betrays you cold the while!   200
Your eyes pursue the bells of foam
Wash'd, eddying, from this bank, their home.
Those gipsies, so your thoughts I scan,
Are less, the poet more, than man.
They feel not, though they move and see;
Deeper the poet feels; but he
Breathes, when he will, immortal air,
Where Orpheus and where Homer are.
In the day's life, whose iron round
Hems us all in, he is not bound;   210
He leaves his kind, o'erleaps their pen,
And flees the common life of men.
He escapes thence, but we abide—
Not deep the poet sees, but wide.

The world in which we live and move
Outlasts aversion, outlasts love,
Outlasts each effort, interest, hope,
Remorse, grief, joy;—and were the scope
Of these affections wider made,
Man still would see, and see dismay'd,   220
Beyond his passion's widest range,
Far regions of eternal change.
Nay, and since death, which wipes out man,
Finds him with many an unsolved plan,
With much unknown, and much untried,
Wonder not dead, and thirst not dried,
Still gazing on the ever full

Eternal mundane spectacle—
This world in which we draw our breath,
In some sense, Fausta, outlasts death.   230

Blame thou not, therefore, him who dares
Judge vain beforehand human cares;
Whose natural insight can discern
What through experience others learn;
Who needs not love and power, to know
Love transient, power an unreal show;
Who treads at ease life's uncheer'd ways—
Him blame not, Fausta, rather praise!
Rather thyself for some aim pray
Nobler than this, to fill the day;   240
Rather that heart, which burns in thee,
Ask, not to amuse, but to set free;
Be passionate hopes not ill resign'd
For quiet, and a fearless mind.
And though fate grudge to thee and me
The poet's rapt security,
Yet they, believe me, who await
No gifts from chance, have conquer'd fate.
They, winning room to see and hear,
And to men's business not too near,   250
Through clouds of individual strife
Draw homeward to the general life.
Like leaves by suns not yet uncurl'd;
To the wise, foolish; to the world,
Weak;—yet not weak, I might reply,
Not foolish, Fausta, in His eye,
To whom each moment in its race,
Crowd as we will its neutral space,
Is but a quiet watershed
Whence, equally, the seas of life and death are fed.   260

Enough, we live!—and if a life,
With large results so little rife,
Though bearable, seem hardly worth
This pomp of worlds, this pain of birth;
Yet, Fausta, the mute turf we tread,
The solemn hills around us spread,

This stream which falls incessantly,
The strange-scrawl'd rocks, the lonely sky,
If I might lend their life a voice,
Seem to bear rather than rejoice.   270
And even could the intemperate prayer
Man iterates, while these forbear,
For movement, for an ampler sphere,
Pierce Fate's impenetrable ear;
Not milder is the general lot
Because our spirits have forgot,
In action's dizzying eddy whirl'd,
The something that infects the world.

for serenity must remain aside from world.

[1849]

SWITZERLAND

1. MEETING

Again I see my bliss at hand,
The town, the lake are here;
My Marguerite smiles upon the strand,
Unalter'd with the year.

I know that graceful figure fair,
That cheek of languid hue;
I know that soft, enkerchief'd hair,
And those sweet eyes of blue.

Again I spring to make my choice;
Again in tones of ire   10
I hear a God's tremendous voice:
"Be counsell'd, and retire."

Ye guiding Powers who join and part,
What would ye have with me?

Switzerland: The poems in this group presumably all refer to Arnold's love
for "Marguerite."

Ah, warn some more ambitious heart,
And let the peaceful be!

[1852]

2. PARTING

Ye storm-winds of Autumn!
Who rush by, who shake
The window, and ruffle
The gleam-lighted lake;
Who cross to the hill-side
Thin-sprinkled with farms,
Where the high woods strip sadly
Their yellowing arms—
Ye are bound for the mountains!
Ah! with you let me go   10
Where your cold, distant barrier,
The vast range of snow,
Through the loose clouds lifts dimly
Its white peaks in air—
How deep is their stillness!
Ah, would I were there!

But on the stairs what voice is this I hear,
Buoyant as morning, and as morning clear?
Say, has some wet bird-haunted English lawn
Lent it the music of its trees at dawn?   20
Or was it from some sun-fleck'd mountain-brook
That the sweet voice its upland clearness took?
            Ah! it comes nearer—
            Sweet notes, this way!

Hark! fast by the window
The rushing winds go,
To the ice-cumber'd gorges,
The vast seas of snow!
There the torrents drive upward
Their rock-strangled hum;   30
There the avalanche thunders
The hoarse torrent dumb.
—I come, O ye mountains!
Ye torrents, I come!

But who is this, by the half-open'd door,
Whose figure casts a shadow on the floor?
The sweet blue eyes—the soft, ash-colour'd hair—
The cheeks that still their gentle paleness wear—
The lovely lips, with their arch smile that tells
The unconquer'd joy in which her spirit dwells—   40
     Ah! they bend nearer—
     Sweet lips, this way!

     Hark! the wind rushes past us!
     Ah! with that let me go
     To the clear, waning hill-side,
     Unspotted by snow,
     There to watch, o'er the sunk vale,
     The frore mountain-wall,
     Where the niched snow-bed sprays down
     Its powdery fall.   50
     There its dusky blue clusters
     The aconite spreads;
     There the pines slope, the cloud-strips
     Hung soft in their heads.
     No life but, at moments,
     The mountain-bee's hum.
     —I come, O ye mountains!
     Ye pine-woods, I come!

Forgive me! forgive me!
    Ah, Marguerite, fain   60
Would these arms reach to clasp thee!
    But see! 'tis in vain.

In the void air, towards thee,
    My stretch'd arms are cast;
But a sea rolls between us—
    Our different past!

To the lips, ah! of others
    Those lips have been prest,

---

48 *frore:* frozen.

And others, ere I was,
　　Were strain'd to that breast;   70

Far, far from each other
　　Our spirits have grown;
And what heart knows another?
　　Ah! who knows his own?

Blow, ye winds! lift me with you!
　　I come to the wild.
Fold closely, O Nature!
　　Thine arms round thy child.

To thee only God granted
　　A heart ever new—   80
To all always open,
　　To all always true.

Ah! calm me, restore me;
　　And dry up my tears
On thy high mountain-platforms,
　　Where morn first appears;

Where the white mists, for ever,
　　Are spread and upfurl'd—
In the stir of the forces
　　Whence issued the world.   90

[1852]

3. A FAREWELL

My horse's feet beside the lake,
Where sweet the unbroken moonbeams lay,
Sent echoes through the night to wake
Each glistening strand, each heath-fringed bay.

The poplar avenue was pass'd,
And the roof'd bridge that spans the stream;
Up the steep street I hurried fast,
Led by thy taper's starlike beam.

I came! I saw thee rise!—the blood
Pour'd flushing to thy languid cheek.   10
Lock'd in each other's arms we stood,
In tears, with hearts too full to speak.

Days flew;—ah, soon I could discern
A trouble in thine alter'd air!
Thy hand lay languidly in mine,
Thy cheek was grave, thy speech grew rare.

I blame thee not!—this heart, I know,
To be long loved was never framed;
For something in its depths doth glow
Too strange, too restless, too untamed.   20

And women—things that live and move
Mined by the fever of the soul—
They seek to find in those they love
Stern strength, and promise of control.

They ask not kindness, gentle ways—
These they themselves have tried and known;
They ask a soul which never sways
With the blind gusts that shake their own.

I too have felt the load I bore
In a too strong emotion's sway;   30
I too have wish'd, no woman more,
This starting, feverish heart away.

I too have long'd for trenchant force,
And will like a dividing spear;
Have praised the keen, unscrupulous course,
Which knows no doubt, which feels no fear.

But in the world I learnt, what there
Thou too wilt surely one day prove,
That will, that energy, though rare,
Are yet far, far less rare than love.   40

Go, then!—till time and fate impress
This truth on thee, be mine no more!

They will!—for thou, I feel, not less
Than I, wast destined to this lore.

We school our manners, act our parts—
But He, who sees us through and through,
Knows that the bent of both our hearts
Was to be gentle, tranquil, true.

And though we wear out life, alas!
Distracted as a homeless wind,   50
In beating where we must not pass,
In seeking what we shall not find;

Yet we shall one day gain, life past,
Clear prospect o'er our being's whole;
Shall see ourselves, and learn at last
Our true affinities of soul.

We shall not then deny a course
To every thought the mass ignore;
We shall not then call hardness force,
Nor lightness wisdom any more.   60

Then, in the eternal Father's smile,
Our soothed, encouraged souls will dare
To seem as free from pride and guile,
As good, as generous, as they are.

Then we shall know our friends!—though much
Will have been lost—the help in strife,
The thousand sweet, still joys of such
As hand in hand face earthly life—

Though these be lost, there will be yet
A sympathy august and pure;   70
Ennobled by a vast regret,
And by contrition seal'd thrice sure.

And we, whose ways were unlike here,
May then more neighbouring courses ply;

May to each other be brought near,
And greet across infinity.

How sweet, unreach'd by earthly jars,
My sister! to maintain with thee
The hush among the shining stars,
The calm upon the moonlit sea!   80

How sweet to feel, on the boon air,
All our unquiet pulses cease!
To feel that nothing can impair
The gentleness, the thirst for peace—

The gentleness too rudely hurl'd
On this wild earth of hate and fear;
The thirst for peace a raving world
Would never let us satiate here.

[1852]

4. ISOLATION. TO MARGUERITE

We were apart; yet, day by day,
I bade my heart more constant be.
I bade it keep the world away,
And grow a home for only thee;
Nor fear'd but thy love likewise grew,
Like mine, each day, more tried, more true.

The fault was grave! I might have known,
What far too soon, alas! I learn'd—
The heart can bind itself alone,
And faith may oft be unreturn'd.   10
Self-sway'd our feelings ebb and swell—
Thou lov'st no more;—Farewell! Farewell!

Farewell!—and thou, thou lonely heart,
Which never yet without remorse
Even for a moment didst depart
From thy remote and spheréd course
To haunt the place where passions reign—
Back to thy solitude again!

Back! with the conscious thrill of shame
Which Luna felt, that summer-night,   20
Flash through her pure immortal frame,
When she forsook the starry height
To hang over Endymion's sleep
Upon the pine-grown Latmian steep.

Yet she, chaste queen, had never proved
How vain a thing is mortal love,
Wandering in Heaven, far removed.
But thou hast long had place to prove
This truth—to prove, and make thine own:
"Thou hast been, shalt be, art, alone."   30

Or, if not quite alone, yet they
Which touch thee are unmating things—
Ocean and clouds and night and day;
Lorn autumns and triumphant springs;
And life, and others' joy and pain,
And love, if love, of happier men.

Of happier men—for they, at least,
Have *dream'd* two human hearts might blend
In one, and were through faith released
From isolation without end   40
Prolong'd; nor knew, although not less
Alone than thou, their loneliness.

[1857]

5. TO MARGUERITE—*Continued*

Yes! in the sea of life enisled,
With echoing straits between us thrown,
Dotting the shoreless watery wild,
We mortal millions live *alone*.
The islands feel the enclasping flow,
And then their endless bounds they know.

---

20 *Luna:* Diana, goddess of the moon, fell in love with Endymion, a shepherd, whom she found asleep on Mt. Latmos.
6 *endless:* eternal.

But when the moon their hollows lights,
And they are swept by balms of spring,
And in their glens, on starry nights,
The nightingales divinely sing;   10
And lovely notes, from shore to shore,
Across the sounds and channels pour—

Oh! then a longing like despair
Is to their farthest caverns sent;
For surely once, they feel, we were
Parts of a single continent!
Now round us spreads the watery plain—
Oh might our marges meet again!

Who order'd, that their longing's fire
Should be, as soon as kindled, cool'd?   20
Who renders vain their deep desire?—
A God, a God their severance ruled!
And bade betwixt their shores to be
The unplumb'd, salt, estranging sea.

[1852]

6. ABSENCE

In this fair stranger's eyes of grey
Thine eyes, my love! I see.
I shiver; for the passing day
Had borne me far from thee.

This is the curse of life! that not
A nobler, calmer train
Of wiser thoughts and feelings blot
Our passions from our brain;

But each day brings its petty dust
Our soon-choked souls to fill,   10
And we forget because we must
And not because we will.

I struggle towards the light; and ye,
Once-long'd-for storms of love!

[1852]

If with the light ye cannot be,
I bear that ye remove.

I struggle towards the light—but oh,
While yet the night is chill,
Upon time's barren, stormy flow,
Stay with me, Marguerite, still!   20

7. THE TERRACE AT BERNE
(composed ten years after the preceding)

Ten years!—and to my waking eye
Once more the roofs of Berne appear;
The rocky banks, the terrace high,
The stream!—and do I linger here?

The clouds are on the Oberland,
The Jungfrau snows look faint and far;
But bright are those green fields at hand,
And through those fields comes down the Aar,

And from the blue twin-lakes it comes,
Flows by the town, the churchyard fair;   10
And 'neath the garden-walk it hums,
The house!—and is my Marguerite there?

Ah, shall I see thee, while a flush
Of startled pleasure floods thy brow,
Quick through the oleanders brush,
And clap thy hands, and cry: *'Tis thou!*

Or hast thou long since wander'd back,
Daughter of France! to France, thy home;
And flitted down the flowery track
Where feet like thine too lightly come?   20

Doth riotous laughter now replace
Thy smile; and rouge, with stony glare,

---

5 *Oberland:* region in the Alps where the chief mountain is the Jungfrau. A short distance from Berne, on the river Aar, is Thun, where Arnold met Marguerite.

Thy cheek's soft hue; and fluttering lace
The kerchief that enwound thy hair?

Or is it over?—art thou dead?—
Dead!—and no warning shiver ran
Across my heart, to say thy thread
Of life was cut, and closed thy span!

Could from earth's ways that figure slight
Be lost, and I not feel 'twas so?   30
Of that fresh voice the gay delight
Fail from earth's air, and I not know?

Or shall I find thee still, but changed,
But not the Marguerite of thy prime?
With all thy being re-arranged,
Pass'd through the crucible of time;

With spirit vanish'd, beauty waned,
And hardly yet a glance, a tone,
A gesture—anything—retain'd
Of all that was my Marguerite's own?   40

I will not know! For wherefore try,
To things by mortal course that live,
A shadowy durability,
For which they were not meant, to give?

Like driftwood spars, which meet and pass
Upon the boundless ocean-plain,
So on the sea of life, alas!
Man meets man—meets, and quits again.

I knew it when my life was young;
I feel it still, now youth is o'er.   50
—The mists are on the mountain hung,
And Marguerite I shall see no more.

[1867]

FADED LEAVES

1. THE RIVER

Still glides the stream, slow drops the boat
Under the rustling poplars' shade;
Silent the swans beside us float—
None speaks, none heeds; ah, turn thy head!

Let those arch eyes now softly shine,
That mocking mouth grow sweetly bland;
Ah, let them rest, those eyes, on mine!
On mine let rest that lovely hand!

My pent-up tears oppress my brain,
My heart is swoln with love unsaid.   10
Ah, let me weep, and tell my pain,
And on thy shoulder rest my head!

Before I die—before the soul,
Which now is mine, must re-attain
Immunity from my control,
And wander round the world again;

Before this teased o'erlabour'd heart
For ever leaves its vain employ,
Dead to its deep habitual smart,
And dead to hopes of future joy.   20

[1852]

2. TOO LATE

Each on his own strict line we move,
And some find death ere they find love;
So far apart their lives are thrown
From the twin soul which halves their own.

Faded Leaves: This group of poems presumably concerns the future Mrs.
Arnold, not "Marguerite," although there is no general agreement of critics
on this point.

And sometimes, by still harder fate,
The lovers meet, but meet too late.
—Thy heart is mine!—*True, true! ah, true!*
—Then, love, thy hand!—*Ah no! adieu!*

[1852]

3. SEPARATION

Stop!—not to me, at this bitter departing,
    Speak of the sure consolations of time!
Fresh be the wound, still-renew'd be its smarting,
    So but thy image endure in its prime.

But, if the stedfast commandment of Nature
    Wills that remembrance should always decay—
If the loved form and the deep-cherish'd feature
    Must, when unseen, from the soul fade away—

Me let no half-effaced memories cumber!
    Fled, fled at once, be all vestige of thee!   10
Deep be the darkness and still be the slumber—
    Dead be the past and its phantoms to me!

Then, when we meet, and thy look strays toward me,
    Scanning my face and the changes wrought there:
Who, let me say, *is this stranger regards me,*
    With the grey eyes, and the lovely brown hair?

[1855]

4. ON THE RHINE

Vain is the effort to forget.
Some day I shall be cold, I know,
As is the eternal moonlit snow
Of the high Alps, to which I go—
But ah, not yet, not yet!

Vain is the agony of grief.
'Tis true, indeed, an iron knot
Ties straitly up from mine thy lot,
And were it snapt—thou lov'st me not!
But is despair relief?   10

Awhile let me with thought have done.
And as this brimm'd unwrinkled Rhine,
And that far purple mountain-line,
Lie sweetly in the look divine
Of the slow-sinking sun;

So let me lie, and, calm as they,
Let beam upon my inward view
Those eyes of deep, soft, lucent hue—
Eyes too expressive to be blue,
Too lovely to be grey.   20

Ah, Quiet, all things feel thy balm!
Those blue hills too, this river's flow,
Were restless once, but long ago.
Tamed is their turbulent youthful glow;
Their joy is in their calm.

                                        [1852]

5. LONGING

Come to me in my dreams, and then
By day I shall be well again!
For then the night will more than pay
The hopeless longing of the day.

Come, as thou cam'st a thousand times,
A messenger from radiant climes,
And smile on thy new world, and be
As kind to others as to me!

Or, as thou never cam'st in sooth,
Come now, and let me dream it truth;   10
And part my hair, and kiss my brow,
And say: *My love! why sufferest thou?*

Come to me in my dreams, and then
By day I shall be well again!
For then the night will more than pay
The hopeless longing of the day.

                                        [1852]

URANIA

I too have suffer'd; yet I know
She is not cold, though she seems so.
She is not cold, she is not light;
But our ignoble souls lack might.

She smiles and smiles, and will not sigh,
While we for hopeless passion die;
Yet she could love, those eyes declare,
Were but men nobler than they are.

Eagerly once her gracious ken
Was turn'd upon the sons of men;   10
But light the serious visage grew—
She look'd, and smiled, and saw them through.

Our petty souls, our strutting wits,
Our labour'd, puny passion-fits—
Ah, may she scorn them still, till we
Scorn them as bitterly as she!

Yet show her once, ye heavenly Powers,
One of some worthier race than ours!
One for whose sake she once might prove
How deeply she who scorns can love.   20

His eyes be like the starry lights—
His voice like sounds of summer nights—
In all his lovely mien let pierce
The magic of the universe!

And she to him will reach her hand,
And gazing in his eyes will stand,
And know her friend, and weep for glee,
And cry: *Long, long I've look'd for thee.*

Urania: the muse of astronomy and, for such poets as Milton, also of poetry.
The Uranian Aphrodite was the goddess of ideal love. Arnold probably in-
tended all three associations. The poem appears to be connected with the
"Switzerland" lyrics.

Then will she weep; with smiles, till then,
Coldly she mocks the sons of men.   30
Till then, her lovely eyes maintain
Their pure, unwavering, deep disdain.

[1852]

EUPHROSYNE

I must not say that thou wast true,
Yet let me say that thou wast fair;
And they, that lovely face who view,
Why should they ask if truth be there?

Truth—what is truth? Two bleeding hearts,
Wounded by men, by fortune tried,
Outwearied with their lonely parts,
Vow to beat henceforth side by side.

The world to them was stern and drear
Their lot was but to weep and moan.   10
Ah, let them keep their faith sincere,
For neither could subsist alone!

But souls whom some benignant breath
Hath charm'd at birth from gloom and care,
These ask no love, these plight no faith,
For they are happy as they are.

The world to them may homage make,
And garlands for their forehead weave;
And what the world can give, they take—
But they bring more than they receive.   20

They shine upon the world! Their ears
To one demand alone are coy;

Euphrosyne: one of the three Graces, daughters of Zeus and givers of
beauty.

They will not give us love and tears,
They bring us light and warmth and joy.

It was not love which heaved thy breast,
Fair child!—it was the bliss within.
Adieu! and say that one, at least,
Was just to what he did not win.

[1852]

DESTINY

Why each is striving, from of old,
To love more deeply than he can?
Still would be true, yet still grows cold?
—Ask of the Powers that sport with man!

They yok'd in him, for endless strife,
A heart of ice, a soul of fire;
And hurl'd him on the Field of Life,
An aimless unallay'd Desire.

[1852]

HUMAN LIFE

What mortal, when he saw,
Life's voyage done, his heavenly Friend,
Could ever yet dare tell him fearlessly:
"I have kept uninfringed my nature's law;
The inly-written chart thou gavest me,
To guide me, I have steer'd by to the end?"

Ah! let us make no claim,
On life's incognisable sea,
To too exact a steering of our way;

Let us not fret and fear to miss our aim, 10
If some fair coast have lured us to make stay,
Or some friend hail'd us to keep company.

Ay! we would each fain drive
At random, and not steer by rule.
Weakness! and worse, weakness bestow'd in vain!
Winds from our side the unsuiting consort rive,
We rush by coasts where we had lief remain;
Man cannot, though he would, live chance's fool.

No! as the foaming swath
Of torn-up water, on the main, 20
Falls heavily away with long-drawn roar
On either side the black deep-furrow'd path
Cut by an onward-labouring vessel's prore,
And never touches the ship-side again;

Even so we leave behind,
As, charter'd by some unknown Powers,
We stem across the sea of life by night,
The joys which were not for our use design'd;—
The friends to whom we had no natural right,
The homes that were not destined to be ours. 30

[1852]

23 *prore:* prow.

TRISTRAM AND ISEULT

I

TRISTRAM

Tristram

Is she not come? The messenger was sure.
Prop me upon the pillows once again—
Raise me, my page! this cannot long endure.
—Christ, what a night! how the sleet whips the pane!
What lights will those out to the northward be?

The Page

The lanterns of the fishing-boats at sea.

Tristram

Soft—who is that, stands by the dying fire?

Tristram and Iseult: Since the Tristram legend was not generally known when he wrote, Arnold prefaced the poem with this quotation from Dunlop's *History of Fiction:*

> In the court of his uncle King Marc, the king of Cornwall, who at this time resided at the castle of Tyntagel, Tristram became expert in all knightly exercises. —The king of Ireland, at Tristram's solicitations, promised to bestow his daughter Iseult in marriage on King Marc. The mother of Iseult gave to her daughter's confidante a philtre, or love-potion, to be administered on the night of her nuptials. Of this beverage Tristram and Iseult, on their voyage to Cornwall, unfortunately partook. Its influence, during the remainder of their lives, regulated the affections and destiny of the lovers.—
>
> After the arrival of Tristram and Iseult in Cornwall, and the nuptials of the latter with King Marc, a great part of the romance is occupied with their contrivances to procure secret interviews. —Tristram, being forced to leave Cornwall, on account of the displeasure of his uncle, repaired to Brittany, where lived Iseult with the White Hands.—He married her—more out of gratitude than love.—Afterwards he proceeded to the dominions of Arthur, which became the theatre of unnumbered exploits.
>
> Tristram, subsequent to these events, returned to Brittany, and to his long-neglected wife. There, being wounded and sick, he was soon reduced to the lowest ebb. In this situation, he despatched a confidant to the queen of Cornwall, to try if he could induce her to follow him to Brittany, etc.

The Page

Iseult.

Tristram

Ah! not the Iseult I desire.

. . . . .

What Knight is this so weak and pale,
Though the locks are yet brown on his noble head,   10
Propt on pillows in his bed,
Gazing seaward for the light
Of some ship that fights the gale
On this wild December night?
Over the sick man's feet is spread
A dark green forest-dress;
A gold harp leans against the bed,
Ruddy in the fire's light.
I know him by his harp of gold,
Famous in Arthur's court of old;   20
I know him by his forest-dress—
The peerless hunter, harper, knight,
Tristram of Lyoness.

What Lady is this, whose silk attire
Gleams so rich in the light of the fire?
The ringlets on her shoulders lying
In their flitting lustre vying
With the clasp of burnish'd gold
Which her heavy robe doth hold,
Her looks are mild, her fingers slight   30
As the driven snow are white;
But her cheeks are sunk and pale.
Is it that the bleak sea-gale
Beating from the Atlantic sea
On this coast of Brittany,
Nips too keenly the sweet flower?
Is it that a deep fatigue
Hath come on her, a chilly fear,
Passing all her youthful hour
Spinning with her maidens here,   40
Listlessly through the window-bars

Gazing seawards many a league,
From her lonely shore-built tower,
While the knights are at the wars?
Or, perhaps, has her young heart
Felt already some deeper smart,
Of those that in secret the heart-strings rive,
Leaving her sunk and pale, though fair?
Who is this snowdrop by the sea?—
I know her by her mildness rare,   50
Her snow-white hands, her golden hair;
I know her by her rich silk dress,
And her fragile loveliness—
The sweetest Christian soul alive,
Iseult of Brittany.

Iseult of Brittany?—but where
Is that other Iseult fair,
That proud, first Iseult, Cornwall's queen?
She, whom Tristram's ship of yore
From Ireland to Cornwall bore,   60
To Tyntagel, to the side
Of King Marc, to be his bride?
She who, as they voyaged, quaff'd
With Tristram that spiced magic draught,
Which since then for ever rolls
Through their blood, and binds their souls,
Working love, but working teen?—
There were two Iseults who did sway
Each her hour of Tristram's day;
But one possess'd his waning time,   70
The other his resplendent prime.
Behold her here, the patient flower,
Who possess'd his darker hour!
Iseult of the Snow-White Hand
Watches pale by Tristram's bed.
She is here who had his gloom,
Where art thou who hadst his bloom?
One such kiss as those of yore
Might thy dying knight restore!

---

67 *teen:* sorrow.

Does the love-draught work no more?   80
Art thou cold, or false, or dead,
Iseult of Ireland?

          .   .   .   .   .

Loud howls the wind, sharp patters the rain,
And the knight sinks back on his pillows again.
He is weak with fever and pain,
And his spirit is not clear.
Hark! he mutters in his sleep,
As he wanders far from here,
Changes place and time of year,
And his closéd eye doth sweep   90
O'er some fair unwintry sea,
Not this fierce Atlantic deep,
While he mutters brokenly:—

                    Tristram

The calm sea shines, loose hang the vessel's sails;
Before us are the sweet green fields of Wales,
And overhead the cloudless sky of May.—
"Ah, would I were in those green fields at play,
Not pent on ship-board this delicious day!
Tristram, I pray thee, of thy courtesy,
Reach me my golden phial stands by thee,   100
But pledge me in it first for courtesy.—"
Ha! dost thou start? are thy lips blanch'd like mine?
Child, 'tis no true draught this, 'tis poison'd wine!
Iseult! . . . .

          .   .   .   .   .

Ah, sweet angels, let him dream!
Keep his eyelids! let him seem
Not this fever-wasted wight
Thinn'd and paled before his time,
But the brilliant youthful knight
In the glory of his prime,   110
Sitting in the gilded barge,
At thy side, thou lovely charge,
Bending gaily o'er thy hand,
Iseult of Ireland!
And she too, that princess fair,
If her bloom be now less rare,

Let her have her youth again—
Let her be as she was then!
Let her have her proud dark eyes,
And her petulant quick replies— 120
Let her sweep her dazzling hand
With its gesture of command,
And shake back her raven hair
With the old imperious air!
As of old, so let her be,
That first Iseult, princess bright,
Chatting with her youthful knight
As he steers her o'er the sea,
Quitting at her father's will
The green isle where she was bred, 130
And her bower in Ireland,
For the surge-beat Cornish strand;
Where the prince whom she must wed
Dwells on loud Tyntagel's hill,
High above the sounding sea.
And that potion rare her mother
Gave her, that her future lord,
Gave her, that King Marc and she,
Might drink it on their marriage-day,
And for ever love each other— 140
Let her, as she sits on board,
Ah, sweet saints, unwittingly!
See it shine, and take it up,
And to Tristram laughing say:
"Sir Tristram, of thy courtesy,
Pledge me in my golden cup!"
Let them drink it—let their hands
Tremble, and their cheeks be flame,
As they feel the fatal bands
Of a love they dare not name, 150
With a wild delicious pain,
Twine about their hearts again!
Let the early summer be
Once more round them, and the sea
Blue, and o'er its mirror kind
Let the breath of the May-wind,
Wandering through their drooping sails,

Die on the green fields of Wales!
Let a dream like this restore
What his eye must see no more!   160

Tristram

Chill blows the wind, the pleasaunce-walks are drear—
Madcap, what jest was this, to meet me here?
Were feet like those made for so wild a way?
The southern winter-parlour, by my fay,
Had been the likeliest trysting-place to-day!
"Tristram!—nay, nay—thou must not take my hand!—
Tristram!—sweet love!—we are betray'd—out-plann'd.
Fly!—save thyself!—save me!—I dare not stay."
One last kiss first!—*" 'T is vain—to horse—away!"*

             .   .   .   .

Ah! sweet saints, his dream doth move   170
Faster surely than it should,
From the fever in his blood!
All the spring-time of his love
Is already gone and past,
And instead thereof is seen
Its winter, which endureth still—
Tyntagel on its surge-beat hill,
The pleasaunce-walks, the weeping queen,
The flying leaves, the straining blast,
And that long, wild kiss—their last.   180
And this rough December-night,
And his burning fever-pain,
Mingle with his hurrying dream,
Till they rule it, till he seem
The press'd fugitive again,
The love-desperate banish'd knight
With a fire in his brain
Flying o'er the stormy main.
—Whither does he wander now?
Haply in his dreams the wind   190
Wafts him here, and lets him find
The lovely orphan child again

---

161 *pleasaunce-walks:* walks in a pleasure garden.

In her castle by the coast;
The youngest, fairest chatelaine,
Whom this realm of France can boast,
Our snowdrop by the Atlantic sea,
Iseult of Brittany.
And—for through the haggard air,
The stain'd arms, the matted hair
Of that stranger-knight ill-starr'd,   200
There gleam'd something, which recall'd
The Tristram who in better days
Was Launcelot's guest at Joyous Gard—
Welcomed here, and here install'd,
Tended of his fever here,
Haply he seems again to move
His young guardian's heart with love;
In his exiled loneliness,
In his stately, deep distress,
Without a word, without a tear.   210
—Ah! 'tis well he should retrace
His tranquil life in this lone place;
His gentle bearing at the side
Of his timid youthful bride;
His long rambles by the shore
On winter-evenings, when the roar
Of the near waves came, sadly grand,
Through the dark, up the drown'd sand,
Or his endless reveries
In the woods, where the gleams play   220
On the grass under the trees,
Passing the long summer's day
Idle as a mossy stone
In the forest-depths alone,
The chase neglected, and his hound
Couch'd beside him on the ground.
—Ah! what trouble's on his brow?
Hither let him wander now;
Hither, to the quiet hours
Pass'd among these heaths of ours   230
By the grey Atlantic sea;

---

194 *chatelaine:* lady of the castle.
203 *Joyous Gard:* Launcelot's castle.

Hours, if not of ecstasy,
From violent anguish surely free!

Tristram

All red with blood the whirling river flows,
The wide plain rings, the dazed air throbs with blows.
Upon us are the chivalry of Rome—
Their spears are down, their steeds are bathed in foam.
"Up, Tristram, up," men cry, "thou moonstruck knight!
What foul fiend rides thee? On into the fight!"
—Above the din her voice is in my ears;   240
I see her form glide through the crossing spears.—
Iseult! . . . .

         .   .   .   .   .

Ah! he wanders forth again;
We cannot keep him; now, as then,
There's a secret in his breast
Which will never let him rest.
These musing fits in the green wood
They cloud the brain, they dull the blood!
—His sword is sharp, his horse is good;
Beyond the mountains will he see   250
The famous towns of Italy,
And label with the blessed sign
The heathen Saxons on the Rhine.
At Arthur's side he fights once more
With the Roman Emperor.
There's many a gay knight where he goes
Will help him to forget his care;
The march, the leaguer, Heaven's blithe air,
The neighing steeds, the ringing blows—
Sick pining comes not where these are.   260
Ah! what boots it, that the jest
Lightens every other brow,
What, that every other breast
Dances as the trumpets blow,
If one's own heart beats not light
On the waves of the toss'd fight,
If oneself cannot get free
From the clog of misery?
Thy lovely youthful wife grows pale

Watching by the salt sea-tide 270
With her children at her side
For the gleam of thy white sail.
Home, Tristram, to thy halls again!
To our lonely sea complain,
To our forests tell thy pain!

Tristram

All round the forest sweeps off, black in shade,
But it is moonlight in the open glade;
And in the bottom of the glade shine clear
The forest-chapel and the fountain near.
—I think, I have a fever in my blood; 280
Come, let me leave the shadow of this wood,
Ride down, and bathe my hot brow in the flood.
—Mild shines the cold spring in the moon's clear light;
God! 'tis *her* face plays in the waters bright.
"Fair love," she says, "canst thou forget so soon,
At this soft hour, under this sweet moon?"—
Iseult! . . . .

.   .   .   .   .

Ah, poor soul! if this be so,
Only death can balm thy woe.
The solitudes of the green wood 290
Had no medicine for thy mood;
The rushing battle clear'd thy blood
As little as did solitude.
—Ah! his eyelids slowly break
Their hot seals, and let him wake;
What new change shall we now see?
A happier? Worse it cannot be.

Tristram

Is my page here? Come, turn me to the fire!
Upon the window-panes the moon shines bright;
The wind is down—but she'll not come to-night. 300
Ah no! she is asleep in Cornwall now,
Far hence; her dreams are fair—smooth is her brow.
Of me she recks not, nor my vain desire.
—I have had dreams, I have had dreams, my page,
Would take a score years from a strong man's age;

And with a blood like mine, will leave, I fear,
Scant leisure for a second messenger.
—My princess, art thou there? Sweet, do not wait!
To bed, and sleep! my fever is gone by;
To-night my page shall keep me company.   310
Where do the children sleep? kiss them for me!
Poor child, thou art almost as pale as I;
This comes of nursing long and watching late.
To bed—good night!

> .   .   .   .   .

She left the gleam-lit fireplace,
She came to the bed-side;
She took his hands in hers—her tears
Down on his wasted fingers rain'd.
She raised her eyes upon his face—
Not with a look of wounded pride,   320
A look as if the heart complained—
Her look was like a sad embrace;
The gaze of one who can divine
A grief, and sympathise.
Sweet flower! thy children's eyes
Are not more innocent than thine.

But they sleep in shelter'd rest,
Like helpless birds in the warm nest,
On the castle's southern side;
Where feebly comes the mournful roar   330
Of buffeting wind and surging tide
Through many a room and corridor.
—Full on their window the moon's ray
Makes their chamber as bright as day.
It shines upon the blank white walls,
And on the snowy pillow falls,
And on two angel-heads doth play
Turn'd to each other—the eyes closed,
The lashes on the cheeks reposed.
Round each sweet brow the cap close-set   340
Hardly lets peep the golden hair;
Through the soft-open'd lips the air
Scarcely moves the coverlet.
One little wandering arm is thrown

At random on the counterpane,
And often the fingers close in haste
As if their baby-owner chased
The butterflies again.
This stir they have, and this alone;
But else they are so still!   350
—Ah, tired madcaps! you lie still;
But were you at the window now,
To look forth on the fairy sight
Of your illumined haunts by night,
To see the park-glades where you play
Far lovelier than they are by day,
To see the sparkle on the eaves,
And upon every giant-bough
Of those old oaks, whose wet red leaves
Are jewell'd with bright drops of rain—   360
How would your voices run again!
And far beyond the sparkling trees
Of the castle-park one sees
The bare heaths spreading, clear as day,
Moor behind moor, far, far away,
Into the heart of Brittany.
And here and there, lock'd by the land,
Long inlets of smooth glittering sea,
And many a stretch of watery sand
All shining in the white moon-beams—   370
But you see fairer in your dreams!
What voices are these on the clear night-air?
What lights in the court—what steps on the stair?

II

ISEULT OF IRELAND

Tristram

Raise the light, my page! that I may see her.—
  Thou art come at last, then, haughty Queen!
Long I've waited, long I've fought my fever;
  Late thou comest, cruel thou hast been.

Iseult

Blame me not, poor sufferer! that I tarried;
  Bound I was, I could not break the band.
Chide not with the past, but feel the present!
  I am here—we meet—I hold thy hand.

Tristram

Thou art come, indeed—thou hast rejoin'd me;
  Thou hast dared it—but too late to save.   10
Fear not now that men should tax thine honour!
  I am dying: build—(thou may'st)—my grave!

Iseult

Tristram, ah, for love of Heaven, speak kindly!
  What, I hear these bitter words from thee?
Sick with grief I am, and faint with travel—
  Take my hand—dear Tristram, look on me!

Tristram

I forgot, thou comest from thy voyage—
  Yes, the spray is on thy cloak and hair.
But thy dark eyes are not dimm'd, proud Iseult!
  And thy beauty never was more fair.   20

Iseult

Ah, harsh flatterer! let alone my beauty!
  I, like thee, have left my youth afar.
Take my hand, and touch these wasted fingers—
  See my cheek and lips, how white they are!

Tristram

Thou art paler—but thy sweet charm, Iseult!
  Would not fade with the dull years away.
Ah, how fair thou standest in the moonlight!
  I forgive thee, Iseult!—thou wilt stay?

Iseult

Fear me not, I will be always with thee;
  I will watch thee, tend thee, soothe thy pain;   30

Sing thee tales of true, long-parted lovers,
    Join'd at evening of their days again.

Tristram

No, thou shalt not speak! I should be finding
    Something alter'd in thy courtly tone.
Sit—sit by me! I will think, we've lived so
    In the green wood, all our lives, alone.

Iseult

Alter'd, Tristram? Not in courts, believe me,
    Love like mine is alter'd in the breast;
Courtly life is light and cannot reach it—
    Ah! it lives, because so deep-suppress'd!   40

What, thou think'st men speak in courtly chambers
    Words by which the wretched are consoled?
What, thou think'st this aching brow was cooler,
    Circled, Tristram, by a band of gold?

Royal state with Marc, my deep-wrong'd husband—
    That was bliss to make my sorrows flee!
Silken courtiers whispering honied nothings—
    Those were friends to make me false to thee!

Ah, on which, if both our lots were balanced,
    Was indeed the heaviest burden thrown—   50
Thee, a pining exile in thy forest,
    Me, a smiling queen upon my throne?

Vain and strange debate, where both have suffer'd,
    Both have pass'd a youth consumed and sad,
Both have brought their anxious day to evening,
    And have now short space for being glad!

Join'd we are henceforth; nor will thy people,
    Nor thy younger Iseult take it ill,
That a former rival shares her office,
    When she sees her humbled, pale, and still.   60

I, a faded watcher by thy pillow,
    I, a statue on thy chapel-floor,

Pour'd in prayer before the Virgin-Mother,
   Rouse no anger, make no rivals more.

She will cry: "Is this the foe I dreaded?
   This his idol? this that royal bride?
Ah, an hour of health would purge his eyesight!
   Stay, pale queen! for ever by my side."

Hush, no words! that smile, I see, forgives me.
   I am now thy nurse, I bid thee sleep.   70
Close thine eyes—this flooding moonlight blinds them!—
   Nay, all's well again! thou must not weep.

Tristram

I am happy! yet I feel, there's something
   Swells my heart, and takes my breath away.
Through a mist I see thee; near—come nearer!
   Bend—bend down!—I yet have much to say.

Iseult

Heaven! his head sinks back upon the pillow—
   Tristram! Tristram! let thy heart not fail!
Call on God and on the holy angels!
   What, love, courage!—Christ! he is so pale.   80

Tristram

Hush, 'tis vain, I feel my end approaching!
   This is what my mother said should be,
When the fierce pains took her in the forest,
   The deep draughts of death, in bearing me.

"Son," she said, "thy name shall be of sorrow;
   Tristram art thou call'd for my death's sake."
So she said, and died in the drear forest.
   Grief since then his home with me doth make.

I am dying.—Start not, nor look wildly!
   Me, thy living friend, thou canst not save.   90

---

85 *sorrow:* the meaning of the Latin *tristis,* from which Tristram's name
derives.

But, since living we were ununited,
   Go not far, O Iseult! from my grave.

Close mine eyes, then seek the princess Iseult;
   Speak her fair, she is of royal blood!
Say I will'd so, that thou stay beside me—
   She will grant it; she is kind and good.

Now to sail the seas of death I leave thee—
   One last kiss upon the living shore!

Iseult

Tristram!—Tristram!—stay—receive me with thee!
Iseult leaves thee, Tristram! never more.   100

    .   .   .   .

   You see them clear—the moon shines bright.
   Slow, slow and softly, where she stood,
   She sinks upon the ground;—her hood
   Had fallen back; her arms outspread
   Still hold her lover's hand; her head
   Is bow'd, half-buried, on the bed.
   O'er the blanch'd sheet her raven hair
   Lies in disorder'd streams; and there,
   Strung like white stars, the pearls still are,
   And the golden bracelets, heavy and rare,   110
   Flash on her white arms still.
   The very same which yesternight
   Flash'd in the silver sconces' light,
   When the feast was gay and the laughter loud
   In Tyntagel's palace proud.
   But then they deck'd a restless ghost
   With hot-flush'd cheeks and brilliant eyes,
   And quivering lips on which the tide
   Of courtly speech abruptly died,
   And a glance which over the crowded floor,   120
   The dancers, and the festive host,
   Flew ever to the door.
   That the knights eyed her in surprise,
   And the dames whispered scoffingly:
   "Her moods, good lack, they pass like showers!
   But yesternight and she would be

As pale and still as wither'd flowers,
And now to-night she laughs and speaks
And has a colour in her cheeks;
Christ keep us from such fantasy!"—   130

Yes, now the longing is o'erpast,
Which, dogg'd by fear and fought by shame,
Shook her weak bosom day and night,
Consumed her beauty like a flame,
And dimm'd it like the desert-blast.
And though the bed-clothes hide her face,
Yet were it lifted to the light,
The sweet expression of her brow
Would charm the gazer, till his thought
Erased the ravages of time,   140
Fill'd up the hollow cheek, and brought
A freshness back as of her prime—
So healing is her quiet now.
So perfectly the lines express
A tranquil, settled loveliness,
Her younger rival's purest grace.

The air of the December-night
Steals coldly around the chamber bright,
Where those lifeless lovers be;
Swinging with it, in the light   150
Flaps the ghostlike tapestry.
And on the arras wrought you see
A stately Huntsman, clad in green,
And round him a fresh forest-scene.
On that clear forest-knoll he stays,
With his pack round him, and delays.
He stares and stares, with troubled face,
At this huge, gleam-lit fireplace,
At that bright, iron-figured door,
And those blown rushes on the floor.   160
He gazes down into the room
With heated cheeks and flurried air,
And to himself he seems to say:
"What place is this, and who are they?

Who is that kneeling Lady fair?
And on his pillows that pale Knight
Who seems of marble on a tomb?
How comes it here, this chamber bright,
Through whose mullion'd windows clear
The castle-court all wet with rain,   170
The drawbridge and the moat appear,
And then the beach, and, mark'd with spray,
The sunken reefs, and far away
The unquiet bright Atlantic plain?
—What, has some glamour made me sleep,
And sent me with my dogs to sweep,
By night, with boisterous bugle-peal,
Through some old, sea-side, knightly hall,
Not in the free green wood at all?
That Knight's asleep, and at her prayer   180
That Lady by the bed doth kneel—
Then hush, thou boisterous bugle-peal!"
—The wild boar rustles in his lair;
The fierce hounds snuff the tainted air;
But lord and hounds keep rooted there.

Cheer, cheer thy dogs into the brake,
O Hunter! and without a fear
Thy golden-tassell'd bugle blow,
And through the glades thy pastime take—
For thou wilt rouse no sleepers here!   190
For these thou seest are unmoved;
Cold, cold as those who lived and loved
A thousand years ago.

III

ISEULT OF BRITTANY

A year had flown, and o'er the sea away,
In Cornwall, Tristram and Queen Iseult lay;
In King Marc's chapel, in Tyntagel old—
There in a ship they bore those lovers cold.

---

175 *glamour:* enchantment, spell.

The young surviving Iseult, one bright day,
Had wander'd forth. Her children were at play
In a green circular hollow in the heath
Which borders the sea-shore—a country path
Creeps over it from the till'd fields behind.
The hollow's grassy banks are soft-inclined,   10
And to one standing on them, far and near
The lone unbroken view spreads bright and clear
Over the waste. This cirque of open ground
Is light and green; the heather, which all round
Creeps thickly, grows not here; but the pale grass
Is strewn with rocks, and many a shiver'd mass
Of vein'd white-gleaming quartz, and here and there
Dotted with holly-trees and juniper.
In the smooth centre of the opening stood
Three hollies side by side, and made a screen,   20
Warm with the winter-sun, of burnish'd green
With scarlet berries gemm'd, the fell-fare's food.
Under the glittering hollies Iseult stands,
Watching her children play; their little hands
Are busy gathering spars of quartz, and streams
Of stagshorn for their hats; anon, with screams
Of mad delight they drop their spoils, and bound
Among the holly-clumps and broken ground,
Racing full speed, and startling in their rush
The fell-fares and the speckled missel-thrush   30
Out of their glossy coverts;—but when now
Their cheeks were flush'd, and over each hot brow,
Under the feather'd hats of the sweet pair,
In blinding masses shower'd the golden hair—
Then Iseult call'd them to her, and the three
Cluster'd under the holly-screen, and she
Told them an old-world Breton history.

Warm in their mantles wrapt the three stood there,
Under the hollies, in the clear still air—
Mantles with those rich furs deep glistering   40
Which Venice ships do from swart Egypt bring.
Long they stay'd still—then, pacing at their ease,

---

²² *fell-fare:* thrush.
²⁶ *stagshorn:* moss.

Moved up and down under the glossy trees.
But still, as they pursued their warm dry road,
From Iseult's lips the unbroken story flow'd,
And still the children listen'd, their blue eyes
Fix'd on their mother's face in wide surprise;
Nor did their looks stray once to the sea-side,
Nor to the brown heaths round them, bright and wide,
Nor to the snow, which, though 't was all away   50
From the open heath, still by the hedgerows lay,
Nor to the shining sea-fowl, that with screams
Bore up from where the bright Atlantic gleams,
Swooping to landward; nor to where, quite clear,
The fell-fares settled on the thickets near.
And they would still have listen'd, till dark night
Came keen and chill down on the heather bright;
But, when the red glow on the sea grew cold,
And the grey turrets of the castle old
Look'd sternly through the frosty evening-air,   60
Then Iseult took by the hand those children fair,
And brought her tale to an end, and found the path,
And led them home over the darkening heath.

And is she happy? Does she see unmoved
The days in which she might have lived and loved
Slip without bringing bliss slowly away,
One after one, to-morrow like to-day?
Joy has not found her yet, nor ever will—
Is it this thought which makes her mien so still,
Her features so fatigued, her eyes, though sweet,   70
So sunk, so rarely lifted save to meet
Her children's? She moves slow; her voice alone
Hath yet an infantine and silver tone,
But even that comes languidly; in truth,
She seems one dying in a mask of youth.
And now she will go home, and softly lay
Her laughing children in their beds, and play
Awhile with them before they sleep; and then
She'll light her silver lamp, which fishermen
Dragging their nets through the rough waves, afar,   80
Along this iron coast, know like a star,
And take her broidery-frame, and there she'll sit

Hour after hour, her gold curls sweeping it;
Lifting her soft-bent head only to mind
Her children, or to listen to the wind.
And when the clock peals midnight, she will move
Her work away, and let her fingers rove
Across the shaggy brows of Tristram's hound
Who lies, guarding her feet, along the ground;
Or else she will fall musing, her blue eyes   90
Fixt, her slight hands clasp'd on her lap; then rise,
And at her prie-dieu kneel, until she have told
Her rosary-beads of ebony tipp'd with gold,
Then to her soft sleep—and to-morrow'll be
To-day's exact repeated effigy.

Yes, it is lonely for her in her hall.
The children, and the grey-hair'd seneschal,
Her women, and Sir Tristram's aged hound,
Are there the sole companions to be found.
But these she loves; and noisier life than this   100
She would find ill to bear, weak as she is.
She has her children, too, and night and day
Is with them; and the wide heaths where they play,
The hollies, and the cliff, and the sea-shore,
The sand, the sea-birds, and the distant sails,
These are to her dear as to them; the tales
With which this day the children she beguiled
She gleaned from Breton grandames, when a child,
In every hut along this sea-coast wild.
She herself loves them still, and, when they are told,   110
Can forget all to hear them, as of old.

Dear saints, it is not sorrow, as I hear,
Not suffering, which shuts up eye and ear
To all that has delighted them before,
And lets us be what we were once no more.
No, we may suffer deeply, yet retain
Power to be moved and soothed, for all our pain,
By what of old pleased us, and will again.
No, 'tis the gradual furnace of the world,

---

97 *seneschal:* steward.

In whose hot air our spirits are upcurl'd 120
Until they crumble, or else grow like steel—
Which kills in us the bloom, the youth, the spring—
Which leaves the fierce necessity to feel,
But takes away the power—this can avail,
By drying up our joy in everything,
To make our former pleasures all seem stale.
This, or some tyrannous single thought, some fit
Of passion, which subdues our souls to it,
Till for its sake alone we live and move—
Call it ambition, or remorse, or love— 130
This too can change us wholly, and make seem
All which we did before, shadow and dream.

And yet, I swear, it angers me to see
How this fool passion gulls men potently;
Being, in truth, but a diseased unrest,
And an unnatural overheat at best.
How they are full of languor and distress
Not having it; which when they do possess,
They straightway are burnt up with fume and care,
And spend their lives in posting here and there 140
Where this plague drives them; and have little ease,
Are furious with themselves, and hard to please.
Like that bald Cæsar, the famed Roman wight,
Who wept at reading of a Grecian knight
Who made a name at younger years than he;
Or that renown'd mirror of chivalry,
Prince Alexander, Philip's peerless son,
Who carried the great war from Macedon
Into the Soudan's realm, and thundered on
To die at thirty-five in Babylon. 150

What tale did Iseult to the children say,
Under the hollies, that bright winter's day?

She told them of the fairy-haunted land
Away the other side of Brittany,

---

143 *Cæsar:* Julius Caesar is said to have wept with envy when he heard that
Alexander the Great had conquered Persia at the age of twenty-five. **Alexan-**
der was the son of Philip of Macedon.
149 *Soudan:* sultan (of Turkey).

Beyond the heaths, edged by the lonely sea;
Of the deep forest-glades of Broce-liande,
Through whose green boughs the golden sunshine creeps,
Where Merlin by the enchanted thorn-tree sleeps.
For here he came with the fay Vivian,
One April, when the warm days first began.   160
He was on foot, and that false fay, his friend,
On her white palfrey; here he met his end,
In these lone sylvan glades, that April-day.
This tale of Merlin and the lovely fay
Was the one Iseult chose, and she brought clear
Before the children's fancy him and her.

Blowing between the stems, the forest-air
Had loosen'd the brown locks of Vivian's hair,
Which play'd on her flush'd cheek, and her blue eyes
Sparkled with mocking glee and exercise.   170
Her palfrey's flanks were mired and bathed in sweat,
For they had travell'd far and not stopp'd yet.
A brier in that tangled wilderness
Had scored her white right hand, which she allows
To rest ungloved on her green riding-dress;
The other warded off the drooping boughs.
But still she chatted on, with her blue eyes
Fix'd full on Merlin's face, her stately prize.
Her 'haviour had the morning's fresh clear grace,
The spirit of the woods was in her face.   180
She look'd so witching fair, that learned wight
Forgot his craft, and his best wits took flight;
And he grew fond, and eager to obey
His mistress, use her empire as she may.

They came to where the brushwood ceased, and day
Peer'd 'twixt the stems; and the ground broke away,
In a sloped sward down to a brawling brook;
And up as high as where they stood to look
On the brook's farther side was clear, but then
The underwood and trees began again.   190
This open glen was studded thick with thorns

---

156 *Broce-liande:* the forest in which Merlin, King Arthur's magician, was
imprisoned by his mistress, Vivian.

Then white with blossom; and you saw the horns,
Through last year's fern, of the shy fallow-deer
Who come at noon down to the water here.
You saw the bright-eyed squirrels dart along
Under the thorns on the green sward; and strong
The blackbird whistled from the dingles near,
And the weird chipping of the woodpecker
Rang lonelily and sharp; the sky was fair,
And a fresh breath of spring stirr'd everywhere.   200
Merlin and Vivian stopp'd on the slope's brow,
To gaze on the light sea of leaf and bough
Which glistering plays all round them, lone and mild,
As if to itself the quiet forest smiled.
Upon the brow-top grew a thorn, and here
The grass was dry and moss'd, and you saw clear
Across the hollow; white anemonies
Starr'd the cool turf, and clumps of primroses
Ran out from the dark underwood behind.
No fairer resting-place a man could find.   210
"Here let us halt," said Merlin then; and she
Nodded, and tied her palfrey to a tree.

They sate them down together, and a sleep
Fell upon Merlin, more like death, so deep.
Her finger on her lips, then Vivian rose,
And from her brown-lock'd head the wimple throws,
And takes it in her hand, and waves it over
The blossom'd thorn-tree and her sleeping lover.
Nine times she waved the fluttering wimple round,
And made a little plot of magic ground.   220
And in that daisied circle, as men say,
Is Merlin prisoner till the judgment-day;
But she herself whither she will can rove—
For she was passing weary of his love.

[1852]

---

197 *dingles:* small wooded valleys.

A SUMMER NIGHT

In the deserted, moon-blanch'd street,
How lonely rings the echo of my feet!
Those windows, which I gaze at, frown,
Silent and white, unopening down,
Repellent as the world;—but see,
A break between the housetops shows
The moon! and, lost behind her, fading dim
Into the dewy dark obscurity
Down at the far horizon's rim,
Doth a whole tract of heaven disclose!   10

And to my mind the thought
Is on a sudden brought
Of a past night, and a far different scene.
Headlands stood out into the moonlit deep
As clearly as at noon;
The spring-tide's brimming flow
Heaved dazzlingly between;
Houses, with long white sweep,
Girdled the glistening bay;
Behind, through the soft air,   20
The blue haze-cradled mountains spread away,
The night was far more fair—
But the same restless pacings to and fro,
And the same vainly throbbing heart was there,
And the same bright, calm moon.

And the calm moonlight seems to say:
Hast thou then still the old unquiet breast,
Which neither deadens into rest,
Nor ever feels the fiery glow
That whirls the spirit from itself away,   30
But fluctuates to and fro,
Never by passion quite possess'd
And never quite benumb'd by the world's sway?—
And I, I know not if to pray

Still to be what I am, or yield and be
Like all the other men I see.

For most men in a brazen prison live,
Where, in the sun's hot eye,
With heads bent o'er their toil, they languidly
Their lives to some unmeaning taskwork give, 40
Dreaming of nought beyond their prison-wall.
And as, year after year,
Fresh products of their barren labour fall
From their tired hands, and rest
Never yet comes more near,
Gloom settles slowly down over their breast;
And while they try to stem
The waves of mournful thought by which they are prest,
Death in their prison reaches them,
Unfreed, having seen nothing, still unblest. 50

And the rest, a few,
Escape their prison and depart
On the wide ocean of life anew.
There the freed prisoner, where'er his heart
Listeth, will sail;
Nor doth he know how there prevail,
Despotic on that sea,
Trade-winds which cross it from eternity.
Awhile he holds some false way, undebarr'd
By thwarting signs, and braves 60
The freshening wind and blackening waves.
And then the tempest strikes him; and between
The lightning-bursts is seen
Only a driving wreck,
And the pale master on his spar-strewn deck
With anguish'd face and flying hair
Grasping the rudder hard,
Still bent to make some port he knows not where,
Still standing for some false, impossible shore.
And sterner comes the roar 70
Of sea and wind, and through the deepening gloom
Fainter and fainter wreck and helmsman loom,
And he too disappears, and comes no more.

Is there no life, but these alone?
Madman or slave, must man be one?

Plainness and clearness without shadow of stain!
Clearness divine!
Ye heavens, whose pure dark regions have no sign
Of languor, though so calm, and, though so great,
Are yet untroubled and unpassionate;   80
Who, though so noble, share in the world's toil,
And, though so task'd, keep free from dust and soil!
I will not say that your mild deeps retain
A tinge, it may be, of their silent pain
Who have long'd deeply once, and long'd in vain—
But I will rather say that you remain
A world above man's head, to let him see
How boundless might his soul's horizons be,
How vast, yet of what clear transparency!
How it were good to abide there, and breathe free;   90
How fair a lot to fill
Is left to each man still!

[1852]

THE BURIED LIFE

Light flows our war of mocking words, and yet,
Behold, with tears mine eyes are wet!
I feel a nameless sadness o'er me roll.
Yes, yes, we know that we can jest,
We know, we know that we can smile!
But there's a something in this breast,
To which thy light words bring no rest,
And thy gay smiles no anodyne.
Give me thy hand, and hush awhile,
And turn those limpid eyes on mine,   10
And let me read there, love! thy inmost soul.

Alas! is even love too weak
To unlock the heart, and let it speak?

Are even lovers powerless to reveal
To one another what indeed they feel?
I knew the mass of men conceal'd
Their thoughts, for fear that if reveal'd
They would by other men be met
With blank indifference, or with blame reproved;
I knew they lived and moved   20
Trick'd in disguises, alien to the rest
Of men, and alien to themselves—and yet
The same heart beats in every human breast!

But we, my love!—doth a like spell benumb
Our hearts, our voices?—must we too be dumb?

Ah! well for us, if even we,
Even for a moment, can get free
Our heart, and have our lips unchain'd;
For that which seals them hath been deep-ordain'd!

Fate, which foresaw   30
How frivolous a baby man would be—
By what distractions he would be possess'd,
How he would pour himself in every strife,
And well-nigh change his own identity—
That it might keep from his capricious play
His genuine self, and force him to obey
Even in his own despite his being's law,
Bade through the deep recesses of our breast
The unregarded river of our life
Pursue with indiscernible flow its way;   40
And that we should not see
The buried stream, and seem to be
Eddying at large in blind uncertainty,
Though driving on with it eternally.

But often, in the world's most crowded streets,
But often, in the din of strife,
There rises an unspeakable desire
After the knowledge of our buried life;
A thirst to spend our fire and restless force
In tracking out our true, original course;   50

A longing to inquire
Into the mystery of this heart which beats
So wild, so deep in us—to know
Whence our lives come and where they go.
And many a man in his own breast then delves,
But deep enough, alas! none ever mines.
And we have been on many thousand lines,
And we have shown, on each, spirit and power;
But hardly have we for one little hour,
Been on our own line, have we been ourselves—   60
Hardly had skill to utter one of all
The nameless feelings that course through our breast,
But they course on for ever unexpress'd.
And long we try in vain to speak and act
Our hidden self, and what we say and do
Is eloquent, is well—but 'tis not true!
And then we will no more be rack'd
With inward striving, and demand
Of all the thousand nothings of the hour
Their stupefying power;   70
Ah yes, and they benumb us at our call!
Yet still, from time to time, vague and forlorn,
From the soul's subterranean depth upborne
As from an infinitely distant land,
Come airs, and floating echoes, and convey
A melancholy into all our day.

Only—but this is rare—
When a belovèd hand is laid in ours,
When, jaded with the rush and glare
Of the interminable hours,   80
Our eyes can in another's eyes read clear,
When our world-deafen'd ear
Is by the tones of a loved voice caress'd—
A bolt is shot back somewhere in our breast,
And a lost pulse of feeling stirs again.
The eye sinks inward, and the heart lies plain,
And what we mean, we say, and what we would, we know.
A man becomes aware of his life's flow.
And hears its winding murmur; and he sees
The meadows where it glides, the sun, the breeze.   90

And there arrives a lull in the hot race
Wherein he doth for ever chase
That flying and elusive shadow, rest.
An air of coolness plays upon his face,
And an unwonted calm pervades his breast.
And then he thinks he knows
The hills where his life rose,
And the sea where it goes.

[1852]

SOHRAB AND RUSTUM

An Episode

And the first grey of morning fill'd the east,
And the fog rose out of the Oxus stream.
But all the Tartar camp along the stream
Was hush'd, and still the men were plunged in sleep;
Sohrab alone, he slept not; all night long

Sohrab and Rustum: To introduce the poem Arnold quoted the following
passage from Sir John Malcolm's *History of Persia:*

> The young Sohrab was the fruit of one of Rustum's early
> amours. He had left his mother, and sought fame under the ban-
> ners of Afrasiab, whose armies he commanded, and soon obtained a
> renown beyond that of all contemporary heroes but his father. He
> had carried death and dismay into the ranks of the Persians, and
> had terrified the boldest warriors of that country, before Rustum
> encountered him, which at last that hero resolved to do, under a
> feigned name. They met three times. The first time they parted by
> mutual consent, though Sohrab had the advantage. The second, the
> youth obtained a victory, but granted life to his unknown father.
> The third was fatal to Sohrab, who, when writhing in the pangs of
> death, warned his conqueror to shun the vengeance that is inspired
> by parental woes, and bade him dread the rage of the mighty
> Rustum, who must soon learn that he had slain his son Sohrab.
> These words, we are told, were as death to the aged hero; and
> when he recovered from a trance, he called in despair for proofs of
> what Sohrab had said. The afflicted and dying youth tore open his
> mail, and showed his father a seal which his mother had placed on
> his arm when she discovered to him the secret of his birth, and
> bade him seek his father. The sight of his own signet rendered
> Rustum quite frantic: he cursed himself, attempted to put an end
> to his existence, and was only prevented by the efforts of his expir-

He had lain wakeful, tossing on his bed;
But when the grey dawn stole into his tent,
He rose, and clad himself, and girt his sword,
And took his horseman's cloak, and left his tent,
And went abroad into the cold wet fog,   10
Through the dim camp to Peran-Wisa's tent.
   Through the black Tartar tents he pass'd, which stood
Clustering like bee-hives on the low flat strand
Of Oxus, where the summer-floods o'erflow
When the sun melts the snows in high Pamere;
Through the black tents he pass'd, o'er that low strand,
And to a hillock came, a little back
From the stream's brink—the spot where first a boat,
Crossing the stream in summer, scrapes the land.
The men of former times had crown'd the top   20
With a clay fort; but that was fall'n, and now
The Tartars built there Peran-Wisa's tent,
A dome of laths, and o'er it felts were spread.
And Sohrab came there, and went in, and stood
Upon the thick piled carpets in the tent,
And found the old man sleeping on his bed
Of rugs and felts, and near him lay his arms.
And Peran-Wisa heard him, though the step
Was dull'd; for he slept light, an old man's sleep;
And he rose quickly on one arm, and said:—   30
   "Who art thou? for it is not yet clear dawn.
Speak! is there news, or any night alarm?"
   But Sohrab came to the bedside, and said:—

---

ing son. After Sohrab's death, he burnt his tents, and all his goods, and carried the corpse to Seistan, where it was interred. The army of Turan was, agreeably to the last request of Sohrab, permitted to cross the Oxus unmolested. It was commanded by Haman: and Zoarrah attended, on the part of Rustum, to see that this engagement was respected by the Persians. To reconcile us to the improbability of this tale we are informed that Rustum could have no idea his son was in existence. The mother of Sohrab had written to him her child was a daughter, fearing to lose her darling infant if she revealed the truth; and Rustum, as before stated, fought under a feigned name, an usage not uncommon in the chivalrous combats of those days.

   Although Sohrab was a Persian, he served in the armies of the Tartar king, Afrasiab, under the command of the general, Peran-Wisa.
2 *Oxus:* Central Asian river flowing from the borders of India to the Aral Sea.
15 *Pamere:* Central Asian plateau.

"Thou know'st me, Peran-Wisa! it is I.
The sun is not yet risen, and the foe
Sleep; but I sleep not; all night long I lie
Tossing and wakeful, and I come to thee.
For so did King Afrasiab bid me seek
Thy counsel, and to heed thee as thy son,
In Samarcand, before the army march'd;   40
And I will tell thee what my heart desires.
Thou know'st if, since from Ader-baijan first
I came among the Tartars and bore arms,
I have still served Afrasiab well, and shown,
At my boy's years, the courage of a man.
This too thou know'st, that while I still bear on
The conquering Tartar ensigns through the world,
And beat the Persians back on every field,
I seek one man, one man, and one alone—
Rustum, my father; who I hoped should greet,   50
Should one day greet, upon some well-fought field,
His not unworthy, not inglorious son.
So I long hoped, but him I never find.
Come then, hear now, and grant me what I ask.
Let the two armies rest to-day; but I
Will challenge forth the bravest Persian lords
To meet me, man to man; if I prevail,
Rustum will surely hear it; if I fall—
Old man, the dead need no one, claim no kin.
Dim is the rumour of a common fight,   60
Where host meets host, and many names are sunk;
But of a single combat fame speaks clear."
  He spoke; and Peran-Wisa took the hand
Of the young man in his, and sigh'd, and said:—
  "O Sohrab, an unquiet heart is thine!
Canst thou not rest among the Tartar chiefs,
And share the battle's common chance with us
Who love thee, but must press for ever first,
In single fight incurring single risk,
To find a father thou hast never seen?   70
That were far best, my son, to stay with us
Unmurmuring; in our tents, while it is war,

---

40 *Samarcand:* Tartar capital.
42 *Ader-baijan:* province of Persia where Sohrab was reared.

And when 'tis truce, then in Afrasiab's towns.
But, if this one desire indeed rules all,
To seek out Rustum—seek him not through fight!
Seek him in peace, and carry to his arms,
O Sohrab, carry an unwounded son!
But far hence seek him, for he is not here.
For now it is not as when I was young,
When Rustum was in front of every fray;   80
But now he keeps apart, and sits at home,
In Seistan, with Zal, his father old.
Whether that his own mighty strength at last
Feels the abhorr'd approaches of old age,
Or in some quarrel with the Persian King.
There go!—Thou wilt not? Yet my heart forebodes
Danger or death awaits thee on this field.
Fain would I know thee safe and well, though lost
To us; fain therefore send thee hence, in peace
To seek thy father, not seek single fights   90
In vain;—but who can keep the lion's cub
From ravening, and who govern Rustum's son?
Go, I will grant thee what thy heart desires."
    So said he, and dropp'd Sohrab's hand, and left
His bed, and the warm rugs whereon he lay;
And o'er his chilly limbs his woollen coat
He pass'd, and tied his sandals on his feet,
And threw a white cloak round him, and he took
In his right hand a ruler's staff, no sword;
And on his head he set his sheep-skin cap,   100
Black, glossy, curl'd the fleece of Kara-Kul;
And rais'd the curtain of his tent, and call'd
His herald to his side, and went abroad.
    The sun by this had risen, and clear'd the fog
From the broad Oxus and the glittering sands.
And from their tents the Tartar horsemen filed
Into the open plain; so Haman bade—
Haman, who next to Peran-Wisa ruled
The host, and still was in his lusty prime.
From their black tents, long files of horse, they stream'd; 110
As when some grey November morn the files,

---

101 *Kara-Kul:* Asian lake on the banks of which lived the sheep from whose
pelts caracul is made.

In marching order spread, of long-neck'd cranes
Stream over Casbin and the southern slopes
Of Elburz, from the Aralian estuaries,
Or some frore Caspian reed-bed, southward bound
For the warm Persian sea-board—so they stream'd.
The Tartars of the Oxus, the King's guard,
First, with black sheep-skin caps and with long spears;
Large men, large steeds; who from Bokhara come
And Khiva, and ferment the milk of mares.   120
Next, the more temperate Toorkmuns of the south,
The Tukas, and the lances of Salore,
And those from Attruck and the Caspian sands;
Light men and on light steeds, who only drink
The acrid milk of camels, and their wells.
And then a swarm of wandering horse, who came
From far, and a more doubtful service own'd;
The Tartars of Ferghana, from the banks
Of the Jaxartes, men with scanty beards
And close-set skull-caps; and those wilder hordes   130
Who roam o'er Kipchak and the northern waste,
Kalmucks and unkempt Kuzzaks, tribes who stray
Nearest the Pole, and wandering Kirghizzes,
Who come on shaggy ponies from Pamere;
These all filed out from camp into the plain.
And on the other side the Persians form'd;—
First a light cloud of horse, Tartars they seem'd,
The Ilyats of Khorassan; and behind,
The royal troops of Persia, horse and foot,
Marshall'd battalions bright in burnish'd steel.   140
But Peran-Wisa with his herald came,
Threading the Tartar squadrons to the front,
And with his staff kept back the foremost ranks.
And when Ferood, who led the Persians, saw
That Peran-Wisa kept the Tartars back,
He took his spear, and to the front he came,
And check'd his ranks, and fix'd them where they stood.
And the old Tartar came upon the sand
Betwixt the silent host, and spake, and said:—
    "Ferood, and ye, Persians and Tartars, hear!   150

---

115 *frore:* frozen.

Let there be truce between the hosts to-day.
But choose a champion from the Persian lords
To fight our champion Sohrab, man to man."
　　As, in the country, on a morn in June,
When the dew glistens on the pearled ears,
A shiver runs through the deep corn for joy—
So, when they heard what Peran-Wisa said,
A thrill through all the Tartar squadrons ran
Of pride and hope for Sohrab, whom they loved.
　　But as a troop of pedlars, from Cabool,　　　　　160
Cross underneath the Indian Caucasus,
That vast sky-neighbouring mountain of milk snow;
Crossing so high, that, as they mount, they pass
Long flocks of travelling birds dead on the snow,
Choked by the air, and scarce can they themselves
Slake their parch'd throats with sugar'd mulberries—
In single file they move, and stop their breath,
For fear they should dislodge the o'erhanging snows—
So the pale Persians held their breath with fear.
　　And to Ferood his brother chiefs came up　　　　170
To counsel; Gudurz and Zoarrah came,
And Feraburz, who ruled the Persian host
Second, and was the uncle of the King;
These came and counsell'd, and then Gudurz said:—
　　"Ferood, shame bids us take their challenge up,
Yet champion have we none to match this youth.
He has the wild stag's foot, the lion's heart.
But Rustum came last night; aloof he sits
And sullen, and has pitch'd his tents apart.
Him will I seek, and carry to his ear　　　　　　　180
The Tartar challenge, and this young man's name.
Haply he will forget his wrath, and fight.
Stand forth the while, and take their challenge up."
　　So spake he; and Ferood stood forth and cried:—
"Old man, be it agreed as thou hast said!
Let Sohrab arm, and we will find a man."
　　He spake: and Peran-Wisa turn'd, and strode
Back through the opening squadrons to his tent.
But through the anxious Persians Gudurz ran,
And cross'd the camp which lay behind, and reach'd,　190
Out on the sands beyond it, Rustum's tents.

Of scarlet cloth they were, and glittering gay,
Just pitch'd; the high pavilion in the midst
Was Rustum's, and his men lay camp'd around.
And Gudurz enter'd Rustum's tent, and found
Rustum; his morning meal was done, but still
The table stood before him, charged with food—
A side of roasted sheep, and cakes of bread,
And dark green melons; and there Rustum sate
Listless, and held a falcon on his wrist,　　　200
And play'd with it; but Gudurz came and stood
Before him; and he look'd, and saw him stand,
And with a cry sprang up and dropp'd the bird,
And greeted Gudurz with both hands, and said:—
　　"Welcome! these eyes could see no better sight.
What news? but sit down first, and eat and drink."
　　But Gudurz stood in the tent-door, and said:—
"Not now! a time will come to eat and drink,
But not to-day; to-day has other needs.
The armies are drawn out, and stand at gaze;　　　210
For from the Tartars is a challenge brought
To pick a champion from the Persian lords
To fight their champion—and thou know'st his name—
Sohrab men call him, but his birth is hid.
O Rustum, like thy might is this young man's!
He has the wild stag's foot, the lion's heart;
And he is young, and Iran's chiefs are old,
Or else too weak; and all eyes turn to thee.
Come down and help us, Rustum, or we lose!"
　　He spoke; but Rustum answer'd with a smile:—　　　220
"Go to! if Iran's chiefs are old, then I
Am older; if the young are weak, the King
Errs strangely; for the King, for Kai Khosroo,
Himself is young, and honours younger men,
And lets the aged moulder to their graves.
Rustum he loves no more, but loves the young—
The young may rise at Sohrab's vaunts, not I.
For what care I, though all speak Sohrab's fame?
For would that I myself had such a son,
And not that one slight helpless girl I have—　　　230

217 *Iran:* Persia.

A son so famed, so brave, to send to war,
And I to tarry with the snow-hair'd Zal,
My father, whom the robber Afghans vex,
And clip his borders short, and drive his herds,
And he has none to guard his weak old age.
There would I go, and hang my armour up,
And with my great name fence that weak old man,
And spend the goodly treasures I have got,
And rest my age, and hear of Sohrab's fame,
And leave to death the hosts of thankless kings,   240
And with these slaughterous hands draw sword no more."
    He spoke, and smiled; and Gudurz made reply:—
"What then, O Rustum, will men say to this,
When Sohrab dares our bravest forth, and seeks
Thee most of all, and thou, whom most he seeks,
Hidest thy face? Take heed lest men should say:
Like some old miser, Rustum hoards his fame,
And shuns to peril it with younger men."
    And, greatly moved, then Rustum made reply:—
"O Gudurz, wherefore dost thou say such words?   250
Thou knowest better words than this to say.
What is one more, one less, obscure or famed,
Valiant or craven, young or old, to me?
Are not they mortal, am not I myself?
But who for men of nought would do great deeds?
Come, thou shalt see how Rustum hoards his fame!
But I will fight unknown, and in plain arms;
Let not men say of Rustum, he was match'd
In single fight with any mortal man."
    He spoke, and frown'd; and Gudurz turn'd, and ran   260
Back quickly through the camp in fear and joy—
Fear at his wrath, but joy that Rustum came.
But Rustum strode to his tent-door, and call'd
His followers in, and bade them bring his arms,
And clad himself in steel; the arms he chose
Were plain, and on his shield was no device,
Only his helm was rich, inlaid with gold,
And, from the fluted spine atop, a plume
Of horsehair waved, a scarlet horsehair plume.
So arm'd, he issued forth; and Ruksh, his horse,   270
Follow'd him like a faithful hound at heel—

Ruksh, whose renown was noised through all the earth,
The horse, whom Rustum on a foray once
Did in Bokhara by the river find
A colt beneath its dam, and drove him home,
And rear'd him; a bright bay, with lofty crest,
Dight with a saddle-cloth of broider'd green
Crusted with gold, and on the ground were work'd
All beasts of chase, all beasts which hunters know.
So follow'd, Rustum left his tents, and cross'd   280
The camp, and to the Persian host appear'd.
And all the Persians knew him, and with shouts
Hail'd; but the Tartars knew not who he was.
And dear as the wet diver to the eyes
Of his pale wife who waits and weeps on shore,   *Keats*
By sandy Bahrein, in the Persian Gulf,
Plunging all day in the blue waves, at night,
Having made up his tale of precious pearls,
Rejoins her in their hut upon the sands—
So dear to the pale Persians Rustum came.   290
     And Rustum to the Persian front advanced,
And Sohrab arm'd in Haman's tent, and came.
And as afield the reapers cut a swath
Down through the middle of a rich man's corn,
And on each side are squares of standing corn,
And in the midst a stubble, short and bare—
So on each side were squares of men, with spears
Bristling, and in the midst, the open sand.
And Rustum came upon the sand, and cast
His eyes toward the Tartar tents, and saw   300
Sohrab come forth, and eyed him as he came.
     As some rich woman, on a winter's morn,
Eyes through her silken curtains the poor drudge
Who with numb blacken'd fingers makes her fire—
At cock-crow, on a starlit winter's morn,
When the frost flowers the whiten'd window-panes—
And wonders how she lives, and what the thoughts
Of that poor drudge may be; so Rustum eyed
The unknown adventurous youth, who from afar
Came seeking Rustum, and defying forth   310

---

277 *Dight:* adorned.

All the most valiant chiefs; long he perused
His spirited air, and wonder'd who he was.
For very young he seem'd, tenderly rear'd;
Like some young cypress, tall, and dark, and straight,
Which in a queen's secluded garden throws
Its slight dark shadow on the moonlit turf,
By midnight, to a bubbling fountain's sound—
So slender Sohrab seem'd, so softly rear'd.
And a deep pity enter'd Rustum's soul
As he beheld him coming; and he stood,   320
And beckon'd to him with his hand, and said:—
   "O thou young man, the air of Heaven is soft,
And warm, and pleasant; but the grave is cold!
Heaven's air is better than the cold dead grave.
Behold me! I am vast, and clad in iron,
And tried; and I have stood on many a field
Of blood, and I have fought with many a foe—
Never was that field lost, or that foe saved.
O Sohrab, wherefore wilt thou rush on death?
Be govern'd! quit the Tartar host, and come   330
To Iran, and be as my son to me,
And fight beneath my banner till I die!
There are no youths in Iran brave as thou."
   So he spake, mildly; Sohrab heard his voice,
The mighty voice of Rustum, and he saw
His giant figure planted on the sand,
Sole, like some single tower, which a chief
Hath builded on the waste in former years
Against the robbers; and he saw that head,
Streak'd with its first grey hairs;—hope filled his soul,   340
And he ran forward and embraced his knees,
And clasp'd his hand within his own, and said:—
   "O, by thy father's head! by thine own soul!
Art thou not Rustum? speak! art thou not he?"
   But Rustum eyed askance the kneeling youth,
And turn'd away, and spake to his own soul:—
   "Ah me, I muse what this young fox may mean!
False, wily, boastful, are these Tartar boys.
For if I now confess this thing he asks,
And hide it not, but say: *Rustum is here!*   350
He will not yield indeed, nor quit our foes,

But he will find some pretext not to fight,
And praise my fame, and proffer courteous gifts,
A belt or sword perhaps, and go his way.
And on a feast-tide, in Afrasiab's hall,
In Samarcand, he will arise and cry:
'I challenged once, when the two armies camp'd
Beside the Oxus, all the Persian lords
To cope with me in single fight; but they
Shrank, only Rustum dared; then he and I   360
Changed gifts, and went on equal terms away.'
So will he speak, perhaps, while men applaud;
Then were the chiefs of Iran shamed through me."
        And then he turn'd, and sternly spake aloud:—
"Rise! wherefore dost thou vainly question thus
Of Rustum? I am here, whom thou hast call'd
By challenge forth; make good thy vaunt, or yield!
Is it with Rustum only thou wouldst fight?
Rash boy, men look on Rustum's face and flee!
For well I know, that did great Rustum stand   370
Before thy face this day, and were reveal'd,
There would be then no talk of fighting more.
But being what I am, I tell thee this—
Do thou record it in thine inmost soul:
Either thou shalt renounce thy vaunt and yield.
Or else thy bones shall strew this sand, till winds
Bleach them, or Oxus with his summer-floods,
Oxus in summer wash them all away."
        He spoke; and Sohrab answer'd, on his feet:—
"Art thou so fierce? Thou wilt not fright me so!   380
I am no girl, to be made pale by words.
Yet this thou hast said well, did Rustum stand
Here on this field, there were no fighting then.
But Rustum is far hence, and we stand here.
Begin! thou art more vast, more dread than I,
And thou art proved, I know, and I am young—
But yet success sways with the breath of Heaven.
And though thou thinkest that thou knowest sure
Thy victory, yet thou canst not surely know.
For we are all, like swimmers in the sea,   390
Poised on the top of a huge wave of fate,
Which hangs uncertain to which side to fall.

And whether it will heave us up to land,
Or whether it will roll us out to sea,
Back out to sea, to the deep waves of death,
We know not, and no search will make us know;
Only the event will teach us in its hour."
   He spoke, and Rustum answer'd not, but hurl'd
His spear; down from the shoulder, down it came,
As on some partridge in the corn a hawk,   400
That long has tower'd in the airy clouds,
Drops like a plummet; Sohrab saw it come,
And sprang aside, quick as a flash; the spear
Hiss'd, and went quivering down into the sand,
Which it sent flying wide;—then Sohrab threw
In turn, and full struck Rustum's shield; sharp rang,
The iron plates rang sharp, but turn'd the spear.
And Rustum seized his club, which none but he
Could wield; an unlopp'd trunk it was, and huge,
Still rough—like those which men in treeless plains   410
To build them boats fish from the flooded rivers,
Hyphasis or Hydaspes, when, high up
By their dark springs, the wind in winter-time
Hath made in Himalayan forests wrack,
And strewn the channels with torn boughs—so huge
The club which Rustum lifted now, and struck
One stroke; but again Sohrab sprang aside,
Lithe as the glancing snake, and the club came
Thundering to earth, and leapt from Rustum's hand.
And Rustum follow'd his own blow, and fell   420
To his knees, and with his fingers clutch'd the sand;
And now might Sohrab have unsheathed his sword,
And pierced the mighty Rustum while he lay
Dizzy, and on his knees, and choked with sand;
But he look'd on, and smiled, nor bared his sword,
But courteously drew back, and spoke, and said:—
   "Thou strik'st too hard! that club of thine will float
Upon the summer-floods, and not my bones.
But rise, and be not wroth! not wroth am I;
No, when I see thee, wrath forsakes my soul.   430
Thou say'st, thou art not Rustum; be it so!
Who art thou then, that canst so touch my soul?
Boy as I am, I have seen battles too—

Have waded foremost in their bloody waves,
And heard their hollow roar of dying men;
But never was my heart thus touch'd before.
Are they from Heaven, these softenings of the heart?
O thou old warrior, let us yield to Heaven!
Come, plant we here in earth our angry spears,
And make a truce, and sit upon this sand,
And pledge each other in red wine, like friends,   440
And thou shalt talk to me of Rustum's deeds.
There are enough foes in the Persian host,
Whom I may meet, and strike, and feel no pang;
Champions enough Afrasiab has, whom thou
Mayst fight; fight *them*, when they confront thy spear!
But oh, let there be peace 'twixt thee and me!"
    He ceased, but while he spake, Rustum had risen,
And stood erect, trembling with rage; his club
He left to lie, but had regain'd his spear   450
Whose fiery point now in his mail'd right-hand
Blazed bright and baleful, like that autumn-star,
The baleful sign of fevers; dust had soil'd
His stately crest, and dimm'd his glittering arms.
His breast heaved, his lips foam'd, and twice his voice
Was choked with rage; at last these words broke way:—
    "Girl! nimble with thy feet, not with thy hands!
Curl'd minion, dancer, coiner of sweet words!
Fight, let me hear thy hateful voice no more!
Thou art not in Afrasiab's gardens now   460
With Tartar girls, with whom thou art wont to dance;
But on the Oxus-sands, and in the dance
Of battle, and with me, who make no play
Of war; I fight it out, and hand to hand.
Speak not to me of truce, and pledge, and wine!
Remember all thy valour; try thy feints
And cunning! all the pity I had is gone;
Because thou hast shamed me before both the hosts
With thy light skipping tricks, and thy girl's wiles."
    He spoke, and Sohrab kindled at his taunts,   470
And he too drew his sword; at once they rush'd
Together, as two eagles on one prey

---

452 *autumn-star:* Sirius, the Dog Star, believed to cause fevers and to make dogs run mad.

Come rushing down together from the clouds,
One from the east, one from the west; their shields
Dash'd with a clang together, and a din
Rose, such as that the sinewy woodcutters
Make often in the forest's heart at morn,
Of hewing axes, crashing trees—such blows
Rustum and Sohrab on each other hail'd.
And you would say that sun and stars took part   480
In that unnatural conflict; for a cloud
Grew suddenly in Heaven, and dark'd the sun
Over the fighters' heads; and a wind rose
Under their feet, and moaning swept the plain,
And in a sandy whirlwind wrapp'd the pair.
In gloom they twain were wrapp'd, and they alone;
For both the on-looking hosts on either hand
Stood in broad daylight, and the sky was pure,
And the sun sparkled on the Oxus stream.
But in the gloom they fought, with bloodshot eyes   490
And labouring breath; first Rustum struck the shield
Which Sohrab held stiff out; the steel-spiked spear
Rent the tough plates, but fail'd to reach the skin,
And Rustum pluck'd it back with angry groan.
Then Sohrab with his sword smote Rustum's helm,
Nor clove its steel quite through; but all the crest
He shore away, and that proud horsehair plume,
Never till now defiled, sank to the dust;
And Rustum bow'd his head; but then the gloom
Grew blacker, thunder rumbled in the air,   500
And lightnings rent the cloud; and Ruksh, the horse,
Who stood at hand, utter'd a dreadful cry;—
No horse's cry was that, most like the roar
Of some pain'd desert-lion, who all day
Hath trail'd the hunter's javelin in his side,
And comes at night to die upon the sand.
The two hosts heard that cry, and quaked for fear,
And Oxus curdled as it cross'd his stream.
But Sohrab heard, and quail'd not, but rush'd on,
And struck again; and again Rustum bow'd   510
His head; but this time all the blade, like glass,
Sprang in a thousand shivers on the helm,
And in the hand the hilt remain'd alone.

Then Rustum raised his head; his dreadful eyes
Glared, and he shook on high his menacing spear,
And shouted: *Rustum!*—Sohrab heard that shout,
And shrank amazed; back he recoil'd one step,
And scann'd with blinking eyes the advancing form;
And then he stood bewilder'd; and he dropp'd
His covering shield, and the spear pierced his side.   520
He reel'd, and staggering back, sank to the ground;
And then the gloom dispersed, and the wind fell,
And the bright sun broke forth, and melted all
The cloud; and the two armies saw the pair—
Saw Rustum standing, safe upon his feet,
And Sohrab, wounded, on the bloody sand.
     Then, with a bitter smile, Rustum began:—
"Sohrab, thou thoughtest in thy mind to kill
A Persian lord this day, and strip his corpse,
And bear thy trophies to Afrasiab's tent.   530
Or else that the great Rustum would come down
Himself to fight, and that thy wiles would move
His heart to take a gift, and let thee go.
And then that all the Tartar host would praise
Thy courage or thy craft, and spread thy fame,
To glad thy father in his weak old age.
Fool, thou art slain, and by an unknown man!
Dearer to the red jackals shalt thou be
Than to thy friends, and to thy father old."
     And, with a fearless mien, Sohrab replied:—   540
"Unknown thou art; yet thy fierce vaunt is vain.
Thou dost not slay me, proud and boastful man!
No! Rustum slays me, and this filial heart.
For were I match'd with ten such men as thee,
And I were that which till to-day I was,
They should be lying here, I standing there.
But that belovèd name unnerved my arm—
That name, and something, I confess, in thee,
Which troubles all my heart, and made my shield
Fall; and thy spear transfix'd an unarm'd foe.   550
And now thou boastest, and insult'st my fate.
But hear thou this, fierce man, tremble to hear:
The mighty Rustum shall avenge my death!
My father, whom I seek through all the world,

He shall avenge my death, and punish thee!"
        As when some hunter in the spring hath found
A breeding eagle sitting on her nest,
Upon the craggy isle of a hill-lake,
And pierced her with an arrow as she rose,
And follow'd her to find her where she fell   560
Far off;—anon her mate comes winging back
From hunting, and a great way off descries
His huddling young left sole; at that, he checks
His pinion, and with short uneasy sweeps
Circles above his eyry, with loud screams
Chiding his mate back to her nest; but she
Lies dying, with the arrow in her side,
In some far stony gorge out of his ken,
A heap of fluttering feathers—never more
Shall the lake glass her, flying over it;   570
Never the black and dripping precipices
Echo her stormy scream as she sails by—
As that poor bird flies home, nor knows his loss,
So Rustum knew not his own loss, but stood
Over his dying son, and knew him not.
        But, with a cold incredulous voice, he said:—
"What prate is this of fathers and revenge?
The mighty Rustum never had a son."
        And, with a failing voice, Sohrab replied:—
"Ah yes, he had! and that lost son am I.   580
Surely the news will one day reach his ear,
Reach Rustum, where he sits, and tarries long,
Somewhere, I know not where, but far from here;
And pierce him like a stab, and make him leap
To arms, and cry for vengeance upon thee.
Fierce man, bethink thee, for an only son!
What will that grief, what will that vengeance be?
Oh, could I live, till I that grief had seen!
Yet him I pity not so much, but her,
My mother, who in Ader-baijan dwells   590
With that old king, her father, who grows grey
With age, and rules over the valiant Koords.
Her most I pity, who no more will see
Sohrab returning from the Tartar camp,
With spoils and honour, when the war is done.

But a dark rumour will be bruited up,
From tribe to tribe, until it reach her ear;
And then will that defenceless woman learn
That Sohrab will rejoice her sight no more,
But that in battle with a nameless foe,   600
By the far-distant Oxus, he is slain."
    He spoke; and as he ceased, he wept aloud,
Thinking of her he left, and his own death.
He spoke; but Rustum listen'd, plunged in thought.
Nor did he yet believe it was his son
Who spoke, although he call'd back names he knew;
For he had had sure tidings that the babe,
Which was in Ader-baijan born to him,
Had been a puny girl, no boy at all—
So that sad mother sent him word, for fear   610
Rustum should seek the boy, to train in arms.
And so he deem'd that either Sohrab took,
By a false boast, the style of Rustum's son;
Or that men gave it him, to swell his fame.
So deem'd he; yet he listen'd, plunged in thought
And his soul set to grief, as the vast tide
Of the bright rocking Ocean sets to shore
At the full moon; tears gather'd in his eyes;
For he remember'd his own early youth,
And all its bounding rapture; as, at dawn,   620
The shepherd from his mountain-lodge descries
A far, bright city, smitten by the sun,
Through many rolling clouds—so Rustum saw
His youth; saw Sohrab's mother, in her bloom;
And that old king, her father, who loved well
His wandering guest, and gave him his fair child
With joy; and all the pleasant life they led,
They three, in that long-distant summer-time—
The castle, and the dewy woods, and hunt
And hound, and morn on those delightful hills   630
In Ader-baijan. And he saw that youth,
Of age and looks to be his own dear son,
Piteous and lovely, lying on the sand,
Like some rich hyacinth which by the scythe
Of an unskilful gardener has been cut,
Mowing the garden grass-plots near its bed,

And lies, a fragrant tower of purple bloom,
On the mown, dying grass—so Sohrab lay,
Lovely in death, upon the common sand.
And Rustum gazed on him with grief, and said:— 640
    "O Sohrab, thou indeed art such a son
Whom Rustum, wert thou his, might well have loved.
Yet here thou errest, Sohrab, or else men
Have told thee false—thou art not Rustum's son.
For Rustum had no son; one child he had—
But one—a girl; who with her mother now
Plies some light female task, nor dreams of us—
Of us she dreams not, nor of wounds, nor war."
    But Sohrab answer'd him in wrath; for now
The anguish of the deep-fix'd spear grew fierce, 650
And he desired to draw forth the steel,
And let the blood flow free, and so to die—
But first he would convince his stubborn foe;
And, rising sternly on one arm, he said:—
    "Man, who art thou who dost deny my words?
Truth sits upon the lips of dying men,
And falsehood, while I lived, was far from mine.
I tell thee, prick'd upon this arm I bear
That seal which Rustum to my mother gave,
That she might prick it on the babe she bore." 660
    He spoke; and all the blood left Rustum's cheeks,
And his knees totter'd, and he smote his hand
Against his breast, his heavy mailed hand,
That the hard iron corslet clank'd aloud;
And to his heart he press'd the other hand,
And in a hollow voice he spake, and said:—
    "Sohrab, that were a proof which could not lie!
If thou show this, then art thou Rustum's son."
    Then, with weak hasty fingers, Sohrab loosed
His belt, and near the shoulder bared his arm, 670
And show'd a sign in faint vermilion points
Prick'd; as a cunning workman, in Pekin,
Pricks with vermilion some clear porcelain vase,
An emperor's gift—at early morn he paints,
And all day long, and, when night comes, the lamp
Lights up his studious forehead and thin hands—
So delicately prick'd the sign appear'd

On Sohrab's arm, the sign of Rustum's seal.
It was that griffin, which of old rear'd Zal,
Rustum's great father, whom they left to die,   680
A helpless babe, among the mountain-rocks;
Him that kind creature found, and rear'd, and loved—
Then Rustum took it for his glorious sign.
And Sohrab bared that image on his arm,
And himself scann'd it long with mournful eyes,
And then he touch'd it with his hand and said:—

   "How say'st thou? Is that sign the proper sign
Of Rustum's son, or of some other man's?"

   He spoke; but Rustum gazed, and gazed, and stood
Speechless; and then he utter'd one sharp cry: 690
O boy—thy father!—and his voice choked there.
And then a dark cloud pass'd before his eyes,
And his head swam, and he sank down to earth.
But Sohrab crawl'd to where he lay, and cast
His arms about his neck, and kiss'd his lips,
And with fond faltering fingers stroked his cheeks,
Trying to call him back to life; and life
Came back to Rustum, and he oped his eyes,
And they stood wide with horror; and he seized
In both his hands the dust which lay around,   700
And threw it on his head, and smirch'd his hair,—
His hair, and face, and beard, and glittering arms;
And strong convulsive groanings shook his breast,
And his sobs choked him; and he clutch'd his sword,
To draw it, and for ever let life out.
But Sohrab saw his thought, and held his hands,
And with a soothing voice he spake, and said:—

   "Father, forbear! for I but meet to-day
The doom which at my birth was written down
In Heaven, and thou art Heaven's unconscious hand.   710
Surely my heart cried out that it was thou,
When first I saw thee; and thy heart spoke too,
I know it! but fate trod those promptings down
Under its iron heel; fate, fate engaged
The strife, and hurl'd me on my father's spear.
But let us speak no more of this! I find
My father; let me feel that I have found!
Come, sit beside me on this sand, and take

My head betwixt thy hands and kiss my cheeks,
And wash them with thy tears, and say: *My son!*   720
Quick! quick! for number'd are my sands of life,
And swift; for like the lightning to this field
I came, and like the wind I go away—
Sudden, and swift, and like a passing wind.
But it was writ in Heaven that this should be."
　So said he, and his voice released the heart
Of Rustum, and his tears broke forth; he cast
His arms round his son's neck, and wept aloud,
And kiss'd him. And awe fell on both the hosts,
When they saw Rustum's grief; and Ruksh, the horse,   730
With his head bowing to the ground and mane
Sweeping the dust, came near, and in mute woe
First to the one then to the other moved
His head, as if inquiring what their grief
Might mean; and from his dark, compassionate eyes,
The big warm tears roll'd down, and caked the sand.
But Rustum chid him with stern voice, and said:—
　"Ruksh, now thou grievest; but, O Ruksh, thy feet
Should first have rotted on their nimble joints,
Or ere they brought thy master to this field!"   740
　But Sohrab look'd upon the horse and said;—
"Is this, then, Ruksh? How often, in past days,
My mother told me of thee, thou brave steed,
My terrible father's terrible horse! and said,
That I should one day find thy lord and thee.
Come, let me lay my hand upon thy mane!
O Ruksh, thou are more fortunate than I;
For thou hast gone where I shall never go,
And snuff'd the breezes of my father's home.
And thou hast trod the sands of Seistan,   750
And seen the River of Helmund, and the Lake
Of Zirrah; and the aged Zal himself
Has often stroked thy neck, and given thee food,
Corn in a golden platter soak'd with wine,
And said: *O Ruksh! bear Rustum well!*—but I
Have never known my grandsire's furrow'd face,
Nor seen his lofty house in Seistan,
Nor slaked my thirst at the clear Helmund stream;
But lodged among my father's foes, and seen

Afrasiab's cities only, Samarcand, 760
Bokhara, and lone Khiva in the waste,
And the black Toorkmun tents; and only drunk
The desert rivers, Moorghab and Tejend,
Kohik, and where the Kalmuks feed their sheep,
The northern Sir; and this great Oxus stream,
The yellow Oxus, by whose brink I die."
　　Then, with a heavy groan, Rustum bewail'd:—
"Oh, that its waves were flowing over me!
Oh, that I saw its grains of yellow silt
Roll tumbling in the current o'er my head!" 770
　　But, with a grave mild voice, Sohrab replied:—
"Desire not that, my father! thou must live.
For some are born to do great deeds, and live,
As some are born to be obscured, and die.
Do thou the deeds I die too young to do,
And reap a second glory in thine age;
Thou art my father, and thy gain is mine.
But come! thou seest this great host of men
Which follow me; I pray thee, slay not these!
Let me entreat for them; what have they done? 780
They follow'd me, my hope, my fame, my star.
Let them all cross the Oxus back in peace.
But me thou must bear hence, not send with them,
But carry me with thee to Seistan,
And place me on a bed, and mourn for me,
Thou, and the snow-hair'd Zal, and all thy friends.
And thou must lay me in that lovely earth,
And heap a stately mound above my bones,
And plant a far-seen pillar over all.
That so the passing horseman on the waste 790
May see my tomb a great way off, and cry:
Sohrab, the mighty Rustum's son, lies there,
Whom his great father did in ignorance kill!
And I be not forgotten in my grave."
　　And, with a mournful voice, Rustum replied:—
"Fear not! as thou hast said, Sohrab, my son,
So shall it be; for I will burn my tents,
And quit the host, and bear thee hence with me,
And carry thee away to Seistan,
And place thee on a bed, and mourn for thee, 800

With the snow-headed Zal, and all my friends.
And I will lay thee in that lovely earth,
And heap a stately mound above thy bones,
And plant a far-seen pillar over all,
And men shall not forget thee in thy grave.
And I will spare thy host; yea, let them go!
Let them all cross the Oxus back in peace!
What should I do with slaying any more?
For would that all whom I have ever slain
Might be once more alive; my bitterest foes,   810
And they who were call'd champions in their time,
And through whose death I won that fame I have—
And I were nothing but a common man,
A poor, mean soldier, and without renown,
So thou mightest live too, my son, my son!
Or rather would that I, even I myself,
Might now be lying on this bloody sand,
Near death, and by an ignorant stroke of thine,
Not thou of mine! and I might die, not thou;
And I, not thou, be borne to Seistan;   820
And Zal might weep above my grave, not thine;
And say: *O son, I weep thee not too sore,*
For willingly, I know, thou met'st thine end!
But now in blood and battles was my youth,
And full of blood and battles is my age,
And I shall never end this life of blood."
    Then, at the point of death, Sohrab replied:—
"A life of blood indeed, thou dreadful man!
But thou shalt yet have peace; only not now,
Not yet! but thou shalt have it on that day,   830
When thou shalt sail in a high-masted ship,
Thou and the other peers of Kai Khosroo,
Returning home over the salt blue sea,
From laying thy dear master in his grave."
    And Rustum gazed in Sohrab's face, and said:—
"Soon be that day, my son, and deep that sea!
Till then, if fate so wills, let me endure."
    He spoke; and Sohrab smiled on him, and took
The spear, and drew it from his side, and eased
His wound's imperious anguish; but the blood   840

Came welling from the open gash, and life
Flow'd with the stream;—all down his cold white side
The crimson torrent ran, dim now and soil'd,
Like the soil'd tissue of white violets
Left, freshly gather'd, on their native bank,
By children whom their nurses call with haste
Indoors from the sun's eye; his head droop'd low,
His limbs grew slack; motionless, white, he lay—
White, with eyes closed; only when heavy gasps,
Deep heavy gasps quivering through all his frame,   850
Convulsed him back to life, he open'd them,
And fix'd them feebly on his father's face;
Till now all strength was ebb'd, and from his limbs
Unwillingly the spirit fled away,
Regretting the warm mansion which it left,
And youth, and bloom, and this delightful world.
  So, on the bloody sand, Sohrab lay dead;
And the great Rustum drew his horseman's cloak
Down o'er his face, and sate by his dead son.
As those black granite pillars, once high-rear'd   860
By Jemshid in Persepolis, to bear
His house, now 'mid their broken flights of steps
Lie prone, enormous, down the mountain side—
So in the sand lay Rustum by his son.
  And night came down over the solemn waste,
And the two gazing hosts, and that sole pair,
And darken'd all; and a cold fog, with night,
Crept from the Oxus. Soon a hum arose,
As of a great assembly loosed, and fires
Began to twinkle through the fog; for now   870
Both armies moved to camp, and took their meal;
The Persians took it on the open sands
Southward, the Tartars by the river marge;
And Rustum and his son were left alone.
  But the majestic river floated on,
Out of the mist and hum of that low land,
Into the frosty starlight, and there moved,
Rejoicing, through the hush'd Chorasmian waste,

---

861 *Jemshid:* legendary king who founded the Persian capital, Persepolis.
878 *Chorasmian waste:* desert of Chorasmia.

Under the solitary moon;—he flow'd
Right for the polar star, past Orgunjè,   880
Brimming, and bright, and large; then sands begin
To hem his watery march, and dam his streams,
And split his currents; that for many a league
The shorn and parcell'd Oxus strains along
Through beds of sand and matted rushy isles—
Oxus, forgetting the bright speed he had
In his high mountain-cradle in Pamere,
A foil'd circuitous wanderer—till at last
The long'd-for dash of waves is heard, and wide
His luminous home of waters opens, bright   890
And tranquil, from whose floor the new-bathed stars
Emerge, and shine upon the Aral Sea.

[1853]

PHILOMELA

Hark! ah, the nightingale—
The tawny-throated!
Hark, from that moonlit cedar what a burst!
What triumph! hark!—what pain!
O wanderer from a Grecian shore,
Still, after many years, in distant lands,
Still nourishing in thy bewilder'd brain
That wild, unquench'd, deep-sunken, old-world pain—
Say, will it never heal?
And can this fragrant lawn   10
With its cool trees, and night,
And the sweet, tranquil Thames,
And moonshine, and the dew,

---

880 *Orgunjè:* a village on the Oxus.
Philomela: Of the several versions of the legend of Tereus, Arnold chose that
in which Tereus, king of Thrace, fell in love with Procne, sister of his queen
Philomela. Tereus cut out Procne's tongue after raping her, but she wove the
story of her outrage into a tapestry for Philomela, who then killed Itylus, the
king's son, and served him as food to his father. The sisters fled Daulis,
Tereus' capital, and when they were pursued, they prayed to become transformed into birds. Philomela became a nightingale, and Procne, a swallow.

To thy rack'd heart and brain
Afford no balm?

Dost thou to-night behold,
Here, through the moonlight on this English grass,
The unfriendly palace in the Thracian wild?
Dost thou again peruse
With hot cheeks and sear'd eyes   20
The too clear web, and thy dumb sister's shame?
Dost thou once more assay
Thy flight, and feel come over thee,
Poor fugitive, the feathery change
Once more, and once more seem to make resound
With love and hate, triumph and agony,
Lone Daulis, and the high Cephissian vale?
Listen, Eugenia—
How thick the bursts come crowding through the leaves!
Again—thou hearest?   30
Eternal passion!
Eternal pain!

                                        [1853]

REQUIESCAT

Strew on her roses, roses,
    And never a spray of yew!
In quiet she reposes;
    Ah, would that I did too!

Her mirth the world required;
    She bathed it in smiles of glee.
But her heart was tired, tired,
    And now they let her be.

Her life was turning, turning,
    In mazes of heat and sound.   10

---

27 *Cephissian vale:* valley of the river Cephissus.
Requiescat: may she rest (in peace).

But for peace her soul was yearning,
And now peace laps her round.

Her cabin'd, ample spirit,
It flutter'd and fail'd for breath.
To-night it doth inherit
The vasty hall of death.

[1853]

THE SCHOLAR-GIPSY *disinterested man*

Go, for they call you, shepherd, from the hill;
Go, shepherd, and untie the wattled cotes!
No longer leave thy wistful flock unfed,
Nor let thy bawling fellows rack their throats,
Nor the cropp'd herbage shoot another head.
But when the fields are still,
And the tired men and dogs all gone to rest,

The Scholar-Gipsy: Arnold prefixed the poem with the following note, drawn from Joseph Glanvil's *Vanity of Dogmatizing*, 1661:

There was very lately a lad in the University of Oxford, who was by his poverty forced to leave his studies there; and at last to join himself to a company of vagabond gipsies. Among these extravagant people, by the insinuating subtilty of his carriage, he quickly got so much of their love and esteem as that they discovered to him their mystery. After he had been a pretty while well exercised in the trade, there chanced to ride by a couple of scholars, who had formerly been of his acquaintance. They quickly spied out their old friend among the gipsies; and he gave them an account of the necessity which drove him to that kind of life, and told them that the people he went with were not such impostors as they were taken for, but that they had a traditional kind of learning among them, and could do wonders by the power of imagination, their fancy binding that of others: that himself had learned much of their art, and when he had compassed the whole secret, he intended, he said, to leave their company, and give the world an account of what he had learned.

The scene of the poem is the countryside around Oxford: the villages of Bab-lock-hithe, Fyfield, Godstow, and Hinksey; the woods of Wychwood, Bagley, and Thessaly; the hills of Cumner and the Hurst; and the river Thames winding through the valley in which these places are located.
2 *wattled cotes:* sheepcotes made of interlaced twigs.

And only the white sheep are sometimes seen
Cross and recross the strips of moon-blanch'd green,
Come, shepherd, and again begin the quest!   10

Here, where the reaper was at work of late—
    In this high field's dark corner, where he leaves
        His coat, his basket, and his earthen cruse,
    And in the sun all morning binds the sheaves,
        Then here, at noon, comes back his stores to use—
            Here will I sit and wait,
        While to my ear from uplands far away
        The bleating of the folded flocks is borne,
        With distant cries of reapers in the corn—
    All the live murmur of a summer's day.   20

Screen'd is this nook o'er the high, half-reap'd field,
    And here till sun-down, shepherd! will I be.
        Through the thick corn the scarlet poppies peep,
    And round green roots and yellowing stalks I see
        Pale pink convolvulus in tendrils creep;
            And air-swept lindens yield
        Their scent, and rustle down their perfumed showers
        Of bloom on the bent grass where I am laid,
        And bower me from the August sun with shade;
    And the eye travels down to Oxford's towers.   30

And near me on the grass lies Glanvil's book—
    Come, let me read the oft-read tale again!
        The story of the Oxford scholar poor,
    Of pregnant parts and quick inventive brain,
        Who, tired of knocking at preferment's door,
            One summer-morn forsook
        His friends, and went to learn the gipsy-lore,
        And roam'd the world with that wild brotherhood,
        And came, as most men deem'd, to little good,
    But came to Oxford and his friends no more.   40

But once, years after, in the country-lanes,
    Two scholars, whom at college erst he knew,

---

10 *quest:* i.e., for the Scholar-Gipsy.
13 *cruse:* jug.

Met him, and of his way of life enquired;
Whereat he answer'd, that the gipsy-crew,
His mates, had arts to rule as they desired
The workings of men's brains,
And they can bind them to what thoughts they will.
"And I," he said, "the secret of their art,
When fully learn'd, will to the world impart;
But it needs heaven-sent moments for this skill."   50

This said, he left them, and return'd no more.—
But rumours hung about the country-side,
That the lost Scholar long was seen to stray,
Seen by rare glimpses, pensive and tongue-tied,
In hat of antique shape, and cloak of grey,
The same the gipsies wore.
Shepherds had met him on the Hurst in spring;
At some lone alehouse in the Berkshire moors,
On the warm ingle-bench, the smock-frock'd boors
Had found him seated at their entering,   60

But, 'mid their drink and clatter, he would fly.
And I myself seem half to know thy looks,
And put the shepherds, wanderer! on thy trace;
And boys who in lone wheatfields scare the rooks
I ask if thou hast pass'd their quiet place;
Or in my boat I lie
Moor'd to the cool bank in the summer-heats,
'Mid wide grass meadows which the sunshine fills,
And watch the warm, green-muffled Cumner hills,
And wonder if thou haunt'st their shy retreats.   70

For most, I know, thou lov'st retired ground!
Thee at the ferry Oxford riders blithe,
Returning home on summer-nights, have met
Crossing the stripling Thames at Bab-lock-hithe,
Trailing in the cool stream thy fingers wet,
As the punt's rope chops round;
And leaning backward in a pensive dream,
And fostering in thy lap a heap of flowers

---

59 *boors*: yokels.

Pluck'd in shy fields and distant Wychwood bowers,
And thine eyes resting on the moonlit stream. 80

And then they land, and thou art seen no more!—
    Maidens, who from the distant hamlets come
        To dance around the Fyfield elm in May,
    Oft through the darkening fields have seen thee roam,
        Or cross a stile into the public way.
            Oft thou hast given them store
    Of flowers—the frail-leaf'd, white anemony,
        Dark bluebells drench'd with dews of summer eves,
        And purple orchises with spotted leaves—
    But none hath words she can report of thee. 90

And, above Godstow Bridge, when hay-time's here
    In June, and many a scythe in sunshine flames,
        Men who through those wide fields of breezy grass
    Where black-wing'd swallows haunt the glittering
            Thames,
        To bathe in the abandon'd lasher pass,
            Have often pass'd thee near
    Sitting upon the river bank o'ergrown;
        Mark'd thine outlandish garb, thy figure spare,
        Thy dark vague eyes, and soft abstracted air—
    But, when they came from bathing, thou wast gone! 100

At some lone homestead in the Cumner hills,
    Where at her open door the housewife darns,
        Thou hast been seen, or hanging on a gate
    To watch the threshers in the mossy barns.
        Children, who early range these slopes and late
            For cresses from the rills,
    Have known thee eying, all an April-day,
        The springing pastures and the feeding kine;
        And mark'd thee, when the stars come out and shine,
    Through the long dewy grass move slow away. 110

In autumn, on the skirts of Bagley Wood—
    Where most the gipsies by the turf-edged way

---

95 *lasher:* pool below a weir or dam.

Pitch their smoked tents, and every bush you see
With scarlet patches tagg'd and shreds of grey,
　　Above the forest-ground called Thessaly—
　　　The blackbird, picking food,
　　Sees thee, nor stops his meal, nor fears at all;
　　　So often has he known thee past him stray,
　　　Rapt, twirling in thy hand a wither'd spray,
　　And waiting for the spark from heaven to fall.　　120

And once, in winter, on the causeway chill
　　Where home through flooded fields foot-travellers go,
　　Have I not pass'd thee on the wooden bridge,
　　Wrapt in thy cloak and battling with the snow,
　　　Thy face tow'rd Hinksey and its wintry ridge?
　　　And thou hast climb'd the hill,
　　And gain'd the white brow of the Cumner range;
　　　Turn'd once to watch, while thick the snowflakes fall,
　　　The line of festal light in Christ-Church hall—
　　Then sought thy straw in some sequester'd grange.　　130

But what—I dream! Two hundred years are flown
　　Since first thy story ran through Oxford halls,
　　　And the grave Glanvil did the tale inscribe
　　That thou wert wander'd from the studious walls
　　　To learn strange arts, and join a gipsy-tribe;
　　　And thou from earth art gone
　　Long since, and in some quiet churchyard laid—
　　　Some country-nook, where o'er thy unknown grave
　　　Tall grasses and white flowering nettles wave,
　　Under a dark, red-fruited yew-tree's shade.　　140

—No, no, thou hast not felt the lapse of hours!
　　For what wears out the life of mortal men?
　　　'Tis that from change to change their being rolls;
　　　'Tis that repeated shocks, again, again,
　　　　Exhaust the energy of strongest souls
　　　　　And numb the elastic powers.
　　Till having used our nerves with bliss and teen,
　　　And tired upon a thousand schemes our wit,

---

129 *Christ-Church hall:* dining hall in Christ Church, an Oxford college.
147 *teen:* suffering.

To the just-pausing Genius we remit
Our worn-out life, and are—what we have been. 150

Thou hast not lived, why should'st thou perish, so?
Thou hadst *one* aim, *one* business, *one* desire;
Else wert thou long since number'd with the dead!
Else hadst thou spent, like other men, thy fire!
The generations of thy peers are fled,
And we ourselves shall go;
But thou possessest an immortal lot,
And we imagine thee exempt from age
And living as thou liv'st on Glanvil's page,
Because thou hadst—what we, alas! have not. 160

For early didst thou leave the world, with powers
Fresh, undiverted to the world without,
Firm to their mark, not spent on other things;
Free from the sick fatigue, the languid doubt,
Which much to have tried, in much been baffled,
brings.
O life unlike to ours!
Who fluctuate idly without term or scope,
Of whom each strives, nor knows for what he strives,
And each half lives a hundred different lives;
Who wait like thee, but not, like thee, in hope. 170

Thou waitest for the spark from heaven! and we,
Light half-believers of our casual creeds,
Who never deeply felt, nor clearly will'd,
Whose insight never has borne fruit in deeds,
Whose vague resolves never have been fulfill'd;
For whom each year we see
Breeds new beginnings, disappointments new;
Who hesitate and falter life away,
And lose to-morrow the ground won to-day—
Ah! do not we, wanderer! await it too? 180

Yes, we await it!—but it still delays,
And then we suffer! and amongst us one,

---

149 *just-pausing Genius:* i.e., the soul of the world, from which man's spirit
comes, scarcely pauses in taking it back at his death.

Who most has suffer'd, takes dejectedly *to Tennyson*
His seat upon the intellectual throne;
   And all his store of sad experience he
      Lays bare of wretched days;
Tells us his misery's birth and growth and signs,
   And how the dying spark of hope was fed,
   And how the breast was soothed, and how the head,
And all his hourly varied anodynes.   190

This for our wisest! and we others pine,
   And wish the long unhappy dream would end,
      And waive all claim to bliss, and try to bear;
   With close-lipp'd patience for our only friend,
      Sad patience, too near neighbour to despair—
         But none has hope like thine!
Thou through the fields and through the woods dost
         stray,
   Roaming the country-side, a truant boy,
   Nursing thy project in unclouded joy,
And every doubt long blown by time away.   200

O born in days when wits were fresh and clear,
   And life ran gaily as the sparkling Thames;
      Before this strange disease of modern life,
   With its sick hurry, its divided aims,
      Its heads o'ertax'd, its palsied hearts, was rife—
         Fly hence, our contact fear!
Still fly, plunge deeper in the bowering wood!
   Averse, as Dido did with gesture stern
   From her false friend's approach in Hades turn,
Wave us away, and keep thy solitude!   210

Still nursing the unconquerable hope,
   Still clutching the inviolable shade,
      With a free, onward impulse brushing through,
   By night, the silver'd branches of the glade—
      Far on the forest-skirts, where none pursue.

---

191 *our wisest:* presumably an ironic reference to Tennyson as one "who most has suffered."
208 *Dido:* In Hades, Dido, queen of Carthage, turned away from the shade of Aeneas, whose faithlessness had caused her suicide.

On some mild pastoral slope
Emerge, and resting on the moonlit pales
Freshen thy flowers as in former years
With dew, or listen with enchanted ears,
From the dark dingles, to the nightingales!   220

[Keats ode to Nightingale]

But fly our paths, our feverish contact fly!
For strong the infection of our mental strife,
Which, though it gives no bliss, yet spoils for rest;
And we should win thee from thy own fair life,
Like us distracted, and like us unblest.
Soon, soon thy cheer would die,
Thy hopes grow timorous, and unfix'd thy powers,
And thy clear aims be cross and shifting made;
And then thy glad perennial youth would fade,
Fade, and grow old at last, and die like ours.   230

Then fly our greetings, fly our speech and smiles!
—As some grave Tyrian trader, from the sea,
Descried at sunrise an emerging prow
Lifting the cool-hair'd creepers stealthily,
The fringes of a southward-facing brow
Among the Ægæan isles;
And saw the merry Grecian coaster come,
Freighted with amber grapes, and Chian wine,
Green, bursting figs, and tunnies steep'd in brine—
And knew the intruders on his ancient home.   240

The young light-hearted masters of the waves—
And snatch'd his rudder, and shook out more sail;
And day and night held on indignantly
O'er the blue Midland waters with the gale,
Betwixt the Syrtes and soft Sicily,
To where the Atlantic raves

217 *pales:* fences.
220 *dingles:* wooded glens.
232 *Tyrian:* from the Phoenician city of Tyre, chief commercial center of the
Mediterranean before the rise of the Greeks.
238 *Chian:* from the Greek island of Chios.
239 *tunnies:* tuna.
245 *Syrtes:* Gulf of Sidra on north coast of Africa.

Outside the western straits; and unbent sails
  There, where down cloudy cliffs, through sheets of
    foam,
Shy traffickers, the dark Iberians come;
And on the beach undid his corded bales.   250

[1853]

Salvation not in committing from — but fleeing untempted 1850's

STANZAS FROM
THE GRANDE CHARTREUSE

Through Alpine meadows soft-suffused
With rain, where thick the crocus blows,
Past the dark forges long disused,
The mule-track from Saint Laurent goes.
The bridge is cross'd, and slow we ride,
Through forest, up the mountain-side.

The autumnal evening darkens round,
The wind is up, and drives the rain;
While, hark! far down, with strangled sound
Doth the Dead Guier's stream complain,   10
Where that wet smoke, among the woods,
Over his boiling cauldron broods.

Swift rush the spectral vapours white
Past limestone scars with ragged pines,
Showing—then blotting from our sight!—
Halt—through the cloud-drift something shines!
High in the valley, wet and drear,
The huts of Courrerie appear.

Strike leftward! cries our guide; and higher
Mounts up the stony forest-way.   20

247 *straits:* of Gibraltar.
249 *Iberians:* people of Iberia, the Spanish peninsula.
Stanzas from the Grande Chartreuse: In 1851 Arnold visited the Carthusian monastery, La Grande Chartreuse, near Grenoble in the French Alps; not far away were the villages of St. Laurent and Courrerie and the river Guiers Mort.

At last the encircling trees retire;
Look! through the showery twilight grey
What pointed roofs are these advance?—
A palace of the Kings of France?

Approach, for what we seek is here!
Alight, and sparely sup, and wait
For rest in this outbuilding near;
Then cross the sward and reach that gate.
Knock; pass the wicket! Thou art come
To the Carthusians' world-famed home.

The silent courts, where night and day
Into their stone-carved basins cold
The splashing icy fountains play—
The humid corridors behold!
Where, ghostlike in the deepening night,
Cowl'd forms brush by in gleaming white.

The chapel, where no organ's peal
Invests the stern and naked prayer—
With penitential cries they kneel
And wrestle; rising then, with bare   40
And white uplifted faces stand,
Passing the Host from hand to hand;

Each takes, and then his visage wan
Is buried in his cowl once more.
The cells!—the suffering Son of Man
Upon the wall—the knee-worn floor—
And where they sleep, that wooden bed,
Which shall their coffin be, when dead!

The library, where tract and tome
Not to feed priestly pride are there,   50
To hymn the conquering march of Rome,
Nor yet to amuse, as ours are!

---

42 *Host:* consecrated wafer in the Mass. Arnold was mistaken in thinking
that it was passed from hand to hand and that it was taken standing.
48 *coffin:* Once more Arnold was wrong in detail, for the Carthusians did not
sleep in their coffins.

They paint of souls the inner strife,
Their drops of blood, their death in life.

The garden, overgrown—yet mild,
See, fragrant herbs are flowering there!
Strong children of the Alpine wild
Whose culture is the brethren's care;
Of human tasks their only one,
And cheerful works beneath the sun.   60

Those halls, too, destined to contain
Each its own pilgrim-host of old,
From England, Germany, or Spain—
All are before me! I behold
The House, the Brotherhood austere!
—And what am I, that I am here?

For rigorous teachers seized my youth,
And purged its faith, and trimm'd its fire,
Show'd me the high, white star of Truth,
There bade me gaze, and there aspire.   70
Even now their whispers pierce the gloom:
What dost thou in this living tomb?

Forgive me, masters of the mind!
At whose behest I long ago
So much unlearnt, so much resign'd—
I come not here to be your foe!
I seek these anchorites, not in ruth,
To curse and to deny your truth;

Not as their friend, or child, I speak!
But as, on some far northern strand,   80
Thinking of his own Gods, a Greek
In pity and mournful awe might stand
Before some fallen Runic stone—
For both were faiths, and both are gone.

---

73 *masters of the mind:* rationalists.
77 *anchorites:* hermits. *ruth:* remorse (for rationalist faith).
83 *Runic stone:* one covered with early Germanic inscriptions.

Wandering between two worlds, one dead,
The other powerless to be born,
With nowhere yet to rest my head,
Like these, on earth I wait forlorn.
Their faith, my tears, the world deride—
I come to shed them at their side.   90

Oh, hide me in your gloom profound,
Ye solemn seats of holy pain!
Take me, cowl'd forms, and fence me round,
Till I possess my soul again;
Till free my thoughts before me roll,
Not chafed by hourly false control!

For the world cries your faith is now
But a dead time's exploded dream;
My melancholy, sciolists say,
Is a pass'd mode, an outworn theme—   100
As if the world had ever had
A faith, or sciolists been sad!

Ah, if it *be* pass'd, take away,
At least, the restlessness, the pain;
Be man henceforth no more a prey
To these out-dated stings again!
The nobleness of grief is gone—
Ah, leave us not the fret alone!

But—if you cannot give us ease—
Last of the race of them who grieve   110
Here leave us to die out with these
Last of the people who believe!
Silent, while years engrave the brow;
Silent—the best are silent now.

Achilles ponders in his tent,
The kings of modern thought are dumb;
Silent they are, though not content,
And wait to see the future come.

---

99 *sciolists:* men of superficial learning.
115 *Achilles:* who sulked in his tent and refused action.

They have the grief men had of yore,
But they contend and cry no more.   120

Our fathers water'd with their tears
This sea of time whereon we sail,
Their voices were in all men's ears
Who pass'd within their puissant hail.
Still the same ocean round us raves,
But we stand mute, and watch the waves.

For what avail'd it, all the noise
And outcry of the former men?—
Say, have their sons achieved more joys,
Say, is life lighter now than then?   130
The sufferers died, they left their pain—
The pangs which tortured them remain.

What helps it now, that Byron bore,
With haughty scorn which mock'd the smart,
Through Europe to the Ætolian shore
The pageant of his bleeding heart?
That thousands counted every groan,
And Europe made his woe her own?

What boots it, Shelley! that the breeze
Carried thy lovely wail away,   140
Musical through Italian trees
Which fringe thy soft blue Spezzian bay?
Inheritors of thy distress
Have restless hearts one throb the less?

Or are we easier, to have read,
O Obermann! the sad, stern page,
Which tells us how thou hidd'st thy head
From the fierce tempest of thine age
In the lone brakes of Fontainebleau,
Or chalets near the Alpine snow?   150

---

133 *Byron:* Cut off from England by his reputation, he died in Missolonghi in the Greek region of Ætolia.
139 *Shelley:* who was drowned in the Bay of Spezzia.
146 *Obermann:* central figure in a philosophic romance of that name by Etienne Pivert de Senancour (1770-1846).

Ye slumber in your silent grave!—
The world, which for an idle day
Grace to your mood of sadness gave,
Long since hath flung her weeds away.
The eternal trifler breaks your spell;
But we—we learnt your lore too well!

Years hence, perhaps, may dawn an age,
More fortunate, alas! than we,
Which without hardness will be sage,
And gay without frivolity.   160
Sons of the world, oh, speed those years;
But, while we wait, allow our tears!

Allow them! We admire with awe
The exulting thunder of your race;
You give the universe your law,
You triumph over time and space!
Your pride of life, your tireless powers,
We laud them, but they are not ours.

We are like children rear'd in shade
Beneath some old-world abbey wall,   170
Forgotten in a forest-glade,
And secret from the eyes of all.
Deep, deep the greenwood round them waves,
Their abbey, and its close of graves!

But, where the road runs near the stream,
Oft through the trees they catch a glance
Of passing troops in the sun's beam—
Pennon, and plume, and flashing lance!
Forth to the world those soldiers fare,
To life, to cities, and to war!   180

And through the wood, another way,
Faint bugle-notes from far are borne,
Where hunters gather, staghounds bay,
Round some fair forest-lodge at morn.

---

154 *weeds:* mourning garments.

Gay dames are there, in sylvan green;
Laughter and cries—those notes between!

The banners flashing through the trees
Make their blood dance and chain their eyes;
That bugle-music on the breeze
Arrests them with a charm'd surprise.   190
Banner by turns and bugle woo:
Ye shy recluses, follow too!

O children, what do ye reply?—
"Action and pleasure, will ye roam
Through these secluded dells to cry
And call us?—but too late ye come!
Too late for us your call ye blow,
Whose bent was taken long ago.

"Long since we pace this shadow'd nave;
We watch those yellow tapers shine,   200
Emblems of hope over the grave,
In the high altar's depth divine;
The organ carries to our ear
Its accents of another sphere.

"Fenced early in this cloistral round
Of reverie, of shade, of prayer,
How should we grow in other ground?
How can we flower in foreign air?
—Pass, banners, pass, and bugles, cease;
And leave our desert to its peace!"   210

[1855]

THYRSIS

A Monody, to Commemorate the Author's Friend,
Arthur Hugh Clough,
Who Died at Florence, 1861

How changed is here each spot man makes or fills!
  In the two Hinkseys nothing keeps the same;
    The village street its haunted mansion lacks,
  And from the sign is gone Sibylla's name,
    And from the roofs the twisted chimney-stacks—
      Are ye too changed, ye hills?
  See, 'tis no foot of unfamiliar men
    To-night from Oxford up your pathway strays!
  Here came I often, often, in old days—
Thyrsis and I; we still had Thyrsis then.   10

Runs it not here, the track by Childsworth Farm,
  Past the high wood, to where the elm-tree crowns
    The hill behind whose ridge the sunset flames?
  The signal-elm, that looks on Ilsley Downs,
    The Vale, the three lone weirs, the youthful Thames?—
      This winter-eve is warm,
  Humid the air! leafless, yet soft as spring,
    The tender purple spray on copse and briers!
  And that sweet city with her dreaming spires,
She needs not June for beauty's heightening,   20

Lovely all times she lies, lovely to-night!—
  Only, methinks, some loss of habit's power
    Befalls me wandering through this upland dim.
  Once pass'd I blindfold here, at any hour;
    Now seldom come I, since I came with him.

Thyrsis: a conventional classical name for a shepherd in pastoral poetry.
Here Arnold applies it to Clough, as he uses Corydon, another such name,
for himself. The poem, a monody (or elegy), should be read in conjunction
with "The Scholar-Gipsy," which sets the background, both physical and
thematic, for this companion-piece.
2 *two Hinkseys:* North and South Hinksey, villages near Oxford. In the latter
Sibella Kerr kept an inn until her death in 1860.
19 *sweet city:* Oxford.

Signal-elm
title of Gipsy-scholar

That single elm-tree bright
Against the west—I miss it! is it gone?
We prized it dearly; while it stood, we said,
Our friend, the Gipsy-Scholar, was not dead;
While the tree lived, he in these fields lived on.   30

Too rare, too rare, grow now my visits here,
But once I knew each field, each flower, each stick;
And with the country-folk acquaintance made
By barn in threshing-time, by new-built rick.
Here, too, our shepherd-pipes we first assay'd.
Ah me! this many a year

no longer writes poetry

My pipe is lost, my shepherd's holiday!
Needs must I lose them, needs with heavy heart
Into the world and wave of men depart;
But Thyrsis of his own will went away.   40

It irk'd him to be here, he could not rest.
He loved each simple joy the country yields,
He loved his mates; but yet he could not keep,
For that a shadow lour'd on the fields,
Here with the shepherds and the silly sheep.
Some life of men unblest

yrs of agnosticism

He knew, which made him droop, and fill'd his head.
He went; his piping took a troubled sound
Of storms that rage outside our happy ground;
He could not wait their passing, he is dead.   50

So, some tempestuous morn in early June,
When the year's primal burst of bloom is o'er,
Before the roses and the longest day—
When garden-walks and all the grassy floor
With blossoms red and white of fallen May
And chestnut-flowers are strewn—
So have I heard the cuckoo's parting cry,

---

35 *shepherd-pipes:* attempts at poetry.
40 *went away:* Clough left Oxford in 1849 in a dispute over his religious orthodoxy.
45 *silly:* simple.
49 *storms:* perhaps European political troubles, but more probably the storms of religious and social controversies.
52 *primal:* of spring.

From the wet field, through the vext garden-trees,
Come with the volleying rain and tossing breeze:
The bloom is gone, and with the bloom go I! 60

Too quick despairer, wherefore wilt thou go? *Cuckoo like Keats nightingale*
Soon will the high Midsummer pomps come on,
Soon will the musk carnations break and swell,
Soon shall we have gold-dusted snapdragon,
Sweet-William with his homely cottage-smell,
And stocks in fragrant blow;
Roses that down the alleys shine afar,
And open, jasmine-muffled lattices,
And groups under the dreaming garden-trees,
And the full moon, and the white evening-star. 70

He hearkens not! light comer, he is flown!
What matters it? next year he will return,
And we shall have him in the sweet spring-days,
With whitening hedges, and uncrumpling fern,
And blue-bells trembling by the forest-ways,
And scent of hay new-mown.
But Thyrsis never more we swains shall see;
See him come back, and cut a smoother reed,
And blow a strain the world at last shall heed— *Thyrsis not*
For Time, not Corydon, hath conquer'd thee! 80 *come back like cuckoo*

Alack, for Corydon no rival now!—
But when Sicilian shepherds lost a mate,
Some good survivor with his flute would go,
Piping a ditty sad for Bion's fate;
And cross the unpermitted ferry's flow,
And relax Pluto's brow,
And make leap up with joy the beauteous head
Of Proserpine, among whose crowned hair
Are flowers first open'd on Sicilian air,
And flute his friend, like Orpheus, from the dead. 90

---

84 *Bion:* Greek poet of Sicily, on whose death his friend Moschus wrote a lament.
85 *unpermitted ferry:* across the river Styx to Hades, ruled by Pluto and his queen, Proserpine, who came from Enna, a region in central Sicily.
90 *Orpheus:* who gained the release from Hades of his wife, Eurydice, by the beauty of his music.

O easy access to the hearer's grace
　　When Dorian shepherds sang to Proserpine!
　　　For she herself had trod Sicilian fields,
　　She knew the Dorian water's gush divine,
　　　She knew each lily white which Enna yields,
　　　　Each rose with blushing face;
　　She loved the Dorian pipe, the Dorian strain.
　　　But ah, of our poor Thames she never heard!
　　　Her foot the Cumner cowslips never stirr'd;
　　And we should tease her with our plaint in vain!　　100

Well! wind-dispersed and vain the words will be,
　　Yet, Thyrsis, let me give my grief its hour
　　　In the old haunt, and find our tree-topp'd hill!
　　Who, if not I, for questing here hath power?
　　　I know the wood which hides the daffodil,
　　　　I know the Fyfield tree,
　　I know what white, what purple fritillaries
　　　The grassy harvest of the river-fields,
　　　Above by Ensham, down by Sandford, yields,
　　And what sedged brooks are Thames's tributaries;　　110

I know these slopes; who knows them if not I?—
　　But many a dingle on the loved hill-side,
　　　With thorns once studded, old, white-blossom'd trees,
　　Where thick the cowslips grew, and far descried
　　　High tower'd the spikes of purple orchises,
　　　　Hath since our day put by
　　The coronals of that forgotten time;
　　　Down each green bank hath gone the ploughboy's
　　　　team,
　　　And only in the hidden brookside gleam
　　Primroses, orphans of the flowery prime.　　120

Where is the girl, who by the boatman's door,
　　Above the locks, above the boating throng,
　　　Unmoor'd our skiff when through the Wytham flats,
　　Red loosestrife and blond meadow-sweet among
　　　And darting swallows and light water-gnats,

---

92 *Dorian:* Bion, Moschus, and Theocritus wrote in simple, straightforward Doric Greek.

We track'd the shy Thames shore?
Where are the mowers, who, as the tiny swell
  Of our boat passing heaved the river-grass,
  Stood with suspended scythe to see us pass?—
They all are gone, and thou art gone as well!   130

Yes, thou art gone! and round me too the night *growing old*
  In ever-nearing circle weaves her shade.
    I see her veil draw soft across the day,
  I feel her slowly chilling breath invade
    The cheek grown thin, the brown hair sprent with
        grey;
      I feel her finger light
  Laid pausefully upon life's headlong train;—
    The foot less prompt to meet the morning dew,
    The heart less bounding at emotion new,
  And hope, once crush'd, less quick to spring again.   140

And long the way appears, which seem'd so short
  To the less practised eye of sanguine youth;
    And high the mountain-tops, in cloudy air,
  The mountain-tops where is the throne of Truth,
    Tops in life's morning-sun so bright and bare!
      Unbreachable the fort
  Of the long-batter'd world uplifts its wall;
    And strange and vain the earthly turmoil grows,
    And near and real the charm of thy repose,
  And night as welcome as a friend would fall.   150

But hush! the upland hath a sudden loss
  Of quiet!—Look, adown the dusk hill-side,
    A troop of Oxford hunters going home,
  As in old days, jovial and talking, ride!
    From hunting with the Berkshire hounds they come.
      Quick! let me fly, and cross
  Into yon farther field!—'Tis done; and see,
    Back'd by the sunset, which doth glorify
    The orange and pale violet evening-sky,
  Bare on its lonely ridge, the Tree! the Tree!   160

---

135 *sprent:* sprinkled.

I take the omen! Eve lets down her veil,
  The white fog creeps from bush to bush about,
    The west unflushes, the high stars grow bright,
And in the scatter'd farms the lights come out.
) I cannot reach the signal-tree to-night,
    Yet, happy omen, hail!
Hear it from thy broad lucent Arno-vale
  (For there thine earth-forgetting eyelids keep
  The morningless and unawakening sleep
Under the flowery oleanders pale),   170

Hear it, O Thyrsis, still our tree is there!—
  Ah, vain! These English fields, this upland dim,
  These brambles pale with mist engarlanded,
That lone, sky-pointing tree, are not for him;
  To a boon southern country he is fled,
    And now in happier air,
Wandering with the great Mother's train divine
  (And purer or more subtle soul than thee,
  I trow, the mighty Mother doth not see)
Within a folding of the Apennine,   180

Thou hearest the immortal chants of old!—
  Putting his sickle to the perilous grain
    In the hot cornfield of the Phrygian king,

---

[167] *Arno-vale:* Clough died in Florence in the valley of the Arno.
[171] *our tree is there:* It has disappeared since Arnold's day.
[177] *Mother:* Nature.
[183] *Phrygian:* Arnold's own note explains this stanza:

Daphnis, the ideal Sicilian shepherd of Greek pastoral poetry,
was said to have followed into Phrygia his mistress Piplea, who had
been carried off by robbers, and to have found her in the power of
the king of Phrygia, Lityerses. Lityerses used to make strangers try
a contest with him in reaping corn, and to put them to death if he
overcame them. Hercules arrived in time to save Daphnis, took
upon himself the reaping-contest with Lityerses, overcame him,
and slew him. The Lityerses-song connected with this tradition
was, like the Linus-song, one of the early plaintive strains of Greek
popular poetry, and used to be sung by corn-reapers. Other traditions represented Daphnis as beloved by a nymph who exacted
from him an oath to love no one else. He fell in love with a princess, and was struck blind by the jealous nymph. Mercury, who was
his father, raised him to Heaven, and made a fountain spring up in
the place from which he ascended. At this fountain the Sicilians
offered yearly sacrifices.

For thee the Lityerses-song again
   Young Daphnis with his silver voice doth sing;
      Sings his Sicilian fold,
His sheep, his hapless love, his blinded eyes—
   And how a call celestial round him rang,
   And heavenward from the fountain-brink he sprang,
And all the marvel of the golden skies.   190

There thou art gone, and me thou leavest here
   Sole in these fields! yet will I not despair.
      Despair I will not, while I yet descry
   'Neath the mild canopy of English air
      That lonely tree against the western sky.
       Still, still these slopes, 'tis clear,
Our Gipsy-Scholar haunts, outliving thee!
   Fields where soft sheep from cages pull the hay,
   Woods with anemonies in flower till May,
Know him a wanderer still; then why not me?   200

A fugitive and gracious light he seeks,
   Shy to illumine; and I seek it too.
      This does not come with houses or with gold,
   With place, with honour, and a flattering crew;
      'Tis not in the world's market bought and sold—
      But the smooth-slipping weeks
Drop by, and leave its seeker still untired;
   Out of the heed of mortals he is gone,
   He wends unfollow'd, he must house alone;
Yet on he fares, by his own heart inspired.   210

Thou too, O Thyrsis, on like quest wast bound;
   Thou wanderedst with me for a little hour!
      Men gave thee nothing; but this happy quest,
   If men esteem'd thee feeble, gave thee power,
      If men procured thee trouble, gave thee rest.
      And this rude Cumner ground,
Its fir-topped Hurst, its farms, its quiet fields,
   Here cam'st thou in thy jocund youthful time,
   Here was thine height of strength, thy golden prime!
And still the haunt beloved a virtue yields.   220

What though the music of thy rustic flute
  Kept not for long its happy, country tone;
    Lost it too soon, and learnt a stormy note
Of men contention-tost, of men who groan,
    Which task'd thy pipe too sore, and tired thy throat—
      It fail'd, and thou wast mute!
  Yet hadst thou alway visions of our light,
    And long with men of care thou couldst not stay,
    And soon thy foot resumed its wandering way,
  Left human haunt, and on alone till night.   230

Too rare, too rare, grow now my visits here!
  'Mid city-noise, not, as with thee of yore,
    Thyrsis! in reach of sheep-bells is my home.
  —Then through the great town's harsh, heart-wearying
      roar,
    Let in thy voice a whisper often come,
      To chase fatigue and fear:
  Why faintest thou? I wander'd till I died.
    Roam on! The light we sought is shining still.
    Dost thou ask proof? Our tree yet crowns the hill,
  Our Scholar travels yet the loved hill-side.   240

                                              [1866]

AUSTERITY OF POETRY

    That son of Italy who tried to blow,
    Ere Dante came, the trump of sacred song,
    In his light youth amid a festal throng
    Sate with his bride to see a public show.

    Fair was the bride, and on her front did glow
    Youth like a star; and what to youth belong—
    Gay raiment, sparkling gauds, elation strong.
    A prop gave way! crash fell a platform! lo,

---

1 *son of Italy:* Giacopone di Todi.

'Mid struggling sufferers, hurt to death, she lay!
Shuddering, they drew her garments off—and found
A robe of sackcloth next the smooth, white skin.

Such, poets, is your bride, the Muse! young, gay,
Radiant, adorn'd outside; a hidden ground
Of thought and of austerity within.

[1867]

DOVER BEACH

The sea is calm to-night.
The tide is full, the moon lies fair
Upon the straits;—on the French coast the light
Gleams and is gone; the cliffs of England stand,
Glimmering and vast, out in the tranquil bay.
Come to the window, sweet is the night-air!
Only, from the long line of spray
Where the sea meets the moon-blanch'd land,
Listen! you hear the grating roar
Of pebbles which the waves draw back, and fling,
At their return, up the high strand,
Begin, and cease, and then again begin,
With tremulous cadence slow, and bring
The eternal note of sadness in.

Sophocles long ago
Heard it on the Ægæan, and it brought
Into his mind the turbid ebb and flow
Of human misery; we
Find also in the sound a thought,
Hearing it by this distant northern sea.

The Sea of Faith
Was once, too, at the full, and round earth's shore
Lay like the folds of a bright girdle furl'd.

---

15 *Sophocles:* The reference is probably to a chorus of *Antigone*, ll. 583 ff.

But now I only hear
Its melancholy, long, withdrawing roar,
Retreating, to the breath
Of the night-wind, down the vast edges drear
And naked shingles of the world.

Ah, love, let us be true
To one another! for the world, which seems   30
To lie before us like a land of dreams,
So various, so beautiful, so new,
Hath really neither joy, nor love, nor light,
Nor certitude, nor peace, nor help for pain;
And we are here as on a darkling plain
Swept with confused alarms of struggle and flight,
Where ignorant armies clash by night.

                                                    [1867]

PALLADIUM

Set where the upper streams of Simois flow
Was the Palladium, high 'mid rock and wood;
And Hector was in Ilium, far below,
And fought, and saw it not—but there it stood!

It stood, and sun and moonshine rain'd their light
On the pure columns of its glen-built hall.
Backward and forward roll'd the waves of fight
Round Troy—but while this stood, Troy could not fall.

So, in its lovely moonlight, lives the soul.
Mountains surround it, and sweet virgin air;   10
Cold plashing, past it, crystal waters roll;
We visit it by moments, ah, too rare!

---

28 *shingles:* beaches covered with coarse stones.
Palladium: statue of Pallas Athena, protectress of Troy (Ilium); while it
stood, Troy was safe, but the city fell when it was stolen.
1 *Simois:* one of the two major rivers of Troy; the other was the Xanthus.

We shall renew the battle in the plain
To-morrow;—red with blood will Xanthus be;
Hector and Ajax will be there again,
Helen will come upon the wall to see.

Then we shall rust in shade, or shine in strife,
And fluctuate 'twixt blind hopes and blind despairs,
And fancy that we put forth all our life,
And never know how with the soul it fares.   20

Still doth the soul, from its lone fastness high,
Upon our life a ruling effluence send.
And when it fails, fight as we will, we die;
And while it lasts, we cannot wholly end.

[1867]

RUGBY CHAPEL

November, 1857

Coldly, sadly descends
The autumn-evening. The field
Strewn with its dank yellow drifts
Of wither'd leaves, and the elms,
Fade into dimness apace,
Silent;—hardly a shout
From a few boys late at their play!
The lights come out in the street,
In the school-room windows;—but cold,
Solemn, unlighted, austere,   10
Through the gathering darkness, arise
The chapel-walls, in whose bound
Thou, my father! art laid.

There thou dost lie, in the gloom
Of the autumn evening. But ah!
That word, *gloom*, to my mind

Rugby Chapel: the burial place of Thomas Arnold, who died in 1842.

Brings thee back, in the light
Of thy radiant vigour, again;
In the gloom of November we pass'd
Days not dark at thy side;   20
Seasons impair'd not the ray
Of thy buoyant cheerfulness clear.
Such thou wast! and I stand
In the autumn evening, and think
Of bygone autumns with thee.

Fifteen years have gone round
Since thou arosest to tread,
In the summer-morning, the road
Of death, at a call unforeseen,
Sudden. For fifteen years,   30
We who till then in thy shade
Rested as under the boughs
Of a mighty oak, have endured
Sunshine and rain as we might,
Bare, unshaded, alone,
Lacking the shelter of thee.

O strong soul, by what shore
Tarriest thou now? For that force,
Surely, has not been left vain!
Somewhere, surely, afar,   40
In the sounding labour-house vast
Of being, is practised that strength,
Zealous, beneficent, firm!

Yes, in some far-shining sphere,
Conscious or not of the past,
Still thou performest the word
Of the Spirit in whom thou dost live—
Prompt, unwearied, as here!
Still thou upraisest with zeal
The humble good from the ground,   50
Sternly repressest the bad!
Still, like a trumpet, dost rouse
Those who with half-open eyes

Tread the border-land dim
'Twixt vice and virtue; reviv'st,
Succourest!—this was thy work,
This was thy life upon earth.

What is the course of the life
Of mortal men on the earth?—
Most men eddy about   60
Here and there—eat and drink,
Chatter and love and hate,
Gather and squander, are raised
Aloft, are hurl'd in the dust,
Striving blindly, achieving
Nothing; and then they die—
Perish;—and no one asks
Who or what they have been,
More than he asks what waves,
In the moonlit solitudes mild   70
Of the midmost Ocean, have swell'd,
Foam'd for a moment, and gone.

And there are some, whom a thirst
Ardent, unquenchable, fires,
Not with the crowd to be spent,
Not without aim to go round
In an eddy of purposeless dust,
Effort unmeaning and vain.
Ah yes! some of us strive
Not without action to die   80
Fruitless, but something to snatch
From dull oblivion, nor all
Glut the devouring grave!
We, we have chosen our path—
Path to a clear-purposed goal,
Path of advance!—but it leads
A long, steep journey, through sunk
Gorges, o'er mountains in snow.
Cheerful, with friends, we set forth—
Then, on the height, comes the storm.   90
Thunder crashes from rock

To rock, the cataracts reply,
Lightnings dazzle our eyes.
Roaring torrents have breach'd
The track, the stream-bed descends
In the place where the wayfarer once
Planted his footstep—the spray
Boils o'er its borders! aloft
The unseen snow-beds dislodge
Their hanging ruin; alas,   100
Havoc is made in our train!
Friends, who set forth at our side,
Falter, are lost in the storm
We, we only are left!
With frowning foreheads, with lips
Sternly compress'd, we strain on,
On—and at nightfall at last
Come to the end of our way,
To the lonely inn 'mid the rocks;
Where the gaunt and taciturn host   110
Stands on the threshold, the wind
Shaking his thin white hairs—
Holds his lantern to scan
Our storm-beat figures, and asks:
Whom in our party we bring?
Whom we have left in the snow?

Sadly we answer: We bring
Only ourselves! we lost
Sight of the rest in the storm.
Hardly ourselves we fought through,   120
Stripp'd, without friends, as we are.
Friends, companions, and train,
The avalanche swept from our side.

But thou would'st not *alone*
Be saved, my father! *alone*
Conquer and come to thy goal,
Leaving the rest in the wild.
We were weary, and we
Fearful, and we in our march

Fain to drop down and to die. 130
Still thou turnedst, and still
Beckonedst the trembler, and still
Gavest the weary thy hand.

If, in the paths of the world,
Stones might have wounded thy feet,
Toil or dejection have tried
Thy spirit, of that we saw
Nothing—to us thou wast still
Cheerful, and helpful, and firm!
Therefore to thee it was given 140
Many to save with thyself;
And, at the end of thy day,
O faithful shepherd! to come,
Bringing thy sheep in thy hand.

And through thee I believe
In the noble and great who are gone;
Pure souls honour'd and blest
By former ages, who else—
Such, so soulless, so poor,
Is the race of men whom I see— 150
Seem'd but a dream of the heart,
Seem'd but a cry of desire.
Yes! I believe that there lived
Others like thee in the past,
Not like the men of the crowd
Who all round me to-day
Bluster or cringe, and make life
Hideous, and arid, and vile;
But souls temper'd with fire,
Fervent, heroic, and good, 160
Helpers and friends of mankind.

Servants of God!—or sons
Shall I not call you? because
Not as servants ye knew
Your Father's innermost mind,
His, who unwillingly sees

One of his little ones lost—
Yours is the praise, if mankind
Hath not as yet in its march
Fainted, and fallen, and died!

170

See! In the rocks of the world
Marches the host of mankind,
A feeble, wavering line.
Where are they tending?—A God
Marshall'd them, gave them their goal.
Ah, but the way is so long!
Years they have been in the wild!
Sore thirst plagues them, the rocks,
Rising all round, overawe;
Factions divide them, their host
Threatens to break, to dissolve.
—Ah, keep, keep them combined!
Else, of the myriads who fill
That army, not one shall arrive;
So they shall stray; in the rocks
Stagger for ever in vain,
Die one by one in the waste.

180

Then, in such hour of need
Of your fainting, dispirited race,
Ye, like angels, appear,
Radiant with ardour divine!
Beacons of hope, ye appear!
Languor is not in your heart,
Weakness is not in your word,
Weariness not on your brow.
Ye alight in our van! at your voice,
Panic, despair, flee away.
Ye move through the ranks, recall
The stragglers, refresh the outworn,
Praise, re-inspire the brave!
Order, courage, return.
Eyes rekindling, and prayers,
Follow your steps as ye go.
Ye fill up the gaps in our files,
Strengthen the wavering line,

19/

200

Stablish, continue our march,
On, to the bound of the waste,
On, to the City of God.

[1867]

George Meredith

[1828-1909]

George Meredith was born in Portsmouth, the only son of intelligent, cultivated parents whose aristocratic appearance belied the fact that Mrs. Meredith was the daughter of an innkeeper, and her husband the son of a tailor who catered chiefly to naval officers. Meredith's father had begun medical training as a young man but was called back to Portsmouth to take over the family shop; he was, unfortunately, a poor businessman, and the family prosperity soon declined. The Merediths had moved in spheres of English society normally closed to tailors and their families, and Meredith himself was abnormally sensitive to social distinctions. In his maturity he successfully conveyed the impression to the world at large that he was the illegitimate son of aristocratic parents, and it was only after his death that the true story of his birth and family became public knowledge.

As a boy, Meredith was brought up in Portsmouth to look and act like a gentleman's son, a rearing which removed him from his contemporaries and made him a lonely child. In 1842 he was sent to a Moravian school on the Rhine, near Coblenz, where he stayed for about two years. After his return to London, where his father had moved the family tailoring establishment, Meredith became articled as a clerk in a solicitor's office in 1846, but he never practiced law. In later years he was a reader for the publishers Chapman and Hall, and he wrote for both the provincial and London newspapers.

In 1849, at the age of twenty-one, Meredith married Mary Ellen Peacock Nicolls, a beautiful widow some nine years older than he, the daughter of the novelist Thomas Love Peacock. The marriage was never a smooth one, although the couple had many tastes in common, including writing, on which they sometimes collaborated. In 1851 Meredith published his first volume, *Poems,* but it was not a great success with either critics or public, although it contained the first version of "Love in the Valley," the most popular of his early poems. Both Merediths were nervous and irritable, and they were miserably poor. Of their several children, only one survived infancy. The couple quarrelled frequently, and Mrs. Meredith may have been unfaithful to her husband. The agony of two intelligent, overly sensitive persons loving but constantly misunderstanding each other prompted Meredith's long poem, *Modern Love,* which is partially a record of his own marriage. In 1858 Mrs. Meredith deserted her husband and small son to run away with a painter. Meredith was deeply hurt and did not forgive his wife even when she returned to England to die. After her death in 1861, he realized that the failure of their marriage was probably as much his fault as that of Mrs. Meredith; there are hints of his awareness of his own guilt in *Modern Love,* as well as in such novels as *The Ordeal of Richard Feverel* and *The Egoist.* The difficulties of marriages between ill-matched couples remained one of his constant themes in the many novels he wrote. Their succession of intellectual, emancipated heroines probably owes something in inspiration to the first Mrs. Meredith.

Although the 1851 volume of poems and *Modern Love and Poems of the English Roadside* were followed by several other major volumes of poetry, Meredith's reputation during his lifetime was made chiefly by his novels. He wrote fiction prolifically, but he deliberately conceded little to the taste of either critics or reading public. His mannered obscurity and his irony alienated many of his contemporaries and have kept his novels from wide popularity even today.

After the death of his wife, Meredith for a time shared a house in Chelsea with Swinburne and Rossetti, but the casual manners of the others soon forced him to move. In 1864 he married Marie Vulliamy and found the happiness he had never known with his first wife. Not long after their marriage, Meredith and his new wife settled in Flint Cottage, Box Hill, Surrey, where the rest of his life was spent. Meredith had always loved the out-of-doors, which gave him the imagery for so much of his poetry, and at Box Hill he could spend hours striding through the woods and over the Surrey hills, finding in nature the calm he too-infrequently saw in persons around him.

In spite of the perplexity which his poetry and novels produced in his readers, Meredith continued writing until almost the end of his life. In 1885 his novel, *Diana of the Crossways*, became his first big popular success. In 1892 he received an honorary degree from St. Andrews University, and in 1905 he was decorated by King Edward. At his death in 1909, he was generally regarded as a great writer, but he remained an enigma to the general public, who could understand neither his reserved personality nor his complex works. Today, when irony and detachment are more common in literature than they were a century ago, Meredith seems less baffling, but it is unlikely that his works will ever be general favorites, for he remains a special and cultivated taste, unfit, by his own claim, for the consumption of "little people or for fools."

Some of the difficulties in Meredith's poetry can be resolved by a knowledge of his essay, *On the Idea of Comedy*, still one of the greatest critical works in English on the comic spirit, "the laughter of the mind." For Meredith, no subject, however tragic or pathetic it might appear from another point of view, was invulnerable to comedy whenever the actions or the characters offended "sound reason, fair justice; are false in humility or mined with conceit," or when they proceeded from egoism. His own first marriage, surely the most disastrous event of his life, provided the inspiration for *Modern Love*. The protagonist (who doubles as third-person narrator) is consumed with sorrow at his own inability and that of his wife to repair their crumbling marriage. Each is tortured by the memory of their happy past, each is racked by physical need for the other, and each seeks happiness in an extra-marital affair. As the husband finally comes to a recognition of his own share of guilt in the wreck of their lives and feels a resurgence of love for his wife, she commits suicide in order to free him for his mistress. Yet, throughout the pathetic tale, Meredith is conscious of the comedy of the pretensions of husband and wife. The laughter is not easy;

it is "often no more than a smile." But behind the tragedy there is always a hint of the high comedy which a detached observer can see in those absurdities of the human race that tug us to our ruin. The mixture of viewpoints is complex, for Meredith found life complex. It was their inability to follow the quick-silver tergiversations of Meredith's mind that so perplexed many of his contemporaries.

If *Modern Love* is in some respects a comedy, it is also much more than that. It is, of course, a narrative told in lyric form, in Meredith's own version of the sonnet sequence. The point of view in the sixteen-line "sonnets" is constantly changing; the many reiterated images shift their meaning and accrue significance of more than one kind. The poem was for the Victorians, too, a study of what modern marriage might become when woman's position gradually became equal with that of her husband. But what has made this a continually fascinating poem is probably the enormous depth of psychological perception Meredith shows into the relations between two persons longing for unity but prevented by their own minds and desires from ever finding it. It is no exaggeration to say that Meredith has put as much insight into these half-hundred lyrics as went into one of his long, complicated novels.

In *Modern Love*, laughing nature says, "I play for Seasons; not Eternities!" For Meredith, coming into maturity with the advent of Darwinism, there were no certainties save the certainty of change. If he could no longer believe in the God of an earlier generation, he looked to nature (which he preferred to call "Earth") for a guide to man's actions. But nature is changeful, even capricious, and man can never hope to understand her completely. "The army of unalterable law" that Lucifer contemplates is "the brain of heaven," yet it is not essentially different from the wilful earth-goddess of "Love in the Valley," who is made to bruise and bless equally. To man, there appears to be only flux; beneath it lies a sureness that he can never understand intellectually but only accept joyously. In "The Woods of Westermain," Meredith is most explicit about the necessity for man to submit to the eternal and inscrutable ways of nature, accepting her processes without either fear or egoism; then will "blood and brain and spirit . . . join for true felicity." Only in this way can man hope to find happiness.

BIBLIOGRAPHY

The standard edition is *The Poetical Works of George Meredith*, With Some Notes by G. M. Trevelyan (Scribner, New York, 1928).

Biography and Criticism:

Kelvin, Norman, *A Troubled Eden: Nature and Society in the Works of George Meredith*. Stanford University Press, Stanford, 1961.

Lindsay, Jack, *George Meredith, His Life and Work*. Bodley Head, London, 1956.

Modern Love, intr. C. Day Lewis. Hart-Davis, London, 1948.

Priestley, J. B., *George Meredith*. Macmillan, London, 1926.

Sassoon, Siegfried, *Meredith*. Constable, London, 1948.

Stevenson, Lionel, *The Ordeal of George Meredith*. Scribner, New York, 1953.

Trevelyan, G. M., *The Poetry and Philosophy of George Meredith*. Constable, London, 1916.

LOVE IN THE VALLEY

Under yonder beech-tree single on the green-sward,
    Couched with her arms behind her golden head,
Knees and tresses folded to slip and ripple idly,
    Lies my young love sleeping in the shade.
Had I the heart to slide an arm beneath her,
    Press her parting lips as her waist I gather slow,
Waking in amazement she could not but embrace me:
    Then would she hold me and never let me go?

      · · · · ·

Shy as the squirrel and wayward as the swallow,
    Swift as the swallow along the river's light   10
Circleting the surface to meet his mirrored winglets,
    Fleeter she seems in her stay than in her flight.
Shy as the squirrel that leaps among the pine-tops,
    Wayward as the swallow overhead at set of sun,
She whom I love is hard to catch and conquer,
    Hard, but O the glory of the winning were she won!

      · · · · ·

When her mother tends her before the laughing mirror,
    Tying up her laces, looping up her hair,
Often she thinks, were this wild thing wedded,
    More love should I have, and much less care.   20
When her mother tends her before the lighted mirror,
    Loosening her laces, combing down her curls,
Often she thinks, were this wild thing wedded,
    I should miss but one for many boys and girls.

      · · · · ·

Heartless she is as the shadow in the meadows
    Flying to the hills on a blue and breezy noon.
No, she is athirst and drinking up her wonder:
    Earth to her is young as the slip of the new moon.
Deals she an unkindness, 'tis but her rapid measure,

Even as in a dance; and her smile can heal no less: 30
Like the swinging May-cloud that pelts the flowers with
 hailstones
Off a sunny border, she was made to bruise and bless.

. . . . .

Lovely are the curves of the white owl sweeping
 Wavy in the dusk lit by one large star.
Lone on the fir-branch, his rattle-note unvaried,
 Brooding o'er the gloom, spins the brown eve-jar.
Darker grows the valley, more and more forgetting:
 So were it with me if forgetting could be willed.
Tell the grassy hollow that holds the bubbling well-spring
 Tell it to forget the source that keeps it filled.   40

. . . . .

Stepping down the hill with her fair companions,
 Arm in arm, all against the raying West,
Boldly she sings, to the merry tune she marches,
 Brave in her shape, and sweeter unpossessed.
Sweeter, for she is what my heart first awaking
 Whispered the world was; morning light is she.
Love that so desires would fain keep her changeless;
 Fain would fling the net, and fain have her free.

. . . . .

Happy happy time, when the white star hovers
 Low over dim fields fresh with bloomy dew,   50
Near the face of dawn, that draws athwart the darkness,
 Threading it with colour, like yewberries the yew.
Thicker crowd the shades as the grave East deepens
 Glowing, and with crimson a long cloud swells.
Maiden still the morn is; and strange she is, and secret;
 Stranger her eyes; her cheeks are cold as cold sea-shells.

. . . . .

Sunrays, leaning on our southern hills and lighting
 Wild cloud-mountains that drag the hills along,
Oft ends the day of your shifting brilliant laughter
 Chill as a dull face frowning on a song.   60

---

36 *eve-jar*: the goatsucker, a nocturnal bird.

Ay, but shows the South-West a ripple-feathered bosom
    Blown to silver while the clouds are shaken and ascend
Scaling the mid-heavens as they stream, there comes a sunset
    Rich, deep like love in beauty without end.

        .   .   .   .   .

When at dawn she sighs, and like an infant to the window
    Turns grave eyes craving light, released from dreams,
Beautiful she looks, like a white water-lily
    Bursting out of bud in havens of the streams.
When from bed she rises clothed from neck to ankle
    In her long nightgown sweet as boughs of May,   70
Beautiful she looks, like a tall garden lily
    Pure from the night, and splendid for the day.

        .   .   .   .   .

Mother of the dews, dark eye-lashed twilight,
    Low-lidded twilight, o'er the valley's brim,
Rounding on thy breast sings the dew-delighted skylark,
    Clear as though the dewdrops had their voice in him.
Hidden where the rose-flush drinks the rayless planet,
    Fountain-full he pours the spraying fountain-showers.
Let me hear her laughter, I would have her ever
    Cool as dew in twilight, the lark above the flowers.   80

        .   .   .   .   .

All the girls are out with their baskets for the primrose;
    Up lanes, woods through, they troop in joyful bands.
My sweet leads: she knows not why, but now she loiters,
    Eyes the bent anemones, and hangs her hands.
Such a look will tell that the violets are peeping,
    Coming the rose: and unaware a cry
Springs in her bosom for odours and for colour,
    Covert and the nightingale; she knows not why.

        .   .   .   .   .

Kerchiefed head and chin she darts between her tulips,
    Streaming like a willow grey in arrowy rain: 90
Some bend beaten cheek to gravel, and their angel
    She will be; she lifts them, and on she speeds again.

---

77 *rose-flush . . . planet:* light of dawn makes the star pale.

Black the driving raincloud breasts the iron gateway:
  She is forth to cheer a neighbour lacking mirth.
So when sky and grass met rolling dumb for thunder
  Saw I once a white dove, sole light of earth.

· · · · ·

Prim little scholars are the flowers of her garden,
  Trained to stand in rows, and asking if they please.
I might love them well but for loving more the wild ones:
  O my wild ones! they tell me more than these.   100
You, my wild one, you tell of honied field-rose,
  Violet, blushing eglantine in life; and even as they,
They by the wayside are earnest of your goodness,
  You are of life's on the banks that line the way.

· · · · ·

Peering at her chamber the white crowns the red rose,
  Jasmine winds the porch with stars two and three.
Parted is the window; she sleeps; the starry jasmine
  Breathes a falling breath that carries thoughts of me.
Sweeter unpossessed, have I said of her my sweetest?
  Not while she sleeps: while she sleeps the jasmine
    breathes,   110
Luring her to love; she sleeps; the starry jasmine
  Bears me to her pillow under white rose-wreaths.

· · · · ·

Yellow with birdfoot-trefoil are the grass-glades;
  Yellow with cinquefoil of the dew-grey leaf;
Yellow with stonecrop; the moss-mounds are yellow;
  Blue-necked the wheat sways, yellowing to the sheaf.
Green-yellow bursts from the copse the laughing yaffle;
  Sharp as a sickle is the edge of shade and shine:
Earth in her heart laughs looking at the heavens,
  Thinking of the harvest: I look and think of mine.   120

· · · · ·

---

113 *birdfoot-trefoil:* a three-lobed fern.
114 *cinquefoil:* plants with five-lobed leaves.
117 *yaffle:* green woodpecker, known by his laughing cry.

This I may know: her dressing and undressing
   Such a change of light shows as when the skies in sport
Shift from cloud to moonlight; or edging over thunder
   Slips a ray of sun; or sweeping into port
White sails furl; or on the ocean borders
   White sails lean along the waves leaping green.
Visions of her shower before me, but from eyesight
   Guarded she would be like the sun were she seen.

     • • • • •

Front door and back of the mossed old farmhouse
   Open with the morn, and in a breezy link   130
Freshly sparkles garden to stripe-shadowed orchard,
   Green across a rill where on sand the minnows wink.
Busy in the grass the early sun of summer
   Swarms, and the blackbird's mellow fluting notes
Call my darling up with round and roguish challenge:
   Quaintest, richest carol of all the singing throats!

     • • • • •

Cool was the woodside; cool as her white dairy
   Keeping sweet the cream-pan; and there the boys from
     school,
Cricketing below, rushed brown and red with sunshine;
   O the dark translucence of the deep-eyed cool!   140
Spying from the farm, herself she fetched a pitcher
   Full of milk, and tilted for each in turn the beak.
Then a little fellow, mouth up and on tiptoe,
   Said, "I will kiss you": she laughed and leaned her cheek.

     • • • • •

Doves of the fir-wood walling high our red roof
   Through the long noon coo, crooning through the coo.
Loose droop the leaves, and down the sleepy roadway
   Sometimes pipes a chaffinch; loose droops the blue.
Cows flap a slow tail knee-deep in the river,
   Breathless, given up to sun and gnat and fly.   150
Nowhere is she seen; and if I see her nowhere,
   Lightning may come, straight rains and tiger sky.

---

130 *link:* land lying near water.

. . . . .

O the golden sheaf, the rustling treasure-armful!
  O the nutbrown tresses nodding interlaced!
O the treasure-tresses one another over
  Nodding! O the girdle slack about the waist!
Slain are the poppies that shot their random scarlet
  Quick amid the wheatears: wound about the waist,
Gathered, see these brides of Earth one blush of ripeness!
  O the nutbrown tresses nodding interlaced!   160

. . . . .

Large and smoky red the sun's cold disk drops,
  Clipped by naked hills, on violet shaded snow:
Eastward large and still lights up a bower of moonrise,
  Whence at her leisure steps the moon aglow.
Nightlong on black print-branches our beech-tree
  Gazes in this whiteness: nightlong could I.
Here may life on death or death on life be painted.
  Let me clasp her soul to know she cannot die!

. . . . .

Gossips count her faults; they scour a narrow chamber
  Where there is no window, read not heaven or her.   170
"When she was a tiny," one aged woman quavers,
  Plucks at my heart and leads me by the ear.
Faults she had once as she learnt to run and tumbled:
  Faults of feature some see, beauty not complete.
Yet, good gossips, beauty that makes holy
  Earth and air, may have faults from head to feet.

. . . . .

Hither she comes; she comes to me; she lingers,
  Deepens her brown eyebrows, while in new surprise
High rise the lashes in wonder of a stranger;
  Yet am I the light and living of her eyes.   180
Something friends have told her fills her heart to brimming,
  Nets her in her blushes, and wounds her, and tames.—
Sure of her haven, O like a dove alighting,
  Arms up, she dropped: our souls were in our names.

. . . . .

Soon will she lie like a white-frost sunrise.
   Yellow oats and brown wheat, barley pale as rye,
Long since your sheaves have yielded to the thresher,
   Felt the girdle loosened, seen the tresses fly.
Soon will she lie like a blood-red sunset.
   Swift with the to-morrow, green-winged Spring!   190
Sing from the South-West, bring her back the truants,
   Nightingale and swallow, song and dipping wing.

         • • • • •

Soft new beech-leaves, up to beamy April
   Spreading bough on bough a primrose mountain, you,
Lucid in the moon, raise lilies to the skyfields,
   Youngest green transfused in silver shining through:
Fairer than the lily, than the wild white cherry:
   Fair as in image my seraph love appears
Borne to me by dreams when dawn is at my eyelids:
   Fair as in the flesh she swims to me on tears.   200

         • • • • •

Could I find a place to be alone with heaven,
   I would speak my heart out: heaven is my need.
Every woodland tree is flushing like the dogwood,
   Flashing like the whitebeam, swaying like the reed.
Flushing like the dogwood crimson in October;
   Streaming like the flag-reed South-West blown;
Flashing as in gusts the sudden-lighted whitebeam:
   All seem to know what is for heaven alone.

                          [1851, 1878]

JUGGLING JERRY

I

Pitch here the tent, while the old horse grazes:
   By the old hedge-side we'll halt a stage.
It's nigh my last above the daisies:
   My next leaf'll be man's blank page.

Yes, my old girl! and it's no use crying:
    Juggler, constable, king, must bow.
One that outjuggles all's been spying
    Long to have me, and he has me now.

II

We've travelled times to this old common:
    Often we've hung our pots in the gorse.   10
We've had a stirring life, old woman!
    You, and I, and the old grey horse.
Races, and fairs, and royal occasions,
    Found us coming to their call:
Now they'll miss us at our stations:
    There's a Juggler outjuggles all!

III

Up goes the lark, as if all were jolly!
    Over the duck-pond the willow shakes.
Easy to think that grieving's folly,
    When the hand's firm as driven stakes!   20
Ay, when we're strong, and braced, and manful,
    Life's a sweet fiddle: but we're a batch
Born to become the Great Juggler's han'ful:
    Balls he shies up, and is safe to catch.

IV

Here's where the lads of the village cricket:
    I was a lad not wide from here:
Couldn't I whip off the bail from the wicket?
    Like an old world those days appear!
Donkey, sheep, geese, and thatched ale-house—I know
        them!
    They are old friends of my halts, and seem,   30
Somehow, as if kind thanks I owe them:
    Juggling don't hinder the heart's esteem.

V

Juggling's no sin, for we must have victual:
    Nature allows us to bait for the fool.

---

²⁷ *whip off the bail from the wicket:* cricketing term, meaning to put out the batsman.

Holding one's own makes us juggle no little;
    But, to increase it, hard juggling's the rule.
You that are sneering at my profession,
    Haven't you juggled a vast amount?
There's the Prime Minister, in one Session,
    Juggles more games than my sins'll count.   40

VI

I've murdered insects with mock thunder:
    Conscience, for that, in men don't quail.
I've made bread from the bump of wonder:
    That's my business, and there's my tale.
Fashion and rank all praised the professor:
    Ay! and I've had my smile from the Queen:
Bravo, Jerry! she meant: God bless her!
    Ain't this a sermon on that scene?

VII

I've studied men from my topsy-turvy
    Close, and, I reckon, rather true.   50
Some are fine fellows: some, right scurvy:
    Most, a dash between the two.
But it's a woman, old girl, that makes me
    Think more kindly of the race:
And it's a woman, old girl, that shakes me
    When the Great Juggler I must face.

VIII

We two were married, due and legal:
    Honest we've lived since we've been one.
Lord! I could then jump like an eagle:
    You danced bright as a bit o' the sun.   60
Birds in a May-bush we were! right merry!
    All night we kiss'd, we juggled all day.
Joy was the heart of Juggling Jerry!
    Now from his old girl he's juggled away.

IX

It's past parsons to console us:
    No, nor no doctor fetch for me:

---

[49] *topsy-turvy:* upside down in his tumbling act.

I can die without my bolus;
　　Two of a trade, lass, never agree!
Parson and Doctor!—don't they love rarely,
　　Fighting the devil in other men's fields!   70
Stand up yourself and match him fairly:
　　Then see how the rascal yields!

X

I, lass, have lived no gipsy, flaunting
　　Finery while his poor helpmate grubs:
Coin I've stored, and you won't be wanting:
　　You shan't beg from the troughs and tubs.
Nobly you've stuck to me, though in his kitchen
　　Many a Marquis would hail you Cook!
Palaces you could have ruled and grown rich in,
　　But your old Jerry you never forsook.   80

XI

Hand up the chirper! ripe ale winks in it;
　　Let's have comfort and be at peace.
Once a stout draught made me light as a linnet.
　　Cheer up! the Lord must have his lease.
May be—for none see in that black hollow—
　　It's just a place where we're held in pawn,
And, when the Great Juggler makes as to swallow,
　　It's just the sword-trick—I ain't quite gone!

XII

Yonder came smells of the gorse, so nutty,
　　Gold-like and warm: it's the prime of May.   90
Better than mortar, brick and putty,
　　Is God's house on a blowing day.
Lean me more up the mound; now I feel it:
　　All the old heath-smells! Ain't it strange?
There's the world laughing, as if to conceal it,
　　But He's by us, juggling the change.

---

67 *bolus:* large pill.
81 *chirper:* cup of drink.

XIII

I mind it well, by the sea-beach lying,
   Once—it's long gone—when two gulls we beheld,
Which, as the moon got up, were flying
   Down a big wave that sparked and swelled.   100
Crack, went a gun: one fell: the second
   Wheeled round him twice, and was off for new luck:
There in the dark her white wing beckon'd:—
   Drop me a kiss—I'm the bird dead-struck!

[1859]

MODERN LOVE

THE PROMISE IN DISTURBANCE

How low when angels fall their black descent,
Our primal thunder tells: known is the pain
Of music, that nigh throning wisdom went,
And one false note cast wailful to the insane.
Now seems the language heard of Love as rain
To make a mire where fruitfulness was meant.
The golden harp gives out a jangled strain,
Too like revolt from heaven's Omnipotent.
But listen in the thought; so may there come
Conception of a newly-added chord,   10
Commanding space beyond where ear has home.
In labour of the trouble at its fount,
Leads Life to an intelligible Lord
The rebel discords up the sacred mount.

[1892]

I

By this he knew she wept with waking eyes:
That, at his hand's light quiver by her head,
The strange low sobs that shook their common bed
Were called into her with a sharp surprise,

The Promise in Disturbance: In the 1892 edition, this sonnet replaced the
original epigraph: "This is not meat/For little people or for fools."

And strangled mute, like little gaping snakes,
Dreadfully venomous to him. She lay   20
Stone-still, and the long darkness flowed away
With muffled pulses. Then, as midnight makes
Her giant heart of Memory and Tears
Drink the pale drug of silence, and so beat
Sleep's heavy measure, they from head to feet
Were moveless, looking through their dead black years,
By vain regret scrawled over the blank wall.
Like sculptured effigies they might be seen
Upon their marriage-tomb, the sword between;
Each wishing for the sword that severs all.   30

II

It ended, and the morrow brought the task.
Her eyes were guilty gates, that let him in
By shutting all too zealous for their sin:
Each sucked a secret, and each wore a mask.
But, oh, the bitter taste her beauty had!
He sickened as at breath of poison-flowers:
A languid humour stole among the hours,
And if their smiles encountered, he went mad,
And raged deep inward, till the light was brown
Before his vision, and the world, forgot,   40
Looked wicked as some old dull murder-spot.
A star with lurid beams, she seemed to crown
The pit of infamy: and then again
He fainted on his vengefulness, and strove
To ape the magnanimity of love,
And smote himself, a shuddering heap of pain.

III

This was the woman; what now of the man?
But pass him. If he comes beneath a heel,
He shall be crushed until he cannot feel,
Or, being callous, haply till he can.   50
But he is nothing:—nothing? Only mark

---

29 *the sword between:* symbolic of their antagonism.
33 *their sin:* loveless physical passion.
44 *fainted:* weakened.
47 *the man:* the wife's lover.

The rich light striking out from her on him!
Ha! what a sense it is when her eyes swim
Across the man she singles, leaving dark
All else! Lord God, who mad'st the thing so fair,
See that I am drawn to her even now!
It cannot be such harm on her cool brow
To put a kiss? Yet if I meet him there!
But she is mine! Ah, no! I know too well
I claim a star whose light is overcast: 60
I claim a phantom-woman in the Past.
The hour has struck, though I heard not the bell!

IV

All other joys of life he strove to warm,
And magnify, and catch them to his lip:
But they had suffered shipwreck with the ship,
And gazed upon him sallow from the storm.
Or if Delusion came, 'twas but to show
The coming minute mock the one that went.
Cold as a mountain in its star-pitched tent,
Stood high Philosophy, less friend than foe: 70
Whom self-caged Passion, from its prison-bars,
Is always watching with a wondering hate.
Not till the fire is dying in the grate,
Look we for any kinship with the stars.
Oh, wisdom never comes when it is gold,
And the great price we pay for it full worth:
We have it only when we are half earth.
Little avails that coinage to the old!

V

A message from her set his brain aflame.
A world of household matters filled her mind,   80
Wherein he saw hypocrisy designed:
She treated him as something that is tame,
And but at other provocation bites.

---

60 *whose light is overcast:* i.e., she is no longer the woman he once loved.
67 *or if Delusion . . . show:* The meaning of this and the following line seems to be that if he succeeds in deluding himself into "other joys of life" the feeling only makes the preceding (or succeeding) misery more intense.
73 *the fire:* passion.
77 *half earth:* half dead.

Familiar was her shoulder in the glass,
Through that dark rain: yet it may come to pass
That a changed eye finds such familiar sights
More keenly tempting than new loveliness.
The "What has been" a moment seemed his own:
The splendours, mysteries, dearer because known,
Nor less divine: Love's inmost sacredness   90
Called to him, "Come!"—In his restraining start,
Eyes nurtured to be looked at scarce could see
A wave of the great waves of Destiny
Convulsed at a checked impulse of the heart.

VI

It chanced his lips did meet her forehead cool.
She had no blush, but slanted down her eye.
Shamed nature, then, confesses love can die:
And most she punishes the tender fool
Who will believe what honours her the most!
Dead! is it dead? She has a pulse, and flow   100
Of tears, the price of blood-drops, as I know,
For whom the midnight sobs around Love's ghost,
Since then I heard her, and so will sob on.
The love is here; it has but changed its aim.
O bitter barren woman! what's the name?
The name, the name, the new name thou hast won?
Behold me striking the world's coward stroke!
That will I not do, though the sting is dire.
—Beneath the surface this, while by the fire
They sat, she laughing at a quiet joke.   110

VII

She issues radiant from her dressing-room,
Like one prepared to scale an upper sphere:
—By stirring up a lower, much I fear!
How deftly that oiled barber lays his bloom!
That long-shanked dapper Cupid with frisked curls
Can make known women torturingly fair;
The gold-eyed serpent dwelling in rich hair
Awakes beneath his magic whisks and twirls.

---

85 *dark rain:* her hair.
107 *the world's coward stroke:* society's condemnation of illicit passion.

His art can take the eyes from out my head,
Until I see with eyes of other men; 120
While deeper knowledge crouches in its den,
And sends a spark up:—is it true we are wed?
Yea! filthiness of body is most vile,
But faithlessness of heart I do hold worse.
The former, it were not so great a curse
To read on the steel-mirror of her smile.

VIII

Yet it was plain she struggled, and that salt
Of righteous feeling made her pitiful.
Poor twisting worm, so queenly beautiful!
Where came the cleft between us? whose the fault? 130
My tears are on thee, that have rarely dropped
As balm for any bitter wound of mine:
My breast will open for thee at a sign!
But, no: we are two reed-pipes, coarsely stopped:
The God once filled them with his mellow breath;
And they were music till he flung them down,
Used! used! Hear now the discord-loving clown
Puff his gross spirit in them, worse than death!
I do not know myself without thee more:
In this unholy battle I grow base: 140
If the same soul be under the same face,
Speak, and a taste of that old time restore!

IX

He felt the wild beast in him betweenwhiles
So masterfully rude, that he would grieve
To see the helpless delicate thing receive
His guardianship through certain dark defiles.
Had he not teeth to rend, and hunger too?
But still he spared her. Once: "Have you no fear?"
He said: 'twas dusk; she in his grasp; none near.
She laughed: "No, surely; am I not with you?" 150
And uttering that soft starry "you," she leaned
Her gentle body near him, looking up;
And from her eyes, as from a poison-cup,

---

[127] *she struggled:* i.e., against her passion for her lover.

He drank until the flittering eyelids screened.
Devilish malignant witch! and oh, young beam
Of heaven's circle-glory! Here thy shape
To squeeze like an intoxicating grape—
I might, and yet thou goest safe, supreme.

X

But where began the change; and what's my crime?
The wretch condemned, who has not been arraigned,   160
Chafes at his sentence. Shall I, unsustained,
Drag on Love's nerveless body thro' all time?
I must have slept, since now I wake. Prepare,
You lovers, to know Love a thing of moods:
Not, like hard life, of laws. In Love's deep woods,
I dreamt of loyal Life:—the offence is there!
Love's jealous woods about the sun are curled;
At least, the sun far brighter there did beam.—
My crime is, that the puppet of a dream,
I plotted to be worthy of the world.   170
Oh, had I with my darling helped to mince
The facts of life, you still had seen me go
With hindward feather and with forward toe,
Her much-adored delightful Fairy Prince!

XI

Out in the yellow meadows, where the bee
Hums by us with the honey of the Spring,
And showers of sweet notes from the larks on wing
Are dropping like a noon-dew, wander we.
Or is it now? or was it then? for now,
As then, the larks from running rings pour showers: 180
The golden foot of May is on the flowers,
And friendly shadows dance upon her brow.
What's this, when Nature swears there is no change
To challenge eyesight? Now, as then, the grace
Of heaven seems holding earth in its embrace.
Nor eyes, nor heart, has she to feel it strange?
Look, woman, in the West. There wilt thou see
An amber cradle near the sun's decline:

156 *circle-glory:* the sun.

Within it, featured even in death divine,
Is lying a dead infant, slain by thee.   190

XII

Not solely that the Future she destroys,
And the fair life which in the distance lies
For all men, beckoning out from dim rich skies:
Nor that the passing hour's supporting joys
Have lost the keen-edged flavour, which begat
Distinction in old times, and still should breed
Sweet Memory, and Hope,—earth's modest seed,
And heaven's high-prompting: not that the world is flat
Since that soft-luring creature I embraced
Among the children of Illusion went: 200
Methinks with all this loss I were content,
If the mad Past, on which my foot is based,
Were firm, or might be blotted: but the whole
Of life is mixed: the mocking Past will stay:
And if I drink oblivion of a day,
So shorten I the stature of my soul.

XIII

"I play for Seasons; not Eternities!"
Says Nature, laughing on her way. "So must
All those whose stake is nothing more than dust!"
And lo, she wins, and of her harmonies   210
She is full sure! Upon her dying rose
She drops a look of fondness, and goes by,
Scarce any retrospection in her eye;
For she the laws of growth most deeply knows,
Whose hands bear, here, a seed-bag—there, an urn.
Pledged she herself to aught, 'twould mark her end!
This lesson of our only visible friend
Can we not teach our foolish hearts to learn?
Yes! yes!—but, oh, our human rose is fair

---

190 *a dead infant:* their love; possibly also the child their estrangement prevented them from having.
200 *Among . . . went:* This line probably means that she has made it apparent that his previous conception of her was an illusion.
217 *visible friend:* Nature.

Surpassingly! Lose calmly Love's great bliss,   220
When the renewed for ever of a kiss
Whirls life within the shower of loosened hair!

XIV

What soul would bargain for a cure that brings
Contempt the nobler agony to kill?
Rather let me bear on the bitter ill,
And strike this rusty bosom with new stings!
It seems there is another veering fit,
Since on a gold-haired lady's eyeballs pure
I looked with little prospect of a cure,
The while her mouth's red bow loosed shafts of wit.   230
Just heaven! can it be true that jealousy
Has decked the woman thus? and does her head
Swim somewhat for possessions forfeited?
Madam, you teach me many things that be.
I open an old book, and there I find
That "Women still may love whom they deceive."
Such love I prize not, madam: by your leave,
The game you play at is not to my mind.

XV

I think she sleeps: it must be sleep, when low
Hangs that abandoned arm toward the floor;   240
The face turned with it. Now make fast the door.
Sleep on: it is your husband, not your foe.
The Poet's black stage-lion of wronged love
Frights not our modern dames:—well if he did!
Now will I pour new light upon that lid,
Full-sloping like the breasts beneath. "Sweet dove,
Your sleep is pure. Nay, pardon: I disturb.
I do not? good!" Her waking infant-stare
Grows woman to the burden my hands bear:
Her own handwriting to me when no curb   250
Was left on Passion's tongue. She trembles through;

---

228 *gold-haired lady:* the husband's mistress; throughout the poem she is
referred to as "Lady" or "my Lady," while the wife is referred to as
"Madam" or "the woman."
243 *black stage-lion:* Othello.
249 *the burden:* an old love letter.

A woman's tremble—the whole instrument:—
I show another letter lately sent.
The words are very like: the name is new.

XVI

In our old shipwrecked days there was an hour,
When in the firelight steadily aglow,
Joined slackly, we beheld the red chasm grow
Among the clicking coals. Our library-bower
That eve was left to us: and hushed we sat
As lovers to whom Time is whispering.   260
From sudden-opened doors we heard them sing:
The nodding elders mixed good wine with chat.
Well knew we that Life's greatest treasure lay
With us, and of it was our talk. "Ah, yes!
Love dies!" I said: I never thought it less.
She yearned to me that sentence to unsay.
Then when the fire domed blackening, I found
Her cheek was salt against my kiss, and swift
Up the sharp scale of sobs her breast did lift:—
Now am I haunted by that taste! that sound!   270

XVII

At dinner, she is hostess, I am host.
Went the feast ever cheerfuller? She keeps
The Topic over intellectual deeps
In buoyancy afloat. They see no ghost.
With sparkling surface-eyes we ply the ball:
It is in truth a most contagious game:
HIDING THE SKELETON, shall be its name.
Such play as this the devils might appal!
But here's the greater wonder; in that we,
Enamoured of an acting nought can tire,   280
Each other, like true hypocrites, admire;
Warm-lighted looks, Love's ephemerioe,
Shoot gaily o'er the dishes and the wine.
We waken envy of our happy lot.
Fast, sweet, and golden, shows the marriage-knot.
Dear guests, you now have seen Love's corpse-light shine.

---

282 *ephemerioe:* May flies, hence short-lived things.

XVIII

Here Jack and Tom are paired with Moll and Meg.
Curved open to the river-reach is seen
A country merry-making on the green.
Fair space for signal shakings of the leg.   290
That little screwy fiddler from his booth,
Whence flows one nut-brown stream, commands the joints
Of all who caper here at various points.
I have known rustic revels in my youth:
The May-fly pleasures of a mind at ease.
An early goddess was a country lass:
A charmed Amphion-oak she tripped the grass.
What life was that I lived? The life of these?
Heaven keep them happy! Nature they seem near.
They must, I think, be wiser than I am;   300
They have the secret of the bull and lamb.
'Tis true that when we trace its source, 'tis beer.

XIX

No state is enviable. To the luck alone
Of some few favoured men I would put claim.
I bleed, but her who wounds I will not blame.
Have I not felt her heart as 'twere my own
Beat thro' me? could I hurt her? heaven and hell!
But I could hurt her cruelly! Can I let
My Love's old time-piece to another set,
Swear it can't stop, and must for ever swell?   310
Sure, that's one way Love drifts into the mart
Where goat-legged buyers throng. I see not plain:—
My meaning is, it must not be again.
Great God! the maddest gambler throws his heart.
If any state be enviable on earth,
'Tis yon born idiot's, who, as days go by,
Still rubs his hands before him, like a fly,
In a queer sort of meditative mirth.

---

292 *stream:* beer.
297 *Amphion-oak:* The music of the mythological Amphion charmed stones
and trees into movement; the girl suggests, by her grace, the stateliness of a
moving oak.
312 *goat-legged:* lustful.

XX

I am not of those miserable males
Who sniff at vice and, daring not to snap,   320
Do therefore hope for heaven. I take the hap
Of all my deeds. The wind that fills my sails
Propels; but I am helmsman. Am I wrecked,
I know the devil has sufficient weight
To bear: I lay it not on him, or fate.
Besides, he's damned. That man I do suspect
A coward, who would burden the poor deuce
With what ensues from his own slipperiness.
I have just found a wanton-scented tress
In an old desk, dusty for lack of use.   330
Of days and nights it is demonstrative,
That, like some aged star, gleam luridly.
If for those times I must ask charity,
Have I not any charity to give?

XXI

We three are on the cedar-shadowed lawn;
My friend being third. He who at love once laughed
Is in the weak rib by a fatal shaft
Struck through, and tells his passion's bashful dawn
And radiant culmination, glorious crown,
When "this" she said: went "thus": most wondrous she.   340
Our eyes grow white, encountering: that we are three,
Forgetful; then together we look down.
But he demands our blessing; is convinced
That words of wedded lovers must bring good.
We question; if we dare! or if we should!
And pat him, with light laugh. We have not winced.
Next, she has fallen. Fainting points the sign
To happy things in wedlock. When she wakes,
She looks the star that thro' the cedar shakes:
Her lost moist hand clings mortally to mine.   350

XXII

What may the woman labour to confess?
There is about her mouth a nervous twitch.

---

[348] *happy things in wedlock:* pregnancy.

'Tis something to be told, or hidden:—which?
I get a glimpse of hell in this mild guess.
She has desires of touch, as if to feel
That all the household things are things she knew.
She stops before the glass. What sight in view?
A face that seems the latest to reveal!
For she turns from it hastily, and tossed   360
Irresolute, steals shadow-like to where
I stand; and wavering pale before me there,
Her tears fall still as oak-leaves after frost.
She will not speak. I will not ask. We are
League-sundered by the silent gulf between.
You burly lovers on the village green,
Yours is a lower, and a happier star!

XXIII

'Tis Christmas weather, and a country house
Receives us: rooms are full: we can but get
An attic-crib. Such lovers will not fret
At that, it is half-said. The great carouse   370
Knocks hard upon the midnight's hollow door,
But when I knock at hers, I see the pit.
Why did I come here in that dullard fit?
I enter, and lie couched upon the floor.
Passing, I caught the coverlet's quick beat:—
Come, Shame, burn to my soul! and Pride, and Pain—
Foul demons that have tortured me, enchain!
Out in the freezing darkness the lambs bleat.
The small bird stiffens in the low starlight.
I know not how, but shuddering as I slept,   380
I dreamed a banished angel to me crept:
My feet were nourished on her breasts all night.

XXIV

The misery is greater, as I live!
To know her flesh so pure, so keen her sense,
That she does penance now for no offence,
Save against Love. The less can I forgive!

---

366 *star:* place in the world.
372 *the pit:* hell.
384 *sense:* moral sense.

The less can I forgive, though I adore
That cruel lovely pallor which surrounds
Her footsteps; and the low vibrating sounds
That come on me, as from a magic shore.   390
Low are they, but most subtle to find out
The shrinking soul. Madam, 'tis understood
When women play upon their womanhood,
It means, a Season gone. And yet I doubt
But I am duped. That nun-like look waylays
My fancy. Oh! I do but wait a sign!
Pluck out the eyes of pride! thy mouth to mine!
Never! though I die thirsting. Go thy ways!

XXV

You like not that French novel? Tell me why.
You think it quite unnatural. Let us see.   400
The actors are, it seems, the usual three:
Husband, and wife, and lover. She—but fie!
In England we'll not hear of it. Edmond,
The lover, her devout chagrin doth share;
Blanc-mange and absinthe are his penitent fare,
Till his pale aspect makes her over-fond:
So, to preclude fresh sin, he tries rosbif.
Meantime the husband is no more abused:
Auguste forgives her ere the tear is used.
Then hangeth all on one tremendous IF:—   410
If she will choose between them. She does choose;
And takes her husband, like a proper wife.
Unnatural? My dear, these things are life:
And life, some think, is worthy of the Muse.

XXVI

Love ere he bleeds, an eagle in high skies,
Has earth beneath his wings: from reddened eve
He views the rosy dawn. In vain they weave
The fatal web below while far he flies.
But when the arrow strikes him, there's a change.
He moves but in the track of his spent pain,   420
Whose red drops are the links of a harsh chain,

---

³⁹⁴ *a Season gone:* love is past.
⁴⁰⁷ *rosbif:* French for roast beef.

Binding him to the ground, with narrow range.
A subtle serpent then has Love become.
I had the eagle in my bosom erst:
Henceforward with the serpent I am cursed.
I can interpret where the mouth is dumb.
Speak, and I see the side-lie of a truth.
Perchance my heart may pardon you this deed:
But be no coward:—you that made Love bleed,
You must bear all the venom of his tooth!   430

XXVII

Distraction is the panacea, Sir!
I hear my oracle of Medicine say.
Doctor! that same specific yesterday
I tried, and the result will not deter
A second trial. Is the devil's line
Of golden hair, or raven black, composed?
And does a cheek, like any sea-shell rosed,
Or clear as widowed sky, seem most divine?
No matter, so I taste forgetfulness.
And if the devil snare me, body and mind,   440
Here gratefully I score:—he seemëd kind,
When not a soul would comfort my distress!
O sweet new world, in which I rise new made!
O Lady, once I gave love: now I take!
Lady, I must be flattered. Shouldst thou wake
The passion of a demon, be not afraid.

XXVIII

I must be flattered. The imperious
Desire speaks out. Lady, I am content
To play with you the game of Sentiment,
And with you enter on paths perilous;   450
But if across your beauty I throw light,
To make it threefold, it must be all mine.
First secret; then avowed. For I must shine
Envied,—I, lessened in my proper sight!
Be watchful of your beauty, Lady dear!

---

427 *side-lie:* lying aspect.
444 *Lady:* his mistress, first referred to in XIV.
454 *lessened in my proper sight:* i.e., lowered in my own estimation.

How much hangs on that lamp you cannot tell.
Most earnestly I pray you, tend it well:
And men shall see me as a burning sphere;
And men shall mark you eyeing me, and groan
To be the God of such a grand sunflower! 460
I feel the promptings of Satanic power,
While you do homage unto me alone.

XXIX

Am I failing? For no longer can I cast
A glory round about this head of gold.
Glory she wears, but springing from the mould;
Not like the consecration of the Past!
Is my soul beggared? Something more than earth
I cry for still: I cannot be at peace
In having Love upon a mortal lease.
I cannot take the woman at her worth! 470
Where is the ancient wealth wherewith I clothed
Our human nakedness, and could endow
With spiritual splendour a white brow
That else had grinned at me the fact I loathed?
A kiss is but a kiss now! and no wave
Of a great flood that whirls me to the sea.
But, as you will! we'll sit contentedly,
And eat our pot of honey on the grave.

XXX

What are we first? First, animals; and next
Intelligences at a leap; on whom 480
Pale lies the distant shadow of the tomb,
And all that draweth on the tomb for text.
Into which state comes Love, the crowning sun:
Beneath whose light the shadow loses form.
We are the lords of life, and life is warm.
Intelligence and instinct now are one.
But nature says: "My children most they seem

---

465 *mould:* earth, hence the completely physical.
478 *pot of honey:* sensual pleasure. *the grave:* of his love for his wife.
482 *all that draweth . . . for text:* i.e., all that takes meaning from the fact of mortality.
484 *shadow:* fear of death.

When they least know me: therefore I decree
That they shall suffer." Swift doth young Love flee,
And we stand wakened, shivering from our dream.   490
Then if we study Nature we are wise.
Thus do the few who live but with the day:
The scientific animals are they.—
Lady, this is my sonnet to your eyes.

XXXI

This golden head has wit in it. I live
Again, and a far higher life, near her.
Some women like a young philosopher;
Perchance because he is diminutive.
For woman's manly god must not exceed
Proportions of the natural nursing size.   500
Great poets and great sages draw no prize
With women: but the little lap-dog breed,
Who can be hugged, or on a mantel-piece
Perched up for adoration, these obtain
Her homage. And of this we men are vain?
Of this! 'Tis ordered for the world's increase!
Small flattery! Yet she has that rare gift
To beauty, Common Sense. I am approved.
It is not half so nice as being loved,
And yet I do prefer it. What's my drift?   510

XXXII

Full faith I have she holds that rarest gift
To beauty, Common Sense. To see her lie
With her fair visage an inverted sky
Bloom-covered, while the underlids uplift,
Would almost wreck the faith; but when her mouth
(Can it kiss sweetly? sweetly!) would address
The inner me that thirsts for her no less,
And has so long been languishing in drouth,
I feel that I am matched; that I am man!
One restless corner of my heart or head,   520
That holds a dying something never dead,
Still frets, though Nature giveth all she can.
It means, that woman is not, I opine,

Her sex's antidote. Who seeks the asp
For serpents' bites? 'Twould calm me could I clasp
Shrieking Bacchantes with their souls of wine!

XXXIII

"In Paris, at the Louvre, there have I seen
The sumptuously-feathered angel pierce
Prone Lucifer, descending. Looked he fierce,
Showing the fight a fair one? Too serene!   530
The young Pharsalians did not disarray
Less willingly their locks of floating silk:
That suckling mouth of his upon the milk
Of heaven might still be feasting through the fray.
Oh, Raphael! when men the Fiend do fight,
They conquer not upon such easy terms.
Half serpent in the struggle grow these worms.
And does he grow half human, all is right."
This to my Lady in a distant spot,
Upon the theme: *While mind is mastering clay,*   540
Gross clay invades it. If the spy you play,
My wife, read this! Strange love-talk, is it not?

XXXIV

Madam would speak with me. So, now it comes:
The deluge or else Fire! She's well; she thanks
My husbandship. Our chain on silence clanks.
Time leers between, above his twiddling thumbs.
Am I quite well? Most excellent in health!
The journals, too, I diligently peruse.
Vesuvius is expected to give news:
Niagara is no noisier. By stealth   550
Our eyes dart scrutinizing snakes. She's glad
I'm happy, says her quivering under-lip.
"And are not you?" "How can I be?" "Take ship!
For happiness is somewhere to be had."
"Nowhere for me!" Her voice is barely heard.

523-4 *woman is not . . . antidote:* i.e., a second woman will not cure the
sickness caused by a first.
526 *Bacchantes:* orgiastic followers of Bacchus, god of wine.
527 *Louvre:* museum where hangs Raphael's painting of St. Michael.
531 *Pharsalians:* Caesar's dandified soldiers at the battle of Pharsalia.

I am not melted, and make no pretence.
With commonplace I freeze her, tongue and sense.
Niagara or Vesuvius is deferred.

XXXV

It is no vulgar nature I have wived.
Secretive, sensitive, she takes a wound   560
Deep to her soul, as if the sense had swooned,
And not a thought of vengeance had survived.
No confidences has she: but relief
Must come to one whose suffering is acute.
O have a care of natures that are mute!
They punish you in acts: their steps are brief.
What is she doing? What does she demand
From Providence or me? She is not one
Long to endure this torpidly, and shun
The drugs that crowd about a woman's hand.   570
At Forfeits during snow we played, and I
Must kiss her. "Well performed!" I said: then she:
" 'Tis hardly worth the money, you agree?"
Save her? What for? To act this wedded lie!

XXXVI

My Lady unto Madam makes her bow.
The charm of women is, that even while
You're probed by them for tears, you yet may smile,
Nay, laugh outright, as I have done just now.
The interview was gracious: they anoint
(To me aside) each other with fine praise: 580
Discriminating compliments they raise,
That hit with wondrous aim on the weak point:
My Lady's nose of Nature might complain.
It is not fashioned aptly to express
Her character of large-browed steadfastness.
But Madam says: Thereof she may be vain!
Now, Madam's faulty feature is a glazed
And inaccessible eye, that has soft fires,
Wide gates, at love-time, only. This admires
My Lady. At the two I stand amazed.   590

---

571 *Forfeits:* game where player redeems a possession by performing a task.

XXXVII

Along the garden terrace, under which
A purple valley (lighted at its edge
By smoky torch-flame on the long cloud-ledge
Whereunder dropped the chariot) glimmers rich,
A quiet company we pace and wait
The dinner-bell in prae-digestive calm.
So sweep up violet banks the Southern balm
Breathes round, we care not if the bell be late:
Though here and there grey seniors question Time
In irritable coughings. With slow foot   600
The low rosed moon, the face of Music mute,
Begins among her silent bars to climb.
As in and out, in silvery dusk, we thread,
I hear the laugh of Madam, and discern
My Lady's heel before me at each turn.
Our tragedy, is it alive or dead?

XXXVIII

Give to imagination some pure light
In human form to fix it, or you shame
The devils with that hideous human game:—
Imagination urging appetite!   610
Thus fallen have earth's greatest Gogmagogs,
Who dazzle us, whom we can not revere:
Imagination is the charioteer
That, in default of better, drives the hogs.
So, therefore, my dear Lady, let me love!
My soul is arrowy to the light in you.
You know me that I never can renew
The bond that woman broke: what would you have?
'Tis Love, or Vileness! not a choice between,
Save petrifaction! What does Pity here?   620
She killed a thing, and now it's dead, 'tis dear.
Oh, when you counsel me, think what you mean!

---

594 *chariot:* sun.
611 *Gogmagogs:* Gogmagog was a giant overthrown by Brute (or Brutus),
the founder of Britain.
616 *arrowy:* speeding like an arrow.

XXXIX

She yields: my Lady in her noblest mood
Has yielded: she, my golden-crownëd rose!
The bride of every sense! more sweet than those
Who breathe the violet breath of maidenhood.
O visage of still music in the sky!
Soft moon! I feel thy song, my fairest friend!
True harmony within can apprehend
Dumb harmony without. And hark! 'tis nigh!   630
Belief has struck the note of sound: a gleam
Of living silver shows me where she shook
Her long white fingers down the shadowy brook,
That sings her song, half waking, half in dream.
What two come here to mar this heavenly tune?
A man is one: the woman bears my name,
And honour. Their hands touch! Am I still tame?
God, what a dancing spectre seems the moon!

XL

I bade my Lady think what she might mean.
Know I my meaning, I? Can I love one,   640
And yet be jealous of another? None
Commits such folly. Terrible Love, I ween,
Has might, even dead, half sighing to upheave
The lightless seas of selfishness amain:
Seas that in a man's heart have no rain
To fall and still them. Peace can I achieve,
By turning to this fountain-source of woe,
This woman, who's to Love as fire to wood?
She breathed the violet breath of maidenhood
Against my kisses once! but I say, No!   650
The thing is mocked at! Helplessly afloat,
I know not what I do, whereto I strive.
The dread that my old love may be alive
Has seized my nursling new love by the throat.

XLI

How many a thing which we cast to the ground,
When others pick it up becomes a gem!
We grasp at all the wealth it is to them;

And by reflected light its worth is found.
Yet for us still 'tis nothing! and that zeal
Of false appreciation quickly fades. 660
This truth is little known to human shades,
How rare from their own instinct 'tis to feel!
They waste the soul with spurious desire,
That is not the ripe flame upon the bough.
We two have taken up a lifeless vow
To rob a living passion: dust for fire!
Madam is grave, and eyes the clock that tells
Approaching midnight. We have struck despair
Into two hearts. O, look we like a pair
Who for fresh nuptials joyfully yield all else? 670

XLII

I am to follow her. There is much grace
In women when thus bent on martyrdom.
They think that dignity of soul may come,
Perchance, with dignity of body. Base!
But I was taken by that air of cold
And statuesque sedateness, when she said
"I'm going"; lit a taper, bowed her head,
And went, as with the stride of Pallas bold.
Fleshly indifference horrible! The hands
Of Time now signal: O, she's safe from me! 680
Within those secret walls what do I see?
Where first she set the taper down she stands:
Not Pallas: Hebe shamed! Thoughts black as death
Like a stirred pool in sunshine break. Her wrists
I catch: she faltering, as she half-resists,
"You love . . . ? love . . . ? love . . . ?" all on an indrawn
    breath.

XLIII

Mark where the pressing wind shoots javelin-like
Its skeleton shadow on the broad-backed wave!
Here is a fitting spot to dig Love's grave;
Here where the ponderous breakers plunge and strike, 690

---

665 *a lifeless vow:* husband and wife have agreed to live together again.
678 *Pallas:* Pallas Athene, maiden goddess of wisdom.
683 *Hebe:* cupbearer to Jupiter, who accused her of immodesty.

And dart their hissing tongues high up the sand:
In hearing of the ocean, and in sight
Of those ribbed wind-streaks running into white.
If I the death of Love had deeply planned,
I never could have made it half so sure,
As by the unblest kisses which upbraid
The full-waked sense; or failing that, degrade!
'Tis morning: but no morning can restore
What we have forfeited. I see no sin:
The wrong is mixed. In tragic life, God wot,   700
No villain need be! Passions spin the plot:
We are betrayed by what is false within.

XLIV

They say, that Pity in Love's service dwells,
A porter at the rosy temple's gate.
I missed him going: but it is my fate
To come upon him now beside his wells;
Whereby I know that I Love's temple leave,
And that the purple doors have closed behind.
Poor soul! if, in those early days unkind,
Thy power to sting had been but power to grieve,   710
We now might with an equal spirit meet,
And not be matched like innocence and vice.
She for the Temple's worship has paid price,
And takes the coin of Pity as a cheat.
She sees through simulation to the bone:
What's best in her impels her to the worst:
Never, she cries, shall Pity soothe Love's thirst,
Or foul hypocrisy for truth atone!

XLV

It is the season of the sweet wild rose,
My Lady's emblem in the heart of me!   720
So golden-crownëd shines she gloriously,
And with that softest dream of blood she glows:
Mild as an evening heaven round Hesper bright!

---

696 *unblest kisses:* passion without love.
700 *wot:* knows.
714 *cheat:* counterfeit.
723 *Hesper:* Venus, the evening star.

I pluck the flower, and smell it, and revive
The time when in her eyes I stood alive.
I seem to look upon it out of Night.
Here's Madam, stepping hastily. Her whims
Bid her demand the flower, which I let drop.
As I proceed, I feel her sharply stop,
And crush it under heel with trembling limbs.   730
She joins me in a cat-like way, and talks
Of company, and even condescends
To utter laughing scandal of old friends.
These are the summer days, and these our walks.

XLVI

At last we parley: we so strangely dumb
In such a close communion! It befell
About the sounding of the Matin-bell,
And lo! her place was vacant, and the hum
Of loneliness was round me. Then I rose,
And my disordered brain did guide my foot   740
To that old wood where our first love-salute
Was interchanged: the source of many throes!
There did I see her, not alone. I moved
Toward her, and made proffer of my arm.
She took it simply, with no rude alarm;
And that disturbing shadow passed reproved.
I felt the pained speech coming, and declared
My firm belief in her, ere she could speak.
A ghastly morning came into her cheek,
While with a widening soul on me she stared.   750

XLVII

We saw the swallows gathering in the sky,
And in the osier-isle we heard them noise.
We had not to look back on summer joys,
Or forward to a summer of bright dye:
But in the largeness of the evening earth
Our spirits grew as we went side by side.
The hour became her husband and my bride.
Love, that had robbed us so, thus blessed our dearth!

---

746 *disturbing shadow:* the wife's lover.
752 *osier-isle:* island covered with willows.

The pilgrims of the year waxed very loud
In multitudinous chatterings, as the flood   760
Full brown came from the West, and like pale blood
Expanded to the upper crimson cloud.
Love, that had robbed us of immortal things,
This little moment mercifully gave,
Where I have seen across the twilight wave
The swan sail with her young beneath her wings.

XLVIII

Their sense is with their senses all mixed in,
Destroyed by subtleties these women are!
More brain, O Lord, more brain! or we shall mar
Utterly this fair garden we might win.   770
Behold! I looked for peace, and thought it near.
Our inmost hearts had opened, each to each.
We drank the pure daylight of honest speech.
Alas! that was the fatal draught, I fear.
For when of my lost Lady came the word,
This woman, O this agony of flesh!
Jealous devotion bade her break the mesh,
That I might seek that other like a bird.
I do adore the nobleness! despise
The act! She has gone forth, I know not where.   780
Will the hard world my sentience of her share?
I feel the truth; so let the world surmise.

XLIX

He found her by the ocean's moaning verge,
Nor any wicked change in her discerned;
And she believed his old love had returned,
Which was her exultation, and her scourge.
She took his hand, and walked with him, and seemed
The wife he sought, though shadow-like and dry.
She had one terror, lest her heart should sigh,
And tell her loudly she no longer dreamed.   790
She dared not say, "This is my breast: look in."
But there's a strength to help the desperate weak.
That night he learned how silence best can speak

---

⁷⁶⁷ *sense:* intelligence.

The awful things when Pity pleads for Sin.
About the middle of the night her call
Was heard, and he came wondering to the bed.
"Now kiss me, dear! it may be, now!" she said.
Lethe had passed those lips, and he knew all.

L

Thus piteously Love closed what he begat:
The union of this ever-diverse pair!   800
These two were rapid falcons in a snare,
Condemned to do the flitting of the bat.
Lovers beneath the singing sky of May,
They wandered once; clear as the dew on flowers:
But they fed not on the advancing hours:
Their hearts held cravings for the buried day.
Then each applied to each that fatal knife,
Deep questioning, which probes to endless dole.
Ah, what a dusty answer gets the soul
When hot for certainties in this our life!—   810
In tragic hints here see what evermore
Moves dark as yonder midnight ocean's force,
Thundering like ramping hosts of warrior horse,
To throw that faint thin line upon the shore!

[1862]

LUCIFER IN STARLIGHT

On a starred night Prince Lucifer uprose.
Tired of his dark dominion swung the fiend
Above the rolling ball in cloud part screened,
Where sinners hugged their spectre of repose.
Poor prey to his hot fit of pride were those.
And now upon his western wing he leaned,

---

798 *Lethe:* river of forgetfulness over which the souls of the dead pass on their way to the underworld. The wife has killed herself, presumably by poison.
808 *dole:* woe.
3 *rolling ball:* the earth.

Now his huge bulk o'er Afric's sands careened,
Now the black planet shadowed Arctic snows.
Soaring through wider zones that pricked his scars
With memory of the old revolt from Awe,   10
He reached a middle height, and at the stars,
Which are the brain of heaven, he looked, and sank.
Around the ancient track marched, rank on rank,
The army of unalterable law.

[1883]

THE STAR SIRIUS

Bright Sirius! that when Orion pales
To dotlings under moonlight still art keen
With cheerful fervour of a warrior's mien
Who holds in his great heart the battle-scales:
Unquenched of flame though swift the flood assails,
Reducing many lustrous to the lean:
Be thou my star, and thou in me be seen
To show what source divine is, and prevails.
Long watches through, at one with godly night,
I mark thee planting joy in constant fire;   10
And thy quick beams, whose jets of life inspire
Life to the spirit, passion for the light,
Dark Earth since she first lost her lord from sight
Has viewed and felt them sweep her as a lyre.

[1883]

---

10 *from Awe:* against God and His angels.
Sirius: the Dog-Star.
1 *Orion:* southern constellation.
13 *her lord:* the sun.

THE WOODS OF WESTERMAIN

I

Enter these enchanted woods,
   You who dare.
Nothing harms beneath the leaves
More than waves a swimmer cleaves.
Toss your heart up with the lark,
Foot at peace with mouse and worm,
   Fair you fare.
Only at a dread of dark
Quaver, and they quit their form:
Thousand eyeballs under hoods   10
   Have you by the hair.
Enter these enchanted woods,
   You who dare.

II

Here the snake across your path
Stretches in his golden bath:
Mossy-footed squirrels leap
Soft as winnowing plumes of Sleep:
Yaffles on a chuckle skim
Low to laugh from branches dim:
Up the pine, where sits the star,   20
Rattles deep the moth-winged jar.
Each has business of his own;
But should you distrust a tone,
   Then beware.
Shudder all the haunted roods,
All the eyeballs under hoods
   Shroud you in their glare.

The Woods of Westermain: near Meredith's home in Surrey; in this poem
they stand for all of Nature, which man can enter safely only with love and
courage. If he fails in either, Nature becomes menacing and terrible.
9 *quit their form:* become horrible.
18 *Yaffles:* green woodpeckers, which make a chuckling sound.
21 *jar:* the nightjar or goatsucker, a nocturnal swift-like bird.
25 *roods:* pieces of land.

Enter these enchanted woods,
  You who dare.

III

Open hither, open hence,   30
Scarce a bramble weaves a fence,
Where the strawberry runs red,
With white star-flower overhead;
Cumbered by dry twig and cone,
Shredded husks of seedlings flown,
Mine of mole and spotted flint:
Of dire wizardry no hint,
Save mayhap the print that shows
Hasty outward-tripping toes,
Heels to terror, on the mould.   40
These, the woods of Westermain,
Are as others to behold,
Rich of wreathing sun and rain;
Foliage lustreful around
Shadowed leagues of slumbering sound.
Wavy tree-tops, yellow whins,
Shelter eager minikins,
Myriads, free to peck and pipe:
Would you better? would you worse?
You with them may gather ripe   50
Pleasures flowing not from purse.
Quick and far as Colour flies
Taking the delighted eyes,
You of any well that springs
May unfold the heaven of things;
Have it homely and within,
And thereof its likeness win,
Will you so in soul's desire:
This do sages grant t' the lyre.
This is being bird and more,   60
More than glad musician this;
Granaries you will have a store
Past the world of woe and bliss;
Sharing still its bliss and woe;

---

⁴⁶ *whins:* gorse or furze.
⁴⁷ *minikins:* tiny creatures.

Harnessed to its hungers, no.
On the throne Success usurps,
You shall seat the joy you feel
Where a race of water chirps,
Twisting hues of flourished steel:
Or where light is caught in hoop 70
Up a clearing's leafy rise,
Where the crossing deerherds troop
Classic splendours, knightly dyes.
Or, where old-eyed oxen chew
Speculation with the cud,
Read their pool of vision through,
Back to hours when mind was mud;
Nigh the knot, which did untwine
Timelessly to drowsy suns;
Seeing Earth a slimy spine, 80
Heaven a space for winging tons.
Farther, deeper, may you read,
Have you sight for things afield,
Where peeps she, the Nurse of seed,
Cloaked, but in the peep revealed;
Showing a kind face and sweet:
Look you with the soul you see 't.
Glory narrowing to grace,
Grace to glory magnified,
Following that will you embrace 90
Close in arms or aëry wide.
Banished is the white Foam-born
Not from here, nor under ban
Phoebus lyrist, Phoebe's horn,
Pipings of the reedy Pan.
Loved of Earth of old they were,

---

68 *race:* channel.
73 *dyes:* colors.
77 *when mind was mud:* i.e., before man and intelligence had developed from the slime of the earth.
79 *Timelessly:* through countless ages.
81 *winging tons:* flying lumps of matter.
84 *the Nurse of seed:* Nature, or Earth.
92 *Foam-born:* Aphrodite, goddess of love, born of the sea.
94 *Phoebus:* Phoebus Apollo, god of song and of the sun. *Phoebe:* Diana, goddess of the moon.
95 *Pan:* god of nature, who played on a reed pipe.

Loving did interpret her;
And the sterner worship bars
None whom Song has made her stars.
You have seen the huntress moon   100
Radiantly facing dawn,
Dusky meads between them strewn
Glimmering like downy awn:
Argent Westward glows the hunt,
East the blush about to climb;
One another fair they front,
Transient, yet outshine the time;
Even as dewlight off the rose
In the mind a jewel sows.
Thus opposing grandeurs live   110
Here if Beauty be their dower:
Doth she of her spirit give,
Fleetingness will spare her flower.
This is in the tune we play,
Which no spring of strength would quell;
In subduing does not slay;
Guides the channel, guards the well:
Tempered holds the young blood-heat,
Yet through measured grave accord
Hears the heart of wildness beat   120
Like a centaur's hoof on sward.
Drink the sense the notes infuse,
You a larger self will find:
Sweetest fellowship ensues
With the creatures of your kind.
Ay, and Love, if Love it be
Flaming over *I* and *ME*,
Love meet they who do not shove
Cravings in the van of Love.
Courtly dames are here to woo,   130
Knowing love if it be true.
Reverence the blossom-shoot

---

102 *meads:* meadows.
103 *awn:* the "beard" of barley or oats.
104 *Argent:* silver.
121 *centaur:* half-man, half-horse.
129 *van:* vanguard, the front.

Fervently, they are the fruit.
Mark them stepping, hear them talk,
Goddess is no myth inane,
You will say of those who walk
In the woods of Westermain.
Waters that from throat and thigh
Dart the sun his arrows back;
Leaves that on a woodland sigh   140
Chat of secret things no lack;
Shadowy branch-leaves, waters clear,
Bare or veiled they move sincere;
Not by slavish terrors tripped;
Being anew in nature dipped,
Growths of what they step on, these;
With the roots the grace of trees.
Casket-breasts they give, nor hide,
For a tyrant's flattered pride,
Mind, which nourished not by light,   150
Lurks the shuffling trickster sprite:
Whereof are strange tales to tell;
Some in blood writ, tombed in hell.
Here the ancient battle ends,
Joining two astonished friends,
Who the kiss can give and take
With more warmth than in that world
Where the tiger claws the snake,
Snake her tiger clasps infurled,
And the issue of their fight   160
Peoples lands in snarling plight.
Here her splendid beast she leads
Silken-leashed and decked with weeds
Wild as he, but breathing faint
Sweetness of unfelt constraint.
Love, the great volcano, flings
Fires of lower Earth to sky;
Love, the sole permitted, sings

---

[148] *Casket-breasts:* those hearts containing treasure. The meaning of this and the three following lines is that women with capabilities should not, for the flattery of man, hide their intelligence, lest it degenerate into a deceptive faculty.
[158] *Where the tiger claws the snake:* i.e., the world of predatory sexual relationships, where man becomes a tiger, woman a snake.

Sovereignly of *ME* and *I*.
Bowers he has of sacred shade,   170
Spaces of superb parade,
Voiceful. . . . But bring you a note
Wrangling, howsoe'er remote,
Discords out of discord spin
Round and round derisive din:
Sudden will a pallor pant
Chill at screeches miscreant;
Owls or spectres, thick they flee;
Nightmare upon horror broods;
Hooded laughter, monkish glee,   180
     Gaps the vital air.
Enter these enchanted woods
     You who dare.

IV

You must love the light so well
That no darkness will seem fell.
Love it so you could accost
Fellowly a livid ghost.
Whish! the phantom wisps away,
Owns him smoke to cocks of day.
In your breast the light must burn   190
Fed of you, like corn in quern
Ever plumping while the wheel
Speeds the mill and drains the meal.
Light to light sees little strange,
Only features heavenly new;
Then you touch the nerve of Change,
Then of Earth you have the clue;
Then her two-sexed meanings melt
Through you, wed the thought and felt.
Sameness locks no scurfy pond   200
Here for Custom, crazy-fond:
Change is on the wing to bud
Rose in brain from rose in blood.
Wisdom throbbing shall you see
Central in complexity;

---

191 *quern:* hand-mill.

From her pasture 'mid the beasts
Rise to her ethereal feasts,
Not, though lightnings track your wit
Starward, scorning them you quit:
For be sure the bravest wing   210
Preens it in our common spring,
Thence along the vault to soar,
You with others, gathering more,
Glad of more, till you reject
Your proud title of elect,
Perilous even here while few
Roam the arched greenwood with you.
    Heed that snare.
Muffled by his cavern-cowl
Squats the scaly Dragon-fowl,   220
Who was lord ere light you drank,
And lest blood of knightly rank
Stream, let not your fair princess
Stray: he holds the leagues in stress,
    Watches keenly there.
Oft has he been riven; slain
Is no force in Westermain.
Wait, and we shall forge him curbs,
Put his fangs to uses, tame,
Teach him, quick as cunning herbs,   230
How to cure him sick and lame.
Much restricted, much enringed,
Much he frets, the hooked and winged,
    Never known to spare.
'Tis enough: the name of Sage
Hits no thing in nature, nought;
Man the least, save when grave Age
From yon Dragon guards his thought.
Eye him when you hearken dumb
To what words from Wisdom come.   240
When she says how few are by
Listening to her, eye his eye.
    Self, his name declare.
Him shall Change, transforming late,

---

[220] *Dragon-fowl:* Self or Egoism, as the poem later explains.
[224] *he holds the leagues in stress:* i.e., he has dominion over the area.

Wonderously renovate.
Hug himself the creature may:
What he hugs is loathed decay.
Crying, slip thy scales, and slough!
Change will strip his armour off;
Make of him who was all maw,   250
Inly only thrilling-shrewd,
Such a servant as none saw
Through his days of dragonhood:
Days when growling o'er his bone,
Sharpened he for mine and thine;
Sensitive within alone;
Scaly as in clefts of pine.
Change, the strongest son of Life,
Has the Spirit here to wife.
Lo, their young of vivid breed   260
Bear the lights that onward speed,
Threading thickets, mounting glades,
Up the verdurous colonnades,
Round the fluttered curves, and down,
Out of sight of Earth's blue crown,
Whither, in her central space,
Spouts the Fount and Lure o' the chase.
Fount unresting, Lure divine!
There meet all: too late look most.
Fire in water hued as wine   270
Springs amid a shadowy host;
Circled: one close-headed mob,
Breathless, scanning divers heaps
Where a Heart begins to throb,
Where it ceases, slow, with leaps:
And 'tis very strange, 'tis said,
How you spy in each of them
Semblance of that Dragon red,
As the oak in bracken-stem.
And, 'tis said, how each and each: 280
Which commences, which subsides:

---

267 *Fount and Lure o' the chase:* Love, according to Meredith's friend and editor, G. M. Trevelyan.
279 *oak in bracken-stem:* reference to rural belief that a section of the stem of the bracken (or fern) shows an oak in miniature.

First my Dragon! doth beseech
Her who food for all provides.
And she answers with no sign;
Utters neither yea nor nay;
Fires the water hued as wine;
Kneads another spark in clay.
Terror is about her hid;
Silence of the thunders locked;
Lightnings lining the shut lid;   290
Fixity on quaking rocked.
Lo, you look at Flow and Drought
Interflashed and interwrought:
Ended is begun, begun
Ended, quick as torrents run.
Young Impulsion spouts to sink;
Luridness and lustre link;
'Tis your come and go of breath;
Mirrored pants the Life, the Death;
Each of either reaped and sown: 300
Rosiest rosy wanes to crone.
See you so? your senses drift;
'Tis a shuttle weaving swift.
Look with spirit past the sense,
Spirit shines in permanence.
That is She, the view of whom
Is the dust within the tomb,
Is the inner blush above,
Look to loathe, or look to love;
Think her Lump, or know her Flame;   310
Dread her scourge, or read her aim;
Shoot your hungers from their nerve;
Or, in her example, serve.
Some have found her sitting grave;
Laughing, some; or, browed with sweat,
Hurling dust of fool and knave
In a hissing smithy's jet.
More it were not well to speak;
Burn to see, you need but seek.
Once beheld she gives the key   320

---

301 *Rosiest rosy wanes to crone:* i.e., the prettiest girl declines into an old woman.

Airing every doorway, she.
Little can you stop or steer
Ere of her you are the seër.
On the surface she will witch,
Rendering Beauty yours, but gaze
Under, and the soul is rich
Past computing, past amaze.
Then is courage that endures
Even her awful tremble yours.
Then, the reflex of that Fount   330
Spied below, will Reason mount
Lordly and a quenchless force,
Lighting Pain to its mad source,
Scaring Fear till Fear escapes,
Shot through all its phantom shapes.
Then your spirit will perceive
Fleshly seed of fleshly sins;
Where the passions interweave,
How the serpent tangle spins
Of the sense of Earth misprised,   340
Brainlessly unrecognized;
She being Spirit in her clods
Footway to the God of Gods.
Then for you are pleasures pure,
Sureties as the stars are sure:
Not the wanton beckoning flags
Which, of flattery and delight,
Wax to the grim Habit-Hags
Riding souls of men to night:
Pleasures that through blood run sane,   350
Quickening spirit from the brain.
Each of each in sequent birth,
Blood and brain and spirit, three
(Say the deepest gnomes of Earth),
Join for true felicity.
Are they parted, then expect
Some one sailing will be wrecked:
Separate hunting are they sped,

---

330 *reflex:* reflection.
333 *Lighting:* tracking.
340 *misprised:* held in contempt.

Scan the morsel coveted.
Earth that Triad is: she hides   360
Joy from him who that divides;
Showers it when the three are one
Glassing her in union.
Earth your haven, Earth your helm,
You command a double realm;
Labouring here to pay your debt,
Till your little sun shall set;
Leaving her the future task:
Loving her too well to ask.
Eglantine that climbs the yew,   370
She her darkest wreathes for those
Knowing her the Ever-new,
And themselves the kin o' the rose.
Life, the chisel, axe and sword,
Wield who have her depths explored:
Life, the dream, shall be their robe,
Large as air about the globe;
Life, the question, hear its cry
Echoed with concordant Why;
Life, the small self-dragon ramped,   380
Thrill for service to be stamped.
Ay, and over every height
Life for them shall wave a wand:
That, the last, where sits affright,
Homely shows the stream beyond.
Love the light and be its lynx,
You will track her and attain;
Read her as no cruel Sphinx
In the woods of Westermain.
Daily fresh the woods are ranged;   390
Glooms which otherwhere appal,
Sounded: here, their worths exchanged,
Urban joins with pastoral:

---

360 *Triad:* blood, brain, and spirit, mentioned seven lines earlier.
363 *Glassing:* reflecting.
374 *chisel, axe and sword:* standing for art, labor, and struggle, the three together representing man's achievements in life.
380 *ramped:* rampant.
384-5 *That, the last . . . stream beyond:* i.e., that even frightening death (the Styx) becomes familiar and comfortable.

Little lost, save what may drop
Husk-like, and the mind preserves.
Natural overgrowths they lop,
Yet from nature neither swerves,
Trained or savage: for this cause:
Of our Earth they ply the laws,
Have in Earth their feeding root,   400
Mind of man and bent of brute.
Hear that song; both wild and ruled.
Hear it: is it wail or mirth?
Ordered, bubbled, quite unschooled?
None, and all: it springs of Earth.
O but hear it! 'tis the mind;
Mind that with deep Earth unites,
Round the solid trunk to wind
Rings of clasping parasites.
Music have you there to feed   410
Simplest and most soaring need.
Free to wind, and in desire
Winding, they to her attached
Feel the trunk a spring of fire,
And ascend to heights unmatched,
Whence the tidal world is viewed
As a sea of windy wheat,
Momently black, barren, rude;
Golden-brown, for harvest meet;
Dragon-reaped from folly-sown;   420
Bride-like to the sickle-blade:
Quick it varies, while the moan,
Moan of a sad creature strayed,
Chiefly is its voice. So flesh
Conjures tempest-flails to thresh
Good from worthless. Some clear lamps
Light it; more of dead marsh-damps.
Monster is it still, and blind,
Fit but to be led by Pain.
Glance we at the paths behind,   430
Fruitful sight has Westermain.
There we laboured, and in turn

---

427 *marsh-damps:* phosphorescent light of decay in swamps.
428 *Monster:* the Dragon-fowl, or Self.

Forward our blown lamps discern,
As you see on the dark deep
Far the loftier billows leap,
   Foam for beacon bear.
Hither, hither, if you will,
Drink instruction, or instil,
Run the woods like vernal sap,
Crying, hail to luminousness!   440
   But have care.
In yourself may lurk the trap:
On conditions they caress.
Here you meet the light invoked:
Here is never secret cloaked.
Doubt you with the monster's fry
All his orbit may exclude;
Are you of the stiff, the dry,
Cursing the not understood;
Grasp you with the monster's claws;   450
Govern with his truncheon-saws;
Hate, the shadow of a grain;
You are lost in Westermain;
Earthward swoops a vulture sun,
Nighted upon carrion:
Straightway venom winecups shout
Toasts to One whose eyes are out:
Flowers along the reeling floor
Drip henbane and hellebore:
Beauty, of her tresses shorn,   460
Shrieks as nature's maniac:
Hideousness on hoof and horn
Tumbles, yapping in her track:
Haggard Wisdom, stately once,
Leers fantastical and trips:
Allegory drums the sconce,
Impiousness nibblenips.
Imp that dances, imp that flits,
Imp o' the demon-growing girl,

---

446 *fry:* offspring.
457 *One whose eyes are out:* Death.
459 *henbane and hellebore:* poisonous plants.
466 *drums the sconce:* beats on the skull.

Maddest! whirl with imp o' the pits   470
Round you, and with them you whirl
Fast where pours the fountain-rout
Out of Him whose eyes are out:
Multitudes on multitudes,
Drenched in wallowing devilry:
And you ask where you may be,
    In what reek of a lair
Given to bones and ogre-broods:
    And they yell you Where.
Enter these enchanted woods,   480
    You who dare.

[1883]

SEED-TIME

I

Flowers of the willow-herb are wool;
Flowers of the briar berries red;
Speeding their seed as the breeze may rule,
Flowers of the thistle loosen the thread.
Flowers of the clematis drip in beard,
Slack from the fir-tree youngly climbed;
Chaplets in air, flies foliage seared;
Heeled upon earth, lie clusters rimed.

II

Where were skies of the mantle stained
Orange and scarlet, a coat of frieze   10
Travels from North till day has waned,
Tattered, soaked in the ditch's dyes;
Tumbles the rook under grey or slate;
Else enfolding us, damps to the bone;
Narrows the world to my neighbour's gate;
Paints me Life as a wheezy crone.

---

⁷ *Chaplets:* wreaths.
⁸ *rimed:* covered with frost.
¹⁰ *frieze:* coarse woolen cloth.

III

Now seems none but the spider lord;
Star in circle his web waits prey,
Silvering bush-mounds, blue brushing sward;
Slow runs the hour, swift flits the ray.   20
Now to his thread-shroud is he nigh,
Nigh to the tangle where wings are sealed,
He who frolicked the jewelled fly;
All is adroop on the down and the weald.

IV

Mists more lone for the sheep-bell enwrap
Nights that tardily let slip a morn
Paler than moons, and on noontide's lap
Flame dies cold, like the rose late born.
Rose born late, born withered in bud!—
I, even I, for a zenith of sun   30
Cry, to fulfil me, nourish my blood:
O for a day of the long light, one!

V

Master the blood, nor read by chills,
Earth admonishes: Hast thou ploughed,
Sown, reaped, harvested grain for the mills,
Thou hast the light over shadow of cloud.
Steadily eyeing, before that wail,
Animal-infant, thy mind began,
Momently nearer me: should sight fail,
Plod in the track of the husbandman.   40

VI

Verily now is our season of seed,
Now in our Autumn; and Earth discerns
Them that have served her in them that can read,
Glassing, where under the surface she burns,
Quick at her wheel, while the fuel, decay,
Brightens the fire of renewal: and we?

---

25 *for the sheep-bell:* because of the sound of the sheep-bell.
40 *husbandman:* farmer, hence wise in the ways of the changes of Nature.

Death is the word of a bovine day,
Know you the breast of the springing To-be.

[1888]

NATURE AND LIFE

I

Leave the uproar: at a leap
Thou shalt strike a woodland path,
Enter silence, not of sleep,
Under shadows, not of wrath;
Breath which is the spirit's bath
In the old Beginnings find,
And endow them with a mind,
Seed for seedling, swathe for swathe.
That gives Nature to us, this
Give we her, and so we kiss.   10

II

Fruitful is it so: but hear
How within the shell thou art,
Music sounds; nor other near
Can to such a tremor start.
Of the waves our life is part;
They our running harvests bear:
Back to them for manful air,
Laden with the woodland's heart!
That gives Battle to us, this
Give we it, and good the kiss.   20

[1888]

---

13 *nor other near:* nor anything else near at hand.

DIRGE IN WOODS

A wind sways the pines,
　　And below
Not a breath of wild air;
Still as the mosses that glow
On the flooring and over the lines
Of the roots here and there.
The pine-tree drops its dead;
They are quiet, as under the sea.
Overhead, overhead
Rushes life in a race,　　　　　　　　10
As the clouds the clouds chase;
　　And we go,
And we drop like the fruits of the tree,
　　Even we,
　　Even so.

[1888]

MEDITATION UNDER STARS

What links are ours with orbs that are
　　So resolutely far:
The solitary asks, and they
Give radiance as from a shield:
　　Still at the death of day,
　　The seen, the unrevealed.
　　Implacable they shine
To us who would of Life obtain,
An answer for the life we strain
　　To nourish with one sign.　　　　10
Nor can imagination throw
The penetrative shaft: we pass
The breath of thought, who would divine
　　If haply they may grow

As Earth; have our desire to know;
If life comes there to grain from grass,
And flowers like ours of toil and pain;
   Has passion to beat bar,
   Win space from cleaving brain;
   The mystic link attain,   20
   Whereby star holds on star.

Those visible immortals beam
   Allurement to the dream:
Ireful at human hungers brook
   No question in the look.
For ever virgin to our sense,
Remote they wane to gaze intense:
Prolong it, and in ruthlessness they smite
The beating heart behind the ball of sight:
   Till we conceive their heavens hoar,   30
   Those lights they raise but sparkles frore,
And Earth, our blood-warm Earth, a shuddering prey
To that frigidity of brainless ray.

   Yet space is given for breath of thought
   Beyond our bounds when musing: more
   When to that musing love is brought,
   And love is asked of love's wherefore.
   'Tis Earth's, her gift; else have we nought:
   Her gift, her secret, here our tie.
   And not with her and yonder sky?   40
   Bethink you: were it Earth alone
   Breeds love, would not her region be
      The sole delight and throne
      Of generous Deity?

   To deeper than this ball of sight
Appeal the lustrous people of the night.
Fronting yon shoreless, sown with fiery sails,
   It is our ravenous that quails,
Flesh by its craven thirsts and fears distraught.
      The spirit leaps alight,   50

---

31 *frore:* frosty.

Doubts not in them is he,
The binder of his sheaves, the sane, the right:
Of magnitude to magnitude is wrought,
To feel it large of the great life they hold:
In them to come, or vaster intervolved,
The issues known in us, our unsolved solved:
That there with toil Life climbs the self-same Tree,
Whose roots enrichment have from ripeness dropped.
So may we read and little find them cold:
Let it but be the lord of Mind to guide   60
Our eyes; no branch of Reason's growing lopped;
Nor dreaming on a dream; but fortified
By day to penetrate black midnight; see,
Hear, feel, outside the senses; even that we,
The specks of dust upon a mound of mould,
We who reflect those rays, though low our place,
      To them are lastingly allied.

So may we read, and little find them cold:
Not frosty lamps illumining dead space,
Not distant aliens, not senseless Powers.   70
The fire is in them whereof we are born;
The music of their motion may be ours.
Spirit shall deem them beckoning Earth and voiced
Sisterly to her, in her beams rejoiced.
Of love, the grand impulsion, we behold
      The love that lends her grace
      Among the starry fold.
Then at new flood of customary morn,
      Look at her through her showers,
      Her mists, her streaming gold,   80
A wonder edges the familiar face:
She wears no more that robe of printed hours;
Half strange seems Earth, and sweeter than her flowers.

                              [1888]

Dante Gabriel Rossetti

[1828-1882]

Like William Blake before him, Dante Gabriel Rossetti presents the rare case of an artist known equally for his mastery of two diverse, if related, arts: poetry and painting. He was born in 1828, the second of the four children of Gabriele Rossetti, an Italian political refugee who was professor of his native language at King's College, London. In a bilingual household bursting with scholarly and artistic talent, Dante Gabriel was understood to be the child who held promise as a painter, and his sister Christina recognized as poetically gifted.

Rossetti's schooling was desultory, for he was not industrious at his studies. Even when he was admitted as a pupil of painting at the Royal Academy, he seldom completed assigned work or paid attention to the teaching that bored him. Both the intellectual discipline he needed for his poetry and the technical skills demanded by painting were neglected; had he not had superb natural, untaught talents in both fields, he would probably have made no mark in either. As it was, Rossetti's self-indulgent attitude toward his work kept him from ever achieving the very top rank in either poetry or painting.

In 1848 Rossetti asked to become a pupil of the young painter Ford Madox Brown, but once more he rebelled against the discipline of his studies. In the autumn of that year, he, Holman Hunt, and John Millais became the ringleaders of a group of young artists who called themselves the Pre-Raphaelite Brotherhood. They took in four other more or less rebellious young men, and the group declared itself in revolt against the prevailing academic standards in art. By their name they intended to signify their rejection of the affectations of the painters who had succeeded Raphael, although they scrupulously denied any intention of primitivism in their techniques. Instead, they were aiming at the emotional directness of the early painters. Their paintings were characterized by close attention to detail conveyed in an emotional manner. The colors were bright, their subjects often literary, and the symbolic details frequently derived from literature. As a school of painting the Pre-Raphaelite Brotherhood never developed, although it was influential in stirring up the convention-bound English artistic world for the few years before the members disbanded to go on to their separate successes. Today, some of their work is in bad condition because the materials and techniques they employed hastened the disintegration of the paintings.

Hunt, Millais, and Rossetti all first exhibited important paintings in 1849. Christina Rossetti was her brother's model for "The Girlhood of Mary Virgin," for which Rossetti wrote two sonnets explaining its symbolism.

In 1850 the Brotherhood issued a short-lived magazine, *The Germ,* notable chiefly for the contributions of Dante and Christina Rossetti. Here appeared the first version of "The Blessed Damozel." The following year the Brotherhood had ceased to function as a group, although many of the members remained friends. While it still formed a cohesive whole, its chief model had been the beautiful young milliner's assistant, Elizabeth Siddal, with whom Rossetti fell in love. Miss Siddal (known to the group as "the Sid") had some talent as painter and poet, but to Rossetti she was something more important, the incarnation of his ideas of physical beauty. By the time the Brotherhood collapsed, Rossetti was engaged to the Sid, but their engagement was to drag on for a weary decade. Miss Siddal's health deteriorated, Rossetti had other feminine companions, and the engagement became a tragically constraining relationship from which neither could get free. In 1860 they were married, but all the excitement of their early love had disappeared, and it was a miserable—if mercifully brief—marriage. Mrs. Rossetti was the slave of drugs and was apparently dying of tuberculosis; Rossetti consoled himself in the arms of other women. Less than two years after their marriage, Mrs. Rossetti died of a self-administered overdose of sleeping draught. Rossetti, overwhelmed by remorse for his own shortcomings as her husband, made what was for him the greatest sacrifice he knew: into her coffin he slipped the manuscript volume containing the only finished copies of all the poems he had so far written. It was buried in the mass of her beautiful hair which had first attracted Rossetti.

By this time, Rossetti had come to know many of the foremost artistic men of his day, among them Swinburne, Ruskin, William Morris, and Edward Burne-Jones. Mrs. Morris was the former Jane Burden, whom Rossetti had met in the middle of his long and frustrating engagement to Miss Siddal. Although he fell in love with Miss Burden, and seems to have loved her to the end of his life, Rossetti felt obligated to marry Miss Siddal, and he urged Morris to marry Jane Burden, in a gesture worthy of the melodrama of the Victorian stage.

After his wife's death, Rossetti moved to Chelsea, where for some years he shared a large and splendid house with a changing series of co-tenants, including Swinburne, George Meredith, and one of Rossetti's mistresses, and a bewildering menage of such exotic pets as wombats, wallabies, chameleons, peacocks, an armadillo, and a zebra.

Rossetti had become well established as a painter, with patrons coming directly to him to purchase or to commission pictures, but he was still relatively unknown as a poet, although he had in 1861 published a group of translations called *The Early Italian Poets* (republished in 1874 as *Dante and His Circle*). In 1869, at the insistence of friends, he had his wife's body exhumed and rescued the poems which had been buried with her. The following year he published *Poems,* which included many of the works for which he is now best known. Some of the sonnets that later made up *The House of Life* first appeared in this volume. A minor literary man, Robert Buchanan, took the publication of the book as the occasion for a pseudonymous attack on Rossetti with an article called "The Fleshly School of Poetry," in which he accused Rossetti of poetic indecency. Rossetti for some years had been addicted to chloral, which he took to combat insomnia. The use of the drug and frequent overindulgence in drink had already disturbed his mind. Buchanan's attack was too much for Rossetti; after this time he suffered from a paranoiac belief that he was persecuted by a conspiracy of those around him.

As his illness deepened, Rossetti withdrew from general society, although he continued painting and writing. The subject of most of his late paintings and poems was the exotic beauty of Jane Morris, and for some time he lived with the Morrises at Kelmscott Manor near Oxford. His paintings still sold well, and in 1881 he reprinted his *Poems* and published *Ballads and Sonnets,* which included the completed *House of Life.* The spring of the next year, 1882, he died, his mind stricken, his body worn out.

Rossetti's poetry has not been easy for critics to deal with because it is in some ways so unlike that of his contemporaries; it would not be unfair to say that it is more Italian than English in inspiration. The diction is heavily Latinate, the imagery lush, hothouse, and occasionally cloying. With the rare exception of a poem like "Jenny," Rossetti's poetry is not concerned with life of England of his day, and he seems to look back to medievalism, or, rather, to the idea of medievalism held by the Victorians. Although Buchanan's attack was far more prurient than the poetry at which it was aimed, it remains true that much of what Rossetti wrote was concerned with an overtly voluptuous sensuousness of a sort unusual in Victorian poetry. Like Poe, whom he greatly admired, Rossetti was fascinated by the idea of the death of a beautiful woman and by the subsequent relationship between the living lover and the dead woman. But, unlike Poe, his idealization of woman was based on a solid tradition. It has often been pointed out that Rossetti was a poetical descendant of the Troubadours, the Provençal poets, and of Dante, and that he had absorbed the medieval ideal of Courtly Love, with its idealization of the lady and its assumption of a link between physical love and divine love. But, to Rossetti, the contemplation, adoration, and possession of feminine beauty were in themselves divine, and he felt no need to think that they reflected a personal divinity beyond themselves. At the same time, in thinking that the unknown can be approached only through the known, he was like the Italian poets he so loved. In sonnet V of *The House of Life,* he is speaking literally:

> Lady, I fain would tell how evermore
> Thy soul I knew not from thy body, nor
> Thee from myself, neither our love from God.

Soul is part of body, and human, physical love is, for him, God, and it is impossible for him to distinguish between the components.

It is therefore natural, but somewhat surprising, to find poems that are essentially totally pagan decorated with the Christian trappings of the Roman Catholic Church, into which Rossetti's father had been baptized, and of the Anglican Church, in which Rossetti himself had been reared and of which his mother and two sisters were devout members (his sister Maria became an Anglican nun in middle life). The externals that, as a child, he had learned to associate with the highest of spiritual experiences were in his manhood attached to a totally different sort of experience, and provided a symbolic framework within which to describe it. In "The Blessed Damozel," for instance, we find a completely un-Christian sense of bereavement for the dead lady manifesting itself in a heaven apparently presided over by the Virgin Mary, and the reunion to which her blessed soul looks forward is expressed in highly physical images. For Rossetti, there was no sense of jar or incongruity in the marriage of two such different points of view.

In the later poetry, the imagery becomes less specific, perhaps more misty. As John Heath-Stubbs has written of Rossetti, "his true merit lies less in direct expressive power, than in his gift for evoking transient and half-defined states of feeling." There is often a sense of only partially realized symbolic significance in the poetry, the exact meaning of which is difficult to translate into other terms. Yet this is probably not to be wondered at when we remember that the visions of which Rossetti is writing are analogous to those mystical perceptions of which poets in the Christian tradition have often written. In each case, the ineffable eludes the concreteness of direct or metaphorical statement, and must be expressed in terms of an apprehension which may be only partial.

The House of Life shows this aspect of Rossetti. Here we have no traditional sonnet sequence with narrative background, or crisis, or clearly marked progression of mood and emotion. Instead, we have a series of considerations (in a Christian mystic, they might be called *meditations*) on love, life, and death, unconnected save in mood and outlook. Nearly every sonnet is literally a "moment's monument," concerned with only one transitory aspect of the poet's general subject. Many deal with instantaneous, fleeting, half-understood states of mind, and the substance of the poem becomes the communication of these states of mind rather than the analysis of them as they are recollected in tranquility. Emotion was the religion of Rossetti, and it is the basis of his best poetry.

BIBLIOGRAPHY

The text of this anthology follows the standard edition, *The Collected Works of Dante Gabriel Rossetti,* ed. William M. Rossetti. 2 vols. (Ellis and Scrutton, London, 1886). Three very useful modern editions are those edited by Paull F. Baum: *Poems, Ballads, and Sonnets* (Odyssey Press, New York, 1937); *The House of Life* (Harvard University Press, Cambridge, 1928); and *The Blessed Damozel* (University of North Carolina Press, Chapel Hill, 1937).

Biography and Criticism:

Bowra, C. M., "The House of Life," *The Romantic Imagination,* Oxford University Press, London, 1950. *[inheritor of previous age]*

Doughty, Oswald, *Dante Gabriel Rossetti: A Victorian Romantic.* Yale University Press, New Haven, 1949.

Heath-Stubbs, John, *The Darkling Plain.* Eyre and Spottiswoode, London, 1950. *[only some good]*

Hough, Graham, *The Last Romantics,* Duckworth, London, 1949. *[good]*

Hueffer, Ford Madox [F. M. Ford], *Rossetti: A Critical Essay on His Art.* Duckworth, London, 1902.

Waugh, Evelyn, *Rossetti: His Life and Works,* Duckworth, London, 1928. *[to be avoided.] [prejudiced]*

Baum, Paul. House of Life Sequence

THE BLESSED DAMOZEL

The blessed damozel leaned out
　　From the gold bar of Heaven;
Her eyes were deeper than the depth
　　Of waters stilled at even;
She had three lilies in her hand,
　　And the stars in her hair were seven.

Her robe, ungirt from clasp to hem,
　　No wrought flowers did adorn,
But a white rose of Mary's gift,
　　For service meetly worn;   10
Her hair that lay along her back
　　Was yellow like ripe corn.

Herseemed she scarce had been a day
　　One of God's choristers;
The wonder was not yet quite gone
　　From that still look of hers;
Albeit, to them she left, her day
　　Had counted as ten years.

(To one, it is ten years of years.
　　. . . Yet now, and in this place,   20
Surely she leaned o'er me—her hair
　　Fell all about my face. . . .
Nothing: the autumn fall of leaves.
　　The whole year sets apace.)

It was the rampart of God's house
　　That she was standing on;

The Blessed Damozel: An interesting comparison can be made to Rossetti's painting of the same name. *Damozel:* damsel.
10 *meetly:* appropriately.
13 *Herseemed:* it seemed to her.

By God built over the sheer depth
   The which is Space begun;
So high, that looking downward thence
   She scarce could see the sun.   30

It lies in Heaven, across the flood
   Of ether, as a bridge.
Beneath, the tides of day and night
   With flame and darkness ridge
The void, as low as where this earth
   Spins like a fretful midge.

Around her, lovers, newly met
   'Mid deathless love's acclaims,
Spoke evermore among themselves
   Their heart-remembered names;   40
And the souls mounting up to God
   Went by her like thin flames.

And still she bowed herself and stooped
   Out of the circling charm;
Until her bosom must have made
   The bar she leaned on warm,
And the lilies lay as if asleep
   Along her bended arm.

From the fixed place of Heaven she saw
   Time like a pulse shake fierce   50
Through all the worlds. Her gaze still strove
   Within the gulf to pierce
Its path; and now she spoke as when
   The stars sang in their spheres.

The sun was gone now; the curled moon
   Was like a little feather
Fluttering far down the gulf; and now
   She spoke through the still weather.
Her voice was like the voice the stars
   Had when they sang together.   60

---

36 *midge:* gnat.

(Ah sweet! Even now, in that bird's song,
   Strove not her accents there,
Fain to be hearkened? When those bells
   Possessed the mid-day air,
Strove not her steps to reach my side
   Down all the echoing stair?)

"I wish that he were come to me,
   For he will come," she said.
"Have I not prayed in Heaven?—on earth,
   Lord, Lord, has he not pray'd?   70
Are not two prayers a perfect strength?
   And shall I feel afraid?

"When round his head the aureole clings,
   And he is clothed in white,
I'll take his hand and go with him
   To the deep wells of light;
As unto a stream we will step down,
   And bathe there in God's sight.

"We two will stand beside that shrine,
   Occult, withheld, untrod,   80
Whose lamps are stirred continually
   With prayer sent up to God;
And see our old prayers, granted, melt
   Each like a little cloud.

"We two will lie i' the shadow of
   That living mystic tree
Within whose secret growth the Dove
   Is sometimes felt to be,
While every leaf that His plumes touch
   Saith His Name audibly.   90

"And I myself will teach to him,
   I myself, lying so,
The songs I sing here; which his voice
   Shall pause in, hushed and slow,

---

87 *the Dove:* the Holy Spirit.

And find some knowledge at each pause,
    Of some new thing to know."

(Alas! We two, we two, thou say'st!
    Yea, one wast thou with me
That once of old. But shall God lift
    To endless unity   100
The soul whose likeness with thy soul
    Was but its love for thee?)

"We two," she said, "will seek the groves
    Where the lady Mary is,
With her five handmaidens, whose names
    Are five sweet symphonies,
Cecily, Gertrude, Magdalen,
    Margaret and Rosalys.

"Circlewise sit they, with bound locks
    And foreheads garlanded;   110
Into the fine cloth white like flame
    Weaving the golden thread,
To fashion the birth-robes for them
    Who are just born, being dead.

"He shall fear, haply, and be dumb:
    Then will I lay my cheek
To his, and tell about our love,
    Not once abashed or weak:
And the dear Mother will approve
    My pride, and let me speak.   120

"Herself shall bring us, hand in hand,
    To Him round whom all souls
Kneel, the clear-ranged unnumbered heads
    Bowed with their aureoles:
And angels meeting us shall sing
    To their citherns and citoles.

107-8 *Cecily . . . Rosalys:* names chosen for their euphony rather than for
any religious or symbolic effect.
126 *citherns and citoles:* medieval stringed instruments.

"There will I ask of Christ the Lord
  Thus much for him and me:—
Only to live as once on earth
  With Love,—only to be,   130
As then awhile, for ever now
  Together, I and he."

She gazed and listened and then said,
  Less sad of speech than mild,—
"All this is when he comes." She ceased.
  The light thrilled towards her, fill'd
With angels in strong level flight.
  Her eyes, prayed, and she smil'd.

(I saw her smile.) But soon their path
  Was vague in distant spheres: 140
And then she cast her arms along
  The golden barriers,
And laid her face between her hands,
  And wept. (I heard her tears.)

                    [1850, 1856, 1870]

TROY TOWN   *celebr. human perfection*

Heavenborn Helen, Sparta's queen,
    (*O Troy Town!*)
Had two breasts of heavenly sheen,
The sun and moon of the heart's desire:
All Love's lordship lay between.
    (*O Troy's down,*   *& all this worth*
    Tall Troy's on fire!)   *gift of Helen*

Helen knelt at Venus' shrine,
    (*O Troy Town!*)

Troy Town: Paris, son of the king of Troy, awarded the golden apple to
Venus in her competition with Minerva and Juno; as a reward she promised
him Helen, most beautiful woman in the world and wife of Menelaus, king
of Sparta. In the war over Helen's abduction, Troy was burned. As a devotee
of Venus, Helen is said to have offered her a cup shaped like one of her
own superb breasts.

Saying, "A little gift is mine,   10
A little gift for a heart's desire.
Hear me speak and make me a sign!
    (*O Troy's down,*
     Tall Troy's on fire!)

"Look, I bring thee a carven cup;
    (*O Troy Town!*)
See it here as I hold it up,—
Shaped it is to the heart's desire,
Fit to fill when the gods would sup.
    (*O Troy's down*   20
     Tall Troy's on fire!)

"It was moulded like my breast:
    (*O Troy Town!*)
He that sees it may not rest,
Rest at all for his heart's desire.
O give ear to my heart's behest!
    (*O Troy's down,*
     Tall Troy's on fire!)

"See my breast, how like it is;
    (*O Troy Town!*)   30
See it bare for the air to kiss!
Is the cup to thy heart's desire?
O for the breast, O make it his!
    (*O Troy's down,*
     Tall Troy's on fire!)

"Yea, for my bosom here I sue;
    (*O Troy Town!*)
Thou must give it where 'tis due,
Give it there to the heart's desire.
Whom do I give my bosom to?   40
    (*O Troy's down,*
     Tall Troy's on fire!)

"Each twin breast is an apple sweet.
    (*O Troy Town!*)
Once an apple stirred the beat

Of thy heart with the heart's desire:—
Say, who brought it then to thy feet?
            (*O Troy's down,*
            Tall Troy's on fire!)

"They that claimed it then were three: 50
            (*O Troy Town!*)
For thy sake two hearts did he
Make forlorn of the heart's desire.
Do for him as he did for thee!
            (*O Troy's down,*
            Tall Troy's on fire!)

"Mine are apples grown to the south,
            (*O Troy Town!*)
Grown to taste in the days of drouth,
Taste and waste to the heart's desire: 60
Mine are apples meet for his mouth."
            (*O Troy's down,*
            Tall Troy's on fire!)

Venus looked on Helen's gift,
            (*O Troy Town!*)
Looked and smiled with subtle drift,
Saw the work of her heart's desire:—
"There thou kneel'st for Love to lift!"
            (*O Troy's down,*
            Tall Troy's on fire!)   70

Venus looked in Helen's face,
            (*O Troy Town!*)
Knew far off an hour and place,
And fire lit from the heart's desire;
Laughed and said, "Thy gift hath grace!"
            (*O Troy's down,*
            Tall Troy's on fire!)

Cupid looked on Helen's breast,
            (*O Troy Town!*)
Saw the heart within its nest,   80
Saw the flame of the heart's desire,—

rejecting notion
that what Helen did
was wrong

Marked his arrow's burning crest.
  (*O Troy's down,*
   Tall Troy's on fire!)

Cupid took another dart,
  (*O Troy Town!*)
Fledged it for another heart,
Winged the shaft with the heart's desire,
Drew the string and said, "Depart!"
  (*O Troy's down,*   90
   Tall Troy's on fire!)

Paris turned upon his bed,
  (*O Troy Town!*)
Turned upon his bed and said,
Dead at heart with the heart's desire,—
"O to clasp her golden head!"
  (*O Troy's down,*
   Tall Troy's on fire!)

[1870]

JENNY

"Vengeance of Jenny's case! Fie on her! Never name her, child!"
         Mrs. Quickly.

Lazy laughing languid Jenny,
Fond of a kiss and fond of a guinea,
Whose head upon my knee to-night
Rests for a while, as if grown light
With all our dances and the sound
To which the wild tunes spun you round:
Fair Jenny mine, the thoughtless queen
Of kisses which the blush between
Could hardly make much daintier;
Whose eyes are as blue skies, whose hair   10
Is countless gold incomparable:

Jenny: See *The Merry Wives of Windsor*, IV, i, 61.

Fresh flower, scarce touched with signs that tell
Of Love's exuberant hotbed:—Nay,
Poor flower left torn since yesterday
Until to-morrow leave you bare;
Poor handful of bright spring-water
Flung in the whirlpool's shrieking face;
Poor shameful Jenny, full of grace
Thus with your head upon my knee;—
Whose person or whose purse may be   20
The lodestar of your reverie?

   This room of yours, my Jenny, looks
A change from mine so full of books,
Whose serried ranks hold fast, forsooth,
So many captive hours of youth,—
The hours they thieve from day and night
To make one's cherished work come right,
And leave it wrong for all their theft,
Even as to-night my work was left:
Until I vowed that since my brain   30
And eyes of dancing seemed so fain,
My feet should have some dancing too:—
And thus it was I met with you.
Well, I suppose 'twas hard to part,
For here I am. And now, sweetheart,
You seem too tired to get to bed.

   It was a careless life I led
When rooms like this were scarce so strange
Not long ago. What breeds the change,—
The many aims or the few years?   40
Because to-night it all appears
Something I do not know again.

   The cloud's not danced out of my brain,—
The cloud that made it turn and swim
While hour by hour the books grew dim.
Why, Jenny, as I watch you there,—
For all your wealth of loosened hair,
Your silk ungirdled and unlac'd
And warm sweets open to the waist,

All golden in the lamplight's gleam,— 50
You know not what a book you seem,
Half-read by lightning in a dream!
How should you know, my Jenny? Nay,
And I should be ashamed to say:—
Poor beauty, so well worth a kiss!
But while my thought runs on like this
With wasteful whims more than enough,
I wonder what you're thinking of.

If of myself you think at all,
What is the thought?—conjectural 60
On sorry matters best unsolved?—
Or inly is each grace revolved
To fit me with a lure?—or (sad
To think!) perhaps you're merely glad
That I'm not drunk or ruffianly
And let you rest upon my knee.

For sometimes, were the truth confess'd,
You're thankful for a little rest,—
Glad from the crush to rest within,
From the heart-sickness and the din 70
Where envy's voice at virtue's pitch
Mocks you because your gown is rich;
And from the pale girl's dumb rebuke,
Whose ill-clad grace and toil-worn look
Proclaim the strength that keeps her weak,
And other nights than yours bespeak;
And from the wise unchildish elf,
To schoolmate lesser than himself
Pointing you out, what thing you are:—
Yes, from the daily jeer and jar, 80
From shame and shame's outbraving too,
Is rest not sometimes sweet to you?—
But most from the hatefulness of man
Who spares not to end what he began,
Whose acts are ill and his speech ill,
Who, having used you at his will,
Thrusts you aside, as when I dine
I serve the dishes and the wine.

Well, handsome Jenny mine, sit up:
I've filled our glasses, let us sup,   90
And do not let me think of you,
Lest shame of yours suffice for two.
What, still so tired? Well, well then, keep
Your head there, so you do not sleep;
But that the weariness may pass
And leave you merry, take this glass.
Ah! lazy lily hand, more bless'd
If ne'er in rings it had been dress'd
Nor ever by a glove conceal'd!

Behold the lilies of the field,   100
They toil not neither do they spin;
(So doth the ancient text begin,—
Not of such rest as one of these
Can share.) Another rest and ease
Along each summer-sated path
From its new lord the garden hath,
Than that whose spring in blessings ran
Which praised the bounteous husbandman,
Ere yet, in days of hankering breath,
The lilies sickened unto death.   110

What, Jenny, are your lilies dead?
Aye, and the snow-white leaves are spread
Like winter on the garden-bed.
But you had roses left in May,—
They were not gone too. Jenny, nay,
But must your roses die, and those
Their purfled buds that should unclose?
Even so; the leaves are curled apart,
Still red as from the broken heart,
And here's the naked stem of thorns.   120

Nay, nay, mere words. Here nothing warns
As yet of winter. Sickness here

---

102 *the ancient text:* "Consider the lilies of the field, how they grow; they
toil not, neither do they spin: and yet I say unto you, that even Solomon in
all his glory was not arrayed like one of these" (*Matthew* 6:28-29).
117 *purfled:* adorned on the edge.

Or want alone could waken fear,—
Nothing but passion wrings a tear.
Except when there may rise unsought
Haply at times a passing thought
Of the old days which seem to be
Much older than any history
That is written in any book;
When she would lie in fields and look   130
Along the ground through the blown grass,
And wonder where the city was,
Far out of sight, whose broil and bale
They told her then for a child's tale.

    Jenny, you know the city now,
A child can tell the tale there, how
Some things which are not yet enroll'd
In market-lists are bought and sold
Even till the early Sunday light,
When Saturday night is market-night   140
Everywhere, be it dry or wet,
And market-night in the Haymarket.
Our learned London children know,
Poor Jenny, all your pride and woe;
Have seen your lifted silken skirt
Advertise dainties through the dirt;
Have seen your coach-wheels splash rebuke
On virtue; and have learned your look
When, wealth and health slipped past, you stare
Along the streets alone, and there,   150
Round the long park, across the bridge,
The cold lamps at the pavement's edge
Wind on together and apart,   .
A fiery serpent for your heart.

    Let the thoughts pass, an empty cloud!
Suppose I were to think aloud,—
What if to her all this were said?
Why, as a volume seldom read
Being opened halfway shuts again,

---

142 *Haymarket:* a major street in the theater district of London, formerly the haunt of prostitutes.

So might the pages of her brain
Be parted at such words, and thence
Close back upon the dusty sense.
For is there hue or shape defin'd
In Jenny's desecrated mind,
Where all contagious currents meet,
A Lethe of the middle street?
Nay, it reflects not any face,
Nor sound is in its sluggish pace,
But as they coil those eddies clot,
And night and day remember not.

   Why, Jenny, you're asleep at last!—
Asleep, poor Jenny, hard and fast,—
So young and soft and tired; so fair,
With chin thus nestled in your hair,
Mouth quiet, eyelids almost blue
As if some sky of dreams shone through!

   Just as another woman sleeps!
Enough to throw one's thoughts in heaps
Of doubt and horror,—what to say
Or think,—this awful secret sway,
The potter's power over the clay!
Of the same lump (it has been said)
For honour and dishonour made,
Two sister vessels. Here is one.

   My cousin Nell is fond of fun,
And fond of dress, and change, and praise,
So mere a woman in her ways:
And if her sweet eyes rich in youth
Are like her lips that tell the truth,
My cousin Nell is fond of love.
And she's the girl I'm proudest of.
Who does not prize her, guard her well?
The love of change, in cousin Nell,
Shall find the best and hold it dear:

160

170

180

190

---

166 *Lethe:* river of oblivion.

The unconquered mirth turn quieter
Not through her own, through others' woe:
The conscious pride of beauty glow
Beside another's pride in her,
One little part of all they share.
For Love himself shall ripen these   200
In a kind soil to just increase
Through years of fertilizing peace.

Of the same lump (as it is said)
For honour and dishonour made,
Two sister vessels. Here is one.

It makes a goblin of the sun.

So pure,—so fall'n! How dare to think
Of the first common kindred link?
Yet, Jenny, till the world shall burn
It seems that all things take their turn;   210
And who shall say but this fair tree
May need, in changes that may be,
Your children's children's charity?
Scorned then, no doubt, as you are scorn'd!
Shall no man hold his pride forewarn'd
Till in the end, the Day of Days,
At Judgment, one of his own race,
As frail and lost as you, shall rise,—
His daughter, with his mother's eyes? *nother fault, but*
result of attitude

How Jenny's clock ticks on the shelf!   220
Might not the dial scorn itself
That has such hours to register?
Yet as to me, even so to her
Are golden sun and silver moon,
In daily largesse of earth's boon,
Counted for life-coins to one tune.
And if, as blindfold fates are toss'd,
Through some one man this life be lost,
Shall soul not somehow pay for soul?

Fair shines the gilded aureole   230
In which our highest painters place
Some living woman's simple face.
And the stilled features thus descried
As Jenny's long throat droops aside,—
The shadows where the cheeks are thin,
And pure wide curve from ear to chin,—
With Raffael's, Leonardo's hand
To show them to men's souls, might stand,
While ages long, the whole world through,
For preachings of what God can do.   240
What has man done here? How atone,
Great God, for this which man has done?
And for the body and soul which by
Man's pitiless doom must now comply
With lifelong hell, what lullaby
Of sweet forgetful second birth
Remains? All dark. No sign on earth
What measure of God's rest endows
The many mansions of his house.

If but a woman's heart might see   250
Such erring heart unerringly
For once! But that can never be.

Like a rose shut in a book
In which pure women may not look,
For its base pages claim control
To crush the flower within the soul;
Where through each dead rose-leaf that clings,
Pale as transparent Psyche-wings,
To the vile text, are traced such things
As might make lady's cheek indeed   260
More than a living rose to read;
So nought save foolish foulness may
Watch with hard eyes the sure decay;
And so the life-blood of this rose,
Puddled with shameful knowledge, flows
Through leaves no chaste hand may unclose:

---

258 *Psyche-wings:* moth wings, here meaning the soul.

Yet still it keeps such faded show
Of when 'twas gathered long ago,
That the crushed petals' lovely grain,
The sweetness of the sanguine stain,   270
Seen of a woman's eyes, must make
Her pitiful heart, so prone to ache,
Love roses better for its sake:—
Only that this can never be:—
Even so unto her sex is she.

Yet, Jenny, looking long at you,
The woman almost fades from view.
A cipher of man's changeless sum
Of lust, past, present, and to come,
Is left. A riddle that one shrinks   280
To challenge from the scornful sphinx.

Like a toad within a stone
Seated while Time crumbles on;
Which sits there since the earth was curs'd
For Man's trangression at the first;
Which, living through all centuries,
Not once has seen the sun arise;
Whose life, to its cold circle charmed,
The earth's whole summers have not warmed;
Which always—whitherso the stone   290
Be flung—sits there, deaf, blind, alone;—
Aye, and shall not be driven out
Till that which shuts him round about
Break at the very Master's stroke,
And the dust thereof vanish as smoke,
And the seed of Man vanish as dust:—
Even so within this world is Lust.

Come, come, what use in thoughts like this?
Poor little Jenny, good to kiss,—
You'd not believe by what strange roads   300
Thought travels, when your beauty goads

---

²⁷⁰ *sanguine:* red.

A man to-night to think of toads!
Jenny, wake up. . . . Why, there's the dawn!

And there's an early waggon drawn
To market, and some sheep that jog
Bleating before a barking dog;
And the old streets come peering through
Another night that London knew;
And all as ghostlike as the lamps.

So on the wings of day decamps   310
My last night's frolic. Glooms begin
To shiver off as lights creep in
Past the gauze curtains half drawn-to,
And the lamp's doubled shade grows blue,—
Your lamp, my Jenny, kept alight,
Like a wise virgin's, all one night! *in Bible.*
And in the alcove coolly spread
Glimmers with dawn your empty bed;
And yonder your fair face I see
Reflected lying on my knee,   320
Where teems with first foreshadowings
Your pier-glass scrawled with diamond rings:
And on your bosom all night worn
Yesterday's rose now droops forlorn
But dies not yet this summer morn.

And now without, as if some word
Had called upon them that they heard,
The London sparrows far and nigh
Clamour together suddenly;
And Jenny's cage-bird grown awake   330
Here in their song his part must take,
Because here too the day doth break.

And somehow in myself the dawn
Among stirred clouds and veils withdrawn
Strikes greyly on her. Let her sleep.
But will it wake her if I heap
These cushions thus beneath her head

Where my knee was? No,—there's your bed,
My Jenny, while you dream. And there
I lay among your golden hair   340
Perhaps the subject of your dreams,
These golden coins.
                    For still one deems
That Jenny's flattering sleep confers
New magic on the magic purse,—
Grim web, how clogged with shrivelled flies!
Between the threads fine fumes arise
And shape their pictures in the brain.
There roll no streets in glare and rain,
Nor flagrant man-swine whets his tusk;
But delicately sighs in musk   350
The homage of the dim boudoir;
Or like a palpitating star
Thrilled into song, the opera-night
Breathes faint in the quick pulse of light;
Or at the carriage-window shine
Rich wares for choice; or, free to dine,
Whirls through its hour of health (divine
For her) the concourse of the Park.
And though in the discounted dark
Her functions there and here are one,   360
Beneath the lamps and in the sun
There reigns at least the acknowledged belle
Apparelled beyond parallel.
Ah Jenny, yes, we know your dreams.

    For even the Paphian Venus seems
A goddess o'er the realms of love,
When silver-shrined in shadowy grove:
Aye, or let offerings nicely placed
But hide Priapus to the waist,
And whoso looks on him shall see   370
An eligible deity.

---

365 *Paphian Venus:* the sensual aspect of love, from Paphos on the island of
Crete, where Venus was believed to have arisen from the sea, and where she
was worshipped with erotic rites.
369 *Priapus:* phallic god of fertility.

Why, Jenny, waking here alone
May help you to remember one,
Though all the memory's long outworn
Of many a double-pillowed morn.
I think I see you when you wake,
And rub your eyes for me, and shake
My gold, in rising, from your hair,
A Danaë for a moment there.

    Jenny, my love rang true! for still   380
Love at first sight is vague, until
That tinkling makes him audible.

    And must I mock you to the last,
Ashamed of my own shame,—aghast
Because some thoughts not born amiss
Rose at a poor fair face like this?
Well, of such thoughts so much I know:
In my life, as in hers, they show,
By a far gleam which I may near,
A dark path I can strive to clear.   390

    Only one kiss. Good-bye, my dear.

           [1870]

THE PORTRAIT

This is her picture as she was:
    It seems a thing to wonder on,
As though mine image in the glass
    Should tarry when myself am gone.
I gaze until she seems to stir,—
Until mine eyes almost aver
    That now, even now, the sweet lips part
To breathe the words of the sweet heart:—
And yet the earth is over her.

---

379 *Danaë:* Greek maiden seduced by Zeus in the form of a golden shower.

Alas! even such the thin-drawn ray 10
   That makes the prison-depths more rude,—
The drip of water night and day
   Giving a tongue to solitude.
Yet only this, of love's whole prize,
Remains; save what in mournful guise
   Takes counsel with my soul alone,—
   Save what is secret and unknown,
Below the earth, above the skies.

In painting her I shrined her face
   Mid mystic trees, where light falls in 20
Hardly at all; a covert place
   Where you might think to find a din
Of doubtful talk, and a live flame
Wandering, and many a shape whose name
   Not itself knoweth, and old dew,
   And your own footsteps meeting you,
And all things going as they came.

A deep dim wood; and there she stands
   As in that wood that day: for so
Was the still movement of her hands 30
   And such the pure line's gracious flow.
And passing fair the type must seem,
Unknown the presence and the dream.
   'Tis she: though of herself, alas!
   Less than her shadow on the grass
Or than her image in the stream.

That day we met there, I and she
   One with the other all alone;
And we were blithe; yet memory
   Saddens those hours, as when the moon 40
Looks upon daylight. And with her
I stooped to drink the spring-water,
   Athirst where other waters sprang;
   And where the echo is, she sang,—
My soul another echo there.

But when that hour my soul won strength
　For words whose silence wastes and kills,
Dull raindrops smote us, and at length
　Thundered the heat within the hills.
That eve I spoke those words again   50
Beside the pelted window-pane;
　　And there she hearkened what I said,
　　With under-glances that surveyed
The empty pastures blind with rain.

Next day the memories of these things,
　Like leaves through which a bird has flown,
Still vibrated with Love's warm wings;
　Till I must make them all my own
And paint this picture. So, 'twixt ease
Of talk and sweet long silences,   60
　　She stood among the plants in bloom
　　At windows of a summer room,
To feign the shadow of the trees.

And as I wrought, while all above
　And all around was fragrant air,
In the sick burthen of my love
　It seemed each sun-thrilled blossom there
Beat like a heart among the leaves.
O heart that never beats nor heaves,
　　In that one darkness lying still,   70
　　What now to thee my love's great will
Or the fine web the sunshine weaves?

For now doth daylight disavow
　Those days,—nought left to see or hear.
Only in solemn whispers now
　At night-time these things reach mine ear,
When the leaf-shadows at a breath
Shrink in the road, and all the heath,
　　Forest and water, far and wide,
　　In limpid starlight glorified,   80
Lie like the mystery of death.

Last night at last I could have slept,
　And yet delayed my sleep till dawn.

Still wandering. Then it was I wept:
    For unawares I came upon
Those glades where once she walked with me:
And as I stood there suddenly,
    All wan with traversing the night,
    Upon the desolate verge of light
Yearned loud the iron-bosomed sea.   90

Even so, where Heaven holds breath and hears
    The beating heart of Love's own breast,—
Where round the secret of all spheres
    All angels lay their wings to rest,—
How shall my soul stand rapt and awed,
When, by the new birth borne abroad
    Throughout the music of the suns,
    It enters in her soul at once
And knows the silence there for God!

Here with her face doth memory sit   100
    Meanwhile, and wait the day's decline.
Till other eyes shall look from it,
Eyes of the spirit's Palestine,
Even than the old gaze tenderer:
While hopes and aims long lost with her
    Stand round her image side by side,
    Like tombs of pilgrims that have died
About the Holy Sepulchre.

[1870]

MARY'S GIRLHOOD

For a Picture

I

This is that blessed Mary, pre-elect
   God's Virgin. Gone is a great while, and she
   Dwelt young in Nazareth of Galilee.
Unto God's will she brought devout respect,
Profound simplicity of intellect,
   And supreme patience. From her mother's knee
   Faithful and hopeful; wise in charity;
Strong in grave peace; in pity circumspect.

So held she through her girlhood; as it were
   An angel-watered lily, that near God   10
     Grows and is quiet. Till, one dawn at home,
She woke in her white bed, and had no fear
   At all,—yet wept till sunshine, and felt awed:
Because the fulness of the time was come.

                        [1870]

II

These are the symbols. On that cloth of red
   I' the center is the Tripoint; perfect each,
   Except the second of its points, to teach
That Christ is not yet born. The books—whose head
Is golden Charity, as Paul hath said—
   Those virtues are wherein the soul is rich;
   Therefore on them the lily standeth, which
Is Innocence, being interpreted.

The seven-thorned briar and the palm seven-leaved
   Are her great sorrow and her great reward.   10
     Until the end be full, the Holy One

Mary's Girlhood: The first of these two sonnets appears to refer to Rossetti's second exhibited picture, "Ecce Ancilla Domini" or "The Annunciation." The second sonnet was inscribed around the frame of his first exhibited picture, "The Girlhood of Mary Virgin."

Abides without. She soon shall have achieved
Her perfect purity; yea, God the Lord
Shall soon vouchsafe His Son to be her Son.

[1886]

From **THE HOUSE OF LIFE**

A Sonnet Sequence

PART I

YOUTH AND CHANGE

[THE SONNET]

A Sonnet is a moment's monument,—
  Memorial from the Soul's eternity
  To one dead deathless hour. Look that it be,
Whether for lustral rite or dire portent,
Of its own arduous fulness reverent:
  Carve it in ivory or in ebony,
  As Day or Night may rule; and let Time see
Its flowering crest impearled and orient.

A Sonnet is a coin: its face reveals
  The soul,—its converse, to what Power 'tis due:—   10
Whether for tribute to the august appeals
  Of Life, or dower in Love's high retinue,
It serve; or, 'mid the dark wharf's cavernous breath,
In Charon's palm it pay the toll to Death.
pays for dieing

[1881]

The House of Life: The title comes from the astrological division of the
heavens into twelve houses, of which one was the house of life. Life, as Rossetti states in the prefatory sonnet, together with Love and Death, form the
subject of the series. In the *Poems* of 1870 Rossetti printed fifty sonnets (sixteen of which had been published the year before in the *Fortnightly Review*)
and eleven songs under the title, "Sonnets and Songs towards a Work to be
Called 'The House of Life'." In the completed version of 1881, the work
was made up of one hundred and one sonnets, with all the songs removed.
It was divided into two parts, "Youth and Change" and "Change and Fate,"
of which the first part is here reprinted.
14 *Charon's palm:* Charon, for a fee, rowed the dead across the river Styx
to the underworld.

SONNET I

Love Enthroned

Love above all

I marked all kindred Powers the heart finds fair:—
  Truth, with awed lips; and Hope, with eyes upcast;
And Fame, whose loud wings fan the ashen Past
To signal-fires, Oblivion's flight to scare;
And Youth, with still some single golden hair
  Unto his shoulder clinging, since the last
  Embrace wherein two sweet arms held him fast;
And Life, still wreathing flowers for Death to wear.

Love's throne was not with these; but far above
  All passionate wind of welcome and farewell   10
He sat in breathless bowers they dream not of;
  Though Truth foreknow Love's heart, and Hope foretell,
And Fame be for Love's sake desirable,
And Youth be dear, and Life be sweet to Love.

[1881]

SONNET II

Bridal Birth

Simile

As when desire, long darkling, dawns, and first
  The mother looks upon the newborn child,
  Even so my Lady stood at gaze and smiled
When her soul knew at length the Love it nurs'd.
Born with her life, creature of poignant thirst
  And exquisite hunger, at her heart Love lay
  Quickening in darkness, till a voice that day
Cried on him, and the bonds of birth were burst.

love full-grown

Now, shadowed by his wings, our faces yearn
  Together, as his full-grown feet now range   10
    The grove, and his warm hands our couch prepare:
Till to his song our bodiless souls in turn
  Be born his children, when Death's nuptial change
    Leaves us for light the halo of his hair.

application of Chr. symbols

[1870]

SONNET III

Love's Testament

O thou who at Love's hour ecstatically
  Unto my heart dost evermore present
  Clothed with his fire, thy heart his testament;
Whom I have neared and felt thy breath to be
The inmost incense of his sanctuary;
  Who without speech hast owned him, and intent
  Upon his will, thy life with mine hast blent,
And murmured, "I am thine, thou'rt one with me!"

O what from thee the grace, for me the prize,
  And what to Love the glory,—when the whole   10
  Of the deep stair thou tread'st to the dim shoal
And weary water of the place of sighs,
And there dost work deliverance, as thine eyes
  Draw up my prisoned spirit to thy soul!

                      [1870]

SONNET IV

Lovesight

When do I see thee most, beloved one?
  When in the light the spirits of mine eyes
  Before thy face, their altar, solemnize
The worship of that Love through thee made known?
Or when in the dusk hours, (we two alone,)
  Close-kissed and eloquent of still replies
  Thy twilight-hidden glimmering visage lies,
And my soul only sees thy soul its own?

O love, my love! if I no more should see
Thyself, nor on the earth the shadow of thee,   10
  Nor image of thine eyes in any spring,—
How then should sound upon Life's darkening slope
The ground-whirl of the perished leaves of Hope,
  The wind of Death's imperishable wing?

                      [1870]

III 12 *place of sighs:* death.

SONNET V

Heart's Hope

By what word's power, the key of paths untrod,
　　Shall I the difficult deeps of Love explore,
　　Till parted waves of Song yield up the shore
Even as that sea which Israel crossed dryshod?
For lo! in some poor rhythmic period,
　　Lady, I fain would tell how evermore
　　Thy soul I know not from thy body, nor
Thee from myself, neither our love from God.

Yea, in God's name, and Love's, and thine, would I
　　When breast to breast we clung, even I and she,—　　　10
As to all hearts all things shall signify;
　　Tender as dawn's first hill-fire, and intense
　　As instantaneous penetrating sense,
In Spring's birth-hour, of other Springs gone by.

[1881]

SONNET VI

The Kiss

What smouldering senses in death's sick delay
　　Or seizure of malign vicissitude
　　Can rob this body of honour, or denude
This soul of wedding-raiment worn to-day?
For lo! even now my lady's lips did play
　　With these my lips such consonant interlude
　　As laurelled Orpheus longed for when he wooed
The half-drawn hungering face with that last lay.

I was a child beneath her touch,—a man
　　Draw from one loving heart such evidence　　　10
　　A spirit when her spirit looked through me,—

V 4 *the sea:* the Red Sea, which miraculously parted to allow the Israelites to leave Egypt (*Exodus* 14).
12 *first hill-fire:* sun's rays upon a hill at dawn.
VI 6 *consonant:* harmonious, without discord.
7 *laurelled Orpheus:* because of his poetic achievements, Orpheus was allowed to try to bring back his wife Eurydice from the dead.

A god when all our life-breath met to fan
Our life-blood, till love's emulous ardours ran,
  Fire within fire, desire in deity.

[1870]

Nuptial Sleep

At length their long kiss severed, with sweet smart:
  And as the last slow sudden drops are shed
  From sparkling eaves when all the storm has fled,
So singly flagged the pulses of each heart.
Their bosoms sundered, with the opening start
  Of married flowers to either side outspread
  From the knit stem; yet still their mouths, burnt red,
Fawned on each other where they lay apart.

Sleep sank them lower than the tide of dreams,
  And their dreams watched them sink, and slid away.   10
Slowly their souls swam up again, through gleams
  Of watered light and dull drowned waifs of day;
Till from some wonder of new woods and streams
  He woke, and wondered more: for there she lay.

[1870]

SONNET VII

Supreme Surrender

To all the spirits of Love that wander by
  Along his love-sown harvest-field of sleep
  My lady lies apparent; and the deep
Calls to the deep; and no man sees but I.
The bliss so long afar, at length so nigh,
  Rests there attained. Methinks proud Love must weep
  When Fate's control doth from his harvest reap
The sacred hour for which the years did sigh.

First touched, the hand now warm around my neck
  Taught memory long to mock desire; and lo!   10

Nuptial Sleep: After Robert Buchanan attacked it in *The Fleshly School
of Poetry,* this sonnet was removed from its place in the series and **was not**
reprinted during Rossetti's lifetime.

Across my breast the abandoned hair doth flow,
Where one shorn tress long stirred the longing ache:
And next the heart that trembled for its sake
    Lies the queen-heart in sovereign overthrow.

[1870]

SONNET VIII

Love's Lovers

Some ladies love the jewels in Love's zone
    And gold-tipped darts he hath for painless play
    In idle scornful hours he flings away;
And some that listen to his lute's soft tone
Do love to vaunt the silver praise their own;
    Some prize his blindfold sight; and there be they
    Who kissed his wings which brought him yesterday
And thank his wings to-day that he is flown.

My lady only loves the heart of Love:
    Therefore Love's heart, my lady, hath for thee   10
    His bower of unimagined flower and tree:
There kneels he now, and all-anhungered of
Thine eyes grey-lit in shadowing hair above,
    Seals with thy mouth his immortality.

[1870]

SONNET IX

Passion and Worship

One flame-winged brought a white-winged harp-player
    Even where my lady and I lay all alone;
    Saying: "Behold, this minstrel is unknown;
Bid him depart, for I am minstrel here:
Only my strains are to Love's dear ones dear."
    Then said I: "Through thine hautboy's rapturous tone
    Unto my lady still this harp makes moan,
And still she deems the cadence deep and clear."

VII 14 *sovereign:* total.
VIII 1 *zone:* girdle.
12 *all-anhungered of:* overcome with hunger for.
IX 6 *hautboy:* oboe.

Then said my lady: "Thou art Passion of Love,
  And this Love's Worship: both he plights to me.   10
Thy mastering music walks the sunlit sea:
But where wan water trembles in the grove
And the wan moon is all the light thereof,
  This harp still makes my name its voluntary."

[1870]

SONNET X

The Portrait

O Lord of all compassionate control,
  O Love! let this my lady's picture glow
  Under my hand to praise her name, and show
Even of her inner self the perfect whole:
That he who seeks her beauty's furthest goal,
  Beyond the light that the sweet glances throw
  And refluent wave of the sweet smile, may know
The very sky and sea-line of her soul.

Lo! it is done. Above the enthroning throat
  The mouth's mould testifies of voice and kiss,   10
    The shadowed eyes remember and foresee.
Her face is made her shrine. Let all men note
  That in all years (O Love, thy gift is this!)
    They that would look on her must come to me.

[1870]

SONNET XI

The Love-letter

Warmed by her hand and shadowed by her hair
  As close she leaned and poured her heart through thee,
  Whereof the articulate throbs accompany
The smooth black stream that makes thy whiteness fair,—
Sweet fluttering sheet, even of her breath aware,—
  Oh let thy silent song disclose to me

---

14 *voluntary:* religious solo.
X 5 *goal:* boundary.
7 *refluent:* flowing back.

That soul wherewith her lips and eyes agree
Like married music in Love's answering air.

Fain had I watched her when, at some fond thought,
  Her bosom to the writing closelier press'd,   10
  And her breast's secrets peered into her breast;
When, through eyes raised an instant, her soul sought
My soul, and from the sudden confluence caught
  The words that made her love the loveliest.

[1870]

SONNET XII

The Lovers' Walk

Sweet twining hedgeflowers wind-stirred in no wise
  On this June day; and hand that clings in hand:—
  Still glades; and meeting faces scarcely fann'd:—
An osier-odoured stream that draws the skies
Deep to its heart; and mirrored eyes in eyes:—
  Fresh hourly wonder o'er the Summer land
Of light and cloud; and two souls softly spann'd
With one o'erarching heaven of smiles and sighs:—

Even such their path, whose bodies lean unto
  Each other's visible sweetness amorously,—   10
  Whose passionate hearts lean by Love's high decree
Together on his heart for ever true,
As the cloud-foaming firmamental blue
  Rest on the blue line of a foamless sea.

[1881]

SONNET XIII

Youth's Antiphony

"I love you, sweet: how can you ever learn
  How much I love you?" "You I love even so,
  And so I learn it." "Sweet, you cannot know

XII 4 *osier:* willow.

How fair you are." "If fair enough to earn
Your love, so much is all my love's concern."
   "My love grows hourly, sweet." "Mine too doth grow,
   Yet love seemed full so many hours ago!"
Thus lovers speak, till kisses claim their turn.

Ah! happy they to whom such words as these
   In youth have served for speech the whole day long,   10
   Hour after hour, remote from the world's throng,
Work, contest, fame, all life's confederate pleas,—
What while Love breathed in sighs and silences
   Through two blent souls one rapturous undersong.

                    [1881]

SONNET XIV

Youth's Spring-tribute

On this sweet bank your head thrice sweet and dear
   I lay, and spread your hair on either side,
   And see the newborn woodflowers bashful-eyed
Look through the golden tresses here and there.
On these debateable borders of the year
   Spring's foot half falters; scarce she yet may know
   The leafless blackthorn-blossom from the snow;
And through her bowers the wind's way still is clear.

But April's sun strikes down the glades to-day;
   So shut your eyes upturned, and feel my kiss   10
Creep, as the Spring now thrills through every spray,
   Up your warm throat to your warm lips: for this
   Is even the hour of Love's sworn suitservice,
With whom cold hearts are counted castaway.

                    [1881]

SONNET XV

The Birth-bond

Have you not noted, in some family
   Where two were born of a first marriage-bed,

XIV 13 *suitservice:* service in a cause.

How still they own their gracious bond, though fed
And nursed on the forgotten breast and knee?—
How to their father's children they shall be
    In act and thought of one goodwill; but each
    Shall for the other have, in silence speech,
And in a word complete community?

Even so, when first I saw you, seemed it, love,
    That among souls allied to mine was yet   10
One nearer kindred than life hinted of.
    O born with me somewhere that men forget,
    And though in years of sight and sound unmet,
Known for my soul's birth-partner well enough!

[1870]

SONNET XVI *characteristic*

A Day of Love

Those envied places which do know her well,
    And are so scornful of this lonely place,
    Even now for once are emptied of her grace:
Nowhere but here she is: and while Love's spell
From his predominant presence doth compel
    All alien hours, an outworn populace,
    The hours of Love fill full the echoing space
With sweet confederate music favourable.

Now many memories make solicitous
    The delicate love-lines of her mouth, till, lit   10
    With quivering fire, the words take wing from it;
As here between our kisses we sit thus
    Speaking of things remembered, and so sit
Speechless while things forgotten call to us.

[1870]

XV 5 *their father's children:* half-brothers and half-sisters.

SONNET XVII

Beauty's Pageant   *varying charges*

What dawn-pulse at the heart of heaven, or last
    Incarnate flower of culminating day,—
    What marshalled marvels on the skirts of May,
Or song full-quired, sweet June's encomiast;
What glory of change by Nature's hand amass'd
    Can vie with all those moods of varying grace
    Which o'er one loveliest woman's form and face
Within this hour, within this room, have pass'd?

Love's very vesture and elect disguise
    Was each fine movement,—wonder new-begot   10
    Of lily or swan or swan-stemmed galiot;
Joy to his sight who now the sadlier sighs,
Parted again; and sorrow yet for eyes
    Unborn, that read these words and saw her not.

[1881]

SONNET XVIII

Genius in Beauty

Beauty like hers is genius. Not the call
    Of Homer's or of Dante's heart sublime,—
    Not Michael's hand furrowing the zones of time,—
Is more with compassed mysteries musical;
Nay, not in Spring's or Summer's sweet footfall
    More gathered gifts exuberant Life bequeaths
    Than doth this sovereign face, whose love-spell breathes
Even from its shadowed contour on the wall.

As many men are poets in their youth,
    But for one sweet-strung soul the wires prolong   10
    Even through all change the indomitable song;
So in likewise the envenomed years, whose tooth

XVII 4 *encomiast:* flatterer.
11 *swan-stemmed galiot:* small fishing-vessel with swan figure-head.
XVIII 3 *Michael:* Michelangelo.
10 *wires:* strings of a musical instrument.

Rends shallower grace with ruin void of ruth,
Upon this beauty's power shall wreak no wrong.

[1881]

SONNET XIX

Silent Noon

Your hands lie open in the long fresh grass,—
The finger-points look through like rosy blooms:
Your eyes smile peace. The pasture gleams and glooms
'Neath billowing skies that scatter and amass.
All round our nest, far as the eye can pass,
Are golden kingcup-fields with silver edge
Where the cow-parsley skirts the hawthorn-hedge.
'Tis visible silence, still as the hour-glass.

Deep in the sun-searched growths the dragon-fly
Hangs like a blue thread loosened from the sky:—   10
So this wing'd hour is dropt to us from above.
Oh! clasp we to our hearts, for deathless dower,
This close-companioned inarticulate hour
When twofold silence was the song of love.

[1881]

SONNET XX

her like moon

Gracious Moonlight

Even as the moon grows queenlier in mid-space
When the sky darkens, and her cloud-rapt car
Thrills with intenser radiance from afar,—
So lambent, lady, beams thy sovereign grace
When the drear soul desires thee. Of that face
What shall be said,—which, like a governing star,
Gathers and garners from all things that are
Their silent penetrative loveliness?

O'er water-daisies and wild waifs of Spring,
There where the iris rears its gold-crowned sheaf   10
With flowering rush and sceptred arrow-leaf,

So have I marked Queen Dian, in bright ring
Of cloud above and wave below, take wing
   And chase night's gloom, as thou the spirit's grief.

[1881]

SONNET XXI

Love-sweetness

Sweet dimness of her loosened hair's downfall
   About thy face; her sweet hands round thy head
   In gracious fostering union garlanded;
Her tremulous smiles; her glances' sweet recall
Of love; her murmuring sighs memorial;
   Her mouth's culled sweetness by thy kisses shed
   On cheeks and neck and eyelids, and so led
Back to her mouth which answers there for all:—

What sweeter than these things, except the thing
   In lacking which all these would lose their sweet:—   10
   The confident heart's still fervour; the swift beat
And soft subsidence of the spirit's wing,
Then when it feels, in cloud-girt wayfaring,
   The breath of kindred plumes against its feet?

[1870]

SONNET XXII

Heart's Haven

Sometimes she is a child within mine arms,
   Cowering beneath dark wings that love must chase,—
   With still tears showering and averted face,
Inexplicably filled with faint alarms:
And oft from mine own spirit's hurtling harms
   I crave the refuge of her deep embrace,—
   Against all ills the fortified strong place
And sweet reserve of sovereign counter-charms.

And Love, our light at night and shade at noon,
   Lulls us to rest with songs, and turns away   10

XX 12 *Queen Dian:* Diana, here referring to the moon.

All shafts of shelterless tumultuous day.
Like the moon's growth, his face gleams through his tune;
And as soft waters warble to the moon,
    Our answering spirits chime one roundelay.

[1881]

SONNET XXIII

Love's Baubles *Fleshly attrib. of*
value

I stood where Love in brimming armfuls bore
    Slight wanton flowers and foolish toys of fruit:
    And round him ladies thronged in warm pursuit,
Fingered and lipped and proffered the strange store. *as*
And from one hand the petal and the core *sanctified*
    Savoured of sleep; and cluster and curled shoot *& worshipped*
    Seemed from another hand like shame's salute,— *by her*
Gifts that I felt my cheek was blushing for.

At last Love bade my Lady give the same:
    And as I looked, the dew was light thereon;   10
    And as I took them, at her touch they shone
With inmost heaven-hue of the heart of flame.
    And then Love said: "Lo! when the hand is hers,
    Follies of love are love's true ministers."

[1870]

SONNET XXIV

youth fr. one love to another

Pride of Youth

Even as a child, of sorrow that we give
    The dead, but little in his heart can find,
    Since without need of thought to his clear mind
Their turn it is to die and his to live:—
Even so the winged New Love smiles to receive
    Along his eddying plumes the auroral wind,
    Nor, forward glorying, casts one look behind
Where night-rack shrouds the Old Love fugitive.

XXIV 6 *auroral wind:* wind of dawn.
8 *night-rack:* clouds of night.

There is a change in every hour's recall,
  And the last cowslip in the fields we see   10
  On the same day with the first corn-poppy.
Alas for hourly change! Alas for all
The loves that from his hand proud Youth lets fall,
  Even as the beads of a told rosary!

                                   [1881]

SONNET XXV

Winged Hours

Each hour until we meet is as a bird
  That wings from far his gradual way along
  The rustling covert of my soul,—his song
Still loudlier trilled through leaves more deeply stirr'd:
But at the hour of meeting, a clear word
  Is every note he sings, in Love's own tongue;
  Yet, Love, thou know'st the sweet strain suffers wrong,
Full oft through our contending joys unheard.

What of that hour at last, when for her sake
  No wing may fly to me nor song may flow;   10
  When, wandering round my life unleaved, I know
The bloodied feathers scattered in the brake,
  And thinks how she, far from me, with like eyes
  Sees through the untuneful bough the wingless skies?

                                   [1869]

SONNET XXVI

Mid-rapture

Thou lovely and beloved, thou my love;
  Whose kiss seems still the first; whose summoning eyes,
  Even now, as for our love-world's new sunrise,
Shed very dawn; whose voice, attuned above
All modulation of the deep-bowered dove,
  Is like a hand laid softly on the soul;
  Whose hand is like a sweet voice to control
Those worn tired brows it hath the keeping of:—

XXV 12 *brake:* thicket.

What word can answer to thy word,—what gaze
   To thine, which now absorbs within its sphere   10
   My worshiping face, till I am mirrored there
Light-circled in a heaven of deep-drawn rays?
   What clasp, what kiss mine inmost heart can prove,
   O lovely and beloved, O my love?

[1881]

SONNET XXVII

Heart's Compass

Sometimes thou seem'st not as thyself alone,
   But as the meaning of all things that are;
   A breathless wonder, shadowing forth afar
Some heavenly solstice hushed and halcyon;
Whose unstirred lips are music's visible tone;
   Whose eyes the sun gate of the soul unbar,
   Being of its furthest fires oracular;—
The evident heart of all life sown and mown.

Even such Love is; and is not thy name Love?
   Yea, by thy hand the Love-god rends apart   10
   All gathering clouds of Night's ambiguous art;
Flings them far down, and sets thine eyes above;
And simply, as some gage of flower or glove,
   Stakes with a smile the world against thy heart.

[1881]

SONNET XXVIII

Soul-light

What other woman could be loved like you,
   Or how of you should love possess his fill?
   After the fulness of all rapture, still,—
As at the end of some deep avenue
A tender glamour of day,—there comes to view

XXVII 4 *solstice:* the time, either midsummer or midwinter, when the sun is
farthest from the equator and appears to pause before returning. *halcyon:*
calm.
13 *gage:* pledge.

Far in your eyes a yet more hungering thrill,—
Such fire as Love's soul-winnowing hands distil
Even from his inmost ark of light and dew.

And as the traveller triumphs with the sun,
   Glorying in heat's mid-height, yet startide brings   10
   Wonder new-born, and still fresh transport springs
From limpid lambent hours of day begun;—
   Even so, through eyes and voice, your soul doth move
   My soul with changeful light of infinite love.

[1881]

SONNET XXIX

The Moonstar

Lady, I thank thee for thy loveliness,
   Because my lady is more lovely still.
   Glorying I gaze, and yield with glad goodwill
To thee thy tribute; by whose sweet-spun dress
Of delicate life Love labours to assess
   My lady's absolute queendom; saying, "Lo!
   How high this beauty is, which yet doth show
But as that beauty's sovereign votaress."

Lady, I saw thee with her, side by side;
   And as, when night's fair fires their queen surround,   10
An emulous star too near the moon will ride,—
   Even so thy rays within her luminous bound
   Were traced no more; and by the light so drown'd,
Lady, not thou but she was glorified.

[1881]

SONNET XXX

Last Fire

Love, through your spirit and mine what summer eve
   Now glows with glory of all things possess'd,
   Since this day's sun of rapture filled the west

XXVIII 8 *ark:* rainbow.
12 *lambent:* radiant.

And the light sweetened as the fire took leave?
Awhile now softlier let your bosom heave,
   As in Love's harbour, even that loving breast,
   All care takes refuge while we sink to rest,
And mutual dreams the bygone bliss retrieve.

Many the days that Winter keeps in store,
   Sunless throughout, or whose brief sun-glimpses   10
   Scarce shed the heaped snow through the naked trees.
This day at least was Summer's paramour,
Sun-coloured to the imperishable core
   With sweet well-being of love and full heart's ease.

[1881]

SONNET XXXI

Her Gifts

High grace, the dower of Queens; and therewithal
   Some wood-born wonder's sweet simplicity;
   A glance like water brimming with the sky
Or hyacinth-light where forest-shadows fall;
Such thrilling pallor of cheek as doth enthral
   The heart; a mouth whose passionate forms imply
   All music and all silence held thereby;
Deep golden locks, her sovereign coronal,
A round reared neck, meet column of Love's shrine
   To cling to when the heart takes sanctuary;   10
   Hands which for ever at Love's bidding be,
And soft-stirred feet still answering to his sign:—
   These are her gifts, as tongue may tell them o'er.
   Breathe low her name, my soul; for that means more.

[1881]

SONNET XXXII

Equal Troth

Not by one measure mayst thou mete our love;
   For how should I be loved as I love thee?—

XXXI 4 *hyacinth:* purple.
8 *coronal:* garland.

I, graceless, joyless, lacking absolutely
All gifts that with thy queenship best behove;—
Thou, throned in every heart's elect alcove,
   And crowned with garlands culled from every tree,
   Which for no head but thine, by Love's decree,
All beauties and all mysteries interwove.

But here thine eyes and lips yield soft rebuke:—
   "Then only," (say'st thou) "could I love thee less,   10
When thou couldst doubt my love's equality."
Peace, sweet! if not to sum but worth we look,—
   Thy heart's transcendence, not my heart's excess,—
Then more a thousandfold thou lov'st than I.

[1881]

SONNET XXXIII

Venus Victrix

Could Juno's self more sovereign presence wear
   Than thou, 'mid other ladies throned in grace?—
   Or Pallas, when thou bend'st with soul-stilled face
O'er poet's page gold-shadowed in thy hair?
Dost thou than Venus seem less heavenly fair
   When o'er the sea of love's tumultuous trance
   Hovers thy smile, and mingles with thy glance
That sweet voice like the last wave murmuring there?

Before such triune loveliness divine
   Awestruck I ask, which goddess here most claims   10
The prize that, howsoe'er adjudged, is thine?
   Then Love breathes low the sweetest of thy names;
And Venus Victrix to my heart doth bring
Herself, the Helen of her guerdoning.

[1881]

Victrix: conquering. The reference is to the choice of Paris between the rival
claims of Juno (power), Pallas (wisdom), and Venus (love). As a reward
for honoring Venus, Paris was promised Helen, most beautiful woman in the
world.
XXXIII 14 *guerdoning:* reward.

SONNET XXXIV

The Dark Glass

Not I myself know all my love for thee:
　　How should I reach so far, who cannot weigh
　　To-morrow's dower by gage of yesterday?
Shall birth and death, and all dark names that be
As doors and windows bared to some loud sea,
　　Lash deaf mine ears and blind my face with spray;
　　And shall my sense pierce love,—the last relay
And ultimate outpost of eternity?

Lo! what am I to Love, the lord of all?
　　One murmuring shell he gathers from the sand,—　　10
　　One little heart-flame sheltered in his hand.
Yet through thine eyes he grants me clearest call
And veriest touch of powers primordial
　　That any hour-girt life may understand.

[1881]

SONNET XXXV

The Lamp's Shrine

Sometimes I fain would find in thee some fault,
　　That I might love thee still in spite of it:
　　Yet how should our Lord Love curtail one whit
Thy perfect praise whom most he would exalt?
Alas! he can but make my heart's low vault
　　Even in men's sight unworthier, being lit
　　By thee, who thereby show'st more exquisite
Like fiery chrysoprase in deep basalt.

Yet will I nowise shrink; but at Love's shrine
　　Myself within the beams his brow doth dart　　10
　　Will set the flashing jewel of thy heart
In that dull chamber where it deigns to shine:

XXXIV 7 *relay:* stopping-place on journey.
14 *hour-girt:* temporal.
XXXV 8 *chrysoprase:* green precious stone. *basalt:* dark green or brown rock.

For lo! in honour of thine excellencies
My heart takes pride to show how poor it is.

[1881]

SONNET XXXVI

Life-in-love

Not in thy body is thy life at all,
   But in this lady's lips and hands and eyes;
   Through these she yields thee life that vivifies
What else were sorrow's servant and death's thrall.
Look on thyself without her, and recall
   The waste remembrance and forlorn surmise
   That lived but in a dead-drawn breath of sighs
O'er vanished hours and hours eventual.

Even so much life hath the poor tress of hair
   Which, stored apart, is all love hath to show   10
   For heart-beats and for fire-heats long ago;
Even so much life endures unknown, even where,
   'Mid change the changeless night environeth,
   Lies all that golden hair undimmed in death.

[1870]

SONNET XXXVII

The Love-moon

"When that dead face, bowered in the furthest years,
   Which once was all the life years held for thee,
   Can now scarce bid the tides of memory
Cast on thy soul a little spray of tears,—
How canst thou gaze into these eyes of hers
   Whom now thy heart delights in, and not see
   Within each orb Love's philtred euphrasy
Make them of buried troth remembrancers?"

XXXVI 1 *thy:* the poet addresses himself.
14 *golden hair:* probably a reference to the unchanged beauty of Mrs.
Rossetti's hair when her husband's poetry was removed from her coffin.
XXXVII 7 *philtred euphrasy:* a philtre is a love-potion; *euphrasy* is eyebright
used medically in the eyes.

"Nay, pitiful Love, nay, loving Pity! Well
    Thou knowest that in these twain I have confess'd   10
Two very voices of thy summoning bell.
    Nay, Master, shall not Death make manifest
In these the culminant changes which approve
The love-moon that must light my soul to Love?"

[1870]

SONNET XXXVIII

The Morrow's Message

"Thou Ghost," I said, "and is thy name To-day?—
    Yesterday's son, with such an abject brow!—
    And can To-morrow be more pale than thou?"
While yet I spoke, the silence answered: "Yea,
Henceforth our issue is all grieved and grey,
    And each beforehand makes such poor avow
    As of old leaves beneath the budding bough
Or night-drift that the sundawn shreds away."

Then cried I: "Mother of many malisons,
    O Earth, receive me to thy dusty bed!"   10
    But therewithal the tremulous silence said:
"Lo! Love yet bids thy lady greet thee once:—
Yea, twice,—whereby thy life is still the sun's;
    And thrice,—whereby the shadow of death is dead."

[1870]

SONNET XXXIX

Sleepless Dreams

Girt in dark growths, yet glimmering with one star,
    O night desirous as the nights of youth!
    Why should my heart within thy spell, forsooth,
Now beat, as the bride's finger-pulses are
Quickened within the girdling golden bar?

---

13 *approve:* give evidence of.
XXXVIII 8 *night-drift:* mists of night.
9 *malisons:* curses.
13 *the sun's:* temporal.

What wings are these that fan my pillow smooth?
And why does Sleep, waved back by Joy and Ruth,
Tread softly round and gaze at me from far?

Nay, night deep-leaved! And would Love feign in thee
   Some shadowy palpitating grove that bears   10
   Rest for man's eyes and music for his ears?
O lonely night! art thou not known to me,
A thicket hung with masks of mockery
   And watered with the wasteful warmth of tears?

[1869]

SONNET XL

Severed Selves

Two separate divided silences,
   Which, brought together, would find loving voice;
   Two glances which together would rejoice
In love, now lost like stars beyond dark trees;
Two hands apart whose touch alone gives ease;
   Two bosoms which, heart-shrined with mutual flame,
   Would, meeting in one clasp, be made the same;
Two souls, the shores wave-mocked of sundering seas:—

Such are we now. Ah! may our hope forecast
   Indeed one hour again, when on this stream   10
   Of darkened love once more the light shall gleam?—
An hour how slow to come, how quickly past,—
Which blooms and fades, and only leaves at last,
   Faint as shed flowers, the attenuated dream.

[1881]

SONNET XLI

Through Death to Love

Like labour-laden moonclouds faint to flee
   From winds that sweep the winter-bitten wold,—
   Like multiform circumfluence manifold

XXXIX 7 *Ruth:* pity.

Of night's flood-tide,—like terrors that agree
Of hoarse-tongued fire and inarticulate sea,—
    Even such, within some glass dimmed by our breath,
    Our hearts discern wild images of Death,
Shadows and shoals that edge eternity.

Howbeit athwart Death's imminent shade doth soar
    One Power, than flow of stream or flight of dove   10
    Sweeter to glide around, to brood above.
Tell me, my heart,—what angel-greeted door
Or threshold of wing-winnowed threshing-floor
    Hath guest fire-fledged as thine, whose lord is Love?

[1881]

SONNET XLII

Hope Overtaken

I deemed thy garments, O my Hope, were grey,
    So far I viewed thee. Now the space between
    Is passed at length; and garmented in green
Even as in days of yore thou stand'st to-day.
Ah God! and but for lingering dull dismay,
    On all that road our footsteps erst had been
    Even thus commingled, and our shadows seen
Blent on the hedgerows and the water-way.

O Hope of mine whose eyes are living love,
    No eyes but hers,—O Love and Hope the same!—   10
    Lean close to me, for now the sinking sun
That warmed our feet scarce gilds our hair above.
    O hers thy voice and very hers thy name!
    Alas, cling round me, for the day is done!

[1881]

SONNET XLIII

Love and Hope

Bless love and hope. Full many a withered year
    Whirled past us, eddying to its chill doomsday;
    And clasped together where the blown leaves lay,

We long have knelt and wept full many a tear.
Yet lo! one hour at last, the Spring's compeer,
  Flutes softly to us from some green byeway:
  Those years, those tears are dead, but only they:—
Bless love and hope, true soul; for we are here.

Cling heart to heart; nor of this hour demand
  Whether in very truth, when we are dead,   10
  Our hearts shall wake to know Love's golden head
Sole sunshine of the imperishable land;
  Or but discern, through night's unfeatured scope,
  Scorn-fired at length the illusive eyes of Hope.

[1881]

SONNET XLIV

Cloud and Wind

Love, should I fear death most for you or me?
  Yet if you die, can I not follow you,
  Forcing the straits of change? Alas! but who
Shall wrest a bond from night's inveteracy,
Ere yet my hazardous soul put forth, to be
  Her warrant against all her haste might rue?—
  Ah! in your eyes so reached what dumb adieu,
What unsunned gyres of waste eternity?

And if I die the first, shall death be then
  A lampless watchtower whence I see you weep?—   10
  Or (woe is me!) a bed wherein my sleep
Ne'er notes (as death's dear cup at last you drain),
The hour when you too learn that all is vain
  And that Hope sows what Love shall never reap?

[1881]

SONNET XLV

Secret Parting

Because our talk was of the cloud-control
  And moon-track of the journeying face of Fate,

XLIV 4 *bond:* pledge.
8 *gyres:* circlings.

Her tremulous kisses faltered at love's gate
And her eyes dreamed against a distant goal:
But soon, remembering her how brief the whole
    Of joy, which its own hours annihilate,
    Her set gaze gathered, thirstier than of late,
And as she kissed, her mouth became her soul.

Thence in what ways we wandered, and how strove
    To build with fire-tried vows the piteous home   10
    Which memory haunts and whither sleep may roam,—
They only know for whom the roof of Love
Is the still-seated secret of the grove,
    Nor spire may rise nor bell be heard therefrom.

[1870]

SONNET XLVI

Parted Love

What shall be said of this embattled day
    And armèd occupation of this night
    By all thy foes beleaguered,—now when sight
Nor sound denotes the loved one far away?
Of these thy vanquished hours what shalt thou say,—
    As every sense to which she dealt delight
    Now labours lonely o'er the stark noon-height
To reach the sunset's desolate disarray?

Stand still, fond fettered wretch! while Memory's art
    Parades the Past before thy face, and lures   10
    Thy spirit to her passionate portraitures:
Till the tempestuous tide-gates flung apart
Flood with wild will the hollows of thy heart,
    And thy heart rends thee, and thy body endures.

[1870]

XLV 4 *against:* toward.
6 *annihilate:* i.e., through pleasure.
14 *Nor . . . therefrom:* This line presumably means that the love of the
grove is totally separate from that sanctified by the Church.
Parted Love: In this sonnet the poet once more addresses himself.

SONNET XLVII

Broken Music

The mother will not turn, who thinks she hears
　　Her nursling's speech first grow articulate;
　　But breathless with averted eyes elate
She sits, with open lips and open ears,
That it may call her twice. 'Mid doubts and fears
　　Thus oft my soul has hearkened; till the song,
　　A central moan for days, at length found tongue,
And the sweet music welled and the sweet tears.

But now, whatever while the soul is fain
　　To list that wonted murmur, as it were　　　　10
The speech-bound sea-shell's low importunate strain,—
　　No breath of song, thy voice alone is there,
O bitterly beloved! and all her gain
　　Is but the pang of unpermitted prayer.

[1869]

SONNET XLVIII

Death-in-love

There came an image in Life's retinue
　　That had Love's wings and bore his gonfalon:
　　Fair was the web, and nobly wrought thereon,
O soul-sequestered face, thy form and hue!
Bewildering sounds, such as Spring wakens to,
　　Shook in its folds; and through my heart its power
　　Sped trackless as the immemorable hour
When birth's dark portal groaned and all was new.

But a veiled woman followed, and she caught
　　The banner round its staff, to furl and cling,—　　　10
　　Then plucked a feather from the bearer's wing,
And held it to his lips that stirred it not,

XLVIII 2 *gonfalon:* banner.
7 *immemorable:* unremembered.

And said to me, "Behold, there is no breath:
I and this Love are one, and I am Death."

[1869]

SONNETS XLIX, L, LI, LII

Willowwood

I

I sat with Love upon a woodside well,
    Leaning across the water, I and he;
    Nor ever did he speak nor looked at me,
But touched his lute wherein was audible
The certain secret thing he had to tell:
    Only our mirrored eyes met silently
    In the low wave; and that sound came to be
The passionate voice I knew; and my tears fell.

And at their fall, his eyes beneath grew hers;
And with his foot and with his wing-feathers   10
    He swept the spring that watered my heart's drouth.
Then the dark ripples spread to waving hair,
And as I stooped, her own lips rising there
    Bubbled with brimming kisses at my mouth.

[1869]

II

And now Love sang: but his was such a song,
    So meshed with half-remembrance hard to free,
    As souls disused in death's sterility
May sing when the new birthday tarries long.
And I was made aware of a dumb throng
    That stood aloof, one form by every tree,
    All mournful forms for each was I or she,
The shades of those our days that had no tongue.

They looked on us, and knew us and were known;
    While fast together, alive from the abyss,   10

Willowwood: the weeping willow, symbol of grief.
3 *souls disused:* souls free of old bodies but not yet reincarnated in new
ones.

Clung the soul-wrung implacable close kiss;
And pity of self through all made broken moan
Which said, "For once, for once, for once alone!"
And still Love sang, and what he sang was this:—

[1869]

III

"O ye, all ye that walk in Willowwood,
  That walk with hollow faces burning white;
What fathom-depth of soul-struck widowhood,
  What long, what longer hours, one lifelong night,
Ere ye again, who so in vain have wooed
  Your last hope lost, who so in vain invite
Your lips to that their unforgotten food,
  Ere ye, ere ye again shall see the light!

Alas! the bitter banks in Willowwood,
  With tear-spurge wan, with blood-wort burning red: 10
Alas! if ever such a pillow could
  Steep deep the soul in sleep till she were dead,—
Better all life forget her than this thing,
That Willowwood should hold her wandering!"

[1869]

IV

So sang he: and as meeting rose and rose
  Together cling through the wind's wellaway
  Nor change it once, yet near the end of day
The leaves drop loosened where the heart-stain glows,—
So when the song died did the kiss unclose;
  And her face fell back drowned, and was as grey
  As its grey eyes; and if it ever may
Meet mine again I know not if Love knows.

Only I know that I leaned low and drank
A long draught from the water where she sank,   10
  Her breath and all her tears and all her soul:

---

10 *spurge:* common English plant. *blood-wort:* "Bloody Dock," plant with red roots or leaves.
2 *wellaway:* grief.

And as I leaned, I know I felt Love's face
Pressed on my neck with moan of pity and grace,
　Till both our heads were in his aureole.

[1869]

SONNET LIII

Without Her

What of her glass without her? The blank grey
　There where the pool is blind of the moon's face.
　Her dress without her? The tossed empty space
Of cloud-rack whence the moon has passed away.
Her paths without her? Day's appointed sway
　Usurped by desolate night. Her pillowed place
　Without her! Tears, ah me! for love's good grace,
And cold forgetfulness of night or day.

What of the heart without her? Nay, poor heart,
　Of thee what word remains ere speech be still?   10
　A wayfarer by barren ways and chill,
Steep ways and weary, without her thou art,
Where the long cloud, the long wood's counterpart,
　Sheds doubled darkness up the labouring hill.

[1881]

SONNET LIV

Love's Fatality

Sweet Love,—but oh! most dread Desire of Love
　Life-thwarted. Linked in gyves I saw them stand,
　Love shackled with Vain-longing, hand to hand:
And one was eyed as the blue vault above:
But hope tempestuous like a fire-cloud hove
　I' the other's gaze, even as in his whose wand
　Vainly all night with spell-wrought power has spann'd
The unyielding caves of some deep treasure-trove.

Also his lips, two writhen flakes of flame,
　Made moan: "Alas O Love, thus leashed with me!   10

LIV 2 *gyves:* fetters.

Wing-footed thou, wing-shouldered, once born free:
And I, thy cowering self, in chains grown tame,—
Bound to thy body and soul, named with thy name,—
   Life's iron heart, even Love's Fatality."

[1881]

SONNET LV

Stillborn Love

The hour which might have been yet might not be,
   Which man's and woman's heart conceived and bore
   Yet whereof life was barren,—on what shore
Bides it the breaking of Time's weary sea?
Bondchild of all consummate joys set free,
   It somewhere sighs and serves, and mute before
   The house of Love, hears through the echoing door
His hours elect in choral consonancy.

But lo! what wedded souls now hand in hand
Together tread at last the immortal strand   10
   With eyes where burning memory lights love home?
Lo! how the little outcast hour has turned
And leaped to them and in their faces yearned:—
   "I am your child: O parents, ye have come!"

[1870]

SONNETS LVI, LVII, LVIII

True Woman   *ideal woman, not in*

I. Herself   *spiritual, but phy.*

To be a sweetness more desired than Spring;
   A bodily beauty more acceptable
   Than the wild rose-tree's arch that crowns the fell;
/ To be an essence more environing
   Than wine's drained juice; a music ravishing
   More than the passionate pulse of Philomel;

---

4 *environing:* enveloping.
6 *Philomel:* nightingale.

To be all this 'neath one soft bosom's swell
That is the flower of life:—how strange a thing!

How strange a thing to be what Man can know
    But as a sacred secret! Heaven's own screen   10
Hides her soul's purest depth and loveliest glow;
    Closely withheld, as all things most unseen,—
    The wave-bowered pearl,—the heart-shaped seal of green
That flecks the snowdrop underneath the snow.

[1881]

II. Her Love

She loves him; for her infinite soul is Love,
    And he her lodestar. Passion in her is
    A glass facing his fire, where the bright bliss
Is mirrored, and the heat returned. Yet move
That glass, a stranger's amorous flame to prove,
    And it shall turn, by instant contraries,
    Ice to the moon; while her pure fire to his
For whom it burns, clings close i' the heart's alcove.

Lo! they are one. With wifely breast to breast
    And circling arms, she welcomes all command   10
    Of love,—her soul to answering ardours fann'd:
Yet as morn springs or twilight sinks to rest,
Ah! who shall say she deems not loveliest
    The hour of sisterly sweet hand-in-hand.

[1881]

III. Her Heaven

If to grow old in Heaven is to grow young,
    (As the Seer saw and said,) then blest were he
    With youth for evermore, whose heaven should be
True Woman, she whom these weak notes have sung.
Here and hereafter,—choir-strains of her tongue,—
    Sky-spaces of her eyes,—sweet signs that flee

---

2 *lodestar:* pole-star or guiding principle.
2 *the Seer:* according to W. M. Rossetti, this refers to Emanuel Swedenborg, eighteenth-century philosopher and mystic.

About her soul's immediate sanctuary,—
Were Paradise all uttermost worlds among.

The sunrise blooms and withers on the hill
    Like any hillflower; and the noblest troth   10
    Dies here to dust. Yet shall Heaven's promise clothe
Even yet those lovers who have cherished still
    This test for love:—in every kiss sealed fast
    To feel the first kiss and forbode the last.

[1881]

SONNET LIX

Love's Last Gift

Love to his singer held a glistening leaf,
    And said: "The rose-tree and the apple-tree
    Have fruits to vaunt or flowers to lure the bee;
And golden shafts are in the feathered sheaf
Of the great harvest-marshal, the year's chief,
    Victorious Summer; aye, and, 'neath warm sea
    Strange secret grasses lurk inviolably
Between the filtering channels of sunk reef.

All are my blooms; and all sweet blooms of love
    To thee I gave while Spring and Summer sang;   10
    But Autumn stops to listen, with some pang
From those worse things the wind is moaning of.
    Only this laurel dreads no winter days:
    Take my last gift; thy heart hath sung my praise."

[1881]

Christina Georgina Rossetti

[*1830-1894*]

Christina Rossetti was born in London in 1830, the youngest of the four remarkable children of Gabriele Rossetti and his half-English wife. Rossetti was a Neapolitan political refugee who earned an inadequate living as a teacher of Italian. In their home the Rossettis spoke English and Italian with equal ease; Christina later mastered French, and knew both Latin and German. It was a bookish, self-contained, and totally unworldly household, which saw little of its neighbors and, indeed, met few outsiders except the fellow-exiles of the father. Of the four children, Christina was easily the slowest at her books, but her flair for poetry was clear when she was a very small child. Her entire education was received at home, but the cultivation of the household was such that this was not the deprivation it might seem.

The elder Rossetti was something of a freethinker, and his wife a devout member of the Church of England. The two sons approximated their father's position; the two daughters were even more religious than their mother. Maria later became an Anglican nun, and there is some evidence that Christina would have liked to do the same. Her religion was High Church in doctrine and devotion, and she was a constant observer of the externals of ceremony. Privately, she seems to have worried all her life over her own state of sinfulness (a state not apparent to others) and to have been in fear of eternal damnation. Like William Cowper of the previous century, she combined a gentle sweetness to others and an obsessive sense of her own inadequacy in matters spiritual. Her somewhat Puritanical code is said to have caused her to paste strips of paper over blasphemous passages in the poetry of Swinburne, whom she otherwise greatly admired, but she was seldom censorious of others. All her life she was devoted to her brother Dante Gabriel, whose life was hardly conducted on Puritan lines.

Because of the family's straitened circumstances, Christina tried briefly the life of a governess, and she also taught Italian; but most of her life was passed uneventfully at home, where she wrote her poetry in her own room. Her first publicly printed poetry appeared in the Pre-Raphaelite magazine, *The Germ*.

Her brother William wrote of Christina that her life had two motive powers, "religion and affection: hardly a third." When she was eighteen, she fell in love with James Collinson, a member of the Pre-Raphaelite Brotherhood and a minor painter. Collinson, who had been converted to Roman Catholicism, proposed to her, but she refused to marry him because of his religion. After Collinson decided that Christina was more important to him than his religion, he re-entered the Anglican Church; when he proposed a second time, he was accepted. Two years later, Collinson changed his religion still another time and rejoined the Roman Catholic Church; Christina reluctantly broke their engagement. The shock of her unhappy romance is said to have overshadowed her life for a decade. Twelve years later, in 1862, Christina began to see a great deal of Charles Bagot Cayley, whom she had probably met before knowing Collinson. Cayley, a scholarly linguist of shy and modest habit, fell deeply in love with her and she with him. In 1866 he proposed, but she declined his offer because, unlike Collinson with too many religions, he had none. Christina's character may be judged by the fact that she refused to marry him, although "she loved the scholarly recluse to the last day of his life . . . and, to the last day of her own, his memory." When personal desire conflicted with religious scruple, she remained loyal to her principles. Neither married, and they remained devoted friends until Cayley's death. Some of the pain of giving him up is indicated in her poetry, particularly in "Monna Innominata."

Through much of her life Christina Rossetti was a partial invalid; the reader who feels that she is unhealthily obsessed with death should remember that she lived under its constant threat for many years before she finally succumbed to cancer in 1894. Her physical condition, her frustrated love for Cayley, and her Christian desire for a final union with God—and with Cayley as well—combined to turn her thoughts to the grave. But her native wit and humor, which so endeared her to her family, frequently lies just beneath the surface of her saddest poetry, keeping it from becoming merely sentimental.

The chief volumes of her poetry were *Goblin Market and Other Poems*, 1862; *The Prince's Progress and Other Poems*, 1866; *A Pageant and Other Poems*, 1881; and *Verses*, 1893. In addition to these, there were charming children's poems and several volumes of prose. All the poems, both those in manuscript and those already printed, were edited and published by her brother William after her death.

The quality of Miss Rossetti's poetry is remarkably constant; it is seldom possible on stylistic evidence alone to determine whether a particular poem is early or late in the canon. Religion, love, and nature (with the three frequently intertwined) are the major subjects of her poetry. Her own residence in the country was brief, but she remembered all she had seen. She had a sharp and loving eye for the external world; giving life to her mystical vision is a warm and somewhat unexpected sensuousness that revels in color, movement, and sound. At other times, her diction is unadorned, gravely dignified, and simple. She has often been called the greatest woman poet in English history, but that is perhaps scant praise. What is more to the point is that she is one of the greatest of lyricists, with a special aptitude for the sonnet, combining sharp imagery and an impeccable sense of rhythm probably equaled among the Victorians only by Tennyson. Her devotional poetry entitles her to a place in the great tradition of Anglican poets with Donne and Herbert.

BIBLIOGRAPHY

The text of the poems follows *The Poetical Works of Christina Georgina Rossetti*, with Memoir and Notes &c. by William Michael Rossetti (Macmillan and Co., London and New York, 1904), the standard edition of Miss Rossetti's poems.

Biography and Criticism:

Bell, Mackenzie, *Christina Rossetti: A Biographical and Critical Study*. Hurst and Blackett, London, 1898.

Birkhead, Edith, *Christina Rossetti and Her Poetry*. Harrap, London, 1930.

Sandars, Mary F., *The Life of Christina Rossetti*. Hutchinson, London, 1930.

Shove, Fredegond, *Christina Rossetti: A Study*. Cambridge University Press, Cambridge, 1931.

Stuart, Dorothy Margaret, *Christina Rossetti*. Clarendon Press, Oxford, 1931.

Thomas, Eleanor W., *Christina Georgina Rossetti*. Columbia University Press, New York, 1931.

Zaturenska, Marya, *Christina Rossetti: A Portrait with Background*. Macmillan and Co., New York, 1949.

SONG

When I am dead, my dearest,
    Sing no sad songs for me;
Plant thou no roses at my head,
    Nor shady cypress tree:
Be the green grass above me
    With showers and dewdrops wet:
And if thou wilt, remember,
    And if thou wilt, forget.

I shall not see the shadows,
    I shall not feel the rain;   10
I shall not hear the nightingale
    Sing on as if in pain:
And dreaming through the twilight
    That doth not rise nor set,
Haply I may remember,
    And haply may forget.

12 December, 1848

SONG

Oh roses for the flush of youth,
    And laurel for the perfect prime;
But pluck an ivy branch for me
    Grown old before my time.

Oh violets for the grave of youth,
    And bay for those dead in their prime;
Give me the withered leaves I chose
    Before in the old time.

6 February, 1849

DREAM LAND

Where sunless rivers weep
Their waves into the deep,
She sleeps a charmèd sleep:
   Awake her not.
Led by a single star,
She came from very far
To seek where shadows are
   Her pleasant lot.

She left the rosy morn,
She left the fields of corn,   10
For twilight cold and lorn
   And water springs.
Through sleep, as through a veil,
She sees the sky look pale,
And hears the nightingale
   That sadly sings.

Rest, rest, a perfect rest
Shed over brow and breast;
Her face is toward the west,
   The purple land.   20
She cannot see the grain
Ripening on hill and plain;
She cannot feel the rain
   Upon her hand.

Rest, rest, for evermore
Upon a mossy shore;
Rest, rest at the heart's core
   Till time shall cease:
Sleep that no pain shall wake;
Night that no morn shall break,   30
Till joy shall overtake
   Her perfect peace.

April, 1849

AFTER DEATH

The curtains were half drawn, the floor was swept
  And strewn with rushes; rosemary and may
  Lay thick upon the bed on which I lay,
Where through the lattice ivy-shadows crept.
He leaned above me, thinking that I slept
  And could not hear him; but I heard him say,
  "Poor child, poor child": and as he turned away
Came a deep silence, and I knew he wept.
He did not touch the shroud, or raise the fold
  That hid my face, or take my hand in his,   10
    Or ruffle the smooth pillows for my head:
    He did not love me living; but once dead
  He pitied me; and very sweet it is
To know he still is warm though I am cold.

28 April, 1849

REST

O Earth, lie heavily upon her eyes;
  Seal her sweet eyes weary of watching, Earth;
  Lie close around her; leave no room for mirth
With its harsh laughter, nor for sound of sighs.
She hath no questions, she hath no replies,
  Hushed in and curtained with a blessèd dearth
  Of all that irked her from the hour of birth;
With stillness that is almost Paradise.
Darkness more clear than noonday holdeth her,
  Silence more musical than any song;   10
Even her very heart has ceased to stir:
Until the morning of Eternity
Her rest shall not begin nor end, but be;
  And when she wakes she will not think it long.

15 May, 1849

REMEMBER

Remember me when I am gone away,
   Gone far away into the silent land;
   When you can no more hold me by the hand,
Nor I half turn to go yet turning stay.
Remember me when no more day by day
   You tell me of our future that you plann'd:
   Only remember me; you understand
It will be late to counsel then or pray.
Yet if you should forget me for a while
   And afterwards remember, do not grieve: 10
   For if the darkness and corruption leave
   A vestige of the thoughts that once I had,
Better by far you should forget and smile
   Than that you should remember and be sad.

25 July, 1849

THE WORLD

By day she woos me, soft, exceeding fair:
   But all night as the moon so changeth she;
   Loathsome and foul with hideous leprosy,
And subtle serpents gliding in her hair.
By day she woos me to the outer air,
   Ripe fruits, sweet flowers, and full satiety:
   But thro' the night a beast she grins at me,
A very monster void of love and prayer.
By day she stands a lie: by night she stands
   In all the naked horror of the truth,   10
With pushing horns and clawed and clutching hands.
Is this a friend indeed, that I should sell
   My soul to her, give her my life and youth,
Till my feet, cloven too, take hold on hell?

27 June, 1854

ECHO

Come to me in the silence of the night;
　Come in the speaking silence of a dream;
Come with soft rounded cheeks and eyes as bright
　As sunlight on a stream;
　　Come back in tears,
O memory, hope, love of finished years.

Oh dream how sweet, too sweet, too bitter sweet,
　Whose wakening should have been in Paradise,
Where souls brimfull of love abide and meet;
　Where thirsting longing eyes   10
　　Watch the slow door
That opening, letting in, lets out no more.

Yet come to me in dreams, that I may live
　My very life again though cold in death:
Come back to me in dreams, that I may give
　Pulse for pulse, breath for breath:
　　Speak low, lean low,
As long ago, my love, how long ago.

18 December, 1854

MAY

I cannot tell you how it was;
But this I know: it came to pass—
Upon a bright and breezy day
When May was young, ah pleasant May!
As yet the poppies were not born
Between the blades of tender corn;
The last eggs had not hatched as yet,
Nor any bird forgone its mate.

I cannot tell you what it was;
But this I know: it did but pass.
It passed away with sunny May,
With all sweet things it passed away,
And left me old, and cold, and grey.

20 November, 1855

A BETTER RESURRECTION

I have no wit, no words, no tears;
   My heart within me like a stone
Is numbed too much for hopes or fears.
   Look right, look left, I dwell alone;
I lift mine eyes, but dimmed with grief
   No everlasting hills I see;
My life is in the falling leaf:
   O Jesus, quicken me.

My life is like a faded leaf,
   My harvest dwindled to a husk:
Truly my life is void and brief
   And tedious in the barren dusk;
My life is like a frozen thing,
   No bud nor greenness can I see;
Yet rise it shall—the sap of Spring;
   O Jesus, rise in me.

My life is like a broken bowl,
   A broken bowl that cannot hold
One drop of water for my soul
   Or cordial in the searching cold;
Cast in the fire the perished thing;
   Melt and remould it, till it be
A royal cup for Him, my King:
   O Jesus, drink of me.

30 June, 1857

ANOTHER SPRING

If I might see another Spring,
  I'd not plant summer flowers and wait:
I'd have my crocuses at once,
My leafless pink mezereons,
    My chill-veined snowdrops, choicer yet
    My white or azure violet,
Leaf-nested primrose; anything
    To blow at once, not late.

If I might see another Spring,
  I'd listen to the daylight birds   10
That build their nests and pair and sing,
Nor wait for mateless nightingale;
    I'd listen to the lusty herds,
    The ewes with lambs as white as snow,
I'd find out music in the hail
    And all the winds that blow.

If I might see another Spring—
  Oh stinging comment on my past
That all my past results in "if"—
    If I might see another Spring   20
I'd laugh to-day, to-day is brief;
I would not wait for anything:
    I'd use to-day that cannot last,
    Be glad to-day and sing.

15 September, 1857

---

4 *mezereons:* flowering shrubs with rose or purple blossoms.
8 *blow:* flower.

A BIRTHDAY

My heart is like a singing bird
    Whose nest is in a watered shoot:
My heart is like an apple-tree
    Whose boughs are bent with thickset fruit;
My heart is like a rainbow shell
    That paddles in a halcyon sea;
My heart is gladder than all these
    Because my love is come to me.

Raise me a dais of silk and down;
    Hang it with vair and purple dyes;   10
Carve it in doves and pomegranates,
    And peacocks with a hundred eyes;
Work it in gold and silver grapes,
    In leaves and silver fleur-de-lys;
Because the birthday of my life
    Is come, my love is come to me.

18 November, 1857

UP-HILL

Does the road wind up-hill all the way?
    Yes, to the very end.
Will the day's journey take the whole long day?
    From morn to night, my friend.

But is there for the night a resting-place?
    A roof for when the slow dark hours begin.
May not the darkness hide it from my face?
    You cannot miss that inn.

---

6 *halcyon:* calm.
10 *vair:* gray squirrel fur.

Shall I meet other wayfarers at night?
  Those who have gone before.   10
Then must I knock, or call when just in sight?
  They will not keep you standing at that door.

Shall I find comfort, travel-sore and weak?
  Of labour you shall find the sum.
Will there be beds for me and all who seek?
  Yea, beds for all who come.

29 June, 1858

GOBLIN MARKET

Morning and evening
Maids heard the goblins cry:
"Come buy our orchard fruits,
Come buy, come buy:
Apples and quinces,
Lemons and oranges,
Plump unpecked cherries,
Melons and raspberries,
Bloom-down-cheeked peaches,

Goblin Market: "The original title of this poem was *A Peep at the Goblins—To M. F. R.—i.e.* Maria Francesca Rossetti. I have more than once heard Christina say that she did not mean anything profound by this fairy tale—it is not a moral apologue consistently carried out in detail. Still the incidents are such as to be at any rate suggestive, and different minds may be likely to read different messages into them. I find at times that people do not see the central point of the story, such as the authoress intended it: and she has expressed it too, but perhaps not with due emphasis. The foundation of the narrative is this: That the goblins tempt women to eat their luscious but uncanny fruits; that a first taste produces a rabid craving for a second taste; but that the second taste is never accorded, and, in default of it, the woman pines away and dies. Then comes the central point: Laura having tasted the fruits once, and being at death's door through inability to get a second taste, her sister Lizzie determines to save her at all hazards; so she goes to the goblins, refuses to eat their fruits, and beguiles them into forcing the fruits upon her with so much insistency that her face is all smeared and steeped with the juices; she gets Laura to kiss and suck these juices off her face, and Laura, having thus obtained the otherwise impossible second taste, rapidly recovers." [W. M. Rossetti]

Swart-headed mulberries,   10
Wild free-born cranberries,
Crab-apples, dewberries,
Pine-apples, blackberries,
Apricots, strawberries;—
All ripe together
In summer weather,—
Morns that pass by,
Fair eves that fly;
Come buy, come buy:
Our grapes fresh from the vine,   20
Pomegranates full and fine,
Dates and sharp bullaces,
Rare pears and greengages,
Damsons and bilberries,
Taste them and try:
Currants and gooseberries,
Bright-fire-like barberries,
Figs to fill your mouth,
Citrons from the South,
Sweet to tongue and sound to eye;   30
Come buy, come buy."

Evening by evening
Among the brookside rushes,
Laura bowed her head to hear,
Lizzie veiled her blushes:
Crouching close together
In the cooling weather,
With clasping arms and cautioning lips,
With tingling cheeks and finger tips.
"Lie close," Laura said,   40
Pricking up her golden head:
"We must not look at goblin men,
We must not buy their fruits:
Who knows upon what soil they fed
Their hungry thirsty roots?"
"Come buy," call the goblins
Hobbling down the glen.

---

22 *bullaces:* small plums.
24 *bilberries:* a species of blueberry.

"Oh," cried Lizzie, "Laura, Laura,
You should not peep at goblin men."
Lizzie covered up her eyes,   50
Covered close lest they should look;
Laura reared her glossy head,
And whispered like the restless brook:
"Look, Lizzie, look, Lizzie,
Down the glen tramp little men.
One hauls a basket,
One bears a plate,
One lugs a golden dish
Of many pounds' weight.
How fair the vine must grow   60
Whose grapes are so luscious;
How warm the wind must blow
Through those fruit bushes."
"No," said Lizzie: "No, no, no;
Their offers should not charm us,
Their evil gifts would harm us."
She thrust a dimpled finger
In each ear, shut eyes and ran:
Curious Laura chose to linger
Wondering at each merchant man.   70
One had a cat's face,
One whisked a tail,
One tramped at a rat's pace,
One crawled like a snail,
One like a wombat prowled obtuse and furry,
One like a ratel tumbled hurry skurry.
She heard a voice like voice of doves
Cooing all together:
They sounded kind and full of loves
In the pleasant weather.   80

Laura stretched her gleaming neck
Like a rush-imbedded swan,
Like a lily from the beck,
Like a moonlit poplar branch,

---

75 *wombat:* badger-like Australian marsupial.
76 *ratel:* South African badger.

Like a vessel at the launch
When its last restraint is gone.

Backwards up the mossy glen
Turned and trooped the goblin men,
With their shrill repeated cry,
"Come buy, come buy."   90
When they reached where Laura was
They stood stock still upon the moss,
Leering at each other,
Brother with queer brother;
Signalling each other,
Brother with sly brother.
One set his basket down,
One reared his plate;
One began to weave a crown
Of tendrils, leaves, and rough nuts brown   100
(Men sell not such in any town);
One heaved the golden weight
Of dish and fruit to offer her:
"Come buy, come buy," was still their cry.
Laura stared but did not stir,
Longed but had no money.
The whisk-tailed merchant bade her taste
In tones as smooth as honey,
The cat-faced purr'd,
The rat-paced spoke a word   110
Of welcome, and the snail-paced even was heard;
One parrot-voiced and jolly
Cried "Pretty Goblin" still for "Pretty Polly";
One whistled like a bird.

But sweet-tooth Laura spoke in haste:
"Good Folk, I have no coin;
To take were to purloin:
I have no copper in my purse,
I have no silver either,
And all my gold is on the furze   120
That shakes in windy weather
Above the rusty heather."
"You have much gold upon your head,"

They answered all together:
"Buy from us with a golden curl."
She clipped a precious golden lock,
She dropped a tear more rare than pearl,
Then sucked their fruit globes fair or red.
Sweeter than honey from the rock,
Stronger than man-rejoicing wine,   130
Clearer than water flowed that juice;
She never tasted such before,
How should it cloy with length of use?
She sucked and sucked and sucked the more
Fruits which that unknown orchard bore;
She sucked until her lips were sore;
Then flung the emptied rinds away
But gathered up one kernel stone,
And knew not was it night or day
As she turned home alone.   140

Lizzie met her at the gate
Full of wise upbraidings:
"Dear, you should not stay so late,
Twilight is not good for maidens;
Should not loiter in the glen
In the haunts of goblin men.
Do you not remember Jeanie,
How she met them in the moonlight,
Took their gifts both choice and many,
Ate their fruits and wore their flowers   150
Plucked from bowers
Where summer ripens at all hours?
But ever in the noonlight
She pined and pined away;
Sought them by night and day,
Found them no more, but dwindled and grew grey;
Then fell with the first snow,
While to this day no grass will grow
Where she lies low:
I planted daisies there a year ago   160
That never blow.
You should not loiter so."
"Nay, hush," said Laura:

"Nay, hush, my sister:
I ate and ate my fill,
Yet my mouth waters still:
To-morrow night I will
Buy more"; and kissed her.
"Have done with sorrow;
I'll bring you plums to-morrow   170
Fresh on their mother twigs,
Cherries worth getting;
You cannot think what figs
My teeth have met in,
What melons icy-cold
Piled on a dish of gold
Too huge for me to hold,
What peaches with a velvet nap,
Pellucid grapes without one seed:
Odorous indeed must be the mead   180
Whereon they grow, and pure the wave they drink
With lilies at the brink,
And sugar-sweet their sap."

Golden head by golden head,
Like two pigeons in one nest
Folded in each other's wings,
They lay down in their curtained bed:
Like two blossoms on one stem,
Like two flakes of new-fall'n snow,
Like two wands of ivory   190
Tipped with gold for awful kings.
Moon and stars gazed in at them,
Wind sang to them lullaby,
Lumbering owls forbore to fly,
Not a bat flapped to and fro
Round their nest:
Cheek to cheek and breast to breast
Locked together in one nest.

Early in the morning
When the first cock crowed his warning,   200
Neat like bees, as sweet and busy,
Laura rose with Lizzie:

Fetched in honey, milked the cows,
Aired and set to rights the house,
Kneaded cakes of whitest wheat,
Cakes for dainty mouths to eat,
Next churned butter, whipped up cream,
Fed their poultry, sat and sewed;
Talked as modest maidens should:
Lizzie with an open heart,   210
Laura in an absent dream,
One content, one sick in part;
One warbling for the mere bright day's delight,
One longing for the night.

At length slow evening came:
They went with pitchers to the reedy brook;
Lizzie most placid in her look,
Laura most like a leaping flame.
They drew the gurgling water from its deep.
Lizzie plucked purple and rich golden flags,   220
Then turning homeward said: "The sunset flushes
Those furthest loftiest crags;
Come, Laura, not another maiden lags.
No wilful squirrel wags,
The beasts and birds are fast asleep."
But Laura loitered still among the rushes,
And said the bank was steep.

And said the hour was early still,
The dew not fall'n, the wind not chill;
Listening ever, but not catching   230
The customary cry,
"Come buy, come buy,"
With its iterated jingle
Of sugar-baited words:
Not for all her watching
Once discerning even one goblin
Racing, whisking, tumbling, hobbling—
Let alone the herds
That used to tramp along the glen,
In groups or single,   240
Of brisk fruit-merchant men.

Till Lizzie urged, "O Laura, come;
I hear the fruit-call, but I dare not look:
You should not loiter longer at this brook:
Come with me home.
The stars rise, the moon bends her arc,
Each glow-worm winks her spark,
Let us get home before the night grows dark:
For clouds may gather
Though this is summer weather, 250
Put out the lights and drench us through;
Then if we lost our way what should we do?"

Laura turned cold as stone
To find her sister heard that cry alone,
That goblin cry,
"Come buy our fruits, come buy."
Must she then buy no more such dainty fruit?
Must she no more such succous pasture find,
Gone deaf and blind?
Her tree of life drooped from the root: 260
She said not one word in her heart's sore ache:
But peering thro' the dimness, nought discerning,
Trudged home, her pitcher dripping all the way;
So crept to bed, and lay
Silent till Lizzie slept;
Then sat up in a passionate yearning,
And gnashed her teeth for baulked desire, and wept
As if her heart would break.

Day after day, night after night,
Laura kept watch in vain 270
In sullen silence of exceeding pain.
She never caught again the goblin cry,
"Come buy, come buy";—
She never spied the goblin men
Hawking their fruits along the glen:
But when the noon waxed bright
Her hair grew thin and grey;

---

258 *succous:* juicy.

She dwindled, as the fair full moon doth turn
To swift decay and burn
Her fire away.   280

One day remembering her kernel-stone
She set it by a wall that faced the south;
Dewed it with tears, hoped for a root,
Watched for a waxing shoot,
But there came none.
It never saw the sun,
It never felt the trickling moisture run:
While with sunk eyes and faded mouth
She dreamed of melons, as a traveller sees
False waves in desert drouth   290
With shade of leaf-crowned trees,
And burns the thirstier in the sandful breeze.

She no more swept the house,
Tended the fowls or cows,
Fetched honey, kneaded cakes of wheat,
Brought water from the brook:
But sat down listless in the chimney-nook
And would not eat.

Tender Lizzie could not bear
To watch her sister's cankerous care,   300
Yet not to share.
She night and morning
Caught the goblins' cry:
"Come buy our orchard fruits,
Come buy, come buy:"—
Beside the brook, along the glen,
She heard the tramp of goblin men,
The voice and stir
Poor Laura could not hear;
Longed to buy fruit to comfort her,   310
But feared to pay too dear.
She thought of Jeanie in her grave,
Who should have been a bride;
But who for joys brides hope to have
Fell sick and died

In her gay prime,
In earliest winter time,
With the first glazing rime,
With the first snow-fall of crisp winter time.

Till Laura dwindling   320
Seemed knocking at Death's door.
Then Lizzie weighed no more
Better and worse;
But put a silver penny in her purse,
Kissed Laura, crossed the heath with clumps of furze
At twilight, halted by the brook:
And for the first time in her life
Began to listen and look.

Laughed every goblin
When they spied her peeping: 330
Came towards her hobbling,
Flying, running, leaping,
Puffing and blowing,
Chuckling, clapping, crowing,
Clucking and gobbling,
Mopping and mowing,
Full of airs and graces,
Pulling wry faces,
Demure grimaces,
Cat-like and rat-like,   340
Ratel- and wombat-like,
Snail-paced in a hurry,
Parrot-voiced and whistler,
Helter-skelter, hurry skurry,
Chattering like magpies,
Fluttering like pigeons,
Gliding like fishes,—
Hugged her and kissed her:
Squeezed and caressed her:
Stretched up their dishes,   350
Panniers, and plates:
"Look at our apples

---

318 *rime:* frost.

Russet and dun,
Bob at our cherries,
Bite at our peaches,
Citrons and dates,
Grapes for the asking,
Pears red with basking
Out in the sun,
Plums on their twigs;   360
Pluck them and suck them,—
Pomegranates, figs."

"Good folk," said Lizzie,
Mindful of Jeanie:
"Give me much and many:"
Held out her apron,
Tossed them her penny.
"Nay, take a seat with us,
Honour and eat with us,"
They answered grinning: 370
"Our feast is but beginning.
Night yet is early,
Warm and dew-pearly,
Wakeful and starry:
Such fruits as these
No man can carry;
Half their bloom would fly,
Half their dew would dry,
Half their flavour would pass by.
Sit down and feast with us,   380
Be welcome guest with us,
Cheer you and rest with us."—
"Thank you," said Lizzie: "But one waits
At home alone for me:
So without further parleying,
If you will not sell me any
Of your fruits though much and many,
Give me back my silver penny
I tossed you for a fee."—
They began to scratch their pates,   390
No longer wagging, purring,
But visibly demurring,

Grunting and snarling.
One called her proud,
Cross-grained, uncivil;
Their tones waxed loud,
Their looks were evil.
Lashing their tails
They trod and hustled her,
Elbowed and jostled her,   400
Clawed with their nails,
Barking, mewing, hissing, mocking,
Tore her gown and soiled her stocking,
Twitched her hair out by the roots,
Stamped upon her tender feet,
Held her hands and squeezed their fruits
Against her mouth to make her eat.

White and golden Lizzie stood,
Like a lily in a flood,—
Like a rock of blue-veined stone   410
Lashed by tides obstreperously,—
Like a beacon left alone
In a hoary roaring sea,
Sending up a golden fire,—
Like a fruit-crowned orange-tree
White with blossoms honey-sweet
Sore beset by wasp and bee,—
Like a royal virgin town
Topped with gilded dome and spire
Close beleaguered by a fleet   420
Mad to tug her standard down.

One may lead a horse to water,
Twenty cannot make him drink.
Though the goblins cuffed and caught her,
Coaxed and fought her,
Bullied and besought her,
Scratched her, pinched her black as ink,
Kicked and knocked her,
Mauled and mocked her,
Lizzie uttered not a word;   430
Would not open lip from lip

Lest they should cram a mouthful in:
But laughed in heart to feel the drip
Of juice that syruped all her face,
And lodged in dimples of her chin,
And streaked her neck which quaked like curd.
At last the evil people,
Worn out by her resistance,
Flung back her penny, kicked their fruit
Along whichever road they took,   440
Not leaving root or stone or shoot;
Some writhed into the ground,
Some dived into the brook
With ring and ripple,
Some scudded on the gale without a sound,
Some vanished in the distance.

In a smart, ache, tingle,
Lizzie went her way;
Knew not was it night or day;
Sprang up the bank, tore thro' the furze,   450
Threaded copse and dingle,
And heard her penny jingle
Bouncing in her purse,—
Its bounce was music to her ear.
She ran and ran
As if she feared some goblin man
Dogged her with gibe or curse
Or something worse:
But not one goblin skurried after,
Nor was she pricked by fear;   460
The kind heart made her windy-paced
That urged her home quite out of breath with haste
And inward laughter.

She cried, "Laura," up the garden,
"Did you miss me?
Come and kiss me.
Never mind my bruises,
Hug me, kiss me, suck my juices
Squeezed from goblin fruits for you,
Goblin pulp and goblin dew.   470

Eat me, drink me, love me;
Laura, make much of me;
For your sake I have braved the glen
And had to do with goblin merchant men."

Laura started up from her chair,
Flung her arms up in the air,
Clutched her hair:
"Lizzie, Lizzie, have you tasted
For my sake the fruit forbidden?
Must your light like mine be hidden,   480
Your young life like mine be wasted,
Undone in mine undoing
And ruined in my ruin,
Thirsty, cankered, goblin-ridden?"—
She clung about her sister,
Kissed and kissed and kissed her:
Tears once again
Refreshed her shrunken eyes,
Dropping like rain
After long sultry drouth;   490
Shaking with anguish, fear, and pain,
She kissed and kissed her with a hungry mouth.

Her lips began to scorch,
That juice was wormwood to her tongue,
She loathed the feast:
Writhing as one possessed she leaped and sung,
Rent all her robe, and wrung
Her hands in lamentable haste,
And beat her breast.
Her locks streamed like the torch   500
Borne by a racer at full speed,
Or like the mane of horses in their flight,
Or like an eagle when she stems the light
Straight toward the sun,
Or like a caged thing freed,
Or like a flying flag when armies run.

Swift fire spread through her veins, knocked at her heart,
Met the fire smouldering there

And overbore its lesser flame;
She gorged on bitterness without a name: 510
Ah fool, to choose such part
Of soul-consuming care!
Sense failed in the mortal strife:
Like the watch-tower of a town
Which an earthquake shatters down,
Like a lightning-stricken mast,
Like a wind-uprooted tree
Spun about,
Like a foam-topped waterspout
Cast down headlong in the sea,   520
She fell at last;
Pleasure past and anguish past,
Is it death or is it life?

Life out of death.
That night long Lizzie watched by her,
Counted her pulse's flagging stir,
Felt for her breath,
Held water to her lips, and cooled her face
With tears and fanning leaves.
But when the first birds chirped about their eaves,   530
And early reapers plodded to the place
Of golden sheaves,
And dew-wet grass
Bowed in the morning winds so brisk to pass,
And new buds with new day
Opened of cup-like lilies on the stream,
Laura awoke as from a dream,
Laughed in the innocent old way,
Hugged Lizzie but not twice or thrice;
Her gleaming locks showed not one thread of grey,   540
Her breath was sweet as May,
And light danced in her eyes.

Days, weeks, months, years
Afterwards, when both were wives
With children of their own;
Their mother-hearts beset with fears,
Their lives bound up in tender lives;

Laura would call the little ones
And tell them of her early prime,
Those pleasant days long gone   550
Of not-returning time:
Would talk about the haunted glen,
The wicked quaint fruit-merchant men,
Their fruits like honey to the throat
But poison in the blood
(Men sell not such in any town):
Would tell them how her sister stood
In deadly peril to do her good,
And win the fiery antidote:
Then joining hands to little hands   560
Would bid them cling together,—
"For there is no friend like a sister
In calm or stormy weather;
To cheer one on the tedious way,
To fetch one if one goes astray,
To lift one if one totters down,
To strengthen whilst one stands."

27 April, 1859

GOOD FRIDAY

Am I a stone and not a sheep
    That I can stand, O Christ, beneath Thy Cross,
    To number drop by drop Thy Blood's slow loss,
And yet not weep?

Not so those women loved
    Who with exceeding grief lamented Thee;
    Not so fallen Peter weeping bitterly;
Not so the thief was moved;

Not so the Sun and Moon
    Which hid their faces in a starless sky,   10
    A horror of great darkness at broad noon—
I, only I.

Yet give not o'er,
   But seek Thy sheep, true Shepherd of the flock;
   Greater than Moses, turn and look once more
And smite a rock.

20 April, 1862

ON THE WING

Once in a dream (for once I dreamed of you)
   We stood together in an open field;
   Above our heads two swift-winged pigeons wheeled,
Sporting at ease and courting full in view:—
When loftier still a broadening darkness flew,
   Down-swooping, and a ravenous hawk revealed;
   Too weak to fight, too fond to fly, they yield;
So farewell life and love and pleasures new.
Then as their plumes fell fluttering to the ground,
   Their snow-white plumage flecked with crimson drops,   10
   I wept, and thought I turned towards you to weep:
   But you were gone; while rustling hedgerow tops
Bent in a wind which bore to me a sound
   Of far-off piteous bleat of lambs and sheep.

17 December, 1862

WHAT WOULD I GIVE!

What would I give for a heart of flesh to warm me through,
Instead of this heart of stone ice-cold whatever I do!
Hard and cold and small, of all hearts the worst of all.

What would I give for words, if only words would come!
But now in its misery my spirit has fallen dumb.
Oh, merry friends, go your way, I have never a word to say.

What would I give for tears! not smiles but scalding tears,
To wash the black mark clean, and to thaw the frost of years,
To wash the stain ingrain, and to make me clean again.

28 January, 1864

WEARY IN WELL-DOING

I would have gone; God bade me stay:
  I would have worked; God bade me rest.
He broke my will from day to day;
  He read my yearnings unexprest,
    And said them nay.

Now I would stay; God bids me go:
  Now I would rest; God bids me work.
He breaks my heart tost to and fro,
  My soul is wrung with doubts that lurk
    And vex it so.   10

I go, Lord, where Thou sendest me;
  Day after day I plod and moil:
But, Christ my God, when will it be
  That I may let alone my toil
    And rest with Thee?

22 October, 1864

BIRDS OF PARADISE

Golden-winged, silver-winged,
  Winged with flashing flame,
Such a flight of birds I saw,
  Birds without a name:
Singing songs in their own tongue—
  Song of songs—they came.

One to another calling,
    Each answering each,
One to another calling
    In their proper speech: 10
High above my head they wheeled,
    Far out of reach.

On wings of flame they went and came
    With a cadenced clang:
Their silver wings tinkled,
    Their golden wings rang;
The wind it whistled through their wings
    Where in heaven they sang.

They flashed and they darted
    Awhile before mine eyes,   20
Mounting, mounting, mounting still,
    In haste to scale the skies,
Birds without a nest on earth,
    Birds of Paradise.

Where the moon riseth not
    Nor sun seeks the west,
There to sing their glory
    Which they sing at rest,
There to sing their love-song
    When they sing their best:—   30

Not in any garden
    That mortal foot hath trod,
Not in any flowering tree
    That springs from earthly sod,
But in the garden where they dwell,
    The Paradise of God.

14 November, 1864

MONNA INNOMINATA

A SONNET OF SONNETS

I

"Lo di che han detto a' dolci amici addio."
DANTE.

"Amor, con quanto sforzo oggi mi vinci!"
PETRARCA.

Come back to me, who wait and watch for you:—
   Or come not yet, for it is over then,
   And long it is before you come again,
So far between my pleasures are and few.
While, when you come not, what I do I do
   Thinking "Now when he comes," my sweetest "when":
   For one man is my world of all the men
This wide world holds; O love, my world is you.
Howbeit, to meet you grows almost a pang
   Because the pang of parting comes so soon;   10
   My hope hangs waning, waxing, like a moon
Between the heavenly days on which we meet:
Ah me, but where are now the songs I sang
   When life was sweet because you called them sweet?

Monna Innominata: the title of the series means "Nameless Lady." Miss Rossetti said that the speaker of the poems was one of the unnamed ladies celebrated by the poets before Dante and Petrarch, who had celebrated Beatrice and Laura. The speaker might be imagined "as sharing her lover's poetic aptitude, while the barrier between them might be one held sacred by both, yet not such as to render mutual love incompatible with mutual honour." W. M. Rossetti was convinced that the sonnets were "intensely personal. . . . The introductory prose-note, about 'many a lady sharing her lover's poetic aptitude,' etc., is a blind—not an untruthful blind, for it alleges nothing that is not reasonable, and on the surface correct, but still a blind interposed to draw off attention from the writer in her proper person." *"Lo . . . addio":* "The day that they have said adieu to their sweet friends." [This and the following translations of the epigraphs are given by W. M. Rossetti.] *"Amor . . . vinci":* "Love with how great a stress dost thou vanquish me to-day!"

II

"Era già l'ora che volge il desio."
DANTE.

"Ricorro al tempo ch'io vi vidi prima."
PETRARCA.

I wish I could remember that first day,
   First hour, first moment of your meeting me,
   If bright or dim the season, it might be
Summer of Winter for aught I can say;
So unrecorded did it slip away,
   So blind was I to see and to foresee,
   So dull to mark the budding of my tree
That would not blossom yet for many a May.
If only I could recollect it, such
   A day of days! I let it come and go   10
   As traceless as a thaw of bygone snow;
It seemed to mean so little, meant so much;
If only now I could recall that touch,
   First touch of hand in hand—Did one but know!

III

"O ombre vane, fuor che ne l'aspetto!"
DANTE.

"Immaginata guida la conduce."
PETRARCA.

I dream of you, to wake: would that I might
   Dream of you and not wake but slumber on;
   Nor find with dreams the dear companion gone,
As, Summer ended, Summer birds take flight.
In happy dreams I hold you full in sight,
   I blush again who waking look so wan;
   Brighter than sunniest day that ever shone,
In happy dreams your smile makes day of night.
Thus only in a dream we are at one,
   Thus only in a dream we give and take   10
   The faith that maketh rich who take or give;

"Era . . . desio": "It was already the hour which turns back the desire."
"Ricorro . . . prima": "I recur to the time when I first saw thee."
"O . . . l'aspetto!": "Oh shades, empty save in semblance!"
"Immaginata . . . conduce": "An imaginary guide conducts her."

If thus to sleep is sweeter than to wake,
    To die were surely sweeter than to live,
Though there be nothing new beneath the sun.

IV

"*Poca favilla gran fiamma seconda.*"
                                    DANTE.
"*Ogni altra cosa, ogni pensier va fore,
E sol ivi con voi rimansi amore.*"
                                    PETRARCA.

I loved you first: but afterwards your love,
    Outsoaring mine, sang such a loftier song
As drowned the friendly cooings of my dove.
    Which owes the other most? My love was long,
    And yours one moment seemed to wax more strong;
I loved and guessed at you, you construed me
And loved me for what might or might not be—
    Nay, weights and measures do us both a wrong.
For verily love knows not "mine" or "thine";
    With separate "I" and "thou" free love has done,   10
    For one is both and both are one in love:
Rich love knows nought of "thine that is not mine";
    Both have the strength and both the length thereof,
Both of us, of the love which makes us one.

V

"*Amor che a nullo amato amar perdona.*"
                                    DANTE.
"*Amor m'addusse in si gioiosa spene.*"
                                    PETRARCA.

O my heart's heart, and you who are to me
    More than myself myself, God be with you,
    Keep you in strong obedience leal and true
To Him whose noble service setteth free;
    Give you all good we see or can foresee,

"*Poca . . . seconda*": "A small spark fosters a great flame."
"*Ogni . . . amore*": "Every other thing, every thought, goes off, and love
alone remains there with you."
"*Amor . . . perdona*": "Love, who exempts no loved one from loving."
"*Amor . . . spene*": "Love led me into such joyous hope."
3 *leal:* loyal.

Make your joys many and your sorrows few,
Bless you in what you bear and what you do,
Yea, perfect you as He would have you be.
So much for you; but what for me, dear friend?
To love you without stint and all I can, 10
To-day, to-morrow, world without an end;
To love you much and yet to love you more,
As Jordan at his flood sweeps either shore;
Since woman is the helpmeet made for man.

VI

*"Or puoi la quantitate
Comprender de l'amor che a te mi scalda."*
DANTE.
"Non vo' che da tal nodo amor mi scioglia."
PETRARCA.

Trust me, I have not earned your dear rebuke,—
I love, as you would have me, God the most;
Would lose not Him, but you, must one be lost,
Nor with Lot's wife cast back a faithless look,
Unready to forego what I forsook;
This say I, having counted up the cost,
This, though I be the feeblest of God's host,
The sorriest sheep Christ shepherds with His crook.
Yet while I love my God the most, I deem
That I can never love you overmuch; 10
I love Him more, so let me love you too;
Yea, as I apprehend it, love is such
I cannot love you if I love not Him,
I cannot love Him if I love not you.

"Or . . . scalda": "Now canst thou comprehend the quantity of the love which glows in me towards thee."
"Non . . . scioglia": "I do not choose that Love should release me from such a tie."
4 *faithless look:* Lot and his family were commanded by God not to look back in their escape from Sodom; Lot obeyed, "But his wife looked back from behind him and she became a pillar of salt" (*Genesis* 19:26).

VII

"Qui primavera sempre ed ogni frutto."
                                        DANTE.
"Ragionando con meco ed io con lui."
                                        PETRARCA.

"Love me, for I love you"—and answer me,
  "Love me, for I love you": so shall we stand
  As happy equals in the flowering land
Of love, that knows not a dividing sea.
Love builds the house on rock and not on sand,
  Love laughs what while the winds rave desperately;
And who hath found love's citadel unmanned?
  And who hath held in bonds love's liberty?—
My heart's a coward though my words are brave—
  We meet so seldom, yet we surely part   10
So often; there's a problem for your art!
  Still I find comfort in his Book who saith,
Though jealousy be cruel as the grave,
  And death be strong, yet love is strong as death.

VIII

"Come dicesse a Dio, D'altro non calme."
                                        DANTE.
"Spero trovar pietà non che perdono."
                                        PETRARCA.

"I, if I perish, perish"—Esther spake:
  And bride of life or death she made her fair
  In all the lustre of her perfumed hair
And smiles that kindle longing but to slake.
She put on pomp of loveliness, to take
  Her husband through his eyes at unaware;

"Qui . . . frutto": "Here always Spring and every fruit."
"Ragionando . . . lui": "Conversing with me, and I with him."
12 *Book: Song of Solomon*. "Set me as a seal upon thine heart, as a seal upon
thine arm; for love is strong as death; jealousy is cruel as the grave: the coals
thereof are coals of fire, which hath a most vehement flame (8:6).
"Come . . . calme": "As if he were to say to God, 'I care for nought else.'"
"Spero . . . perdono": "I hope to find pity, and not only pardon."
1 *Esther*: in spite of warnings against so doing, Esther, the Jewish queen of
Ahasuerus, King of Persia, went to plead with him for her people's freedom,
saying, "If I perish, I perish." Her beauty secured the success of her mission.
Her story is told in the Book of *Esther*.

She spread abroad her beauty for a snare,
Harmless as doves and subtle as a snake.
She trapped him with one mesh of silken hair,
   She vanquished him by wisdom of her wit,   10
      And built her people's house that it should stand:—
   If I might take my life so in my hand,
And for my love to Love put up my prayer,
   And for love's sake by Love be granted it!

IX

"O dignitosa coscienza e netta!"
                              DANTE.
"Spirto piu acceso di virtuti ardenti."
                              PETRARCA.

Thinking of you, and all that was, and all
   That might have been and now can never be,
   I feel your honoured excellence, and see
Myself unworthy of the happier call;
For woe is me who walk so apt to fall,
   So apt to shrink afraid, so apt to flee,
   Apt to lie down and die (ah woe is me!)
Faithless and hopeless turning to the wall.
And yet not hopeless quite nor faithless quite,
Because not loveless; love may toil all night,   10
But take at morning; wrestle till the break
   Of day, but then wield power with God and man:—
   So take I heart of grace as best I can,
Ready to spend and be spent for your sake.

X

"Con miglior corso e con migliore stella."
                              DANTE.
"La vita fugge e non s'arresta un'ora."
                              PETRARCA.

Time flies, hope flags, life plies a wearied wing;
   Death following hard on life gains ground apace;

"*O . . . netta!*": "O dignified and pure conscience!"
"*Spirto . . . ardenti*": "Spirit more lit with burning virtues."
"*Con . . . stella*": "With better course and with better star."
"*La . . . o.a*": "Life flees, and stays not an hour."

Faith runs with each and rears an eager face,
Outruns the rest, makes light of everything,
Spurns earth, and still finds breath to pray and sing;
    While love ahead of all uplifts his praise,
    Still asks for grace and still gives thanks for grace,
Content with all day brings and night will bring.
Life wanes; and when love folds his wings above
    Tired hope, and less we feel his conscious pulse,   10
        Let us go fall asleep, dear friend, in peace;
        A little while, and age and sorrow cease;
    A little while, and life reborn annuls
Loss and decay and death, and all is love.

XI

"Vien dietro a me e lascia dir le genti."
                  DANTE.
"Contando i casi della vita nostra.'"
                  PETRARCA.

Many in aftertimes will say of you
    "He loved her"—while of me what will they say?
    Not that I loved you more than just in play,
For fashion's sake as idle women do.
Even let them prate; who know not what we knew
    Of love and parting in exceeding pain,
    Of parting hopeless here to meet again,
Hopeless on earth, and heaven is out of view.
But by my heart of love laid bare to you,
    My love that you can make not void nor vain,   10
Love that foregoes you but to claim anew
Beyond this passage of the gate of death,
    I charge you at the Judgment make it plain
My love of you was life and not a breath.

"*Vien . . . genti*": "Come after me, and leave folk to talk."
"*Contando . . . nostra*": "Relating the casualties of our life."

XII

"Amor che ne la mente mi ragiona."
                              DANTE.
"Amor vien nel bel viso di costei."
                              PETRARCA.

If there be any one can take my place
    And make you happy whom I grieve to grieve,
    Think not that I can grudge it, but believe
I do commend you to that nobler grace,
That readier wit than mine, that sweeter face;
    Yea, since your riches make me rich, conceive
    I too am crowned, while bridal crowns I weave,
And thread the bridal dance with jocund pace.
For if I did not love you, it might be
    That I should grudge you some one dear delight;   10
        But since the heart is yours that was mine own,
    Your pleasure is my pleasure, right my right,
    Your honourable freedom makes me free,
        And you companioned I am not alone.

XIII

"E drizzeremo glí occhi al Primo Amore."
                              DANTE.
"Ma trovo peso non da le mie braccia."
                              PETRARCA.

If I could trust mine own self with your fate,
    Shall I not rather trust it in God's hand?
    Without Whose Will one lily doth not stand,
Nor sparrow fall at his appointed date;
    Who numbereth the innumerable sand,
Who weighs the wind and water with a weight,
To Whom the world is neither small nor great,
    Whose knowledge foreknew every plan we planned.
Searching my heart for all that touches you,
    I find there only love and love's goodwill   10
Helpless to help and impotent to do,

"Amor . . . ragiona": "Love, who speaks within my mind."
"Amor . . . costei": "Love comes in the beautiful face of this lady."
"E . . . Amore": "And we will direct our eyes to the Primal Love."
"Ma . . . braccia": "But I find a burden to which my arms suffice not."

Of understanding dull, of sight most dim;
And therefore I commend you back to Him
　Whose love your love's capacity can fill.

XIV

"E la Sua Volontade è nostra pace."
DANTE.
"Sol con questi pensier, con altre chiome."
PETRARCA.

Youth gone, and beauty gone if ever there
　Dwelt beauty in so poor a face as this;
　　Youth gone and beauty, what remains of bliss?
I will not bind fresh roses in my hair,
To shame a cheek at best but little fair,—
　Leave youth his roses, who can bear a thorn,—
I will not seek for blossoms anywhere,
　Except such common flowers as blow with corn.
Youth gone and beauty gone, what doth remain?
　The longing of a heart pent up forlorn,　　　10
　　A silent heart whose silence loves and longs;
　　The silence of a heart which sang its songs
While youth and beauty made a summer morn,
Silence of love that cannot sing again.

Before 1882

DE PROFUNDIS

Oh why is heaven built so far,
　Oh why is earth set so remote?
I cannot reach the nearest star
　That hangs afloat.

I would not care to reach the moon,
　One round monotonous of change;
Yet even she repeats her tune
　Beyond my range.

"*E . . . pace*": "And His will is our peace."
"*Sol . . . chiome*": "Only with these thoughts, with different locks."

I never watch the scattered fire
   Of stars, or sun's far-trailing train,   10
But all my heart is one desire,
   And all in vain:

For I am bound with fleshly bands,
   Joy, beauty, lie beyond my scope;
I strain my heart, I stretch my hands,
   And catch at hope.

Before 1882

EASTER DAY

Words cannot utter
   Christ His returning:
Mankind, keep jubilee,
   Strip off your mourning,
Crown you with garlands,
   Set your lamps burning.

Speech is left speechless;
   Set you to singing,
Fling your hearts open wide,
   Set your bells ringing: 10
Christ the Chief Reaper
   Comes, His sheaf bringing.

Earth wakes her song-birds,
   Puts on her flowers,
Leads out her lambkins,
   Builds up her bowers:
This is man's spousal day,
   Christ's day and ours.

Before 1886

OUT OF THE DEEP HAVE I CALLED
UNTO THEE, O LORD

Alone Lord God, in Whom our trust and peace,
  Our love and our desire, glow bright with hope;
  Lift us above this transitory scope
Of earth, these pleasures that begin and cease,
This moon which wanes, these seasons which decrease:
  We turn to Thee; as on an eastern slope
  Wheat feels the dawn beneath night's lingering cope,
Bending and stretching sunward ere it sees.
Alone Lord God, we see not yet we know;
  By love we dwell with patience and desire,   10
    And loving so and so desiring pray;
    Thy Will be done in earth as heaven to-day;
As yesterday it was, to-morrow so;
  Love offering love on love's self-feeding fire.

Before 1893

SLEEPING AT LAST

Sleeping at last, the trouble and tumult over,
  Sleeping at last, the struggle and horror past,
Cold and white, out of sight of friend and of lover,
  Sleeping at last.

No more a tired heart downcast or overcast,
No more pangs that wring or shifting fears that hover,
  Sleeping at last in a dreamless sleep locked fast.

Sleeping at Last: W. M. Rossetti regarded these verses "as being the very last that Christina ever wrote."

Fast asleep. Singing birds in their leafy cover
   Cannot wake her, nor shake her the gusty blast.
Under the purple thyme and the purple clover   10
   Sleeping at last.

Circa 1893

Algernon Charles Swinburne

[*1837-1909*]

Alone among the great Victorian poets, Algernon Charles Swinburne was, in the strict sense, an aristocrat. His mother was the daughter of the Earl of Ashburnham; his father, an admiral, was the second son of a baronet. The sensitivity and cultivation of his mind were like those of his mother, and he resembled his bluff father little save in his love of the sea.

Swinburne was brought up as a High Church Anglican and as a child showed an excessive and emotional religious devotion that tapered off into the atheism (and militant anti-Christianity) of his adult life. He was thin and physically frail, with tiny hands and feet, and a big head with a mop of red hair above a body so short that, even as a man, he was the size of a boy of twelve or thirteen. As a child he disliked all sports except the three at which he surprisingly excelled, riding, mountain climbing, and swimming. All three required physical courage and a certain recklessness, but swimming was most important to him because it brought him into contact with the ocean, the "green-girdled mother," that was to be the central image of his poetry. At times, the sea was to represent to him by its lashing a special kind of punitive lover; at others, it became the birthplace of the sea-born Aphrodite or the timeless, imperturbable mother of all living things, standing, by its agelessness, for refuge against temporal disappointment.

When he went to Eton at twelve, Swinburne already knew French and Italian well, and he was as widely read in some directions as were his masters. At school he was somewhat apart from the other boys, but his physical courage kept him from the bullying that his size would normally have invited. The corporal punishment then common in English public schools was no cruelty to him, for it only aggravated his abnormal pleasure in pain. Most of his spare time at Eton was spent in the library with the volumes of Elizabethan and Jacobean dramatists with whom he was familiar before he was fourteen, and by then he had already begun a fine collection of rare editions of their works. He wrote good poetry in schoolboy Greek and won prizes in French and Italian, but he constantly chafed against discipline and so left school early to prepare for Oxford.

In 1856 Swinburne matriculated at Balliol College, Oxford, where he stayed intermittently for nearly four years, becoming increasingly republican in politics and atheistic in religion. What had been a dislike of discipline at Eton now became a full revolt against authority in state and church. Rather more to his immediate disadvantage, Swinburne rebelled against the moral codes of his society and began at Oxford a life of dissipation, involving drink and, probably, the irregular sexual practices with which his name has become involved. As he had done at school, he frequently neglected his studies, but his private reading was wide in at least four languages, and his friends said admiringly that there seemed to be nothing written in English or French that Swinburne had not read. To his stay in Oxford he owed the beginning of the most influential literary friendship of his life, that with Rossetti, who helped and guided his work for more than a decade. Walter Pater, Benjamin Jowett, William Morris, and Edward Burne-Jones were among the men of talent with whom he formed friendships at Oxford. Aside from his poetic interests, much of his time was spent in political talk and thinking. His idols were the Italian revolutionaries, while Napoleon III represented everything he hated. Because of his radical tendencies, Swinburne became an embarrassment to Balliol, but when he withdrew in 1860 without a degree, it was apparently of his own accord. He continued through his life the habit of reading constantly, and became probably the most learned poet of the century. But though his information increased, Swinburne's intellect cannot be said to have developed greatly, and his opinions and attitudes were in large part set by the time he left Oxford.

With the allowance given to him by his wealthy parents, Swinburne was able to live in London and begin at once devoting himself to a lifetime of writing. His first book, containing two plays, *The Queen-Mother and Rosamund*, was published in 1860, but it was scarcely noticed by either reviewers or public. For a time, he shared a house with Rossetti and Meredith in Chelsea, while he continued writing both poetry and prose tales. In 1865 he published his first success, *Atalanta in Calydon*. As his first plays had been Elizabethan in inspiration, *Atalanta* was a tragedy in the Greek manner. Dazzled by its rhythmic and metrical splendor, few critics noticed in it a deep anti-Christian feeling and a revolt against Victorian morality.

What had gone unnoticed in *Atalanta* was rammed into the face of the reader with the appearance of *Poems and Ballads* in 1866. The poems were the quintessence of the "Swinburne music"—sensuous, ornate, filled with the hypnotic sensuality of rhythms unfamiliar to English ears. But the poems were also profoundly anti-Christian, with Christ told that "the world has grown grey from thy breath," and the poems were full of implications of perverse forms of sexuality, of which the most openly stated were masochism and sadism. To his startled contemporaries the book seemed alive with blood, whips, snakes, tongues, and hints of unmentionable vices. In the most famous review of the volume, John Morley said that Swinburne (whom he called "the libidinous laureate of a pack of satyrs") was "tuning his lyre in a stye" and "grovelling down among the nameless shameless abominations which inspire him with such frenzied delight."

In truth, today the volume seems a curious mixture of a genuine revolt against the narrow-minded hypocrisy of his age and a schoolboyish desire to shock, shouting aloud those aspects of life that polite society normally ignores. While working on "Dolores," he wrote to a friend that he was adding spurt after spurt to his "perennial and poisonous fountain"; the phrase suggests more a desire to pile up shocking stanzas than an attempt to write a cohesive serious poem. It would be unfair, however, to indicate that Swinburne did not know what he was doing, and still more unfair to deny him the impish sense of humor that delighted in excess, in both statement and style, of which the poem is probably the result. (Some indication of Swinburne's awareness of his own poetic liabilities is shown in his self-parodies, including the delightful "Nephelidia," written many years later.) But even his most outraged contemporaries could not deny that the 1866 volume was the work of a genuine poet with an inner ear of a kind unique in the language. Morley himself was constrained to commend Swinburne for "the fervour of his imagination, the beauty of his melody, the splendour of many phrases and pictures." The reception accorded *Poems and Ballads* was indicative of the mingled admiration and dislike which Swinburne's poetry aroused for the rest of his life.

In 1871 he published *Songs Before Sunrise*, chiefly inspired by worship of a more respectable form of liberty, the Italian Risorgimento; this volume and *Poems and Ballads* remain the high-water marks of his enormous poetic production, although there were magnificent poems scattered through the other volumes.

During the 1870's Swinburne's personal life became more hectic, and, naturally, his health crumbled until, in 1879, a friend, Theodore Watts (who later called himself Watts-Dunton), saved him from almost certain death by taking him to live in a London suburb, Putney. The screaming macaw to which Swinburne had been compared in his youth became a tame bird under the anxious eye of Watts-Dunton. He was cut off from his old friends and haunts, his health improved, and his habits became more conventional. All that was lacking now was the poetic instinct. Whether the guarded life he led in Putney prevented the flame from visiting him often or whether it would have been smothered in any case, we shall probably never know. His long interest in the Elizabethans remained, and with the knowledge of years of omnivorous reading, he began concentrating on literary criticism, much of it of a high order. As one writer has said of him, "In his early work he was a poet of amazing promise, and in his later work he was a great man of letters." In 1909, thirty years after going to Putney, Swinburne died there of influenza.

It would be impossible to trace simply the influences that converged in the works of a man so widely read: the Elizabethans and Greeks in his dramas; Poe and Baudelaire in his imagery;

Shelley, Landor, Hugo, and Whitman in his ideals of personal and political liberty; and a host of others as well. Although he was the descendant of many streams of literary tradition, Swinburne left no poetic progeny. Of all the great Victorians, he has suffered most from the inevitable reaction against the idols of a preceding age, and, so far, there is no indication of a renewed adoration of his work. In our own day there is a deep distrust of the gorgeousness of sheer sound at which Swinburne excelled. Indeed, his metrical perfection was his own worst enemy, so far as posthumous fame goes, for it would be impossible to proceed further in that direction than did Swinburne. There is little growth of development in his style after *Atalanta;* the rhythms of the later poems are reminiscent if not repetitive, and the ideas and symbols show small change. Perhaps, too, his reputation has suffered because what shocked his contemporaries in his poetry has become so commonplace in our own literature, and his defiance of a narrow Victorian morality has become a twentieth-century cliché.

But when all the adverse criticism has been made, there remains the stubborn fact that Swinburne was the creator of some of the best-remembered poetry of his century. Critical tastes vary as to his best poems or as to the poetic qualities for which he should be honored, but hardly any sensitive reader can escape the fascination of his rhythms or deny his ability to create his own world, one at once recognizably *Swinburnian.*

BIBLIOGRAPHY

The standard edition is *Complete Works of Algernon Charles Swinburne,* 20 vols. ed. Edmund Gosse and T. J. Wise. (Gabriel Wells, New York, 1925-1927).

Biography and Criticism:

Chew, Samuel C., *Swinburne.* John Murray, London, 1931. *stand. brog., cursory*

Eliot, T. S., "Swinburne as Poet," in *The Sacred Wood.* Methuen, London, 1920.

Gosse, Edmund, *The Life of Algernon Charles Swinburne.* Macmillan, New York, 1917. *mostly about Gosse, avoid*

Hare, Humphrey, *Swinburne: A Biographical Approach.* H. F. and G. Wetherby, London, 1949. *seeks sexual absorption*

Lafourcade, Georges, *Swinburne: A Literary Biography.* G. Bell and Son, London, 1932. *out of date*

Lang, Cecil Y., ed., *The Swinburne Letters*. 6 vols. Yale University Press, New Haven, 1959-1962.

Nicolson, Harold G., *Swinburne*. Macmillan, New York, 1926. *good but out of date*

Rutland, William R., *Swinburne: A Nineteenth Century Hellene*. Blackwell, Oxford, 1931.

Welby, T. Earle, *A Study of Swinburne*. Faber and Gwyer, London, 1926. *little better than above, somewhat ltd.*

From ATALANTA IN CALYDON

I. WHEN THE HOUNDS OF SPRING

When the hounds of spring are on winter's traces,
  The mother of months in meadow or plain
Fills the shadows and windy places
  With lisp of leaves and ripple of rain;
And the brown bright nightingale amorous
Is half assuaged for Itylus,
For the Thracian ships and the foreign faces,
  The tongueless vigil, and all the pain.

Come with bows bent and with emptying of quivers,
  Maiden most perfect, lady of light,   10
With a noise of winds and many rivers,
  With a clamour of waters, and with might;
Bind on thy sandals, O thou most fleet,
Over the splendour and speed of thy feet;
For the faint east quickens, the wan west shivers,
  Round the feet of the day and the feet of the night.

Where shall we find her, how shall we sing to her,
  Fold our hands round her knees, and cling?
O that man's heart were as fire and could spring to her,
  Fire, or the strength of the streams that spring!   20
For the stars and the winds are unto her
As raiment, as songs of the harp-player;
For the risen stars and the fallen cling to her,
  And the southwest-wind and the west-wind sing.

For winter's rains and ruins are over,
  And all the season of snows and sins;
The days dividing lover and lover,

When the Hounds of Spring: the first song of the chorus in Swinburne's
tragedy in Greek form, *Atalanta in Calydon.*
2 *mother of months:* Artemis, goddess of the moon, addressed by the chorus.
6 *Itylus:* See note to Swinburne's poem of that name (p. 685).

The light that loses, the night that wins;
And time remembered is grief forgotten,
And frosts are slain and flowers begotten,   30
And in green underwood and cover
    Blossom by blossom the spring begins.

The full streams feed on flower of rushes.
    Ripe grasses trammel a travelling foot,
The faint fresh flame of the young year flushes
    From leaf to flower and flower to fruit;
And fruit and leaf are as gold and fire,
And the oat is heard above the lyre,
And the hoofèd heel of a satyr crushes
    The chestnut-husk at the chestnut-root.   40

And Pan by noon and Bacchus by night,
    Fleeter of foot than the fleet-foot kid,
Follows with dancing and fills with delight
    The Mænad and the Bassarid;
And soft as lips that laugh and hide
The laughing leaves of the trees divide,
And screen from seeing and leave in sight
    The god pursuing, the maiden hid.

The ivy falls with the Bacchanal's hair
    Over her eyebrows hiding her eyes;   50
The wild vine slipping down leaves bare
    Her bright breast shortening into sighs;
The wild vine slips with the weight of its leaves,
But the berried ivy catches and cleaves
To the limbs that glitter, the feet that scare
    The wolf that follows, the fawn that flies.

II. BEFORE THE BEGINNING OF YEARS

Before the beginning of years
    There came to the making of man

---

38 *oat:* shepherd's pipe of straw.
41 *Pan:* patron of shepherds. *Bacchus:* god of wine.
44 *Mænad and the Bassarid:* feminine worshippers of Bacchus in nocturnal rites involving wild dances.
49 *Bacchanal:* follower of Bacchus.
Before the Beginning of Years: the second chorus of *Atalanta*.

Time, with a gift of tears;
   Grief, with a glass that ran;
Pleasure, with pain for leaven;
   Summer, with flowers that fell;
Remembrance fallen from heaven,
   And madness risen from hell;
Strength without hands to smite;
   Love that endures for a breath: 10
Night, the shadow of light,
   And life, the shadow of death.
And the high gods took in hand
   Fire, and the falling of tears,
And a measure of sliding sand
   From under the feet of the years;
And froth and drift of the sea;
   And dust of the labouring earth;
And bodies of things to be
   In the houses of death and of birth;   20
And wrought with weeping and laughter,
   And fashioned with loathing and love,
With life before and after
   And death beneath and above,
For a day and a night and a morrow,
   That his strength might endure for a span
With travail and heavy sorrow,
   The holy spirit of man.

From the winds of the north and the south
   They gathered as unto strife;   30
They breathed upon his mouth,
   They filled his body with life;
Eyesight and speech they wrought
   For the veils of the soul therein,
A time for labour and thought,
   A time to serve and to sin;
They gave him light in his ways,
   And love, and a space for delight,
And beauty and length of days,
   And night, and sleep in the night.   40
His speech is a burning fire;
   With his lips he travaileth;

In his heart is a blind desire,
  In his eyes foreknowledge of death;
He weaves, and is clothed with derision;
  Sows, and he shall not reap;
His life is a watch or a vision
  Between a sleep and a sleep.

[1865]

THE TRIUMPH OF TIME

Before our lives divide for ever,
  While time is with us and hands are free,
(Time, swift to fasten and swift to sever
  Hand from hand, as we stand by the sea)
I will say no word that a man might say
Whose whole life's love goes down in a day;
For this could never have been; and never,
  Though the gods and the years relent, shall be.

Is it worth a tear, is it worth an hour,
  To think of things that are well outworn?   10
Of fruitless husk and fugitive flower,
  The dream foregone and the deed forborne?
Though joy be done with and grief be vain,
Time shall not sever us wholly in twain;
Earth is not spoilt for a single shower;
  But the rain has ruined the ungrown corn.

It will grow not again, this fruit of my heart,
  Smitten with sunbeams, ruined with rain
The singing seasons divide and depart,

The Triumph of Time: This poem was perhaps inspired by the events of
1862, when Swinburne is said to have proposed to Miss Jane Faulkner and
to have been rejected rather rudely for another suitor. The poem was composed the following year. Whether or not the proposal actually was made,
the poem seems to allude to a rejection as the cause of—or, at least, the
failure of the last bastion against—degradation and the speaker's sexual ab-
normality.

Winter and summer depart in twain.   20
It will grow not again, it is ruined at root,   *grafter*
The bloodlike blossom, the dull red fruit;
Though the heart yet sickens, the lips yet smart,
    With sullen savour of poisonous pain.

I have given no man of my fruit to eat;
    I trod the grapes, I have drunken the wine.   *own fault*
Had you eaten and drunken and found it sweet,
    This wild new growth of the corn and vine,
This wine and bread without lees or leaven,
We had grown as gods, as the gods in heaven,   30
Souls fair to look upon, goodly to greet,
    One splendid spirit, your soul and mine.

In the change of years, in the coil of things,
    In the clamour and rumour of life to be.
amar We, drinking love at the furthest springs,
    Covered with love as a covering tree,
We had grown as gods, as the gods above,   *this didn't happen.*
Filled from the heart to the lips with love,
Held fast in his hands, clothed warm with his wings,
    O love, my love, had you loved but me!   40

We had stood as the sure stars stand, and moved
    As the moon moves, loving the world; and seen
Grief collapse as a thing disproved,
    Death consume as a thing unclean.
Twain halves of a perfect heart, made fast
Soul to soul while the years fell past;
Had you loved me once, as you have not loved;
    Had the chance been with us that has not been.

I have put my days and dreams out of mind,
    Days that are over, dreams that are done.   50
Though we seek life through, we shall surely find
    There is none of them clear to us now, not one.
But clear are these things; the grass and the sand,
Where, sure as the eyes reach, ever at hand,
With lips wide open and face burnt blind,
    The strong sea-daisies feast on the sun.

The low downs lean to the sea; the stream,
    One loose thin pulseless tremulous vein,
Rapid and vivid and dumb as a dream,
    Works downward, sick of the sun and the rain;   60
No wind is rough with the rank rare flowers;
The sweet sea, mother of loves and hours,
Shudders and shines as the grey winds gleam
    Turning her smile to a fugitive pain.

Mother of loves that are swift to fade,
    Mother of mutable winds and hours.
A barren mother, a mother-maid,
    Cold and clean as her faint salt flowers
I would we twain were even as she,
Lost in the night and the light of the sea,   70
Where faint sounds falter and wan beams wade,
    Break, and are broken, and shed into showers.

The loves and hours of the life of a man,
    They are swift and sad, being born of the sea.
Hours that rejoice and regret for a span,
    Born with a man's breath, mortal as he;
Loves that are lost ere they come to birth,
Weeds of the wave, without fruit upon earth.
I lose what I long for, save what I can,
    My love, my love, and no love for me!   80

It is not much that a man can save
    On the sands of life, in the straits of time,
Who swims in sight of the great third wave
    That never a swimmer shall cross or climb.
Some waif washed up with the strays and spars
That ebb-tide shows to the shore and the stars;
Weed from the water, grass from a grave,
    A broken blossom, a ruined rhyme.

There will no man do for your sake, I think,
    What I would have done for the least word said.   90
I had wrung life dry for your lips to drink,

---

83 *great third wave:* allusion to the legend that each third wave is larger than the two preceding it.

Broken it up for your daily bread:
Body for body and blood for blood,
As the flow of the full sea risen to flood
That yearns and trembles before it sink,
 I had given, and lain down for you, glad and dead.

Yea, hope at highest and all her fruit,
 And time at fullest and all his dower,
I had given you surely, and life to boot,
 Were we once made one for a single hour.   100
But now, you are twain, you are cloven apart,
Flesh of his flesh, but heart of my heart;
And deep in one is the bitter root,
 And sweet for one is the lifelong flower.

To have died if you cared I should die for you, clung
 To my life if you bade me, played my part
As it pleased you—these were the thoughts that stung,
 The dreams that smote with a keener dart
Than shafts of love or arrows of death;
These were but as fire is, dust, or breath,   110
Or poisonous foam on the tender tongue
 Of the little snakes that eat my heart.

I wish we were dead together to-day,
 Lost sight of, hidden away out of sight,
Clasped and clothed in the cloven clay,
 Out of the world's way, out of the light,
Out of the ages of worldly weather,
Forgotten of all men altogether,
As the world's first dead, taken wholly away,
 Made one with death, filled full of the night.   120

How we should slumber, how we should sleep,
 Far in the dark with the dreams and the dews!
And dreaming, grow to each other, and weep,
 Laugh low, live softly, murmur and muse;
Yea, and it may be, struck through by the dream,
Feel the dust quicken and quiver, and seem
Alive as of old to the lips, and leap
 Spirit to spirit as lovers use.

Sick dreams and sad of a dull delight;
   For what shall it profit when men are dead   130
To have dreamed, to have loved with the whole soul's
      might,
   To have looked for day when the day was fled?
Let come what will, there is one thing worth,
To have had fair love in the life upon earth:
To have held love safe till the day grew night,
   While skies had colour and lips were red.

Would I lose you now? would I take you then,
   If I lose you now that my heart has need?
And come what may after death to men,
   What thing worth this will the dead years breed?   140
Lose life, lose all; but at least I know,
O sweet life's love, having loved you so,
Had I reached you on earth, I should lose not again,
   In death nor life, nor in dream or deed.

Yea, I know this well: were you once sealed mine,
   Mine in the blood's beat, mine in the breath,
Mixed into me as honey in wine,
   Not time, that sayeth and gainsayeth,
Nor all strong winds had severed us then;
Not wrath of gods, nor wisdom of men,   150
Nor all things earthly, nor all divine,
   Nor joy nor sorrow, nor life nor death.

I had grown pure as the dawn and the dew,
   You had grown strong as the sun or the sea.
But none shall triumph a whole life through:
   For death is one, and the fates are three.
At the door of life, by the gate of breath,
There are worse things waiting for men than death;
Death could not sever my soul and you,
   As these have severed your soul from me.   160

---

156 *the fates are three:* the three goddesses of Greek myth who controlled man's fate: Clotho, who holds the distaff; Lachesis, who spins the thread of life; and Atropos, who cuts it off.

You have chosen and clung to the chance they sent you,
　Life sweet as perfume and pure as prayer.
But will it not one day in heaven repent you?
　Will they solace you wholly, the days that were?
Will you lift up your eyes between sadness and bliss,
Meet mine, and see where the great love is,
And tremble and turn and be changed? Content you;
　The gate is strait; I shall not be there. *is crooked sexadly*

But you, had you chosen, had you stretched hand,
　Had you seen good such a thing were done,   170
I too might have stood with the souls that stand
　In the sun's sight, clothed with the light of the sun;
But who now on earth need care how I live?
Have the high gods anything left to give,
Save dust and laurels and gold and sand?
　Which gifts are goodly; but I will none.

O all fair lovers about the world,
　There is none of you, none, that shall comfort me.
My thoughts are as dead things, wrecked and whirled
　Round and round in a gulf of the sea;   180
And still, through the sound and the straining stream,
Through the coil and chafe, they gleam in a dream,
The bright fine lips so cruelly curled,
　And strange swift eyes where the soul sits free.

Free, without pity, withheld from woe,
　Ignorant; fair as the eyes are fair.
Would I have you change now, change at a blow,
　Startled and stricken, awake and aware?
Yea, if I could, would I have you see
My very love of you filling me,   190
And know my soul to the quick, as I know
　The likeness and look of your throat and hair?

I shall not change you. Nay, though I might,
　Would I change my sweet one love with a word?
I had rather your hair should change in a night,

---

168 *I shall not be there:* i.e., because of his sins he will be damned.

Clear now as the plume of a black bright bird;
Your face fail suddenly, cease, turn grey,
Die as a leaf that dies in a day.
I will keep my soul in a place out of sight,
   Far off, where the pulse of it is not heard.   200

Far off it walks, in a bleak blown space,
   Full of the sound of the sorrow of years.
I have woven a veil for the weeping face,
   Whose lips have drunken the wine of tears;
I have found a way for the failing feet,
A place for slumber and sorrow to meet;
There is no rumour about the place,
   Nor light, nor any that sees or hears.

I have hidden my soul out of sight, and said
   "Let none take pity upon thee, none   210
Comfort thy crying: for lo, thou art dead,
   Lie still now, safe out of sight of the sun.
Have I not built thee a grave, and wrought
Thy grave-clothes on thee of grievous thought,
With soft spun verses and tears unshed,
   And sweet light visions of things undone?

"I have given thee garments and balm and myrrh,
   And gold, and beautiful burial things.
But thou, be at peace now, make no stir;
   Is not thy grave as a royal king's?   220
Fret not thyself though the end were sore;
Sleep, be patient, vex me no more.
Sleep; what hast thou to do with her?
   The eyes that weep, with the mouth that sings?"

Where the dead red leaves of the years lie rotten,
   The cold old crimes and the deeds thrown by,
The misconceived and the misbegotten,
   I would find a sin to do ere I die,
Sure to dissolve and destroy me all through,
That would set you higher in heaven, serve you   230
And leave you happy, when clean forgotten,
   As a dead man out of mind, am I.

since she has turned him down, only death to look for

Your lithe hands draw me, your face burns through me,
  I am swift to follow you, keen to see;
But love lacks might to redeem or undo me;
  As I have been, I know I shall surely be;
"What should such fellows as I do?" Nay,
My part were worse if I chose to play;
For the worst is this after all; if they knew me,
  Not a soul upon earth would pity me. 240

And I play not for pity of these; but you,
  If you saw with your soul what man am I,
You would praise me at least that my soul all through
  Clove to you, loathing the lives that lie;
The souls and lips that are bought and sold,
The smiles of silver and kisses of gold,
The lapdog loves that whine as they chew,
  The little lovers that curse and cry.

There are fairer women, I hear; that may be;
  But I, that I love you and find you fair, 250
Who are more than fair in my eyes if they be,
  Do the high gods know or the great gods care?
Though the swords in my heart for one were seven,
Should the iron hollow of doubtful heaven,
That knows not itself whether night-time or day be,
  Reverberate words and a foolish prayer?

I will go back to the great sweet mother,
  Mother and lover of men, the sea.
I will go down to her, I and none other,
  Close with her, kiss her and mix her with me; 260
Cling to her, strive with her, hold her fast:
O fair white mother, in days long past
Born without sister, born without brother,
  Set free my soul as thy soul is free.

O fair green-girdled mother of mine,
  Sea, that art clothed with the sun and the rain,

---

237 *"What . . . do?"*: see *Hamlet*, III, i.
253 *seven:* The Seven Sorrows of the Virgin Mary are represented by seven swords.

Thy sweet hard kisses are strong like wine,
　　Thy large embraces are keen like pain.
Save me and hide me with all thy waves,
Find me one grave of thy thousand graves,　　　　270
Those pure cold populous graves of thine
　　Wrought without hand in a world without stain.

I shall sleep, and move with the moving ships,
　　Change as the winds change, veer in the tide;
My lips will feast on the foam of thy lips,
　　I shall rise with thy rising, with thee subside;
Sleep, and not know if she be, if she were,
Filled full with life to the eyes and hair,
As a rose is fulfilled to the roseleaf tips
　　With splendid summer and perfume and pride.　　280

This woven raiment of nights and days,
　　Were it once cast off and unwound from me,
Naked and glad would I walk in thy ways,
　　Alive and aware of thy ways and thee;
Clear of the whole world, hidden at home,
Clothed with the green and crowned with the foam,
A pulse of the life of thy straits and bays,
　　A vein in the heart of the streams of the sea.

Fair mother, fed with the lives of men,
　　Thou art subtle and cruel of heart, men say.　　290
Thou hast taken, and shalt not render again;
　　Thou art full of thy dead, and cold as they.
But death is the worst that comes of thee;
Thou art fed with our dead, O mother, O sea,
But when hast thou fed on our hearts? or when,
　　Having given us love, hast thou taken away?

O tender-hearted, O perfect lover,
　　Thy lips are bitter, and sweet thine heart.
The hopes that hurt and the dreams that hover,
　　Shall they not vanish away and apart?　　300
But thou, thou art sure, thou art older than earth;
Thou art strong for death and fruitful of birth;

Thy depths conceal and thy gulfs discover;
    From the first thou wert; in the end thou art.

And grief shall endure not for ever, I know.
    As things that are not shall these things be;
We shall live through seasons of sun and of snow,
    And none be grievous as this to me.
We shall hear, as one in a trance that hears,
The sound of time, the rhyme of the years;   310
Wrecked hope and passionate pain will grow
    As tender things of a spring-tide sea.

Sea-fruit that swings in the waves that hiss,
    Drowned gold and purple and royal rings.
And all time past, was it all for this?
    Times unforgotten, and treasures of things?
Swift years of liking and sweet long laughter,
That wist not well of the years thereafter
Till love woke, smitten at heart by a kiss,
    With lips that trembled and trailing wings?   320

There lived a singer in France of old
    By the tideless dolorous midland sea.
In a land of sand and ruin and gold
    There shone one woman, and none but she.
And finding life for her love's sake fail,
Being fain to see her, he bade set sail,
Touched land, and saw her as life grew cold,
    And praised God, seeing; and so died he.

Died, praising God for his gift and grace:
    For she bowed down to him weeping, and said   330
"Live;" and her tears were shed on his face
    Or ever the life in his face was shed.
The sharp tears fell through her hair, and stung
Once, and her close lips touched him and clung
Once, and grew one with his lips for a space;
    And so drew back, and the man was dead.

---

321 *singer:* Geoffrey Rudel, Provençal poet of the twelfth century, sailed the
Mediterranean to Tripoli to see the beauty of a lady of that country. When
he reached port he was dying, but he revived briefly when the lady came
aboard his ship.

O brother, the gods were good to you.
  Sleep, and be glad while the world endures.
Be well content as the years wear through;
  Give thanks for life, and the loves and lures;   340
Give thanks for life, O brother, and death,
For the sweet last sound of her feet, her breath,
For gifts she gave you, gracious and few,
  Tears and kisses, that lady of yours.

Rest, and be glad of the gods; but I,
  How shall I praise them, or how take rest?
There is not room under all the sky
  For me that know not of worst or best,
Dream or desire of the days before,
Sweet things or bitterness, any more.   350
Love will not come to me now though I die,
  As love came close to you, breast to breast.

I shall never be friends again with roses;
  I shall loathe sweet tunes, where a note grown strong
Relents and recoils, and climbs and closes,
  As a wave of the sea turned back by song.
There are sounds where the soul's delight takes fire,
Face to face with its own desire;
A delight that rebels, a desire that reposes;
  I shall hate sweet music my whole life long.   360

The pulse of war and the passion of wonder,
  The heavens that murmur, the sounds that shine,
The stars that sing and the loves that thunder,
  The music burning at heart like wine,
An armed archangel whose hands raise up
All senses mixed in the spirit's cup
Till flesh and spirit are molten in sunder—
  These things are over, and no more mine.

These were a part of the playing I heard
  Once, ere my love and my heart were at strife;   370
Love that sings and hath wings as a bird,
  Balm of the wound and heft of the knife.
Fairer than earth is the sea, and sleep

Than overwatching of eyes that weep,
   Now time has done with his one sweet word,
      The wine and leaven of lovely life.

I shall go my ways, tread out my measure,
    Fill the days of my daily breath
With fugitive things not good to treasure,
    Do as the world doth, say as it saith;   380
But if we had loved each other—O sweet,
Had you felt, lying under the palms of your feet,
The heart of my heart, beating harder with pleasure
    To feel you tread it to dust and death—

Ah, had I not taken my life up and given
    All that life gives and the years let go,
The wine and honey, the balm and leaven,
    The dreams reared high and the hopes brought low?
Come life, come death, not a word be said;
Should I lose you living, and vex you dead?   390
I never shall tell you on earth; and in heaven,
    If I cry to you then, will you hear or know?

                            [1866]

ITYLUS

   Swallow, my sister, O sister swallow,
     How can thine heart be full of the spring?
      A thousand summers are over and dead.
   What hast thou found in the spring to follow?
   What has thou found in thine heart to sing?
      What wilt thou do when the summer is shed?

   O swallow, sister, O fair swift swallow,
     Why wilt thou fly after spring to the south,
      The soft south whither thine heart is set?

Itylus: son of Tereus, king of Thrace, and his wife Procne. Tereus violated
Procne's sister Philomela and tore out her tongue to prevent her telling of
the rape. In revenge, the sisters killed Itylus and served him as food to his
father. Procne was transformed into a swallow, Philomela into a nightingale.

Shall not the grief of the old time follow? 10
   Shall not the song thereof cleave to thy mouth?
     Hast thou forgotten ere I forget?

Sister, my sister, O fleet sweet swallow,
   Thy way is long to the sun and the south;
     But I, fulfilled of my heart's desire,
Shedding my song upon height, upon hollow,
   From tawny body and sweet small mouth
     Feed the heart of the night with fire.

I the nightingale all spring through,
   O swallow, sister, O changing swallow, 20
     All spring through till the spring be done,
Clothed with the light of the night on the dew,
   Sing, while the hours and the wild birds follow,
     Take flight and follow and find the sun.

Sister, my sister, O soft light swallow,
   Though all things feast in the spring's guest-chamber,
     How hast thou heart to be glad thereof yet?
For where thou fliest I shall not follow,
   Till life forget and death remember,
     Till thou remember and I forget. 30

Swallow, my sister, O singing swallow,
   I know not how thou hast heart to sing.
     Hast thou the heart? is it all past over?
Thy lord the summer is good to follow,
   And fair the feet of thy lover the spring:
     But what wilt thou say to the spring thy lover?

O swallow, sister, O fleeting swallow,
   My heart in me is a molten ember
     And over my head the waves have met,
But thou wouldst tarry or I would follow, 40
   Could I forget or thou remember,
     Couldst thou remember and I forget.

O sweet stray sister, O shifting swallow,
   The heart's division divideth us.

Thy heart is light as a leaf of a tree;
But mine goes forth among sea-gulfs hollow
    To the place of the slaying of Itylus,
        The feast of Daulis, the Thracian sea.

O swallow, sister, O rapid swallow,
    I pray thee sing not a little space.   50
        Are not the roofs and the lintels wet?
The woven web that was plain to follow,
    The small slain body, the flowerlike face,
        Can I remember if thou forget?

O sister, sister, thy first-begotten!
    The hands that cling and the feet that follow,
        The voice of the child's blood crying yet
Who hath remembered me? who hath forgotten?
    Thou hast forgotten, O summer swallow,
        But the world shall end when I forget.   60

[1866]

HYMN TO PROSERPINE

After the Proclamation in Rome of the Christian Faith
Vicisti, Galilæe.

I have lived long enough, having seen one thing, that love
    hath an end;
Goddess and maiden and queen, be near me now and be-
    friend.
Thou art more than the day or the morrow, the seasons that
    laugh or that weep;

---

48 *Daulis:* Tereus' capital city, where he ate the flesh of his son.
52 *woven web:* tapestry which Philomela wove to tell Procne her story.
Hymn to Proserpine: The poem is supposed to be addressed by a Roman
pagan of the fourth century to Proserpine, the earth-goddess who was queen
of the underworld, presiding over death and change. The Edict of Milan
by the emperor Constantine in 313 gave recognition and toleration to Christianity. The dying words of the emperor Julian are said to have been,
"*Vicisti, Galilæe*" ("Thou hast conquered, Galilean").

For these give joy and sorrow; but thou, Proserpina, sleep.
Sweet is the treading of wine, and sweet the feet of the
    dove; *death wish*
But a goodlier gift is thine than foam of the grapes or love.
Yea, is not even Apollo, with hair and harpstring of gold,
A bitter God to follow, a beautiful God to behold?
I am sick of singing: the bays burn deep and chafe: I am
    fain
To rest a little from praise and the grievous pleasure and
    pain.   10
For the Gods we know not of, who give us our daily breath,
We know they are cruel as love or life, and lovely as death.
O Gods dethroned and deceased, cast forth, wiped out in a
    day!
From your wrath is the world released, redeemed from
    your chains, men say.
New Gods are crowned in the city; their flowers have broken
    your rods;
They are merciful, clothed with pity, the young compassion-
    ate Gods.
But for me their new device is barren, the days are bare;
Things long past over suffice, and men forgotten that were.
Time and the Gods are at strife; ye dwell in the midst
    thereof,
Draining a little life from the barren breasts of love.   20
I say to you, cease, take rest; yea, I say to you all, be at
    peace,
Till the bitter milk of her breast and the barren bosom shall
    cease,
Wilt thou yet take all, Galilean? but these thou shalt not
    take,
The laurel, the palms and the pæan, the breasts of the
    nymphs in the brake;
Breasts more soft than a dove's, that tremble with tenderer
    breath;
And all the wings of the Loves, and all the joy before death;

---

7 *Apollo:* god of song.
9 *bays:* laurel leaves in poet's crown.
15 *New Gods:* saints of Christianity.
24 *brake:* thicket.

All the feet of the hours that sound as a single lyre,
Dropped and deep in the flowers, with strings that flicker like fire.
More than these wilt thou give, things fairer than all these things?
Nay, for a little we live, and life hath mutable wings.   30
A little while and we die; shall life not thrive as it may?
For no man under the sky lives twice, outliving his day.
And grief is a grievous thing, and a man hath enough of his tears:
Why should he labour, and bring fresh grief to blacken his years?
Thou hast conquered, O pale Galilean; the world has grown grey from thy breath;
We have drunken of things Lethean, and fed on the fullness of death.
Laurel is green for a season, and love is sweet for a day;
But love grows bitter with treason, and laurel outlives not May.
Sleep, shall we sleep after all? for the world is not sweet in the end;
For the old faiths loosen and fall, the new years ruin and rend.   40
Fate is a sea without shore, and the soul is a rock that abides;
But her ears are vexed with the roar and her face with the foam of the tides.
O lips that the live blood faints in, the leavings of racks and rods!
O ghastly glories of saints, dead limbs of gibbeted Gods!
Though all men abase them before you in spirit, and all knees bend,
I kneel not neither adore you, but standing, look to the end.
All delicate days and pleasant, all spirits and sorrows are cast
Far out with the foam of the present that sweeps to the surf of the past:
Where beyond the extreme sea-wall, and between the remote sea-gates,

---

[36] *Lethean:* referring to the river Lethe, the boundary of the world of the dead. Crossing it brought forgetfulness.

Waste water washes, and tall ships founder, and deep death
  waits: 50
Where, mighty with deepening sides, clad about with the
  seas as with wings,
And impelled of invisible tides, and fulfilled of unspeakable
  things,
White-eyed and poisonous-finned, shark-toothed and serpen-
  tine-curled,
Rolls, under the whitening wind of the future, the wave of
  the world.
The depths stand naked in sunder behind it, the storms flee
  away;
In the hollow before it the thunder is taken and snared as a
  prey;
In its sides is the north-wind bound; and its salt is of all
  men's tears;
With light of ruin, and sound of changes, and pulse of
  years:
With travail of day after day, and with trouble of hour upon
  hour;
And bitter as blood is the spray; and the crests are as fangs
  that devour: 60
And its vapour and storm of its steam as the sighing of spirits to be;
And its noise as the noise in a dream; and its depth as the
  roots of the sea:
And the height of its heads as the height of the utmost stars
  of the air;
And the ends of the earth at the might thereof tremble, and
  time is made bare.
Will ye bridle the deep sea with reins, will ye chasten the
  high sea with rods?
Will ye take her to chain her with chains, who is older than
  all ye Gods?
And ye as a wind shall go by, as a fire shall ye pass and be
  past;
Ye are Gods, and behold, ye shall die, and the waves be
  upon you at last.
In the darkness of time, in the deeps of the years, in the
  changes of things,

rel. of
aphrodite
will prevail,
is best

Ye shall sleep as a slain man sleeps and the world shall forget you for kings.
Though the feet of thine high priests tread where thy lords
and our forefathers trod,
Though these that were Gods are dead, and thou being dead
art a God,
Though before thee the throned Cytherean be fallen, and
hidden her head,
Yet thy kingdom shall pass, Galilean, thy dead shall go down
to thee dead.
Of the maiden thy mother men sing as a goddess with grace
clad around;
Thou art throned where another was king; where another
was queen she is crowned.
Yea, once we had sight of another: but now she is queen,
say these.
Not as thine, not as thine was our mother, a blossom of flow-
ering seas,
Clothed round with the world's desire as with raiment, and
fair as the foam,
And fleeter than kindled fire, and a goddess, and mother of
Rome.   80
For thine came pale and a maiden, and sister to sorrow; but
ours,
Her deep hair heavily laden with odour and colour of flow-
ers,
White rose of the rose-white water, a silver splendour, a
flame,
Bent down unto us that besought her, and earth grew sweet
with her name.
For thine came weeping, a slave among slaves, and rejected;
but she
Came flushed from the full-flushed wave, and imperial, her
foot on the sea.
And the wonderful waters knew her, the winds and the
viewless ways,

---

73 *Cytherean:* Venus, or Aphrodite, who appeared from the foam of the
sea on the shores of the island of Cythera.
80 *mother of Rome:* Aphrodite was believed to be the mother of Aeneas,
who built Lavinium near the present site of Rome.

And the roses grew rosier, and bluer the sea-blue stream of
the bays.

Ye are fallen, our lords, by what token? we wist that ye
should not fall.

Ye were all so fair that are broken; and one more fair than
ye all.   90

But I turn to her still, having seen she shall surely abide in
the end;

Goddess and maiden and queen, be near me now and be-
friend.

O daughter of earth, of my mother, her crown and blossom
of birth,

I am also, I also, thy brother; I go as I came unto earth.

In the night where thine eyes are as moons are in heaven,
the night where thou art,

Where the silence is more than all tunes, where sleep over-
flows from the heart,

Where the poppies are sweet as the rose in our world, and
the red rose is white,

And the wind falls faint as it blows with the fume of the
flowers of the night,

And the murmur of spirits that sleep in the shadow of Gods
from afar

Grows dim in thine ears and deep as the deep dim soul of a
star,   100

In the sweet low light of thy face, under heavens untrod by
the sun,

Let my soul with their souls find place, and forget what is
done and undone.

Thou art more than the Gods who number the days of our
temporal breath;

For these give labour and slumber; but thou, Proserpina,
death.

Therefore now at thy feet I abide for a season in silence. I
know

I shall die as my fathers died, and sleep as they sleep; even
so.

For the glass of the years is brittle wherein we gaze for a
span;

---

97 *poppies:* flowers of oblivion, sacred to Proserpine.

A little soul for a little bears up this corpse which is man.
So long I endure, no longer; and laugh not again, neither
    weep.
For there is no God found stronger than death; and death
    is a sleep.   110

[1866]

DOLORES

Notre-Dame des Sept Douleurs

    Cold eyelids that hide like a jewel
        Hard eyes that grow soft for an hour;
    The heavy white limbs, and the cruel
        Red mouth like a venomous flower;
    When these are gone by with their glories,
        What shall rest of thee then, what remain
    O mystic and sombre Dolores,
        Our Lady of Pain?

    Seven sorrows the priests give their Virgin;
        But thy sins, which are seventy times seven,   10
    Seven ages would fail thee to purge in,
        And then they would haunt thee in heaven:
    Fierce midnights and famishing morrows,
        And the loves that complete and control
    All the joys of the flesh, all the sorrows
        That wear out the soul.

    O garment not golden but gilded,
        O garden where all men may dwell,
    O tower not of ivory, but builded

---

108 *A little soul . . . which is man:* quotation from the Stoic philosopher
Epictetus.
Notre-Dame des Sept Douleurs: Our Lady of the Seven Sorrows. The title
properly belongs to the Virgin Mary, but here Swinburne is deliberately in-
verting the meaning, so as to apply it to Dolores.
17 *O garment . . . gilded:* this stanza is an inversion of the Litany of the
Blessed Virgin. See also *Song of Solomon* 7:4.

By hands that reach heaven from hell;   20
O mystical rose of the mire,
    O house not of gold but of gain,
O house of unquenchable fire,
    Our Lady of Pain!

O lips full of lust and of laughter,
    Curled snakes that are fed from my breast,
Bite hard, lest remembrance come after
    And press with new lips where you pressed.
For my heart too springs up at the pressure,
    Mine eyelids too moisten and burn;   30
Ah, feed me and fill me with pleasure,
    Ere pain come in turn.

In yesterday's reach and to-morrow's,
    Out of sight though they lie of to-day,
There have been and there yet shall be sorrows
    That smite not and bite not in play.
The life and the love thou despisest,
    These hurt us indeed, and in vain,
O wise among women, and wisest,
    Our Lady of Pain.   40

Who gave thee thy wisdom? what stories
    That stung thee, what visions that smote?
Wert thou pure and a maiden, Dolores,
    When desire took thee first by the throat?
What bud was the shell of a blossom
    That all men may smell to and pluck?
What milk fed thee first at what bosom?
    What sins gave thee suck?

We shift and bedeck and bedrape us,
    Thou art noble and nude and antique;   50
Libitina thy mother, Priapus
    Thy father, a Tuscan and Greek.
We play with light loves in the portal,
    And wince and relent and refrain;

---

51 *Libitina:* Roman goddess of death. *Priapus:* Greek God of sexuality and fertility, son of Bacchus and Aphrodite.

Loves die, and we know thee immortal,
    Our Lady of Pain.

Fruits fail and love dies and time ranges;
    Thou art fed with perpetual breath,
And alive after infinite changes,
    And fresh from the kisses of death;   60
Of languors rekindled and rallied,
    Of barren delights and unclean,
Things monstrous and fruitless, a pallid
    And poisonous queen.

Could you hurt me, sweet lips, though I hurt you?
    Men touch them, and change in a trice
The lilies and languors of virtue
    For the raptures and roses of vice;
Those lie where thy foot on the floor is,
    These crown and caress thee and chain,   70
O splendid and sterile Dolores,
    Our Lady of Pain.

There are sins it may be to discover,
    There are deeds it may be to delight.
What new work wilt thou find for thy lover,
    What new passions for daytime or night?
What spells that they know not a word of
    Whose lives are as leaves overblown?
What tortures undreamt of, unheard of,
    Unwritten, unknown?   80

Ah beautiful passionate body
    That never has ached with a heart!
On thy mouth though the kisses are bloody,
    Though they sting till it shudder and smart,
More kind than the love we adore is,
    They hurt not the heart or the brain,
O bitter and tender Dolores,
    Our Lady of Pain.

As our kisses relax and redouble,
    From the lips and the foam and the fangs   90

Shall no new sin be born for men's trouble,
    No dream of impossible pangs?
With the sweet of the sins of old ages
    Wilt thou satiate thy soul as of yore?
Too sweet is the rind, say the sages,
    Too bitter the core.

Hast thou told all thy secrets the last time,
    And bared all thy beauties to one?
Ah, where shall we go then for pastime,
    If the worst that can be has been done?   100
But sweet as the rind was the core is;
    We are fain of thee still, we are fain,
O sanguine and subtle Dolores,
    Our Lady of Pain.

By the hunger of change and emotion,
    By the thirst of unbearable things,
By despair, the twin-born of devotion,
    By the pleasure that winces and stings,
The delight that consumes the desire,
    The desire that outruns the delight,   110
By the cruelty deaf as a fire
    And blind as the night,

By the ravenous teeth that have smitten
    Through the kisses that blossom and bud,
By the lips intertwisted and bitten
    Till the foam has a savour of blood,
By the pulse as it rises and falters,
    By the hands as they slacken and strain,
I adjure thee, respond from thine altars,
    Our Lady of Pain.   120

Wilt thou smile as a woman disdaining
    The light fire in the veins of a boy?
But he comes to thee sad, without feigning,
    Who has wearied of sorrow and joy;
Less careful of labour and glory
    Than the elders whose hair has uncurled:

And young, but with fancies as hoary
   And grey as the world.

I have passed from the outermost portal
   To the shrine where the <u>sin</u> is a prayer;   *reversed* 130
What care though the service be mortal?
   O our Lady of Torture, what care?
All thine the last wine that I pour is,
   The last in the chalice we drain, ·
O fierce and luxurious Dolores,
   Our Lady of Pain.

All thine the new wine of desire,
   The fruit of four lips as they clung
Till the hair and the eyelids took fire,
   The foam of a serpentine tongue,   140
The froth of the serpents of pleasure,
   More salt than the foam of the sea,
Now felt as a flame, now at leisure
   As wine shed for me.

Ah thy people, thy children, thy chosen,
   Marked cross from the womb and perverse!
They have found out the secret to cozen
   The gods that constrain us and curse;
They alone, they are wise, and none other;
   Give me place, even me, in their train,   150
O my sister, my spouse, and my mother,
   Our Lady of Pain.

For the crown of our life as it closes
   Is darkness, the fruit thereof dust;
No thorns go as deep as a rose's,   *world of perversion*
   And love is more cruel than lust.
Time turns the old days to derision,
   Our loves into corpses or wives;
And marriage and death and division
   Make barren our lives.   160

---

129 *I . . . portal:* This stanza has overtones of the Black Mass.
135 *luxurious:* voluptuous.
146 *cross:* abnormal.

And pale from the past we draw nigh thee,
 And satiate with comfortless hours;
And we know thee, how all men belie thee,
 And we gather the fruit of thy flowers;
The passion that slays and recovers,
 The pangs and the kisses that rain
On the lips and the limbs of thy lovers,
 Our Lady of Pain.

The desire of thy furious embraces
 Is more than the wisdom of years,   170
On the blossom though the blood lie in traces,
 Though the foliage be sodden with tears.
For the lords in whose keeping the door is
 That opens on all who draw breath
Gave the cypress to love, my Dolores,
 The myrtle to death.

And they laughed, changing hands in the measure.
 And they mixed and made peace after strife;
Pain melted in tears, and was pleasure;
 Death tingled with blood, and was life. 180
Like lovers they melted and tingled,
 In the dusk of thine innermost fane;
In the darkness they murmured and mingled,
 Our Lady of Pain.

In a twilight where virtues are vices,
 In thy chapels, unknown of the sun,
To a tune that enthralls and entices,
 They are wed, and the twain were as one.
For the tune from thine altar hath sounded
 Since God bade the world's work begin, 190
And the fume of thine incense abounded,
 To sweeten the sin.

175-6 *cypress . . . myrtle:* The perverse gods reverse the normal association of cypress with death and of myrtle with love.
182 *fane:* shrine.
185 *In a twilight . . . vices:* once more the stanza is reminiscent of the Black Mass.

Love listens, and paler than ashes,
  Through his curls as the crown on them slips,
Lifts languid wet eyelids and lashes,
  And laughs with insatiable lips.
Thou shalt hush him with heavy caresses,
  With the music that scares the profane;
Thou shalt darken his eyes with thy tresses,
  Our Lady of Pain.   200

Thou shalt blind his bright eyes though he wrestle,
  Thou shalt chain his light limbs though he strive;
In his lips all thy serpents shall nestle,
  In his hands all thy cruelties thrive.
In the daytime thy voice shall go through him,
  In his dreams he shall feel thee and ache;
Thou shalt kindle by night and subdue him
  Asleep and awake.

Thou shalt touch and make redder his roses
  With juice not of fruit nor of bud;   210
When the sense in the spirit reposes,
  Thou shalt quicken the soul through the blood,
Thine, thine the one grace we implore is,
  Who would live and not languish or feign,
O sleepless and deadly Dolores,
  Our Lady of Pain.

Dost thou dream, in a respite of slumber,
  In a lull of the fires of thy life,
Of the days without name, without number,
  When thy will stung the world into strife;   220
When, a goddess, the pulse of thy passion
  Smote kings as they revelled in Rome;
And they hailed thee re-risen, O Thalassian,
  Foam-white, from the foam?

When thy lips had such lovers to flatter;
  When the city lay red from thy rods,
And thine hands were as arrows to scatter

---

223 *Thalassian:* of the sea. Swinburne is associating Venus and Dolores.

The children of change and their gods;
When the blood of thy foemen made fervent
   A sand never moist from the main,   230
As one smote them, their lord and thy servant,
   Our Lady of Pain.

On sands by the storm never shaken,
   Nor wet from the washing of tides;
Nor by foam of the waves overtaken,
   Nor winds that the thunder bestrides;
But red from the print of thy paces,
   Made smooth for the world and its lords,
Ringed round with a ring of fair faces,
   And splendid with swords.   240

There the gladiator, pale for thy pleasure,
   Drew bitter and perilous breath;
There torments lay hold on the treasure
   Of limbs too delicious for death;
When thy gardens were lit with live torches,
   When the world was a steed for thy rein;
When the nations lay prone in thy porches,
   Our Lady of Pain.

When, with flame all around him aspirant,
   Stood flushed, as a harp-player stands,   250
The implacable beautiful tyrant,
   Rose-crowned, having death in his hands;
And a sound as the sound of loud water
   Smote far through the flight of the fires,
And mixed with the lightning of slaughter
   A thunder of lyres.

Dost thou dream of what was and no more is,
   The old kingdoms of earth and the kings?
Dost thou hunger for these things, Dolores,
   For these, in a world of new things?   260
But thy bosom no fasts could emaciate,

---

245 *live torches:* as Nero is said to have burned Christians alive for illumination.
251 *tyrant:* Nero, who burned Rome to the sound of music.

No hunger compel to complain
Those lips that no bloodshed could satiate,
   Our Lady of Pain.

As of old when the world's heart was lighter,
   Through thy garments the grace of thee glows,
The white wealth of thy body made whiter
   By the blushes of amorous blows,
And seamed with sharp lips and fierce fingers,
   And branded by kisses that bruise;   270
When all shall be gone that now lingers.
   Ah, what shall we lose?

Thou wert fair in the fearless old fashion,
   And thy limbs are as melodies yet,
And move to the music of passion
   With lithe and lascivious regret.
What ailed us, O gods, to desert you
   For creeds that refuse and restrain?
Come down and redeem us from virtue,
   Our Lady of Pain.   280

All shrines that were Vestal are flameless,
   But the flame has not fallen from this;
Though obscure be the god, and though nameless
   The eyes and the hair that we kiss;
Low fires that love sits by and forges
   Fresh heads for his arrows and thine;
Hair loosened and soiled in mid orgies
   With kisses and wine.

Thy skin changes country and colour,
   And shrivels or swells to a snake's.   290
Let it brighten and bloat and grow duller,
   We know it, the flames and the flakes,
Red brands on it smitten and bitten,
   Round skies where a star is a stain,
And the leaves with thy litanies written,
   Our Lady of Pain.

---

281 *Vestal:* referring to the shrine of Vesta, where her virgins tended a
sacred flame.

On thy bosom though many a kiss be,
   There are none such as knew it of old.
Was it Alciphron once or Arisbe,
   Male ringlets or feminine gold,   300
That thy lips met with under the statue,
   Whence a look shot out sharp after thieves
From the eyes of the garden-god at you
   Across the fig-leaves?

Then still, through dry seasons and moister,
   One god had a wreath to his shrine;
Then love was the pearl of his oyster,
   And Venus rose red out of wine.
We have all done amiss, choosing rather
   Such loves as the wise gods disdain;   310
Intercede for us thou with thy father,
   Our Lady of Pain.

In spring he had crowns of his garden,
   Red corn in the heat of the year,
Then hoary green olives that harden
   When the grape-blossom freezes with fear;
And milk-budded myrtles with Venus
   And vine-leaves with Bacchus he trod;
And ye said, "We have seen, he hath seen us,
   A visible God."   320

What broke off the garlands that girt you?
   What sundered you spirit and clay?
Weak sins yet alive are as virtue
   To the strength of the sins of that day.
For dried is the blood of thy lover,
   Ipsithilla, contracted the vein;
Cry aloud, "Will he rise and recover,
   Our Lady of Pain?"

---

299 *Alciphron . . . Arisbe:* respectively, Greek rhetorician and one of Priam's wives; aside from the fact of their being male and female, the reference is obscure.

303 *garden-god:* Priapus, whose phallic image was set in gardens as an emblem of fertility.

306 *One god:* Priapus.

326 *Ipsithilla:* lover mentioned by Catullus in *Carmina*, XXXII.

Chr. as perversion

Cry aloud; for the old world is broken:
    Cry out; for the Phrygian is priest,   330
And rears not the bountiful token
    And spreads not the fatherly feast.
From the midmost of Ida, from shady
    Recesses that murmur at morn,
They have brought and baptized her, Our Lady,
    A goddess new-born.

And the chaplets of old are above us,
    And the oyster-bed teems out of reach;
Old poets outsing and outlove us,
    And Catullus makes mouths at our speech,   340
Who shall kiss, in thy father's own city,
    With such lips as he sang with, again?
Intercede for us all of thy pity,
    Our Lady of Pain.

Out of Dindymus heavily laden
    Her lions draw bound and unfed
A mother, a mortal, a maiden,
    A queen over death and the dead.
She is cold, and her habit is lowly,
    Her temple of branches and sods;   350
Most fruitful and virginal, holy,
    A mother of gods.

She hath wasted with fire thine high places,
    She hath hidden and marred and made sad
The fair limbs of the Loves, the fair faces
    Of gods that were goodly and glad.
She slays, and her hands are not bloody;
    She moves as a moon in the wane,

---

330 *the Phrygian:* contemptuous reference to the unsexed priests of Cybele, a goddess of fecundity and mother of the gods, worshipped in Phrygia. The poet is, of course, implying a parallel to Christianity.
333 *Ida:* mountain where Cybele was worshipped.
337 *chaplets:* garlands.
340 *Catullus:* Roman poet of the first century B.C., who wrote passionate lyrics.
345 *Dindymus:* Phrygian mountain associated with Cybele.
346 *lions:* drawing Cybele's chariot.

White-robed, and thy raiment is ruddy,
    Our Lady of Pain.   360

They shall pass and their places be taken,
    The gods and the priests that are pure.
They shall pass, and shalt thou not be shaken?
    They shall perish, and shalt thou endure?
Death laughs, breathing close and relentless
    In the nostrils and eyelids of lust,
With a pinch in his fingers of scentless
    And delicate dust.

But the worm shall revive thee with kisses;
    Thou shalt change and transmute as a god,   370
As the rod to a serpent that hisses,
    As the serpent again to a rod.
Thy life shall not cease though thou doff it;
    Thou shalt live until evil be slain,
And good shall die first, said thy prophet,
    Our Lady of Pain.

Did he lie? did he laugh? does he know it,
    Now he lies out of reach, out of breath,
Thy prophet, thy preacher, thy poet,
    Sin's child by incestuous Death?   380
Did he find out in fire at his waking,
    Or discern as his eyelids lost light,
When the bands of the body were breaking
    And all came in sight?

Who has known all the evil before us,
    Or the tyrannous secrets of time?
Though we match not the dead men that bore us
    At a song, at a kiss, at a crime—
Though the heathen outface and outlive us,
    And our lives and our longings are twain—   390
Ah, forgive us our virtues, forgive us,
    Our Lady of Pain.

---

[371] *rod to a serpent:* see *Exodus* 7:8-10 for reference to Aaron's rod. Swinburne is using the transformation of rod into serpent and back again for his own purposes of eroticism.

Who are we that embalm and embrace thee
    With spices and savours of song?
What is time, that his children should face thee?
    What am I, that my lips do thee wrong?
I could hurt thee—but pain would delight thee;
    Or caress thee—but love would repel;
And the lovers whose lips would excite thee
    Are serpents in hell.   400

Who now shall content thee as they did,
    Thy lovers, when temples were built
And the hair of the sacrifice braided
    And the blood of the sacrifice spilt,
In Lampsacus fervent with faces,
    In Aphaca red from thy reign,
Who embraced thee with awful embraces,
    Our Lady of Pain?

Where are they, Cotytto or Venus,
    Astarte or Ashtaroth, where?   410
Do their hands as we touch come between us?
    Is the breath of them hot in thy hair?
From their lips have thy lips taken fever,
    With the blood of their bodies grown red?
Hast thou left upon earth a believer
    If these men are dead?

They were purple of raiment and golden,
    Filled full of thee, fiery with wine,
Thy lovers, in haunts unbeholden,
    In marvellous chambers of thine.   420
They are fled, and their footprints escape us,
    Who appraise thee, adore, and abstain,
O daughter of death and Priapus,
    Our Lady of Pain.

405-6 *Lampsacus . . . Aphaca:* centers of the worship of Priapus and Venus.
409 *Cotytto:* Thracian goddess associated with Cybele and worshipped in licentious rites.
410 *Astarte or Ashtaroth:* alternative names of the Asiatic goddess equivalent to Venus or Aphrodite.

What ails us to fear overmeasure,
   To praise thee with timorous breath,
O mistress and mother of pleasure,
   The one thing as certain as death?
We shall change as the things that we cherish,
   Shall fade as they faded before,   430
As foam upon water shall perish,
   As sand upon shore.

We shall know what the darkness discovers,
   If the grave-pit be shallow or deep;
And our fathers of old, and our lovers,
   We shall know if they sleep not or sleep.
We shall see whether hell be not heaven,
   Find out whether tares be not grain,
And the joys of thee seventy times seven,
   Our Lady of Pain.   440

[1866]

THE GARDEN OF PROSERPINE

Here, where the world is quiet;
   Here, where all trouble seems
Dead winds' and spent waves' riot
   In doubtful dreams of dreams;
I watch the green field growing
For reaping folk and sowing,
For harvest-time and mowing,
   A sleepy world of streams.

I am tired of tears and laughter,
   And men that laugh and weep;   10
Of what may come hereafter
   For men that sow to reap:

Proserpine: goddess of the underworld, without whose permission no man could die. She spent half of each year in the outer world with her mother, the earth goddess Demeter. She was associated with the change of seasons, as well as with death.

I am weary of days and hours,
Blown buds of barren flowers,
Desires and dreams and powers
    And everything but sleep.

Here life has death for neighbour,
    And far from eye or ear
Wan waves and wet winds labour,
    Weak ships and spirits steer;   20
They drive adrift, and whither
They wot not who make thither;
But no such winds blow hither,
    And no such things grow here.

/ No growth of moor or coppice,
    No heather-flower or vine,
But bloomless buds of poppies,
    Green grapes of Proserpine,
Pale beds of blowing rushes
Where no leaf blooms or blushes   30
Save this whereout she crushes
    For dead men deadly wine.

unnatural is
growth of this
garden

Pale, without name or number,
    In fruitless fields of corn,
They bow themselves and slumber
    All night till light is born;
And like a soul belated,
In hell and heaven unmated,
By cloud and mist abated
    Comes out of darkness morn.   40

Though one were strong as seven,
    He too with death shall dwell,
Nor wake with wings in heaven,
    Nor weep for pains in hell;
Though one were fair as roses,
His beauty clouds and closes;
And well though love reposes,
    In the end it is not well.

Pale, beyond porch and portal,
    Crowned with calm leaves, she stands   50
Who gathers all things mortal
    With cold immortal hands;
Her languid lips are sweeter
Than love's who fears to greet her
To men that mix and meet her
    From many times and lands.

She waits for each and other,
    She waits for all men born;
Forgets the earth her mother,
    The life of fruits and corn;   60
And spring and seed and swallow
Take wing for her and follow
Where summer song rings hollow
    And flowers are put to scorn.

There go the loves that wither,
    The old loves with wearier wings;
And all dead years draw thither,
    And all disastrous things;
Dead dreams of days forsaken,
Blind buds that snows have shaken,   70
Wild leaves that winds have taken,
    Red strays of ruined springs.

We are not sure of sorrow,
    And joy was never sure;
To-day will die to-morrow;
    Time stoops to no man's lure;
And love, grown faint and fretful,
With lips but half regretful
Sighs, and with eyes forgetful
    Weeps that no loves endure.   80

From too much love of living,
    From hope and fear set free,
We thank with brief thanksgiving

---

49 *beyond porch and portal:* within the entrance to Hades.

/   Whatever gods may be *(Henley)*
    That no life lives for ever;
    That dead men rise up never;
    That even the weariest river
        Winds somewhere safe to sea.

Then star nor sun shall waken,
    Nor any change of light: 90
Nor sound of waters shaken,
    Nor any sound or sight:
Nor wintry leaves nor vernal,
Nor days nor things diurnal;
Only the sleep eternal
    In an eternal night.

                                        [1866]

AVE ATQUE VALE

In memory of Charles Baudelaire

Nous devrions pourtant lui porter quelques fleurs;
Les morts, les pauvres morts, ont de grandes douleurs,
Et quand Octobre souffle, émondeur des vieux arbres,
Son vent mélancolique à l'entour de leurs marbres,
Certe, ils doivent trouver les vivants bien ingrats.
                            LES FLEURS DU MAL.

I

Shall I strew on thee rose or rue or laurel,
    Brother, on this that was the veil of thee?
    Or quiet sea-flower moulded by the sea,

Ave Atque Vale: "Hail and Farewell." This gravely moving poem is Swinburne's tribute to the great French poet who so influenced his own writing; he thought Baudelaire "one of the most exquisite, most delicate, and most perfect poets of the century." The epigraph is from Baudelaire's *Les Fleurs du Mal* ("The Flowers of Evil"):
    Moreover, we must bring him some flowers;
    The dead, the poor dead, have great sorrows,
    And when October, pruner of old trees, blows
    His melancholy wind around their tombs,
    They must think the living very ungrateful indeed.
[1] *rose or rue or laurel:* symbols of love, regret, and poetry.

Or simplest growth of meadow-sweet or sorrel,
　　Such as the summer-sleepy Dryads weave,
　　Waked up by snow-soft sudden rains at eve?
Or wilt thou rather, as on earth before,
　　Half-faded fiery blossoms, pale with heat
　　And full of bitter summer, but more sweet
To thee than gleamings of a northern shore　　　　10
　　Trod by no tropic feet?

II

For always thee the fervid languid glories
　　Allured of heavier suns in mightier skies;
　　Thine ears knew all the wandering watery sighs
Where the sea sobs round Lesbian promontories,
　　The barren kiss of piteous wave to wave
　　That knows not where is that Leucadian grave
Which hides too deep the supreme head of song.
　　Ah, salt and sterile as her kisses were,
　　The wild sea winds her and the green gulfs bear　　20
Hither and thither, and vex and work her wrong,
　　Blind gods that cannot spare.

III

Thou sawest, in thine old singing season, brother,
　　Secrets and sorrows unbeheld of us:
　　Fierce loves, and lovely leaf-buds poisonous,
Bare to thy subtler eye, but for none other
　　Blowing by night in some unbreathed-in clime;
　　The hidden harvest of luxurious time,
Sin without shape, and pleasure without speech;
　　And where strange dreams in a tumultuous sleep　　30
　　Make the shut eyes of stricken spirits weep;
And with each face thou sawest the shadow on each,
　　Seeing as men sow men reap.

---

5 *Dryads:* wood nymphs.
15 *Lesbian:* Sappho, the Greek poet, according to legend threw herself into
the sea from a cliff on the island of Leucas.
33 *as men . . . reap:* "Whatsoever a man soweth, that shall he also reap"
(*Galatians* 6:7).

IV

O sleepless heart and sombre soul unsleeping,
    That were athirst for sleep and no more life
    And no more love, for peace and no more strife!
Now the dim gods of death have in their keeping
    Spirit and body and all the springs of song,
    Is it well now where love can do no wrong,
Where stingless pleasure has no foam or fang   40
    Behind the unopening closure of her lips?
    Is it not well where soul from body slips
And flesh from bone divides without a pang
    As dew from flower-bell drips?

V

It is enough; the end and the beginning
    Are one thing to thee, who art past the end.
    O hand unclasped of unbeholden friend,
For thee no fruits to pluck, no palms for winning,
    No triumph and no labour and no lust,
    Only dead yew-leaves and a little dust.   50
O quiet eyes wherein the light saith nought,
    Whereto the day is dumb, nor any night
    With obscure finger silences your sight,
Nor in your speech the sudden soul speaks thought,
    Sleep, and have sleep for light.

VI

Now all strange hours and all strange loves are over,
    Dreams and desires and sombre songs and sweet,
    Hast thou found place at the great knees and feet
Of some pale Titan-woman like a lover,
    Such as thy vision here solicited,   60
    Under the shadow of her fair vast head,
The deep division of prodigious breasts,
    The solemn slope of mighty limbs asleep,
    The weight of awful tresses that still keep
The savour and shade of old-world pine-forests
    Where the wet hill-winds weep?

---

[59] *Titan-woman:* reference to Baudelaire's "La Géante" (The Giantess).

VII

Hast thou found any likeness for thy vision?
    O gardener of strange flowers, what bud, what bloom,
    Hast thou found sown, what gathered in the gloom?
What of despair, of rapture, of derision,   70
    What of life is there, what of ill or good?
    Are the fruits grey like dust or bright like blood?
Does the dim ground grow any seed of ours,
    The faint fields quicken any terrene root,
    In low lands where the sun and moon are mute
And all the stars keep silence? Are there flowers
    At all, or any fruit?

VIII

Alas, but though my flying song flies after,
    O sweet strange elder singer, thy more fleet
    Singing, and footprints of thy fleeter feet,   80
Some dim derision of mysterious laughter
    From the blind tongueless warders of the dead,
    Some gainless glimpse of Proserpine's veiled head,
Some little sound of unregarded tears
    Wept by effaced unprofitable eyes,
    And from pale mouths some cadence of dead sighs—
These only, these the hearkening spirit hears,
    Sees only such things rise.

IX

Thou art far too far for wings of words to follow,
    Far too far off for thought or any prayer.   90
    What ails us with thee, who art wind and air?
What ails us gazing where all seen is hollow?
    Yet with some fancy, yet with some desire,
    Dreams pursue death as winds a flying fire,
Our dreams pursue our dead and do not find.
    Still, and more swift than they, the thin flame flies,
    The low light fails us in elusive skies,
Still the foiled earnest ear is deaf, and blind
    Are still the eluded eyes.

---

83 *Proserpine:* See note to "The Garden of Proserpine" (p. 706).

X

Not thee, O never thee, in all time's changes,   100
    Not thee, but this the sound of thy sad soul,
    The shadow of thy swift spirit, this shut scroll
I lay my hand on, and not death estranges
    My spirit from communion of thy song—
    These memories and these melodies that throng
Veiled porches of a Muse funereal—
    These I salute, these touch, these clasp and fold
    As though a hand were in my hand to hold,
Or through mine ears a mourning musical
    Of many mourners rolled.   110

XI

I among these, I also, in such station
    As when the pyre was charred, and piled the sods,
    And offering to the dead made, and their gods,
The old mourners had, standing to make libation,
    I stand, and to the gods and to the dead
    Do reverence without prayer or praise, and shed
Offering to these unknown, the gods of gloom,
    And what of honey and spice my seedlands bear,
    And what I may of fruits in this chilled air,
And lay, Orestes-like, across the tomb   120
    A curl of severed hair.

XII

But by no hand nor any treason stricken,
    Not like the low-lying head of Him, the King,
    The flame that made of Troy a ruinous thing,
Thou liest, and on this dust no tears could quicken
    There fall no tears like theirs that all men hear
    Fall tear by sweet imperishable tear
Down the opening leaves of holy poets' pages.
    Thee not Orestes, not Electra mourns;
    But bending us-ward with memorial urns   130

---

[120] *Orestes-like:* Orestes laid a lock of his own hair as a sacrifice on the tomb of his father, Agamemnon.
[123] *the King:* Agamemnon.
[129] *Electra:* sister of Orestes and daughter of Agamemnon.

The most high Muses that fulfil all ages
　　Weep, and our God's heart yearns.

XIII

For, sparing of his sacred strength, not often
　　Among us darkling here the lord of light
　　Makes manifest his music and his might
In hearts that open and in lips that soften
　　With the soft flame and heat of songs that shine.
　　Thy lips indeed he touched with bitter wine,
And nourished them indeed with bitter bread;
　　Yet surely from his hand thy soul's food came,　　140
　　The fire that scarred thy spirit at his flame
Was lighted, and thine hungering heart he fed
　　Who feeds our hearts with fame.

XIV

Therefore he too now at thy soul's sunsetting,
　　God of all suns and songs, he too bends down
　　To mix his laurel with thy cypress crown,
And save thy dust from blame and from forgetting.
　　Therefore he too, seeing all thou wert and art,
　　Compassionate, with sad and sacred heart,
Mourns thee of many his children the last dead,　　150
　　And hallows with strange tears and alien sighs
　　Thine unmelodious mouth and sunless eyes,
And over thine irrevocable head
　　Sheds light from the under skies.

XV

And one weeps with him in the ways Lethean,
　　And stains with tears her changing bosom chill:
　　That obscure Venus of the hollow hill,
That thing transformed which was the Cytherean,

---

134 *the lord of light:* Apollo, god of poetry and of the sun.
146 *laurel . . . cypress:* the laurel of poetry mingled with the cypress of death.
155 *ways Lethean:* paths of forgetfulness.
157 *obscure Venus:* The meaning of this and the following three lines is that Venus has become transformed from the foam-born goddess of Cythera and the goddess of heavenly love celebrated at Mt. Eryx in Sicily to the sensual temptress of medieval legend, holding licentious court in a German mountain cave.

With lips that lost their Grecian laugh divine
    Long since, and face no more called Erycine;   160
A ghost, a bitter and luxurious god.
    Thee also with fair flesh and singing spell
    Did she, a sad second prey, compel
Into the footless places once more trod.
    And shadows hot from hell.

XVI

And now no sacred staff shall break in blossom,
    No choral salutation lure to light
    A spirit sick with perfume and sweet night
And love's tired eyes and hands and barren bosom.
    There is no help for these things; none to mend   170
    And none to mar; not all our songs, O friend,
Will make death clear or make life durable.
    Howbeit with rose and ivy and wild vine
    And with wild notes about this dust of thine
At least I fill the place where white dreams dwell
    And wreathe an unseen shrine.

XVII

Sleep; and if life was bitter to thee, pardon,
    If sweet, give thanks; thou hast no more to live;
    And to give thanks is good, and to forgive.
Out of the mystic and the mournful garden   180
    Where all day through thine hands in barren braid
    Wove the sick flowers of secrecy and shade,
Green buds of sorrow and sin, and remnants grey,
    Sweet-smelling, pale with poison, sanguine-hearted,
    Passions that sprang from sleep and thoughts that
        started,
Shall death not bring us all as thee one day
    Among the days departed?

XVIII

For thee, O now a silent soul, my brother,
    Take at my hands this garland, and farewell.

---

166 *sacred staff:* Tannhauser, after a year of dalliance with Venus in her
cave, repented his sins; as token of Divine forgiveness of Tannhauser, the
sacred staff of the Pope broke into bloom.

Thin is the leaf, and chill the wintry smell,   190
   And chill the solemn earth, a fatal mother,
     With sadder than the Niobean womb,
     And in the hollow of her breasts a tomb.
Content thee, howsoe'er, whose days are done;
   There lies not any troublous thing before,
   Nor sight nor sound to war against thee more,
For whom all winds are quiet as the sun,
   All waters as the shore.

[1868]

life force here,
force of all universe

HERTHA

swing not devote of Eastern, mystic

I am that which began;
   Out of me the years roll;
Out of me God and man;
   I am equal and whole;
God changes, and man, and the form of them bodily;
   I am the soul.

Before ever land was,
   Before ever the sea,
Or soft hair of the grass,
   Or fair limbs of the tree,
Or the flesh-coloured fruit of my branches, I was, and thy
   soul was in me.   10

First life on my sources
   First drifted and swam;
Out of me are the forces
   That save it or damn;

---

192 *Niobean:* To humble the pride of Niobe, Apollo and Artemis killed her fourteen children.
Hertha: Germanic goddess of earth and growth, here considered as the source of all being. Swinburne thought this poem his greatest single piece because it contained "the most of lyric force and music combined with the most of condensed and clarified thought."
4 *equal:* being of one nature only.

Out of me man and woman, and wild-beast and bird; before God was, I am.
         Beside or above me
            Nought is there to go;
         Love or unlove me,
            Unknow me or know,
I am that which unloves me and loves; I am stricken, and I
   am the blow.   20

         I the mark that is missed
            And the arrows that miss,
         I the mouth that is kissed
            And the breath in the kiss,
The search, and the sought, and the seeker, the soul and
   the body that is.

         I am that thing which blesses
            My spirit elate;
         That which caresses
            With hands uncreate
My limbs unbegotten that measure the length of the measure of fate.   30

         But what thing dost thou now,
            Looking Godward, to cry,
         "I am I, thou art thou,
            I am low, thou art high"?
I am thou, whom thou seekest to find him; find thou but
   thyself, thou art I.

         I the grain and the furrow,
            The plough-cloven clod
         And the ploughshare drawn thorough,
            The germ and the sod,
The deed and the doer, the seed and the sower, the dust
   which is God.   40

---

¹⁵ *before God was, I am:* ironic echo of Christ's words, "Before Abraham
was, I am" (*John* 8:58).
²⁹ *uncreate:* uncreated.

Hast thou known how I fashioned thee,
   Child, underground?
Fire that impassioned thee,
   Iron that bound,
Dim changes of water, what thing of all these hast thou
   known of or found?

Canst thou say in thine heart
   Thou hast seen with thine eyes
With what cunning of art
   Thou wast wrought in what wise,
By what force of what stuff thou wast shapen, and shown
   on my breast to the skies?   50

Who hath given, who hath sold it thee,
   Knowledge of me?
Hath the wilderness told it thee?
   Hast thou learnt of the sea?
Hast thou communed in spirit with night? have the winds
   taken counsel with thee?

Have I set such a star
   To show light on thy brow
That thou sawest from afar
   What I show to thee now?
Have ye spoken as brethren together, the sun and the moun-
   tains and thou?   60

What is here, dost thou know it?
   What was, hast thou known?
Prophet or poet
   Nor tripod nor throne
Nor spirit nor flesh can make answer, but only thy mother
   alone.

Mother, not maker,
   Born, and not made;
Though her children forsake her,
   Allured or afraid,

---

64 *Nor tripod nor throne:* neither priest nor king. The priestess of Apollo at
Delphi sat on a three-legged altar.

Praying prayers to the God of their fashion, she stirs not for
   all that have prayed. 70

> A creed is a rod,
>   And a crown is of night;
> But this thing is God,
>   To be man with thy might,
> To grow straight in the strength of thy spirit, and live out
>   thy life as the light.

> I am in thee to save thee,
>   As my soul in thee saith;
> Give thou as I gave thee,
>   Thy life-blood and breath,
> Green leaves of thy labour, white flowers of thy thought, and
>   red fruit of thy death. 80

> Be the ways of thy giving
>   As mine were to thee;
> The free life of thy living,
>   Be the gift of it free;
> Not as servant to lord, nor as master to slave, shalt thou give
>   thee to me.

> O children of banishment,
>   Souls overcast,
> Were the lights ye see vanish meant
>   Alway to last,
> Ye would know not the sun overshining the shadows and
>   stars overpast. 90

> I that saw where ye trod
>   The dim paths of the night
> Set the shadow called God
>   In your skies to give light;
> But the morning of manhood is risen, and the shadowless
>   soul is in sight.

> The tree many-rooted

---

96 *tree many-rooted:* in Germanic mythology, the tree of life, Igdrasil.

That swells to the sky
    With frondage red-fruited,
      The life-tree am I;
In the buds of your lives is the sap of my leaves: ye shall
    live and not die.   100

    But the Gods of your fashion
      That take and that give,
    In their pity and passion
      That scourge and forgive,
They are worms that are bred in the bark that falls off; they
    shall die and not live.

    My own blood is what stanches
      The wounds in my bark;
    Stars caught in my branches
      Make day of the dark,
And are worshipped as suns till the sunrise shall tread out
    their fires as a spark.   110

    Where dead ages hide under
      The live roots of the tree,
    In my darkness the thunder
      Makes utterance of me;
In the clash of my boughs with each other ye hear the
    waves sound of the sea.

    That noise is of Time,
      As his feathers are spread
    And his feet set to climb
      Through the boughs overhead,
And my foliage rings round him and rustles, and branches
    are bent with his tread.   120

    The storm-winds of ages
      Blow through me and cease,
    The war-wind that rages,
      The spring-wind of peace,
Ere the breath of them roughen my tresses, ere one of my
    blossoms increase.

All sounds of all changes,
    All shadows and lights
  On the world's mountain-ranges
    And stream-riven heights,
Whose tongue is the wind's tongue and language of storm-
    clouds on earth-shaking nights; 130

  All forms of all faces,
    All works of all hands
  In unsearchable places
    Of time-stricken lands,
All death and all life, and all reigns and all ruins, drop
    through me as sands.

  Though sore be my burden
    And more than ye know,
  And my growth have no guerdon
    But only to grow,
Yet I fail not of growing for lightnings above me or death-
    worms below. 140

  These too have their part in me,
    As I too in these;
  Such fire is at heart in me,
    Such sap is this tree's,
Which hath in it sounds and all secrets of infinite lands and
    of seas.

  In the spring-coloured hours
    When my mind was as May's,
  There brake forth of me flowers
    By centuries of days,
Strong blossoms with perfume of manhood, shot out from
    my spirit as rays. 150

  And the sound of them springing
    And smell of their shoots
  Were as warmth and sweet singing
    And strength to my roots;
And the lives of my children made perfect with freedom
    of soul were my fruits.

I bid you but be;
　　I have need not of prayer;
　　I have need of you free
　　　　As your mouths of mine air;
That my heart may be greater within me, beholding
　　the fruits of me fair.　　　　　　　　　　　　160

　　More fair than strange fruit is
　　　　Of faiths ye espouse;
　　In me only the root is
　　　　That blooms in your boughs;
Behold now your God that ye made you, to feed him with
　　faith of your vows.

　　In the darkening and whitening
　　　　Abysses adored,
　　With dayspring and lightning
　　　　For lamp and for sword,
God thunders in heaven, and his angels are red with the
　　wrath of the Lord.　　　　　　　　　　　　170

　　O my sons, O too dutiful
　　　　Toward Gods not of me,
　　Was not I enough beautiful?
　　　　Was it hard to be free?
For behold, I am with you, am in you and of you; look
　　forth now and see.

　　Lo, winged with world's wonders,
　　　　With miracles shod,
　　With the fires of his thunders
　　　　For raiment and rod,
God trembles in heaven, and his angels are white with the
　　terror of God.　　　　　　　　　　　　180

　　For his twilight is come on him,
　　　　His anguish is here;
　　And his spirits gaze dumb on him,
　　　　Grown grey from his fear;

---

181 *twilight:* parallel to the Germanic myth of the destruction (or twilight)
of the gods as a necessary prelude to regeneration.

And his hour taketh hold on him stricken, the last of his in-
    finite year.

      Thought made him and breaks him,
        Truth slays and forgives;
      But to you, as time takes him,
        This new thing it gives,
Even love, the beloved Republic, that feeds upon freedom
    and lives.   190

      For truth only is living,
        Truth only is whole,
      And the love of his giving
        Man's polestar and pole;
Man, pulse of my centre, and fruit of my body, and seed of
    my soul.

      One birth of my bosom;
        One beam of mine eye;
      One topmost blossom
        That scales the sky;
Man, equal and one with me, man that is made of me, man
    that is I.   200

           [1871]

COR CORDIUM

O heart of hearts, the chalice of love's fire,
    Hid round with flowers and all the bounty of bloom;
    O wonderful and perfect heart, for whom
The lyrist liberty made life a lyre;
O heavenly heart, at whose most dear desire
    Dead love, living and singing, cleft his tomb,
    And with him risen and regent in death's room

---

190 *Republic:* Hertha, said Swinburne, was a "good republican," for only
in liberty "can man's soul reach its full stature and growth."
Cor Cordium: "Heart of Hearts." The title is taken from the inscription on
Shelley's tomb in Rome.

All day thy choral pulses rang full choir;
O heart whose beating blood was running song,
   O sole thing sweeter than thine own songs were,   10
   Help us for thy free love's sake to be free,
True for thy truth's sake, for thy strength's sake strong,
   Till very liberty make clean and fair
   The nursing earth as the sepulchral sea.

[1871]

A FORSAKEN GARDEN

In a coign of the cliff between lowland and highland,
   At the sea-down's edge between windward and lee,
Walled round with rocks as an inland island,
   The ghost of a garden fronts the sea.
A girdle of brushwood and thorn encloses
   The steep square slope of the blossomless bed
Where the weeds that grew green from the graves of its roses
     Now lie dead.

The fields fall southward, abrupt and broken,
   To the low last edge of the long lone land.   10
If a step should sound or a word be spoken,
   Would a ghost not rise at the strange guest's hand?
So long have the grey bare walks lain guestless,
   Through branches and briars if a man make way,
He shall find no life but the sea-wind's, restless
     Night and day.

The dense hard passage is blind and stifled
   That crawls by a track none turn to climb
To the strait waste place that the years have rifled
   Of all but the thorns that are touched not of time.   20
The thorns he spares when the rose is taken;
   The rocks are left when he wastes the plain.
The wind that wanders, the weeds wind-shaken,
     These remain.

Not a flower to be pressed of the foot that falls not;
  As the heart of a dead man the seed-plots are dry;
From the thicket of thorns whence the nightingale calls not,
  Could she call, there were never a rose to reply.
Over the meadows that blossom and wither
  Rings but the note of a sea-bird's song;
Only the sun and the rain come hither
    All year long.

The sun burns sere and the rain dishevels
  One gaunt bleak blossom of scentless breath.
Only the wind here hovers and revels
  In a round where life seems barren as death.
Here there was laughing of old, there was weeping,
  Haply, of lovers none ever will know,
Whose eyes went seaward a hundred sleeping
    Years ago.

Heart handfast in heart as they stood, "Look thither."
  Did he whisper? "look forth from the flowers to the sea;
For the foam-flowers endure when the rose-blossoms wither,
  And men that love lightly may die—but we?"
And the same wind sang and the same waves whitened,
  And or ever the garden's last petals were shed,
In the lips that had whispered, the eyes that had lightened,
    Love was dead.

Or they loved their life through, and then went whither?
  And were one to the end—but what end who knows?
Love deep as the sea as a rose must wither,
  As the rose-red seaweed that mocks the rose.
Shall the dead take thought for the dead to love them?
  What love was ever as deep as a grave?
They are loveless now as the grass above them
    Or the wave.

All are at one now, roses and lovers,
  Not known of the cliffs and the fields and the sea.
Not a breath of the time that has been hovers
  In the air now soft with a summer to be.
Not a breath shall there sweeten the seasons hereafter

Of the flowers or the lovers that laugh now or weep,
When as they that are free now of weeping and laughter
　　　We shall sleep.

Here death may deal not again for ever;
　　Here change may come not till all change end.
From the graves they have made they shall rise up never,
　　Who have left nought living to ravage and rend.
Earth, stones, and thorns of the wild ground growing,
　　While the sun and the rain live, these shall be;　　　　70
Till a last wind's breath upon all these blowing
　　　Roll the sea.

Till the slow sea rise and the sheer cliff crumble,
　　Till terrace and meadow the deep gulfs drink,
Till the strength of the waves of the high tides humble
　　The fields that lessen, the rocks that shrink,
Here now in his triumph where all things falter,
　　Stretched out on the spoils that his own hand spread,
As a god self-slain on his own strange altar,
　　　Death lies dead.　　　　　　　　　　　80

We never existed

[1878]

THE HIGHER PANTHEISM
IN A NUTSHELL

Satire on Tennyson pg. 194

One, who is not, we see: but one, whom we see not, is:
Surely this is not that: but that is assuredly this.

What, and wherefore, and whence? for under is over and
　　under:
If thunder could be without lightning, lightning could be
　　without thunder.

The Higher Pantheism in a Nutshell: This parody and the two following it
were published anonymously in *The Heptalogia, or The Seven Against
Sense, A Cap with Seven Bells,* a set of seven parodies on Victorian men-of-
letters. This poem is, of course, a parody of Tennyson's "The Higher Pantheism."

Doubt is faith, in the main: but faith, on the whole, is doubt.
We cannot believe by proof: but could we believe without?

Why, and whither, and how? for barley and rye are not
    clover:
Neither are straight lines curves: yet over is under and
    over.

Two and two may be four: but four and four are not eight:
Fate and God may be twain: but God is the same thing as
    fate.   10

Ask a man what he thinks, and get from a man what he
    feels:
God, once caught in the fact, shows you a fair pair of heels.

Body and spirit are twins: God only knows which is which:
The soul squats down in the flesh, like a tinker drunk in a
    ditch.

More is the whole than a part: but half is more than the
    whole:
Clearly, the soul is the body: but is not the body the soul?

One and two are not one: but one and nothing is two:
Truth can hardly be false, if falsehood cannot be true.

Once the mastodon was: pterodactyls were common as
    cocks:
Then the mammoth was God: now is He a prize ox.   20

Parallels all things are: yet many of these are askew:
You are certainly I: but certainly I am not you.

Springs the rock from the plain, shoots the stream from the
    rock:
Cocks exist for the hen: but hens exist for the cock.

God, whom we see not, is: and God, who is not, we see:
Fiddle, we know, is diddle: and diddle, we take it, is dee.

[1880]

SONNET FOR A PICTURE

That nose is out of drawing. With a gasp,
  She pants upon the passionate lips that ache
  With the red drain of her own mouth, and make
A monochord of colour. Like an asp,
One lithe lock wriggles in his rutilant grasp.
  Love's white warm shrewbread to a browner cake.
  Her bosom is an oven of myrrh, to bake
The lock his fingers clench has burst its hasp.
The legs are absolutely abominable.
  Ah! what keen overgust of wild-eyed woes   10
  Flags in that bosom, flushes in that nose?
Nay! Death sets riddles for desire to spell,
  Responsive. What red hem earth's passion sews,
But must be ravenously unripped in hell?

[1880]

NEPHELIDIA *parody / satire on own stuff*

From the depth of the dreamy decline of the dawn through
  a notable nimbus of nebulous noonshine,
  Pallid and pink as the palm of the flag-flower that flickers
    with fear of the flies as they float,
Are they looks of our lovers that lustrously lean from a mar-
  vel of mystic miraculous moonshine,
  These that we feel in the blood of our blushes that thicken
    and threaten with throbs through the throat?
Thicken and thrill as a theatre thronged at appeal of an ac-
  tor's appalled agitation,
  Fainter with fear of the fires of the future than pale with
    the promise of pride in the past;

Sonnet for a Picture: a parody of the style of his good friend Dante Gabriel
Rossetti.
Nephelidia: "cloudlets." This is probably the best-known self-parody in the
English language.

Flushed with the famishing fullness of fever that reddens
    with radiance of rathe recreation,
  Gaunt as the ghastliest of glimpses that gleam through
    the gloom of the gloaming when ghosts go aghast?
Nay, for the nick of the tick of the time is a tremulous touch
    on the temples of terror,
  Strained as the sinews yet strenuous with strife of the
    dead who is dumb as the dust-heaps of death: 10
Surely no soul is it, sweet as the spasm of erotic emotional
    exquisite error,
  Bathed in the balms of beatified bliss, beatific itself by
    beatitude's breath.
Surely no spirit or sense of a soul that was soft to the spirit
    and soul of our senses
  Sweetens the stress of suspiring suspicion that sobs in the
    semblance and sound of a sigh;
Only this oracle opens Olympian, in mystical moods and tri-
    angular tenses—
  "Life is the lust of a lamp for the light that is dark till the
    dawn of the day when we die."
Mild is the mirk and monotonous music of memory, melodi-
    ously mute as it may be,
  While the hope in the heart of a hero is bruised by the
    breach of men's rapiers, resigned to the rod;
Made meek as a mother whose bosom-beats bound with the
    bliss-bringing bulk of a balm-breathing baby,
  As they grope through the grave-yard of creeds, under
    skies growing green at a groan for the grimness of God. 20
Blank is the book of his bounty beholden of old, and its bind-
    ing is blacker than bluer:
  Out of blue into black is the scheme of the skies, and their
    dews are the wine of the bloodshed of things;
Till the darkling desire of delight shall be free as a fawn
    that is freed from the fangs that pursue her,
  Till the heart-beats of hell shall be hushed by a hymn
    from the hunt that has harried the kennel of kings.

                              [1880]

---

7 *rathe:* speedy.
17 *mirk:* dark.

Thomas Hardy

[1840-1928]

More than any other of the great Victorians, Thomas Hardy unites the last century and our own. When he was born, Queen Victoria had been on the throne only three years, Southey was poet laureate, Wordsworth was still writing, and Poe was in mid-career. Among the new writers were Tennyson, Browning, Dickens, and Thackeray. At Hardy's death, he had outlasted Victoria, her son, and was near the end of her grandson's reign; Joyce, Eliot, Pound, Frost, and Hemingway were already established as major writers. The tremendous span of his life is perhaps less remarkable, however, than the fact that his artistic creativity lasted until just before his death; he was a first-rate artist for over sixty years. So timeless is his best work that it is usually impossible to guess the date of a poem's composition unless it is concerned with a specific historical event.

Like Meredith, Hardy was a writer most famous during his lifetime for his novels, and, like Meredith once more, he thought of himself as a poet, a judgment posterity has only slowly begun to accept.

Hardy, the son of a Dorset builder and stonemason, was born near Dorchester in the southwestern part of England, in the heart of what had been the ancient kingdom of Wessex, a name he preferred to use for the locale of many of his poems and novels. When Hardy was a child, Dorset was still lightly settled and totally non-urban. The natives spoke with a distinct accent; the members of the lower classes were ill-educated and superstitious. Beneath the veneer of their Christianity lay the pagan traditions of the countryside; around them lay the ruins of temples and amphitheatres from prehistoric and Roman times. Vestigial fire worship was still practiced on the tops of lonely hills. Country fairs, rural weddings and funerals, hangings, rustic dancing to rusty fiddles: these were the occasions of ceremonial, sadness, or celebration. The way of a man with a maid, jealousy, sudden violence, the threat of primitive ways coming into conflict with modern law, the reflection of man's brief life in nature surrounding him: these were the constant concerns. Small wonder that modern civilization seemed transitory to Hardy, and that the country life, tied to the enduring earth, seemed reality. To few writers have the scenes of childhood had such importance as the Wessex life had for Hardy.

Hardy's formal schooling was slight, but he managed to educate himself well. At sixteen he was apprenticed to an architect, and in 1862 he went to London to work as an architect himself. For some years he specialized in the restoration of old country churches.

In 1867 Hardy showed his first novel to the publishers Chapman and Hall, whose reader, George Meredith, rejected it. However, Meredith did encourage the younger man to continue his writing, and from 1871 until 1896 Hardy turned out a series of novels now numbered among the masterpieces of the late nineteenth century. Culminating the series were his great tragic novels, *Tess of the D'Urbervilles*, 1891, and *Jude the Obscure*, 1896. These two powerful works were attacked as immoral, both in their treatment of sexual mores and in their reflection of Hardy's somber view of the universe and the forces that control it. The latter novel was promptly nicknamed "Jude the Obscene." At least partly because of the abuse that the books attracted, Hardy gave up the writing of novels, which he had once called "mere journeywork," and returned to his first love, poetry. *Wessex Poems*, his first volume of poetry, appeared in 1898 and was followed by a half dozen other volumes before his death.

In his old age England recognized Hardy as a great literary man, forgetting the charges of obscenity and blasphemy that had been levelled at his novels. The last few years of his life were

passed in a glow of fame, prosperity, and honors seldom accorded a writer. His first wife, to whom he had been married for
almost forty years, died in 1912, and in 1914, at the age of seventy-
four, he married his secretary, with whom he lived contentedly
until his death. He died quietly in 1928 in the house he had built
near Dorchester in 1883. His heart was buried with his first wife,
his ashes interred in Westminster Abbey.

Externally, much of Hardy's life was happy, but beneath the
surface there was a persistent melancholy, although he never allowed it to spoil his relations with other persons. Even as a boy of
five or six he was so aware of the difficulties of the life of man
that he would lie with his hat over his face, wishing that he
might never grow up. It would be an oversimplification to say
that this characteristic of his personality dictated the pattern of
his thinking, but undoubtedly the so-called "Hardy pessimism"
fitted into his own emotional cast. As a boy he was religious, and
it was expected that he would become a clergyman; but as he
matured, he lost all orthodox faith. Curiously enough, he never
became actively hostile to organized religion (indeed, he frequently went to church), but he did entertain the quixotic desire
to rid the Church of England of all supernatural belief, retaining only liturgical services with no affirmations and no supplica-
tions.

The labels of "pessimist" and "atheist" Hardy protested, for
his own definition of those terms was not that of most people. Of
the "fifty meanings" that are attached to the word "God," he
wrote, the only reasonable meaning is that of "the Cause of
Things," or their "invariable antecedent." In that sense, he said,
no modern thinker can be an atheist.

For the "Cause of Things" Hardy used a variety of names,
including "Unconscious Will," "Immanent Will," "Supreme
Mover," "Prime Force," "Doom," and "Spinner of the Years." By
all the terms he signified the chain of causation operating in
the affairs of man and nature. On occasion he said that "the Cause
of Things" must obviously be "either limited in power, unknow-
ing, or cruel," but usually he regarded this force as less malign
than blind and mindless, unaware of man but moving him in
such a way as to make mockery of his free will. In more hopeful moments, Hardy called himself a meliorist, believing that the
Unconscious Will was becoming aware of itself and that it might

in time develop the attributes of beneficence and sympathy toward man.

Since man was at best a pawn of the Unconscious Will, Hardy advocated ignoring what he could not control and concentrating on love, kindness, and decency, both to his fellows and to the lower creatures of the earth. In these terms, man, Hardy felt, has done better with his raw materials "than God has done with his." His own sensitivity to the sufferings of others was intense, and such poems as "The Puzzled Game-Birds" and "The Blinded Bird" are evidence of his horror at the mistreatment of the animal kingdom. To him, cruelty to dumb, uncomprehending creatures was a terrible parallel to the undeserved suffering of man in a universe oblivious of his needs.

Although Hardy's world view constantly comes through his writings, he specifically discounted himself as a philosopher, holding that the purpose of art is "to record impressions, not convictions." But it was his convictions which caused his choice of impressions, and many of his poems take on their final meaning because the deliberately simple events have a symbolic sense of universal importance. A poem as limpid as "In Time of 'The Breaking of Nations,' " for instance, was inspired by the sight of a horse ploughing a field in 1870, although the verses were not written until 1914; what is important in the poem is surely neither a reflection on the Franco-Prussian War nor direct comment on the First World War, but a cosmic awareness of the relationship of men and animals to events beyond their control. "The Convergence of the Twain" owes its staggering impact not to the sinking of the *Titanic* but to the brooding sense of the impersonal fate that caused it to go down.

The diction of Hardy's poetry is deliberately simple and unadorned, full of country phrases and almost totally innocent of "literary" language; part of its sense of timelessness is due to this simplicity, occasionally so reminiscent of Biblical language. Undoubtedly Hardy learned some of his mastery of colloquial, rough speech from the poetry of Browning, whom he greatly admired. Many of the situations in the poems derive from the minute records of incidents in rustic life that Hardy kept throughout his life. He may be said to have succeeded in fulfilling Wordsworth's object of choosing "incidents and situations from common life," relating them in "language really used by man," and "tracing in them, truly though not ostentatiously, the primary laws of our nature."

BIBLIOGRAPHY

The text of the poems follows the most satisfactory edition, *Collected Poems of Thomas Hardy* (Macmillan, New York, 1958), which contains all the shorter poems except those in the posthumous volume *Winter Words*, 1929.

Biography and Criticism:

Guerard, Albert J., ed., *Hardy: A Collection of Critical Essays.* Prentice-Hall, Englewood Cliffs, N.J., 1963.

Hardy, Florence Emily, *The Life of Thomas Hardy, 1840-1928.* Macmillan, London (St. Martin's Press, New York), 1962.

Hynes, Samuel L., *The Pattern of Hardy's Poetry.* University of North Carolina Press, Chapel Hill, 1961.

Southern Review, Summer 1940 (Thomas Hardy Centennial Issue).

Weber, Carl J., *Hardy of Wessex: His Life and Literary Career.* Columbia University Press, New York, 1940.

NEUTRAL TONES

We stood by a pond that winter day,
And the sun was white, as though chidden of God,
And a few leaves lay on the starving sod;
   —They had fallen from an ash, and were grey.

Your eyes on me were as eyes that rove
Over tedious riddles of years ago;
And some words played between us to and fro
   On which lost the more by our love.

The smile on your mouth was the deadest thing
Alive enough to have strength to die;   10
And a grin of bitterness swept thereby
   Like an ominous bird a-wing. . . .

Since then, keen lessons that love deceives,
And wrings with wrong, have shaped to me
Your face, and the God-curst sun, and a tree,
   And a pond edged with grayish leaves.

1867   [1898]

AT AN INN

When we as strangers sought
   Their catering care,
Veiled smiles bespoke their thought
   Of what we were.
They warmed as they opined
   Us more than friends—
That we had all resigned
   For love's dear ends.

And that swift sympathy
   With living love   10
Which quicks the world—maybe
   The spheres above,
Made them our ministers,
   Moved them to say,
"Ah, God, that bliss like theirs
   Would flush our day!"

And we were left alone
   As love's own pair;
Yet never the love-light shone
   Between us there!   20
But that which chilled the breath
   Of afternoon,
And palsied unto death
   The pane-fly's tune.

The kiss their zeal foretold,
   And now deemed come,
Came not: within his hold
   Love lingered numb.
Why cast he on our port
   A bloom not ours?   30
Why shaped us for his sport
   In after-hours?

As we seemed we were not
   That day afar,
And now we seem not what
   We aching are.
O severing sea and land,
   O laws of men,
Ere death, once let us stand
   As we stood then!   40

[1898]

---

24 *pane-fly's tune:* buzz of a fly in the window.

DRUMMER HODGE

I

They throw in Drummer Hodge, to rest
  Uncoffined—just as found:
His landmark is a kopje-crest
  That breaks the veldt around;
And foreign constellations west
  Each night above his mound.

II

Young Hodge the Drummer never knew—
  Fresh from his Wessex home—
The meaning of the broad Karoo,
  The Bush, the dusty loam,   10
And why uprose to nightly view
  Strange stars amid the gloam.

III

Yet portion of that unknown plain
  Will Hodge for ever be;
His homely Northern breast and brain
  Grow to some Southern tree,
And strange-eyed constellations reign
  His stars eternally.

[1901]

Drummer Hodge: fictional drummer boy in the Boer war.
3 *kopje:* South African hillock.
4 *veldt:* prairie.
5 *foreign constellations west:* Constellations of the Southern hemisphere move westward.
9 *Karoo:* dry plateau in South Africa.

SHELLEY'S SKYLARK

The Neighbourhood of Leghorn: March 1887

Somewhere afield here something lies
In Earth's oblivious eyeless trust
That moved a poet to prophecies—
A pinch of unseen, unguarded dust:

The dust of the lark that Shelley heard,
And made immortal through times to be;—
Though it only lived like another bird,
And knew not its immortality:

Lived its meek life; then, one day, fell—
A little ball of feather and bone;   10
And how it perished, when piped farewell,
And where it wastes, are alike unknown.

Maybe it rests in the loam I view,
Maybe it throbs in a myrtle's green,
Maybe it sleeps in the coming hue
Of a grape on the slopes of yon inland scene.

Go find it, faeries, go and find
That tiny pinch of priceless dust,
And bring a casket silver-lined,
And framed of gold that gems encrust;   20

And we will lay it safe therein,
And consecrate it to endless time;
For it inspired a bard to win
Ecstatic heights in thought and rhyme.

[1901]

Leghorn: In 1820 Shelley wrote "To a Skylark" near Leghorn.

"I SAID TO LOVE"

I said to Love,
"It is not now as in old days
When men adored thee and thy ways
    All else above;
Named thee the Boy, the Bright, the One
Who spread a heaven beneath the sun,"
    I said to Love.

I said to him,
"We now know more of thee than then;
We were but weak in judgment when,   10
    With hearts abrim,
We clamoured thee that thou would'st please
Inflict on us thine agonies,"
    I said to him.

I said to Love,
"Thou art not young, thou art not fair,
No elfin darts, no cherub air,
    Nor swan, nor dove
Are thine; but features pitiless,
And iron daggers of distress,"   20
    I said to Love.

"Depart then, Love! . . .
—Man's race shall perish, threatenest thou,
Without thy kindling coupling-vow?
The age to come the man of now
    Know nothing of?—
We fear not such a threat from thee;
We are too old in apathy!
Mankind shall cease.—So let it be,"
    I said to Love.   30

[1901]

---

[1] *Love:* here represented as the boy Cupid, son of Venus.

GOD-FORGOTTEN

I towered far, and lo! I stood within
The presence of the Lord Most High,
Sent thither by the sons of Earth, to win
    Some answer to their cry.

—"The Earth, sayest thou? The Human race?
By Me created? Sad its lot?
Nay: I have no remembrance of such place:
    Such world I fashioned not."—

—"O Lord, forgive me when I say
Thou spakest the word that made it all."—   10
"The Earth of men—let me bethink me. . . . Yea!
    I dimly do recall

"Some tiny sphere I built long back
(Mid millions of such shapes of mine)
So named . . . It perished, surely—not a wrack
    Remaining, or a sign?

"It lost my interest from the first,
My aims therefor succeeding ill;
Haply it died of doing as it durst?"—
    "Lord, it existeth still."—   20

"Dark, then, its life! For not a cry
Of aught it bears do I now hear;
Of its own act the threads were snapt whereby
    Its plaints had reached mine ear.

"It used to ask for gifts of good,
Till came its severance, self-entailed,
When sudden silence on that side ensued,
    And has till now prevailed.

"All other orbs have kept in touch;
Their voicings reach me speedily: 30

Thy people took upon them overmuch
  In sundering them from me!

"And it is strange—though sad enough—
  Earth's race should think that one whose call
Frames, daily, shining spheres of flawless stuff
  Must heed their tainted ball! . . .

"But sayest it is by pangs distraught,
  And strife, and silent suffering?—
Sore grieved am I that injury should be wrought
  Even on so poor a thing!   40

"Thou shouldst have learnt that *Not to Mend*
  For Me could mean but *Not to Know:*
Hence, Messengers! and straightway put an end
  To what men undergo." . . .

Homing at dawn, I thought to see
  One of the Messengers standing by.
—Oh, childish thought! . . . Yet often it comes to me
  When trouble hovers nigh.

[1901]

SONG OF HOPE

O sweet To-morrow!—
  After to-day
  There will away
This sense of sorrow.
Then let us borrow
Hope, for a gleaming
Soon will be streaming,
  Dimmed by no gray—
  No gray!

While the winds wing us   10
  Sighs from The Gone,

Nearer to dawn
Minute-beats bring us;
When there will sing us
Larks, of a glory
Waiting our story
　Further anon—
　　Anon!

Doff the black token,
　Don the red shoon,　　　　　　　　　　　20
　Right and retune
Viol-strings broken:
Null the words spoken
In speeches of rueing,
The night cloud is hueing,
　To-morrow shines soon—
　　Shines soon!

[1901]

THE PUZZLED GAME-BIRDS

Triolet

They are not those who used to feed us
When we were young—they cannot be—
These shapes that now bereave and bleed us?
They are not those who used to feed us,
For did we then cry, they would heed us.
—If hearts can house such treachery
They are not those who used to feed us
When we were young—they cannot be!

[1901]

---

20 *shoon:* shoes.
Triolet: stanza of eight lines in which the first line is the same as the fourth and seventh, and the second the same as the eighth; the rhyme scheme is abaaabab.

THE DARKLING THRUSH

I leant upon a coppice gate
    When Frost was spectre-gray,
And Winter's dregs made desolate
    The weakening eye of day.
The tangled bine-stems scored the sky
    Like strings of broken lyres,
And all mankind that haunted nigh
    Had sought their household fires.

The land's sharp features seemed to be
    The Century's corpse outleant,   10
His crypt the cloudy canopy,
    The wind his death-lament.
The ancient pulse of germ and birth
    Was shrunken hard and dry,
And every spirit upon earth
    Seemed fervourless as I.

At once a voice arose among
    The bleak twigs overhead
In a full-hearted evensong
    Of joy illimited;   20
An aged thrush, frail, gaunt, and small,
    In blast-beruffled plume,
Had chosen thus to fling his soul
    Upon the growing gloom.

So little cause for carolings
    Of such ecstatic sound
Was written on terrestrial things
    Afar or nigh around,
That I could think there trembled through
    His happy good-night air   30

---

[1] *coppice:* thicket.
[5] *bine:* climbing plant.
[10] *Century's corpse:* end of the nineteenth century.

Some blessed Hope, whereof he knew
And I was unaware.

December, 1900   [1901]

THE SELF-UNSEEING

Here is the ancient floor,
Footworn and hollowed and thin,
Here was the former door
Where the dead feet walked in.

She sat here in her chair,
Smiling into the fire;
He who played stood there,
Bowing it higher and higher.

Childlike, I danced in a dream;
Blessings emblazoned that day;   10
Everything glowed with a gleam;
Yet we were looking away!

                                        [1901]

THE CURATE'S KINDNESS

A WORKHOUSE IRONY

I

I thought they'd be strangers aroun' me,
  But she's to be there!
Let me jump out o' waggon and go back and drown me
  At Pummery or Ten-Hatches Weir.

II

I thought: "Well, I've come to the Union—
  The workhouse at last—

After honest hard work all the week, and Communion
  O' Zundays, these fifty years past.

III

" 'Tis hard; but," I thought, "never mind it:
  There's gain in the end:
And when I get used to the place I shall find it
  A home, and may find there a friend.

10

IV

"Life there will be better than t'other,
  For peace is assured.
The men in one wing and their wives in another
  Is strictly the rule of the Board."

V

Just then one young Pa'son arriving
  Steps up out of breath
To the side o' the waggon wherein we were driving
  To Union; and calls out and saith:

20

VI

"Old folks, that harsh order is altered,
  Be not sick of heart!
The Guardians they poohed and they pished and they
    paltered
  When urged not to keep you apart.

VII

" 'It is wrong,' I maintained, 'to divide them,
  Near forty years wed.'
'Very well, sir. We promise, then, they shall abide them
  In one wing together,' they said."

VIII

Then I sank—knew 'twas quite a foredone thing
  That misery should be
To the end! . . . To get freed of her there was the one
    thing
  Had made the change welcome to me.

30

IX

To go there was ending but badly;
  'Twas shame and 'twas pain;
"But anyhow," thought I, "thereby I shall gladly
  Get free of this forty years' chain."

X

I thought they'd be strangers aroun' me,
  But she's to be there!
Let me jump out o' waggon and go back and drown me
  At Pummery or Ten-Hatches Weir.   40

[1909]

1967

In five-score summers! All new eyes,
New minds, new modes, new fools, new wise;
New woes to weep, new joys to prize;

With nothing left of me and you
In that live century's vivid view
Beyond a pinch of dust or two;

A century which, if not sublime,
Will show, I doubt not, at its prime,
A scope above this blinkered time.

—Yet what to me how far above?   10
For I would only ask thereof
That thy worm should be my worm, Love!

1867   [1909]

THE DIVISION

Rain on the windows, creaking doors,
  With blasts that besom the green,
And I am here, and you are there,
  And a hundred miles between!

O were it but the weather, Dear,
  O were it but the miles
That summed up all our severance,
  There might be room for smiles.

But that thwart thing betwixt us twain,
  Which nothing cleaves or clears,   10
Is more than distance, Dear, or rain,
  And longer than the years!

[1909]

THE MAN HE KILLED

"Had he and I but met
  By some old ancient inn,
We should have sat us down to wet
  Right many a nipperkin!

"But ranged as infantry,
  And staring face to face,
I shot at him as he at me,
  And killed him in his place.

"I shot him dead because—
  Because he was my foe,   10
Just so: my foe of course he was;
  That's clear enough; although

---

2 *besom:* sweep.
4 *nipperkin:* half-pint of beer.

"He thought he'd 'list, perhaps,
    Off-hand like—just as I—
Was out of work—had sold his traps—
    No other reason why.

"Yes; quaint and curious war is!
    You shoot a fellow down
You'd treat if met where any bar is,
    Or help to half-a-crown."   20

1902   [1909]

CHANNEL FIRING

That night your great guns, unawares,
Shook all our coffins as we lay,
And broke the chancel window-squares,
We thought it was the Judgment-day

And sat upright. While drearisome
Arose the howl of wakened hounds:
The mouse let fall the altar-crumb,
The worms drew back into the mounds,

The glebe cow drooled. Till God called, "No;
It's gunnery practice out at sea   10
Just as before you went below;
The world is as it used to be:

"All nations striving strong to make
Red war yet redder. Mad as hatters
They do no more for Christés sake
Than you who are helpless in such matters.

"That this is not the judgment-hour
For some of them's a blessed thing,

---

13 *'list:* enlist.
9 *glebe cow:* cow kept on land attached to a rectory or vicarage.

For if it were they'd have to scour
Hell's floor for so much threatening. . . .   20

"Ha, ha. It will be warmer when
I blow the trumpet (if indeed
I ever do; for you are men,
And rest eternal sorely need)."

So down we lay again. "I wonder,
Will the world ever saner be,"
Said one, "than when He sent us under
In our indifferent century!"

And many a skeleton shook his head.
"Instead of preaching forty year,"   30
My neighbour Parson Thirdly said,
"I wish I had stuck to pipes and beer."

Again the guns disturbed the hour,
Roaring their readiness to avenge,
As far inland as Stourton Tower,
And Camelot, and starlit Stonehenge.

April, 1914   [1914]

THE CONVERGENCE OF THE TWAIN

Lines on the Loss of the Titanic

I

In a solitude of the sea
Deep from human vanity,
And the Pride of Life that planned her, stilly couches she.

35-6 *Stourton Tower . . . Stonehenge:* three places connected with England's remote past. Stourton is an ancient tower, Camelot the legendary seat of King Arthur, and Stonehenge a group of prehistoric stones with pre-Christian religious associations.
Titanic: The S. S. *Titanic,* reputed to be unsinkable, went down in April, 1912, when she struck an iceberg on her maiden voyage.

II

Steel chambers, late the pyres
　　Of her salamandrine fires,
Cold currents thrid, and turn to rhythmic tidal lyres.

III

Over the mirrors meant
　　To glass the opulent
The sea-worm crawls—grotesque, slimed, dumb, indifferent.

IV

Jewels in joy designed   10
　　To ravish the sensuous mind
Lie lightless, all their sparkles bleared and black and blind.

V

Dim moon-eyed fishes near
　　Gaze at the gilded gear
And query: "What does this vaingloriousness down here?"

VI

Well: while was fashioning
　　This creature of cleaving wing,
The Immanent Will that stirs and urges everything

VII

Prepared a sinister mate
　　For her—so gaily great—   20
A Shape of Ice, for the time far and dissociate.

VIII

And as the smart ship grew
　　In stature, grace, and hue,
In shadowy silent distance grew the Iceberg too.

---

5 *salamandrine:* The salamander was believed to be able to live in fire.
6 *thrid: thread.*

IX

Alien they seemed to be:
No mortal eye could see
The intimate welding of their later history,

X

Or sign that they were bent
By paths coincident
On being anon twin halves of one august event.   30

XI

Till the Spinner of the Years
Said "Now!" And each one hears,
And consummation comes, and jars two hemispheres.

[1914]

"AH, ARE YOU DIGGING ON MY GRAVE?"

"Ah, are you digging on my grave,
    My loved one?—planting rue?"
—"No: yesterday he went to wed
One of the brightest wealth has bred.
'It cannot hurt her now,' he said,
    'That I should not be true.'"

"Then who is digging on my grave?
    My nearest dearest kin?"
—"Ah, no: they sit and think, 'What use!
What good will planting flowers produce?   10
No tendance of her mound can loose
    Her spirit from Death's gin.'"

"But some one digs upon my grave?
    My enemy?—prodding sly?"

---

12 *gin:* snare.

—"Nay: when she heard you had passed the Gate
That shuts on all flesh soon or late,
She thought you no more worth her hate,
   And cares not where you lie."

"Then, who is digging on my grave?
   Say—since I have not guessed!"   20
—"O it is I, my mistress dear,
Your little dog, who still lives near,
And much I hope my movements here
   Have not disturbed your rest?"

"Ah, yes! *You* dig upon my grave . . .
   Why flashed it not on me
That one true heart was left behind!
What feeling do we ever find
To equal among human kind
   A dog's fidelity!"   30

"Mistress, I dug upon your grave
   To bury a bone, in case
I should be hungry near this spot
When passing on my daily trot.
I am sorry, but I quite forgot
   It was your resting-place."

                              [1914]

THE NEWCOMER'S WIFE

He paused on the sill of a door ajar
That screened a lively liquor-bar,
For the name had reached him through the door
Of her he had married the week before.

"We call her the Hack of the Parade;
But she was discreet in the games she played;
If slightly worn, she's pretty yet,
And gossips, after all, forget:

"And he knows nothing of her past;
I am glad the girl's in luck at last;   10
Such ones, though stale to native eyes,
Newcomers snatch at as a prize."

"Yes, being a stranger he sees her blent
Of all that's fresh and innocent,
Nor dreams how many a love-campaign
She had enjoyed before his reign!"

That night there was the splash of a fall
Over the slimy harbour-wall:
They searched, and at the deepest place
Found him with crabs upon his face.   20

[1914]

A POET

Attentive eyes, fantastic heed,
Assessing minds, he does not need,
Nor urgent writs to sup or dine,
Nor pledges in the rosy wine.

For loud acclaim he does not care
By the august or rich or fair,
Nor for smart pilgrims from afar,
Curious on where his hauntings are.

But soon or later, when you hear
That he has doffed this wrinkled gear,   10
Some evening, at the first star-ray,
Come to his graveside, pause and say:

"Whatever his message—glad or grim—
Two bright-souled women clave to him";

---

[14] *two bright-souled women:* presumably referring to Hardy's two marriages.

Stand and say that while day decays;
It will be word enough of praise.

[1914]

IN CHURCH

"And now to God the Father," he ends,
And his voice thrills up to the topmost tiles:
Each listener chokes as he bows and bends,
And emotion pervades the crowded aisles.
Then the preacher glides to the vestry-door,
And shuts it, and thinks he is seen no more.

The door swings softly ajar meanwhile,
And a pupil of his in the Bible class,
Who adores him as one without gloss or guile,
Sees her idol stand with a satisfied smile   10
And re-enact at the vestry-glass
Each pulpit gesture in deft dumb-show
That had moved the congregation so.

[1914]

THE BLINDED BIRD

So zestfully canst thou sing?
And all this indignity,
With God's consent, on thee!
Blinded ere yet a-wing
By the red-hot needle thou,
I stand and wonder how
So zestfully thou canst sing!

Resenting not such wrong,
Thy grievous pain forgot,

Eternal dark thy lot,   10
Groping thy whole life long,
After that stab of fire;
Enjailed in pitiless wire;
Resenting not such wrong!

Who hath charity? This bird.
Who suffereth long and is kind,
Is not provoked, though blind
And alive ensepulchred?
Who hopeth, endureth all things?
Who thinketh no evil, but sings?   20
Who is divine? This bird.

[1917]

THE OXEN

Christmas Eve, and twelve of the clock.
    "Now they are all on their knees,"
An elder said as we sat in a flock
    By the embers in hearthside ease.

We pictured the meek mild creatures where
    They dwelt in their strawy pen,
Nor did it occur to one of us there
    To doubt they were kneeling then.

So fair a fancy few would weave
    In these years! Yet, I feel,   10
If someone said on Christmas Eve,
    "Come; see the oxen kneel

"In the lonely barton by yonder coomb
    Our childhood used to know,"

The Oxen: According to an ancient belief, domestic oxen kneel at the hour of Christ's birth as the oxen knelt around the manger at Bethlehem.
13 *barton:* farmyard. *coomb:* ravine.

　　I should go with him in the gloom,
　　　Hoping it might be so.

[1917]

AT A COUNTRY FAIR

At a bygone Western country fair
I saw a giant led by a dwarf
With a red string like a long thin scarf;
How much he was the stronger there
　　The giant seemed unaware.

And then I saw that the giant was blind,
And the dwarf a shrewd-eyed little thing;
The giant, mild, timid, obeyed the string
As if he had no independent mind,
　　Or will of any kind.　　　　　　　　　　10

Wherever the dwarf decided to go
At his heels the other trotted meekly,
(Perhaps—I know not—reproaching weakly)
Like one Fate bade that it must be so,
　　Whether he wished or no.

Various sights in various climes
I have seen, and more I may see yet,
But that sight never shall I forget,
And have thought it the sorriest of pantomimes,
　　If once, a hundred times!　　　　　　　20

[1917]

HE FEARS HIS GOOD FORTUNE

There was a glorious time
At an epoch of my prime;
Mornings beryl-bespread,
And evenings golden-red;
   Nothing gray:
And in my heart I said,
"However this chanced to be,
It is too full for me,
Too rare, too rapturous, rash,
Its spell must close with a crash   10
   Some day!"

The radiance went on
Anon and yet anon,
And sweetness fell around
Like manna on the ground.
   "I've no claim,"
Said I, "to be thus crowned:
I am not worthy this:—
Must it not go amiss?—
Well . . . let the end foreseen   20
Come duly!—I am serene."
   —And it came.

[1917]

---

³ *beryl-bespread:* strewn with blue-green gems.

IN TIME OF
"THE BREAKING OF NATIONS"

I

Only a man harrowing clods
    In a slow silent walk
With an old horse that stumbles and nods
    Half asleep as they stalk.

II

Only thin smoke without flame
    From the heaps of couch-grass;
Yet this will go onward the same
    Though Dynasties pass.

III

Yonder a maid and her wight
    Come whispering by: 10
War's annals will fade into night
    Ere their story die.

[1917]

SNOW IN THE SUBURBS

Every branch big with it,
    Bent every twig with it;
Every fork like a white web-foot;
Every street and pavement mute:
Some flakes have lost their way, and grope back upward, when
Meeting those meandering down they turn and descend again.
    The palings are glued together like a wall,
    And there is no waft of wind with the fleecy fall.

A sparrow enters the tree,
    Whereon immediately   10

"The Breaking of Nations": Jeremiah 51:20.

A snow-lump thrice his own slight size
Descends on him and showers his head and eyes,
  And overturns him,
  And near inurns him,
And lights on a nether twig, when its brush
Starts off a volley of other lodging lumps with a rush.

  The steps are a blanched slope,
  Up which, with feeble hope,
A black cat comes, wide-eyed and thin;
  And we take him in.   20

[1925]

EPITAPH ON A PESSIMIST

  I'm Smith of Stoke, aged sixty-odd,
    I've lived without a dame
  From youth-time on; and would to God
    My dad had done the same.

(*From the French and Greek*)
[1925]

Gerard Manley Hopkins

[1844-1889]

To say that Hopkins was born in the middle of the nineteenth century, that he was influenced by the poetry of Keats, Tennyson, the Rossettis, and Swinburne, and by the aesthetic theory of Pater, and that his chief subject matter was the relationship between nature and religion is to suggest that he was a typical Victorian poet. Victorian he certainly was; typical, never. It is probably one of the great pieces of luck in literary history that Hopkins' poems were never widely known during his lifetime and that most of them remained unpublished until three decades after his death. To a generation used to the style of Tennyson and Browning, they might have seemed totally incomprehensible. When they were finally published in 1918, they burst upon a poetic world that was already aware of Yeats, Pound, and Eliot; the strangeness of Hopkins' diction and rhythms, his compression of whole sentences into a few words, and his deliberate disregard of normal syntax brought his poems almost immediate admiration, if not always for the right reasons. Within a dozen years after their publication, Hopkins was a model for a whole movement in English poetry. Today, experimental poetry no longer needs the sanction of the past, and it is easier to see that, however admirable his own achievement was, Hopkins' poetry has not been a great model for other poets to emulate. He remains unique, a Victorian in many of his ideas, a great and idiosyncratic experimenter in some of his forms.

Hopkins was born in a London suburb, one of seven artistically gifted children in a cultivated and religious household, Anglican in its persuasion. In 1863, after attending a school in London, Hopkins went to Balliol College, Oxford, to study classics. Walter Pater was, for a time, his tutor, and at Oxford Hopkins came to know Dr. Pusey, one of the leaders of the Oxford Movement, the Broad Church classicist Benjamin Jowett, and Robert Bridges, who later became Poet Laureate and who was the first (and somewhat reluctant) editor of Hopkins' poetry. Hopkins, who had always been devout, became increasingly interested in the High Church movement at Oxford, at least partially because it offered him a satisfactory form of the discipline he felt he so badly needed. Typical of the restraint he imposed upon himself is the regimen he undertook during Lent, 1866: "No pudding on Sundays. No tea except to keep one awake, and then without sugar. . . . Not to sit in armchair except I can work in no other way. Ash Wednesday and Good Friday bread and water." In the autumn of 1866 he was received into the Roman Catholic Church by John Henry Newman. His conversion was the cause of great anguish to his family, and the consequent partial estrangement was deeply painful to Hopkins.

In the autumn of 1867, after taking a first-class degree in classics at Oxford, he went to Birmingham to work under Newman at the Oratory School, with the idea of eventually taking Holy Orders. A year later he became a novice in the Jesuit order; the record of his next decade is largely the history of his novitiate in London, Lancashire, and, most notably, St. Beuno's College in North Wales. He acted as priest at several churches in England after his ordination, taught classics at a Roman Catholic college in Lancashire, and in 1884 became Professor of Classics in the Catholic University College in Dublin. He died of typhoid fever in Dublin shortly before his forty-fifth birthday.

As a boy Hopkins had written a good deal of poetry, some of which is most accomplished. He continued his writing at Oxford, producing, among others, the beautiful little poems "Heaven-Haven" and "The Habit of Perfection." When he became a Jesuit, he determined to give up the writing of poetry as a voluntary self-denial, in order that he might achieve the discipline and selflessness prescribed for Jesuits by their founder, St. Ignatius

Loyola. The poetry written before this time, he said, "I burnt
. . . and resolved to write no more, as not belonging to my profession, unless it were by the wish of my superiors." Fortunately,
copies of many of these poems had been made and were saved.
For seven years he endured the abstention from poetry, surely
the most painful discipline he could know. The renunciation is
typical of the man and of his priesthood; there is no question of
Hopkins' faith or sense of duty, but his whole life as a priest was
difficult because he was consumed with a need to give himself
up wholly to his religion. When he felt spiritual dryness, or when
he became aware of his own very human failings, the sense of
the disparity between aspiration and achievement threw him into
an agony that few men can know. The pain he felt is indicated
in such poems as "No worst, there is none": "O the mind, mind
has mountains; cliffs of fall / Frightful, sheer, no-man-fathomed.
Hold them cheap / May who ne'er hung there."

After becoming a Jesuit, Hopkins resumed writing poetry
with an ode on the sinking of the ship *Deutschland*. At the time,
he was studying theology at St. Beuno's, "Away in the loveable
west, / On a pastoral forehead of Wales." His own account of the
writing of the poem shows how little poetry had been out of his
mind during the silence of seven years:

> When in the winter of '75 the *Deutschland* was wrecked
> in the mouth of the Thames and five Franciscan nuns, exiles
> from Germany by the Falck Laws, aboard of her were
> drowned I was affected by the account and happening to say
> so to my rector he said that he wished some one would write
> a poem on the subject. On this hint I set to work and, though
> my hand was out at first, produced one. I had long had
> haunting my ear the echo of a new rhythm, which now I real-
> ized on paper.

He offered the poem to the Jesuit magazine, the *Month*, but its
"oddnesses could not but dismay an editor's eye, so that . . .
though at first they accepted it, after a time they withdrew and
dared not print it."

"The Wreck of the Deutschland" has been to many readers,
as it was to Robert Bridges, "a great dragon folded in the gate
to forbid all entrance" to the poetry of Hopkins, but like his
other poems, it most easily yields itself when read aloud. It will
probably always occupy a central position in his poetry, for it considers almost everything that he ever used as themes in his other

works. Hopkins was always occupied with the quality of paradox in nature and God; or, it might be more accurate to say, he
was fascinated that they, like coins, display two totally different
aspects. The poem considers nature as both beautiful and terrible; God as both comforter and destroyer; religious experience
as both meditation and sudden conversion, as both private and
public.

There are four major sections in the poem. The first section
(Part the First) introduces the theme of man's difficulty in accepting the terror and dread that he finds in God, and Hopkins
gives as an example his own perception of the frown of God's
face "Before me, the hurtle of hell / Behind." From this he proceeds to the parallel of Christ's own Passion, and he concludes
the section with a supplication to be mastered by God. The second section (stanzas 11-17) gives an impressionistic but fairly
straightforward account of the physical circumstances of the
wreck. The third section (stanzas 18-31) moves to the consideration of the "tall nun," the meaning of her emotions and cries, the
realization that her suffering parallels his own and that of Christ's
Passion, and the likeness between the nun and the Virgin Mary
in her having given figurative birth to Christ in her acceptance
of His purpose. The final section (stanzas 32-35) triumphantly
states the mercy of God in what seems terrible, and concludes
with a prayer to the nun to intercede with God for the recon-
version of England.

"The echo of a new rhythm" that had been haunting Hopkins' ear and that was introduced for the first time in this poem
is what he called Sprung Rhythm. Actually, Hopkins did not intend to imply that the principle was a totally new one, although
it had largely fallen out of use in English poetry for two centuries. Some of the sources on which he drew for his practice
were the choruses of Milton's *Samson Agonistes,* the rhythms of
nursery rhymes, the wide variation of syllabification in Shakespeare's blank verse, the musical setting of texts, Old English
poetry, and Greek verse. In all of them a line may contain a vary-
ing number of actual syllables while retaining a constant number
of accents. Thus, for instance, in such sonnets as "The Windhover," there are five primary accents in each line, although there
is great variation in the number of syllables. In scanning lines of
Sprung Rhythm, Hopkins marked only the stresses, putting them
at the beginning of each foot and letting the unaccented syllables

fall as they would. For example, the final stress in the first line of "The Windhover" is on "king-," so the first two syllables of the second line are part of the same foot, and the first full foot of the second line begins with "daylight's." A careful study of the "Author's Preface" will explain the system sufficiently for the reader who is willing to follow his ear. Hopkins explained that he used Sprung Rhythm because it came closest to "the rhythm of prose, that is the native and natural rhythm of speech, the least forced, the most rhetorical and emphatic of all possible rhythms." It is interesting to notice that though Hopkins allowed himself such freedom with rhythm, he seldom used any but standard verse forms; many poems which at first glance seem anarchical turn out to be strict sonnets in the number of lines used, the rhyme pattern, and the rhetorical structure. (He called "Spelt from Sibyl's Leaves"—in which the lines have as many as nineteen or twenty syllables—"the longest sonnet ever written.")

The range of subject and emotion in his poetry is not great, but Hopkins put such compression of thought into his poems that it has been said he alone of the great Victorian poets would still be interesting for his thought if his poems were paraphrased in prose. His startling imagery, rhyme, assonance, and alliteration were always at the service of the idea that he had in mind.

If it is frustrating to search for Hopkins' poetic progenitors in formal matters, it is at least easy to isolate the philosopher to whom he is most indebted in both thought and aesthetic conceptions. Duns Scotus ("the Subtle Doctor"), a medieval Franciscan, provided Hopkins with the theological and philosophical sanction he needed for his own way of thinking. Scotus said that each created thing has its own *haecceitas* ("thisness") or individuality, while at the same time it is mysteriously like all other members of its species and, indeed, like all creation. Or, to put it another way, each created thing partakes of both the individual and the general. The perception of both individual natures and general natures is a simultaneous act of the intellect and the senses. For Hopkins this was important because it meant that perception of external nature is not a lower form of knowledge but is at one with intellectual and spiritual knowledge. Love of nature is therefore not a clog on man's spiritual nature and it need not be a hindrance to his spiritual duties.

Hopkins' own turn of mind was toward the individual: his notebooks are full of minute descriptions of trees, clouds, or rocks, in each case trying to record an accurate account of the particular specimen at hand; his drawings are as minutely faithful to particulars as his extremely accomplished pencil could make them. Applied to poetic description, this means that he seeks to find what is particular in each thing he describes. For instance, in "As kingfishers catch fire," he seeks the special quality inherent in kingfishers, dragonflies, stones, or bells:

> Each mortal thing does one thing and the same:
> Deals out that being indoors each one dwells;
> Selves—goes itself; *myself* it speaks and spells

But if "each mortal thing" speaks "*myself*," it is also doing "one thing and the same" as all other mortal things. It is thus both individual and general. Hopkins' interest in the dual nature of all life is implicit in his constant consideration of things, creatures, and events as compounded of unity and diversity, of change and stability, and of order and haphazardness, even in his fondness for words indicating duality or plurality of appearance, such as "pied," "dappled," and "brindled." In the world of particularity and change, God "fathers-forth whose beauty is past change."

The pattern of *haecceitas* (or individuality) Hopkins liked to call "inscape," and the feeling that the perception of inscape aroused in him he called "instress." Frequently he used "instress" (or "stress") in an extended sense to mean "understanding" or "to cause to understand." His constant search for unusual, dialectal, archaic, or even coined words was not undertaken in love of strangeness for its own sake, but rather that the freshness of the words might convey the inscape of what he was describing, to create instress for the reader. Some of the greatest nineteenth-century poetry was poetry of nature; Hopkins is perhaps unique in that the persistent vividness of his natural description is actually a logical extension of his theological and philosophical beliefs.

Much of Hopkins' early poetry has a Keats-like lushness of imagery; the exuberance of his experimental middle period pushes the sensuous qualities of nature to an extreme in his joy (even in "The Wreck of the Deutschland") in the revelation of God in the phenomenal world. In his late "terrible" sonnets, he moves into a much more austere, stark form of poetry. Most of these sonnets deal with Hopkins' sensitive horror at his inability to live up to his own impossibly high standards in religion and poetry, but in all their agony there is no disbelief in God, only consternation at the poet's inability to understand Him. The diction of these late poems is comparatively direct and simple; their whole mood of suffering is almost always completely intelligible at first reading. Probably, like Donne, whose religious poetry grew out of the erotic poetry of his young manhood, Hopkins could never have written these taut, spare, splendid lyrics of suffering without the experimentation that preceded them. To proceed from the serenity of the early poems through the dazzling beauty of Hopkins' middle period to the frightening magnificence of the "terrible" sonnets is an experience that leaves few sensitive readers without a permanent alteration of their poetic perceptions.

BIBLIOGRAPHY

The best and most complete edition is *Poems of Gerard Manley Hopkins,* ed. Robert Bridges and W. H. Gardner. Third edition. (Oxford University Press, New York and London, 1948).

Biography and Criticism:

Gardner, W. H., *Gerard Manley Hopkins (1844-1889): A Study of Poetic Idiosyncrasy in Relation to Poetic Tradition.* 2 vols. Secker and Warburg, London, 1948-1949.

Kenyon Critics, *Gerard Manley Hopkins.* New Directions, Norfolk, Conn., 1945.

Pick, John, *Gerard Manley Hopkins, Priest and Poet.* Oxford University Press, London, New York, Toronto, 1942.

Ruggles, Eleanor, *Gerard Manley Hopkins.* John Lane, The Bodley Head, London, 1947.

Weyand, Norman, ed., *Immortal Diamond: Studies in Gerard Manley Hopkins,* Sheed and Ward, New York, 1949.

HEAVEN-HAVEN

A Nun Takes the Veil

I have desired to go
　　Where springs not fail,
To fields where flies no sharp and sided hail
　　And a few lilies blow.

And I have asked to be
　　Where no storms come,
Where the green swell is in the havens dumb,
　　And out of the swing of the sea.

1866

THE HABIT OF PERFECTION

　　Elected Silence, sing to me
　　And beat upon my whorlèd ear,
　　Pipe me to pastures still and be
　　The music that I care to hear.

　　Shape nothing, lips; be lovely-dumb:
　　It is the shut, the curfew sent
　　From there where all surrenders come
　　Which only makes you eloquent.

　　Be shellèd, eyes, with double dark
　　And find the uncreated light:
　　This ruck and reel which you remark
　　Coils, keeps, and teases simple sight.

10

---

2 *whorlèd:* coiled, or in loops.
11 *ruck and reel:* throng and spiral (of material existence).
12 *Coils, keeps:* snares, emprisons.

Palate, the hutch of tasty lust,
Desire not to be rinsed with wine:
The can must be so sweet, the crust
So fresh that come in fasts divine!

Nostrils, your careless breath that spend
Upon the stir and keep of pride,
What relish shall the censers send
Along the sanctuary side!　　　　　　　　　　　20

O feel-of-primrose hands, O feet
That want the yield of plushy sward,
But you shall walk the golden street
And you unhouse and house the Lord.

And, Poverty, be thou the bride
And now the marriage feast begun,
And lily-coloured clothes provide
Your spouse not laboured-at nor spun.

1866

AUTHOR'S PREFACE*

The poems in this book are written some in Running Rhythm, the common rhythm in English use, some in Sprung Rhythm, and some in a mixture of the two. And those in the common rhythm are some counterpointed, some not.

Common English rhythm, called Running Rhythm above, is measured by feet of either two or three syllables and (putting

---

13 *hutch:* cupboard.
18 *keep:* maintenance.
22 *want:* lack.
24 *unhouse and house:* remove (the consecrated wafer) from the tabernacle and consume.
27 *lily-coloured:* see *Matthew* 6:28-29.
* *Preface:* written about 1883 for the manuscript book of Hopkins' poems which was kept by Robert Bridges. Bridges said that it applied only to those poems after Hopkins had become a Jesuit (i.e., "The Wreck of the Deutschland" and those poems which succeeded it).

aside the imperfect feet at the beginning and end of lines and also some unusual measures, in which feet seem to be paired together and double or composite feet to arise) never more or less.

Every foot has one principal stress or accent, and this or the syllable it falls on may be called the Stress of the foot and the other part, the one or two unaccented syllables, the Slack Feet (and the rhythms made out of them) in which the stress comes first are called Falling Feet and Falling Rhythms, feet and rhythm in which the slack comes first are called Rising Feet and Rhythms, and if the stress is between two slacks there will be Rocking Feet and Rhythms. These distinctions are real and true to nature; but for purposes of scanning it is a great convenience to follow the example of music and take the stress always first, as the accent or the chief accent always comes first in a musical bar. If this is done there will be in common English verse only two possible feet—the so-called accentual Trochee and Dactyl, and correspondingly only two possible uniform rhythms, the so-called Trochaic and Dactylic. But they may be mixed and then what the Greeks called a Logaoedic Rhythm arises. These are the facts and according to these the scanning of ordinary regularly-written English verse is very simple indeed and to bring in other principles is here unnecessary.

But because verse written strictly in these feet and by these principles will become same and tame the poets have brought in licences and departures from rule to give variety, and especially when the natural rhythm is rising, as in the common ten-syllable or five-foot verse, rhymed or blank. These irregularities are chiefly Reversed Feet and Reversed or Counterpoint Rhythm, which two things are two steps or degrees of licence in the same kind. By a reversed foot I mean the putting the stress where, to judge by the rest of the measure, the slack should be and the slack where the stress, and this is done freely at the beginning of a line and, in the course of a line, after a pause; only scarcely ever in the second foot or place and never in the last, unless when the poet designs some extraordinary effect; for these places are characteristic and sensitive and cannot well be touched. But the reversal of the first foot and of some middle foot after a strong pause is a thing so natural that our poets have generally done it, from Chaucer down, without remark and it commonly passes unnoticed and cannot be said to amount to a formal change of rhythm, but rather is that irregularity which all natural growth and motion shews. If however the reversal is repeated in two feet running, especially so as to include the sensitive second foot, it must be due either to great want of ear or else is a calculated effect, the superinducing or *mounting* of a new rhythm upon the old; and since the new or mounted rhythm is actually heard and at the same time the mind naturally supplies the natural or standard foregoing rhythm, for we do not forget what the rhythm is that by rights we should be hearing, two rhythms are in some manner running at once and we have something answerable to counterpoint in music, which is two or more strains of tune going on together, and this is Counterpoint Rhythm. Of this kind of verse Milton is the great master and the choruses of *Samson Agonistes* are written throughout in it—but with the disadvantage that he does not let the reader clearly know what the ground-rhythm is meant to be and so they have struck most readers as merely irregular. And in fact if you counterpoint throughout, since one only of the counter rhythms is actually heard, the other is really destroyed or cannot come to exist, and what is written is one rhythm only and probably Sprung Rhythm, of which I now speak.

Sprung Rhythm, as used in this book, is measured by feet of from one to four syllables, regularly, and for particular effects any number of weak or slack syllables may be used. It has one stress, which falls on the only syllable, if there is only one, or, if there are more, then scanning as above, on the first, and so gives rise to four sorts of feet, a monosyllable and the so-called accentual Trochee, Dactyl, and the First Paeon. And there will be four corresponding natural rhythms; but nominally the feet are mixed and any one may follow any other. And hence Sprung Rhythm differs from Running Rhythm in having or being only one nominal rhythm, a mixed or "logaoedic" one, instead of three, but on the other hand in having twice the flexibility of foot, so that any two stresses may either follow one another running or be divided by one, two, or three slack syllables. But strict Sprung Rhythm cannot be counterpointed. In Sprung Rhythm, as in logaoedic rhythm generally, the feet are assumed to be equally long or strong and their seeming inequality is made up by pause or stressing.

Remark also that it is natural in Sprung Rhythm for the lines to be *rove over*, that is for the scanning of each line immediately to take up that of the one before, so that if the first has one or more syllables at its end the other must have so many the less at its beginning; and in fact the scanning runs on without break from the beginning, say, of a stanza to the end and all the stanza is one long strain, though written in lines asunder.

Two licences are natural to Sprung Rhythm. The one is rests, as in music; but of this an example is scarcely to be found in this book, unless in the *Echos*, second line. The other is *hangers* or *outrides*, that is one, two, or three slack syllables added to a foot and not counting in the nominal scanning. They are so called because they seem to hang below the line or ride forward or backward from it in another dimension than the line itself, according to a principle needless to explain here. These outriding half feet or hangers are marked by a loop underneath them, and plenty of them will be found.

The other marks are easily understood, namely accents, where the reader might be in doubt which syllable should have the stress; slurs, that is loops *over* syllables, to tie them together into the time of one; little loops at the end of a line to shew that the rhyme goes on to the first letter of the next line; what in music are called pauses ⌒, to shew that the syllable should be dwelt on; and twirls ⁓, to mark reversed or counterpointed rhythm.

Note on the nature and history of Sprung Rhythm—Sprung Rhythm is the most natural of things. For (1) it is the rhythm of common speech and of written prose, when rhythm is perceived in them. (2) It is the rhythm of all but the most monotonously regular music, so that in the words of choruses and refrains and in songs written closely to music it arises. (3) It is found in nursery rhymes, weather saws, and so on; because, however these may have been once made in running rhythm, the terminations having dropped off by the change of language, the stresses come together and so the rhythm is sprung. (4) It arises in common verse when reversed or counterpointed, for the same reason.

But nevertheless in spite of all this and though Greek and Latin lyric verse, which is well known, and the old English verse seen in "Pierce Ploughman" are in sprung rhythm, it has in fact ceased to be used since the Elizabethan age, Greene being the last writer who can be said to have recognized it. For perhaps there was not, down to our days, a single, even short, poem in English in which sprung rhythm is employed—not for single effects or in fixed places—but as the governing principle of the scansion. I say this because the contrary has been asserted: if it is otherwise the poem should be cited.

Some of the sonnets in this book are in five-foot, some in six-foot or Alexandrine lines.

Nos. 13* and 22 are Curtal-Sonnets, that is they are constructed in proportions resembling those of the sonnet proper, namely, 6+4 instead of 8+6, with however a halfline tailpiece (so that the equation is rather $1\frac{2}{3} + \frac{3}{4} = 2\frac{1}{4} = 10\frac{1}{2}$).

THE WRECK OF THE DEUTSCHLAND

To the Happy Memory of Five Franciscan Nuns
Exiles by the Falk Laws
Drowned Between Midnight and Morning of
Dec. 7th, 1875

PART THE FIRST

1

Thou mastering me
  God! giver of breath and bread;
World's strand, sway of the sea;
  Lord of living and dead;
Thou hast bound bones and veins in me, fastened me
    flesh,
And after it almost unmade, what with dread,
  Thy doing: and dost thou touch me afresh?
Over again I feel thy finger and find thee.

2

I did say yes
  O at lightning and lashed rod;   10

---

* 13: "Pied Beauty."
Falk Laws: The nuns had been forced to leave Germany because of the decrees against Roman Catholics passed under Bismarck's government in 1873. They were drowned when their ship struck sandbanks near the mouth of the Thames; the ship was en route to America.
3 World's . . . sea: border of the world, mover of the sea.

Thou heardst me truer than tongue confess
    Thy terror, O Christ, O God;
Thou knowest the walls, altar and hour and night:
    The swoon of a heart that the sweep and the hurl of
        thee trod
      Hard down with a horror of height:
And the midriff astrain with leaning of, laced with fire of
    stress.

3

    The frown of his face
    Before me, the hurtle of hell
Behind, where, where was a, where was a place?
    I whirled out wings that spell   20
And fled with a fling of the heart to the heart of the Host.
My heart, but you were dovewinged, I can tell,
    Carrier-witted, I am bold to boast,
To flash from the flame to the flame then, tower from the
    grace to the grace.

4

    I am soft sift
    In an hourglass—at the wall
Fast, but mined with a motion, a drift,
    And it crowds and it combs to the fall;
I steady as a water in a well, to a poise, to a pane,
But roped with, always, all the way down from the tall   30
    Fells or flanks of the voel, a vein
Of the gospel proffer, a pressure, a principle, Christ's gift.

---

16 *laced:* girdled. *stress:* For this word, see the introduction to Hopkins.
20 *that spell:* meaning either "that time" or "(wings) that help."
23 *Carrier-witted:* with the homing instinct like that of the carrier pigeon.
24 *tower:* to rise.
25 *sift:* as of sand. The contrast in this stanza is between the constantly falling motion of sand in an hourglass and the steadiness of the surface of the water in a well.
28 *combs:* drifts.
29 *pane:* glassy surface.
30 *roped:* fed with twisting streams.
31 *fells:* ridges. *voel:* bare hill.

5

I kiss my hand
  To the stars, lovely-asunder
Starlight, wafting him out of it; and
  Glow, glory in thunder;
Kiss my hand to the dappled-with-damson west:
Since, tho' he is under the world's splendour and
    wonder,
  His mystery must be instressed, stressed;
For I greet him the days I meet him, and bless when I
    understand.   40

6

Not out of his bliss
  Springs the stress felt
Nor first from heaven (and few know this)
  Swings the stroke dealt—
Stroke and a stress that stars and storms deliver,
That guilt is hushed by, hearts are flushed by and
    melt—
  But it rides time like riding a river
(And here the faithful waver, the faithless fable and miss).

7

It dates from day
  Of his going in Galilee;   50
Warm-laid grave of a womb-life grey;
  Manger, maiden's knee;
The dense and the driven Passion, and frightful sweat;
Thence the discharge of it, there its swelling to be,
  Though felt before, though in high flood yet—

---

37 *damson:* red-purple, the color of damson plums and of the sunset.

38-9 *Since . . . stressed:* i.e., the nature of God, behind the physical world, must be brought home to man's mind.

41-4 *Not out . . . dealt:* The meaning of these four lines is that the nature of God is not to be comprehended in the happiness of Christ on earth; it is, instead, made manifest in His Incarnation and Passion, mentioned in the next stanza.

47 *rides time . . . river:* i.e., is timeless, or is above time, which flows by like a river.

What none would have known of it, only the heart, being
       hard at bay,

8

    Is out with it! Oh,
      We lash with the best or worst
    Word last! How a lush-kept plush-capped sloe
      Will, mouthed to flesh-burst,   60
Gush!—flush the man, the being with it, sour or sweet
Brim, in a flash, full!—Hither then, last or first,
      To hero of Calvary, Christ's feet—
Never ask if meaning it, wanting it, warned of it—men go.

9

    Be adored among men,
      God, three-numberèd form;
    Wring thy rebel, dogged in den,
      Man's malice, with wrecking and storm.
Beyond saying sweet, past telling of tongue,
Thou art lightning and love, I found it, a winter and
      warm;   70
      Father and fondler of heart thou hast wrung:
Hast thy dark descending and most art merciful then.

10

    With an anvil-ding
      And with fire in him forge thy will
    Or rather, rather then, stealing as Spring
      Through him, melt him but master him still:
Whether at once, as once at a crash Paul,
Or as Austin, a lingering-out swéet skíll,
      Make mercy in all of us, out of us all
Mastery, but be adored, but be adored King.   80

---

59 *sloe:* fruit with pungent flavor.
77 *Paul:* the conversion of St. Paul in an instant is compared to the slower
conversion of St. Augustine (Austin).

PART THE SECOND

11

"Some find me a sword; some
    The flange and the rail; flame,
Fang, or flood" goes Death on drum,
    And storms bugle his fame.
But wé dream we are rooted in earth—Dust!
Flesh falls within sight of us, we, though our flower the
        same,
    Wave with the meadow, forget that there must
The sour scythe cringe, and the blear share come.

12

On Saturday sailed from Bremen,
    American-outward-bound,   90
Take settler and seamen, tell men with women,
    Two hundred souls in the round—
O Father, not under thy feathers nor ever as guessing
The goal was a shoal, of a fourth the doom to be
        drowned;
    Yet did the dark side of the bay of thy blessing
Not vault them, the millions of rounds of thy mercy not
        reeve even them in?

13

Into the snows she sweeps,
    Hurling the haven behind,
The Deutschland, on Sunday; and so the sky keeps,
    For the infinite air is unkind,   100
And the sea flint-flake, black-backed in the regular
        blow,
    Sitting Eastnortheast, in cursed quarter, the wind;
    Wiry and white-fiery and whirlwind-swivellèd snow
Spins to the widow-making unchilding unfathering deeps.

---

82 *flange and the rail:* These words seem to suggest instruments of torture.
88 *scythe cringe:* i.e., either that the scythe will bend to us (the grasses) or
that the scythe will make us cringe. *blear share:* lusterless plowshare.
95 *bay:* architectural recess or shelter.
96 *reeve:* fasten, as with the ropes of a ship.

14

She drove in the dark to leeward,
        She struck—not a reef or a rock
But the combs of a smother of sand: night drew her
        Dead to the Kentish Knock;
And she beat the bank down with her bows and the
        ride of her keel:
The breakers rolled on her beam with ruinous shock;   110
        And canvas and compass, the whorl and the wheel
Idle for ever to waft her or wind her with, these she
        endured.

15

Hope had grown grey hairs,
        Hope had mourning on,
Trenched with tears, carved with cares,
        Hope was twelve hours gone;
And frightful a nightfall folded rueful a day
Nor rescue, only rocket and lightship, shone,
        And lives at last were washing away:
To the shrouds they took,—they shook in the hurling and
        horrible airs.   120

16

One stirred from the rigging to save
        The wild woman-kind below,
With a rope's end round the man, handy and brave—
        He was pitched to his death at a blow,
For all his dreadnought breast and braids of thew:
They could tell him for hours, dandled the to and fro
        Through the cobbled foam-fleece, what could he do
With the burl of the fountains of air, buck and the flood of
        the wave?

---

111 *whorl:* propeller.
125 *thew:* muscle.
127 *cobbled:* hurled like a stone.
128 *burl:* fullness.

17

They fought with God's cold—
And they could not and fell to the deck   130
(Crushed them) or water (and drowned them) or
    rolled
With the sea-romp over the wreck.
Night roared, with the heart-break hearing a heart-
    broke rabble,
The woman's wailing, the crying of child without
    check—
Till a lioness arose breasting the babble,
A prophetess towered in the tumult, a virginal tongue told.

18

Ah, touched in your bower of bone
Are you! turned for an exquisite smart,
Have you! make words break from me here all alone,
Do you!—mother of being in me, heart.   140
O unteachably after evil, but uttering truth,
Why tears! is it? tears; such a melting, a madrigal start!
Never-eldering revel and river of youth,
What can it be, this glee? the good you have there of your
    own?

19

Sister, a sister calling
A master, her master and mine!—
And the inboard seas run swirling and hawling;
The rash smart sloggering brine
Blinds her; but she that weather sees one thing, one;
Has one fetch in her: she rears herself to divine   150
Ears, and the call of the tall nun
To the men in the tops and the tackle rode over the storm's
    brawling.

---

141 *after:* in search of.
144 *glee:* in the sense both of joy and of a vocal composition resembling a
madrigal.
147 *hawling:* veering.
148 *sloggering:* hitting with heavy blows.
150 *fetch:* contrivance, dodge.

20

She was first of a five and came
Of a coifèd sisterhood.
(O Deutschland, double a desperate name!
O world wide of its good!
But Gertrude, lily, and Luther, are two of a town,
Christ's lily and beast of the waste wood:
From life's dawn it is drawn down,
Abel is Cain's brother and breasts they have sucked the
    same.)   160

21

Loathed for a love men knew in them,
Banned by the land of their birth,
Rhine refused them. Thames would ruin them;
Surf, snow, river and earth
Gnashed: but thou art above, thou Orion of light;
Thy unchancelling poising palms were weighing the
    worth,
Thou martyr-master: in thy sight
Storm flakes were scroll-leaved flowers, lily showers—sweet
    heaven was astrew in them.

22

Five! the finding and sake
And cipher of suffering Christ.   170
Mark, the mark is of man's make
And the word of it Sacrificed.
But he scores it in scarlet himself on his own bespoken,
Before-time-taken, dearest prizèd and priced—

---

154 *coifèd:* wearing nun's headpieces.
157 *town:* Eisleben, where lived both St. Gertrude, German Roman Catholic
mystic, and Martin Luther.
165 *Orion:* the constellation of the Hunter, here standing for God, who
hunted the nuns out of their "chancel" in order that they might find their
salvation.
169 *Five:* Hopkins makes poetic capital from the number of the nuns, for it
parallels the five wounds of Christ. Some holy persons such as St. Francis of
Assisi have received the stigmata of Christ's wounds on their own bodies.
169-70 *finding . . . cipher:* symbols or emblems.

Stigma, signal, cinquefoil token
For lettering of the lamb's fleece, ruddying of the rose-flake.

23

Joy fall to thee, father Francis,
Drawn to the Life that died;
With the gnarls of the nails in thee, niche of the
lance, his
Lovescape crucified   180
And seal of his seraph-arrival! and these thy daughters
And five-livèd and leavèd favour and pride,
Are sisterly sealed in wild waters,
To bathe in his fall-gold mercies, to breathe in his all-fire
glances.

24

Away in the loveable west,
On a pastoral forehead of Wales,
I was under a roof here, I was at rest,
And they the prey of the gales;
She to the black-about air, to the breaker, the thickly
Falling flakes, to the throng that catches and quails   190
Was calling "O Christ, Christ, come quickly":
The cross to her she calls Christ to her, christens her wild-
worst Best.

25

The majesty! what did she mean?
Breathe, arch and original Breath.
Is it love in her of the being as her lover had been?
Breathe, body of lovely Death.
They were else-minded then, altogether, the men
Woke thee with a *we are perishing* in the weather of
Gennesareth.
Or is it that she cried for the crown then,
The keener to come at the comfort for feeling the
combating keen?   200

---

175 *cinquefoil:* having five leaves.
195 *lover:* Christ.
197 *They:* Christ's disciples, who were frightened by the storm on the sea
of Gennesareth and by Christ's walking on the waves (*Matthew* 14: 22-33).

26

For how to the heart's cheering
　The down-dugged ground-hugged grey
Hovers off, the jay-blue heavens appearing
　Of pied and peeled May!
Blue-beating and hoary-glow height; or night, still
　　higher,
　With belled fire and the moth-soft Milky Way,
　What by your measure is the heaven of desire,
The treasure never eyesight got, nor was ever guessed
　　what for the hearing?

27

No, but it was not these.
　The jading and jar of the cart,   210
Time's tasking, it is fathers that asking for ease
　Of the sodden-with-its-sorrowing heart,
Not danger, electrical horror; then further it finds
　The appealing of the Passion is tenderer in prayer
　　apart:
　Other, I gather, in measure her mind's
Burden, in wind's burly and beat of endragonèd seas.

28

But how shall I . . . make me room there:
　Reach me a . . . Fancy, come faster—
Strike you the sight of it? look at it loom there,
　Thing that she . . . there then! the Master,   220
Ipse, the only one, Christ, King, Head:
　He was to cure the extremity where he had cast her;
　Do, deal, lord it with living and dead;

---

202 *grey:* mist or fog.

208 *The treasure . . . hearing:* "Eye hath not seen, nor ear heard, neither
have entered into the heart of man, the things which God hath prepared for
them that love him" (1 *Corinthians* 2: 9).

211 *fathers:* begets.

213 *electrical horror:* perhaps a reference to lightning.

214 *The appealing . . . apart:* i.e., the tender aspects of the Passion are
felt in quiet prayer; in the shipwreck the nun's perceptions are totally different.

221 *Ipse:* Himself.

Let him ride, her pride, in his triumph, despatch and have
        done with his doom there.

29

Ah! there was a heart right!
    There was single eye!
Read the unshapeable shock night
    And knew the who and the why;
Wording it now but by him that present and past,
Heaven and earth are word of, worded by?—   230
    The Simon Peter of a soul! to the blast
Tarpeian-fast, but a blown beacon of light.

30

Jesu, heart's light,
    Jesu, maid's son,
What was the feast followed the night
    Thou hadst glory of this nun?—
Feast of the one woman without stain.
    For so conceivèd, so to conceive thee is done;
    But here was heart-throe, birth of a brain,
Word, that heard and kept thee and uttered thee outright.   240

31

Well, she has thee for the pain, for the
    Patience; but pity of the rest of them!
Heart, go and bleed at a bitterer vein for the
    Comfortless unconfessed of them—
No not uncomforted: lovely-felicitous Providence
Finger of a tender of, O of a feathery delicacy, the
        breast of the
    Maiden could obey so, be a bell to, ring of it, and
Startle the poor sheep back! is the shipwrack then a
        harvest, does tempest carry the grain for thee?

---

231 *Simon Peter:* whose faith in Christ allowed him to walk on the water.
232 *Tarpeian-fast:* probably meaning as steady as the Tarpeian rock on the
Capitoline hill in Rome.
235 *feast:* The Feast of the Immaculate Conception of the Virgin Mary is on
8 December, the day following the shipwreck.

32

I admire thee, master of the tides,
    Of the Yore-flood, of the year's fall;   250
The recurb and the recovery of the gulf's sides,
    The girth of it and the wharf of it and the wall;
Stanching, quenching ocean of a motionable mind;
Ground of being, and granite of it: past all
    Grasp God, throned behind
Death with a sovereignty that heeds but hides, bodes but
    abides;

33

With a mercy that outrides
    The all of water, an ark
For the listener; for the lingerer with a love glides
    Lower than death and the dark;   260
A vein for the visiting of the past-prayer, pent in
    prison,
The-last-breath penitent spirits—the uttermost mark
    Our passion-plungèd giant risen,
The Christ of the Father compassionate, fetched in the
    storm of his strides.

34

Now burn, new born to the world,
    Doubled-naturèd name,
The heaven-flung, heart-fleshed, maiden-furled
    Miracle-in-Mary-of-flame,
Mid-numbered He in three of the thunder-throne!
Not a dooms-day dazzle in his coming nor dark as he
    came;   270
    Kind, but royally reclaiming his own;

---

[256] *bodes:* presages.
[259] *love glides:* i.e., love (that) glides.
[260] *dark:* Purgatory.
[261] *vein:* See "vein/Of the gospel proffer" in stanza 4.
[262-4] *uttermost mark . . . his strides:* The reference appears to be to those souls in extremity who show how far out the mercy of the resurrected Christ can reach; "giant" is the subject of the sentence, "fetched" the verb.
[266] *Doubled-naturèd:* Christ as both man and God.
[269] *Mid-numbered:* second of the Trinity.

A released shower, let flash to the shire, not a lightning of
    fire hard-hurled.

35

  Dame, at our door
  Drowned, and among our shoals,
Remember us in the roads, the heaven-haven of the
    Reward:
    Our King back, oh, upon English souls!
Let him easter in us, be a dayspring to the dimness of
    us, be a crimson-cresseted east,
More brightening her, rare-dear Britain, as his reign
    rolls,
    Pride, rose, prince, hero of us, high-priest,
Our hearts' charity's hearth's fire, our thoughts' chivalry's
    throng's Lord.   280

1876

GOD'S GRANDEUR

The world is charged with the grandeur of God.
  It will flame out, like shining from shook foil;
  It gathers to a greatness, like the ooze of oil
Crushed. Why do men then now not reck his rod?
Generations have trod, have trod, have trod;
  And all is seared with trade; bleared, smeared with toil;
  And wears man's smudge and shares man's smell: the soil
Is bare now, nor can foot feel, being shod.

And for all this, nature is never spent;
  There lives the dearest freshness deep down things;   10
And though the last lights off the black West went
  Oh, morning, at the brown brink eastward, springs—

---

275 *roads:* sheltered harbors.
276 *back:* verb meaning "return."
277 *crimson-cresseted:* lighted crimson as with torches.
2 *shook foil:* tinsel or goldfoil shaken.
3 *oil:* olive oil.

Because the Holy Ghost over the bent
　World broods with warm breast and with ah! bright
　　wings.

1877

THE STARLIGHT NIGHT

Look at the stars! look, look up at the skies!
　O look at all the fire-folk sitting in the air!
　The bright boroughs, the circle-citadels there!
Down in dim woods the diamond delves! the elves'-eyes!
The grey lawns cold where gold, where quickgold lies!
　Wind-beat whitebeam! airy abeles set on a flare!
　Flake-doves sent floating forth at a farmyard scare!
Ah well! it is all a purchase, all is a prize.

Buy then! bid then!—What?—Prayer, patience, alms, vows.
Look, look: a May-mess, like on orchard boughs!　　　　　10
　Look! March-bloom, like on mealed-with-yellow sallows!
These are indeed the barn; withindoors house
The shocks. This piece-bright paling shuts the spouse
　Christ home, Christ and his mother and all his hallows.

1877

---

⁵ *quickgold:* The word is probably Hopkins' coinage, meaning a combination of the gold of the stars and the fluidity of quicksilver.
⁶ *whitebeam:* tree whose leaves show their white undersides in wind. *abeles:* poplars.
¹⁰ *May-mess:* intended to recall both the likeness of the starlight to fruit blossoms and the sacramental nature of the light (May is the month of the Virgin Mary, and "mess" is a variant of "Mass").
¹¹ *mealed-with-yellow sallows:* yellow-spotted willows.
¹³ *shocks:* sheaves. The sentence is intended to recall the parable of the sower and the seed: "Gather ye together first the tares, and bind them in bundles to burn them: but gather the wheat into my barn" (*Matthew* 13: 30). *piece-bright paling:* bright fence of stars.

SPRING

Nothing is so beautiful as spring—
   When weeds, in wheels, shoot long and lovely and lush;
   Thrush's eggs look little low heavens, and thrush
Through the echoing timber does so rinse and wring
The ear, it strikes like lightnings to hear him sing;
   The glassy peartree leaves and blooms, they brush
   The descending blue; that blue is all in a rush
With richness; the racing lambs too have fair their fling.

What is all this juice and all this joy?
   A strain of the earth's sweet being in the beginning   10
In Eden garden.—Have, get, before it cloy,
   Before it cloud, Christ, lord, and sour with sinning,
Innocent mind and Mayday in girl and boy,
   Most, O maid's child, thy choice and worthy the win-
      ning.

1877

THE WINDHOVER

To Christ Our Lord

I caught this morning morning's minion, king-
   dom of daylight's dauphin, dapple-dawn-drawn Falcon, in
     his riding
Of the rolling level underneath him steady air, and strid-
     ing
High there, how he rung upon the rein of a wimpling wing
In his ecstasy! then off, off forth on swing,

Windhover: kestrel or hawk that hovers in the wind.
1 *minion:* favorite.
4 *rung . . . wing:* i.e., swung around in a circle whose center was the feathered wing of the bird. "Rung upon the rein" is a term from the training of horses.

As a skate's heel sweeps smooth on a bow-bend: the hurl and
  gliding
Rebuffed the big wind. My heart in hiding
Stirred for a bird,—the achieve of, the mastery of the thing!

Brute beauty and valour and act, oh, air, pride, plume here
  Buckle! AND the fire that breaks from thee then, a billion   10
Times told lovelier, more dangerous, O my chevalier!

No wonder of it: shéer plód makes plough down sillion
Shine, and blue-bleak embers, ah my dear,
  Fall, gall themselves, and gash gold-vermilion.

1877

PIED BEAUTY

Glory be to God for dappled things—
  For skies of couple-colour as a brinded cow;
    For rose-moles all in stipple upon trout that swim;
Fresh-firecoal chestnut-falls; finches' wings;
  Landscape plotted and pieced—fold, fallow, and plough;
    And áll trádes, their gear and tackle and trim.

All things counter, original, spare, strange;
  Whatever is fickle, freckled (who knows how?)

---

6 *bow-bend:* figure eight.
7 *in hiding:* The meaning is probably "in humble station," although it may refer to the heart encased in the body.
8 *achieve:* achievement.
9 *here:* probably both in the bird and in the poet's heart.
10 *Buckle:* The meaning of this word is much disputed, but the primary meanings suggested have been: *clasp, fasten, sag, crumple.*
11 *chevalier:* Christ.
12 *sillion:* furrow.
2 *brinded:* brindled.
5 *plotted and pieced:* laid out in fields and farms. *fallow:* unplanted land.
8 *fickle:* changeable.

With swift, slow; sweet, sour; adazzle, dim;
He fathers-forth whose beauty is past change: 10
Praise him.

1877

HURRAHING IN HARVEST

Summer ends now; now, barbarous in beauty, the stooks arise
    Around; up above, what wind-walks! what lovely behaviour
    Of silk-sack clouds! has wilder, wilful-wavier
Meal-drift moulded ever and melted across skies?

I walk, I lift up heart, eyes,
    Down all that glory in the heavens to glean our Saviour;
    And, éyes, heárt, what looks, what lips yet gave you a
Rapturous love's greeting of realer, of rounder replies?

And the azurous hung hills are his world-wielding shoulder
    Majestic—as a stallion stalwart, very-violet-sweet!—   10
These things, these things were here and but the beholder
    Wanting; which two when they once meet,
The heart réars wíngs bold and bolder
    And hurls for him, O half hurls earth for him off under his feet.

1877

THE CAGED SKYLARK

As a dare-gale skylark scanted in a dull cage
    Man's mounting spirit in his bone-house, mean house, dwells—
    That bird beyond the remembering his free fells;
This in drudgery, day-labouring-out life's age.

---

1 *stooks:* sheaves or shocks.
6 *Down:* draw in, ingest, pull down.
12 *Wanting:* lacking.
3 *fells:* hills.

Though aloft on turf or perch or poor low stage,
   Both sing sometímes the sweetest, sweetest spells,
   Yet both droop deadly sómetimes in their cells
Or wring their barriers in bursts of fear or rage.

Not that the sweet-fowl, song-fowl, needs no rest—
Why, hear him, hear him babble and drop down to his nest, 10
   But his own nest, wild nest, no prison.

Man's spirit will be flesh-bound when found at best,
But uncumbered: meadow-down is not distressed
   For a rainbow footing it nor he for his bónes rísen.

1877

THE LOSS OF THE EURYDICE

Foundered March 24, 1878

The Eurydice—it concerned thee, O Lord:
Three hundred souls, O alas! on board,
   Some asleep unawakened, all un-
warned, eleven fathoms fallen

Where she foundered! One stroke
Felled and furled them, the hearts of oak!
   And flockbells off the aerial
Downs' forefalls beat to the burial.

For did she pride her, freighted fully, on
Bounden bales or a hoard of bullion?—   10
   Precious passing measure,
Lads and men her lade and treasure.

---

⁵ *turf . . . stage:* various platforms in the bird's cage. "Stage" also suggests, in relation to man, the idea of all the world's being a stage.
¹³ *uncumbered:* unlimited, as the resurrected physical body will be.
Eurydice: Hopkins took the occasion of the sinking of the ship for a meditation on the state of Protestant England, broken away from the Roman Catholic Church.
⁷⁻⁸ *flockbells . . . forefalls:* sheepbells from the slopes of the coastal cliffs.
¹² *lade:* cargo.

She had come from a cruise, training seamen—
Men, boldboys soon to be men:
    Must it, worst weather,
Blast bole and bloom together?

No Atlantic squall overwrought her
Or rearing billow of the Biscay water:
    Home was hard at hand
And the blow bore from land.   20

And you were a liar, O blue March day.
Bright sun lanced fire in the heavenly bay;
    But what black Boreas wrecked her? he
Came equipped, deadly-electric,

A beetling baldbright cloud thorough England
Riding: there did storms not mingle? and
    Hailropes hustle and grind their
Heavengravel? wolfsnow, worlds of it, wind there?

Now Carisbrook keep goes under in gloom;
Now it overvaults Appledurcombe;   30
    Now near by Ventnor town
It hurls, hurls off Boniface Down.

Too proud, too proud, what a press she bore!
Royal, and all her royals wore.
    Sharp with her, shorten sail!
Too late; lost; gone with the gale.

This was that fell capsize,
As half she had righted and hoped to rise
    Death teeming in by her portholes
Raced down decks, round messes of mortals.   40

---

16 *bole:* trunk.
22 *lanced fire:* lightning.
23 *Boreas:* north wind.
29 *keep:* castle. The places mentioned are on the Isle of Wight.
33 *press:* full sail; also, crowd (of crew).
34 *royals:* sails.

And he boards her in Oh! such joy
He has lost count what came next, poor boy.—

They say who saw one sea-corpse cold
He was all of lovely manly mould,
   Every inch a tar,
Of the best we boast our sailors are.

Look, foot to forelock, how all things suit! he
Is strung by duty, is strained to beauty,
   And brown-as-dawning-skinned
With brine and shine and whirling wind.   80

O his nimble finger, his gnarled grip!
Leagues, leagues of seamanship
   Slumber in these forsaken
Bones, this sinew, and will not waken.

He was but one like thousands more,
Day and night I deplore
   My people and born own nation,
Fast foundering own generation.

I might let bygones be—our curse
Of ruinous shrine no hand or, worse,   90
   Robbery's hand is busy to
Dress, hoar-hallowèd shrines unvisited;

Only the breathing temple and fleet
Life, this wildworth blown so sweet,
   These daredeaths, ay this crew, in
Unchrist, all rolled in ruin—

Deeply surely I need to deplore it,
Wondering why my master bore it,
   The riving off that race
So at home, time was, to his truth and grace   100

89-90 *our curse . . . shrine:* reference to the English Reformation and the
consequent desecration of Roman Catholic shrines.

Then a lurch forward, frigate and men;
"All hands for themselves" the cry ran then;
   But she who had housed them thither
Was around them, bound them or wound then

Marcus Hare, high her captain,
Kept to her—care-drowned and wrapped in
   Cheer's death, would follow
His charge through the champ-white water-in-a-

All under Channel to bury in a beach her
Cheeks: Right, rude of feature,
   He thought he heard say
"Her commander! and thou too, and thou this way.'

It is even seen, time's something server,
In mankind's medley a duty-swerver,
   At downright "No or yes?"
Doffs all, drives full for righteousness.

Sydney Fletcher, Bristol-bred,
(Low lie his mates now on watery bed)
   Takes to the seas and snows
As sheer down the ship goes.

Now her afterdraught gullies him too down;
Now he wrings for breath with the deathgush brown;
   Till a lifebelt and God's will
Lend him a lift from the sea-swill.

Now he shoots short up to the round air;
Now he gasps, now he gazes everywhere;
   But his eye no cliff, no coast or
Mark makes in the rivelling snowstorm.

Him, after an hour of wintry waves,
A schooner sights, with another, and saves,

---

[47] *Cheer's death:* despair.
[50] *Right:* a personified abstract noun, the object of "heard."
[53] *It is . . . server:* i.e., it is seen that even one acting out of self-interest.
[68] *rivelling:* furrowing.

That a starlight-wender of ours would say
The marvellous Milk was Walsingham Way
   And one—but let be, let be:
More, more than was will yet be.—

O well wept, mother have lost son;
Wept, wife; wept, sweetheart would be one:
   Though grief yield them no good
Yet shed what tears sad truelove should.

But to Christ lord of thunder
Crouch; lay knee by earth low under: 110
   "Holiest, loveliest, bravest,
Save my hero, O Hero savest.

And the prayer thou hearst me making
Have, at the awful overtaking,
   Heard; have heard and granted
Grace that day grace was wanted."

Not that hell knows redeeming,
But for souls sunk in seeming
   Fresh, till doomfire burn all,
Prayer shall fetch pity eternal.   120

1878

THE MAY MAGNIFICAT

May is Mary's month, and I
Muse at that and wonder why:
   Her feasts follow reason,
   Dated due to season—

[101-2] *That . . . Way:* i.e., that a pilgrim in the starlight would say that the Milky Way was a guide to the shrine of the Virgin at Walsingham.

[103] *one:* Duns Scotus, who championed the doctrine of the Immaculate Conception (see "Duns Scotus's Oxford," p. 796).

[105] *mother . . . son:* i.e., mother (you who) have lost a son.

[106] *sweetheart . . . one:* i.e., sweetheart (who) would be one (in marriage).

[114] *Have:* i.e., (You) have.

Magnificat: song of praise (of the Virgin Mary).

Candlemas, Lady Day;
But the Lady Month, May,
   Why fasten that upon her,
   With a feasting in her honour?

Is it only its being brighter
Than the most are must delight her?   10
   Is it opportunest
   And flowers finds soonest?

Ask of her, the mighty mother:
Her reply puts this other
   Question: What is Spring?—
   Growth in every thing—

Flesh and fleece, fur and feather,
Grass and greenworld all together;
   Star-eyed strawberry-breasted
   Throstle above her nested   20

Cluster of bugle blue eggs thin
Forms and warms the life within;
   And bird and blossom swell
   In sod or sheath or shell.

All things rising, all things sizing
Mary sees, sympathising
   With that world of good,
   Nature's motherhood.

Their magnifying of each its kind
With delight calls to mind   30
   How she did in her stored
   Magnify the Lord.

Well but there was more than this:
Spring's universal bliss

---

5 *Candlemas, Lady Day:* Feast of the Purification of the Virgin Mary, 2
February, and Feast of the Annunciation, 25 March.
21 *bugle blue:* color of the bugle flower, the Ajuga.
32 *Magnify the Lord:* For the original Magnificat, the hymn of the Virgin
Mary, see *Luke* 1: 46-55.

Much, had much to say
To offering Mary May.

When drop-of-blood-and-foam-dapple
Bloom lights the orchard-apple
And thicket and thorp are merry
With silver-surfèd cherry   40

And azuring-over greybell makes
Wood banks and brakes wash wet like lakes
And magic cuckoocall
Caps, clears, and clinches all—

This ecstasy all through mothering earth
Tells Mary her mirth till Christ's birth
To remember and exultation
In God who was her salvation.

1878

BINSEY POPLARS

Felled 1879

My aspens dear, whose airy cages quelled,
Quelled or quenched in leaves the leaping sun,
All felled, felled, are all felled;
    Of a fresh and following folded rank
        Not spared, not one
        That dandled a sandalled
    Shadow that swam or sank
On meadow and river and wind-wandering weed-
    winding bank.

    O if we but knew what we do
        When we delve or hew—   10

---

³⁹ *thorp:* farm.
⁴² *brakes:* thickets.
Binsey: village near Oxford.

Hack and rack the growing green!
Since country is to tender
To touch, her being só slender,
That, like this sleek and seeing ball
But a prick will make no eye at all,
Where we, even where we mean

To mend her we end her,
When we hew or delve:
After-comers cannot guess the beauty been.
Ten or twelve, only ten or twelve   20
Strokes of havoc únselve
The sweet especial scene,
Rural scene, a rural scene,
Sweet especial rural scene.

1879

DUNS SCOTUS'S OXFORD

Towery city and branchy between towers;
Cuckoo-echoing, bell-swarmèd, lark-charmèd, rook-racked,
    river-rounded;
The dapple-eared lily below thee; that country and town did
Once encounter in, here coped and poisèd powers;

Thou hast a base and brickish skirt there, sours
That neighbour-nature thy grey beauty is grounded
Best in; graceless growth, thou hast confounded
Rural rural keeping—folk, flocks, and flowers.

Yet ah! this air I gather and I release
He lived on; these weeds and waters, these walls are what   10
He haunted who of all men most sways my spirits to peace;

Duns Scotus: Johannes Duns Scotus, 1274?-1308, Scholastic philosopher
who championed the doctrine of the Immaculate Conception. He is thought
to have been in Oxford at the beginning of the fourteenth century.
4 *coped:* equally matched.

Of realty the rarest-veinèd unraveller; a not
Rivalled insight, be rival Italy or Greece;
Who fired France for Mary without spot.

1879

THE BUGLER'S FIRST COMMUNION

A bugler boy from barrack (it is over the hill
There)—boy bugler, born, he tells me, of Irish
    Mother to an English sire (he
Shares their best gifts surely, fall how things will),

This very very day came down to us after a boon he on
My late being there begged of me, overflowing
    Boon in my bestowing,
Came, I say, this day to it—to a First Communion.

Here he knelt then ín regimental red.
Forth Christ from cupboard fetched, how fain I of feet   10
    To his youngster take his treat!
Low-latched in leaf-light housel his too huge godhead.

There! and your sweetest sendings, ah divine,
By it, heavens, befall him! as a heart Christ's darling,
    dauntless;
    Tongue true, vaunt- and tauntless;
Breathing bloom of a chastity in mansex fine.

Frowning and forefending angel-warder
Squander the hell-rook ranks sally to molest him;
    March, kind comrade, abreast him;
Dress his days to a dexterous and starlight order.   20

How it dóes my heart good, visiting at that bleak hill,
When limber liquid youth, that to all I teach

---

12 *realty:* reality.
10 *cupboard:* tabernacle of the altar.
12 *housel:* the wafer in the Communion. *his:* Christ's.
18 *Squander:* disperse. *ranks sally:* i.e., troops (that) come forth.

Yields tender as a pushed peach,
Hies headstrong to its wellbeing of a self-wise self-will!

Then though I should tread tufts of consolation
Dáys áfter, só I in a sort deserve to
    And do serve God to serve to
Just such slips of soldiery Christ's royal ration.

Nothing élse is like it, no, not all so strains
Us: fresh youth fretted in a bloomfall all portending   30
    That sweet's sweeter ending;
Realm both Christ is heir to and thére réigns.

O now well work that sealing sacred ointment!
O for now charms, arms, what bans off bad
    And locks love ever in a lad!
Let mé though see no more of him, and not disappointment

Those sweet hopes quell whose least me quickenings lift,
In scarlet or somewhere of some day seeing
    That brow and bead of being,
An our day's God's own Galahad. Though this child's drift   40

Seems by a divíne doom chánnelled, nor do I cry
Disaster there; but may he not rankle and roam
    In backwheels though bound home?—
That left to the Lord of the Eucharist, I here lie by;

Recorded only, I have put my lips on pleas
Would brandle adamantine heaven with ride and jar, did
    Prayer go disregarded:

---

29 *all so strains:* i.e., all (that) so strains.
30 *fretted:* ornamented.
36-8 *not disappointment . . . seeing:* i.e., let not disappointment quell those
sweet hopes, whose least stirrings uplift me, of some day seeing, in scarlet, or
elsewhere.
40 *drift:* future path.
42-3 *but may . . . home?:* i.e., but may he not sin (fret and turn backwards)
although his destination is Heaven?
46 *brandle:* shake. *ride and jar:* assault and clash.

Forward-like, but however, and like favourable heaven
    heard these.

1879

FELIX RANDAL

Felix Randal the farrier, O he is dead then? my duty all
    ended,
Who have watched his mould of man, big-boned and hardy-
    handsome
Pining, pining, till time when reason rambled in it and some
Fatal four disorders, fleshed there, all contended?

Sickness broke him. Impatient he cursed at first, but mended
Being anointed and all; though a heavenlier heart began
    some
Months earlier, since I had our sweet reprieve and ransom
Tendered to him. Ah well, God rest him all road ever he of-
    fended!

This seeing the sick endears them to us, us too it endears.
My tongue had taught thee comfort, touch had quenched
    thy tears,   10
Thy tears that touched my heart, child, Felix, poor Felix
    Randal;

How far from then forethought of, all thy more boisterous
    years,
When thou at the random grim forge, powerful amidst
    peers,

---

[48] *Forward-like . . . these:* i.e., perhaps it is both premature and presumptuous of me to feel so, but I do, and like enough Heaven has heard my prayers.
[1] *farrier:* shoer of horses.
[6] *Being anointed:* having received Extreme Unction.
[7] *reprieve and ransom:* sacrament, either of confession or of Communion.
[8] *all road ever:* however.
[13] *random:* built of unmatched stones.

Didst fettle for the great grey drayhorse his bright and bat-
tering sandal!

1880

As kingfishers catch fire, dragonflies dráw fláme;
As tumbled over rim in roundy wells
Stones ring; like each tucked string tells, each hung bell's
Bow swung finds tongue to fling out broad its name;
Each mortal thing does one thing and the same:
Deals out that being indoors each one dwells;
Selves—goes itself; *myself* it speaks and spells,
Crying *Whát I dó is me: for that I came.*

I say móre: the just man justices;
Kéeps gráce: thát keeps all his goings graces;   10
Acts in God's eye what in God's eye he is—
Chríst—for Christ plays in ten thousand places,
Lovely in limbs, and lovely in eyes not his
To the Father through the features of men's faces.

1881?

THE LEADEN ECHO AND
THE GOLDEN ECHO

Maidens' Song from St. Winefred's Well

THE LEADEN ECHO

How to kéep—is there ány any, is there none such, nowhere
known some, bow or brooch or braid or brace, láce, latch
or catch or key to keep
Back beauty, keep it, beauty, beauty, beauty, . . . from
vanishing away?

---

14 *fettle:* make ready.
1 *kingfishers:* small brilliantly blue birds.
3 *tucked:* plucked.
6 *being indoors each:* i.e., being (that) inside each.

Ó is there no frowning of these wrinkles, rankèd wrinkles
   deep,
Dówn? no waving off of these most mournful messengers,
   still messengers, sad and stealing messengers of grey?
No there's none, there's none, O no there's none,
Nor can you long be, what you now are, called fair,
Do what you may do, what, do what you may,
And wisdom is early to despair:
Be beginning; since, no, nothing can be done
To keep at bay   10
Age and age's evils, hoar hair,
Ruck and wrinkle, drooping, dying, death's worst, winding
   sheets, tombs and worms and tumbling to decay;
So be beginning, be beginning to despair.
O there's none; no no no there's none:
Be beginning to despair, to despair,
Despair, despair, despair, despair.

THE GOLDEN ECHO

   Spare!

There is one, yet I have one (Hush there!);
Only not within seeing of the sun,
Not within the singeing of the strong sun,   20
Tall sun's tingeing, or treacherous the tainting of the earth's
   air,
Somewhere elsewhere there is ah well where! one,
Oñe. Yes I cán tell such a key, I dó know such a place,
Where whatever's prized and passes of us, everything that's
   fresh and fast flying of us, seems to us sweet of us and
   swiftly away with, done away with, undone,
Úndone, done with, soon done with, and yet dearly and
   dangerously sweet
Of us, the wimpled-water-dimpled, not-by-morning-matchéd
   face,
The flower of beauty, fleece of beauty, too too apt to, ah! to
   fleet,

---

³ *frowning:* followed syntactically by "Dówn" in the next line.
¹¹ *hoar:* gray or white.
¹² *Ruck:* crease.
¹⁷ *Spare·* wait.

Never fleets móre, fastened with the tenderest truth
To its own best being and its loveliness of youth: it is an
　　everlastingness of, O it is an all youth!
Come then, your ways and airs and looks, locks, maiden
　　gear, gallantry and gaiety and grace,　　　　　　　　30
Winning ways, airs innocent, maiden manners, sweet looks,
　　loose locks, long locks, lovelocks, gaygear, going gallant,
　　girlgrace—
Resign them, sign them, seal them, send them, motion them
　　with breath,
And with sighs soaring, soaring síghs deliver
Them; beauty-in-the-ghost, deliver it, early now, long be-
　　fore death
Give beauty back, beauty, beauty, beauty, back to God,
　　beauty's self and beauty's giver.
See; not a hair is, not an eyelash, not the least lash lost;
　　every hair
Is, hair of the head, numbered.
Nay, what we had lighthanded left in surly the mere mould
Will have waked and have waxed and have walked with the
　　wind what while we slept,
This side, that side hurling a heavyheaded hundredfold　　40
What while we, while we slumbered.
O then, weary then whý should we tread? O why are we so
　　haggard at the heart, so care-coiled, care-killed, so fagged,
　　so fashed, so cogged, so cumbered,
When the thing we freely fórfeit is kept with fonder a care,
Fonder a care kept than we could have kept it, kept
Far with fonder a care (and we, we should have lost it)
　　finer, fonder
A care kept.—Where kept? Do but tell us where kept,
　　where.—
Yonder.—What high as that! We fallow, now we follow.—
　　Yonder, yes yonder, yonder,
Yonder.

1882

38-9 *Naÿ, what . . . slept:* Explained by Hopkins: "Nay more: the seed that
we so carelessly and freely flung into the dull furrow, and then forgot it, will
have come to ear meantime, etc."
42 *fashed:* perplexed. *cogged:* cheated.

SPELT FROM SIBYL'S LEAVES

Earnest, earthless, equal, attuneable, ˈvaulty, voluminous, . . .
stupendous
Evening strains to be tíme's vást, ˈwomb-of-all, home-of-all,
hearse-of-all night.
Her fond yellow hornlight wound to the west, ˈher wild hollow hoarlight hung to the height
Waste; her earliest stars, earl-stars, ˈstárs principal, overbend us,
Fíre-féaturing heaven. For earth ˈher being has unbound,
her dapple is at an end, as-
tray or aswarm, all throughther, in throngs; ˈself ín self
steepèd and páshed—qúite
Disremembering, dísmémbering ˈáll now. Heart, you round
me right
With: Óur évening is over us; óur night ˈwhélms, whélms,
ánd will end us.
Only the beak-leaved boughs dragonish ˈdamask the tool-
smooth bleak light; black,
Ever so black on it. Óur tale, O óur oracle! ˈLét life, wáned,
ah lét life wind   10
Off hér once skéined stained véined varíety ˈupon, áll on twó
spools; párt, pen, páck
Now her áll in twó flocks, twó folds—black, white; ˈright,
wrong; reckon but, reck but, mind
But thése two; wáre of a wórld where bút these ˈtwó tell,
each off the óther; of a rack

Sibyl's Leaves: The Cumaean Sibyl wrote her prophecies on leaves and **threw**
them to the winds.
1 *attuneable:* capable of harmony.
3 *hornlight:* light of a horned moon that is like the light from a lantern
(lanthorn). *hoarlight:* cold, frosty light.
4 *earl-stars:* major stars.
6 *throughther:* through-other, or through each other. *páshed:* violently
broken.
7 *round:* counsel.
9 *damask:* etch with intricate pattern.
11 *párt, pen, páck:* separate, as sheep from goats.
13 *wáre:* beware, be aware of. *tell:* matter.

Where, selfwrung, selfstrung, sheathe- and shelterless, |
    thóughts agaínst thoughts ín groans grínd.

1885

(CARRION COMFORT)

Not, I'll not, carrion comfort, Despair, not feast on thee;
Not untwist—slack they may be—these last strands of man
In me ór, most weary, cry *I can no more.* I can;
Can something, hope, wish day come, not choose not to be.
But ah, but O thou terrible, why wouldst thou rude on me
Thy wring-world right foot rock? lay a lionlimb against me?
        scan
With darksome devouring eyes my bruisèd bones? and fan,
O in turns of tempest, me heaped there; me frantic to avoid
        thee and flee?

  Why? That my chaff might fly; my grain lie, sheer and
        clear.
Nay in all that toil, that coil, since (seems) I kissed the rod,   10
Hand rather, my heart lo! lapped strength, stole joy, would
        laugh, chéer.
Cheer whom though? the hero whose heaven-handling
        flung me, fóot tród
Me? or me that fought him? O which one? is it each one?
        That night, that year
Of now done darkness I wretch lay wrestling with (my
        God!) my God.

1885?

No worst, there is none. Pitched past pitch of grief,
More pangs will, schooled at forepangs, wilder wring.

---

[10] *coil:* trouble in which one is tangled. *kissed the rod:* accepted discipline
(of the Church).
[11] *Hand rather:* refers to ordination of the priest.
[2] *schooled at forepangs:* taught by earlier sorrow.

Comforter, where, where is your comforting?
Mary, mother of us, where is your relief?
My cries heave, herds-long; huddle in a main, a chief
Woe, wórld-sorrow; on an áge-old anvil wince and sing—
Then lull, then leave off. Fury had shrieked "No ling-
ering! Let me be fell: force I must be brief."

   O the mind, mind has mountains; cliffs of fall
Frightful, sheer, no-man-fathomed. Hold them cheap   10
May who ne'er hung there. Nor does long our small
Durance deal with that steep or deep. Here! creep,
Wretch, under a comfort serves in a whirlwind: all
Life death does end and each day dies with sleep.

1885

               ❧

   I wake and feel the fell of dark, not day.
What hours, O what black hoúrs we have spent
This night! what sights you, heart, saw; ways you went!
And more must, in yet longer light's delay.
     With witness I speak this. But where I say
Hours I mean years, mean life. And my lament
Is cries countless, cries like dead letters sent
To dearest him that lives alas! away.

     I am gall, I am heartburn. God's most deep decree
Bitter would have me taste: my taste was me;   10
Bones built in me, flesh filled, blood brimmed the curse.
     Selfyeast of spirit a dull dough sours. I see
The lost are like this, and their scourge to be
As I am mine, their sweating selves; but worse.

1885

---

[5] *herds-long:* as frightened bleating runs along a herd of sheep.
[8] *fell:* cruel. *force:* perforce.
[12] *Durance:* endurance, imprisonment.
[1] *fell:* used to mean both cruelty and pelt or hide.

Patience, hard thing! the hard thing but to pray,
But bid for, Patience is! Patience who asks
Wants war, wants wounds; weary his times, his tasks;
To do without, take tosses, and obey.
    Rare patience roots in these, and, these away,
Nowhere. Natural heart's ivy, Patience masks
Our ruins of wrecked past purpose. There she basks
Purple eyes and seas of liquid leaves all day.

We hear our hearts grate on themselves: it kills
To bruise them dearer. Yet the rebellious wills   10
Of us we do bid God bend to him even so.
    And where is he who more and more distils
Delicious kindness?—He is patient. Patience fills
His crisp combs, and that comes those ways we know.

1885

My own heart let me more have pity on; let
Me live to my sad self hereafter kind,
Charitable; not live this tormented mind
With this tormented mind tormenting yet.
    I cast for comfort I can no more get
By groping round my comfortless, than blind
Eyes in their dark can day or thirst can find
Thirst's all-in-all in all a world of wet.

Soul, self; come, poor Jackself, I do advise
You, jaded, let be; call off thoughts awhile   10
Elsewhere; leave comfort root-room; let joy size
At God knows when to God knows what; whose smile

2-3 *Patience who asks . . . wounds:* i.e., whoever asks for patience must accept strife and pain.
14 *combs:* honeycombs.
9 *Jackself:* everyday self.

's not wrung, see you; unforeseen times rather—as skies
Betweenpie mountains—lights a lovely mile.

1885

HARRY PLOUGHMAN

Hard as hurdle arms, with a broth of goldish flue
Breathed round; the rack of ribs; the scooped flank; lank
Rope-over thigh; knee-nave; and barrelled shank—
    Head and foot, shoulder and shank—
By a grey eye's heed steered well, one crew, fall to;
Stand at stress. Each limb's barrowy brawn, his thew
That onewhere curded, onewhere sucked or sank—
    Soared or sank—,
Though as a beechbole firm, finds his, as at a roll-call, rank
And features, in flesh, what deed he each must do—
    His sinew-service where do.

He leans to it, Harry bends, look. Back, elbow, and liquid
    waist
In him, all quail to the wallowing o' the plough: 's cheek
    crimsons; curls   10
Wag or crossbridle, in a wind lifted, windlaced—
    See his wind- lilylocks -laced;
Churlsgrace, too, child of Amansstrength, how it hangs or
    hurls
Them—broad in bluff hide his frowning feet lashed! raced

13-14 *skies . . . mountains:* i.e., dappled (pied) skies seen between mountains.
1 *hurdle:* wooden gate. *broth of goldish flue:* foam of golden fluff (hair).
3 *knee-nave:* kneecap.
4 *one crew:* unified, acting as one.
5-8 *Each limb's . . . where do:* This sentence might be roughly paraphrased: "The mountainous strength of each limb (the muscles in some places bunched together in a lump and elsewhere hollowed out), though strong as a beech trunk, finds its subservient place (as at a roll-call) and carries out the task appointed for it, wherever necessary."
11 *See . . . laced:* i.e., see his hair, beautiful as lilies, blown by the wind.
12-14 *Churlsgrace . . . furls:* The approximate meaning is: "How his rustic grace (derivative from manly strength) directs the movement of his feet (laced into shoes of rough hide) as they are pitted in a race against the plow along the furrows gleaming with dampness."

With, along them, cragiron under and cold furls—
    With-a-fountain's shining-shot furls.

1887

                   ❦

---

*Justus quidem tu es, Domine, si disputem tecum: verum-
tamen justa loquar ad te: Quare via impiorum prosper-
atur? &c.*

Thou art indeed just, Lord, if I contend
With thee; but, sir, so what I plead is just.
Why do sinners' ways prosper? and why must
Disappointment all I endeavour end?
    Wert thou my enemy, O thou my friend,
How wouldst thou worse, I wonder, than thou dost
Defeat, thwart me? Oh, the sots and thralls of lust
Do in spare hours more thrive than I that spend,
Sir, life upon thy cause. See, banks and brakes
Now, leavèd how thick! lacèd they are again   10
With fretty chervil, look, and fresh wind shakes
Them; birds build—but not I build; no, but strain,
Time's eunuch, and not breed one work that wakes.
Mine, O thou lord of life, send my roots rain.

1889

Justus . . . &c.: The epigraph (which is translated in the first three lines
of the poem) is from *Jeremiah* 12:1, in the Latin Vulgate, and the rest of the
chapter is echoed through the rest of the sonnet.
⁹ *brakes:* thickets.
¹¹ *fretty chervil:* aromatic herb with carrot-like leaves.

Alfred Edward Housman

[1859-1936]

Few poets have achieved a reputation so high as that of A. E. Housman on such a meager output of verse. Three slender volumes, *A Shropshire Lad,* 1896; *Last Poems,* 1922; and the posthumous *More Poems,* 1936; and some two dozen brief poems subsequently published: on the strength of these, Housman became one of the most popular poets since the death of Tennyson.

The externals of his life were as restricted as the limits of his poetry, and the glaring disparity between the romantic emotions of the poems and the uneventful life and austerely controlled figure of the man who wrote them has tempted critics and biographers into unprofitable Freudian speculation about the nature of his personality and the hidden sources of his emotions.

Housman was born near Bromsgrove, Worcestershire, the eldest of the seven talented children of a prosperous solicitor and his wife, both members of old families of the locality. After studying at Bromsgrove School, he went as scholar to St. John's College, Oxford, where, after a brilliant start, he failed to take a degree with honors. The following year he became a clerk in the Patent Office, and in his spare time resumed his classical studies. In the course of ten years he published a series of papers which attracted such wide scholarly attention that in 1892 he was made Professor of Latin at University College, London, a position that would normally have been denied him because of the low standing of his Oxford degree. For nearly twenty years he taught at University College and increased his reputation as a great scholar with uncompromising standards and devastatingly destructive critical wit, writing chiefly of Propertius, Ovid, Manilius, and Juvenal. In 1911 he was elected Professor of Latin at Cambridge, where he lived quietly in Trinity College until his death at seventy-six.

Not only the scholarly world but even Housman's family were startled by the depth of emotion revealed in the poems of *A Shropshire Lad* and the succeeding volumes. The relative simplicity of his ideas of the fading of beauty, the fickleness of affection, the brevity of youth, and the unfairness of life's burdens has often prompted a critical charge of too-easy emotion, but Housman's pastoral limpidity conceals the profound disillusionment of a man who grew up with evolution and said that he had become "a deist at 13 and an atheist at 21."

The melodious names of Shropshire—Ludlow and Wenlock, Hughley and Clee—chime like bells through his poems, but Housman was no man of Shropshire, nor had he spent much time in that county, although he retained an affection for it because its hills had been "the western horizon" of his childhood. Indeed, the topographical details of Shropshire are sometimes quite wrong, as Housman freely admitted in later years. And just as he was not personally to be associated with Shropshire, so he tried to disavow any connection between himself and the Shropshire Lad, who was, he wrote, an imaginary figure with only a trace of his own temper and outlook on life. To try to find a biographical parallel would, of course, be nonsensical, but in the poems the reader can easily find the personality that Housman tried to hide from the world. Although he insisted that the poems in *A Shropshire Lad* were not autobiographical, in the later volumes the mask was slightly lifted, and in such poems as "Because I liked you better" the reader feels the reverberation of Housman's own sorrow, the sorrow of a man condemned to live without comfort or love in a world not of his own making. Using a domesticated version of the pastoral tradition of his beloved classical poets, Housman made the sadness of the life of the Shropshire rustic a metaphor for the insupportable lot of all men.

But Housman insisted that poetry was "not the thing said

but a way of saying it," and it is the unstrained lyricism of his poetry, the felicity of phrase, the apparent ease of diction, and the effortless variety of his meters which will undoubtedly ensure him his place in English poetry.

When the "occasion" of the poem seems inadequate to provoke the poet's response of black despair; when, that is, his response seems out of all proportion to the stimulus, one must remember that Housman was writing out of a sense of injury by the world so deeply engrained that any injustice apparent in man's lot seemed to him adequate demonstration of the injustice of the entire universe. What have been called his sentimentality and melodrama are probably only the reverse of the symbolic process of perception that allowed Wordsworth to see a field of daffodils as the cause for solemn joy at the harmony of the world. Housman saw the bridal beauty of the cherry tree in flower as evidence of the poignance of brief beauty doomed to die in an unheeding world. Whether Hardy's attitude or Wordsworth's is preferable is, as Housman would have pointed out, a question for philosophy, not for the study of poetry.

BIBLIOGRAPHY

The best edition is *Complete Poems of A. E. Housman*, ed. T. B. Haber (Holt, Rinehart and Winston, New York, 1959), which the text of this anthology follows.

Biography and Criticism:

Carter, John, and Sparrow, John, *A. E. Housman: An Annotated Hand-List.* Rupert Hart-Davis, London, 1952.

Gow, A. S. F., *A. E. Housman.* Cambridge University Press, Cambridge, 1936.

Haber, Tom Burns, *The Manuscript Poems of A. E. Housman.* University of Minnesota Press, Minneapolis, 1955.

Housman, Laurence, *A. E. H.: Some Poems, Some Letters and a Personal Memoir,* Jonathan Cape, London, 1937.

Richards, Grant, *Housman, 1897-1936.* Oxford University Press, Oxford, 1941.

Watson, George L., *A. E. Housman: A Divided Life.* Rupert Hart-Davis, London, 1957.

Wilson, Edmund, "A. E. Housman," *The Triple Thinkers,* Harcourt, Brace, New York, 1938.

FROM A Shropshire Lad (*1896*)

II

Loveliest of trees, the cherry now
Is hung with bloom along the bough,
And stands about the woodland ride
Wearing white for Eastertide.

Now, of my threescore years and ten,
Twenty will not come again,
And take from seventy springs a score,
It only leaves me fifty more.

And since to look at things in bloom
Fifty springs are little room,   10
About the woodlands I will go
To see the cherry hung with snow.

VII

When smoke stood up from Ludlow,
    And mist blew off from Teme,
And blithe afield to ploughing
    Against the morning beam
    I strode beside my team,

The blackbird in the coppice
    Looked out to see me stride,
And hearkened as I whistled
    The trampling team beside,
    And fluted and replied: 10

"Lie down, lie down, young yeoman;
    What use to rise and rise?
Rise man a thousand mornings
    Yet down at last he lies,
    And then the man is wise."

I heard the tune he sang me,
  And spied his yellow bill;
I picked a stone and aimed it
  And threw it with a will:
  Then the bird was still.   20

Then my soul within me
  Took up the blackbird's strain,
And still beside the horses
  Along the dewy lane
  It sang the song again:

"Lie down, lie down, young yeoman;
  The sun moves always west;
The road one treads to labour
  Will lead one home to rest,
  And that will be the best."   30

XIII

When I was one-and-twenty
  I heard a wise man say,
"Give crowns and pounds and guineas
  But not your heart away;
Give pearls away and rubies
  But keep your fancy free."
But I was one-and-twenty,
  No use to talk to me.

When I was one-and-twenty
  I heard him say again,   10
"The heart out of the bosom
  Was never given in vain;
'Tis paid with sighs a plenty
  And sold for endless rue."
And I am two-and-twenty,
  And oh, 'tis true, 'tis true.

XIX

TO AN ATHLETE DYING YOUNG

The time you won your town the race
We chaired you through the market-place;
Man and boy stood cheering by,
And home we brought you shoulder-high.

To-day, the road all runners come,
Shoulder-high we bring you home,
And set you at your threshold down,
Townsman of a stiller town.

Smart lad, to slip betimes away
From fields where glory does not stay   10
And early though the laurel grows
It withers quicker than the rose.

Eyes the shady night has shut
Cannot see the record cut,
And silence sounds no worse than cheers
After earth has stopped the ears:

Now you will not swell the rout
Of lads that wore their honours out,
Runners whom renown outran
And the name died before the man.   20

So set, before its echoes fade,
The fleet foot on the sill of shade,
And hold to the low lintel up
The still-defended challenge-cup.

And round that early-laurelled head
Will flock to gaze the strengthless dead,
And find unwithered on its curls
The garland briefer than a girl's.

XXI

BREDON HILL

In summertime on Bredon
  The bells they sound so clear;
Round both the shires they ring them
  In steeples far and near,
  A happy noise to hear.

Here of a Sunday morning
  My love and I would lie,
And see the coloured counties,
  And hear the larks so high
  About us in the sky.   10

The bells would ring to call her
  In valleys miles away:
"Come all to church, good people;
  Good people, come and pray."
  But here my love would stay.

And I would turn and answer
  Among the springing thyme,
"Oh, peal upon our wedding,
  And we will hear the chime,
  And come to church in time."   20

But when the snows at Christmas
  On Bredon top were strown,
My love rose up so early
  And stole out unbeknown
  And went to church alone.

They tolled the one bell only,
  Groom there was none to see,

---

1 *Bredon:* (pronounced "Bree-don") hill in Worcestershire, near the border of Gloucestershire; from it five counties can be seen in good weather. According to Housman, the poem was written before he had decided upon a Shropshire locale for the volume.

The mourners followed after,
 And so to church went she,
 And would not wait for me.   30

The bells they sound on Bredon,
 And still the steeples hum.
"Come all to church, good people,"—
 Oh, noisy bells, be dumb;
 I hear you, I will come.

XXIII

The lads in their hundreds to Ludlow come in for the fair,
 There's men from the barn and the forge and the mill and
  the fold,
The lads for the girls and the lads for the liquor are there,
 And there with the rest are the lads that will never be old.

There's chaps from the town and the field and the till and
  the cart,
 And many to count are the stalwart, and many the brave,
And many the handsome of face and the handsome of heart,
 And few that will carry their looks or their truth to the
  grave.

I wish one could know them, I wish there were tokens to tell
 The fortunate fellows that now you can never discern;   10
And then one could talk with them friendly and wish them
  farewell
 And watch them depart on the way that they will not return.

But now you may stare as you like and there's nothing to scan;
 And brushing your elbow unguessed-at and not to be told
They carry back bright to the coiner the mintage of man,
 The lads that will die in their glory and never be old.

XXVII

"Is my team ploughing,
 That I was used to drive
And hear the harness jingle
 When I was man alive?"

Ay, the horses trample,
The harness jingles now;
No change though you lie under
The land you used to plough.

"Is football playing
Along the river shore,
With lads to chase the leather,
Now I stand up no more?"

Ay, the ball is flying,
The lads play heart and soul;
The goal stands up, the keeper
Stands up to keep the goal.

"Is my girl happy,
That I thought hard to leave,
And has she tired of weeping
As she lies down at eve?"

Ay, she lies down lightly,
She lies not down to weep:
Your girl is well contented.
Be still, my lad, and sleep.

"Is my friend hearty,
Now I am thin and pine,
And has he found to sleep in
A better bed than mine?"

Yes, lad, I lie easy,
I lie as lads would choose;
I cheer a dead man's sweetheart,
Never ask me whose.

XXXI

On Wenlock Edge the wood's in trouble;
His forest fleece the Wrekin heaves;

1 *Wenlock Edge:* range of hills in Shropshire.
2 *Wrekin:* extinct volcano in that county.

The gale, it plies the saplings double,
    And thick on Severn snow the leaves.

'Twould blow like this through holt and hanger
    When Uricon the city stood:
'Tis the old wind in the old anger,
    But then it threshed another wood.

Then, 'twas before my time, the Roman
    At yonder heaving hill would stare: 10
The blood that warms an English yeoman,
    The thoughts that hurt him, they were there.

There, like the wind through woods in riot,
    Through him the gale of life blew high;
The tree of man was never quiet:
    Then 'twas the Roman, now 'tis I.

The gale, it plies the saplings double,
    It blows so hard, 'twill soon be gone:
To-day the Roman and his trouble
    Are ashes under Uricon.   20

XXXVI

White in the moon the long road lies,
    The moon stands blank above;
White in the moon the long road lies
    That leads me from my love.

Still hangs the hedge without a gust,
    Still, still the shadows stay:
My feet upon the moonlit dust
    Pursue the ceaseless way.

The world is round, so travellers tell,
    And straight though reach the track,   10
Trudge on, trudge on, 'twill all be well,
    The way will guide one back.

---

6 *Uricon:* Roman city in Shropshire.

But ere the circle homeward hies
Far, far must it remove:
White in the moon the long road lies
That leads me from my love.

LIV

With rue my heart is laden
For golden friends I had,
For many a rose-lipt maiden
And many a lightfoot lad.

By brooks too broad for leaping
The lightfoot boys are laid;
The rose-lipt girls are sleeping
In fields where roses fade.

LXI

HUGHLEY STEEPLE

The vane on Hughley steeple
Veers bright, a far-known sign,
And there lie Hughley people,
And there lie friends of mine.
Tall in their midst the tower
Divides the shade and sun,
And the clock strikes the hour
And tells the time to none.

To south the headstones cluster,
The sunny mounds lie thick;   10
The dead are more in muster
At Hughley than the quick.
North, for a soon-told number,
Chill graves the sexton delves,
And steeple-shadowed slumber
The slayers of themselves.

To north, to south, lie parted,
    With Hughley tower above,
The kind, the single-hearted,
    The lads I used to love.   20
And, south or north, 'tis only
    A choice of friends one knows,
And I shall ne'er be lonely
    Asleep with these or those.

LXII

"Terence, this is stupid stuff:
You eat your victuals fast enough;
There can't be much amiss, 'tis clear,
To see the rate you drink your beer.
But oh, good Lord, the verse you make,
It gives a chap the belly-ache.
The cow, the old cow, she is dead;
It sleeps well, the horned head:
We poor lads, 'tis our turn now
To hear such tunes as killed the cow.   10
Pretty friendship 'tis to rhyme
Your friends to death before their time
Moping melancholy mad:
Come, pipe a tune to dance to, lad."

    Why, if 'tis dancing you would be,
There's brisker pipes than poetry.
Say, for what were hop-yards meant,
Or why was Burton built on Trent?
Oh many a peer of England brews
Livelier liquor than the Muse,   20
And malt does more than Milton can
To justify God's ways to man.
Ale, man, ale's the stuff to drink
For fellows whom it hurts to think:

---

1 *Terence:* Housman's original title for *A Shropshire Lad* was *The Poems of Terence Hearsay.*
18 *Burton:* chief brewing center in England; many of its brewers were made peers.
21-2 *And . . . man:* see *Paradise Lost,* I, 25-26.

Look into the pewter pot
To see the world as the world's not.
And faith, 'tis pleasant till 'tis past:
The mischief is that 'twill not last.
Oh I have been to Ludlow fair
And left my necktie God knows where, 30
And carried half-way home, or near,
Pints and quarts of Ludlow beer:
Then the world seemed none so bad,
And I myself a sterling lad;
And down in lovely muck I've lain,
Happy till I woke again.
Then I saw the morning sky:
Heigho, the tale was all a lie;
The world, it was the old world yet,
I was I, my things were wet, 40
And nothing now remained to do
But begin the game anew.

Therefore, since the world has still
Much good, but much less good than ill,
And while the sun and moon endure
Luck's a chance, but trouble's sure,
I'd face it as a wise man would,
And train for ill and not for good.
'Tis true, the stuff I bring for sale
Is not so brisk a brew as ale: 50
Out of a stem that scored the hand
I wrung it in a weary land.
But take it: if the smack is sour,
The better for the embittered hour;
It should do good to heart and head
When your soul is in my soul's stead;
And I will friend you, if I may,
In the dark and cloudy day.

There was a king reigned in the East:
There, when kings will sit to feast, 60

---

59 *king:* Mithridates VI, King of Pontus, *circa* 122-64 B.C., is said to have taken poison in increasingly large portions until he developed total immunity to its effects.

They get their fill before they think
With poisoned meat and poisoned drink.
He gathered all that springs to birth
From the many-venomed earth;
First a little, thence to more,
He sampled all her killing store;
And easy, smiling, seasoned sound,
Sate the king when healths went round.
They put arsenic in his meat
And stared aghast to watch him eat;   70
They poured strychnine in his cup
And shook to see him drink it up:
They shook, they stared as white's their shirt:
Them it was their poison hurt.
—I tell the tale that I heard told.
Mithridates, he died old.

FROM Last Poems (1922)

IV

ILLIC JACET

Oh hard is the bed they have made him,
    And common the blanket and cheap;
But there he will lie as they laid him:
    Where else could you trust him to sleep?

To sleep when the bugle is crying
    And cravens have heard and are brave,
When mothers and sweethearts are sighing
    And lads are in love with the grave.

Oh dark is the chamber and lonely,
    And lights and companions depart;   10
But lief will he lose them and only
    Behold the desire of his heart.

And low is the roof, but it covers
    A sleeper content to repose;
And far from his friends and his lovers
    He lies with the sweetheart he chose.

IX

The chestnut casts his flambeaux, and the flowers
    Stream from the hawthorn on the wind away,
The doors clap to, the pane is blind with showers.
    Pass me the can, lad; there's an end of May.

Illic Jacet: there lies.
1 *flambeaux:* candle-shaped blossoms.

There's one spoilt spring to scant our mortal lot,
    One season ruined of our little store.
May will be fine next year as like as not:
    Oh ay, but then we shall be twenty-four.

We for a certainty are not the first
    Have sat in taverns while the tempest hurled   10
Their hopeful plans to emptiness, and cursed
    Whatever brute and blackguard made the world.

It is in truth iniquity on high
    To cheat our sentenced souls of aught they crave,
And mar the merriment as you and I
    Fare on our long fool's-errand to the grave.

Iniquity it is; but pass the can.
    My lad, no pair of kings our mothers bore;
Our only portion is the estate of man:
    We want the moon, but we shall get no more.   20

If here to-day the cloud of thunder lours
    To-morrow it will hie on far behests;
The flesh will grieve on other bones than ours
    Soon, and the soul will mourn in other breasts.

The troubles of our proud and angry dust
    Are from eternity, and shall not fail.
Bear them we can, and if we can we must.
    Shoulder the sky, my lad, and drink your ale.

XIV

THE CULPRIT

The night my father got me
    His mind was not on me;
He did not plague his fancy
    To muse if I should be
    The son you see.

The day my mother bore me
  She was a fool and glad,
For all the pain I cost her,
  That she had borne the lad
  That borne she had.   10

My mother and my father
  Out of the light they lie;
The warrant would not find them,
  And here 'tis only I
  Shall hang so high.

Oh let not man remember
  The soul that God forgot,
But fetch the county kerchief
  And noose me in the knot,
  And I will rot.   20

For so the game is ended
  That should not have begun.
My father and my mother
  They had a likely son,
  And I have none.

XVIII

The rain, it streams on stone and hillock,
  The boot clings to the clay.
Since all is done that's due and right
Let's home; and now, my lad, good-night,
  For I must turn away.

Good-night, my lad, for nought's eternal;
  No league of ours, for sure.
To-morrow I shall miss you less,
And ache of heart and heaviness
  Are things that time should cure.   10

Over the hill the highway marches
  And what's beyond is wide:
Oh soon enough will pine to nought

Remembrance and the faithful thought
That sits the grave beside.

The skies, they are not always raining
 Nor grey the twelvemonth through;
And I shall meet good days and mirth,
And range the lovely lands of earth
 With friends no worse than you.   20

But oh, my man, the house is fallen
 That none can build again;
My man, how full of joy and woe
Your mother bore you years ago
 To-night to lie in the rain.

XXXVI

REVOLUTION

West and away the wheels of darkness roll,
 Day's beamy banner up the east is borne,
Spectres and fears, the nightmare and her foal,
 Drown in the golden deluge of the morn.

But over sea and continent from sight
 Safe to the Indies has the earth conveyed
The vast and moon-eclipsing cone of night,
 Her towering foolscap of eternal shade.

See, in mid heaven the sun is mounted; hark,
 The belfries tingle to the noonday chime.   10
'Tis silent, and the subterranean dark
 Has crossed the nadir, and begins to climb.

FROM More Poems (1936)

[INTRODUCTORY]

They say my verse is sad: no wonder.
Its narrow measure spans
Tears of eternity, and sorrow
Not mine, but man's.

This is for all ill-treated fellows
Unborn and unbegot,
For them to read when they're in trouble
And I am not.

VII

Stars, I have seen them fall,
   But when they drop and die
No star is lost at all
   From all the star-sown sky.
The toil of all that be
   Helps not the primal fault;
It rains into the sea,
   And still the sea is salt.

XVIII

Delight it is in youth and May
   To see the morn arise,
And more delight to look all day
   A lover in the eyes.
Oh maiden, let your distaff be,
And pace the flowery meads with me,
   And I will tell you lies.

'Tis blithe to see the sunshine fail,
   And hear the land grow still

And listen till the nightingale   10
    Is heard beneath the hill.
Oh follow me where she is flown
Into the leafy woods alone,
    And I will work you ill.

XXV

Yon flakes that fret the eastern sky
    Lead back my day of birth;
The far, wide-wandered hour when I
    Came crying upon earth.

Then came I crying, and to-day,
    With heavier cause to plain,
Depart I into death away,
    Not to be born again.

XXXI

Because I liked you better
    Than suits a man to say,
It irked you and I promised
    To throw the thought away.

To put the world between us
    We parted, stiff and dry;
"Good-bye," said you, "forget me";
    "I will, no fear," said I.

If e'er, where clover whitens
    The dead man's knoll, you pass,   10
And no tall flower to meet you
    Starts in the trefoiled grass,

Halt by the headstone naming
    The heart no longer stirred,
And say the lad that loved you
    Was one that kept his word.

XXXVII

I did not lose my heart in summer's even,
   When roses to the moonrise burst apart:
When plumes were under heel and lead was flying,
   In blood and smoke and flame I lost my heart.

I lost it to a soldier and a foeman,
   A chap that did not kill me, but he tried;
That took the sabre straight and took it striking
   And laughed and kissed his hand to me and died.

Index of Authors, Titles of Poems, and First Lines

(The names of authors are set in capitals, titles in italics, and first lines in roman type. When the title of a poem is the initial part, or all, of the first line, only the first line is given.)

ABOUT THE AUTHOR

ROBERT BERNARD MARTIN is Associate Professor of English at Princeton University, where he has taught since 1951. Professor Martin received his A.B. from the University of Iowa, his A.M. from Harvard University, and his B. Litt. from Oxford University. A specialist in Victorian literature, he is the author of *Charles Kingsley's American Notes*, *The Dust of Combat: A Life of Charles Kingsley*, and *Enter Rumor: Four Early Victorian Scandals*, and co-author of *A Companion to Victorian Literature*.

A NOTE ON THE TYPE

The text of this book is set in Caledonia, a Linotype face designed by W. A. Dwiggins, the man responsible for so much that is good in contemporary book design and typography. Caledonia belongs to the family of printing types called "modern face" by printers—a term used to mark the change in style of type-letters that occurred about 1800. Caledonia borders on the general design of Scotch Modern but is more freely drawn than that letter.